# HELLENISM IN BYZANTIUM

This is the first systematic study of what it meant to be "Greek" in late antiquity and Byzantium, an identity that could alternately become national, religious, philosophical, or cultural. Through close readings of the sources – including figures such as Julian, Psellos, and the Komnenian scholars – Professor Kaldellis surveys the space that Hellenism occupied in each period; the broader debates in which it was caught up; and the historical causes of its successive transformations. The first part (100–400) shows how Romanization and Christianization led to the abandonment of Hellenism as a national label and its restriction to a negative religious sense and a positive, albeit rarefied, cultural one. The second (1000–1300) shows how Hellenism was revived in Byzantium and contributed to the evolution of its culture. The discussion looks closely at the reception of the classical tradition, which was the reason why Hellenism was always desirable and dangerous in Christian society, and presents a new model for understanding Byzantine civilization.

ANTHONY KALDELLIS is Professor of Greek and Latin at The Ohio State University. He has published many articles and monographs on late antiquity and Byzantium, and is currently completing a related book on the subject of the Christian Parthenon. His most recent titles are *Mothers and Sons, Fathers and Daughters: The Byzantine Family of Michael Psellos* (2006) and *Procopius of Caesarea: Tyranny, History and Philosophy at the End of Antiquity* (2004).

GREEK CULTURE IN THE ROMAN WORLD

*Editors*
SUSAN E. ALCOCK, University of Michigan
JAŚ ELSNER, Corpus Christi College, Oxford
SIMON GOLDHILL, University of Cambridge

The Greek culture of the Roman Empire offers a rich field of study. Extraordinary insights can be gained into processes of multicultural contact and exchange, political and ideological conflict, and the creativity of a changing, polyglot empire. During this period, many fundamental elements of Western society were being set in place: from the rise of Christianity, to an influential system of education, to long-lived artistic canons. This series is the first to focus on the response of Greek culture to its Roman imperial setting as a significant phenomenon in its own right. To this end, it will publish original and innovative research in the art, archaeology, epigraphy, history, philosophy, religion, and literature of the empire, with an emphasis on Greek material.

Titles in series:

*Athletics and Literature in the Roman Empire*
Jason König

*Describing Greece: Landscape and Literature in the* Periegesis *of Pausanias*
William Hutton

*The Making of Roman India*
Grant Parker

*Hellenism in Byzantium: The Transformations of Greek Identity and the Reception of the Classical Tradition*
Anthony Kaldellis

*Religious Identity in Late Antiquity: Greeks, Jews and Christians in Antioch*
Isabella Sandwell

# HELLENISM IN BYZANTIUM

*The Transformations of Greek Identity and the
Reception of the Classical Tradition*

ANTHONY KALDELLIS

CAMBRIDGE
UNIVERSITY PRESS

CAMBRIDGE UNIVERSITY PRESS
Cambridge, New York, Melbourne, Madrid, Cape Town, Singapore, São Paulo

Cambridge University Press
The Edinburgh Building, Cambridge CB2 8RU, UK

Published in the United States of America by Cambridge University Press, New York

www.cambridge.org
Information on this title: www.cambridge.org/9780521876889

First published 2007

Printed in the United Kingdom at the University Press, Cambridge

*A catalogue record for this publication is available from the British Library*

ISBN 978-0-521-87688-9 hardback

*I dedicate this book to my uncle Christophoros,*
*in gratitude and admiration.*

# Contents

*Preface*                                                                 *page* ix

Introduction                                                                    1

PART I  GREEKS, ROMANS, AND CHRISTIANS
IN LATE ANTIQUITY                                                              11

1  "We too are Greeks!": the legacies of Hellenism                            13
   Classical Greece                                                           14
   The Hellenistic world                                                      21
   The Second Sophistic                                                       30

2  "The world a city": Romans of the East                                    42
   Becoming Roman                                                            45
   The translation of Romania                                                61
   Byzantium as a nation-state                                               74
   The myth of the "multi-ethnic empire"                                     82
   The fictions of ecumenical ideology                                      100
   Where did all the Greeks go?                                             111

3  "Nibbling on Greek learning": the Christian
   predicament                                                              120
   Between Greeks and Barbarians, within Hellenism                          121
   The challenge of Hellenism                                               131
   The legacy of Julian                                                     143
   Ours or theirs? The uneasy patristic settlement                         154
   Conclusion: the end of ancient Hellenism                                166

*Interlude.*  Hellenism in limbo: the middle years (400–1040)               173

PART II   HELLENIC REVIVALS IN BYZANTIUM                189

4   Michael Psellos and the instauration of philosophy      191
    "Unblocking the streams of philosophy"                  193
    Science and dissimulation                               202
    Between body and soul: a new humanism                   209
    Hellenes in the eleventh century?                       219

5   The Third Sophistic: the performance of Hellenism
    under the Komnenoi                                      225
    Anathema upon philosophy                                225
    Emperors and sophists                                   233
    Hellenism as an expansion of moral and aesthetic
        categories                                          241
    Hellenic fantasy worlds: the new Romance novels         256
    A philosopher's novel: Prodromos on religion and war    270
    Hellenic afterworlds: the *Timarion*                    276
    Toward a new Hellenic identity                          283
    Anti-Latin Hellenism                                    295
    Ioannes Tzetzes: professional classicism                301
    Eustathios of Thessalonike: scholar, bishop, humanist   307

6   Imperial failure and the emergence of national Hellenism  317
    Michael Choniates and the "blessed" Greeks              317
    Athens: a Christian city and its classicist bishop      323
    East and West: negotiating labels in 1204               334
    *Moderni Graeci* or Romans? Byzantines under Latin
        occupation                                          345
    Roman nationalism in the successor states               360
    Imperial Hellenism: Ioannes III Batatzes and
        Theodoros II Laskaris                                368
    The intellectuals of Nikaia                             379

General conclusions                                         389

*Bibliography*                                              398
*Index*                                                     453

# *Preface*

This book attempts to mediate among different fields, different methodologies within those fields, and my own personal interests and backgrounds. It combines intellectual, cultural, and literary history to answer the following questions: what did it mean to be Greek in Byzantium, how and why did those meanings change over time and across different sites of the culture, and how were those changes related to the reception of the classical tradition? Obviously, its primary audience will be those who are interested in late antiquity and Byzantium, but it also attempts to build bridges to (and between) Classics and Modern Greek Studies. Classicists are increasingly looking beyond the narrow definitions of their field that prevailed in the past and into the extension and reception of Greek culture in later societies (from the Second Sophistic to late antiquity, the Renaissance, and modern Greece). This book offers them a guide to how some familiar ancient themes continued to evolve in Byzantium. Students of modern Greece, on the other hand, have long been intrigued by the way in which Greek modernity has defined itself in terms of classical antiquity, sounding alternating notes of tension and harmony, but ideologies and institutions have not favored giving the same attention to Byzantium, and nonexperts are understandably intimidated by the alien, overdocumented, and understudied millennium that stands between the two canonical poles. This book offers them a study of how the Byzantines coped with many of the same problems that the modern Greeks would face (and still do), especially regarding the contested spaces of Greek identity. My position as a Byzantinist in a classics department that includes a program of Modern Greek has proven an advantage for thinking through these fundamental questions.

Methodologically the book likewise stands in the middle. It basically tells a narrative and rests on research that is primarily philological: reading through thousands of pages of arcane and mostly untranslated sources and examining what they say. At the same time, Hellenic identity is treated as a historically and discursively constructed entity, not a stable "essence," and therefore as always being reimagined and contested. This is now a conventional approach in the humanities. The parameters and modalities of identity – memory, performance, polarity, rhetoric, ritual, reception, community, nationality, ethnicity, continuity, and many others – have now generated a vast theoretical literature and no longer appear as straightforward as our sources wish to represent them. And to "deconstruct" a text is not merely to refute its truth-claims or to historicize it, but to show what parts of the world it must forget in order to have a presence and how these exclusions are often reinscribed within its basic assumptions. I have, therefore, tried to combine philological, historical, and more theoretical approaches in this study, though I have tried never to deviate from the rule that anything worth saying can be said in lucid English. Too much theory can sometimes make it impossible to say anything straightforward at all, and I have a story to tell.

The study of Hellenism is also caught up in a personal narrative. The Greek educational system taught me biology and physics but caused me to hate ancient Greek. Somehow I ended up a Byzantinist in Ohio. The encouragement of student choice in American colleges and the vastly different approach to the humanities that prevails here contributed to this conversion. It was here that I devoted myself to the Greek literary and philosophical tradition and grasped its challenge to the modern predicament. However, the dialectical tension between modernity and the classics, and among national, philosophical, and professional ideas of Hellenism, superimposed onto a renewed polarization between East and West, has produced in me a series of displacements: I am always outside looking in or inside looking out at what matters. Here I glimpse the Byzantine dynamic of "inner" and "outer" wisdom, that fusion of ideal and alienation. This is the experience that I read in Gregorios of Nazianzos, Michael Psellos, Michael Choniates, and others. In their personal engagement with Greece, they too were neither here nor there. Byzantium has become for me a crucible, as among all historical societies it poses in the most intriguing way the challenge of negotiating the Greek, Roman, and Christian traditions, which challenge most of us face still. This book attempts to tell the story of that Byzantine predicament.

The greatest pleasure in writing is thanking people at the end of a long work. My department has promoted Byzantine Studies, harbored intellectual diversity, and provided friends for debate and discussion. Giorgos Anagnostou and Carolina López-Ruiz deserve special mention here. As department chairs, David Hahm and Fritz Graf have supported my work in many ways, research trips to Greece and flexible teaching schedules being the most important. The College of Humanities should also be thanked for making all this possible. I am grateful to all who read and commented on parts of this book while it was in preparation, including Mark Anderson, Patrick Baker, Garth Fowden, Gregory Jusdanis, Dimitris Krallis, and Bryan Lauer. Stephanos Efthymiades is the best friend a Byzantinist could hope for and has given me more than I can acknowledge. Ian Mladjov helped me with medieval names, titles, and genealogies. I should thank separately the Press's two readers, whose learned reports and astute criticisms led to improvements on many fronts; their sympathy is appreciated all the more given the rough state of the original submission. Michael Sharp, the editor at the Cambridge University Press, saw the book through the publication process with exemplary professionalism and efficiency. I am very grateful to them all.

Also, I owe an enormous debt to my colleagues in the field from so many countries who publish the primary sources that I use and write the books and critical studies I rely on. This work would not be possible without theirs. It is a further pleasure to know that many of them have supported me personally or professionally over the years, as teachers, friends, or models of scholarship. I want to recognize here Panagiotis Agapitos, Polymnia Athanassiadi, John Fine, Garth Fowden, Traianos Gagos, Timothy Gregory, Antony Littlewood, Paul Magdalino, Paul Stephenson, Warren Treadgold, and Ray Van Dam.

I dedicate *Hellenism in Byzantium* to my uncle Christophoros Kaldellis, in gratitude and admiration. His Hellenism is rather that of Eupalinos and Euclid; still, it is because of him that I understood what Sokrates meant when he said that the richest man is the one with the fewest needs. Our conversations have been wide-ranging and stimulating. I hope this answers some of his questions.

# Introduction

Defining Europe and "the West" more generally has become a difficult and contentious project, as political as it is theoretical and as pressing as it is unlikely to result in a broad consensus. Now that boundaries are being tested and former certainties are becoming obsolete in both theory and practice, to define anything at this level of abstraction, with so much at stake for so many, is to enter a debate where theory is immediately translated into politics (or vice versa). For example, one recent trend of thought looks to the Roman tradition as the basis of European identity, but given how it understands "Rome" this position inevitably reflects a Latin bias. Are the Slavic, Germanic, and Greek traditions and contributions – to name only a few – so marginal? In a more sophisticated version, the Roman basis is perceived as fundamentally engaged with the Greek and Hebrew pasts and so both defined by them and in a self-conscious, secondary relation to them. Yet this ignores the degree to which ancient Hellenism and Judaism were themselves also defined through constructed oppositions, and it also tends to conflate "Roman" with "Latin" and even "Catholic," choices that, as we will see, are anything but ideologically neutral.[1] Others insist that Christendom is the true crucible of the modern West. But this too imposes discomforting exclusions, and challenges the secular enterprise of modernity. How *much* of Christendom anyway? In drawing battle lines for the next century, one foreign-policy theorist placed the orthodox world outside the West. Many Greeks, on the other hand, believe that their small country was included in the EEC at such an early stage largely (or only) because of the centrality of Hellas to "western civilization," and are frustrated when that tradition is excluded from proposed definitions.

Definitions have unintended and even ironic consequences. We could, for instance, define the West as including all nations that share in the

---

[1] Brague (2002); see Gourgouris (1996) 155 for recent debates.

following three patrimonies: all believe (or did until recently) that their cultures and ideals have been shaped by Greek literature and philosophy; by Roman law and systems of governance; and by Christianity. Lawyers in these countries study Roman jurisprudence regardless of whether their laws stem directly from the Roman tradition; their Academies include departments devoted to the study of classical antiquity; and their towns are full of Christian churches, regardless of whether they are attended. Certainly, these institutions are waning, and it is unclear what, if anything, will take their place. Moreover, other nations such as Turkey may (or may not) "join the club," but when they do it will be in awareness of the fact that their histories have been shaped by a different set of cultural coordinates.

Is this, then, the "essence" of the West? Perhaps it is, as long as we heed the lesson of the past century of scholarship: such essences are not immutable entities but rather sites of contestation. The reception of the Greek, Roman, and Christian traditions has unfolded in different circumstances and diverse cultures, resulting in a wide array of values and priorities. More importantly, Athens, Rome, and Jerusalem themselves stand for ideals whose essences are always contested and often at variance. Wars and philosophical battles have been fought over the true meaning of Christianity and over the mantle of Rome in Europe. So, on the one hand, the relationship between the Church and classical culture has always been tense, but, on the other, it is now impossible to speak of "authentic" Hellenism or Christianity. There is little fixity to be found here: the West is rather a basic set of problems followed by a multitude of answers. Still, there is something to be said for the fact that at least the fundamental problems of authority have remained recognizably the same, that passions can still be aroused over ancient things. If that ceases, the basic questions themselves will have become obsolete.

This study will complicate matters considerably by identifying something in the margins that has traditionally been excluded from the debate through a combination of ignorance and prejudice, and setting it squarely in the middle. In the process it will uncover forgotten alternatives and challenge familiar ones. After all, an unintended consequence of our definition of the basic cultural parameters of "the West" is that Byzantium emerges as the quintessentially western civilization. This is not how Byzantium is usually understood – far from it – but there is the irony too.

Without intending to contribute to these wider debates, modern historians of Byzantium have defined its civilization as the convergence of

"Roman political concepts, Greek culture, and Christian faith."[2] These are not modern categories; they reflect how some Byzantine thinkers perceived the composite nature of their culture. For example, in an oration on the Crucifixion, the orator and philosopher Michael Psellos of the eleventh century commented on the trilingual inscription placed on the Cross. Latin, he explains, stands for practical excellence and political strength, as the Romans were the most energetic and powerful people; Greek stands for the study of nature, as the Greeks surpassed all with regard to knowledge of the nature of beings; and Hebrew stands for infallible theology, as the Jews were the first to understand God.[3] In another cultural sphere, it was the confluence of Greek medicine, Christian charity, and the Roman welfare state that led in Byzantium to the invention of the hospital as we know it today.[4] This heuristic model can help us understand the dynamics of Byzantine culture in many of its expressions. Synesios of Kyrene (ca. AD 400) was at once a Platonist philosopher, Christian bishop, and orator-statesman in his local province and Constantinople. Consider his statement to Anysios that "I have not chosen an apolitical philosophy ... given that the most philanthropic religion leads us to a character that cares for the polity." It has been noted that "his praise of Anysios as a soldier is typically Roman, while his ethical and political statements imply the possibility of achieving harmony between the values of Greek philosophy and the Christian religion."[5]

This book will trace the Byzantines' attempts to come to terms with these competing elements and chart their evolving reflections on the relative worth of each in the complex patrimony that they inherited from late antiquity. It was in fact the only time in history when these three cultural components ever fused together so powerfully and so clearly. It is ironic in light of this that Byzantium has not been studied with more sympathy in the West but has been dismissed as a fundamentally non-western, oriental, "other." How has this been done? First, its Roman identity has been denied or suppressed, and claimed as an exclusive possession of the West; second, Orthodoxy has been cast as oriental based on its unfamiliar (because more ancient) practices and cruel fate under the Ottomans, which shaped the biases of western travelers and early modern scholars; and, third, when it has

[2] Ostrogorsky (1969) 27. Cf. Zambelios (1857) 30–35, 490, 650, 683–691, who anticipated the attempt by modern Greek historiography to Hellenize Byzantium by downplaying its Roman component (see pp. 111–114 below). For the evolution of his thought, see Matalas (2002) 149–159.
[3] Psellos, *Oration on the Crucifixion of our Lord Jesus Christ* 359–378 (*Or. Hag.* 3). This cultural genealogy has nothing to do with the western medieval notion of the three sacred languages.
[4] Miller (1997).    [5] Synesios, *Katastasis* 1.305a–b; Bregman (1982) 168; cf. Lauxtermann (2003) 246.

not been appropriated and distorted by modern nationalism, Byzantine Hellenism has been reduced to a matter of manuscripts and Atticizing prose, which no one *wants* to read (or so we are told) and which few can anyway. In fact, many of the texts that will be studied here had not yet been published when formative views about Byzantium were put in place. But this fact does not excuse the level of the bias. For the past 500 years the West has imagined its relation to ancient Greece as a dynamic and vitally intellectual one, but even recent work continues to cast Byzantium not as a genuine participant but only as the caretaker of the classical tradition for the ultimate benefit of the West, its "true" heir.[6] So the history of *manuscripts* passes through Byzantium and the Arabs, but the history of *ideas* and *literature* routinely jumps from St. Augustine to the Renaissance. This is forgetfulness in the service of ideology.

In one sense, then, this study aims to fill in that huge gap for the benefit of all who are interested. The classical tradition was never lost in Byzantium, which is why it could not be rediscovered. There were periodic revivals, but there could be no Byzantine Renaissance, at least not in the western sense. In another sense, this study aims to correct an injustice. Byzantium has so far been represented through modern and western ideologies. That will here be reversed: cultural aspects and practices that are taken as definitively western will here be presented as basically Byzantine.

The first part of this book aims to define the cultural space occupied by Hellenism within the constitutive elements of Byzantine civilization. Specifically, the first chapter surveys the Hellenic legacies that the Byzantines inherited from antiquity, with attention to ideals and original social contexts. The emphasis is on notions of Hellenism embedded in canonical texts. Commentary and in-depth analysis have been kept to a minimum here, as this ground has been covered by others. The second and third chapters define the increasingly limited cultural space occupied by notions of Hellenism in relation especially to the Roman and Christian components of Byzantine identity. It is only against that background that we can understand the Hellenic "revivals" that occurred later, starting in the eleventh century, which were, in turn, philosophical, literary, and protonational. Specifically, the second chapter takes a new and close look at the Roman identity of Byzantium, which has amazingly been bypassed in the scholarship. Why did the Byzantines, the majority of whose ancestors

---

[6] One should compare here the Arabic reception of Greek thought, which is only now receiving serious and sympathetic attention in scholarship written for general audiences; see Gutas (1998), who, however, is hostile to Byzantium.

had been Greek, call and firmly believe themselves to be Romans? A new thesis will be advocated: Byzantium was not "a universal, Christian, multi-ethnic empire," as all think today, but a nation-state like most modern nation-states, in this case the nation-state of the Romans. The ancient Greeks, along with many other peoples and cultures, were assimilated to it and kept its identity, in various forms, for almost two thousand years.

The third chapter will examine the tensions between Christianity and the dominant Hellenic culture of late antiquity (in ca. AD 100–400). The identification of Hellenes and pagans was less accidental than it might seem at first: the Fathers of the Church knew that classical culture was contaminated not only by the gods and theology of the Greeks but also by their "worldly" values. It will be argued here that they never satisfactorily resolved those tensions which, moreover, were not primarily theological (as is usually assumed) but ethical.

The revivals of Hellenism in the middle period will be the subject of the second part of the book, a narrative of intellectual and cultural history that explores the gradual transformations of Byzantine identity that took place after the eleventh century, with emphasis on the role played in them by the reception of the classical tradition. The rise of independent philosophical thought and the aggression of the western (Latin) "Romans" challenged the Christian faith and the Roman identity of the empire. For some, philosophical Hellenism spurred the displacement of traditional Orthodoxy, in both metaphysics and ethics (Chapter 4); for others, classicizing performance (understood broadly) was energized as a cultural and existential ideal that pushed against the boundaries of its former confinement (Chapter 5); while in the thirteenth century Hellenism acquired the weight of national discourse and complemented the rhetoric of New Rome (Chapter 6). Throughout this period, the advancement of learning made high culture (*paideia*) a prominent pursuit for many, including emperors, bishops, scholars, philosophers, and high officials. The classical Greek legacy converted many to a cultural vision of Hellenism through the intense personal involvement and even enthusiasm it has always been able to generate. Through their cultivation of Attic Greek, Byzantine Hellenists had closer access and a greater stylistic affinity to the classics than has been possible ever since.

The two parts of the book are, therefore, separated by what appears to be a quite substantial gap, which stretches from the end of late antiquity to the mid-eleventh century. Hellenism was a burning question in late antiquity and became a preoccupation after the eleventh century. But between AD 400 and 1050 there was little interest in Greek identity, despite the flourishing of scholarship and classicism in the years 400–640 and their revival after the late eighth century. On the question of what it could mean to be Greek in a more personal or collective sense, thinkers of the later period had to rediscover what had lain dormant in their texts and come to terms with it anew. As they picked up where late antiquity had left off, the two parts of the book are joined in a kind of counterpoint. The intermediate period is surveyed in a brief Interlude.

"Hellenism" is, of course, a huge and, in its totality, an unmanageable historical category. Depending on how we define it – linguistically, ethnically, nationally, culturally, or whether in terms of manuscripts, ideas, and identities – it encompasses such a vast body of evidence that no book will ever do it justice. Preliminary studies of its history in Byzantium lump together speech, literature, *paideia*, rhetoric, philosophy, art, and heresy.[7] Some methodological comments are therefore in order. This book is a study of Hellenic identity and will examine what it meant to be Greek at different times in Byzantium and why and how those ideas and their social context changed. It focuses on identity as discursively constructed and therefore on writers and intellectuals, who were admittedly a minority among the Byzantines, though an effort will also be made to determine the social scope of these ideas, especially in the thirteenth century. Studies of this specific problem to date consist of articles in which detailed theoretical analysis and the close reading of texts have not been feasible, as well as one dated, short, and inaccessible German dissertation that sweeps through the centuries.[8]

For reasons that will become clear, before the thirteenth century Hellenic identity in Byzantium was largely derived from one's stance toward the classical tradition, whose many aspects were not always harmonious, for example poetic, philosophical, or rhetorical. These, in turn, could be valorized and integrated into social and literary life in different and even contradictory ways. This explains the subtitle of this book, in which the conjunction "and" should be understood as limiting the second term: the reception of the classical tradition is studied only to the degree that it was implicated in the transformations of Hellenic identity. My aim has not been to compile catalogues of manuscripts, commentaries, lexika, or necessarily to determine who read what and how, or evaluate Byzantine

---

[7] E.g., Garzya (1985).

[8] Lechner (1954), limited to historical and patristic sources; cf. Jüthner (1923), a solid summary of the ancient evidence; more recently Garzya (1985) and (1992); Magdalino (1991a); Gounaridis (1996); Koder (2003); Dagron (2005b), all brief articles.

classical scholarship, though these were the basic modes and instruments of the reception of the classical tradition in Byzantium.[9]

Other topics of historical inquiry are more rigorously excluded by my focus. The reader will not find here an objective history of the "Greek-speakers," which would have to cope with many more "Hellenisms" than are studied here (e.g., the demography and languages of medieval southern Italy and Asia Minor after the Turkish inroads).[10] Nor will I discuss here the fascinating question of how Byzantines interpreted and reused the physical monuments of ancient Greece. This is the subject of a complementary and forthcoming book on *The Christian Parthenon: Classicism and Pilgrimage in Byzantine Athens* (to appear in 2008), where I demonstrate how those monuments claimed a prominent place in the landscape and local identities of Byzantium, albeit a place that is not always discursively defined in our sources.

Therefore, for all that it testifies to the vitality of the Hellenic tradition, this book is not concerned primarily with the question of Greek continuity, which involves diverse areas of research such as linguistics, settlement patterns, and folklore. These are valuable fields of study, but land demarcations, grammar, patterns of myth and metaphor in folklore, and customs such as bull sacrifices and ritual laments that have survived from antiquity to the present, were not understood by the Byzantines to be essentially Hellenic. Even animal sacrifices could be rededicated to saints and thereby take on an anti-pagan significance, which in the mind of some Byzantines would have made them anti-Hellenic by definition. We must "differentiate between ancient evidence of certain social and textual practices and ancient evidence that explicitly attests those practices as constitutive or expressive of a collective identity."[11] In other words, continuity of practice – which separate research leads me to believe was in fact considerable – is not the same as continuity of identity. Still, the history presented here, much of it for the first time, and the conclusions drawn from it, will surely be of interest to those who do study the more general questions of Greek continuity.

Many studies give the impression that Hellenism is an immutable entity that must be discovered behind the changing appearances of history, a

[9] Wilson (1983); Lemerle (1986); and Lauxtermann (2003), esp. ch. 3, for poetry.
[10] Cf. the titles of Vryonis (1971) and Martin (2005).
[11] McCoskey (2003) 98. Myth and metaphor: Alexiou (2002), also revisiting her study of the ritual lament. Folklore – both the discipline and its subject – was not recruited into the construction of Greek identity prior to the nineteenth century: ibid. 33; Herzfeld (1986); Skopetea (1988) 173, 194–196. Sacrifices: Kaldellis (2002) 179–181. For similar survivals, see Constantelos (1998) ch.3.

quasi-metaphysical assumption that has affected a variety of fields. For example, in the past historians tried to ascertain whether certain theological positions were more "Hellenic" in their "essence," say, whether the Iconophiles were more Hellenic compared to the "oriental" Iconoclasts, and so on. Such readings, now largely discredited, have had a long career but there now seems to be little prospect for their revival. They have no basis in the sources. This is a more delicate issue when it comes to the arguments advanced by modern Greek nationalism, which have not always respected the theoretical distinctions among biological continuity, cultural profiles, and national identity. Some Greek scholars cite later Byzantine claims of Hellenic identity as proof of the empire's underlying Hellenic "essence" throughout its history.[12] This methodology should be resisted, for those claims were the products of specific historical circumstances and need to be examined on their own terms; they presuppose the developments that are studied in this book. It is not our job (or right) as historians to tell our subjects whether they "really were" Greeks, but to understand *what* they may have meant by it when they said it and, if possible, *why* they said it. Besides, many Greek intellectuals and historians are now less interested in ethnic continuity, however strong the arguments in its favor may appear to be, than in the diverse historical forms of their national culture; and national pride has more to gain anyway from recognizing the adaptability of the Greek tradition and the power of its canonical literature to seduce even the most unreceptive of cultures.

Unfortunately, it has not been possible in this book to trace the history of Byzantine Hellenism all the way to the end of the empire's existence. Three main movements have been identified: Hellenism as philosophy in the eleventh century; as elite culture (*paideia*) and rhetorical performance in the twelfth; and as protonationalism in the thirteenth. The effort to describe these developments, along with the conflicts and transformations of late antiquity, has resulted in a long monograph already, and even there coverage has been too dense in places. Much remains to be done. Most of the authors discussed in the second part of this study have not been translated and so have not generated much secondary bibliography. There is often none to cite at all. Along with the limitations of my own expertise, these are some reasons why 1261 was chosen as a terminal date, though many exciting chapters in the history of Byzantine Hellenism occurred afterwards. In particular, two major figures stand at either end of that later period,

---

[12] E.g., Vryonis (1999); Missiou (2000). See pp. 111–112 below.

Theodoros Metochites and Georgios Gemistos "Plethon," who require separate monographs. I have no claim on them.

By the late thirteenth century the labels and reception of Hellenism had experienced such transformations (and ironies) as to make the period covered here conceptually satisfying. The Hellenic nationalism of the emperor Theodoros II Laskaris (d. 1258), with which I conclude, stands philosophically between the anti-barbarian Hellenism of the Persian Wars described by Herodotos and the Romanticism of the Greek Revolution.

PART I

*Greeks, Romans, and Christians
in late antiquity*

CHAPTER I

# *"We too are Greeks!": the legacies of Hellenism*

People speaking the language we call Greek have lived continually in the Aegean region since at least 1600 BC, and possibly earlier. Greek is, moreover, one of the most conservative and enduring languages in history. Among those still spoken it has probably changed the least in the past three and a half thousand years, by any indicator. This is an astonishing feat of continuity and provides an obvious and fair point of national pride. But historians should be cautious of arguments for national continuity whose main foundation is language. Granted, there have been Greek-speakers in the mainland since the age of the Mycenaean palaces, but they have not always regarded themselves as Greeks – as *Hellenes*. On the basis of Hittite evidence and Homer, it now seems certain that the Mycenaeans called themselves Achaians, a term arising from historical circumstances and encoding values that we cannot now recover. The ethnonym *Hellenes* did not emerge until much later, roughly at the time of Homer in the eighth century BC, as even ancient historians such as Thucydides realized. Greek identity is a historical and social construct: it arose at a particular moment in history in accordance with a particular set of social and ideological coordinates; it then changed and evolved, as all human things do; and then went into abeyance for about a thousand years, the period that will be covered in this study.[1]

The fact that Hellenic identity was in fact reconstituted in modern times – roughly two centuries ago, and very successfully at that – complicates inquiries into its historical evolution. Interest in the history of Hellenism among historians today is usually inspired by a fascination with classical culture or a concern with the national identity of modern Greece, which is usually a personal concern. As it happens, however, only in those two relatively brief periods – namely before the international diffusion of Greek culture in the fourth century BC and then after the foundation of

---

[1] Achaians: Latacz (2004); Hellenes: Hall (2002).

the modern Greek state in the 1830s – do we find what may be called a national Greek consciousness, namely the belief that being Greek entails sharing a common language, religion, way of life, and ethnic descent. Despite huge differences in historical context, these two views, ancient and modern, are certainly more similar to each other than to the permutations of Hellenism that prevailed in the intervening period. The result is a degree of interference, as students and exponents of "classical" and "modern" Greece echo each other, for instance by taking their bearings from that very polarity. This has in turn given rise to a misleading picture of continuity, especially among historians who know little of Byzantium. National Hellenism is valorized and extended backwards and forwards to include that long, unknown, and unliked period (which happens to make up the single largest block of Greek historical time). However, as we will see, in the 2,000 years that separated the Revolution of 1821 from Alexander the Great, very different versions of Hellenism emerged and took hold.

The present chapter summarizes how notions of Hellenic identity evolved between classical times and the cultural movement of the Second Sophistic. Its aim is twofold: first, to present the variety of ideas, images, symbols, and associations of Hellenism to which the Byzantines were exposed in the literary tradition that they inherited from antiquity. Many of the texts discussed below were known to Byzantine scholars and contributed to the revival of Hellenism that began in the eleventh century, though not all ancient constructions were recycled in the Christian empire. We will present the full range of options from which the scholars of Byzantium selected and modified what best served their needs. Second, by sketching the evolution of Hellenism in antiquity, this survey will offer a diachronic context against which the Byzantine revival itself can best be appreciated by those interested in the broader history of the topic, including both its impressive continuities and its surprising ruptures. Emphasis, then, will be placed on how Hellenic identity was constructed and deconstructed in texts that later came to constitute the Hellenic legacy of Byzantium. Attention will also be given to the particular historical circumstances that propelled the ongoing debate in antiquity.

CLASSICAL GREECE

A broad sense of a common Hellenic identity had developed among the Greek-speaking city-states and loosely federated tribal nations of the Aegean region even before they found themselves in the path of Persian imperialism. Though they did not provide a common ethnonym, the epic poems of Homer offered a framework for cultural convergence – which we call Panhellenism – that was based on language, religion, shared tales, and an aristocratic competitive ethos. Myths and heroic genealogies could then supply the putative link of common descent, and common institutions in neutral locations, especially the oracle of Delphi and the games at Olympia, focalized the sharing of religion and culture. But it was really the threat of Persian conquest in 480 BC that forced some of the warring cities and kingdoms to develop a stronger and active sense of Hellenic unity. The need for it was made all the more urgent by the dramatic failure of the Greeks to unite against the invader. With the fate of Greece in the balance, the Spartans sent envoys to the Athenians to dissuade them against the pro-Persian counsel of Alexandros I of Makedonia. The Athenians' response, recorded by Herodotos, contains a famous and virtually unique definition of Hellenism as an ethnic and national identity: "There is our common Greekness (τὸ Ἑλληνικόν): we are one in blood and one in language; those shrines of the gods belong to us all in common, and the sacrifices in common, and then there are our customs, bred of a common upbringing. It would be indecent for the Athenians to prove traitors to all these" (8.144.2). Though the words were no doubt rhetorical and the context diplomatic, the Athenians thereby acknowledged a patriotic duty to the rest of Greece. And a number of cities later presented the defeat of Xerxes as a victory for all the Greeks.[2]

It was belief in blood-links that made Hellenism an ethnic identification, even if the Greeks had no word that corresponded exactly with our (very recent) neologism "ethnicity." *Ethnos* itself was too ambiguous, given that it could refer to any kind of group with a common identity, including the citizens of a polis or the members of the female sex. When used in connection with populations larger than a polis that were believed to have a common descent, for example (and in ascending order of inclusiveness) Thessalians, Aiolians, or Hellenes, the basis of *ethnos* was *genos* and *syngeneia* (birth and kinship).[3] Herodotos does sometimes call the Greeks collectively a *genos* (1.143.2), yet, in contrast to the rhetoric of modern nationalism, "blood" is rarely invoked in our texts. It was remembered in crisis and diplomacy, if not always successfully. Desperately seeking support for the Ionian revolt against Persia, Aristagoras of Miletos reminded the Spartan king Kleomenes in 499 BC that the Ionians are "of your blood" (5.49.2). In any case, such claims could only be established through heroic

[2] Hall (2002) 182–183; for Homer and Panhellenism, Nagy (1990) chs. 2–3.
[3] Jones (1996); Hall (1997) 34–40; for *ethnos* as a polis grown huge, Aristotle, *Politics* 7.4 (1326b3–5).

genealogies, which were very malleable. Xerxes himself appealed to the citizens of Argos as distant relatives, citing their connection through the hero Perseus. This could be seen as a mere diplomatic overture, but genealogy had its place. As only Greeks defined by descent were allowed to compete at Olympia, the games became a functional definition of who was and who was not Greek at any time. When Alexandros I of Makedonia, known by the disarmingly ambiguous name "Philhellene," wished to compete, he was required to prove his ethnicity, which he did by showing, to the organizers' satisfaction, that his royal ancestors had come from Argos. But in this case the "proof" probably applied only to the king, not his subjects.[4] Other functional standards existed in Greece and abroad, for example membership in the Hellenion, a common temple for Greeks established in 570 BC in the trading post of Naukratis in Egypt.

Hellenic *syngeneia* was mostly established through myth. The eponymous founders of cities, royal lines, and nations (*ethnê*), were integrated into a single (though constantly evolving) genealogy that began with Hellen, the son of Deukalion (the hero who survived the flood). A consensus has now emerged among historians that these heroic genealogies represented not dim memories of the Bronze Age and the migrations that followed it but attempts by historical Greeks to exploit the past by fashioning heroic connections to serve them now and in the future.[5] Blood was therefore less important in times of peace than the symbolic relationships established in legend and varied to suit circumstance. In the Archaic age, genealogical grafting had served more the desire of ruling clans to be heroized than of whole peoples to be Hellenized, but in later periods the heroes were believed to have sired whole nations. Genealogy also had a "scientific" function, as it enabled the Greeks to make sense of foreign peoples, regardless of whether the latter even knew their Greek heroic ancestors, e.g., the Persians who were supposedly descended from Perseus.[6]

Recent scholarship has rightly viewed Hellenic identity as a constantly evolving historical construct, reinforced by discourses that served the needs and ambitions of the moment. Yet this does not mean that it did not reflect very real cultural commonalities. Almost any, say, Theban who traveled abroad would quickly realize that he had far more in common in terms of language, worship, politics, and culture with the Athenian he killed in last

---

[4] Xerxes: Herodotos 7.150.2; Alexandros: 5.22; cf. 8.137–139. Olympia and Panhellenism: Renfrew (1988) 23; Ioakimidou (2000) 75–80. Makedonians: Stoppie (2003), citing previous bibliography.
[5] Hall (1997); (2002); McInerney (1999); and Malkin (2001); cf. Braund (1994) ch. 1, for myth in early Georgian–Greek relations.
[6] Malkin (1998) 19, 135–136, 154, 170, and *passim*.

year's border skirmish than with any Phoenician or Egyptian. Yet the contours of Panhellenism hardly worried the average Greek most of the time. Other overlapping and competing identities – civic, gender, class, religious, tribal, mercantile, and philosophical – were usually more pressing. History and personality decided which of these roles was operational at any moment. But we need not linger on them here, for they had disappeared by Byzantine times, when the need to define Hellenism in relation to Christianity and the Roman order suppressed the internal complexity of ancient Greek society and gave its cultural monuments a compelling (if to us historically spurious) homogeneity. What remained was mostly the texts, their constructions and deconstructions. Besides, even in classical times the imagined coherence of the Hellenic people was not shaken by the existence of subordinate ethnic groupings, such as Dorians or Ionians, or by the fact that the cities were often at war against each other.

The challenge to ethnic Panhellenism was issued instead by those who recognized that blood was as fictitious as the myths that proved it and that only custom and law were in the end paramount. Herodotos, after all, mentions blood not in his own voice but in speeches that he ascribes to others. It has been suggested that in his account of the famous response of the Athenians to the Spartans, he ranked the components of Hellenism in what *he* took to be an order of increasing importance: blood, language, religion, and custom.[7] Herodotos elsewhere claims (albeit in a confusing passage) that the residents of Attica were originally Pelasgians who spoke a barbarian language but later "became one with the Greeks" when they learned Greek (1.56–58). This drives a wedge between the Athenians' mythistory of autochthony and their claim to represent the pinnacle of Hellenic culture and to be blood-relatives of other Greeks.[8] Herodotos could separate the historical question of origins from the political acts by which cities established a social consensus around valorized cultural artifacts and myths and thereby created ethnic identities. That consensus, he knew, was malleable and changed in response to new challenges. He also suspected that the term "barbarian" basically encoded alterity as such and was culturally relative: the Egyptians, he says, likewise called barbarians those who do not speak Egyptian (2.158.5).

---

[7] Hall (2002) 190–194.
[8] Thomas (2000) 117 122; (2001) 222 225. Herodotos' position on the Pelasgian question is complicated by what he says in 2.51, 6.137–139, and 8.44. For his view that Ionian ethnic identity was malleable, see McInerney (1999) 31–33, 159; (2001) 57–59. For Euripides' deconstruction of the Greek–barbarian polarity, see Saïd (2002).

The same deconstructive insight shapes the brilliant argument that Thucydides presents in the introduction of his *History* (1.2–18). The original inhabitants of Greece, he argues, were Pelasgian, and the coming of Hellen and his sons did not result in a common Hellenic identity. Thucydides famously notes that even Homer, who lived long after the Trojan War, did not call the enemies of Troy "Greeks." The poet seems to have been unaware of the division of mankind into Greeks and barbarians (1.3).[9] The Greeks, therefore, were once no different from barbarians and only gradually developed their distinctively Greek cultural characteristics. Thus, those who developed less in this direction offer glimpses into what Greeks used to be in the distant past, namely barbarians (1.5–6; cf. 2.68.2: the Amphilochian Argives learned Greek – ἡλληνίσθησαν – from the Ambrakiots).[10] Needless to say, Thucydides despised patriotic myths, even those of his own city (1.20). This fact has generally been forgotten in the recent attack on the Greek "canon" as encoding hegemonic ideologies: most Greek authors – especially poets, historians, and philosophers – critique and even refute rather than promote the ideologies that structured their societies, including notions of Hellenic identity.

Isokrates, a key author in the Byzantine curriculum, was therefore being more eloquent than original when he declared famously in his *Panegyrikos* (ca. 380 BC) that Athens has "so outdistanced the rest of mankind in thought and speech that its students have become the teachers of everyone else; Athens has made it so that the name of the Greeks designates not a race (*genos*) but a mindset, and those are called Greeks who share in our culture rather than our common stock (*physis*)" (50). This claim, which seems to advocate an inclusive and non-racial Hellenic identity, has often been taken as a prescient formulation of what was about to occur in the wake of Alexander's conquests. But in fact its author was no true champion of universal Hellenism. Isokrates was advocating a Panhellenic expedition against "the barbarian" that would solve the domestic problems of Greece, such as the excess of unemployed mercenaries, an idea that he admitted was a rhetorical cliché (15). Greeks owed it to themselves to become rich on barbarian backs (173–174). Isokrates had little interest in spreading Greek culture to all-out barbarians; what he was aiming at in formulating this famous definition was for *other Greeks* to recognize the supremacy of *Athenian culture* and specifically of his own school, which he was constantly

---

[9] Thucydides forgot that the poet called the Karians "barbarian in speech" (*Iliad* 2.867) or else his text did not include the line: see Strabon 14.2.28 (and below).

[10] See Malkin (1998) 144–145 for this passage.

advertising. To be a true Greek, one had to study with Isokrates.[11] It is in the orators, then, more than in any other place, that we find ideologies being promoted at Athens.

Beyond Isokrates, the "cultural" definition of Hellenism, in fact the very notion of "the" barbarian, seem to have been of Athenian design. It was Athens that defined itself as the antithesis of this newly imagined barbarism, whether prompted by the memory of Marathon and Salamis or by a civic ideology that relied heavily on the contrast between a supposedly autochthonous citizen body and slaves who were of mostly barbarian origin. Yet Athens was so large a city that Herodotos called the inhabitants of Attica an *ethnos* unto themselves (1.57.3). Their policy of granting citizenship liberally to thousands, including Samians, Plataians, and the children of resident foreigners, led the Athenians to found their unity more on culture than on their myth of a common descent, which few, perhaps, took to be more than a symbol.[12] At the same time, Athens also felt the need to justify its exploitative hegemony over other Greeks. To a degree, then, the unity of "Hellas" in the classical age was a mirror fashioned by Athens to reflect its own imperial glory: Greece was invented and projected precisely so that Athens could be its Capital, its Savior, and its School. By comparison even other Greeks, such as the Spartans, were implicitly barbaric, for "the barbarian" was, after all, only the inversion of Athenian ideals.[13] And the centrality of the Athenians in the canon of classical literature – indeed, the fact that Athenians created that canon and set its language – ensured that this image of Athens and the barbarian was fixed before the eyes of posterity. One of the most influential speeches studied in Byzantium was the *Panathenaic Oration* of the second-century AD orator Ailios Aristeides. Its main thesis, following Isokrates, was that all Greeks owed their character and achievements to Athens.[14] It is slightly surreal to imagine how different the Greek legacy would have been had the texts of,

---

[11] Cf. Isokrates, *Philippos* 106–108; see Bloom (1995) in general. For Isokrates' intentions and complex view of Hellenism and barbarism, see Usher (1993); Flower (2000) 124; Saïd (2001) 276–286; in Byzantium, Voliotis (1988) pt. 2. The cliché of Greeks uniting against barbarians can also be found in Plato's quasi-parodic *Menexenos* 239a–243c.

[12] Cohen (2000).

[13] Athens and Greece: Perikles in Thucydides 2.41.1; Isokrates, *Panegyrikos* 78–81; *Antidosis* 295–296, 299; Hippias in Plato, *Protagoras* 337d–e; "Thucydides" in the *Greek Anthology* 7.45: "Athens, the Greece of Greece." See Most (1997); Hall (2002) 8, 186–187. Sparta: Too (1995) 147; Thomas (2001) 218. Athens and "the" barbarian: Coleman (1997) 189, 192–193, 196. According to Herodotos 9.11, the Spartans differentiated between foreign Greeks and barbarians.

[14] Ailios Aristeides, *Or.* 1. For Athens in Aristeides, see Saïd (2001) 293–294; in Byzantium, Hunger (1978) v. I, 75.

say, Lesbos survived rather than those of Athens, with Alkaios and Sappho instead of Aischylos and Sophokles, and Hellanikos instead of Thucydides.

Civic patriotism was, in the end, more important than Hellenism, which explains why Panhellenism was never translated into political reality, though such a reality was perfectly conceivable. Aristotle showed how close the Greeks were to imagining themselves as a politically unified nation when he said that they could rule the world if only they had a single state.[15] Beyond even that degree of intra-Hellenic universality, philosophy had proven that the distinction between Greeks and barbarians was also culturally constructed. Herodotos knew from the Sophists that Hellenism, by whatever definition, was a function of custom (*nomos*), not nature (*physis*). Antiphon had explicitly taught that "we are all by nature alike fully made to be either barbarians or Hellenes."[16]

Plato took philosophy itself to the point where it transcended Hellenism. Ironically, he has been accused of chauvinism by making Sokrates argue in the *Republic* that the Greeks are kin and should treat each other and the barbarians accordingly (469b–471b) – yet another expression of the latent national idea. But it is missed that this is only one step in the gradual process by which Sokrates educates Glaukon away from his initial Athenocentric bias. Later in the dialogue he suggests that the conjunction of philosophy and political power proposed in the *Republic* may have already occurred "in some barbarian place, far outside our field of vision" (499c). And when, in the *Phaedo*, Sokrates addresses the question of the survival of philosophy after his death, he suggests to his companions that they seek a guide wherever they may find him: "Greece is a spacious land and there are many virtuous men in it, but many too are the races of the barbarians that you must search through" (78a). True philosophy knew neither ethnic nor even narrowly cultural boundaries. Much later, during the reign of Hadrian, a notable of the Lykian town of Oinoanda named Diogenes had a stoa built with a massive inscription 80 meters long on it that laid out the tenets of the philosophy of Epikouros. Diogenes addressed his message to "all Greeks and barbarians," noting that "all people have a single fatherland, the entire earth, and a single home, the cosmos."[17] It does not matter here exactly what Diogenes meant by a Greek; what is

---

[15] Aristotle, *Politics* 7.7 (1327b30–33). For Panhellenism in the fourth century, see Flower (2000) esp. 98, 105, citing previous bibliography. Cf. Poseidippos fr. 28.

[16] Text, translation, and discussion in Thomas (2000) 131–132.

[17] Gordon (1996) 29–33. Cf. Demokritos fr. 247; Euripides fr. 777 and 1047; Sokrates in Cicero, *Tusculan Disputation* 5.37; Plutarch, *On Exile* 7 (*Moralia* 600f–601a); Arrianos, *The Discourses of Epiktetos* 1.9.1; also Dion Chrysostomos, *Or.* 13.32 (*In Athens*); Marcus Aurelius, *Meditations* 6.44.

important is that his aim was to transcend that distinction. The temptation to overcome the polarity of Greeks and barbarians was one that Greek philosophy flirted with down to late antiquity, often with mixed results, as we will see when we turn to the Neoplatonists.

## THE HELLENISTIC WORLD

Diogenes the Epicurean compels our attention. What draws it is less the content of his manifesto than the fact that it was inscribed for all to see in the highlands of Lykia. What made it possible for Lykia to produce a man such as he? Compare the epigrammatist Meleagros (ca. 100 BC), who was raised in Tyre and retired to Kos, but had been born in Gadara, "an Attic land, but among the Assyrians ... If I am a Syrian, what wonder is there in that? It is only one world that we inhabit, stranger: the world."[18] Though he wrote excellent Greek verse, he seems to have known Aramaic and Phoenician as well, or at least boasted that he could greet people in foreign languages (as would later the Byzantine poet Ioannes Tzetzes, perhaps imitating Meleagros).

To account for such men in places that would have been regarded as irredeemably barbaric in the fifth century BC, we must turn to the diffusion abroad of Greek culture and power. Before the reign of Alexander this was balanced out by the importation of foreign cultural elements into Greece, but export and colonization greatly expanded in scope after the foundation of the Hellenistic kingdoms and continued apace under Roman rule. There is no need to discuss here the details of a process that produced thousands and perhaps millions of new "Greeks" as it extinguished dozens of local identities around the Mediterranean. The general contours of this history are known, though regional diversity complicates matters and the mechanisms of cultural negotiation and fusion on the ground elude us. Still, by the later empire, people who would have been considered barbarians in the time of Perikles had exchanged their native languages for Greek and had taken on a thoroughly Greek cultural profile. Their societies adapted to the institutions of the city-state. Public art and architecture followed Greek norms. The council hall, gymnasium, temple, and stoa became the focal points of public life along with the culturally determinative activities that took place in them.[19] Local gods and legends of national origin were

---

[18] *Greek Anthology* 7.417–419; cf. 4.1. See Hengel (1974) v. I, 84–85; Millar (1987a) 130; and Geiger (2002) 233–234 for language and identity in his poems.
[19] Surveys in A. H. M. Jones (1940) and (1971).

"translated" into their Greek equivalents or grafted directly onto the Greek genealogy. The citizens of Tyre and other Phoenician cities were allowed to compete in the Olympic games. Local histories were often forgotten, except by a few erudite scholar-priests, and even they disappeared during the empire, even in Egypt. Above all, the education of the elite consisted of Greek *paideia*: Homer, rhetoric, and philosophy sublimated the cultural homogeneity of the Hellenistic and later of the eastern Roman world.[20]

We will leave for later certain conceptual problems regarding the nature and extent of Hellenization to outline first the mechanisms of this gradual but unmistakable transformation. Colonies and royal foundations transplanted thousands of Greeks to Asia Minor and the Near East. In sufficient numbers and density these alone could stimulate crucial changes in neighboring barbarian societies. Writing about the indigenous inhabitants of his native Sicily, the historian Diodoros noted that "on account of the multitude of Greeks who sailed there, the natives both learned their speech and, being acculturated in their way of life, in the end changed their barbarian speech and even their name, being called Sikeliotai," i.e., Sicilian Greeks (5.6.5). The fact that this happened at all is more important for our purposes than whether they were "active" or "passive" agents in their own Hellenization.[21] No matter how the words are parsed, we are clearly dealing with cultures that failed to maintain their identity in the face of powerful and more seductive Hellenic models. We should also note that in Sicily this occurred even though the land was not unified politically nor governed by a Greek court. In regions that by contrast were under Greek power, many native communities converted out of self-interest. By learning Greek and presenting a Greek cultural profile they could communicate more effectively with the bureaucracies in the new centers of power like Alexandria and Antioch, prove their loyalty to the kings, and even join the ranks of the elite themselves. It was only a matter of time before this persona, assumed at first for purposes of exchange and advancement, was internalized. For their part, the kings and their officers favored those who respected Greek cultural codes, and the favor of the kings was coveted. In the lands that would later form the core of the Byzantine empire, people such as Phrygians, Kappadokians, and Thrakians, had formerly derived whatever coherence they had from their native dynasties. When these were overthrown, their

[20] For education, see Marrou (1956) esp. part 2. Games and other aspects of Hellenization: Sartre (2005) 7–10, 86–87 (the Nabataeans), 152 (Syrian cities), 161–162 (myths), 187–188 (nomenclature) and ch. 9: "Hellenization and Indigenous Cultures." On Phoenician athletes, see also Hengel (1974) v. I, 71.
[21] Debated by many, e.g., Antonaccio (2001) 126–127.

languages replaced or complemented by Greek, and their communal cults Hellenized, there was not much left to differentiate them from each other or even from the new Greek colonies, their neighbors.

Summaries inevitably simplify. The process described above occurred neither uniformly nor immediately. But, again, we are not interested here in the multiplicity of overlapping and evolving identities that emerged in the vast new Greek kingdoms, whether ethnic, political, religious, or philosophical. They are the subject of a large and sophisticated scholarly bibliography. Rather, we must look at this world from the later viewpoint of Byzantium, which was its direct heir, and focus on the transformations of Hellenism that it promoted. The key development of the new world created by Alexander and his successors was that it was now possible and easy for both individuals and entire communities to become Greek, often to the point of completely losing their native traditions. To be sure, the most ancient and the more primitive peoples of the Near East could absorb foreign culture without disrupting their sense of identity, which was, like that of the Greeks, complex in practice, diverse in origin, and greatly changed from centuries of Persian rule, as Plato had noted in the *Laws* (692e–693a). They too could do what the author of the Platonic *Epinomis* boasted: "whatever the Greeks receive from the barbarians, this they elevate to a higher perfection" (987d). The Karians, for instance, borrowed much from the Greeks in classical times and were extensively urbanized and Hellenized by their Hekatomnid rulers, but the latter, especially Maussollos, managed to create a bilingual dynastic culture that fused Greek, Persian, and Karian elements in a unique way.[22]

But it was not to last. The Hekatomnid dynasty passed into history along with the Persian empire, while Hellenization accelerated under Makedonian and Roman rule.[23] For instance, there was nothing notably Karian about Euthydemos and Hybreas, described by Strabon as leading "citizens and orators" of Mylasa in the first century BC (14.2.24). Their social roles were thoroughly determined by the expectations of Greek *paideia*. Yet in Hekatomnid times Mylasa had been one of the chief non-Greek cities of Karia. In other regions, historians can sometimes track the gradual disappearance of non-Hellenic identities, especially when a continuous body of evidence is available, such as in the papyri of Egypt. "The Thrakians of Egypt," for example, "adopted Greek names, they used the

[22] Hornblower (1982) 11–12, 250 ff., 352–353; Ruzicka (1992) 6–7, 29–32, 35–38, 42–44, 48–49, 52–53; Boardman (2000) 14. So too the kings of Kommagene: Sartre (2005) 24, 75.

[23] Hornblower (1982) ch. 12, esp. 343 ff.; Ruzicka (1992) 156.

Greek language, the army made them familiar with the Greek way of life. They worshipped the same gods as the Greeks . . . In the end, there was no cultural feature left by which they could (or, for that matter, would) distinguish themselves from the Greeks. At that moment they vanished from history."[24] The antiquarian Pausanias would later mention the Hellenistic athlete Nikostratos from Kilikia, "who had nothing in common with the Kilikians except the name" (5.21.10).

This new world called for a new terminology. The polarity of Greek and barbarian was adjusted to accommodate widespread cultural conversion. Strabon of Amaseia in Pontos, a geographer and historian of the age of Augustus and Tiberius, notes in his discussion of the term "barbarian" that "we," i.e., presumably Greeks, "misused the word as though it were an ethnic label, setting up a distinction between Greeks and all others." In his eyes it made little sense to lump everyone together just because they spoke "thickly or harshly." He further suggests that Karians were called "barbarian in speech" by Homer (*Iliad* 2.867) not because their language was foreign but because they spoke Greek with a harsh accent. The Karians, he adds, were among the first to come into contact with Greeks "at a time when all the others had *not yet* seriously engaged with the Greeks nor tried to live in a Greek way or learn *our* language" (14.2.28).

So far so good. But what, then, did it mean to be Greek? In his polemic against Eratosthenes of Kyrene, Strabon notes that the third-century BC scholar rejected the division of mankind into Greeks and barbarians as well as the advice given to Alexander (presumably by Aristotle) to treat Greeks as friends and barbarians as enemies. Eratosthenes had reasoned that the proper division should be between good and bad people and that both could be found among *both* Greeks *and* barbarians. But, Strabon countered somewhat speciously, what else does it mean to be Greek than to "have lawful and civil qualities and to be familiar with *paideia* and the art of speaking?" Alexander was therefore right to accept Aristotle's advice because by definition barbarians are uncivilized and Greeks civilized.[25] Strabon thereby suggests that Eratosthenes was not really saying anything different from Alexander's advisors but attacks him for thinking he was saying something different. We should not view this dispute as a quibble, saying with Voltaire that "Greeks were cunning people, and split hairs in four,"[26] for the two views were ultimately quite different. Eratosthenes was not claiming that the two divisions, good and bad people on the one hand

[24] Goudriaan (1992) 79.    [25] Strabon 1.4.9; see the sources cited by Coleman (1997) 193.
[26] Voltaire, *Philosophical Dictionary*, 47.

and Greeks and barbarians on the other, produced extensionally identical groups, but rather that good and bad people are distributed among different ethnic or cultural groups. Human worth is, in this schema, independent of specific cultural forms, and has to do with universal moral standards. For Strabon, however, only those who possess Greek *paideia* can be virtuous and so, conversely, no one immoral or uneducated can be a true Greek. Granted, Strabon's definition does eliminate ethnicity as a formal factor, but what people, after all, were more likely to lack Greek *paideia* but those barbarians whom Alexander was advised to treat with hostility on ethnic and cultural grounds? In practice, then, Strabon's "ethical" Hellenism verges close to the ethnic criteria rejected by Eratosthenes, in addition to having a strong class bias (reinscribed as a moral distinction), for *paideia* could not be acquired even by all ethnic Greeks.

Hellenization – and its reverse – were discussed extensively in antiquity. The literary critic Dionysios of Halikarnassos, who moved in the same circles as Strabon, argued in his antiquarian history that Rome was originally founded by Greeks but over time they mixed with barbarians who spoke other languages and practiced different customs and so eventually forgot their ancient manners. He then goes on to generalize, noting that many "who live among barbarians quickly forget their Greekness (τὸ Ἑλληνικόν)," which consists, he notes, of the Greek language, customs, gods, and just laws, "those things, in other words, by which the nature of Greeks and barbarians is most differentiated." The omission of "blood" from a list that otherwise seems closely modeled on the Athenian speech in Herodotos has been noted.[27] Just as barbarians can become Greeks, then, Greeks can become barbarians. Dionysios cites as additional proof the cities on the Black Sea. Regarding one of these, Borysthenes (Olbia), the Bithynian orator and philosopher Dion Chrysostomos noted in ca. AD 100 that its citizens knew Homer by heart "even though they no longer speak Greek well on account of living among barbarians."[28] As worries in other texts reveal, Hellenism may have been the dominant direction of cultural change, especially after Alexander, but it was not irreversible.[29] This anxiety, as we will see, was similar to that felt by the Byzantine scholars who revived Hellenism

---

[27] Dionysios of Halikarnassos, *Roman Antiquities* 1.89.4; see Gabba (1991) 98–118; Hall (2002) 224.

[28] Dion Chrysostomos, *Or.* 36.9 (*Borysthenic Oration, which he delivered in his native land*). Dion visited Olbia: see C. P. Jones (1978) 61–64.

[29] The book has not yet been written on de-Hellenization. See also Cyprian Salamis in Isokrates' *Euagoras*: the Phoenician ἐξεβαρβάρωσεν the city (20, also 47), but Evagoras "made the citizens Greeks from barbarians" (66); and *Letter* 9 (to Archidamos) on "those Greeks who speak our language but follow the customs of barbarians." Also pseudo-Plato, *Letter* 8.353d–e on the threat to Greek in Sicily; Strabon 5.4.4 on the faint survival of Greek customs at Cumae, on which also Diodoros 12.76.4,

in the twelfth century. They had a strong sense of the fragility of their cultural accomplishments, being very conscious of the fact that they lived amid an ocean of barbarism, which included the majority of other Byzantines and the actual barbarians beyond the frontiers, which were often poorly defended.

In antiquity, at least, Hellenizing the barbarians was often understood as the achievement of great statesmen. Long after the events in question, Plutarch consolidated for posterity the legend of Alexander, the king who had "tamed" the barbarians and taught them the brotherhood of man by building Greek cities in their lands, teaching them Greek laws, customs, and religion, and by making them read Homer and recite tragedies. Plutarch compared Alexander to the philosopher Karneades, who "Hellenized" a man who was a Carthaginian by birth (Καρχηδόνιον τὸ γένος, ἑλληνίζειν ἐποίησεν). Plutarch agreed with Strabon that the mark of τὸ Ἑλληνικόν was not Greek clothing but rather virtue, just as τὸ βαρβαρικὸν was marked by vice. Recent discoveries have made Plutarch's view of Hellenization seem less ridiculous, though it is certainly fantastic as an account of Alexander's career and motivation.[30] But the biographical habit was difficult to break. The fourth-century AD orator Libanios of Antioch ascribed the same role to king Seleukos, the founder of his beloved native city: it was he who had "Hellenized (ἑλληνίζων) the barbarians" in Mesopotamia. Libanios hoped that his friend the emperor Julian would do the same to the Persians, listing all the policies that modern scholars associate today with Hellenization.[31]

Likewise, the Jewish philosopher Philon of Alexandria praised Augustus "for increasing Greece by so many more Greeces" and "Hellenizing" (ἀφελληνίσας) the barbarians.[32] Philon is himself an interesting case of Hellenic hybridity. Though loyal to his faith and people, he did not know Hebrew and was as versed in Greek philosophy as in the Septuagint. A sign of his Hellenization was his inability to decide whether the world was divided into Jews and gentiles or into Greeks and barbarians, the latter

---

Livius 4.44.12, and Dionysios of Halikarnassos, *Roman Antiquities* 15.6.4; Plutarch, *Pyrrhos* 1.4 on the barbarization and re-Hellenization of Epeiros; *Timoleon* 20.7 on Syracuse; Polybios 34.14.5 and Livius 38.17.11 on Alexandria; Athenaios, *Dinner-Sophists* 14.632a on Poseidonia (Paestum); Julian, *Letter* 3/ 8.441b–c (Wright/Bidez and Cumont) on himself in Gaul; Priskianos, *Solutions for Chosroes* 8 (p. 93) foreign places denature Greeks; Agathias, *Histories* 1.2.2 on the barbarization of Massilia. For Thucydides on the Makedonian kings, see Athanassiadi-Fowden (1977) 337; in tragedy, Euripides, *Orestes* 485. For loss of Attic accent, Solon fr. 36.10; Demosthenes, *Or.* 57.18 (*Against Euboulides*).

[30] Plutarch, *On the Fortune or Virtue of Alexander* 4–6 (*Moralia* 328a–329d); cf. *Alexander* 47.3 on teaching Persian recruits Greek letters and Makedonian arms. Recent discoveries: Parsons (1993) 152–153; for Plutarch's conception in general, Humbert (1991).

[31] Libanios, *Or.* 11.103 (*Antiochene Oration*); *Or.* 18.282 (*Funeral Oration for Julian*).

[32] Philon, *On the Embassy to Gaius* 147.

polarity being symptomatic of his Greek *paideia*. He had mixed views regarding the Greeks, to whom he owed more than he was willing to admit: "our" law was for him the Torah but "our" language was Greek.[33] The Jewish historian Josephos noted in his *Jewish Antiquities* that "when the Greeks rose to power they adorned all the nations with the names that seemed good to them and imposed on them orders of government, as though they were descended from them." The Greeks thereby "Hellenized (ἐξελληνίσαντες)" the names and regimes of other peoples. Josephos was not immune from this. Writing in Greek himself, he admitted that he too had "Hellenized" the names of people in his work "for the pleasure of my readers" (1.121, 128–129). We have here a good instance of Hellenization through market pressure, of how *readers* were active agents in the assimilation of *writers*.

Beyond what hybrids like Philon and Josephos had to say about the cultural history of the Roman world, the case of the Jews is especially relevant here. First, the Jewish community, held together (to whatever degree it was) by religious observance and the collective memory of a national history, was the only ancient people whose identity partially survived the Roman empire, i.e., it survived both Hellenization and Romanization. Second, only among Jews do we find a rejection of Greek culture expressed ideologically, in *texts* rather than only in practice, which is owed to the textual and theological basis of the community's coherence. Interestingly, the first Greeks who wrote about them labeled them a nation of philosophers (a view that would soon be revoked).[34] And finally, the complex reception of Hellenism by these Jews prefigured the Christian debate over the value of Greek culture. The pious Maccabean zealots who preferred martyrdom over what they called "Hellenism" were regarded as forerunners of the later Christian martyrs who also refused to submit to paganism, which the Church likewise began to call "Hellenism," for reasons that we will examine closely.

The Jewish experience was complicated by the diversity of conditions in which the community lived and the manifold streams of thought and political factions within it. At one extreme, many chose to assimilate fully to the dominant culture and ceased to be Jews; at the other, small groups of zealots continued the study of Hebrew and anxiously avoided the pollution of foreign customs. The majority lay in between. In the diaspora, most spoke Greek and conformed to the culture of their cities, deriving

[33] Goudriaan (1992) 82–86; Gruen (2002) 215–221, 227. Other Jews used *Hellen* to mean gentiles: Geiger (2002) 241.
[34] Hengel (1974) v. I, 255–261.

their distinctiveness from religious practice, a selective adherence to the Law, and their memory of a shared history. Some even expressed pride in their traditions through Greek literary forms such as tragedies and epic poetry. Jewish superiority was here proved at the cost of playing by Greek rules, for instance by arguing that the glories of Hellenism were really Jewish in origin, thus basically accepting, if only tacitly, that Greek culture was the standard of worth. Philon is a good example of this: he was "essentially" both Greek and Jewish. Other Hellenistic Jewish writers had an entirely Greek *paideia* and their concepts for discussing history, religion, and ethics were derived less from the Septuagint than from Greek philosophy. A few went so far as to suggest that the Jewish God may have been equivalent to some of the chief deities of other religious traditions, e.g., the Greek Zeus.[35]

These developments occurred also in Palestine, though the linguistic balance there tipped more in favor of Aramaic than Greek and the population included groups who opposed foreign customs and insisted on strict adherence to the Law (albeit selectively interpreted). Still, as early as the beginning of the third century Hekataios of Abdera could report that the Jews had changed many of their ancestral traditions through mingling with foreigners.[36] By 175 BC, high priests and notables in Jerusalem had perceived the attractions and advantages of Greek culture with sufficient clarity to initiate an ambitious reform of the city and cult in a push to end their nation's self-imposed separation from the rest of the world. Jerusalem was to be a Greek polis, its youth given a Greek *paideia* in gymnasia. Key aspects of the Law, including circumcision, were abolished. These reforms seem to have enjoyed considerable support among the populace (as even the texts opposing them concede). Motives, of course, cannot be known with any degree of certainty, as our witnesses are hostile. Against a complex background of factional strife, ideological polarization, and military instability, the reform led to a civil war in which the conflict between traditional Judaism and Hellenism played only a part. The Hellenizing faction bribed the Seleukid king, Antiochos IV, to intervene, but his heavy-handed involvement in the 160s – plundering the Temple and installing garrisons – roused conservative reaction. The Hellenizers reformed the Temple along Greek and Phoenician lines, equating its deity with Zeus or Baal. As is well known, the Maccabean revolt and ensuing civil war put a bloody end to this experiment and wrote its history from the victors' viewpoint.

---

[35] The latest surveys are Gruen (1998) and (2002); for theological syncretism, also Hengel (1974) v. I, 264–266, 308.
[36] In Diodoros of Sicily 40.8.

A summary of a history by a certain Iason of Kyrene (which we know as 2 Maccabees) denounces the "extreme of Hellenism (ἀκμὴ Ἑλληνισμοῦ)" of the traitors; also their introduction of gentile practices (τὰ Ἑλληνικά); and the attempt to "convert their own people to a Hellenic mentality (ἐπὶ τὸν Ἑλληνικὸν χαρακτῆρα τοὺς ὁμοφύλους μετῆγε)."[37] This was the first time that these terms were given such a meaning, at least in our extant sources, reflecting the hard-liners' insecurity in the face of a foreign culture that was both dominant and appealing.

In the long run, the Maccabean revolt and conservative reaction saved the Jews from going the way of, say, the Phoenicians, but this was hardly the end of Jewish Hellenism. The Hasmonean dynasty that ruled Judaea for the following century basically adopted the modes of Hellenistic king-ship and lifestyle. Even the gymnasium was retained in Jerusalem, and one king, Aristoboulos, took on the epithet of "the Philhellene."[38] This brought on new rounds of conservative opposition. King Herod (37–4 BC) was a thoroughly Hellenized and secular ruler, though he usually respected his subjects' religious scruples. Hellenism was by then the common political and cultural language of the eastern Mediterranean, and no power could function that did not speak it. In the short term, then, the effect of the revolt was to create a defensive hypersensitivity to certain aspects of the Law (e.g., the Temple and images), but this apparently sufficed to maintain the sense of a distinctive identity in some circles. It would also result in extreme hostility being shown to insensitive Roman officials and reformers such as the early Christians, who did not respect or sought to change certain taboos. It is the latter who interest us, for they inherited the distinctively religious ambivalence toward Hellenism that was created through all this turmoil. They too struggled to define just what part of "Hellenism" was incompatible with their faith. It was never entirely clear which aspects of the surrounding culture were implicated in paganism and which were safe to use. Like their Jewish predecessors, they tried to use Hellenic "forms" to express Christian "content," but the line could not be drawn so neatly. For example, the pro-Maccabean historian Iason of Kyrene used a Greek medium to record his outrage against the Hellenists, but he too seems to have absorbed some of their underlying mental categories, as when he called his opponents, without a trace of irony, the "barbarians."[39]

---

[37] 2 Maccabees 4.10, 4.13, 6.9, 11.24. See Hengel (1974) v. I *passim*, esp. 58–61 for Greek in Palestine; 73 77, 277 303 for the reform movement; v. II, 95 100 for Iason of Kyrene; cf. 184 185 for parallel Egyptian evidence.

[38] For Hasmonean Hellenism, see Gruen (1998) 9–40; Philhellene: Josephos, *Jewish Antiquities* 13.318.

[39] 2 Maccabees 2.21, 4.25, and *passim*.

The parallels between Jewish and Christian Hellenism (or anti-Hellenism) are curious. Hellenistic Jews chose Greek names such as Theodoros, Theodosios, and Theophilos, which pointed to their religion albeit under Hellenic guise; this also pointed forward to the nomenclature of Christian Byzantium, a *Byzance avant Byzance*. Likewise, among all the people of antiquity it was Jewish hard-liners who first condemned Greek literature and cursed philosophy and the autonomous life of the mind as contrary to their faith. These attitudes would later form one wing of Christian opinion in the Roman empire.[40] Here we see the origins and the crux, as it were, of the problem of Hellenism in Byzantium. For over a thousand years the fate of the Greek tradition was in the hands of those who saw themselves as its opponents in a fundamental sense, albeit in a sense that was always negotiable. This basic continuity also shaped the reception of Hellenistic Judaism, and continues to do so even today. We have the writings of Philon, Josephos, and others only because Byzantines like Eusebios of Kaisareia (ca. AD 300) were also struggling to define the relationship between Scripture and Greek *paideia*, between the history of the Jewish nation and that of the rest of the ancient world. Otherwise, these writings seem to have had little impact on the development of Greek or Jewish culture in antiquity, a fact that usually goes unnoticed. "Philon and Josephos," wrote the Byzantine statesman and essayist Theodoros Metochites in the early fourteenth century, "became more famous than any other Jews from time immemorial for having acquired Greek wisdom in addition to their ancestral beliefs" – famous, we should add, only among Greek-speaking Christians.[41]

## THE SECOND SOPHISTIC

The evidence reviewed so far refutes the belief that Hellenization is a modern notion and that "there is not even a word for it in classical or Byzantine Greek."[42] Ancient writers had a number of terms for the process that has also fascinated modern historians, "Hellenization" being one of them. Let us consider some men from different points on the compass who are noted as having *become* Greek. The focus on individuals, especially educated ones, anticipates the argument that will be made regarding the

---

[40] Names: Hengel (1974) v. I, 63–64; Homer etc.: 75–76, 139.
[41] Theodoros Metochites, *Moral Maxims* 16.1.9.
[42] Bowersock (1990) 7; cf. xi: "Hellenism ... was a concept the ancients talked about, whereas Hellenization was not." The point is not clear. Cf. also Ailios Aristeides, *Or.* 1.324 (*Panathenaic Oration*).

revival of Hellenism in Byzantium, for it was scholars in Constantinople who first began to call themselves Greeks based on their *paideia* before the label was used in a more general sense. In addition, some of the men discussed here and their experiences would have been familiar to the Byzantines and perhaps provided models for them.

The second-century AD satirist Lucian hailed from Samosata, a city on the Euphrates, and his native language was a form of Aramaic. Still, he mastered the conventions of Attic prose through hard work and went on to become one of the most widely traveled lecturers and successful writers in the empire. In one of his works, personified Rhetoric describes his career: "I found this man wandering in Ionia when he was a young boy, still speaking in a barbarous manner and all but wearing a caftan in Assyrian fashion; he didn't know what to do with himself, so I took him in and gave him a proper *paideia*."[43] Lucian could refer to himself as either a Greek or a "Syrian," but his fluid use of these terms was often ironic or polemical; besides, an outsider's perspective suited his satirical take on imperial society. Still, he noted that even though he and other sophists were of "barbarian birth (*genos*)," this made no difference to their "*paideia* and manners."[44] Celts and Skythians, he knew, could become indistinguishable from native Athenians through education.[45] At forty, Lucian – or the carefully constructed persona that emerges from his works – converted to philosophy,[46] which he regarded as the most perfect *paideia* and which he defended with wit and passion against its shallow professors.

Learned men also became Greeks in the West, usually in the process of becoming learned. Cicero called Titus Albucius, a senator of ca. 105 BC, "learned in Greek or rather almost a Greek himself . . . he spent his youth at Athens and became a complete Epicurean."[47] When exiled, he returned to Athens. Cicero's own friend Titus Pomponius spoke Attic so well that "you

---

[43] Lucian, *Twice Accused* 27; for his origins, see the literary account in *The Dream, or the Life of Lucian*, with discussion in Swain (1996) 298–311, citing previous bibliography. For skepticism about his native language, see Millar (1993) 454–456.

[44] Lucian, *The Dead Come to Life, or the Fisherman* 19; "Syrian" in *The Skythian, or the Proxenos* 9; and *To the one without* paideia *who collects many books* 19. For Lucian's insecurities, see Swain (1996) 46–49, 311–312.

[45] Lucian, *The Skythian, or the Proxenos* 1, 3; *Toxaris, or on Friendship* 57; *Herakles* 4.

[46] Cf. Lucian, *Twice Accused* 32; *Hermotimos* 13. There is always more going on in Lucian than meets the eye, and his multiple levels of irony and allusion resist succinct exposition. For his destabilization of the discourse of Hellenism, see Whitmarsh (2001) 122–128; Goldhill (2002) 89.

[47] Cicero, *Brutus* 131; see Kaimio (1979) 239–240; and Gruen (1992) 257–258, 290–291. For Roman love of Greek *paideia*, see, e.g., Plutarch, *Marcus Cato* 22.1–3; for the Roman reception of Greek *paideia* in Plutarch, see Swain (1996) 141–143, 406; in general, Kaimio (1979) ch. 5. See also the more famous statements by Cicero, *Brutus* 254 and Horace, *Epistles* 2.1.156, on how conquered Greece conquered Rome.

would have thought that he had been born in Athens"; this earned him the name Atticus.[48] Likewise, the emperor Hadrian was known as *Graeculus* because of his enthusiasm for *graecis studiis*.[49] But *Graeculus* was not quite *Graecus*, and even Atticus refused Athenian citizenship. The Romans, after all, had not conquered the Greeks to surrender their sense of distinctiveness and superiority. The masters of the world set the scope and the limits of their Hellenization and developed subtle social and communicative codes by which they made their use and even love of Greek things complicit in the ongoing maintenance of their own Roman identity.[50] The latter, as we will see in the following chapter, finally prevailed over Hellenism, even in Greece itself.

Turning to Lucian's "Celts," we meet the notorious Favorinus of Arelate, who studied Greek at Massilia, went on speaking tours in Greece, and penned philosophical works. According to his biographer Philostratos, he claimed that his life was marked by three paradoxes: "though a Gaul, he Hellenized; though a eunuch, he was tried for adultery; and though he fell out with an emperor, he yet lived."[51] The emperor was Hadrian; Favorinus was not exactly a eunuch, but had undescended testicles (some called him a hermaphrodite);[52] and the second and third paradoxes presumably had nothing to do with the first. A skilled performer, Favorinus used a remarkable argument to persuade the Corinthians to reinstate his statue:

If someone is a Roman, not of the masses but of the equestrian order, and has studied to perfect not only the language but the mentality, manners, and dress of the Greeks, and has done this more masterfully and brilliantly than any past Romans or present Greeks (I must say); and when one sees the best of the Greeks in Rome inclining toward Roman things, while he inclines toward Greek things and on account of this is sacrificing his property, his civic status, and everything else in order that he not only seem to be Greek but actually be Greek as well ... ought this man not have a statue here in Corinth? Indeed so, and in every city. But in yours especially, because even though he is a Roman he has been thoroughly Hellenized (ἀφηλληνίσθη), just as your city has been;[53] in Athens too, because he Atticizes in his speech ... In fact, it seems that he has been specifically equipped by the gods for this very purpose, namely to furnish an example to the inhabitants of

[48] Nepos, *Atticus* 4.1. Plinius, *Letters* 4.3.5, 7.25.4, praises Romans for being equal to Athenians. See also the sophist Ailianos "who Atticized like the Athenians of the midlands even though he was a Roman": Philostratos, *Lives of the Sophists* 624.

[49] *Historia Augusta: Hadrian* 1.5. For Livius Andronicus and Ennius as *semigraeci*, see Suetonius, *On Teachers of Grammar and Rhetoric* 1 (with commentary at 48–51).

[50] Gruen (1992); Wallace-Hadril (1998).

[51] Philostratos, *Lives of the Sophists* 489. For Favorinus and his lost philosophical works, see Holford-Strevens (1997); Whitmarsh (2001) 119–121.

[52] Gleason (1995) 3, and *passim* for his persona, both personal and rhetorical, and its social context.

[53] Corinth was a Roman *colonia*; for its Hellenization, see Engels (1990) 35, 71–73.

Greece that education is not at all different from birth with respect to fame; ... and to the Celts, so that no barbarian ever despairs of attaining Greek *paideia*, by looking at him.[54]

This passage merits discussion, especially from the point of view of the later Byzantine accommodation of Rome and Greece. We observe, first, a contrast between lower- and upper-class Romans: it is the latter, whose status in imperial society was secure, who were most tempted to indulge in "becoming Greek." The variety of Hellenism championed by Favorinus is therefore a function of elite *paideia* (again, we note the prominence of Athens in this curriculum, highlighted by the fact that Favorinus is actually speaking in Corinth). Conversely, the orator admits that while he was studying to become Greek, many Greeks were moving in the opposite direction and were trying to become as Roman as possible. This choice, which we will discuss in the next chapter, was entirely comprehensible as a reaction by a conquered people seeking advancement in a still-foreign empire. We already observe, then, in this configuration another *Byzance avant Byzance*: the subject population seeks to assimilate itself to the Roman order, while a section of the elite, regardless of its ethnic origin, incurs great expenses to cultivate an idealized Hellenism.

Favorinus' oration also sets limits upon a recent and now popular view of Hellenization, namely that the latter provided only a formal "medium" through which non-Hellenic cultural "content" could be expressed, just as it had formerly been expressed through native media. According to this view, pervasive contact with Hellenism stimulated native traditions and gave them a new vitality and new modes of expression. Studies that follow this approach, however, are not relevant to men – or whatever he was exactly – such as Favorinus, for whom Hellenism entailed a personal engagement with Greek *paideia*. Their subject matter is defined as "the more pedestrian Greek elements that were at the heart of Near Eastern Hellenism."[55] They focus on religion and on those regions where Hellenization did not in the long run eliminate native traditions and languages, for example Egypt. There a strong sense of local identity in a large sector of the native population created a counterweight to the rulers' Greek culture and made ethnicity fluid in the middle, as people crossed the gray area that lay between the two poles (three, if one includes Jews). There it was possible for one to complain that

---

[54] Favorinus, *Corinthian Oration* 25–27 (pseudo-Dion Chrysostomos, *Or.* 37).
[55] Bowersock (1990) 81; for the "medium" thesis, see 5, 7, 15, 58, 61, 67–68, 72; Fowden (1986) 43–44; Cameron (1997) 6–7, 14 (summary); Gruen (1998) *passim*; and Frankfurter (1998) 103, 106–111, 176, 221–254.

he was not being paid because "they see that I am a barbarian . . . and do not speak Greek," and for another to complain that he was being attacked "because I am a Hellene."[56] In Syria, also, a native tongue flourished and eventually became enshrined in the practices and literature of the Syriac Church. These studies also focus on Arabia, though this was certainly a peripheral region from a Byzantine, i.e., a Graeco-Roman, point of view.

This recent work is very insightful, for it is based on neglected evidence and explains how Hellenic forms were often adapted to native traditions, which in some cases were indeed strengthened rather than abolished in the process. It corrects silences in our sources regarding the non-classical aspects of the ancient world, but its thesis should not be applied indiscriminately across the empire. It focuses on regions that did not become part of the Byzantine state and on aspects of daily life and worship that did not much concern Hellenizers in the first place. More importantly, the medium cannot be so easily separated from the content as is often assumed.[57] The forms of one culture cannot immaculately "translate" the content of another, either on the linguistic level or more generally.[58] Moreover, it has rightly been stressed that Hellenism too was "a carrier of quite definite and unique religious, moral and cultural values,"[59] so native traditions were certainly altered when they expressed themselves through its media. Favorinus, at least, was explicit that *paideia* could fundamentally change one's identity. Our texts, as we have

---

[56] Goudriaan (1992); Thompson (2001); complaints cited in Hengel (1974) v. I, 39; late antiquity: Fowden (1986) 13–14.

[57] E.g., Bowersock (1990) too casually brushes aside the change from aniconic to anthropomorphic representation in Nabataean religion by claiming that just because the new face "was a local face" Hellenization did not "annihilate" local traditions (8–9, 20, 75). "Annihilation" is a straw man. Also, the institution of athletic games at Bostra cannot be explained away just because they were dedicated to a local god and enhanced the status of the city (9). This was true in every Greek city. By contrast, Sartre (2005) 366 calls the adoption of images by Arabs and Jews "revolutionary." The Arabs, in any case, were unrepresentative of the empire's population; cf. Trombley (2001) v. II, 164. Frankfurter (1998) employs subjective criteria in evaluating the "democratizing" effect of the use of Greek in Egypt, which effected a major change in the economy of religious knowledge: where does one draw the line around what was "authentically Egyptian" (224)? Egyptian scribes felt that by using Greek they were betraying their traditions and begged divine approval before proceeding (238–239, 244–246). Horapollon, who came from a distinguished priestly family and wrote a book in Greek on the interpretation of hieroglyphics, could scarcely read them and lied about having translated it from Egyptian. To his credit, Frankfurter discusses these problems at length. See pp. 28–30 above for Hellenistic Judaism.

[58] The *Prologos* to the translation of the *Wisdom of Sirach* 21–22 notes the lack of direct equivalence between Greek and Jewish concepts; cf. Cicero, *Against Verres* 2.154: *sôter* has no Latin equivalent; Diogenes Laertios 1.4 on philosophy; *Corpus Hermeticum* 16.1–2 on Egyptian words; and Iamblichos, *On the Mysteries* 7.5 on divine names; see Fowden (1986) 37–38 for more; and p. 64 below for Latin legal terms put into Greek. The Christological controversies revealed that Greek theological vocabulary lacked exact Latin equivalents.

[59] Athanassiadi-Fowden (1977) 325 and *passim*.

often seen, specify when someone "was a Hellene not only in his speech but in his soul" despite being, say, an Ioudaios by *genos*. When they meant less, they said less: for instance, the Greeks saw in the Roman general Flamininus a man who was Greek "in voice and language" – so presumably not in his "soul" too.[60]

We are here less interested in Egypt, Syria, and Arabia, which were lost to the empire in the seventh century, and more in the Balkans and Asia Minor. We are also more interested in the Hellenized upper classes of the empire, because it was they who created the classical texts that the Byzantines inherited and who, indeed, were the very paragons of ancient Hellenism. On their level, it is wrong to separate form from content, for that occludes the profoundly transformative experience that was the acquisition of Greek *paideia*. Favorinus, as we saw, stressed that mentality and manners were as important as language and dress. Accordingly, we find that there was nothing especially "Gallic" about him, or "Syrian" about the satires of Lucian and "Bithynian" about the orations of Dion of Prousa. Nor, a century later, was there anything recognizably "Phoenician," "Syrian," or "Semitic" about the philosopher Porphyrios of Tyre, though those terms are used rather freely by modern scholars in connection with him. We do not even know whether he could speak the *patrios dialektos* that produced his native name, Malchos.[61] Moreover, despite their varied origins all these men were far more alike in terms of education and values than each was to the less Hellenized people of his own native land. For Dion this international group consisted of "those who partake of Hellas" – the same verb (κοινωνοῦντες) that Christians were using to express their relationship to Christ.[62] Byzantine scholars who later rediscovered or, rather, reinvented Hellenism, such as Eustathios of Thessalonike and Michael Choniates, would have found the company of these men more congenial on the level of *paideia* than that of their own contemporaries, religious and social differences notwithstanding.

This affinity was not accidental; it had deep roots in the reception of the classical tradition in later antiquity and Byzantium. Dion, Favorinus, and Lucian all belonged to a dazzling revival of classical culture that peaked in the second century AD and indelibly marked the legacy of Hellenism. Philostratos called its rhetorical (and probably dominant) aspect the "Second Sophistic," because he viewed it as a direct sequel of the "First" Sophistic of the classical age. We do not have to credit his opinion that it was founded by the Athenian orator Aischines in his spare time, but the

---

[60] Cf. Klearchos in Josephos, *Against Apion* 1.180 with Plutarch, *Life of Flamininus* 5.7.
[61] Millar (1997).    [62] Dion Chrysostomos, *Or.* 12.42 (*Olympic Oration*).

name Philostratos coined has caught on, and his need to find a classical
pedigree is typical of the movement as a whole.[63] The literary critic and
Roman antiquarian Dionysios Halikarnassos had already, in the late first
century BC, advocated a return to rhetorical Atticism, by which he meant
the language used in Athens in the fifth and fourth centuries BC.[64]

The new sophists were powerful men in their local communities, as was
Dion at Prousa, and often enormously wealthy, as were Antonios Polemon
and Herodes Attikos. Their training as orators emphasized purist Attic
diction and their themes were drawn from classical history (which ended
with Alexander). Aristeides, regarded in Byzantium as a model of style, left
behind dozens of such declamations, including the (invented) speeches that
Demosthenes would have delivered at such-and-such a moment. At provincial festivals, in theatrical halls, before the provincial governors on
behalf of their cities, or before the emperors in Rome, the sophists would
put on performances replete with classical imitations, elaborate gestures,
and voice modulations.[65] They were the new celebrities of the Roman
world and acted like it. The ascetic strictures and analytical reasoning of
Greek philosophy were not for them, and they fully deserved Lucian's
acerbic and ironical wit.

The Second Sophistic seduced its heirs, including Byzantium, with its
normative model of cultural Hellenism, a model that Byzantine scholars
who overcame their Christian inhibitions could fully embrace. A true
Hellene, in this sense, embodied the *paideia* of a Dion or an Aristeides.
Like them, he was a master of pure Attic diction and could speak like Plato
or Demosthenes with no admixture of later, vulgar, or foreign expressions.
This served to set him apart and above his own less-educated contemporaries and established a social class based on linguistic skill.[66] He knew
ancient history and literature intimately and could grasp classical allusions
and the nuanced hints that they contained. He was often an accomplished
classical scholar, textual editor, or antiquarian. Social status, prestige, and
imperial favor were expected to attend upon this level of attainment, as
were ethical qualities such as urbanity, refinement, moderation, generosity,
wit, and the ability to secure favors for oneself and one's city through
rhetorical performance.[67] The elegance of rhetoric beautified the world (or
an emperor) and presented audiences with an orderly, rational cosmos.

---

[63] Philostratos, *Lives of the Sophists* 480–484, 507; for cautionary comments, see Reardon (1984).
[64] Swain (1996) 17–31.    [65] Gleason (1995).    [66] Swain (1996) chs. 1–2.
[67] For Hellenism and refinement, see Dion Chrysostomos, *Or.* 44.10 (*A salute to his fatherland for proposing honors for him*); cf. Saïd (2001) 290.

Sophists were only the most spectacular performers in a broader cult of classicism that flourished in the second century. There were other venues and forms, and we should expand our focus to include them, as the cultural activity of this age shaped subsequent notions of "the classical." For instance, it set the chronological limits of "ancient" Greece between Homer and Alexander, and made this period into a model of both ethical and aesthetic imitation. Plutarch wrote the lives of Greek heroes from Theseus to the Roman conquest to provide models of virtue.[68] For him the anti-Roman Achaian general Philopoimen was a "late born child of Hellas," even "the last of the Greeks."[69] Pausanias, who wrote an antiquarian guidebook to Greece, suppressed most monuments and events that postdated the Roman conquest. There was a consensus that the glory of Greece had peaked with Alexander. Historical novels, mostly romances, became a fully fledged genre and were set in unspecified periods of the classical, definitely pre-Roman past. The classical legacy was also codified in encyclopedic collections. Athenaios produced his massive *Dinner-Sophists*, a compilation of trivia and quotations from ancient and Hellenistic authors. Diogenes Laertios wrote the *Lives and Opinions of the Best Philosophers*, ending with the teachings of his own favorite Epikouros, a contemporary of Alexander. Diogenes believed that both philosophy and the human race had begun with the Greeks and not, as others thought, among barbarians (1.3).

Classical Greece became a normative standard and conferred legitimacy.[70] Civic benefactors were compared in public inscriptions to figures from ancient history and literature, who were in turn placed proudly on local coins. Sculpture imitated ancient masterpieces, and classical monuments were copied, restored, or, in the case of the Olympieion in Athens, completed by the *Graeculus* emperor Hadrian. The oracle at Delphi revived as did classical and Homeric names. The Roman consul and historian Arrianos of Nikomedeia modeled his life and works on Xenophon and even took his name, writing an *Anabasis of Alexander*; he even named his dogs after Xenophon's. Aristeides had dreams about Sophokles and Plato. For those enchanted by Greek culture, the Second Sophistic was a time of extravagant, almost baroque, beauty.

The glorification and social prestige of *paideia* in the high Roman empire did not, however, entirely obliterate the ethnic dimension of ancient Hellenism. Inter-city relationships were still forged on the basis of putative consanguinity, a diplomatic habit that was adopted throughout

---

[68] Plutarch, *Perikles*, preface; *Timoleon*, preface.    [69] Plutarch, *Philopoimen* 1.6–7.
[70] Summary in Gordon (1996) 8–13 (with citations). The basic survey is Bowie (1970).

the East after Alexander and that still flourished under the empire. Mythic founders were grafted onto the Hellenic genealogy and previously native ancestors were reimagined as colonists from Greece.[71] The learned and the great traced their family origin to heroes of old, for example Herodes Attikos from Miltiades, Plutarch from the heroes of his native Boiotia, and others from Perikles or Alkibiades.[72] The reign of Hadrian also witnessed the institution of the Panhellenion, an association of Greek cities housed in Athens. The requirements for admission stressed Greek descent and included loyalty to Rome. Hadrian's own philhellenism has been seen at work here as well as the oddly racial view of Hellenism held by his friend, the sophist Polemon.[73] Yet we should not conclude from this that the Greeks of the empire had a strong sense of ethnic unity. Consanguinity was not a belief that could inspire action but a rhetorical strategy that was adopted by cities to deal with greater powers. It was a convenient and fluid diplomatic tool that offered no sure standard by which to know exactly who was Greek. Besides, it could easily seem artificial or absurd, as was only to be expected among elites who had long since learned the slipperiness and polysemy of myth. As we saw above, even Xerxes had tried to forge a myth of common descent with Argos (based on Perseus) during his invasion of Greece, and Hellenistic Jews had later claimed kinship with the Spartans.[74] These overtures bore little fruit, but even less fanciful claims were greeted with skepticism. The orator Aristeides noted in his praise of Athens that others "are looking for some way to trace themselves back to you."[75] Polemon's racialism was an exception among his colleagues and rivals, whose own genealogical pretensions smacked of antiquarianism, as did the quickly forgotten rules of the Panhellenion.

The broad extension and consequent rarefaction of Greek ethnicity may be viewed as part of the process that led ultimately to the general loss of ethnicity among many of the empire's subjects. This complex process, the corollary of their acceptance of a Roman national identity, will be discussed in the next chapter. The Roman context, however, has been implicated in modern discussions of the Second Sophistic. Two basic views have been proposed. The first entangles the movement in the modes of Roman rule,[76]

---

[71] The standard survey of epigraphic sources is Curty (1995). For the Hellenistic period, see Habicht (1998) 66–71; Scheer (2003); for the second century AD, Gordon (1996) 31; Swain (1996) 76 (and n. 25). See below for Hadrian's Panhellenion.

[72] Gordon (1996) 31 n. 106; Swain (1996) 86; Habicht (1998) 127 n. 41.

[73] Romeo (2002), esp. 34–35.    [74] Herodotos 7.150.2; Gruen (1998) 253–268.

[75] Ailios Aristeides, *Or.* 1.334 (*Panathenaic Oration*); for cynicism, see Hall (2002) 223–224; for artificiality, Musti (1963) 237–239.

[76] Bowersock (1969), esp. 58; but his prosopography must yield to Bowie (1982).

arguing that the Second Sophistic was made possible only by the settled conditions of the empire and by Roman receptivity to literary culture, especially philhellenism. Like many modern philhellenes, the Romans were less interested in contemporary Greece than in their own idealized vision of the classical past that they found in books and which Greek "guides" encouraged them to find in the present. As today, this process was facilitated by a flourishing tourist trade. Thus, the Roman preference for pre-monarchical and non-eastern Hellenism stimulated or at least reinforced the classicizing trends of the Greek-speaking elite. Dionysios of Halikarnassos, who pioneered Atticism, was explicit on this.[77] Besides, the policy of Roman philhellenism aimed as much to promote Roman power as to celebrate Greek culture.[78] By extension, it is very likely that the Byzantines, who were themselves Romans, were drawn to the legacy of the Second Sophistic partly for this reason, that as a rhetorical movement it had originally responded and catered to an imperial culture directly related to their own.

On the other hand, one cannot deny an element of resentment toward Roman power in the great Greek nostalgia of the second century.[79] Hellenism, both cultural and national, thrived on the old distinction between Greeks and barbarians, and Rome could as easily slip into the latter category as the former. Political impotence was felt acutely in some circles and discussed with dismay. Cultural pride and ancestral links, fueled by the Roman rhetoric of freedom and self-determination, could not but have entertained national dreams. But these, we know, could not result in political action because they lacked institutions to back them up, a clear conception of national identity and territory, as well as a consensus of values between the elite and the rapidly Romanizing masses of greater "Greece." As late as the Roman era it was still not decided whether the Makedonians and their legacy were fully Greek or not. In practice, therefore, and beyond the rhetoric, nostalgia bred little more than local or elite snobbery. And the conditions of empire were anyway not such as to stir thoughts of revolt. To the contrary, many of the exponents of cultural Hellenism were themselves complicit in Roman rule, had in fact benefited from it personally as they were gradually identifying with it politically. The Greeks were by then well on the way to becoming Byzantines, that is, Romans.

---

[77] Dionysios of Halikarnassos, *On the Ancient Orators* 3. Cf. Swain (1996) 66, 73, with modern comparisons, Spawforth (2001) 376-379.

[78] For Hadrian, see Boatwright (2000) 152-153.

[79] Chiefly Swain (1996). Whitmarsh (2001) complicates our readings of the texts, but accepts the same framework.

The Second Sophistic merits our attention not only because it codified an attractive if excessive vision of cultural Hellenism, but because the stance toward the classical heritage that combined reverence, imitation, and innovation represented one of few possible alternatives and would recur in later periods. In particular, the revival of Hellenism in twelfth-century Byzantium was not merely based on the models provided by the Second Sophistic, it took a strikingly similar path, for example in the revival of the romantic novel set in an unspecified but definitely pre-Roman past. As in the second century, we will witness in the twelfth the rise of showmanship in performance to complement the emphasis on panegyric and the emergence of authorial egos of epic proportions, yet all this in the context of a Christian society and (often) ecclesiastical careers. Komnenian Byzantium, as we will see, fully deserves the label of a "Third Sophistic."

Let us conclude, then, with some reflections on the significance of the Second Sophistic for the long-term evolution of Hellenic classicism. Whether we like it or not (and many do not), the Second Sophistic fundamentally shaped the perception and reception of Hellenism in Byzantium and in early modern times. As a social and broadly based cultural movement it may have fizzled in the third century, when imperial instability changed the relationship between Rome and the provinces along with the dynamics of social prestige, while other concurrent developments undermined the valorization of classical antiquity that was its mainspring. But as a rhetorical movement it still flourished in the later empire: Libanios, Himerios, the orators of Gaza, and others, have left more declamations and panegyrics than survive from the second century. The Church Fathers were also products of this movement, in fact one may even say that Sophistic detoured into homiletics. The sophists' orations and manuals provided the models that later Byzantines were trained to imitate, with considerable success.[80] Unlike most modern classicists, the Byzantines were not embarrassed to learn style or history from Dion, Aristeides, and Athenaios.[81] This gave them a comprehensive view of antiquity – from Homer to the Church Fathers – that still contained within itself the worshipful and self-consciously derivative outlook of the Roman period as a "supplement" to the Attic classics.

[80] Kennedy (1983); Wilken (1983) ch. 4. In some ways the Second Sophistic is still alive in the official rhetoric of modern Greece, for example in the avoidance of proper names in polemical discourse.
[81] Treadgold (1984) *passim*, esp. 89–91 for Photios' *Bibliotheke*.

The Byzantines, then, recognized a Greek past that included the canonical authors, the Hellenistic commentaries, the Sophistic modulations, and what was for many of them the patristic culmination of antiquity. Byzantium bequeathed this holistic view to western Europe along with most of the apparatus of Greek classical scholarship, where it held sway until the Enlightenment. It was only in recent times that the narrow definition of the "classical," the one that prevailed in the second century AD itself, was revived and institutionalized in western Academies. Modern classicism affected to despise "later" literature while fully adhering to its verdicts and canonical constructions and relying on its scholarly tools. There is considerable scope for ideological deconstruction here. Our Classical Studies are in many respects still caught up in these nineteenth-century tangles. We have had to laboriously rediscover – in reality invent – "the Hellenistic world" and "late antiquity," whose discreteness as disciplines, however, is debatable. Slowly, we are working our way back to a more holistic Byzantine view of Greek antiquity.

# CHAPTER 2

# *"The world a city": Romans of the East*

It is well known that the people we call Byzantines today called themselves Romans (Romaioi). In the middle period of Byzantium's history, with which the second and more narrative part of this study will be chiefly concerned, this "national" label appears or is pervasive in virtually all texts and documents (excluding the strictly theological) regardless of the geographical and social origins of their authors, which, in Byzantium, were diverse. ("Byzantines" were for them only the residents of Constantinople, archaically styled after the City's classical name.) These Romans called their state Romania ('Ρωμανία) or Romaïs, its capital New Rome (among other names, titles, and epithets), and its rulers the *basileis* of the Romans, whom we call "emperors." This Roman identity survived the fall of the empire and Ottoman rule, though it was greatly changed by those events. While in Byzantium the Romans were a highly unified nation, under the Porte they were redefined so as to encompass a multi-ethnic and linguistically diverse religious community. Later, with the foundation of the modern Greek state, *romiosyne* came to represent the orthodox and demotic aspects of the new Hellenic national persona, complementing the classical and idealistic aspect that was projected abroad. Continuity and change are alike illustrated in a story remembered by Peter Charanis, born on the island of Lemnos in 1908 and later a professor of Byzantine history at Rutgers University.

When the island was occupied by the Greek navy [in 1912], Greek soldiers were sent to the villages and stationed themselves in the public squares. Some of us children ran to see what these Greek soldiers, these Hellenes, looked like. "What are you looking at?" one of them asked. "At Hellenes," we replied. "Are you not Hellenes yourselves?" he retorted. "No, we are Romans."[1]

---

[1] Barker (1979) 2, abbreviated. I thank Prof. Barker for the story and reference. For the dualism of Hellenic and Roman in modern Greece, see Herzfeld (1986); Leontis (1995) 189–194.

Thus was the most ancient national identity in all of history finally absorbed and ended. Charanis, as we will see, eventually came to regard himself as a Hellene.

And yet this most indisputable and central fact, that the Byzantines firmly believed themselves to be Romans, has not received in scholarship the attention and emphasis that it deserves. That is because both Greek and western European scholars have had an interest in downplaying it, the former, as we will see at the end of this chapter, because they desire to find a core of national "Greekness" behind what they take to be only a Roman façade, while the latter hold that the Roman legacy is fundamentally western and Latin and cannot bring themselves to accept that Byzantium "really was" Roman. In doing so both sides have perpetuated the western medieval bias against the eastern empire, according to which the Byzantines were only Greeklings, not true Romans. Rome belongs to the West, it is instinctively assumed, and to the Latin-speaking world, and so other "essences" have had to be imagined for Byzantium, for example Greek Orthodoxy or Ecumenical Orthodoxy or oriental despotism or even medieval Hellenism. For many western historians Rome also belongs to antiquity and so anything later than it can at best constitute a "reception," despite the fact that in the case of Byzantium *alone* are we dealing with direct political, social, and cultural continuity from Julius Caesar to Konstantinos XI Palaiologos. But the existence of a single state and political community with a continuous history lasting over two thousand years defeats scholarly specialization. Periodization, in this case arbitrary, requires new names such as "Byzantium" and new names suggest a different "essence."

The aim of this chapter is to explore what it meant to be a Roman in Byzantium, for that identity temporarily restricted, in fact entirely suppressed, the possibility of national Hellenism. As we will see, the latter would be revived only when the former entered a phase of severe crisis, in the thirteenth century, and then only to complement it, not to replace it. So who were these Byzantine Romans and why have they not been recognized as one of the historical nations of the world? Contrary to one myth, the Roman identity of Byzantium was *not* a function of its official faith, though the latter was certainly mobilized in support of it, as had other gods in earlier times. Nor was it a function of ethnicity, since it was not kinship or a belief in common descent that made one a Roman. Rather, it was a social consensus that all belonged to a single historical political community defined by laws, institutions, religion, language, and customs, in other words to a nation, that provided the foundation of Romania. The

Romans, either of Old or New Rome, formed a coherent and continuous society unified and defined by the institutions of their state, the most longevous in history, and the customs of their society.

We should not allow later developments to obscure this picture. The Roman name was redefined by the Ottomans after 1453 to include all who were subject ecclesiastically to the orthodox patriarch of Constantinople, regardless of their cultural, historical, or linguistic differences and regardless of whether they had any memory of once belonging to the Roman state that the Ottomans had supplanted. These Romans of the millet of Rum – millets were the religious groupings of the subjects of the Ottoman empire – were not simply the Romans of Byzantium under new management. These were not only two extensionally different groups, they were different *kinds* of groups. Ironically, it was the Ottomans who began the process, perpetuated by many modern historians, of identifying Romania with its religion. But this is a politically motivated error, then as now, that occludes the real foundations of Roman society. In Byzantium the overlap of Church and society was basically an accident of history, for most Byzantines recognized that being Roman was not the same as being orthodox (e.g., barbarians could be orthodox; heretical or even pagan emperors were still legitimate emperors of the Romans). However, the (contingent) overlap of the two within the empire inevitably resulted in occasionally vague equations which we should no longer view uncritically.

Nor, as we have mentioned, did the Romans of Byzantium define themselves ethnically. It was only after centuries of Ottoman rule that a segment of the Greek-speaking portion of the millet of Rum began to experiment with notions of Hellenic nationality, involving a variety of linguistic, cultural, religious, and ethnic criteria. It was precisely the extremely diverse membership of their millet that made the Roman label unusable to the leaders of this new movement, for, contrary to what is stated or implied in many studies, there was no "Greek millet," only a Roman one at times dominated by Greek-speakers.[2] Herein, then, lies the origin of the modern Greek misunderstanding of Byzantium, which projects modern national definitions onto the non-national religious community of the millet of Rum and, from there, back onto the politically defined community of the medieval Romans.

The present chapter offers the first-ever modern account of Byzantium as Romania, focusing on how the Greek-speaking East gradually came to identify with Romania and how this new order limited the scope of

---

[2] *Pace*, e.g., Smith (1986) 66, 108–109, 114; (1991) 35; for the difficulty of imagining the nation from within the millet, see Skopetea (1988) 24–25; Matalas (2002) 13, 22–29, 167, 218–227.

Hellenic identity; how Romania was gradually converted to the Greek language in late antiquity without any diminution, however, in the coherence and normative power of its Roman identity; and what relationship existed between Romania as a politically defined community and any ethnic groups that may have existed within and outside of its borders. In short, unless we pay close attention to the Roman basis of Byzantine identity it will prove impossible to make sense of the later *revival* of Hellenism, for we will have mistaken the character and loyalties of the men who engaged in that project. It made a difference whether these later Hellenists believed that their newfound Greekness complemented or supplanted their Roman identity.

BECOMING ROMAN

During the course of late antiquity the Greeks ceased to think of themselves as Greeks in any national sense and became Romans. The empire "constituted a new world-view, a Roman 'state of things' which *replaced* the Greek state of things."[3] But how did this happen? Unfortunately, few modern discussions of Romanization are helpful since most deal with the empire's western provinces, reflecting the bias which claims the Roman tradition for the West. Romanization, according to this view, was the process by which the West learned Latin and became urbanized. As the Greeks did not learn Latin and did not need to be urbanized, they were not Romanized. This is one distortion of the history of the early empire that a modicum of knowledge about Byzantium would set straight. Why did the Greek-speaking subjects of the empire exit antiquity not only calling but deeply believing themselves to be Romans? A common answer is that the Greek label was barred by Christianity, which identified it with paganism. The Greeks were thus "forced to yield any sense of an internal identity based on their heritage."[4] But this will not do. The conversion to Romania occurred before the one to Christianity, and, more importantly, it was an independent process with different causes; the pagan Hellenes of late antiquity were as Roman as their Christian fellow citizens; finally, this explanation cannot account for the sincerity and earnestness of the Roman identity. The Roman name was not a label slapped onto a deeper Greek identity. The religious explanation also cannot account for the fact that there were no attempts after ca. 400 to articulate a national Hellenic

[3] Reardon (1974) 25.
[4] Swain (1996) 36. This view is popular among Greek historians, e.g., Zambelios (1857) 44, 54; Constantelos (1998) ix, 3, 170.

identity even without using the ethnonym, to find other labels and criteria by which to separate Greeks from other Romans. It was not as though "the Greeks" wanted to maintain their national distinctiveness but lacked the vocabulary due to an accident of religious terminology; rather, by the end of antiquity no one wanted even to attempt this.

To be sure, Romanization in the East did not obliterate local memories, religions, or the Greek language, nor did it entirely alter the ambitions of the elite and living conditions of the population, as it had, for instance, in Gaul.[5] But those were not necessary effects of Romanization, as that process will be understood here. They occurred in some regions; in others not. Romanization will be defined here as the process by which the former conquered came to identify with the Roman order and participate actively in its social and political institutions, accepting Rome as their chief *patria* or *patris* and subordinating all local allegiances to it or allowing them to lapse if they were in conflict with it. Only secondarily, or as a concomitant of this deeper process, did they accept changes to their material lives. In most of the scholarship, however, these latter material changes have been taken to be definitive of Romanization rather than merely indicative of it. Naturally, Roman orders were in constant evolution, in Byzantium as in the Republic and early empire, but the following account will suggest that there was a continuity in national consensus between Cicero and, say, the orators of twelfth-century Byzantium such as cannot, ironically, be claimed for the medieval West. The focus here, then, will be on political and national identity and not on material culture (revealed through archaeology), or on economic development or urbanization, for otherwise disastrous conclusions may result, for example that "the East needed no Romanizing, nor accepted it"[6] – as though Byzantium never existed. This process is so little understood that historians of Hellenism can presently say nothing more specific than that the name *Romaios* "attached itself to the occupants of the Greek peninsula at some unspecified time after the Romans destroyed Corinth (146 BC)."[7] Ignorance of Byzantium and its late-antique antecedents can benefit ancient historians too for it reveals in their fully developed form trends that were in their infancy and perhaps scarcely detectable in earlier periods. Periodization here again interferes.

---

[5] Woolf (1998) 67, 74, 142, 229, 247.

[6] MacMullen (1990) 57. Brunt (1976) 163 flatly acknowledges the Romanization of the East, but does not explain it. His focus is on the West. An archaeological view of Romanization is assumed in many publications, e.g., Millett (1990) 1–2 ("An Essay in Archaeological Interpretation"), citing previous bibliography.

[7] Leontis (1995) 80 n. 30.

The fact is not in dispute: the Byzantines were Romans. The conventional notion that Rome was for them only an adopted (and so implicitly foreign) ideal of empire can probably be ascribed to the bias of past diplomatic historians who were looking for manufactured "ideologies" in official documents and who did not feel obligated to take a longer and deeper view to explain the continuity and coherence of Roman society for almost two millennia.[8] This notion also reflects a western bias, as it makes Rome into something external to the Byzantines which they only laid claim to in the abstract for political purposes. In reality, abundant evidence indicates that in late antiquity and Byzantium the idea of the Roman *res publica* "was not only the legitimizing element at the center of political ideology and self-representation at the imperial court but had also become the point of reference in the personal field of self-consciousness of the normal citizen."[9] "We" are Romans in most texts written after the late third century, whether by pagans or Christians, in Greek or Latin. The equation is unselfconscious. But what does it mean?

Citizenship by itself does not hold the answer. As is well known, in 212 the emperor M. Aurelius Antoninus (nicknamed Caracalla) granted citizenship to all free men and women of the empire. Thus was the Roman policy of gradual and liberal enfranchisement consummated, in a single act that probably created more Romans than had yet existed.[10] But the legal fact of citizenship entailed both more and less than is commonly assumed. Less, because it was not the mere possession of certain legal rights that persuaded Greeks and others to identify with the Roman order. Scholarly emphasis on citizenship is understandable as it can be documented, roughly quantified, and its social and legal consequences known. It is a more tricky matter, however, to know what people felt about the empire and why they eventually accepted its claim to constitute a normative political community and did so regardless of whether they were its legal citizens. It was those underlying attitudes that ultimately determined the coherence and resilience of Romania, not a legal fact and its judicial and fiscal consequences. It is therefore misleading to say, as one historian has regarding the early empire, that the bestowal of citizenship made "citizens feel a sense of obligation to the Roman state very much like that inspired by patriotism of the European nations of modern times." That sense resulted from a deeper identification, which alone can explain why

---

[8] E.g., Dölger (1953) 71.  [9] Chrysos (1996) 8.
[10] Buraselis (1989) 120–148; Honoré (2004) 114–115.

these new "citizens" went on fighting for New Rome with battle cries of the sort "remember that you are Romans" for a thousand years after 212. It is, then, wrong to say, as does the same historian regarding Byzantium, that when citizenship later lost its value "Roman identity survived in a non-political form ... The concept was now a cultural, and increasingly a religious one, which involved no consciousness of an obligation to maintain the Roman empire against its enemies."[11] No Byzantine would ever subscribe to this statement, which is made possible by an ignorance of the history of New Rome. Roman identity became fiercely patriotic precisely when it no longer rested on the mere fact of citizenship, when it became a pervasive instinct that is too easily taken for granted and therefore missed in the more superficial search for legal facts.

This brings us to the sense in which citizenship entailed more than a set of legal rights held in an otherwise foreign system. Romanization was complete when the formerly conquered peoples realized a "consensus regarding Rome's right to maintain social order and to establish a normative political culture."[12] By then, the majority of the subjects of Byzantine Romania lacked the need, the vocabulary, and the mental categories with which to assert an identity that was not integrated into the Roman order. They accepted the claim broadcast by Rome that authority was legitimate only when it served the welfare of the provincials. It was, after all, an expansive and egalitarian conception of Roman community and of Rome as the common fatherland of all peoples, conjoined perhaps with the myth of Alexander the Great as the apostle of the brotherhood of man, that inspired the aforementioned edict of Caracalla, himself the scion of a provincial dynasty.[13] He and his jurists were not alone. In many texts from late antiquity – Greek and Latin, Christian and pagan – Rome is hailed as the common *patria* of all people. Rome was The City, a city made into a world. Ethnicity was irrelevant as community was now defined by consensus, law, and custom.[14] And, as many sources testify, after 212 there was only one law throughout the empire. Menandros' rhetorical manual repeatedly notes that it is "now" useless to praise a city for its excellent laws, since all are governed by the same Roman laws. In the late fourth century, Ioannes Chrysostomos noted that in the time of St. Paul the Athenians

[11] Liebeschuetz (2001) 344 and 346–351. Many studies are distracted by citizenship, e.g., Chrysos (1996) 9–10.
[12] Ando (2000) xi, and 10 for citizenship. I am indebted to Ando's account.   [13] Buraselis (1989).
[14] Sources cited and discussed in Ando (2000) 11, 15, 49, 63–69; for Christian authors, 346–351; see also Buraselis (1989) 188.

were not governed by their own laws but by those of the Romans, to a degree projecting back onto that time what obtained in his own.[15]

What were the mechanisms by which Greeks and others became Romans in this sense? It should be borne in mind that this process was almost but not entirely completed before the end of late antiquity (ca. 610), when many less Romanized areas of the empire were lost. This book studies the loss and revival of *Byzantine* Hellenism, and therefore the focus is on those lands that would form the core of the middle empire, mainly Greece and Asia Minor. But the emphasis on late antiquity in the pages that follow is justified by the fact that it was in late antiquity when the basic modes and orders of the later "national" Romania were established. Romanization, as it is understood here, took centuries to work its effects, but centuries are in abundance in Roman history.

One aspect of the transformation was ideological and, though it might seem banal to us and unlikely to compel loyalty, it was in fact a striking departure from the modes of ancient kingship and of Hellenistic royal authority in particular. Down to AD 1453 the Roman emperor was understood as subordinate to the polity that he governed, indeed as the head of the state he was in fact its servant, despite the occasional boasts of over-zealous flatterers. The polity, in turn, whether called *res publica, politeia*, or the *koinon*, was defined by law but grounded in universal consensus and therefore theoretically instituted by popular will. For instance, soldiers fought and died for their *patria* Rome and not for the emperor personally. Their oaths of loyalty to him notwithstanding, they were Romans, not the king's men. The emperor swore an oath of office like everyone else.[16] That is why he was always the emperor *of the Romans*, and not, like a Hellenistic monarch who simply was the state, a *basileus* plain and simple, answerable to no one but his own genius. It was a characteristically Roman notion that one had to be the king *of something*, namely of the corporate body that empowered magistrates to act with authority, in this case the *res publica*.[17] In theory, an emperor could be and sometimes was deposed for failing in his duties toward his subjects.

---

[15] Menandros Rhetor, *Treatise I* (*Division of Epideictic Speeches*) 60.10–16, 67.11–14, 68.10–14; Ioannes Chrysostomos, *Homily on Acts* 38.2; for these and similar statements, see Buraselis (1989) 167–172, to which should be added Bardesanes in MacMullen (1990) 33; for a study of this process, Garnsey (2004) 145–149. For earlier statements, see Strabon 10.4.22 (regarding Crete); Aristeides, *Or.* 26.102 (*Roman Oration*); see below for this oration.

[16] Beck (1970) 13 17, 22 23, and *passim*, esp. 24 for AD 1453; (1982) 38 45; Chrysos (2003) 129 130. I prefer 'polity' (from *politeia*) to 'commonwealth' because the latter connotes loose multi-ethnic groupings.

[17] Ando (1999) 15–17.

This may seem to be "mere ideology," but it was not, even if only because provincials subscribed to it and thereby consented to a regime that was defined by it. Even "fiction . . . can be an important spiritual force, if it is accepted by everyone. The history of Rome knew several fictions of a *longue durée*, which contributed, through their influence on morale and mentality, to the continuity of the social order of the Romans."[18] What we are dealing with here, however, was no fiction, and provincials did not accept it by default or coercion. The empire had been created through arms but was maintained in large part through a consensus as freely given as that of any modern nation-state (which is not to ignore the mechanisms of social control and manufacture of consent operative in *both*). The *koinon*, the "sharing" of the *politeia*, rested on a moral consensus that was grounded in the qualities that had made Rome both different and ultimately superior to other cities, at least in the eyes of Dionysios of Halikarnassos: Rome was the most generous and "communal" of cities (*koinotatê*), whose community rested upon a horizontal moral consensus.[19] New Romans had reason to believe in the sincerity of that consensus. The late Roman and Byzantine emperors – drawn from all provinces and all social levels – for their part proclaimed that they were bound by law and authorized to rule solely for the benefit of all their subjects (and not only the citizens among them, at least before 211).[20] This was imposed on them by principle and was not the arbitrary whim of personal benevolence. The emperors accordingly implemented utilitarian building projects in every province and granted tax remissions, subsidies for local projects, and disaster relief. To these were added later the works of Christian charity, including hospitals, orphanages, and ransom for those captured by barbarians. The provincials could see their taxes at work for them. The state improved the way they traveled, bathed, and ate, and thereby defined their loyalties.

We need, then, to reverse the picture that is painted for us in so many surveys of Byzantine culture, according to which the emperor was an absolute ruler who reigned by the grace of God and whose subjects simply had to accept that fact. The opposite seems to have been the case, namely that the emperor was believed to rule by the grace of God only if he was responsive to the needs of his subjects, as some twelfth-century petitions imply and, in one case, directly state. The emperors probably answered thousands of petitions each year, and did so because it was

[18] Alföldy (2001) 16.   [19] Dionysios of Halikarnassos, *Roman Antiquities* 1.89.1.
[20] Sources in Karagiannopoulos (1992); non-citizens: Ando (2000) 148, 330 ff.; Liebeschuetz (2001) 345.

their job.[21] In their vast totality these acts gave overwhelming physical realization to imperial ideology and created a unified community based on reciprocal expectations. Precedents were established and documentation gave individuals legal power over the bureaucracy. Ideology was not a fiction in this system, but a constantly enacted reality. Official statements such as tax receipts, imperial rescripts, birth certificates, property assessments, annual loyalty oaths, the census, and others, defined new Roman identities in all contexts, collective and individual. Only philosophers or fanatics could resist. These new Romans, from Britain to Arabia, eventually came to share the same calendar, weights and measures, coinage, census and taxes, public monuments, loyalty rituals, festivals, games and imperial cult, camps and armies, courts and laws, social and political opportunities, public archives, *paideia*, and language(s), all of which were effectively deployed by the authorities so as to constantly remind the provincial population of its increasingly equal stake in the *politeia* and elicit its active participation. Crucially, the provincials *knew* that they all belonged to the same global community precisely by the fact that they shared all these things.[22] "Rallies, parades, festivals: all aim to consolidate the symbolic unity of a people and their subservience to a dominant set of objectives."[23] Milestones along standardized roads created a vast imaginary grid that bound the periphery to the political and ideological center. The degree of uniformity (and therefore predictability) at work was astonishing: the same festivals were celebrated from the Euphrates frontier to Britain; military camps were built according to specification with such undeviating regularity that gates were built even when they opened directly onto steep ravines. And, in late antiquity, it is even possible to speak of a "nationalized" organization of the circus games and acclamations, which promoted imperial ideology and brought citizens into transcivic empire-wide loyalties, reinforcing "identification with a broader provincial and imperial society."[24] Only in the late nineteenth or early twentieth century did modern nations achieve this level of uniformity.

Naturally there was discontent with corruption and class injustice, as there is always and everywhere. But the crucial point is that this was

[21] Macrides (2004) 368–369; for the early period, Millar (1977), whose famous conclusion that they did not initiate policy is, however, doubtful.

[22] Ando (2000) *passim*, is fundamental; see esp. 8, 41, 119, 337, 411; for standardized weights in the early Byzantine period, Gittings (2003) 38, citing previous bibliography; for personal archives in the middle Byzantine period (and their limitations), Neville (2004) ch. 6.

[23] Whitmarsh (2001) 296.

[24] Festivals: Fink, Hoey, and Snyder (1940) 202–210; camps: Burns (2003) 166; circus: Liebeschuetz (2001) 203 n. 1 and 216; Holum (2005) 104.

discontent with the partial failure of an ideal of political justice, not a rejection of it in favor of another, perhaps more local, alternative. With few exceptions before the late twelfth century, armed uprisings were understood as civil wars, not secessionist native revolts. To be sure, regions such as Wales, Egypt, and Isauria were not assimilated until very late or before they were lost. Yet by the second century the empire was well on its way toward becoming a single nation as integrated as any modern nation-state, an imagined community "conceived as a deep, horizontal comradeship,"[25] despite obvious class differences. Never before had this been done, though Greeks at any rate were not entirely unprepared. Discussing the achievements of his native Achaian League, Polybios noted that by using the same laws, measures, weights, coins, magistrates, senators, and judges, the Peloponnese had nearly become a unified polis, lacking only a single protective wall. Recall that Aristotle had rejected the notion that the Peloponnese could form a single polis if only it were surrounded by a wall.[26] When later Byzantine thinkers looked back upon late antiquity and reflected on what had happened to the ancient Greeks, they realized that the latter had become Romans in this very way. Witness Georgios Akropolites writing in the late 1250s:

No other nations were ever as harmonious as the Greeks (*Graikoi*) and the Italians. And this was only to be expected, for science and learning came to the Italians from the Greeks. And after that point, so that they need not use their ethnic names, a New Rome was built to complement the Elder one, so that all were called Romans after the common name of such great cities, and have the same faith and the same name for it. And just as they received that most noble name from Christ, so too did they take upon themselves the national (*ethnikon*) name [i.e., Romans]. And everything else was common to them: magistracies, laws, literature, city councils, law courts, piety itself.[27]

The creation of this Roman *oikoumenê* was the deliberate goal of imperial policy, chiefly of Augustus, Hadrian, and the Severan jurists. "This vast extension of *romanitas* was not made in a fit of absence of mind. It was a deliberate imperial commitment."[28] From the start, imperial ideology sought to build a consensus in the provinces by using all media of communication at its disposal to rally local loyalties, no matter how diverse initially,

---

[25] For imagined communities in the modern era, see Anderson (1991), here 7. For Byzantium as a nation-state, see below. For Wales, see, e.g., Snyder (2003) 54, 75.

[26] Polybios 2.37.9–11; Aristotle, *Politics* 3.3.

[27] Georgios Akropolites, *Against the Latins* 2.27 (v. II, p. 64). For the context, see p. 382 below.

[28] Millar (1987b) 146.

behind the person of the emperor.[29] But the emperor was a symbol: an image malleable and adaptable, he was consumed by the world which he came to define. In Byzantium, he acted as a chief executive and functional definition of Roman identity, a form of symbolic shorthand, but he did not constitute the *essence* of that identity; the latter was constructed socially and historically by a consensus that did not require him.[30] The Romans were a people, not a class of legally defined servants.

Turning back to the origins of Romania, provincials were not passively incorporated into the Roman order. They were offered the opportunity to promote their own assimilation and contribute to the expanding polity. As we will see, this was recognized at the time as the most original aspect of Roman rule and has been well discussed by historians. The small administration of the early empire depended on the support and active participation of local notables, who were often rewarded with citizenship. At first, like Pompeius' man from Mytilene, Theophanes, they served as propagandists and local instruments. Theophanes followed the general on campaign, wrote his praises, and helped secure Mytilene for him. Similar opportunities existed under the emperors, only in more formal guise. Greeks obtained posts in the secretarial departments of the administration, where they shaped the communication between center and periphery.[31] With citizenship, families eventually claimed high office and before long are attested as governors and consuls. Among the first were the descendants of Theophanes himself, who did not forget Mytilene from their Roman *domus*.[32] The rise of provincials to the Senate has been well studied as part of the process that gradually eliminated the differences between center and periphery even before 212, as did the shift in military recruitment from Italy to the provinces. The career of the centurion Gaius Iulius Saturninus from Chios, who served under the Flavians in a unit of Spaniards in Egypt, well reflects the globalizing effect of office.[33] From the third century we have the Bithynian senator Kassios Dion, who wrote a history of Rome. It was in Greek, but reflected a thoroughly Roman point of view. It was in fact through this work that many Byzantines knew their Roman history: one called its author "Dion the Roman" to distinguish him

[29] Boatwright (2000) 4–6; for Hadrian, see also Ando (2000) 40–41, 278, 316–320, 330–331, 410.
[30] *Pace* Cheynet (2002) 25, 28, among many others.
[31] Theophanes: Kaldellis (2002) 65–66, citing previous bibliography; posts: Millar (1977) 83 ff.
[32] Labarre (1996) 148 153; Kaldellis (2002) 90–91.
[33] For the Senate, see the works cited by Buraselis (1989) 73. Chios: Sarikakis (1998) 251–252; cf. the complex cultural loyalties of the Hellenized Kolchian Amazaspos: Braund (1994) 230–231. For the army and Romanization, see Woolf (1998) 243–245.

from Dion Chrysostomos, whose negotiation of Hellenism and Rome a century earlier was more ambiguous than that of Kassios Dion.[34]

These well-known developments are mentioned here because Byzantium was their offspring and heir. The dynamism and longevity of Roman society in all periods were predicated on its ability to assimilate new peoples, to make its *res publica* attractive to them. The Byzantines had even less interest in ethnicity than had the Romans of old; after all, there had been an old guard of blue-bloods in the Rome of the Caesars such as never existed in New Rome.[35] Assimilation in Byzantium occurred faster, and the religious requirements had changed. We will return to this issue below, when we consider the danger of trying to identify ethnic groups – including "the Greeks" – in Byzantium. For now, let us turn directly to the accommodation reached between Hellenism and Rome in late antiquity.

As we have seen, ignorance of Byzantium vitiates many discussions of Romanization in the Greek East. The fact itself is either ignored or acknowledged but reduced to material culture and mere legal status, as though baths and a choice of court could ever persuade a population to bear a Roman identity for over a millennium. The Greeks in particular were overaware of their distinctive history and culture. Only the most powerful and enticing prospects could lead them to subordinate it or give it up for a foreign, initially "barbaric" alternative. Given this, the Romanization of Greece is at once one of the most fascinating and understudied transformations in history. What room was left for Hellenism in Romania? In the cultural articulation that we call Byzantium, what existential space was allotted to being Roman and what to being Greek?[36] We should not be distracted by the terminological confusion introduced by Christianity nor view Hellenism in Byzantium exclusively from a Christian standpoint, as is usually done, for its first accommodation was with Rome; we will examine the Christian modulation of the issue in the next chapter.

A stable Byzantine symbiosis between "Greece" and "Rome" was already in place by the late third and early fourth century (though still not without some dissent), as Rome lay exclusive claim to citizenship and to social and national allegiance, while Athens claimed *paideia*. Because the two defined themselves in relation to different aspects of life, they were not in conflict.

---

[34] Kekaumenos, *Strategikon* 5; for the Diones, see Swain (1996) chs. 6 and 13.

[35] E.g., Suetonius, *Augustus* 40.3–4 and Kassios Dion 56.7.5 (Augustus); Tacitus, *Annals* 11.23; Herodianos, *History of the Empire after Marcus* 7.7.5 (referring to events after 212); and the sources cited by Alföldy (1988) 113, 233 n. 117.

[36] Woolf (1994) insightfully discusses the problem (esp. 128–130), dealing with an earlier period and not considering the trends leading to the Byzantine solution.

Sacrifices, however, had to be made on both sides: Rome lost much of the Latin tradition (though not all), while Greece lost ethnicity, history, and the polis (though Romania used the rhetoric of the Greek polis to focalize loyalty).[37] History and community went to Rome, while language and intellectual life, especially rhetoric and philosophy, went to Athens. Material life, prominent in modern discussions, was ultimately unimportant. Even at the peak of the Second Sophistic there does not seem to have been much concern on the part of ardent Hellenists over the Roman origin of baths, hippodromes, roads, villas, cement, arches, and gladiatorial games. Greeks and Romans did not really define their identity that way. It is modern archaeology that has tended to equate ethnicity with material culture, though this methodology has come under increasing criticism.

An initial Hellenic reaction to Romanization there certainly was, which we mentioned briefly in the previous chapter in connection with the Second Sophistic. Trivially, some Greeks were abused by the Hellenists for imitating the Romans, for instance by shaving their beards.[38] Others realized that far broader issues were at stake. Despite his general admiration for the Romans, acceptance of the empire, and personal possession of Roman citizenship, Plutarch regarded Greeks as irreducibly different from Romans, who were *allophyloi*, and he did not approve of Greek integration into Roman society. A proud citizen of Chaironeia claiming descent from the ancient heroes of Boiotia, he ridiculed provincial elites who lusted after Roman office, and championed the small polis: "I choose to live in a small town lest it become even smaller."[39] He also wrote an insightful and somewhat bitter treatise on the state of politics in the Greek world. Opportunities for great actions, he notes, are a thing of the past. All one can do is try to make powerful Roman friends, because the Romans look after their friends. "Now, when the affairs of the cities no longer involve leadership in wars nor the dissolution of tyrannies nor alliances, what kind of a beginning may one make of a brilliant political career? Well, public trials remain, and embassies to the emperor." Seeing as "they have a boot on their head," Greeks should not be encouraged to "imitate the deeds

---

[37] For Romania as a polis, see p. 57 below.

[38] Beards: Dion Chrysostomos, *Or.* 36.17 (*Borysthenic Oration, which he delivered in his native land*); Apollonios (?), *Letter* 70; Roman names: Philostratos, *Regarding Apollonios of Tyana* 4.5; in general, Favorinus, *Corinthian Oration* 25 (pseudo-Dion Chrysostomos, *Or.* 37); food: Palladas in *Greek Anthology* 9.502. For other forms of imitation, see Price (1984) 89–91.

[39] *Allophyloi*: Plutarch, *Flamininus* 2.5; local patriotism: e.g., *Demosthenes* 1.2; descent: *On the Slowness of God to Punish* 13 (*Moralia* 558a–b); provincial ambitions: *On Contentment* 10 (470c–d); *On Exile* 14 (605b–c); in general, see Gabba (1991) 55–56, and Swain (1996) ch. 5; cf. ibid. 362 for Galenos' defense of small-town life.

of their ancestors."[40] Such advice could be given only by one who did not, ultimately, regard himself as a Roman. And there is some evidence to indicate that, despite Plutarch's pessimistic picture, many other Greek notables like him preferred to live in their own cities and occupy themselves with local or regional affairs rather than take up service with Rome. That would explain why the Greeks were among the last provincials to make their mark in the Senate or the army or on the throne.[41] Still, even as Plutarch was writing, Arrianos of Nikomedeia, one of the first Greek senators from Bithynia, was blazing a glorious military and civil career in Roman service. Interestingly, it was not only for Rome that Arrianos left his native city, but also for Athens, where he retired, became a citizen, and served as *archôn*.

Rome and Athens could be reconciled on the basis of their respective strengths, which were generally compatible. An anecdote told by Lucian, whose devotion to his native Samosata took third place to his love of Greek *paideia* and his membership in the global Roman community, indicates how this could be done: "A certain Polybios, altogether lacking *paideia* and ungrammatical, said, 'The emperor has honored me with Roman citizenship.' 'If only,' said the philosopher Demonax, 'he had made you a Greek rather than a Roman!' "[42] The distinction here is asymmetrical, as Hellenism involves only *paideia*. Polybios could conceivably have "become" both a Greek (in terms of higher culture) and a Roman (politically), as was after all Lucian himself, one of the first Greek writers to use the first-person plural in referring to Romans. More philosophical or even mystical definitions of Hellenism were equally compatible with the Roman order.[43]

The most interesting text that may be discussed in this connection is the often-quoted *Roman Oration* of Ailios Aristeides (*Or.* 26), which is important because it is the only systematic exposition of the structure *and* ideology of the empire and was written by a very conservative Hellenist who was also a Roman citizen and would become hugely popular in Byzantium. The grounds for caution are obvious: the work is panegyrical and was delivered at the court. But Aristeides' extensive knowledge of history and political thought enabled him to compare the empire intelligently to its

[40] Plutarch, *Political Precepts* 10, 17 (*Moralia* 805a, 814a) and *passim*; similarly in Dion Chrysostomos, see Swain (1996) 219.
[41] Salmeri (2000) 56–63.
[42] Lucian, *Demonax* 40; cf. *On service in a rich household* 25; and Kassios Dion 69.3.5: "Caesar can give you money and honor but cannot make you an orator."
[43] E.g., in Philostratos, *Regarding Apollonios of Tyana* 3.43.

predecessors and define its innovations in governance, while his rhetorical skill enabled him to devise thoughtful images for the new modes of Roman rule, which became those of Byzantium too. His *Roman Oration* is usually studied by classicists who are working at the chronological limits of their field and whose training causes them read it while looking *back* to classical antiquity. Here the conventional periodization of our disciplines will be flouted: Aristeides is offered as a remarkably prescient look *forward* to Byzantium.

Whatever his complicated personal feelings about the relative worth of Roman and Hellenic identities, Aristeides testifies to the powerful ideological appeal of the Roman polity. The entire *oikoumenê*, he says, is governed for the protection of its subjects as though it were a single city (36): the extension of citizenship, a conception unlike anything imagined in the past, has established a common and global *demokratia* (59–60). "Democracy" for him was not, as with us, the antithesis of monarchy but a fundamental aspect of the *res publica* (*politeia* in Greek) that had survived the change of the regime. "You have made the word Roman apply not to a city, but to a common *genos*." The division between Greeks and barbarians has given way to that between Romans and non-Romans (63). An imagined community of Romans has been created in every city, where there can be no thought of or interest in rebellion (64; cf. 68). The governed have in fact become the governors, as the *politeia* is common to all (65–66). And if the world has become a single city (cf. 61), its walls are the legions on the frontiers (79–84) – thus indicating the superior union of Rome compared to Polybios' Achaian Peloponnese.

The Romans occupied an ambiguous position between Greeks and barbarians, destabilizing both categories; they were a sort of *tertium quid*.[44] The reason for this is to be sought in the Romans' own efforts to represent themselves to the peoples of the eastern Mediterranean through Greek media, which made them always "inside-outsiders." But stronger efforts to assimilate them to Greek history and ethnicity, as that by Dionysios of Halikarnassos, did not go far; the Romans did not become Greeks. To the contrary, by late antiquity, the Romans had created a distinctive and unprecedented universal *oikoumenê* under their own name in which local identities, including the Greek, were submerged and eventually disappeared. Thus Romans eventually replaced Greeks as the polar opposite of the barbarians. In Byzantium, it is "Romans and barbarians" that usually means "everyone"

---

[44] See the texts cited by Jüthner (1923) ch. 7; Browning (2002) 262 and the discussion in Hartog (2001) ch. 5.

and it is a sign of Hellenic revival when we again find "Greeks and barbarians" in our texts. Aristeides, however, was not yet ready to surrender his Hellenic identity. Rome he may have regarded as supreme in war, law, and governance – in what we call "nation-building" – but in his *Panathenaic Oration* he praised Athens for retaining its cultural primacy. Athens still instructs the world how to be Greek through its *paideia* – "not by establishing garrisons," a curious phrase. So, then, just as the *Roman Oration* explains how all people have come together in the Roman *politeia*, the *Panathenaic Oration* explains how they have embraced the wisdom and beauty of Athens and the Attic tongue as a sign of true *paideia*.[45] We have here already a prefiguration of the cultural articulation of Byzantium.

To further illustrate the Byzantine accommodation of Hellenism and Rome I have chosen for discussion two men from late antiquity, the pagan emperor Julian and the philosopher-bishop Synesios, whose attitudes toward *paideia* were traditional but who are highlighted here precisely because their view of Christianity was, at least from a later perspective, unconventional. They show that the accommodation between Rome and Greece was not of Christian manufacture.

Julian we will discuss more fully in the next chapter. He was in many ways the first Byzantine emperor: he was the first to be born in Constantinople (in the year after its foundation) and his native language was Greek, though he had Latin. He called himself a Roman emperor, though he never visited Rome (the decline of the City's importance inversely reflected the Romanization of the provinces). He believed that his rise to the throne was the work of God and that his duties included promulgating Orthodoxy. He was not interested in his ethnicity, noting that his family was Thrakian in *genos*, referring to the Illyrian origins of the Constantinian dynasty. But he never assigned any importance to this, adding in the same passage that despite it his way of life was Greek: *logos* displaces *genos*.[46] As we will see, Julian vaguely recognized the existence of a Greek nation, but for him personally Hellenism was a matter of *paideia*. Like the emperor Hadrian, he too was called *Graeculus* and *Asianus* by his Gallic troops (who were not trying to flatter him).[47] The eunuch to whom Julian gratefully owed his *paideia*, and his love of Homer in particular, was

---

[45] Ailios Aristeides, *Or.* 1 (*Panathenaic Oration*), esp. 322–327; for Rome and Athens in Aristeides, see Saïd (2001) 293. Even in the *Roman Oration* he notes that it was the Athenians who first began to live in a civilized way (101). Romans and barbarians in Byzantium: Lechner (1954) 73–83.
[46] Julian, *Misopogon* 367c; in 348c–d his ancestors are "Mysian." Cf. Julian's friend Libanios, *Or.* 11.184 (*Antiochene Oration*): a man should be called a Greek because of *logoi* and not *genos*.
[47] Ammianus Marcellinus 17.9.3.

by *genos* a "Skythian" barbarian, i.e., probably a Goth.[48] When his friend and colleague Saloustios, like Favorinus a native of Gaul and a philosopher, was recalled by the suspicious court of Constantius II, Julian wrote a farewell piece saying that "I now enroll myself among the Celts on your behalf, you who should be among the first of the Greeks on account of your lawfulness and the rest of virtue, the peak of oratory, and familiarity with philosophy."[49] In another work written in the same period, he calls Greece, which he visited as a student, "my true fatherland" on account of its preeminence in *paideia*. He especially loved Athens.[50] But in many comments elsewhere he reveals that he is also a Roman and that his city is Rome, or New Rome, though the Greeks, he adds, are related to "us" Romans (nicely inverting Dionysios' Hellenocentrism).[51] Roman *politeia* displaces also local ethnicity: all people, "even if they are from elsewhere, by participating in Rome's constitution and by using the customs and laws that we devise there, become members of our political order."[52] From these passages we obtain a relatively coherent sense of what Julian believed it meant to be Greek and what it meant to be Roman: they were different albeit perfectly compatible sites of identity.

Of course, Julian meant more by Hellenism than any Byzantines could accept. But religion aside, the respective space that he assigned to Greece and Rome was typical. Rome – whether Old or New Rome, or Romania as a whole – was a *patria* of law and custom, while Athens was the homeland of those educated in Hellenic *paideia*. So too the Platonist Synesios of Kyrene, a student of the pagan martyr Hypatia and later bishop of Ptolemaïs in the early fifth century. His works, like those of Julian, were prized as models of philosophy and style by later Byzantines even though the precise contents of his faith were hazy. Chosen as bishop for his leadership against the barbarians despite not being baptized, Synesios agreed on the condition that he keep his wife and that he not have to believe in doctrines like the Resurrection. To be sure, he was not impressed

---

[48] Julian, *Misopogon* 352a ff.

[49] Julian, *Or.* 8.252a–b (*Consolation to himself upon the departure of the most excellent Saloustios*). The precise form of the name is disputed.

[50] Greece: Julian, *Or.* 3.118d (*Panegyric for the Empress Eusebia*); Athens: *Letter to Themistios the Philosopher* 260a–b; *Misopogon* 348b–c. See Huart (1978) 101.

[51] Julian, *Or.* 1.41a (*Panegyric for the Emperor Constantius*); *Or.* 4.152d–153d, 154c, 155a (*Hymn to King Helios for Saloustios*): Rome, our city, is Greek; *Or.* 5.180b (*Hymn to the Mother of the Gods*); *Letter to a Priest* 302d; *Letter* 47.433d; *Against the Galilaeans* 200a b: the Greeks are related to us Romans, but cf. *Symposium, or Kronia* 324a; cf. *Misopogon* 357b: the Antiochenes are also Romans. In *Letter* 48 to the Alexandrians, Constantinople is his native city. In general, see Bouffartigue (1992) 661–665.

[52] Julian, *Or.* 1.5c (*Panegyric for the Emperor Constantius*).

with contemporary Athens, finding it a depressing ruin, and liked to trace his ancestry to the sons of Herakles who led the Dorians into Sparta.[53] This genealogical conceit was a rare leftover from the affectations of the Second Sophistic. When his devotion to Hellenism was questioned by Christian polemicists, Synesios responded by writing a treatise on Dion Chrysostomos entitled *Dion, or on My Way of Life*, in which he argued that "a philosopher should not be evil in any way or boorish, but should be initiated in the mysteries of the Graces and be a Hellene in a most precise sense, namely that he should be able to hold converse with humanity through his familiarity with every work of literature."[54]

A Roman, on the other hand, was something different. In his speech *On Kingship*, presented before like-minded conservatives in Constantinople in 398, Synesios defended the "ancient institutions" of the Romans (15). He condemned the granting of exemptions from military service to farmers in order to hire barbarians, urging the exclusive recruitment of native troops and the exclusion of barbarians from office (19–20). His argument is based not on race but on Plato's *Republic* (*Politeia* in Greek) and his own loyalty to the Roman order. Soldiers must be "guardians" of the "laws by which they were nurtured and educated, for they are the men whom Plato likened to watch-dogs." Those must be excluded who do not respect "our" values.[55] The presence of foreigners in a well-regulated city had, after all, presented Aristotle with a political challenge not on racial grounds but because they were "raised according to different laws."[56]

Julian and Synesios were Platonist philosophers who fought at the court and on the battlefield to defend the empire from barbarians. They could be both Hellenes and Romans, but how few Romans could afford to be Greeks in this way! In its basic articulation, then, Byzantium resembled the ancient Republic: a Roman *res publica* in which only a few leading men could indulge their Greek tastes. That the citizens actually spoke Greek had

[53] Conditions of ordination: Synesios, *Letter* 105; Athens: *Letters* 54, 136; ancestry: *Letters* 41 (239 ff.), 113; *Katastasis* 2.303a. The best study remains that of Bregman (1982). The philosopher Hegias claimed descent from Solon: Marinos, *Proklos, or on Happiness* 26. Basileios of Patras (ca. 500) from Oxylos: Bingen (1954) 74.

[54] Synesios, *Dion, or on My Way of Life* 4.42b and *passim*; cf. Bregman (1982) 127–137; Cameron and Long (1993) 62 ff.

[55] See Heather (1988); Cameron and Long (1993) ch. 4 and 301–310 against the strict "Hellenist" reading of Synesios' works by Dagron (1969) 29–33. See also p. 171 below.

[56] Aristotle, *Politics* 7.6 (1327a11–15). Cf. the episode under Theodosius I in Zosimos, *New History* 4.30, where the violence of barbarian recruits is deemed inappropriate for men "who wish to live according to the Roman laws." See Kaldellis (2004b).

little to do with Greek identity, as we will see. Diglossia persisted, only a Latinized demotic Greek took the place of Latin as the social inferior to Attic. Byzantine history was born already under the Republic; Roman history continued to the end of Byzantium.

## THE TRANSLATION OF ROMANIA

*Romania* was neither a name artificially superimposed by the Byzantines on their state in a purely formal recognition of their political origins and legal system nor a default label used by medieval Greeks blocked by Christianity from using their "true" name. It represented a primary identification with a social and political community that was both directly continuous with that of ancient Rome and required the abandonment or subordination of any ethnic or local identities that diminished or fractured the unity of the Roman polity. This conception was not changed by the transfer of empire from Old to New Rome during late antiquity. For the scholar-emperor Konstantinos VII in the tenth century – or his ghost-writers – "the Roman empire (*archê*) in Byzantion" was nothing other than the ancient "Roman *politeia*" (*politeia* was Greek for *res publica*).[57] Only the location of the capital had changed, but the "capital" in the third and fourth centuries AD had effectively accompanied the emperors on their campaigns and tours and had ceased to be at Rome before Constantinople was even founded. "Rome" was not a mere city, but an ecumenical community. The foundation of New Rome, then, represented a *return* to imperial stability: it was a deliberate transplantation of the former seat of empire to eastern Romania, a branch-office of Rome that contained all of its defining institutions, whose parity with the original fell short only in honor, not in rank or identity. The eleventh-century historian Michael Attaleiates knew that when Constantine had transferred the *basileia* from Rome to Byzantion he took many distinguished families with him and built palaces for them like those in Rome. The emperors added landmarks to mirror those of Rome and the writers even imagined seven hills. In the early sixth century, the historian Hesychios of Miletos rewrote the history of ancient Byzantion to make it parallel the history of ancient Rome and thereby prefigure its future imperial greatness. In the twelfth century, Anna Komnene, daughter of the emperor Alexios I, imagined that the porphyry marble that lined the

---

[57] Theophanes Continuatus, Book 5: *Life of Basileios I* 1 (pp. 211–212).

room in which she and so many other Byzantine princes had been born, and from which they derived the rank of porphyrogennetos and the legitimacy of their rule, had been brought from Rome by the emperors of old. Constantinople *was* Rome.[58]

As Christians, the Byzantines traced the grounds of their community to the Chosen People of the Old Testament, but as a nation their consciousness was thoroughly Roman. Institutional continuity and excellent historical records easily established the authentic Roman origin and imperial legitimacy of their state and society. Nor was this done defensively, as though anyone seriously doubted it. In the sixth century, the emperor Justinian traced the "ancient history of the government" back to "Aeneas, the King of Troy, Prince of the Republic, from whom we are said to descend," adding that "Romulus and Numa founded the government."[59] The antiquarian Ioannes Lydos, promoted by Justinian to a chair of Latin in Constantinople, believed that the offices of the early Byzantine state had their origin in the time of Romulus and also that the Republic was the only period of true freedom in Roman history.[60] This was not a function of Latin bias, which both Justinian and Lydos had in abundance; later Byzantines, who knew no Latin, also believed that their political history – as distinct from their religious origins – began with Aeneas. After narrating the Trojan War, for example, most Byzantine chronicles follow him to Italy and then leap ahead to Caesar, evincing little interest in Greek history.[61] Certainly, they are more concerned with the succession of emperors, though a strong interest in the Republic can be adduced too, especially for the eleventh and twelfth centuries. The historian Attaleiates looked back to the Republic for the origins of Byzantine law and for models of virtuous warfare and statecraft that could be imitated by present-day Romans. The chronicler Ioannes Zonaras had no doubts that he himself belonged to the *ethnos* of the Romans, whose history stretched without interruption from the days of the ancient kings to the period of the Komnenoi; this nation had conquered in the past almost the entire world despite changing

[58] Dagron (1974); Calderone (1993) 733–744; Dölger (1953) 83–98 provides many citations but is wrongly skeptical ("auf einer Fiktion," etc.), being engaged in a legal rather than a historical inquiry. Michael Attaleiates, *History* 217–218; for Hesychios, see Kaldellis (2005c); Anna Komnene, *Alexiad* 7.2.4.

[59] Justinian, *Novel* 47, preface.    [60] Kaldellis (2005a). For Lydos, see also pp. 73–74 below.

[61] Jeffreys (1979) esp. 203–207, 213–215, and 227–228 for Manasses and Malalas; Dagron (2005b) 199. A series of vignettes by the eleventh-century polymath Michael Psellos begins with the kings, includes the first consuls, and then follows the sequence of emperors after Julius Caesar: *Historia Syntomos* 1–16. For its authenticity, see Duffy and Papaioannou (2003); for its omission of Biblical history, Ljubarskij (2004a) 286.

its constitution many times.[62] In the late eleventh century, Ioannes Xiphilinos (a nephew of the patriarch) wrote an epitome of sections of the Roman history of Kassios Dion, noting at one place in the reign of Augustus that those events were very relevant because "our lives and *politeuma*" still entirely depend on them.[63]

Just as the Byzantines referred to foreign peoples by classical names, making the Goths into Skythians and the Arabs into Medes, so too did they regularly call themselves Ausones, an ancient name for the original inhabitants of *Italy*. This was the standard "classicizing" name that the Byzantines used for themselves, not "Hellenes."[64] In short, the depth and seriousness of the Byzantines' Roman identity should not be denied lightly or on false premises. For instance, it does not matter what they were called by their neighbors. That is no way to approach a culture to begin with: suppose we tried to understand those others based on what the Byzantines called them! In addition, the Arabic (or Semitic in general), Armenian, Slavic, and Latin terminology for Byzantium was idiosyncratic, inconsistent, and reflected historical, antiquarian, linguistic, and political biases that do not reflect Byzantine self-ascriptions.[65] Some modern Greek scholars actually *prefer* foreign usage, which they use selectively to imply that the Byzantines "really were Greeks, but had not realized it themselves."[66] To the contrary, the Byzantines sometimes corrected foreign usage in translating texts, changing "Greek" to "Roman."[67] Medieval western perceptions in particular may

---

[62] Republic: Magdalino (1983) esp. 343 n. 109; Macrides and Magdalino (1992) 127–129; Kaldellis (2005a) 12–13. Attaleiates: Kaldellis (2007b). Ioannes Zonaras, *Chronicle* 6.29. For the meaning of *ethnos* and related words, see below.

[63] Ioannes Xiphilinos, *Epitome of Dion of Nikaia* 53.22 (v. III, p. 526).

[64] E.g., Michael Attaleiates, *History* 31, 214; Alexios I Komnenos, *Muses, passim*; Theodoros Prodromos, *Poems, passim*; Niketas Choniates, *History* 150. See Pitsakis (1995) 26–27. Countless more such references exist.

[65] Armenian: Bartikian (1993) 731–733; Arabic: El Cheikh (2004) 22–24, 86–89, 104–106, 192–193; Persian: Asatrian (1996); Persian, Arabic, and Turkoman in the twelfth and thirteenth centuries: Shukurov (2001) 266–270; Slavic: Nikolov (2006).

[66] Vakalopoulos (1974) 87, the pioneer of Greek historiography on the question.

[67] The *Apocalypse* of pseudo-Methodios refers to "the empire of the Hellenes, namely that of the Romans" (9.7, 11.3, 13.11; v. I, pp. 124, 136, 174). Tăpkova-Zaimova (1993) seems to offer this as proof that the "essence" of Byzantium was Greek. This conclusion can hardly be proven by such a text, but here the evidence actually proves the opposite. We are dealing with a text written in Syriac, in the seventh century in Mesopotamia; it was translated into Greek before 800. Alexander (1985) 56, notes that "the Greek [i.e., Byzantine] translator has replaced the words 'of the Greeks' by 'of the Romans' or has added the latter expression ... to make it absolutely clear that pseudo-Methodios' prophesies referred to the Roman (Byzantine) Empire." In short, the Byzantine translator believed that "Greek" in Syriac meant "Roman" in Greek. He added the glosses quoted at the top of this note to explain that Hellene "really means" Roman. And this is to say nothing of the fantastic contents of the work, which derive Greek and Roman dynasties from an Ethiopian bloodline, etc.; see Reinink (1992).

satisfy modern Greek expectations, but they perpetuate the bias according to which the Byzantines were "mere" Greeks, or "Greeklings," i.e., the illegitimate heirs of Rome. Some Greek historians swallow this insult because it helps establish "continuity" with *ancient Greece*, a modern nationalist obsession to which their Latin sources were in fact utterly indifferent.

There are two qualifications, however, that merit further discussion. The first is that most Byzantines spoke Greek rather than Latin, especially after the sixth century, whereas being Roman in the Republic and early empire required some engagement with the Latin tradition. The second is the widespread belief that the Byzantine empire really consisted of a number of separate ethnicities, for instance Slavic, Greek, and Armenian, which were brought under the authority of what was in reality a multi-ethnic imperial state. Byzantine history can then be carved up into the constituent histories of these groups according to the logic of the modern nationalisms that claim them. This second view will be discussed in detail in the next section; we will first discuss the question of language.

We will not pretend that nothing is lost, gained, or at any rate altered when the linguistic balance of a national and political system gradually shifts from one language to another, especially when its coherence rests to some degree on ideological assumptions about civic consensus and a body of law. An ancient jurist, for example, noted that some Latin legal terms "cannot properly be translated," even though their etymology was originally Greek. The Senator and historian Kassios Dion acknowledged that "it is entirely impossible to render the force of the word *auctoritas* into Greek."[68] An important task for the future (though still unrecognized in the field of Byzantine Studies, because it crosses disciplinary boundaries) is to determine how *romanitas* changed when it was transferred from a mostly Latin environment to a mostly Greek one, even if that shift was effected slowly over the course of many centuries. For instance, one historian has perceptively noted that the Republic known to the Byzantines was that of Polybios and Kassios Dion and not that of Cicero and Livius.[69] This clearly made a difference, but what? We need more studies of the effect that translation had on Roman identity.

Two preliminary considerations can be offered here. First, the Hellenization of imperial rule in the East began much earlier than is usually

---

[68] Gaius, *Institutes* 3.93; cf. Ulpianus in Justinian, *Digest* 45.1.1.6. Kassios Dion 55.3.4–5. From the legal side, see Troianos (2004b) 166–168; Honoré (2004) 115.

[69] Magdalino (1983) 344. Ioannes Tzetzes, *Histories* 5.100–110 (pp. 170–171), cites Dionysios of Halikarnassos and Kassios Dion for the story of Kakos and Herakles, not Virgil, though he also mentions "many other writers who wrote of Rome."

recognized and so the modes of Roman rule and consensus-building had many centuries in which to adapt to the Greek environment of the East. Second, the Latinization of Byzantium was more extensive than is usually granted.

Rome was always part of the broader Greek world and its aristocracy had been culturally and linguistically Hellenized from the days of the Republic, if not before. And yet, paradoxically, Julius Caesar and Marcus Aurelius (a Stoic who kept his diaries in Greek) were far more Hellenized than, say, Justinian, who had no interest in Greek culture and whose contribution to the evolution of the Byzantine *politeia* was the codification of Roman law.[70] Before the founding of Constantinople, the city with the largest Greek-speaking population after Alexandria was in fact Rome, which was proven to have been a Greek city from its origins by the immigrant intellectual Dionysios of Halikarnassos. Our aim here is not to see in early imperial Rome the later articulation of Byzantium, again a *Byzance avant Byzance*, though that can be done. What is important is that the Romans were content from early on to use Greek in governing the East albeit always in accordance with Roman institutions. "There is ample evidence for official use of Greek by Roman administrators in Greek language areas," in fact even in the West and in Rome itself.[71] Some governors even drew attention in their edicts to the fact that they were using Greek. Already under Claudius there was trouble with judges from the East who could not speak Latin despite being Roman citizens. And the Hellenist Philostratos in the early third century makes his hero Apollonios argue explicitly that good emperors should appoint Greek-speakers to rule Greek lands and Latins to Latin lands, noting that one governor of Hellas had failed because he did not know Greek. This advice perhaps reflected Antonine policy.[72] The early empire was already close to Byzantium here, though no less Roman.

Most surveys of Byzantine history assert that the seventh-century emperor Herakleios "changed the official language from Latin to Greek" and link this to his simplification and alleged Hellenization of the imperial title to *basileus*.[73] But the fact, if it is a fact, does not support the inter- pretation. First, the title: emperors after Herakleios still styled themselves

---

[70] Romans and Greek: Kaimio (1979). Justinian: Honoré (1975) esp. 121–123.
[71] Swain (1996) 41; also Kaimio (1979) ch. 3 and 21–25 for Greeks in Rome; Rochette (1997) 160 n. 420, and 83 144 for official use of Latin in the East; Ando (2000) 83; Adams (2004) 186, 197; and Sartre (2005) 251 for coins.
[72] Claudius: MacMullen (2000) 12–13. Apollonios: Kaimio (1979) 110–129, here 117; Swain (1996) 389.
[73] See, e.g., Ostrogorsky (1969) 106–107, among many others.

*autokratôr* and *Sebastos* (i.e., *imperator* and *Augustus*). There was no clean break nor any "constitutional change." Moreover, *basileus* had been used to designate the emperor unofficially in Greek-speaking lands for centuries and even when used by itself was always understood to really mean "*basileus* of the Romans," a conception that was, as we saw, fundamentally Roman and antithetical to Hellenistic usage.[74] Consider the explanation given by the preacher Ioannes Chrysostomos for why the *basileus* in Psalm 44 must be God. The Psalmist

does not say which *basileus*, thereby making clear that he means the God of all. For just as when we are talking about the *basileus* of the Persians, we do not call him simply the *basileus*, but add "of the Persians," and likewise in the case of the one of the Armenians; when, then, we are talking about our own [i.e., the Roman *basileus*] we do not need the addition because it suffices to call him *basileus*. So too is it sufficient for the prophet, given that he is talking about the real *basileus*, to call him *basileus* simply.[75]

From a Roman point of view, *basileia* had to refer to a particular nation, and this was as true for the emperor of the Romans as it was for Persia, though common usage abbreviated the title when the referent was obvious. If, then, in everyday life *basileus* was the emperor of the Romans, in the Psalm he must be God. And the full form βασιλεὺς ῾Ρωμαίων would in fact be used officially from the seventh century and especially in the ninth, when westerners usurped it.[76] Herakleios, then, changed nothing in the conceptualization of the imperial office or even the language in which the majority of his subjects had spoken of it for centuries.

Second, no source claims that Herakleios changed the official language, which is only to be expected given that there is nothing in Roman law that corresponds to our notion of an official language. The Romans of the Republic eventually accepted all forms of Italian Latin as equally indicative of *romanitas* as the idiom of Rome itself, and under the empire they opened that field to any form of Latin and even Greek as well. "There was never any legal requirement that citizens should learn Latin."[77] The emperor Claudius even praised a barbarian for mastering "our two languages," namely Greek and Latin.[78] As we saw above, the East could be governed

---

[74] For imperial titles before and after Herakleios, see Rösch (1978) *passim*, esp. App. 1 and 2 for lists and tables; *basileus*: ibid. 37, 112; Chrysos (1978) 70, and *passim* for the international context of Herakleian usage, though unnecessarily accepting Hellenistic influence (on 72). *Pace* Shahîd (1981), I am not convinced of Christian influences.
[75] Ioannes Chrysostomos, *Homily on Psalm 44* 1.    [76] Rösch (1978) 112–116.
[77] Adams (2004) 188 and *passim*.    [78] Suetonius, *Claudius* 42.

officially in Greek from as early as the Republic. Bureaucratic restrictions on the official use of languages other than Latin were gradually abolished. The jurist Ulpianus noted that public notices should be posted in the language, Greek or Latin, known to their addressees, and wrote elsewhere that legally binding responses could be given in Greek or Latin, and perhaps in Punic or Aramaic given that "all tongues can produce a verbal obligation, provided that both parties understand each other's language." He observed that *fideicommissa* "may be left in any language, not only Greek or Latin but Punic, Gallic, or that of any other nation." By 439, Roman citizens could leave their wills in Greek.[79] But of a single "official language of the state" there is no trace in the record.

We should think rather in terms of the language that, for whatever contingent historical and cultural reasons, happened to be predominant in certain periods and in specific contexts, such as the army, the courts, or in legislation. Paradoxically, it was the Latinist Justinian who in 535 began to issue edicts mainly in Greek, a change that, equally paradoxically, would not have been to the liking of his *quaestor* Tribonianus, who preferred Latin despite the fact that his native tongue was probably Greek and his outlook Platonic.[80] Their contemporary Ioannes Lydos, also a Greek-speaker from Asia Minor and a student of the Platonists, accused Kyros of Panopolis, prefect of Constantinople in the mid-fifth century, of being the first "to transgress the ancient practice and issue his decrees in Greek." A professor of Latin, Lydos no doubt had a personal and professional stake in the matter. Yet elsewhere in the same work he accuses Justinian's prefect Ioannes the Kappadokian of (again?) changing the law from "the language of the Italians" to Greek. Overall, there was no official change of language because there were many different official settings and no one official language.[81]

To be sure, sometime after ca. 600 Latin went out of use in Byzantium, or at any rate was confined to very small circles, though minor counter-trends may be observed still in the seventh century as aristocrats in the East, affecting Roman traditionalism, clung to Latin, while conversely the

[79] Ulpianus in Justinian, *Digest* 14.3.11.3, 45.1.1.6, and 32.1.11.1; wills, etc.: Kelly (2004) 32–33; for the official use of Latin in the East, see Rochette (1997) 83–144; for the use of Greek, Troianos (2004b) 156–161; Rapp (2004) 1232–1235.

[80] Honoré (1978) 39, 41–42, 124; Plato: Lanata (1984), esp. pt. 2., ch. 4, and (1989). For Latin as "the ancestral language" (according to Justinian), see Dagron (1969) 44 n. 7; Basilikopoulou (1993) 106.

[81] Ioannes Lydos, *On the Magistracies of the Roman State* 2.12 = 3.42, 3.68; for Lydos in general, see Maas (1992); for his intellectual background, Kaldellis (2003); for Kyros, Cameron (1982) 221–270; for progressive steps in the course of linguistic change, Dagron (1969) 38–46.

Roman Church was ruled by Greek-speakers.[82] Those trends soon spent their force. In sum, we are dealing with a gradual process. Greek was one of the languages in which Romania could conduct its business from as early as the Republic. The empire did not suddenly switch from Latin to Greek in the seventh century, though the loss of Latin was a very important development. In the tenth century, Konstantinos VII could look back and say that after Herakleios emperors "Hellenized even more and cast off their ancestral Roman language," i.e., Latin.[83] But the same point had been made already, for example by Ioannes Lydos, about other spheres of the administration. In reality, Romans had long "Hellenized," i.e., spoken Greek, and are referred to as ἑλληνίζοντες Ῥωμαῖοι in the sixth century by Prokopios.[84]

For a while, then, there were within the same empire Romans who spoke Latin and Romans who spoke Greek; other languages were, of course, spoken as well, but these were not usually employed by the institutions of government and were rarely noted in our sources. In middle Byzantium, at any rate, Roman identity was negotiated between Greek and Latin. For the sake of convention and to avoid confusion, Latin-speaking Romans could be called *Latinoi* or *Italoi* while Greek-speaking Romans could be called *Graikoi*. Byzantine writers of the middle centuries could use the latter term to refer to their language without implying all the negative qualities that it could acquire when used in a hostile way by Latin-speaking westerners. Still, there were moments when these differences excited passions, especially in ecclesiastical debates. Ancient Greek writers, after all, had little favorable to say about Latin (when they deigned to notice it at all), and their attitudes lay at hand for the Byzantines to use in a heated moment. In the mid-860s, Michael III sent a notorious (albeit lost) letter to pope Nicolaus I, in which he (or its probable ghost-writer, the patriarch Photios) called Latin a "barbarous and Skythian tongue." "Why then do you call yourself emperor of the Romans?" the pope wondered in his angry response. So whereas ordinarily the Byzantines regarded Latin as their "ancestral language," in times of tension with Old Rome they could switch codes and deride it by reviving the attitudes of the sophists of late antiquity toward the impoverished and barbarous language of the West. The

---

[82] Eclipse of Latin: Troianos (2004a) and (2004b) 173–181, but cf. Rapp (2004) 1226; counter-trends: Leontsini (2001).
[83] Konstantinos VII, *On the Themes* I pr. (p. 60).    [84] E.g., Prokopios, *Wars* 2.29.25, 3.21.2, 7.1.28.

exchange between pope and emperor was a rarity in the middle period, but these tensions would explode after 1204.[85]

So much for the Hellenization of Romania. On the other hand, looking at the linguistic evolution of the eastern empire, one may argue that, parallel to this Hellenization, the period leading up to Herakleios was – again, paradoxically – also one in which the Greek language itself was heavily Latinized. Latin had been spoken and studied in the East under the first emperors,[86] but with the new capital and larger bureaucracy inaugurated in the early fourth century interest in the study of Latin peaked and loan-words steadily began to work their way into Greek by the thousands. The origin of these words, hundreds of which are still in use, lay in the provincials' need to advance in the expanded army, court, administration, and judiciary, in short, in those structures that lent institutional and ideological coherence to Romania. Moreover, this happened, as we will see, at precisely that time when local identities, including forms of Hellenism, were rapidly yielding to the universal orders of New Rome. Greek became Latinized just when Greeks and others were finally being Romanized.

In Byzantium, the "wisdom" or "science of the Romans" or "Italians" was a way of referring to the study of law, as Byzantine law was basically Roman law by another name.[87] Latin and Latin loan-words are accordingly most prevalent in Byzantine works on law, on offices (e.g., by Ioannes Lydos), ceremonies (e.g., by Konstantinos VII), ranks and precedence (e.g., by Philotheos), the military (e.g., by the emperor Maurikios), sports (e.g., the hippodrome and its factions), and in technical treatises written by government employees, for instance the *hippiatrika* written by army

---

[85] Michael III quoted by Nicolaus I, *Letter to the emperor Michael III* (*Letter* 86 in *PL* 119 [1880] 926–962, here 932a ff. = *Letter* 88 in *MGH Epistolarum* v. VI, pp. 454–487, here 459). For context, see Dvornik (1948) ch. 4 (esp. 105: "This is the first time that we see Greek patriotism at odds with Roman and Latin nationalism"); also Fögen (1998) 17–21. Photios calls Latin a "barbarous tongue" in *Letter* 291.75–80 to the bishop of Aquileia. Ancient Greek views of Latin: Rochette (1997) 258–269. Negative views were expressed in canonical late-antique sources: for the poverty of Latin, Gregorios of Nazianzos, *Or.* 21.35 (*In Honor of Athanasios, Bishop of Alexandria*); barbarism: Synesios, *Letter* 66 (p. 119) and Libanios (below). Themistios considered Greek to be sufficient, until he had to address an emperor who did not speak it: *Or.* 6.71c (*Brotherly Love, or on* Philanthropia). For negative views of Latin in Byzantium after 1204 (and some before), see Maltezou (1993) 93–97 (more may be added); see p. 297 below for Eustathios' debate. Isaakios II Angelos sent a letter to the pope ascribing the confusion over *filioque* to the poverty of Latin: Demetrios Tornikes, *Letter* 33 (p. 339). After 1204, Michael Choniates called Italians *barbarophonoi*, *Letter* 148.4.

[86] See, e.g., MacMullen (2000) 13. Plutarch, *Platonic Questions* 10.3 (*Moralia* 1010d) attests widespread knowledge of Latin; the basic study is Rochette (1997).

[87] Pitsakis (1995) 28–29; Stolte (1999) 82.

doctors. But many words used in daily life were also of Latin origin.[88] In fact, the medieval West would accept many ancient Roman terms not directly from the Latin tradition but from the East: "Byzantium as the mediator of imperial Roman culture presents a most interesting problem, still largely unexplored, for the historian of language; much of the western terminology of administration, bureaucracy, and court ceremonial that seems Latin, may, in reality, represent a Latin filtered through Greek."[89] The fourth century in particular saw the widespread availability of Latin instruction in the East, focused on centers of legal studies like Berytos, which was a largely Roman and Latin city; the translation of many Latin works into Greek; and the irony that the last great secular Latin writers, the historian Ammianus Marcellinus and the poet Claudianus, hailed from Antioch and Alexandria respectively and were native Greek speakers.[90] The careers of the African Priscianus and Corippus (late fifth and sixth centuries respectively) attest that Latin epic and panegyric still had an audience in sixth-century Constantinople, which was in many ways still a Latin city, while some Greek-speaking Byzantines after 600 still accepted Latin as the ancestral tongue of the Romans.[91] In short, the transition to Greek in Byzantium was not an abrupt change, representing a "civilizational" change, but emerged gradually from a long period during which the empire as a whole (as opposed to its individual subjects) was basically bilingual. Romania had a long time in which to adjust to its Greek setting, over seven hundred years in fact.

The absorption of Latin by the East complemented a general accelera-tion of Romanization in late antiquity that further eroded ethnic and local civic identities. The institutions of government became far more pervasive and penetrated deeper into provincial life as the new empire of Diocletian and Constantine deployed a far larger army and imposed higher taxes, a thorough census, and a huge bureaucracy. Resources became scarcer for

---

[88] For loan-words by category, see Zilliacus (1935) and (1937), anachronistically concerned with "nationality," i.e., ethnicity, in the later period; in law, Troianos (2004b) 165–173; for bibliography and statistics, see the works cited by Kahane and Kahane (1982) 128–129 n. 5, with lists of their own; and MacMullen (1990) 282–283 n. 7; for the *hippiatrika*, Fisher (1982) 207.

[89] Kahane and Kahane (1981) 410.

[90] For Latin in the East in late antiquity, see Cameron (1982) 233; Jones (1986) 988–991; Rochette (1997) 116–144 (official use), 248–254 (prosopography); Rapp (2004) 1228–1232; for Berytos, Hall (1999); for translations (not comprehensive), Fisher (1982); Rochette (1997) 293–319 (all periods). For a summary of sources on the language question, see Basilikopoulou (1993). No Byzantinist can agree with the verdict of Brunt (1976) 162, that "what was specifically Latin in the common civilization of the empire made little impact in the East," though he allows (163 n. 9) a brief vogue after the transfer of government.

[91] E.g., Theophylaktos Simokattes, *History* 6.9.14; Theophanes the Confessor, *Chronographia* s.a. 6079 (p. 258). See below for Konstantinos VII. Sixth-century Constantinople: Mango (2005) 322.

local projects, leading to urban decline and a flight of notables to the central administration, whether civil, military, or ecclesiastical, where they found salaries, opportunities, and exemptions. New Rome and its vast new Senate duplicated the effect in the East as it too drained the resources and personnel of the cities, and not without protest.[92] There emerged a largely "international" cadre of peripatetic officials more loyal to Roman institutions than to their own cities. A constant flow of legislation sought to regulate an ever broader range of issues, replacing local norms. Eventually, there were few or no institutions left that were not complicit in the ordering and maintenance of Romania. To complement the process on the religious side, a universal faith sponsored and even imposed by the state largely succeeded in eliminating the religious diversity of the ancient world, establishing more or less the same doctrines, temples, rituals, and men throughout the Roman world.

There were protests on the Greek side against all this and a crisis within Hellenism that went beyond the Christian challenge, though the struggle on both fronts was in vain. Libanios, the great orator of Antioch, the friend of Julian and of Julian's memory, protested to the emperors on behalf of the temples against the monks and, like a latter-day Plutarch, on behalf of the cities against the parasitic growth of New Rome. He decried the growing popularity of Latin and use of its legal jargon by a class of rootless officials, developments that he feared would undermine the linguistic and civic basis of Hellenism.[93] Globalization was eliminating local diversity and the independence of true Hellenes. Ironically, his own career was based largely on the administration's need for men who excelled at Greek *paideia*,[94] and Antioch was, after all, nothing like Plutarch's Chaironeia. Libanios' notion of Hellenism was moreover diffuse: in his orations he agreed with Julian that eloquence is inextricably linked with religion, yet in his correspondence, perhaps with Christian students in mind, he projected a vaguer aesthetic, literary, and moral view, closer to that of his much younger contemporary, the philosopher and future bishop Synesios.[95]

---

[92] For a summary, see Van Dam (2002) 55–57; for protests, Dagron (1969) 27–29; (1974) 37, 53–54, 56, 64, 75–76, 134–135.

[93] For the temples, see esp. Libanios, *Or.* 30 (*To the Emperor Theodosios, On Behalf of the Temples*), also his works about and for Julian; against Constantinople: Dagron (1974) 56, 64 (citing Zosimos also); against Latin: Fisher (1982) 175; Rochette (1997) 130–135; Troianos (2004b) 161–165.

[94] Brown (1992) ch. 1, relying heavily on the testimony and outlook of Libanios.

[95] For religion, see, e.g., Libanios, *Or.* 62.8 (*To those who jeered at his* paideia). "I believe that these two things, the worship of the gods and the study of letters, are akin to each other"; also *Or.* 1.234 (*My Life, or Regarding His Own Fortune*); *Or.* 12.27, 33 (*An Address to the Emperor Julian as Consul*): learning contains the seeds of religion; *Or.* 13.1, 8, 13 (*An Address to Julian*); and *Or.* 18.157, 161

Libanios feared that the new Christian, bureaucratic, and Latin empire would undermine the civic, literary, and religious aspects of Hellenism, and so he eloquently fought what would be the last stand of Hellenic independence from Romania, though his Hellenism could not muster or articulate a national objective (at most he could refer to "the cities of the Greeks," though in his time even they were rapidly becoming Roman and Christian). Libanios' defense of Hellenism was basically a professional skirmish that revolved around the career of the court orator and Aristotelian professor Themistios, who, though not a Christian and ignorant of Latin, notoriously served all the emperors of the fourth century except the Hellenist Julian. To him was entrusted the illustrious task of recruiting a Senate for New Rome, which drew thousands of able and wealthy men to the center from the cities, and the role of spokesman for imperial policy, which he played well behind a façade of philosophical independence. A recent study has cast him as a sophisticated but subservient propagandist. His opponents viewed him as an ambitious opportunist and traitor to the cause, rewarded for putting a Hellenic face on the new regime. And we do not know whether his delicate pleas for religious toleration had any effect on the policies of his Christian masters. For his part, Themistios argued that philosophy must engage with power and use the arts of rhetoric to guide its policies, though against the accusation of abandoning his home city he would have done better to champion Rome as the highest and common *patria* of all than to insist, as he did, that Constantinople was a polis just like any other. He did, however, lift some sonorous phrases about the unity of empire from Aristeides' *Roman Oration*. When he was promoted to the Senate, Constantius II noted, in words probably ghost-written by Themistios himself, that "in receiving from us a Roman rank, he offers us Hellenic wisdom in exchange."[96]

In this, the last albeit asymmetrical struggle between Rome and Hellenism in antiquity, Rome won decisively, though assisted at the end by the collapse of civic life in the seventh century and the transformation of the empire into a vast Roman city-state. The Second Sophistic ideal of the cultivated and urbane orator was confined to the capital and henceforth

---

(*Funeral Oration for Julian*). But cf. *Letters* 347.2, 357.1, 411.4, 1544.1 on ethical and literary Hellenism. For the latter conception, see Schouler (1991) and Athanassiadi (1992) 206–207, citing previous bibliography.

[96] Constantius II, *Address to the Senate concerning Themistios* 21a. For the fourth-century struggle within Hellenism, see the brilliant reconstruction by Dagron (1968), where Themistios' position is discussed at length; for his use of Aristeides: 90 n. 40–40bis; for his career and personas, Heather (1998); Heather and Moncur (2001) 1–42. For Ammianus' *Roman* dislike of Constantinople, see Kelly (2003), citing other hostile fourth-century observers on 588–589.

thrived mostly on imperial patronage: Greek wisdom in exchange for Roman ranks, as Constantius had put it. Libanios was admired by posterity as a model of style, but it was Themistios' career that was envied as a model of political and philosophical responsibility, for example by two leading Byzantine writers we will examine later, Michael Psellos and Michael Choniates.[97] Hellenism had finally been tamed and appropriated by the court, and its fortunes would thereafter be tied to the fate of the court, as was made painfully clear to those who sought *paideia* and offices in Asia Minor and Epeiros after the terrible events of 1204, when the center collapsed. Yet there was one – and only one – arena in which Hellenism did fight back successfully in the world of New Rome, and that was language. Though completely accepting the Roman order, many Byzantine writers adhered to the linguistic strictures of Attic purity established by the Second Sophistic; they even purged Latinism from their new editions of ancient texts, for example in Symeon Metaphrastes' late tenth-century rewriting of saints' lives. Linguistic purity was the mainstay of Byzantine Hellenism. One historian has even suggested that popular Latinized Greek was the precursor of the later demotic, the "Romaic" language that would struggle for recognition against Attic purity even down to the 1980s (and still does).[98]

But we are getting ahead of ourselves; we will return to these questions below. Late antiquity witnessed the triumph of Rome as the primary recipient of provincial loyalty and the exclusive beneficiary of their political ambitions, and the establishment of the concomitant right of the *res publica* to shape virtually all aspects of its subjects' lives. This transformation can be strikingly illustrated by comparing two Greek-speaking antiquarians from either end of the period we have reviewed. In the second century Pausanias of Magnesia (in Lydia) traveled throughout Greece and wrote about its ancient monuments, pointedly neglecting its history under Rome and all Latin writers. A Greek patriot, he valued national freedom and believed that the Romans were essentially foreign conquerors, even if, like the emperor Hadrian, they could be philhellenic. Pausanias was among the last to really believe in the contemporary existence of a Greek nation.[99] In the sixth century, by contrast, Ioannes Lydos from Philadelpheia (likewise in Lydia) moved to Constantinople and obtained a series of posts in the administration. He wrote in Greek about ancient Rome in an effort to

[97] Kaldellis (1999a) 169–170 n. 349.
[98] Symeon: Zilliacus (1937); demotic: Dagron (1969) 55; for the literary reaction against Latin influence in late antiquity, Rochette (1997) 75–83; for Libanios, see above.
[99] Habicht (1998) 104–105, 134.

demonstrate the continuity of the Roman political system from Romulus to Justinian. He too did this out of a concern for national freedom, by which, however, he meant that of the Roman Republic. He cited dozens of Latin authors and, as we saw, lamented the decline of Latin in his own age. In fact, he claimed that before the vile prefect Ioannes the Kappadokian authorized the use of Greek, the inhabitants of "Europe" used to speak "the language of the Italians," especially in official contexts, "even though most of them were Greek."[100]

## BYZANTIUM AS A NATION-STATE

Pausanias was among the last ancient Hellenes who felt a strong sense of "national" difference from the Romans. Over sixteen hundred years later, the founders of modern Greece would pick up where he left off, with a love for ancient monuments and hatred of foreign domination. Where he omitted all reference to post-classical monuments on the Akropolis, they systematically tore them down, making his imagination a reality. But what had happened to the Greeks in the meantime, from the second to the nineteenth century? Whatever degree and manner of "continuity" we allow to pass through those years – and I believe it was considerable – it existed at a level of practice that did not typically generate discourses of identity. Like almost all other subjects of the empire, the Greeks became, i.e., firmly believed themselves to be, Romans. Being "Greek" in Byzantium was a matter either of religion (a negative quality) or high culture (a positive one). The revival of Hellenism in the eleventh and twelfth centuries took place between those two poles. In the thirteenth century, by contrast, Hellenism was implicated in a different kind of discourse and almost attained the level of a national identification, interestingly linked here too with an interest in ancient monuments and a hatred for foreign oppression (by the Crusaders). So whereas in the previous chapter we gave an account of Hellenism as high culture, and in the next we will explain why it was identified with paganism by the Christians, this section will account for the Roman aspect of Byzantine identity in a way that will make intelligible both the extinction of national Hellenism in late antiquity and its flickering revival after 1204. What did it mean to be a Roman in Byzantium?

---

[100] Ioannes Lydos, *On the Magistracies of the Roman State* 3.68, with Bandy's comment (p. 339); for Lydos' idea of freedom, see Kaldellis (2005a).

The opinion that currently prevails, the one that I too held before I began to investigate this problem – indeed before I even realized that it was in fact a problem – is that Byzantium was a "multi-ethnic empire" whose subjects were united loosely by religion and by loyalty to the emperor and whose common identity was grounded in abstract ecumenical and Christian notions. In other words, there was nothing more to being "a Roman" than the mere fact of being a (Christian) subject of the emperor. I have come to realize that this picture is in part misleading and in part simply false. Orthodoxy was certainly an important component of Roman unity and solidarity, but it does not go far enough. The Byzantines did not accept as Romans the orthodox people who lived outside their borders, but instead looked down on them as barbarians. Orthodoxy was not the "content" of Byzantium's Roman identity, as many historians imply or state. Nor was the emperor that content; he was not the power that arbitrarily united an allegedly heterogeneous assembly of peoples, without whom they would go their separate national, ethnic, or geographic ways. Quite the contrary, the emperor, as we saw, was defined in terms of his people, the Romans, and was beholden to them. Traitors, usurpers, and dissidents were no less Roman.[101] Moreover, Byzantine intellectuals knew that Rome had once been governed by a Republic, possibly better than it was now being governed by the emperors, and believed that the Republic was the same (Roman) community as theirs, only governed differently. The emperor at times functioned as a shorthand *symbol* for the Byzantines' collective loyalty to Romania, but he himself was not that to which they were primarily and ultimately loyal. He was the head, servant, and symbol of what counted: the nexus of faith, law, history, custom, and language called the *politeia*, the ancient *res publica*, the shared national polity.

In the mid-fifth century the historian Priskos claimed to have met a man from Greece at the court of Attila who had willingly taken up with the Huns and had negative things to say about how the Romans governed themselves. Priskos replied that their governance by this or that emperor was one thing; their *politeia*, however, was the ultimate standard by which the empire should be judged. This (probably invented) scene allowed the historian to air some serious criticisms of how his own *patria* was being governed, but we should note that the debate presupposes a distinction between the governance of the state and its moral and national basis, namely the *politeia* and the laws, which even Priskos' expatriate Greek

---

[101] *Pace* Greatrex (2000) 268, whose definition would exclude his chief source, Prokopios.

had to concede were good.[102] The *res publica*, Cicero had maintained, "is the property of a people. But a people is not just any collection of human beings brought together in any sort of way, but an assemblage of people in large numbers associated in an agreement (*consensus*) with respect to justice and a partnership for the common good."[103] This definition prefigures modern definitions of the nation as "the goal of citizen loyalties and the expression of the common will of the citizens."[104] Romans could decry abuse and break laws without thereby calling the *res publica* into question, just as one can wallow in sin without ceasing to be a Christian – though it was possible for the Roman state to alienate its subjects through bad policy and undermine their loyalty.

Conversely, Romans could not long retain their identity as captives in foreign states, unless they redefined themselves as a religious group or a true *genos*, options that were considered in the West after the fifth century and in the East as the empire lost ground after 1071. But this denatured their identity as Romans; usually they simply adapted to their new circumstances and were lost to Rome. Maurikios noted in his *Strategikon* (ca. 600) that refugees from Slavic lands "must be very closely watched. Even some Romans have given in to the times, forget their own people, and prefer to gain the good will of the enemy" (11.4). Unlike Christianity and cultural Hellenism, which as identities were constituted by different existential markers, Roman identity did not travel well beyond the borders of the *politeia*, its constitutive environment.[105] In 1142 Ioannes II Komnenos encountered some former imperial subjects in southern Asia Minor who, while still Christian, had come to an agreement with the Turks and "looked upon the Romans as their enemies. So much greater is custom, strengthened by time, than race (*genos*) or faith," observed the historian Niketas Choniates.[106]

Byzantium, as the natural continuation of the later Roman empire, is here for the first time defined as the nation-state of the Romans, a unified political community held together by a common "custom" (*ethos*). This view may

---

[102] Priskos fr. 11.2.407–510; see Maas (1995) esp. 149–154, citing previous discussions.
[103] Cicero, *On the Republic* 1.39.    [104] Smith (1986) 167.
[105] Cf. Woolf (1998) 248–249, without discussing Byzantium.
[106] Niketas Choniates, *History* 37; the idea was a commonplace: see Nikephoros Blemmydes, *Basilikos Andrias* 124 (and the sources cited on p. 82). For the events in question, see Foss (1998) 158–160; in general, Vryonis (1971) 184, 210–216, 223–244. For Roman identity surviving prolonged captivity, see Greatrex (2000) 279 n. 12. Examples can also be adduced from later centuries, e.g., *The Miracles of Saint Demetrios* 284 ff. (v. I, pp. 227 ff.), on which see Anagnostakis (2001); and Theophanes Continuatus, Book 5: *Life of Basileios I* 4–5 (pp. 216 ff.). For "post-Roman" Britain, see Chrysos (2003) 124–125.

later have to be modified or varied, but it offers, I believe, the best starting-point than the definition currently in use. Byzantium was a very tightly knit national state whose coherence did not derive primarily from its religion or its ruler and whose alleged universal ideology was in fact limited to a more restricted rhetorical space than is commonly realized. This view will doubt-less meet with resistance among both Byzantinists and modern theorists of the nation. But the former have discussed the nature of Romania in an imprecise way and have generally not studied modern discussions of nations and national identity, while the latter are generally unaware of the evidence for pre-modern states and hold to the modernist fallacy, namely the belief that some historical developments such as national identity (or religious skepticism for that matter) are exclusive features of modernity. Though the projection of (allegedly) modern phenomena onto the past distorts history, the same is true when we allow the fear of anachronism to be used pre-emptively as an indiscriminate rhetorical topos that prevents us from under-standing genuine parallels, especially now that it is becoming increasingly clear that national identity is not an exclusively modern (far less industrial) development. "All in all, there is little reason to hold dogmatically to the conventional view that nationalism came into existence for the first time in the modern world. At the very least, the possibility of premodern national-ism should not be ruled out *a priori*."[107] An interesting argument has recently been made that ancient Athens fits modern definitions of the nation.[108] The present chapter will offer a preliminary formulation of the thesis that Byzantium was closer to a nation-state than to any of the alter-natives that have been proposed. The material from the sources that can be used to document this thesis has proven to be far more abundant than I had first anticipated, and a monograph-length treatment of the issue may be forthcoming. For now, it is hoped that this preliminary version will stir debate and lead to a more precise (and historical) understanding than is currently available.

In the middle period of its history, Byzantium was understood to be the state of the Roman people: Romania was just the *archê* of the Romans. The vast majority of its population identified themselves as Romans and knew,

---

[107] Poole (1999) 34; cf. Reynolds (1998) 21–25. Poole continues: "There is however a more modest version of the conventional wisdom available: that it was developments in the early modern world which marked the beginning of the *age of nationalism*." In arguing that Byzantium was a nation-state, I will not insist that it was nationalistic. *Nationalism* is the movement that seeks to unite (or "awaken") the nation and assert its identity, consolidate its territory, usually in competition with other nations. Such a movement was not necessary in Byzantium, where the effects of nationalism were produced by centuries of assimilation to the Roman *politeia*.

[108] Ober (1996) 117; Cohen (2000); Anderson (2003) esp. 215–216.

regardless of whether they were from Naupaktos or Attaleia and of whether they knew each other personally, that they were all Romans precisely because they shared the same religion, language, art and architecture, history, state and laws, customs, and probably material conditions. They were not split into ethnic groups or social castes. They were subject to the same laws and each of them could theoretically occupy any office in the state. Official power derived from the state and its offices and not from clan or caste.[109] All this makes the Byzantines a nation. Also, their state was not a federation of tribes or regional states. Its borders, beyond which lived hostile barbarians, were coterminous with the reach and jurisdiction of their national institutions, namely their Church, army, courts, social hierarchies, and bureaucracy. All this makes Byzantium a nation-state. Given the concession that even in modern times "national identity is fundamentally multi-dimensional and can never be reduced to a single element," as well as that any one particular element may be absent from the makeup of a particular nation, we have here a perfect fit between Byzantium and modern definitions of the nation-state. The latter require a sense of political community, "however tenuous," and "at least some common institutions and a single code of rights and duties for all the members of the community"; a territory controlled by the state and valorized by religious or historic associations; and "a measure of common values and traditions among the population, or at any rate its 'core' community." Byzantium flies past these minimal requirements, with its single dominant language, religion, state apparatus, and fairly homogeneous culture.[110]

On what grounds, then, may the Byzantine claim to nationality be denied? The objections of modernists, who, following E. Gellner, believe that the possibility of imagining the nation is restricted to the modern world, are vitiated by an almost total ignorance on their part of the powerful means that lay at the disposal of the Roman authorities when they made Romans of their subjects in late antiquity, and the deep penetration into the life and minds of all Romans of the ideology and institutions of the Byzantine state in later times.[111] The cultural, political,

---

[109] Holmes (2003) and (2005) 463–465.

[110] Smith (1991) 8–15; see also Miller (1995) 21–27; Poole (1999) 10–18. For Roman national identity in Byzantium, see Arrigoni (1972) 138–140 and Ahrweiler (1975a) 32–36, who do not explain what they mean. The latter exaggerates the importance of Christianity, which, however, served largely in conflicts with the non-Christian East.

[111] Ignorance of ancient conditions likewise vitiates the arguments of those who qualify the modernist position, e.g., Smith (1991) 69, esp. (1986) 10, 69–70 (with notes), 105, 131. No one grappling with this problem can henceforth ignore Ando (2000). Conversely, within their own period, modernists are hard-pressed to explain the emergence of modern Greek nationalism: Gellner (1997) 41.

and especially *ideological* penetration of Greece by the Romans during the empire exceeded that by the modern Greek state before the early twentieth century (when wars and massive conscription allowed it to consummate the nationalist project). In fact, it took centuries for the allegedly modern "revolution in the control of administration and in cultural co-ordination" to attain Roman imperial levels. What we must not forget is that, even *if* levels of control and ideological penetration in Roman antiquity were inferior and slower than those of early modernity, our focus is on the middle Byzantine period, by which time Rome would have had *one thousand years* in which to work its effect, starting in the age of Polybios. What modernists also ignore is that the governing ideology of the empire was not "imperial" in the sense of being self-consciously multi-ethnic; rather, under the direction of Augustus, Hadrian, the Severan jurists, Diocletian, and Constantine, it aimed to create a Romanocentric consensus in the provinces that subsumed or replaced local allegiances, including ethnicities. We have already surveyed the means and ends of this policy, which made Romania different from any other empire in world history. Likewise, in Byzantium "political rituals fostered links of loyalty and identification with the greater whole... A system drawn from distant Constantinople structured the subtle gradations of elite society in the provinces,"[112] even the most distant.

The most important obstacle to this new thesis comes not from theorists of the modern nation but from two conventional notions about Byzantine identity that have been taken for granted in scholarship (though, as we will see, they have never been systematically advocated, far less proven). We need to consider, then, *first* the notion that it was a "multi-ethnic empire" and, *second* its "universalism." The first stems from a misunderstanding of the alleged ethnonyms used in the sources (such as Thrakian, Kappadokian, etc.), but more importantly from the need of modern nationalists to pull their own ancestors out of the Byzantine melting-pot. The second fiction was formulated chiefly by legal and diplomatic historians who were looking for precisely such abstract definitions of Christian statehood and were not much interested in the constitution of a historical society. Before we turn to these obstacles, however, let us briefly consider what appears to be the only

---

[112] McCormick (1998) 46, 50–51; see Neville (2004) 23 for another illustration; Holmes (2003) 37, 46–48, 55, for the reign of Basileios II; Kazhdan and Epstein (1985) 64–67 for the eleventh century, Dagron (2003) 21–24 in general. Matters were obviously different in recently conquered or only nominally controlled territories, such as the northern Balkans; see Stephenson (2000a) *passim* and below; for the possible limits of this system, see Cheynet (2003a).

objection to Byzantine nationhood that has been formulated by a modern historian of Byzantium on theoretical grounds.

Paul Magdalino, who otherwise recognizes a Byzantine nationalism of sorts, has denied that Byzantium was a true nation not only on the usual grounds that we will examine shortly but also because of the importance of its capital. "Byzantium never became a nation-state because it never lost the mentality of a city-state."[113] But it is not clear in what way we are to understand Byzantium as a "city-state" that conflicts with it being a nation-state. City-states are notoriously unified and homogeneous entities; anything the size of Byzantium that attained that level of unity certainly qualifies as a nation-state.

The problem with city-states in this context is that we associate them with ancient Greece. In ancient Greece, it is true, what Professor Magdalino calls the "parochialism" of the "city-state mentality" hindered the emergence of a single nation and a historically effective sense of Greek national unity. But Byzantium was not an assembly of disunited city-states. A "parochial" mentality would be relevant if it involved multiple and dispersed loci of civic identity in the context of a hypothetical nation that failed to create a unified state, as in classical Greece. That is how city-states are incompatible with nations. But there is no theoretical reason why an individual city-state cannot be considered a nation in its own right, like Singapore. As mentioned, recent studies have compared democratic Athens to a nation-state. It was too big to be a city-state as even ancient writers recognized when they said that the Athenians were more of an *ethnos* than a polis.[114]

Historically and administratively the capital was the most important city, and the Byzantines' fixation with keeping it even at the cost of provincial regions made strategic sense. Constantinople was defensible and could control both the Balkans and Asia Minor in a way that no other center could. But the importance of the capital did not diminish the extension of Roman identity to the provinces. The vast majority of Romans did not live in New Rome yet were no less Roman on that count, Constantinopolitan snobbery notwithstanding. "The parochialism of a pre-industrial society which lacked the technical means to grow out of a city-state mentality"[115] is counter-balanced by the ability of the center to transmit its "mentality"

---

[113] Magdalino (1991a) 6–7 and (1991b) 190, 196–197; also Angold (1999) 38. Despite the title, Alexander (1962) does not discuss this problem. I wish to declare here my enormous admiration for Professor Magdalino's work, and my debt to him is evident in the notes of the second part of this book. What I am taking issue with is a paragraph-length comment in one of his papers. But so few have debated the points in question that I have had to fall back on comments made in passing by great scholars.
[114] Ober (1996) 117; Cohen (2000); Anderson (2003) esp. 215–216.    [115] Magdalino (1993) 111, 153.

throughout the provinces, to create a unified city-state out of what had begun as a multi-ethnic empire. This is the antithesis of parochialism and should lead us to revise modernist beliefs about the technical basis of national identity.[116] As a center of power, then, Constantinople was not *historically* more important than, say, Athens for modern Greece, Vienna for Austria, or Cairo for Egypt. Magdalino is not on safe ground when he says that it should be the nation that creates the capital rather than vice versa, even (or especially) when he cites France.[117] But it is not even correct to say that Romania was created by its capital, given that the idea of the Roman *res publica* predated Constantinople, in fact it was Romania – "the world a city" – that created New Rome at precisely the time when elder Rome itself was losing its historical importance.

Roman identity was ideologically independent of any city. Rome itself had been abandoned by the emperors and then New Rome founded without altering what it meant to be Roman, because the latter was now invested in an entire world, not merely one city. The Byzantines never forgot that event and knew well how it justified their claim to be true Romans. When the new capital was lost in 1204 the Byzantines simply regrouped by moving "the *archê* of the Romans" to the city of Nikaia, just as they had once moved it from Rome to New Rome. Nikaia was then praised as Constantinople had been formerly.[118] In short, the nation was prior to the capital.[119] As we will see in the final chapter of this book, the loss of New Rome forced the Byzantines to think hard about what made them Romans and what united them, in a way that was independent of the capital. That is why the evidence from 1204–1261 is so crucial.[120]

As Ioannes III Doukas Batatzes declared to pope Gregorius IX in 1239, "he who is emperor rules over a nation (*ethnos*) and a people (*laos*) ... not over rocks and wooden beams, of which walls and towers are made [i.e., of a city]."[121] The Romans loved their City and often treated it as a symbol of the nation and its territory, but they knew that conceptually it was not its essence. In an *Encomium* for his teacher Georgios Akropolites (ca. 1252),

---

[116] Magdalino shows how this was possible: (1993) 310–315.
[117] Cf. Armstrong (1982) 170, and 168 on the city as a focus; Jusdanis (2001) 39–41. Consider the *ideological* importance of Kosovo for Serbia or Jerusalem for Israel. For modern Athens, Bastéa (2000) esp. xvii–xviii, 9.
[118] E.g., Theodoros II Laskaris, *Praise of Nikaia* 1, 7 (*op. rh.* pp. 68, 78–79). For transferring the capital's institutions, see Nikephoros Blemmydes, *A Partial Account* 1.12. See also pp. 360, 367 below. Modern Neo-Romans agree on this point. Romanides (2002) 232. just as Constantine moved Rome from West to East, so too can it still be moved again today; "Constantinople is not necessary for this to happen."
[119] Cf. Koder (2005) 157.    [120] Cf. Eastmond (2004) 4–5.
[121] Ioannes III Doukas Batatzes, *Letter to pope Gregorius IX* (p. 375).

Theodoros II Laskaris praised "his *patris*, the imperial city of Constantine, which is now enslaved and named in diverse ways, as it has been divided into parts and is named after those parts." Laskaris here slides from the City to Romania and treats them as equivalent.[122] But the conflation of the two – "the world a city" – had begun already, as we have seen, in Aristeides' *Roman Oration*.

### THE MYTH OF THE "MULTI-ETHNIC EMPIRE"

The fiction of Byzantium as a multi-ethnic empire owes its existence to a number of factors operative in modern historiography. First, as we saw, Romanization has been viewed misleadingly as a process of urbanization and legal change, not as one of national assimilation. The early Roman empire was indeed multi-ethnic and multi-cultural, but because ancient historians have generally known little of Byzantium their view of Romanization, on which Byzantinists must then rely, is very deficient. One cannot see where Romanization was going without looking at the later centuries. Unfortunately, there has been no dialogue between the two fields and, indeed, almost zero theoretical discussion of what it really meant to be Roman in Byzantium as an extension of the developments of late antiquity. We have addressed this deficiency in the previous two sections, though only in a partial and preliminary way.

Second, nineteenth-century scholars were obsessed with racial groups and tribes and believed them to be the building-blocks of history. The idea that they could be assimilated into broader nations and effectively go extinct went against the grain of most research. This was and still is especially the case in scholarship produced in countries where the urgent search for origins has to pass through Byzantium. Following this model, the empire is carved up along ethnic lines that correspond to modern nations and the bits are then distributed to each according to need. Historiography became deeply implicated in the creation of ideologies of histories that served modern nations. The empire was presented as an artificial system that held diverse groups together at various times, with or without their consent. Some groups, however, are difficult to discover in the sources, resulting in nations that are ancient and modern but lacking a Middle Age.[123] "Greeks" are among the most difficult to identify in this

---

[122] Theodoros II Laskaris, *Encomium for Georgios Akropolites* 4 (*op. rh.* p. 101).
[123] Romanides (2002) 233–234 puts it well.

historiographical mess, as their ethnic label was not in use (allegedly for religious reasons).

At first, the pioneers of the national imagination that awoke around the time of the Greek War of Independence had to persuade a large segment of the new nation to set aside its Byzantine (Roman) memories and loyalties in order to embrace the Greeks as its ancestors and legitimators of its national aspirations. These ancient Greeks were seen as one of the many nations enslaved by the wicked Roman Byzantines (and later by the Turks), but this required a belief in a nation that left no trace of itself for over a thousand years. National historians gradually worked their way over to the opposite position, seeing the Greeks as those very Romans who had governed the Byzantine empire, which was now viewed as not quite so wicked.[124] There is still no solid consensus on this issue in Greece (much depends on how one feels about the Church), but among many historians the opinion prevails that after all other groups have been identified and removed, e.g., Armenians and Bulgarians, those who remain must be Greek, though disguised under the alienating label of Roman.[125] (Not surprisingly, no one cares about groups like the Phrygians, whose ethnonyms have no seat on the UN.) In works by Greek and many Greek-American scholars, the Byzantines are presumed to have "really been" Greeks – unless they are suspected of belonging to an ethnic minority. The racial basis of such identifications is revealed by the fact that these latter groups often do not lose their "minority" status in Greek eyes even when they are deemed to have been "Hellenized." We will discuss this below, when we consider the fate of the Greeks in the Roman melting-pot.

This ethnic dismemberment of Byzantium requires that the seriousness of its Roman identity as a historical force be minimized and occluded behind ethnic rhetoric. As we will see, however, ethnic identities may well have existed within the empire's borders but were limited to small groups and were generally lost when they came into close contact with the Roman polity. They played little role in the shaping of Byzantine history. This

---

[124] For the first realignment, see Politis (1998); for the second, Skopetea (1988) 175–189; Matalas (2002) 108–111, 146, 151–159. I have found one voice of Roman resistance in all of this, Romanides (2002), whose insights are fascinating, given how little he knew about the history in question.

[125] E.g., in Vryonis (1971) 22, 53, and *passim*; Svoronos (2004) 33. See pp. 111–117 below. It should be noted that racial criteria in the twentieth century became more narrow than they had been in the nineteenth, when other Balkan groups (not yet nations in Greek eyes) were deemed Greek by blood, religion, or culture (though not language), and whose true (Greek) national consciousness had to be awakened. The political motivation for this belief, which was terminated by Bulgarian nationalism, requires little comment. It is no longer even remembered in Greece.

section, then, will discuss how ethnicity operated in medieval Byzantium and will argue that it played a small role in the construction of Roman identity. The goal is to clear the ground for a new look at Byzantine Hellenism, because, as we saw above, a *potentially* ethnic and even national idea was inherited as a part of the classical Greek legacy. In Byzantium, however, at least until a late date, the few declarations of ethnic Hellenism that are attested operated generally as rhetorical amplifiers of high culture and therefore as claims by *individuals* to high status; they were not an effort to establish or even imply the continued existence of a Greek nation in Byzantine times. Besides, the significance of national Greek revivals, when they did occur, would make little sense if they did not take place against a thoroughly Roman background.

The process was well underway in late antiquity. As provincials became Romans, regional, tribal, and ethnic identities gradually disappeared from the record or were converted into purely geographic labels. Looking at the regions that would later form the core of the Byzantine empire, we see that neither their languages nor regional identities survived the Hellenization of their cultures and the Romanization of their societies. Already in the first century, the geographer Strabon noted that languages and ethnonyms were being lost because of Roman rule (12.4.6). Karian and Lydian went extinct. The evidence that has recently been adduced for a Lydian identity in the early empire is meager and points toward a local antiquarian revival that did not impinge on the discursive construction of identity and so did not compete with Rome.[126] The distinctiveness of Kappadokia in late antiquity was represented only by a (negative) provincial stereotype and a thick accent. Its most famous scion, Gregorios of Nazianzos, cared so little for the name that he branded a theological opponent as a "Kappadokian monster."[127] By the early fifth century (and probably long earlier), the fact that a holy man in Syria spoke Greek rather than Syriac was explained by his origin in Kilikia.[128] Scholars have tracked down every reference to the survival of the indigenous languages of Asia Minor, e.g., Mysian, Lykaonian, and Celtic (its Hellenized speakers already long known as *Gallograeci*). Except for neo-Phrygian, the results are unimpressive and ambiguous. These languages were generally not used for writing, were

[126] Karian: Hornblower (1982) 343 n. 98; Lydia: Spawforth (2001). For this process in general in Asia Minor, see Mitchell (2000).

[127] Stereotypes: Van Dam (2002) I, 13–16, 24–28; Gregorios of Nazianzos, *Or.* 21.16 (*In Honor of Athanasios, Bishop of Alexandria*).

[128] Theodoretos, *History of the Monks in Syria* 28.4 (Thalaleios).

confined to rural areas, and were probably spoken by people who also knew Greek. Moreover, they were (apparently) not linked to any collective identity, which is what the present argument is really about. In any case, none are heard from again after ca. 600, though the scarcity of our sources permits that they were perhaps still used for some time afterwards.[129]

Regardless of the survival or not of these languages, the important thing is that there is no trace in our sources of any ethnic or regional identity that was incompatible with assimilation into Romania, excepting perhaps the Isaurians, "the internal barbarians" of southern Asia Minor who were never fully pacified, and, in part, the Jews, who seem, however, to have largely assimilated in the period after the great revolts of the first and second centuries but were later forced by the Christian turn of Roman society to fashion a specifically Jewish solidarity.[130] Looking beyond the regions that would form the core of the Byzantine empire, one study of the Roman Near East could find no groups beyond the Jews and Samaritans that were unified by the memory of a national past and no collective identities to correspond with the cultural diversity that we observe through archaeology and epigraphy and the region's native languages. It seems that these languages and "cultures" did not really impede assimilation to Romania. The emergence of Syriac literature in late antiquity, at any rate, does not seem to correspond to any observable underlying ethnicity, nationality, or even relatively distinct cultural group, to say nothing of the doctrinal divisions that its texts reflect. Whether these groups, if they were that in any self-conscious sense, set themselves apart somehow from the emerging Roman *oikoumenê*, is yet unknown. This is a controversial area of research, though not directly relevant to the regions of Byzantium. Unfortunately, the question of Romanization, which is here understood as the acceptance of Rome as a normative political community and not as the spread of baths, villas, and "citizenship," is too often confused with the different question of Hellenization, and scholars slide too easily from "cultural background," "history," and "heritage" to "identity," "ethnicity,"

---

[129] Surveys in Brunt (1976) 170–172; Mitchell (1993) 50–51, 58, 172–175, citing previous works; (2000) 129. *Gallograeci*: Mitchell (2003) 280; cf. the *Gothograikoi* in Asia Minor in Theophanes the Confessor, *Chronographia* s.a. 6207 (p. 385). Extinction: Vryonis (1971) 45–49; Charanis (1972) II 25–26.

[130] It is unclear how the Isaurians were constituted as a group and how the events of the fifth and early sixth centuries should be interpreted: Burgess (1990); Shaw (1990) esp. 261; Elton (2000); for the emperor Zenon (an Isaurian) hated as a "foreigner," see Petros Patrikios in Konstantinos VII, *Book of Ceremonies* 1.92 (v. I, p. 420); but political enemies were often cast as ethnic foreigners: see below. Jews as pagan Graeco-Romans: Schwartz (2001) part 2, esp. 104, 142, 175–176, 190–191.

and even "national identity," as though these terms all mean the same thing or directly imply each other.[131]

Whatever ethnicities and national allegiances survived the Hellenistic period, at least in the Balkans and Asia Minor, seem to have been lost during the Roman centuries or, at any rate, ceased to produce evidence of their existence. In his *Roman Oration* Aristeides (second century AD) noted that new soldiers from the provinces were ashamed to use their prior national labels now that they were Romans (75). This means that they at least remembered such loyalties, but after four more centuries of Roman rule there is no evidence for them at all, not even indirect. Recent studies that have questioned the coherence of Roman identity in late antiquity, arguing for a more fluid condition by dismantling the distinction between Romans and barbarians who came from or lived outside the frontiers, have focused *exclusively* on the frontiers, on client states, and the army, in other words on precisely those sites where the norms of the *res publica* were contested, while *entirely* leaving out of the picture the millions of Romans living within the empire who set the standard.[132]

As with the Lydians mentioned above, we should not be misled by the fanciful conceits of antiquarianism, such as the Doric pedigree of Synesios, or by its politics, such as the effort by Justinian's *quaestor* Tribonianus to invent national histories to match the artificial provinces newly reorganized by his master. Those histories had no reality on the ground and no basis in history, while Synesios' affectation was hardly incompatible with his being a Roman in the first place, since one was not a Roman by virtue of descent. Ethnic inclusiveness defined the Roman polity from the days of its legendary foundation and can be demonstrated for all subsequent periods of its history. To be sure, there always was racial prejudice against outsiders but it evaporated in the face of successful integration. It was understood in antiquity that Rome was eager to assimilate the discoveries of others and

---

[131] Near East: Millar (1987b) and (1993) 6, 76, 124, 220; Syriac: ibid. 492–493 and (1998); Cameron (1997) 5; Hoyland (2004) 188–189 (instances of Syriac pride are few, ambiguous, and postdate the Arab conquests). Jones (1959) demonstrated that heresies were not national movements in disguise; cf. Millar (1998) 168. For direct Roman architectural influence in the East, see Sartre (2005) 171–174, 225–226. Hall (1999) fails to establish a Phoenician ethnic identity in late antiquity (e.g., she assumes it on the basis of the retention of the geographic name by the administration). Dirven (1997) moves casually from the "Syrian heritage" (163) of the author of the *De Dea Syria* to his "Syrian identity" (164) and "national culture ... a patriotic work by a member of a subjected nation" (169). No justification is offered for this semantic slide. See Lightfoot (2003) 182 ff., 200 ff.

[132] Among many works, see Amory (1997); Greatrex (2000); Pohl (2005) esp. 453–454 for the military bias. But see Kaldellis (2004b).

even their populations.[133] This was possible because the Romans, and later the Byzantines, did not define their national community in terms of ethnicity. With the exception of social snobbery (mostly during the Republic) and occasional rhetorical flourishes, "*romanitas* is precisely not an ethnic identification ... it was predicated from an early date on the notion of ethnic heterogeneity between Latin, Sabine and Etruscan populations."[134] (Trojans may be added.) Again, it was not so much biological descent that the Byzantines traced to ancient Italy as it was the institutions that defined their society.

What existential space, then, did notions of ethnicity occupy in Byzantine society? First, let us scrutinize the terminology by which the Byzantines might have referred to such groups, either among themselves or outside the empire, because its uncritical use causes confusion. *Ethnos*, for instance, contains the root of the modern neologism "ethnicity," but in Byzantine usage it could signify the Romans themselves or any barbarian group no matter how it was constituted, as well as any other kind of group, such as women, philosophers, and Christians. In the Septuagint, the plural *ethnê* is used for what we call "gentiles." In Byzantium, *ethnê* and *ethnikoi* could refer to pagans (instead of "Hellen"[135] – *ethnikos* would be revived in modern Greece, which obviously required a term for pagans that avoided this ambiguity!); they could also refer to all non-Romans. These words, then, combined the exclusivity of the faith with the classical distinction between barbarians and Greeks/Romans. *Ethnikoi* were "political gentiles." Even if they were Christian, they were not Roman, but they could become Romans just as pagans could become Christians.

*Genos* suggested biological relation and often designated one's family, while *phylon* suggested "race." Yet both were used by historians interchangeably with *ethnos* and, beyond ethnography, all three words could also designate any category of things regardless of how they were constituted as a group. Georgios Akropolites refers to the *genos* of Muslims and then to their *phyla*. Eustathios calls Christians a *phylon*, while Anna states that her father ordered his men to miss when shooting the Crusaders in order to avoid an *emphylios phonos*, a murder of one's own, given that

---

[133] Sources in Swain (1996) 248. For prejudice, see p. 54 above. But cf. Statius, *Silvae* 4.5.45–48. For Tribonianus, see Maas (1986); Mitchell (2000) 135; cf. Millar (1998) 163–164 for "ethnonyms" formed from imperial provinces.

[134] Hall (2002) 23.

[135] Lechner (1954) 22–23, 31; and Ahrweiler (1998) 2, citing Theodoros the Stoudite; for the ideology of the "nations," see Nicol (1972) I 317; (1979a) 74.

they were Christians.[136] That some individuals are called in our sources "Romans by *genos*" does not mean that the Byzantines considered themselves an ethnic group, only that the individuals in question were at least second-generation Romans. When Michael Attaleiates declared that he had made it in Constantinople despite being from a different *genos* he meant only that he was a provincial; conversely, when Gregorios Antiochos insisted (defensively) that he was a true native (*authigenês*) he was expressing only Constantinopolitan snobbery toward provincials, though it may have also contained an element of anti-Latin xenophobia (in that age of tension between East and West).[137] In any case, no assertions of what we call "ethnicity" were operative here, nor did a multitude of such internal *genê* and *ethnê* imply the empire's "ethnic" division. For example, our sources mention men whose *genos* was from Boukellarioi, a province in central Asia Minor created in the eighth century and named after an army unit; it had never been an *ethnos* in any other sense.[138] So too with being "a Kilikian by *genos*": whether there had ever been such a *genos* (which is doubtful), here it meant only that one hailed from Kilikia.[139]

We must, then, admit the vagueness of this terminology. The Byzantines did not view themselves collectively as a *genos* in the strong sense of being biologically related to each other.[140] For them, Muslims and Christians, Romans and the inhabitants of Attaleia, as well as Turks, women, and turtles, could all be called a *genos*, an *ethnos*, or a *phylon*. This means that any of these terms may stand for what I am calling a "nation," though, conversely, the latter's existence can neither be proven nor refuted by these terms. This was illustrated by the thirteenth-century philosopher Nikephoros Blemmydes, according to whom *genos* can refer either to one's parents or to one's *patris*, "as for instance we say that Paul's *genos* is from Tarsos," rather than, say, that he was Jewish (which he also was, but in a very different sense). Blemmydes goes

---

[136] Interchangeable use: Michael Attaleiates, *History* 30–31 (cf. 57 for civil war as *emphylios*); Georgios Akropolites, *History* 41–42; Eustathios, *Against an Overachieving Stylite in Thessalonike* 59 (*Or.* 22, Tafel p. 192); cf. also his *Funeral Oration for the Emperor Manuel Komnenos* 45 (*Or.* 23, Tafel p. 207); Anna Komnene, *Alexiad* 10.9.6–7. For Christian conflicts as civil wars, see Ahrweiler (1998) 5; for *ethnos, genos, et al.*, in the *Chronicle of the Morea*, Sansaridou-Hendrickx (1999) ch. 4; in the historian Gregoras, Blachakin (2003) 197–207.

[137] Gregorios Antiochos, *Encomium for the Patriarch Basileios Kamateros* 3 (p. 51). For both authors, see Magdalino (2000) 152; Kazhdan (1984b) 198; for the similar boast of the canonist Theodoros Balsamon, see Pitsakis (1991) 107.

[138] Skylitzes Continuatus (p. 155): the eunuch Nikephoros.

[139] Theodoretos, *History of the Monks of Syria* 28.4.

[140] Ahrweiler (1975a) 50–51; Chrysos (1996) 8; Greatrex (2000) 268–269; and Papoulia (2003) 51 ff., rely too much on the strong sense of *genos* and related words in texts such as Prokopios, *Wars* 2.6.23; and Ioannes Kinnamos, *History* 6.2. For the Greek vocabulary of inclusion and exclusion, see Ahrweiler (1984) 344–345.

on to explain that nations may be *genê* regardless of whether they are constituted by a common biological descent or by political union.[141]

The few attempts that the Byzantines made to establish ancient genealogies support the conclusion that at least until the end of the middle period they did not regard a common descent as constitutive of Roman identity. A rich cultural and historical heritage gave them a broad range of genealogical options, though time and population movements ensured that all connections were fictitious while the context, usually panegyrical, ensured that they were also rhetorical. Significantly, ancient Roman families and especially Aeneas seem to be most frequently invoked. For example, Basileios I (867–886) was flattered by a genealogy that included Philip and Alexander, Arsakes the Parthian, Tiridates the Armenian, and the Roman emperor Constantine. The Doukas family claimed descent from a cousin of Constantine I who moved with him from Italy to Constantinople and was also a descendant of Aeneas. Aeneas was also the putative ancestor of at least one aristocrat in late-antique Rome; of all the Romans, according to Justinian; and of the civil official Alexios Aristenos, according to the twelfth-century orator Nikephoros Basilakes. In order to praise the emperor Nikephoros III Botaneiates (1078–1081), the historian Michael Attaleiates traced his descent to the Byzantine Phokas family and from there back to the Roman Fabii, including Scipio Africanus and Aemilius Paulus. This Roman pedigree was later turned by the historian Nikephoros Bryennios into a favorable rhetorical comparison for Alexios I Komnenos, whence it was copied by the emperor's daughter Anna. The twelfth-century orator Gregorios Antiochos predictably claimed descent from the Seleukid king Antiochos I.[142] The Greek element, we observe, was only one among many options; the Roman element predominated, with Aeneas in the lead, but this was only a figurative way of stressing the Roman identity of the nation.

The Byzantines did not articulate an idea of common ethnicity, as some western medieval writers did regarding their own people.[143] The basis of their unity clearly lay elsewhere. Consider Kekaumenos, the eleventh-century

---

[141] Nikephoros Blemmydes, *Epitome Logica* 10.1–4, in *PG* CXLII (1885) 687–1004, here 753. For Paul's *genos* as Jewish, see Photios below.

[142] Basileios I: Genesios, *On the Reigns of the Emperors* 4.24 (and pp. 94–95 for the other sources); also Dagron (2003) 201. Doukas: Nikephoros Bryennios, *Materials for a History* pr. 9; Aeneas: *Timarion* 8; also Toxotius in Jerome, *Letter* 108.4; Justinian, *Novel* 47, preface; and Nikephoros Basilakes, *Oration for Alexios Aristenos* 9 (*Or. et ep.* p. 13); for the problem of Aeneas in the twelfth century, see p. 299 below. Michael Attaleiates, *History* 217–220 (cf. Bryennios, *Materials for a History* 2.3; Anna Komnene, *Alexiad* 1.1.3). Antiochos: Darrouzès (1962) 76.

[143] See Hall (2002) 10–11, without discussing Byzantium; Chrysos (2003) 134.

author of a book of maxims. He had served in the military and as governor of the province of Hellas. His book is fascinating for many reasons, but what interests us is the information that this man who spent his life in imperial service gives about his ancestors, of whom he was proud. He does not hide the fact that some of them had been enemies of the empire or independent chiefs on the periphery. His grandfather Demetrios Polemarchios had fought with Samuel of Bulgaria against Basileios II, but was later given ranks by that emperor. His other grandfather, Kekaumenos, had fought *against* Samuel as governor of Hellas and may have been the same as an ancestor who had been an independent chief (*toparchês*) on the Armenian border and, Kekaumenos admits, an "enemy of Romania." Attempts to determine which of these men "were really" Bulgarians or Armenians who defected to the Romans are irrelevant and impossible to resolve. If they had defected once, they – or their ancestors – may have defected once or twice already. All we know is that Kekaumenos was fully Roman in his own outlook and did not feel that his ancestry was relevant to that allegiance. In fact, he argued passionately that emperors should not promote foreigners (*ethnikoi*) who were not of royal birth to high rank because that was unfair to the Romans themselves and made Roman offices seem cheap. It is unclear how he reconciled this with his own family history.[144]

The majority of the elite in middle Byzantium had one or more ancestors of German, Latin, Norman, Scandinavian, Rus', Bulgarian (or other Slavic), Armenian, Alanic, Arabic, Turkish, "Assyrian," Georgian, or Abchasian descent. Sometimes this was reflected in their surnames, such as Eudokia Ingerina, the wife of Basileios I; Konstantinos Oumbertopoulos, "whose surname was based on his *genos*," as Anna Komnene noted; Ioannes Italos, the student of Psellos, possibly of Norman descent; and Ouzas, "whose name was based on his *genos*."[145] Roman names were taken with baptism, for convenience, or, as in the case of brides from the West, upon entry into their new families. Egilbald, for example, became Georgios; Bertha, a daughter of the king of Italy married to Romanos II, "was renamed Eudokia after the name of the grandmother and the sister of Konstantinos [VII]," as the latter, her father-in-law, proudly noted.[146] Nor was mixed ethnicity limited to the upper class (whose ranks were constantly

[144] Kekaumenos, *Strategikon* 30, 31, 73 (ancestors), 81 (policy toward *ethnikoi*); he may have known some Bulgarian: 2, 31, but cf. Mullett (1997) 272 n. 262; for his view of foreigners, Roueché (2000).
[145] Ingerina: Mango (1973); for the rest, Anna Komnene, *Alexiad* 4.4.3, 5.8.1–2, 5.7.3.
[146] Egilbald: McCormick (1998) 19; Bertha: Konstantinos VII, *De administrando imperio* 26.

being turned over). A later *vita* of the emperor Constantine has him populate the new capital "not only with Romans but with people of all *ethnê*."[147] A list of known population transfers, settlements, and migrations, would fill many pages.[148] In the twelfth century, the court orator Eustathios praised Manuel I for settling so many barbarians on Roman land that it could now be renamed New Persia or European Persia, comparing it to the Greek settlement of southern Italy in antiquity. But his indifference to the barbarians' ethnicity does not mean that their presence was unproblematic, for no Roman would consent to a settlement whose purpose was merely to increase the manpower available to the emperor at the expense of Roman unity. Eustathios notes elsewhere that those who had the best character among these settled barbarians enlisted in the army while the rest changed their former savagery against the Romans to mildness and began to contribute to life in Roman towns. Here we can observe the first stages of their assimilation.[149] Interestingly, Eustathios' account echoes nearly verbatim a Latin oration of 297 praising the emperor Constantius I for his settlement of barbarian tribes on Roman soil.[150] This parallel is a testament not to Eustathios' knowledge of Latin but to the continuity of Roman policy.

The subsequent careers of those recruits and the sons of the barbarians who were settled in towns can be glimpsed in Byzantine narratives. Prosouch, who served under Manuel I, is described by the historian Ioannes Kinnamos as a "Persian by *genos*, but having a Roman upbringing and *paideia*." *Paideia* does not here mean that he was classically educated, only that his customs were Roman. Ioannes Ises, also a "Persian by *genos*, had a Roman upbringing and way of life (*diaita*)."[151] These men may have been *mixobarbaroi*, but their sons would be Romans with no qualification. Unfortunately, the mechanisms of assimilation and acculturation by which this happened have not yet received the attention they deserve.[152] Byzantine writers are clear that one had to learn the language and adapt to Roman

---

[147] *The Life of the Great Emperor Constantine, He who Is among the Saints and Equal to the Apostles* 10 (p. 87). For other texts that acknowledged that the capital was multi-racial, see n. 160 below.

[148] Vryonis (1971) 49–55; Charanis (1972) *passim*, esp. III; Wirth (1979); Ditten (1993); and Koder (2005) 188–202.

[149] New Persia: Eustathios, *Address to the Emperor Manuel Komnenos* (*Or.* 14, Wirth pp. 247–248). Assimilation: *Funeral Oration for the Emperor Manuel Komnenos* 18–19 (*Or.* 23, Tafel p. 200). In general, see Magdalino (1993) 175–176.

[150] *Panegyrici Latini* 8.9; for tr. and commentary, Nixon and Rodgers (1994) 121–122; Burns (2003) 299–300.

[151] Ioannes Kinnamos, *History* 2.14, 5.13; for Turks in imperial service, Bádenas (1998).

[152] For a good start, see Laiou (1991a) 91–96, and (1998); for Armenians, Garsoïan (1998) esp. 103; for Turks, Bádenas (1998) esp. 184–188; for Latins, Nicol (1979b).

manners. Ethnicity was not a factor. Romanos II praised his wife Bertha-Eudokia for quickly learning Greek and "our customs." Western princesses who married young into the imperial family required interpreters when the Crusaders arrived in 1203. Nor was there a theoretical limit to how high one could rise. Theodora, the Norman wife of Michael II Doukas, ruler of Epeiros in the thirteenth century, ended up the patron saint of the capital city of Arta.[153] A boy, "Persian by *genos*," captured by the Crusaders in Asia Minor in 1097 and presented to Alexios I Komnenos, became a playmate of his son Ioannes; when the latter ascended the throne, our Persian, now Ioannes Axouch, rose to become second-in-command of the empire, the arbiter of the succession in 1143, and the founder of a powerful family. "Many of the emperor's distinguished relatives, on meeting him by chance, would dismount and make obeisance," noted the historian Niketas Choniates. "The nobility and liberality of his mind quite overshadowed his humble origins and made Axouch beloved by all" (9–10). It was the rise from humble, not specifically from Turkish, origins, that impressed Niketas.

It is, then, wrong to declare that "racial exclusivity, at least among the upper classes, was part of the Byzantine belief in their innate superiority."[154] This statement erroneously implies that the upper classes defined themselves racially. But few or none did this. No doubt there was considerable prejudice, especially against newcomers and barbarians and other groups who would not assimilate to the Roman way of life, such as the Vlachs, about whom Kekaumenos had some nasty comments (74–75), or the Jews, whom Christians had non-racial reasons to dislike. The rhetoric of racial exclusion, as we will see, could also be deployed against personal and political opponents who were otherwise quite Roman. These were not political attacks against foreigners but purely internal disputes exploiting racist rhetoric. Regarding actual foreigners, the Byzantines had reason to think that virtually anyone could be assimilated. Even the New Testament offered the striking example of Paul, who was a Roman citizen despite being a Jew by *genos*, a point that Photios stressed in his letters. Unfortunately, he did not elaborate on what he thought it meant for Paul to be a Roman beyond the legal fact of citizenship, because he was interested in making a technical point to absolve the Apostle of mendacity.[155] Consider also the inclusive definition of "indigenous inhabitants" (*autochthones*) offered by the

[153] Romanos II, *Funeral Oration for his Wife Bertha* (p. 271); Lock (1995) 291. For the training that future empresses required, see also Theophanes the Confessor, *Chronographia* s.a. 6274 (p. 455), with Connor (2004) 213. Theodora: Konstantakopoulou (2002) 346, citing previous bibliography.
[154] Angold (1975b) 67.    [155] Photios, *Letters* 103, esp. 44–65; also *Letters* 246, and esp. 247.

twelfth-century Aristotelian commentator Stephanos: "those who are not migrants or colonists from another land, or who, if they come from another land, have lived in this land long enough to be old-timers and in this respect resemble the indigenous inhabitants, like those who resemble the indigenous inhabitants of Constantinople."[156]

A brief discussion must be devoted at this point to Konstantinos VII's famous treatise on the empire's foreign policy (known as the *De administrando imperio*) because it is often cited to show Byzantine racial exclusivity. This work, however, really proves the opposite conclusion (if, in fact, it can be used reliably at all). Here is the argument that Konstantinos advises his son Romanos II to use in rebuffing foreign demands for imperial brides: "never shall an emperor of the Romans ally himself in marriage with a nation whose customs differ from and are alien to those of the Roman order, especially with a nation that is infidel and unbaptized." Here we see a fundamentally cultural definition of Roman national unity. The emperor repeats the same point two pages later, focusing on "laws and institutions," but here he adds a passage that has caused much mischief: "it is right that each nation should marry and cohabit not with those of another race (*phylon*) and tongue but with those of the same tribe (*genos*) and speech." Beyond the ambiguity in the Byzantine usage of those terms, if we follow the course of Konstantinos' argument we see that for him racial difference is constituted *by* difference in customs. The comparison of nations to animal species is specious and, in the context of this mendacious work, a deliberate falsehood advanced for political reasons.[157] The Byzantines knew well from their own society – and many from their own ancestors – what Isokrates taught them in their studies, that "men assimilate to those customs in which they have been raised."[158]

We have seen that Byzantine aristocrats had no difficulty acknowledging their foreign origins. In another sense, however, "ethnicity" could be a negative quality in Byzantium, when it denoted internal regional stereotypes or, for recent arrivals, a failure to fully assimilate. Often it was used to disparage personal enemies, so we must carefully distinguish between rhetoric that aimed to cast political enemies as outsiders from rhetoric that aimed to exclude first-generation Romans, who were vulnerable because they were undergoing assimilation. In the late fourth century, for

---

[156] Stephanos (possibly Skylitzes), *Commentary on Aristotle's* Rhetoric 1360b31 (p. 270); tr. (slightly modified) by Magdalino (2000) 156.
[157] Konstantinos VII, *De administrando* ... 13; for the mendacity, see Lounghis (1990); Magdalino (2002) 177–181; Dagron (2003) 214–215. "Racism": Ahrweiler (1975a) 50–51.
[158] Isokrates, *Areopagitikos* 40.

example, intrigue at the court led to a temporary ban on Lykians in public office because that province was believed to have supported the losing side. The sixth century likewise saw much hostile rhetoric directed against Kappadokians on account of Justinian's hated prefect Ioannes.[159] But in neither case can nations of Lykians and Kappadokians with separate collective identities be postulated; all we have here are flimsy regional stereotypes and politically motivated rhetoric. The same was probably true of political attacks that invoked foreign origins, e.g., calling someone a Skythian.[160] It is possible that there was no "ethnic" truth whatsoever behind such accusations.

A way to repel these attacks and reestablish one's Roman status was by a display of Greek *paideia*, for no barbarian could possess that. The early tenth-century exile Niketas Magistros was hardly staking a claim to Greek ethnicity when he said that he was a Spartan on his mother's side and an Athenian on his father's; he was only a Roman who happened to have been born in Sparta. What is more important is that his claim occurs in a rhetorical display of classical learning by a man who was out of favor at the court and had been reviled for having "a Slavic face."[161] Whereas ethnic insults cast political losers as outsiders, classicism could confer, or reconfirm, insider status (yet too much classicism could incur the charge of religious "Hellenism"). Conversely, ethnic imputations could be used to challenge an opponent's *paideia* and, by extension, his suitability for office. In the early fourteenth century, the scholar Ioannes Katrares attacked the cultural credentials of a Bulgarian candidate for the patriarchal throne by, among other things, calling him a Vlach by birth and an Albanian in appearance, in sum, a "Bulgaralbanitovlachos."[162] Again, ethnicity here was being used to reinforce more crucial deficiencies. It was not the

---

[159] Lykians: Kelly (2004) 48–49. Kappadokians: e.g., Ioannes Lydos, *On the Magistracies of the Roman State* 2.17, 2.20–21, 3.38, and esp. 3.57–72; for Kappadokians, see n. 168 below.

[160] For ethnicity in rhetorical denunciations, see, e.g., Brokkaar (1972) 199 n. 3 against Basileios Lakapenos; Nikephoros Basilakes, *Against Bagoas* 12–13 (*Or. et ep.* pp. 99–100), on which Magdalino (1993) 283. For more, see Konstantakopoulou (2002) 345–346. In his attack on the Constantinopolitan mob, Niketas Choniates does not fail to mention that it was composed of "diverse *genē*" (*History* 234), but the main point of his tirade is fundamentally political. See also the Nikaian patriarch Germanos II, *Oration against the official in charge of the kanikleios, who insulted his* genos (*Or.* 10; pp. 281–287), whose point is to attack Constantinopolitan aristocratic snobbery; see Magdalino (1984) 65; Angold (1995) 541.

[161] Niketas Magistros, *Letter* 2; face: Konstantinos VII, *On the Themes* 2.7 (p. 91). *Pace* Vryonis (1978) 252 n. 2, Niketas does not call himself a Greek. Lakonia: Pratsch (2005). Cf. the political matrix of ethnic imputations in modern Greece: Gourgouris (1996) 151 n. 22.

[162] Ioannes Katrares, *Anakreontic Verses against the Philosopher among Philosophers and Most Eloquent Neophytos* 50–54 (p. 677). *Pace* Vryonis (1999) 28–29, Katrares does not attack Neophytos for not being ethnically Greek. For Ioannes Bekkos and Gregorios of Cyprus, see p. 385 below.

motivating source of hostility and seems in some cases to have been invented purely for polemical purposes. By the same token, ethnicity could be an asset to those who *wanted* to appear as outsiders or as exotic. Psellos claimed that magicians and charlatans (like ancient magicians who posed as Persian *magoi* and our "Gypsy" fortune-tellers) did not possess any real art but adduced as credentials their "ethnic origins, the one claiming to be an Illyrian, the other a Persian."[163]

In short, Byzantium was not multi-ethnic in the way that some modern states aspire to be, namely multi-cultural, where ethnic diversity is recognized and even highlighted; rather, ethnic origins were irrelevant and usually forgotten after the requirements of assimilation were met. "Empire," then, is a misleading term because it tends to group Romania along with "multi-ethnic states" such as the Persian, Holy Roman, or Ottoman empires, which were explicitly understood as encompassing different ethnic groups or nations ruled by a single authority. The early Roman empire also falls within this category. Byzantium, then, was not an empire, if current terminology presupposes "the inner incompatibility of empire and nation."[164] The *res publica* was not a federation of ethnic groups or a dominion by one of the rest. In his lament for the fall of Constantinople in 1204, Niketas Choniates complained that the Latin aggressors were "not true nations (*ethnē*) but indistinct and scattered tribes (*genē*)" (577); presumably, he believed that Romania constituted a distinct and unified *ethnos*. When Theodoros Laskaris praised his father, Ioannes III Doukas Batatzes (in the early 1250s), for "smashing the image of the nations, that is mixed, multi-limbed, much-compounded, and many-headed, and setting up a Roman image for them to worship," he implies that that image was unified in every way, not only politically.[165] Thus, although they could (casually) admit their ethnic origins, the Byzantines did not take this logic to its conclusion and *define* their society as *essentially* multi-ethnic. Their defining criteria were language, laws, customs, and religious belief – *paideia*, *diaita*, and *doxa* – and these had nothing to do with *genos* (strictly defined). What we call ethnicity was only a curiosity about first- or second-generation Romans or an antiquarian construction, as we saw above with the nations invented by Tribonianus and the genealogies of the panegyrists.

---

[163] Psellos, *Accusation of the Archpriest before the Synod* 2659–2661 (*OFA* I). See the Syrian woman in Theodoros Prodromos, *Letter* 5 (1252a). Cf. Lucian, *Lover of Lies* 11–13; in general, Graf (1997).

[164] Anderson (1991) 93; cf. also Zakythinos (1980) 314: "the main features of an empire are … multiracial composition"; also Gounaridis (1986) 248; Pitsakis (1997) 79–80. But cf. Armstrong (1982) 131.

[165] Theodoros II Laskaris, *Encomium for Ioannes III Doukas Batatzes* 6 (*op. rh.* p. 33).

Consider again Konstantinos VII, who noted in his survey of the empire's provinces (called themes) that "the theme now called Anatolikon is inhabited by five *ethnê*, the Phrygians, Lykaonians, Isaurians, Pamphilians, and Pisidians ... But when they fell under the Roman yoke ... they all fused together under one authority."[166] These *ethnê* had no real existence in Konstantinos' time other than purely geographical (if they ever had). These terms, which were geographical and not ethnic, rhetorical and not existential, were inherited from classical ethnography and lacked contemporary relevance. They hardly reflected, as is sometimes asserted, "ethnic divisions" within Byzantine society.[167] At most, they conveyed vague regional stereotypes (as we say today of people from the Midwest, East Coast, or Deep South of the US). After the end of the empire's life, Gennadios Scholarios again affirmed how little these so-called internal divisions signified: "it makes no difference whether I am from Thessaly or Byzantion, given that Thessalians and Byzantioi differ neither in their language nor in belief nor in customs, as perhaps they once did,"[168] presumably in pre-Roman times. Now they were all just Romans. When the early eleventh-century general Eustathios Daphnomeles pleaded with his Bulgarian attackers, he denied blinding their lord out of hatred "because he is a Bulgarian and I Roman; for I am not a Roman from among those who inhabit Thrake and Makedonia, but rather from Asia Minor." One was a Roman from somewhere in the empire, like the theologian Demetrios: "he was Roman by *genos*, from the town of Lampe."[169]

For these reasons, attempts to identify the ethnic origins of individual Byzantines are misleading as well as tiresome, especially regarding families that were established in the empire for centuries and which took no interest in their ethnic origins, which were certainly mixed. They would not have understood modern obsessions and would have assumed, if asked these questions, that their Roman patriotism was being called into question.

---

[166] Konstantinos VII, *On the Themes* 1.1.

[167] *Pace* Obolensky (1971) 355; Kazhdan and Epstein (1985) 173; the verdict in ibid. 170 that "despite their ethnic pride, the Byzantines did not represent a unified 'nation'," must be reversed: despite being a unified nation, the Byzantines had little by way of ethnic pride.

[168] Gennadios Scholarios, *Refutation of Judaism* (pp. 252–253). For "Kappadokians," etc., see, e.g., Michael Attaleiates, *History* 170, 246. For regional stereotypes, see, e.g., Magdalino (1998) on Paphlagonians; Michael Psellos, *Chronographia* 6.99, 6.110 on Makedonians; Leon the Deacon, *History* 3.1 and n. 159 on Kappadokians. For *genos* used by Prokopios in connection with what are in fact geographically defined groups, see Greatrex (2000) 268. For the meaning of Makedonia in Byzantium, see Tarnanidis (2000). For the transformation of ethnic labels to geographical terms, see Mitchell (2000) 134 for Asia Minor, and Papoulia (1993) esp. 291–294 for Thrake and Makedonia.

[169] Ioannes Skylitzes, *Historical Synopsis: Basileios II and Konstantinos VIII* 42 (p. 362). Ioannes Kinnamos, *History* 6.2.

After so many studies on the putative Armenian origin of the emperor Herakleios it is both disarming and refreshing to see Konstantinos VII refer to him simply as "the Libyan," because he began his career in Carthage, where his family had its base.[170] Geography again replaces ethnicity. If we must talk about ethnicity in Byzantium, we should think in terms of degrees of assimilation, from recent arrivals to full Romans. The most heated modern debates tend to concern families that belong to the latter end of the spectrum. About them it is beside the point to ask who "was really" an Armenian or a Bulgarian and attempt the dismemberment of Byzantium into ethnic groups, with the lines usually drawn in accordance with the scholar's own national purposes. Too much paper has been wasted on such efforts, whose futility and contentiousness are more appropriate for the internet.

The Byzantines, then, were Romans, not Greeks or Armenians in disguise, or, for that matter, Pisidians or Paphlagonians, "ethnic groups" that no one cares about today because no one happens to bear their name. We should not view Romania as a multi-ethnic empire but as the nation-state of the Romans that happened at times to include a number of partially assimilated minorities within its borders, as have *all* modern nation-states, indeed all states, throughout history. If, then, it is false to say that the empire was fundamentally split into ethnic groups – because these simply did not exist – it is a wild exaggeration to say of its "ethnic minorities" that "their very existence challenged the concept of Byzantine uniformity."[171] I, at least, am aware of no such challenge, at least outside the army, and even there only at specific moments and rarely with great impact – except in the fifth century, in the West!

On the other hand, "it is important not to overemphasize the degree of cultural homogeneity required by the nation-state."[172] The claims of medieval people to constitute nations are often rejected if only one of their members can be shown to have set his personal interests above those of the nation in question or switched sides in a war. By such standards, there have never been nations, not even in modern times. There were and always will be ambiguities. The Venetians and some of the residents of southern Italy before the eleventh century were a liminal case, sometimes Roman and sometimes not, eventually not. Regions along the Danube

---

[170] Konstantinos VII, *On the Themes* I pr. (p. 60).
[171] Kazhdan and Constable (1982) 153–154; Svoronos (2004) 61–62. Cf. Nicol (1972) I 317: "the heterogeneous mixture of races that made up the Byzantine empire."
[172] Poole (1999) 35.

became "semi-barbaric" when the "Skythians" who had been settled there introduced their own way of life.[173] Larger groups, such as the Bulgarians, could not be assimilated easily or completely even when conquered, and were placed under special measures that recognized their difference. Some Byzantines believed that by accepting Christianity the Bulgarians were civilized and "almost" assimilated to "Roman customs." But many clearly were not "pure Romans."[174] One such pure Roman, Theophylaktos Hephaistos, appointed their bishop in the late eleventh century, argued that the Bulgarians were no longer a barbarian *ethnos* but a people of God, civilized and yet distinct from the Romans. His was an optimistic view, but did not quite disguise the fact that the Bulgarians posed a problem of categorization, compounded by the fact that their "identity" had never been as coherent as that of the Romans.[175] There were other minorities, such as Armenians, many of whom were suddenly absorbed in the mid-eleventh century. They neither spoke Greek nor were orthodox, at any rate according to the protests of one Eustathios Boïlas.[176] Greek was by far the dominant language in the empire and its knowledge was a key factor in acculturation, but it was not the only one. And an army active in so many lands inevitably produced oddities: Ioannes Gilakios in the sixth century, commanding a unit of fellow Armenians in Italy against the Goths, spoke neither Greek, nor Latin, nor Gothic; Petros Libellios from Antioch in the eleventh century, "an Assyrian by his *genos*," knew the "wisdom" (i.e., languages) of both Romans and Saracens and led a contingent of Varangians (Northmen) in Syria.[177] First-generation Romans would also have experienced alienation. Men like Gregorios Pakourianos, a general of Armenian or Georgian origin who rose high in the Roman army but founded a monastery from which all Romans were excluded as "violent and greedy," must have held an ambiguous position indeed in Roman society.[178]

---

[173] Venetians: Laiou (1991a) 85–88; Danube: Michael Attaleiates, *History* 204–205; and Stephenson (2000a) 107–114, on other Byzantine writers.

[174] Ahrweiler (1998) 7, 9; for categories of exclusion (1984) 345–348.

[175] For Theophylaktos and others, see Kazhdan (1984b) 219–221; Mullett (1997) 235–239, 261, 266–277; Stephenson (2000b) 249–252.

[176] Garsoïan (1998) 109–110; in general, Seibt (2003); for Byzantine treatment of minorities, Konstantakopoulou (2002) 340 ff. (though I disagree with her view of Roman identity as exclusively religious).

[177] Gilakios: Prokopios, *Wars* 7.26.24–26; Libellios: Michael Attaleiates, *History* 205. Languages: Dagron (1993) and (1994); Oikonomides (1999) esp. 12, 16 for Greek.

[178] Gregorios Pakourianos, *Typikon* 24 (p. 105).

There were perennial internal tensions as well. The fisc and the law treated Jews more or less equally,[179] but the Church, and therefore society, did not. Constantinopolitans were notoriously arrogant and regarded provincials as a lesser breed. "I am no alien here," wrote Gregorios Antiochos defensively, "I did not come from elsewhere; I am locally born and I belong here." Provincials were a different *genos*.[180] But it does not seem – at any rate not before the late twelfth century – that local loyalties conflicted with the unity of Roman identity. Cicero had long since explained that many Romans had two *patriae*, but supreme devotion always went to the one that represented the *res publica*.[181] In Byzantium there is some evidence for tension between the *oikos* – the large household – and Romania, but not the village, town, or city, at least not between the seventh and twelfth centuries. Certainly there were local loyalties, but they made little mark in our sources. There was nothing comparable to what we observe in, say, the later Ottoman empire, where "the Greek rarely speaks of his nation, yet he speaks continually, and with enthusiasm, of his country – an epithet which he applies to his native village."[182]

To conclude, the Byzantines did not believe that Romania was ethnically divided, therefore it was not. Though they did recognize the presence of ethnic minorities, this did not undermine the unity of Romania. More importantly, they did not define themselves as a group along ethnic lines, except in a few rhetorical contexts, for instance when they claimed to be the descendants of Aeneas. In giving up the idea of the multi-ethnic empire, however, we should not swing to the opposite extreme and deny that Romania was a nation just because it was not ethnic in conception. Many modern nations lack an ethnic aspect (or claim to lack it). Theorists of the nation are divided as to the precise importance of this factor, but an agreement seems to have emerged that nations do not *have* to be ethnic in nature.[183] One may be tempted to compare Byzantium in this regard to the US, which is also republican and imperial and has been proclaimed a "civic nation," given that, in theory, belonging does not depend on ethnicity. But that notion regarding the US has been shown to be largely a

---

[179] Pitsakis (1997) 85–91; Laiou (1998); Neville (2004) 132–133, for the positive side of integration.
[180] See p. 88 above.
[181] Cicero, *Laws* 2.2.5; cf. *For Balbus* 28–29; *For Caecina* 100; Modestinus in Justinian, *Digest* 50.1.33; cf. Ando (2000) 10–11. For the pride of the jurist Ulpianus in his native Tyre, see Justinian, *Digest* 50.15.1.1; cf. Millar (1993) 290–295.
[182] G. Finlay in Peckham (2001) 30–31, 62. For the tension between *oikos* and Romania, see Magdalino (1989) 184–185; for a late example of local patriotism, Eustathios, *The Capture of Thessalonike* 69 (pp. 88–89).
[183] Smith (1991) 11–13; Miller (1995) 19–21; Poole (1999) 34–43.

fiction – albeit still a politically powerful one. The rulers of Byzantium were not – and were not perceived to be – drawn overwhelmingly from one ethnic group, nor did its society have to cope with the legacy of race-based slavery and the ethnic enthusiasms that pervade the population and shape its behavior.[184]

## THE FICTIONS OF ECUMENICAL IDEOLOGY

Having disposed of the "multi-ethnic empire" and the idea that the Byzantines "were really" Greeks (or whatever) beneath the thin surface of a Roman label, we can now interrogate the second pole of the modern view of Byzantium, namely that it "was not a national state but a polity which, by virtue of its Roman and Christian inheritance, claimed to be universal." The amply attested nationalist tendencies of its subjects are accordingly dismissed as "aberrant"[185] – though how they were possible at all is not explained. It is odd how often historians who are discussing this problem go out of their way to reject the national interpretation when no one has in fact propounded it, and how defensively they do it. Still, no rigorous argumentation has been offered on this issue, and the methodology by which the "universalist" interpretation has been constructed is problematic. First, it rests on the fiction of the "multi-ethnic empire," which was partly devised to serve the needs of *modern* national identities competing *against* that of Byzantium itself. Second, it is based on a tiny number of tendentious claims in the sources, namely those made by a sacerdotally minded emperor (Justinian), an ambitious canonist (Theodoros Balsamon), and a desperate patriarch (Antonios IV). These claims are taken out of their circumscribed ideological or rhetorical contexts and transformed into an existential and historical reality. All of them were made in unique circumstances in defense of idiosyncratic and self-serving ambitions. They point, as we expect from such men, to a Byzantium that is all abstraction: an ecumenical, Christian, and imperial ideal that explains little about how the vast majority of Byzantines actually thought and behaved, at least beyond the narrow ideological or diplomatic contexts in which these statements were made.

[184] For a historical approach, see Jusdanis (2001) 155–162; cf. Smith (1986) 216; Anagnostou (2004) 30 ff.
[185] Obolensky (1972) 1; Angold (1999) 37. Countless similar statements can be cited. For Byzantine nationalism, see also Magdalino (1991a); for the period of the Nikaian empire, see pp. 360–368 below. For the fantasy of "universalism" as the historical essence of Byzantium, see Armstrong (1982) 145–151.

It is important to note that it has never been *proven* that the Byzantines were not a nation, despite the frequent claims that are made to the contrary, nor has an "ecumenical" Byzantium ever been systematically demonstrated. The idea has rather been inherited and recycled from the prehistory of the field, and never scrutinized. It has even been granted by its proponents that "perhaps because it has always seemed cut and dried the question of the Byzantine identity has only excited occasional interest."[186] This should arouse our suspicion, especially when it is also granted that when we turn to the sources this "basic political theory" of the Byzantines "is seldom spelled out in so many words for the simple reason that it was taken for granted."[187] We might draw the opposite conclusion from this silence. This "basic theory," it turns out, was set in place by modern legal and diplomatic historians, along with the odd theologian, in other words by scholars who deal with those texts in which historical reality least impinges. Looking for precise and universal definitions, they found them, but did not then interrogate their sources. The exercise is comparable to taking a few partisan commentaries on the US constitution and treating them as definitive statements of what it means to actually be an American, while at the same time ignoring all historical, social, and cultural realities.

What, then, were these universalist commitments that allegedly prevented the Byzantines from being a nation? The notion of "ecumenicity" that has been so important in shaping our view of Byzantium has not been examined with regard to either its precise ideological content and commitments or its impact on the realities of Byzantine history and the maintenance of the *politeia*. The papers of a recent conference on the topic reveal just how little critical analysis has gone into the making of this notion: the contributors one by one admit that "ecumenicity" was more confined to the sphere of diplomacy than was previously realized (and was often used in cynical defiance of reality); that rhetoric and propaganda operated on a different "register" than that of actual politics and foreign policy; that by *oikoumenê* many (most?) Byzantines of the middle period meant nothing more than Romania itself, in both the political and the ecclesiastical spheres (in other words that a nation had inherited and been invested with a universalizing rhetoric); and that most Byzantines realized full well that this ideological conceit did not correspond to the usually well-demarcated territorial limits of their state.[188] In sum, it is time for modern notions of Byzantine identity to engage with reality.

---

[186] Angold (1999) 36.    [187] Nicol (1972) I 317.
[188] See the papers by J. Koder, G. Dagron, and E. Chrysos in Chrysos (2005a).

Let us consider the Byzantines' universal commitments. There was, first, the universalism of Roman law, but this served precisely to define the horizontal nature of their society and mark its boundaries with the outside. Unlike the West, social status was not legally defined in Byzantium, resulting in considerable mobility and a tacit or active identification on the part of the population with all state institutions, making it effectively a nation.[189] The Byzantines believed that their legal system was superior to all others, in fact that theirs was one of the few "legal" societies in existence, and they knew from the history of late antiquity that their laws could sustain a universal polity; however, at any point in their history, real or imagined, that polity extended no further than the borders of their state. "Universalism" in practice was therefore a promise, a once and possibly future ideal that did (and could do) nothing to disrupt the national basis of Roman identity. In practice, Roman law set the Roman nation apart from its neighbors; its universal applicability was a matter of potential, not identity.[190]

Then there was the idea of "empire without limits," a rhetorical conceit of the early principate that did echo in Byzantium, albeit faintly and without engaging with the constitutive elements of Roman identity given that, in the scope of its territorial ambitions, it was never engaged with reality to begin with. It was easy for orators and religious enthusiasts to claim that God had appointed the Roman emperor to rule over "the entire world," but that was on a level of discourse that dispensed with the realities of that world and, with it, the basis of Roman identity. In the early empire, Rome in practice recognized the legitimacy of foreign states and acknowledged the equality of the Persians; this recognition would later be extended to the Caliphate.[191] Later, "empire without limits" was basically a rhetorical amplification of the theme of "restoration," whose origin lay in the crises of late antiquity and the emergence of a theoretically ecumenical Christian community. But Justinian was perhaps the only emperor who took its logic seriously, that is who pursued a foreign policy based on the vision of a culturally, linguistically, and nationally heterogeneous population united only by his own authority and the Christian faith. He was, as a result,

---

[189] Neville (2004) 78, noting the exception of slavery (which seems to have been unlike its ancient predecessor).

[190] Pitsakis (2005) presents evidence that Byzantine (as opposed to late Roman) law was influential in other medieval and even modern societies, but "influence" does not establish "ecumenicity," as we are not dealing with the same *politeia*.

[191] Pitsakis (1997) 78–79 and n. 16; Kaldellis (2004a) 72–73, citing previous bibliography; Schmalzbauer (2004).

unique among the emperors in regarding his Roman subjects as no different than the barbarians whom he conquered, putting his writers in the awkward position of having to justify the forced inclusion within the *res publica* of culturally alien peoples. That is why *all* historians who believe that the Byzantines were by definition merely "the subjects of the Christian Roman emperor to whom God had entrusted the direction of worldly affairs" cite Justinian, and just about *only* Justinian,[192] falling into the ideological trap prepared by that emperor in his legal works. It is now being recognized that from an ideological point of view Justinian was a radical, and not above lying to promote his authoritarian vision. In fact, no emperor generated more ideological opposition among his own subjects. Further research will no doubt reveal that his impact on later Byzantines was limited to the sphere of occasional rhetoric, and was probably dominant not even there. After the failure of Justinian's wars, the ideal of ecumenical restoration was confined to the realm of diplomacy, especially, or exclusively, regarding Italy and the union of Churches. In practice, it functioned as rhetorical jubilation for the small-scale reconquest of lands in the Balkans and Asia Minor.[193]

It is, finally, the Christian component of Byzantine universalism that provides the main foundation for scholarly discussions. Christianity certainly has universal ambitions, though it has never achieved them and is quite compatible with fiercely national and other partisan movements. The early Christians hoped to convert the world, abolish religious differences, and transcend national ones,[194] but after the sixth century few Byzantines were inspired by this vision. They did what they could to spread the faith to others, though generally only when invited to do so. Only a minority, especially in monastic circles, was animated by the vision of a Christian *oikoumenê* that transcended Romania. Other Christians could naturally feel an affinity with their coreligionists elsewhere (there being neither Greek nor Jew in Christ) but this feeling has rarely or never broken

---

[192] E.g., Angold (1999) 37.

[193] For Justinian and his subjects, see Kaldellis (2004a) 133, *passim* for ideological opposition; also (2005a). Justinian as a radical: Honoré (2004) 129–132; Pazdernik (2005). During his reign, imperial propaganda extended the discourse of assimilation based on *diaita*, *êthê*, and *doxa*, to conquered people on the periphery: Maas (2003) 160–174. For Manuel I's notion and use of restoration, see Magdalino (1993) 23–24, 419–422, 460–462 (Manuel looked back to Justinian); cf. Shepard (2006) 40 for the Italian limits of imperial universalism. Ahrweiler (1975a) 46 offers no proof that world-rule expressed the "deepest convictions" of the "average Byzantine" nor defines the mental, emotional, and national spaces that such visions occupied. Ecumenicity had powerful ideological opponents even within Byzantium, at least according to Lounghis (1990).

[194] Cf. Dagron (2005a) 50–53.

down national boundaries on a historical scale. The ecumenical vision of the Church ultimately had no impact on Roman identity, which is proven by the fact that the Byzantines quite simply did not regard barbarian Christians as Romans. Being orthodox (in a formal sense, at any rate) was perhaps necessary but not sufficient to make one a Roman.

This is established by the consistent record over a thousand years of dealings between the Byzantines and their "barbarian" Christian neighbors. All of *two* statements have been uncovered that seem to contradict this picture and they have been touted in the literature, indeed they are often made the basis for definitions of what it meant to be a Roman despite the fact that both were made under highly unusual circumstances, had no practical effect, and bore no relation to what anyone else believed. The first was a response by the canon lawyer of the twelfth century, Theodoros Balsamon, to questions posed to the Constantinopolitan Church by Markos, the patriarch of Alexandria, regarding the legal status of the orthodox Christians in Egypt. Clearly this is not something that worried most Byzantines, but it provided Balsamon with an opportunity to expand the jurisdiction of Roman law (i.e., of his area of expertise). He declared accordingly that all orthodox people were Romans wherever they may live. But this was a legal fiction invented on the spot to answer a theoretical question of canon law that bore little relation to the historical and cultural basis of Roman identity and did not reflect the consensus of Roman society. In fact, we possess an earlier redaction of the answer to Markos drawn up by a certain Ioannes of Chalkedon in which the Egyptian Christians are deemed to be separate from "our Romans." And the true limits of Romania were revealed by the patriarch of Alexandria himself, when he confessed that the *Basilika*, the Byzantine law-code, was not available in Egypt.[195]

The second and more famous statement was issued in 1393 by the patriarch Antonios IV in an appeal to the Grand Prince of Moscow at a time when the empire was nearing its end. He there asserts the universal authority of the emperor over all the Romans, "by which I mean over all the Christians"[196] – note: he says all *Christians*, not merely all the orthodox!

[195] Theodoros Balsamon, *Answers to questions regarding canon law posed by Markos of Alexandria*, Quest. 3 (956); see Pitsakis (1991) 108–109 (citing previous scholarship) who takes Balsamon's answer as indicative of Byzantine opinion; also (1995) 29–30, 31; (1997) 80–81; (2005) 141–142; Konstantakopoulou (2002) 332; Dagron (2003) 257. For the circumstances, see Angold (1995) 507–508.

[196] Antonios, patriarch of Constantinople, *Letter to the Grand Prince of Moscow* (esp. p. 191). Countless scholars cite this as a standard formulation of the Byzantine perspective.

The rhetoric is moving and the statement accordingly cited in all discussions of Byzantine identity that affirm its ecumenicity. Again, while we should not deny that the Byzantines felt some spiritual link with other Christians, this last-minute desperate appeal, contradicting everything that we know from a thousand years of history, should not be taken at face value. Never had Byzantines before even implied that the Rus' were Romans, and only in equally desperate appeals had they claimed to know from "history books" that Romania and the Christian West had once been united.[197] Antonios' plea finds a modern parallel in the occasional appeals to the West made by modern Greeks on the basis of Europe's common Hellenic legacy. This rhetoric is not cynical – there is clearly something there – but one would be mistaken to conclude from it that modern Greeks regard other Europeans as Greek, Hellenic legacies notwithstanding.

Balsamon and Antonios' formulations were essentially without real precedent because they operated in highly circumscribed ideological spaces. It comes then as no surprise that they had little or no effect – except on modern scholars of Byzantium. This reveals how influential legal, diplomatic, and ecclesiastical historians have been in forging the definitions that underlie modern ideas of Byzantium. It is time now for cultural historians to assert their right to look beyond the rhetoric of those fields. To belong to the polity of New Rome required more than mere conversion to Christianity or nominal submission to the emperor: Byzantium was not a Church or a vague entity like the Holy Roman empire. The "emperor of the Romans" was not the "commander of the faithful," even though his subjects were supposed to belong to one Church. Granted, the Byzantines never forgot that their emperor had once ruled the entire Christian world and recognized that his position entailed ecumenical rights and responsibilities. But after the rest of the world had gone its own way, the gap between that ideal and what it actually meant to be a Roman yawned to the point where it could not be bridged by words. The Byzantines knew this, of course, and certainly did not believe the fantasy imputed to them by historians, who then ridicule them for believing that "myth" of ecumenicity, the "monstrous fable," "ostrich-like attitude," "beliefs that contradicted reality," etc.[198] No: during the transition from late antiquity to the middle period this ecumenical ideal ceased to have any relation to what it actually

---

[197] E.g., Michael VII to Robert Guiscard in Michael Psellos, *Letter S* 144, cf. Nicol (1972) I 327. For the irrelevance of Photios' Patriarchal Ecumenism, see Dagron (2003) 232–234. For Akropolites, see p. 382 below.
[198] The phrases are from Nicol (1972) I.

meant to be a Roman. In practice, the *basileus* became the ruler of a people that defined itself by what we can only call national criteria. To that degree it would probably be better to call him the "king of the Romans," which is what *basileus* meant, after all. That would occlude the preeminence that he was supposed to enjoy with respect to his barbarian colleagues, though this had meaning only within a limited diplomatic space. The Byzantines may have regarded themselves as the only true heirs of the ecumenical Christian and Roman empire, and theoretically entitled to possess it again, but a restoration would have required not merely conversion but the spread of Roman "customs" and laws, in short of national unity. In practice, this was impossible and so hardly pursued.

Consider, for example, the tension between Anna Komnene's declaration that "the empire of the Romans is by nature the sovereign of the other nations (*ethnē*)," which clearly implies some kind of "universality," with her sheer hatred of the Latin Christians who were "of a different race (*phylon*), barbarous, and incompatible with our customs."[199] We are dealing with two different approaches to reality here: the one was a diplomatic and ideological fiction inherited from late antiquity, while the other reflected the actual grounds on which the vast majority of Byzantines differentiated themselves from others. I am not advocating that we discard the former altogether. But its place in the overall picture should be fixed only after we have ascertained the historical grounds of Byzantine national identity. In the current scheme, the latter have been completely discarded and the former put in their place, with, as we have seen, absurd results. Byzantium has been turned into a playground for idealism.

In fact, of the major peoples of Christendom the Byzantines were individually and collectively the *least* receptive to pleas for common cause among Christians, and the *least* likely to set the interests of Christendom above those of their *patria*. Let us repeat that, for all its universal ambitions, Christianity historically has proven itself quite capable of buttressing and even creating very particularistic national identities, both in the Middle Ages and later.[200] In many of its activities, the Byzantine Church was more of a national than an ecumenical institution, as our argument would predict. It mobilized morale in wars against other Christians and was used as a platform of imperial propaganda.[201] It was fully integrated into

---

[199] Cf. Anna Komnene, *Alexiad* 14.7.2 with 1.10.2. Cf. Nicol (1972) I 327; Garzya (1992) 31.
[200] Smith (2003).
[201] See, e.g., Leon VI, *Taktika*, epilogue 62; cf. McCormick (1986) 244–251; Magdalino (1993) 457; in general, Charanis (1982) 102. Cf. Armstrong (1982) 180, 203, for the complicity of nation and Church.

the structures of provincial administration that unified the nation, as the Crusaders discovered to their chagrin when they tried to take them over in 1204. Frederick II Hohenstaufen, that great enemy of ecclesiastical independence, thought Byzantium a model of Church–state relations: *O felix Asia!* he proclaimed.[202]

When we look beyond the legal and theological aberrations of Justinian and the pleas of Antonios IV that have so dominated historians' perspectives, we find that in everyday life the Byzantines identified foreigners by what they called "customs," for example by their dress and speech, as the eleventh-century mystic Symeon the New Theologian reveals in an analogy. In the fourteenth century, the historian Nikephoros Gregoras wrote that in order to become a Latin a Byzantine would have to change his "attitude, faith, dress, beard, and all his customs." This is probably how most Byzantines identified who was one of their own, and not by turning to the commentaries of Balsamon. To attack his theological opponent Gregorios of Cyprus in the 1280s, Ioannes Bekkos argued that while he himself "had been born and raised among Romans and from Romans," Gregorios "was born and raised among Italians, and not only that, he merely affects our dress and speech." The poet of *Digenes* implied that conversion to Christianity and adoption of Roman clothes and customs was supposed to have a civilizing effect: the word is *gnôme*, which we might also translate as "mindset."[203] This existed at the most intangible edge of "custom," but, as with any nation whose coherence stems from a common culture, the Byzantines seem to have been able to identify such intangibles along with more visible "ethnic" *indicia*.[204] What counts, at any rate, is that they *thought* that they could.

According to the historian Georgios Pachymeres, after 1204, when the capital was seized by the Crusaders, some of its residents "who had

---

[202] Martin (2002) 483.

[203] Symeon the New Theologian, *Ethical Discourse* 9.275 (v. II, p. 240); cf. Eustathios, *Oration for the Emperor Manuel Komnenos* (*Or.* 16, Wirth pp. 263–264). Nikephoros Gregoras, *Roman History* 9.1. Bekkos: Georgios Pachymeres, *History* 7.34 (v. III, p. 101); see p. 385 below. *Digenes Akrites G* 2.22–25 and 3.257 for Roman clothes, on which de Boel (2003).

[204] The Franks differed from the Romans mainly in language and dress, according to Agathias, *Histories* 1.2.1–5. For Arabs identified by dress, see *The Life of Saint Andreas the Fool* 12.799–800 (v. II, p. 66); *Timarion* 33, 37. To escape from Constantinople, Alousianos "dressed himself as an Armenian," according to Ioannes Skylitzes, *Historical Synopsis: Michael IV* 27 (p. 413); see also ibid., *Basileios II and Konstantinos VII* (p. 329): Boris was shot "because he was wearing a Roman uniform," on which cf. Garsoïan (1998) 102–103 n. 187. The emperor Romanos IV Diogenes changes from barbarian to Roman clothes in Ioannes Zonaras, *Chronicle* 18.14. In Georgios Pachymeres, *History* 12.26 both dress and mentality were involved. For ethnographic aspects of foreignness, see Pohl (1998) for the early period; Simeonova (2001) for the middle period.

accommodating convictions could incline either toward the Romans or toward the Italians; other Romans approached them because they were Roman, while Italians were at ease on account of their familiarity with them."²⁰⁵ These "accommodators (*thelêmatarioi*)" are not identified here as being Roman because they were subjects of the Byzantine emperor (as they were not). Nor was it only their language, or the church that they attended (if any), or their clothes, or any other *one* factor; it was rather the entire matrix of customs, practices, beliefs, and histories that identified them as part of the same nation as the Romans of nearby Nikaia who were, at that very moment, about to reclaim their City. We should, then, be cautious in using our sources on this point, because they sometimes focus on only one or two elements of this broader constitutive matrix of identity, which has misled some scholars into supposing that the specific elements that are mentioned on any occasion were the only ones that mattered. So when a text happens to present a Byzantine as a Christian because the context calls for him to be differentiated from an infidel, scholars (wrongly) deduce that the "essence" of Byzantine identity was Christianity; when it presents him as orthodox as against other Christians, then that becomes the essence; and so on with "loyalty to the emperor" and other attributes.²⁰⁶ There are even instances where Byzantines use the word "language" to *mean* "nation" (which indicates that for them national unity required a common language).²⁰⁷

We must be careful here, because it was not the intention of our sources to give full accounts of Byzantine identity; on any particular occasion, they list the attributes that were most relevant to the narrative, but far more than what they say was required in practice. In the final chapter of this study we will examine the evidence for Byzantine nationalism after 1204. There it emerges with clarity that the Byzantines knew that being Roman and being Christian were different things: the former was a matter of religion, yes, but

---

²⁰⁵ Georgios Pachymeres, *History* 2.14 (v. I, p. 157).

²⁰⁶ E.g., Gregorios Dekapolites was asked what his faith was and he replied Christian orthodox. Mango (1980) 31 concludes dramatically (the last sentence of his chapter): "It did not occur to him to describe himself as a Roman." This illogical argument has caused much confusion (given the incidence of its citation by later historians).

²⁰⁷ E.g., Michael Attaleiates, *History* 43; Theodoros II Laskaris, *On Christian Theology* 7.3 (p. 138); Gregorios of Cyprus, *Letter* 131 (p. 109); *Chronicle of the Morea* 1269. As we have seen, imperial ideology included a transnational component that was occasionally asserted in theory, though without practical consequence. The emperor was theoretically responsible for the whole Church, which included many nations and languages. Laskaris elsewhere promised that at a Council he would show no bias for Greek-speakers: *To the Bishop of Kotrone, Against the Latins regarding the Holy Spirit* 529–538 (p. 181). But was he believed on this point? Can we imagine him awarding victory to Latin-speaking papalists over his own strident Hellenism (for which, see p. 374 below)?

also of language, culture, and especially of the social consensus of a historical community. The evidence for the period after 1204 is especially important as the state had been fragmented and in many places abolished, which temporarily forced the Byzantines to talk about their nation independently of the state and the emperor, thereby revealing the assumptions that had formerly been subsumed under political unity. But the essential criteria for being regarded as a Roman remained the same as before.

Obviously, the "customs" of the Byzantine court were different from those of the peasants, and the customs of the fifth century were different from those of the fifteenth. Unfortunately, we know little about the ethnographic *indicia* of Byzantine identity, in part because misleading abstractions such as "multi-ethnic empire" and "ecumenical Christian society" have come between us and our subjects. Still, it seems that Roman society could accommodate – even insisted on – internal complexity in these matters (as do modern nations), and cultural and historical change did not outstrip the nation's ability to keep pace and maintain a continuous sense of its identity.[208]

In short, there is little evidence that the rhetorical fantasy of universal empire, the diplomatic fiction of the "family of nations,"[209] and the thoroughly modern notion of a "Byzantine Commonwealth" embracing all (Slavic) orthodox peoples, shaped how the Byzantines thought of themselves or treated outsiders. Dimitri Obolensky's book of that title, cited by all who believe in the "multi-ethnic empire," may be ambitious in scope and brilliant in execution but it is fundamentally flawed in conception. Its basic notion corresponds to nothing in the Byzantine world-view (as he admits: pp. 14–15), being the product of a modern Slavic and orthodox bias. Obolensky could imagine nations only on a racial basis (355, 398) and viewed Byzantium as "supranational and universal" (202), though without discussing the evidence for its internal constitution. He was therefore taken in by the diplomatic fiction of the family of nations and, accordingly, could not make sense of actual Byzantine behavior. For example, his valorization of universalism led him to believe that the Byzantines should have accepted converted barbarians as fully Roman, so he was greatly puzzled that they did not, setting it down to inexplicable – Greek! – cultural chauvinism (15, 353–356). Note that in his epilogue, Obolensky goes to some length to

---

[208] For an attempt to trace changes in "the daily regime," see Kazhdan and Epstein (1985) 74–83. For "ethnic" fashions, see, e.g., Prokopios, *Secret History* 7.8–14; for dress (specifically hats) and Roman identity in the later period: Kiousopoulou (2004) esp. 195. "Deconstructions" of Roman identity in late antiquity based on ethnographic evidence rely too much on the military and the frontier: e.g., Amory (1997) 338–347; see p. 86 above.

[209] See now Chrysos (2005b) 74–77.

argue that despite adopting many of the concepts and images of Byzantine universalism, Russia remained a fully *national* state.[210]

The strongest expression that Obolensky could find of Byzantine solidarity *in practice* with other members of his proposed Commonwealth was penned by the fourteenth-century statesman Demetrios Kydones. In looking for allies in the war against the Turks, Kydones considered first the "Mysioi" and the "Tribaloi" (i.e., the Balkan Slavs), who "are similar to us, devoted to God, and at times have shared many things in common with us." This is a tepid endorsement of orthodox ecumenicity; moreover, Kydones goes on to *reject* them as allies because they are untrustworthy, grasping, and hate the Romans.[211] Far from revealing the supranational character of the Byzantine mentality, it shows exactly the opposite, namely how irrelevant such factors were to nationally minded Byzantine politicians. To be sure, Kydones was extremely pro-western, but this only highlights one of the ways in which Christendom as such did not matter in practice. His opponents (let us say those who preferred an alliance with the Slavs) would have made their case on the basis of the same national premises as did he: what is in *our* interest as Romans? Kydones leaves no doubt about who "we" are at the very beginning of his work, when he lists all the lands and resources currently within the Roman state.

The universal ideals that historians have defined as the core of Byzantine identity are so rarefied that they cannot explain the mechanisms and rhetoric of exclusion that characterized Byzantine society in practice. Those ideals operated on a different level than the social consensus that created and sustained Romania in the first place. Besides, when pressed to define their identity many modern nations also cite highly universalist "core values." This is as true for such "civic" nations as Canada as for those like Greece where ethnicity is a key component of identity. This does not mean, however, that they are predisposed to merge with other nations on the basis of those abstract values or that they wish to extend their identity and citizenship to the world. The ideal of Roman and Christian ecumenism probably occupied the same space in the rhetoric of Byzantium as does the ideal of Hellenism as universal humanism in the rhetoric of modern Greece:

[210] Obolensky (1971); cf. Meyendorff (1993) 230: "The difference was that the Roman Empire of Justinian was, at least in principle, universal, whereas the new Slavic empires were, in fact, nation states." If Byzantine cultural influence were to be viewed without Slavic bias, we would include the early medieval West, the early Caliphate, the Caucasus states, and Nubia as within its orbit. For a more diffuse and plausible version of Obolensky's thesis, see Shepard (2006) 17–20.

[211] Demetrios Kydones, *Advice to the Romans* 972–976, esp. 972. The passages in Lechner (1954) 102–104 hardly strengthen the case, as they too involve putting a good face on bad situations and can be countered by other expressions in the same authors (see ibid. 107–114).

both are inherited from the legitimating past yet are disembodied from the actual sources of community coherence, though they can stir passions in the proper context. A theoretical commitment to universal ideals is no obstacle to a strong and particularistic national identity, but ultimately the latter is grounded in a different set of historical and cultural factors.[212]

In the course of its long history, Byzantium certainly experienced diversity, change, and the presence of large unassimilated minorities. And yet the fact remains that its society managed to survive the thousand most turbulent years of history when so many other ventures such as the barbarian kingdoms, the empire of Charlemagne, and the Caliphate, failed. Romania outlived its own "heirs" precisely because it was the institutional expression of a society with a strong sense of collective identity and because it continued to invest its resources in those institutions that had created a universal Roman identity in late antiquity. Byzantine Romania had the most sophisticated administrative apparatus in Christendom and could mobilize resources with greater efficiency and recover from greater setbacks largely because it claimed the active loyalty of a people.[213] Arab visitors, closer to the Byzantines than we are, admitted that in comparison with their states "the Roman nation" was extremely "united."[214]

## WHERE DID ALL THE GREEKS GO?

So where does this leave the Greeks? The challenge to national historians is greater in their case than with other groups whose ethnonym and language have survived into our times. The Greeks were among the original peoples converted to Romania, leaving none of their kind outside the empire to which those inside, if they could be identified, could be compared (unlike, say, the Armenians); and those inside not only refused after a certain point to be called Hellenes for religious reasons, they positively insisted on calling themselves Romans for all the reasons we have explained. Yet the Greeks are at the same time the only one among those original peoples whose language, culture, and even identity have been reconstituted in modern times to form a nation (no one cares anymore for Thrakians, Phrygians, etc.).

This brings us back to the young boy from Lemnos in 1912 who thought he was a Roman when the Greek soldier thought he "was really" a Greek.

[212] For Canada, see Jusdanis (2001) 29 and n. 12; for modern Greece, Skopetea (1988) 211; Leontis (1995) 88–89, 107, 119–124, Gourgouris (1996) 172, Matalas (2002) 316–317, 352.
[213] For the ability of Byzantium to muster resources on a scale that western kingdoms could not match, see Treadgold (2005).
[214] Cited in El Cheikh (2004) 111.

Peter Charanis did eventually accept the national identity offered to him by his new state. To be sure, by 1912 the difference was purely verbal. But as a Byzantinist he would later go on to argue that, like him, the Byzantines also "were really" Greeks who only called themselves Romans, "i.e., Greeks in language and in culture," and that the Greek element was the "reality" and "basis" of Roman identity. That culture may shape identity is a blow against racial determinism, but the schema is not applied consistently: it is used to account for the Hellenization of the Slavs but not the Romanization of the Greeks. From the modern Greek standpoint, the latter event never happened at all – or never "really" happened – and there is not even a word for it. Byzantine "culture," in which the political, historical, and even national components of identity apparently play no role, was Greek regardless of whether the Byzantines thought so or not. Culture, then, may trump race, but it is also used to trump identity; it is then narrowed to language, which is easily shown to have been "Greek." In making this equation Charanis was not alone among both Greek and western scholars.[215] One of the former has concluded that the Byzantines "were not Romans, but Greeks. They had not realized this themselves, but the Franks did."[216] Hence most Greek discussions of Byzantine identity end up talking about Hellenism. But many western historians have followed along. One says that in the seventh century "Byzantium became a fully Greek state" as "the remaining remnants of Roman tradition were the most part relinquished" (in reality, no such thing ever happened). Another has denied that the Byzantines were Roman in any significant sense,[217] while translators of Byzantine sources render the "Romans" as "Greeks," perhaps to avoid confusion with the "true" Romans of antiquity (i.e., of the West).

We should be skeptical of these equations. There is, no doubt, considerable continuity in language and culture between ancient and modern

---

[215] Charanis (1978) 88–89; also (1972) *passim*, esp. I 19, II 44, VI 417, XI 258, XXI 34, and XXII 116; also Zambelios (1857) 15–16, 35; Vryonis (1978) 248–249; Bryer (1983) 96; Tsougarakis (1995); Constantelos (1998) 1–8, 171, 196–197. The last scholar pays lip service to cultural Hellenism and Hellenization, but always refers to Hellenized foreigners as "minorities," which gives away his racial preconceptions. Cf. Barker (1979) 3: Charanis believed that "his ethnic consciousness had been pointing him in what was to become his life's ultimate direction," the study of Byzantium. The basic assumption of Greek scholarship is that from Mycenae to the present we are dealing with a single nation (*ethnos*) that has had many names. This was formulated in the nineteenth century by K. Paparrigopoulos; see the prefaces reprinted in (1970); also Zakythinos (1980) *passim*, esp. 325: "in the psychology of the Greeks, there exists that permanent substructure that can always be traced"; Christou (2003) 7–8, 145, 154; Svoronos (2004) 25; and in Bastéa (2000) 181–182. Non-Greek scholars are taken in, e.g., Smith (1991) 30, when they do not choose guides carefully.

[216] Vakalopoulos (1974) 87.

[217] Respectively: Cameron (1991) 310, referring to the "Greek administration" (313); and Vryonis (1992) 20–21; cf. also Smith (1986) 90, 108.

Greece and many fine studies are devoted to this intriguing question. There is also no reason to deny that there was not also considerable biological continuity, which is what many Greeks really want when they say "language and culture," disclaimers to the contrary notwithstanding. Yet even an exclusive biological continuity would not suffice to make the Byzantines into Greeks, so long, that is, as we are serious about setting aside racial history. The Roman name, I have argued, reflected a profound transformation in identity and consciousness. We cannot just brush aside the most powerful and longevous political and national identity in history and assume that we can understand the Byzantines better than they understood themselves. One might then say that the Presidents of the US "are really" Englishmen (or what not), regardless of the fact that they consider themselves Americans. Whatever truth there may be in such an equation at the level of language, culture, and genes – considerable, perhaps – this is a profound misunderstanding of what it means to be an American. Few who speak English today are English. Likewise, the Byzantines were Romans who happened to speak Greek and not Greeks who happened to call themselves Romans.

Language and "culture" are not racially determined. They are socially constructed and evolving practices whose historical meaning is determined by the communities that valorize them. Many Byzantine practices were inherited from Greek antiquity, but this does not entitle us to call them Greek when the Byzantines understood them as Roman. It is the way in which they are implicated in the discursive construction of identity that enables us to understand any culture that practices them, not what antiquarian research may tell us about their origins (or what modern national interests want proven regarding their "true" significance). We have seen that assimilation required the adoption of "Roman customs." Consider the seventh-century Slav Perboundos who, according to many modern scholars, "was living in Thessalonike, wearing Greek dress and speaking Greek." But what our source actually says is that he was "wearing Roman dress and speaking *our* language" – there is no reference to anything "Greek." Besides, it is likely that Perboundos "really was" wearing Roman rather than Greek dress. As for his language, so little did the author care about it being "Greek" that he did not name it, leading one editor of the text to postulate (wrongly) an otherwise unknown Thessalonikan dialect.[218] "Our"

---

[218] *The Miracles of Saint Demetrios* 235 (v. I, p. 209); "Greek dress": Lemerle in v. II, p. 113; Browning (1989b) 303; Toynbee (1973) 97; Laiou (2000) 4; Moorhead (2001) 178. For the alleged dialect, see Grigoriou-Ioannidou (2000).

language probably refers to what *we* call Greek, but what it *means* is "the language of the Romans." After the sixth century, "the Roman language" or "the language of the Romans" could signify Greek as well as Latin. In other words, what we call "Greek" the Byzantines could call "Roman," simply because they were Romans and that was their language. For Anna Komnene *hellenizein* and *romaïzein* meant the same thing, i.e., to speak "Greek" or "Roman."[219] So, the evidence marshaled today to prove that Byzantium "was really" Greek had already been redeployed in Byzantium to prove that it was Roman. But Greek scholars tend to intrude the ethnonym "Greek" into texts where it does not occur. This is not dishonest; but it is done in good faith by historians who have failed to recognize the depth of Byzantium's Roman identity. Their insistence on the name, however, to the point of using it when they believe that it "really means" the same thing as Roman, is indicative of their participation in a nationally oriented discourse that valorizes modern ethnonyms.[220]

What, then, happened to the ancient Greeks? Late-antique sources rarely mention them as a currently existing nation (as opposed to a religious group), which accords with the silence in those sources regarding all such "national" groups. Everyone, or almost everyone, was now basically a Roman. Former national or ethnic groups now designated only regional origins; for example, in the fifth century we have a reference to "a Roman woman from the region of Epeiros." Libanios could refer to the "cities of the Greeks," but he means by this the cities of Greece and Asia Minor as opposed to those of Palestine and Sicily, which might also have been called Greek but in another sense. But that other sense was hard to define, and its continued survival was a doubtful matter. By the time we reach the *Miracles of Saint Demetrios*, in the late sixth and early seventh centuries, "the land of the Greeks" really does mean nothing more than the Roman territory of

---

[219] Anna Komnene, *Alexiad* 7.3.4 and 7.8.3; cf. *Digenes Akrites* G 1.115: Greek is called the Roman language; see de Boel (2003) 175–180, who does not realize that this usage was not limited to this text; Lasithiotakis (2005) 49–56; for "the Roman language," Dagron (1994) 220; Grigoriou-Ioannidou (2000) 97–101; de Boel (2003) 175–177 for Latin.

[220] See, e.g., n. 161 and n. 162 above for Vryonis on Niketas Magistros and Ioannes Katrares. That Vryonis refers to Byzantines as "the Greeks" throughout his *magnum opus* (1971) is problematic; that he makes the sources that he quotes talk about Greeks or the Greek nation (when they do not) is troubling. Constantelos (1998) 155 calls Ostrogorsky's "two brothers" (the apostles to the Slavs) "the two Greek brothers." Elsewhere he says that "properly speaking the Byzantine Empire was the Mediaeval Greek Empire" (171). Yet not a single source calls it that. Even Dagron (1993) 86 n. 23 attributes to Psellos the claim that charlatans try to pass themselves off as non-Greek in order to be credible, but what Psellos actually says is that they claim to possess insider "ethnic" knowledge such as Illyrian or Persian: see p. 95 above. Such "shorthand" confuses the issues. For the importance of ethnonyms, see Hall (2002) 125.

Greece.[221] Like other formerly or pseudo-national groups in late antiquity, the Greeks had no collective identity but only a geographical one, as we see also in the works of the sixth-century historian Prokopios. For him the Greeks were the inhabitants of the Greek mainland and not a nation, for such a "Greek" nation as would be defined by language, culture, history, and perhaps putative descent would have to include most of the eastern Mediterranean, including Prokopios himself, who was from Kaisareia in Palestine. But Prokopios identifies fully with Romania and nowhere calls himself a Greek on the basis of his ethnicity, *paideia*, or religion (whatever that was). He was, of course, familiar with Christian usage, as he also refers to pagans as the "so-called Hellenes," clearly a different group – a different *kind* of group – than the Hellenes who lived in Greece.[222] Likewise, the monk Paulos "the Greek" who appears in the pages of Ioannes Moschos (early seventh century), was simply a monk from Greece, in accordance with Moschos' casual geographic use of ethnonyms throughout his work.[223]

What did the Byzantines think about these Greeks? Setting aside the religious polemic against the pagan "Hellenes," which we will examine in the next chapter, some early Byzantines attached negative stereotypes to Greeks, by which in this period we mean Romans who came from Greece. Prokopios says that officials would abuse soldiers from Greece by calling them *Graikoi*, a Latin name with pejorative connotations, as ancient Greek sources known to the Byzantines complained. It is called a "racial slur" in Ioannes Zonaras' epitome of Kassios Dion while in Prokopios' *Wars* it is used often by western foes to insult all Roman soldiers collectively.[224] "It is

---

[221] Epeiros: Malchos fr. 20.266–267. Libanios, *Or.* 18.292 (*Funeral Oration for Julian*). *The Miracles of Saint Demetrios* 284 (v. I, p. 137).

[222] Prokopios, *Secret History* 11.31, 26.30; *Wars* 2.4.11, 5.15.24. For Hellas in Prokopios, see Charanis (1972) XVIII 162–164; for the integration of the Greeks into Romania, Koder (1990) 104.

[223] Ioannes Moschos, *Spiritual Meadow* 163. "Greeks" in western sources of the sixth century, alongside Goths, Syrians, and Jews, are those who speak Greek or come from Greece; for sources, Harris (2003) 61.

[224] Prokopios, *Secret History* 24.7; cf. *Wars* 4.27.38, 5.18.40, 5.29.11, 7.9.12, 7.21.4, 7.21.12–14, 8.23.25. Ancient sources: Swain (1996) 79 n. 35, and 405 for Zonaras. For the origin of *Graecus*, see Hall (2002) 70, 170, citing previous bibliography; for its negative value, Hunger (1987) 15–31; Dubuisson (1991); in early medieval usage, Moorhead (2001) 127; for later Byzantine dislike of it, Mauromatis (1987) 190; Maltezou (1999) 113; Papoulia (2003) 49 n. 37. Cf. Claudianus, *Against Eutropius* 2.135: *Byzantinos proceres Graiosque Quirites*, and this from an Alexandrian poet, albeit in western service. For the linguistic and cultural sense of Ammianus' defensive claim to be *Graecus*, see Matthews (1989) 461–463, 551 n. 23; (1994) 268 n. 75; and Shahîd (1998), who uses *ethnikon* too loosely. Ammianus was Roman in outlook. One of the last (potential) claims to Greek ethnicity was by the man Priskos met at the court of Attila (see pp. 75–76 above), identified as a "*Graikos by genos*" (fr. 11.2.423). But we have seen that *genos* is an unreliable word (and note that he used the Latin, i.e., Roman, version of the name, though he spoke Greek).

surely no accident that the opprobrious meaning of *Graecus* makes its appearance in Prokopios at about the same time when the term *Romania* is first found in the more popular language of Malalas to designate the Byzantine empire."[225] Yet this pejorative Latin term for the Greeks was used casually in Byzantium, another striking sign of its continuity with the ancient Romans. Where modern historians say that the empire "Hellenized" the Slavs who settled in Greece in the seventh and eighth centuries by teaching them to speak Greek, what our source, Leon VI, actually says is that his father Basileios I (867–886) persuaded them to abandon their ancient customs, accept Roman rule and take baptism, and that he "Graecized" them – γραικώσας, i.e., he taught them Greek. Leon did not have to use this Latin word here to avoid confusion with the religious meaning of *Hellen*, given that when it referred to language *hellenizein* had no religious connotations. It was rather that he viewed all Greek things, including his own language, from a Roman point of view.[226]

In his treatise *On the Themes*, Leon's son Konstantinos VII promoted the thesis that "Hellenic" was not the name of a people to begin with but rather the name of a language that later came to be used to refer to the Graikoi. In the antiquarian ethnography of this work, these Hellenic Graikoi are only one of many *ethnê* that were absorbed into the Roman world in antiquity. Far from showing any particular attachment to them, Konstantinos frequently denigrates their (pagan) mythistories. His outlook too is therefore Roman and Christian. Describing the state of the empire after Herakleios, he says that the emperors "Hellenized even more and cast off their ancestral Roman language," i.e., Latin. When he wants to refer to the population of the Peloponnese harassed by the Slavs he calls them not *Hellenes* but *Graikoi*. Here he may have wanted to avoid implying that the Slavs were harassing pagans, for a few pages later he mentions some inhabitants of the Mani in the Peloponnese who were still called Hellenes because they worshiped in the manner of "the ancient Hellenes." In other words, they were Hellenes because of their religion and not their ethnicity. But were they national Greeks as well? No: Konstantinos tells us that they were not of the same *genos* as the Slavs because they were descended from "ancient Romans"! Even here we fail to find any clear notion that the Greek nation

---

[225] Alexander (1962) 340–341. Romania is attested earlier in other kinds of texts.

[226] Leon VI, *Taktika* 18.101, on which Koder (1990) 107–108 and (2000). For a reconstruction of this "Hellenization," see Herrin (1973); Dunn (1977) for a different model. Cf. Theophanes the Confessor, *Chronographia* s.a. 6274 (p. 455): "the language of the *Graikoi* and the customs of the Romans."

had survived into Byzantine times. The "ancient Greeks" are mentioned only in order to explain the *religion* of these pagan *Romans*.[227]

I have found only two texts which indicate that the Byzantines may have recognized the survival of a Hellenic nation into the recent past, though both are highly problematic as sources. The first is the so-called *Chronicle of Monembasia*, an anonymous three-page summary of events in the Peloponnese during the sixth and then in the early ninth centuries. The first section recounts that during the reign of Maurikios, the Avars (not the Slavs) invaded and settled Greece as far as the Peloponnese, where "they expelled and destroyed the noble [or, more probably, "native"] Hellenic *ethnê*," who then fled to Italy, to the islands, and to Monembasia. This text has always annoyed nationalist Greek scholars, who have labored to minimize its value regarding the settlement of *Slavs* (not Avars!) in Greece, but from this point of view it may, paradoxically, be hailed as proof that at least one Byzantine recognized the survival of *Greeks* until a relatively late date (even if they had then been scattered by the Avars).

But we should be cautious. One vague reference cannot make up for the silence of all our other sources. Moreover, the text is incoherent, switching from Avars to Slavs, and from ca. 600 to ca. 800, without explanation. It is anonymous, possibly a forgery to benefit the see of Patras, and cannot be dated precisely (ca. 900 is likely). Above all, it is unclear what it means by "Hellenic *ethnê*": were they Hellenic by virtue of religion, of descent from the ancient Greeks, or just because they lived in Hellas? The last alternative is more likely, as the text, in standard fashion, refers throughout to "Romans" who are differentiated by locale (e.g., Thrakians, Makedonians, Hellenes). Byzantine texts often refer to the inhabitants of Hellas as "Hellenes" in a geographical sense, as the inhabitants of Kappadokia were called Kappadokians. It stands to reason therefore that the Hellenes in this text were only the Romans who lived in Hellas. This interpretation is reinforced by the variant reading "native (ἐγγενῆ)," which has gained wide support, against the reading "noble (εὐγενῆ)," which implies continuity with, and valorization of, classical antiquity. The latter reading faces additional problems, as it reveals a classicizing mentality that, at this time, was found in very few. Indeed, one of the candidates who has been proposed for the authorship of this text is the classical scholar Arethas, a native of

---

[227] Name: Konstantinos VII, *On the Themes* 2.5 (p. 89); Herakleios: ibid. I pr. (p. 60); *Graikoi* and *Hellenes*: *De administrando imperio* 49, 50. For the *Hellenes* of Mani, see Arrigoni (1972) 122–133, who involves notions of Greek descent not in the text; Anagnostakis (1993).

Patras and later bishop of Kaisareia in Kappadokia. His view – if a single, possibly corrupt, word can be called a view – that the Greeks were a "noble" race would prefigure the developments of the twelfth and thirteenth centuries that we will study in the second part of this book.[228]

The second passage occurs in another odd place, an anti-Christian polemic by the ninth-century Arab essayist al-Jāḥiẓ. In arguing that the Byzantines (Romans) are worthless, he notes that none of the ancient writers was either a Christian or a Roman. The ancients "were individuals of one nation; they have perished but the traces of their minds live on: they are the Greeks. Their religion was different from the religion of the Romans, and their culture was different from the culture of the Romans. They were scientists, while these people [i.e., the Byzantines] are artisans who appropriated the books of the Greeks on account of geographical proximity ... claiming that the Greeks were but one of the Roman tribes." It would be fascinating to know what that last claim looked like on the Byzantine side and who made it. But Arab formulations of the relationship between Greeks and Byzantines served the polemical needs of Arab intellectuals, who were philhellenic but anti-Christian and anti-Byzantine. It is unlikely that they reflect actual East–West debates on the ownership of the classical tradition or the survival of the Hellenic nation.[229]

To conclude, the casual equation of Greeks and Byzantines perpetrated in modern Greek scholarship prevents us from actually making sense of Hellenism in Byzantium, for if we see it everywhere on putative ethnic grounds we will not see it where it mattered most. If it existed always then it makes no sense to say that at some point and in response to specific historical circumstances it was revived. At least before the thirteenth century, Hellenism in Byzantium was something that only a few engaged in, risking societal condemnation. It was exclusive, seductive, and could be subversive. It was not a matter of everyday practice or mere "language." One was not born into it, for it required hard work and patient training. As Erasmus would put it defensively, "anyone is a Greek who has worked hard

---

[228] The key phrase occurs only in the earliest version of the text, found in the Iveron ms. The *Chronicle of Monembasia* has generated a specialized critical literature, focusing on the accuracy of the text's historical information. To my knowledge, no one has wondered what it means exactly by "Hellenic *ethnê.*" There is no reason to give an exhaustive bibliography here: see Curta (2004) 535–538; for Arethas' authorship, Koder (1976) and (1990) 105, 109. His emendation is accepted by the text's editor, Dujčev (1980) 54, and others: Turlej (1998) 448. For the inhabitants of Hellas as Hellenes, see pp. 184–185 below.

[229] Translation in Gutas (1998) 87; polemical context: 84–95.

and successfully at Greek literature, though he may not wear a beard."[230] The Hellenes of Byzantium were not those who merely spoke Greek; those were only the Romans. They were rather those who engaged in a study of classical thought and forged, on the basis of *paideia*, a new Hellenic identity, as did the scholars of Erasmus' Europe. What form that would take remains to be seen.

---

[230] Cited in Goldhill (2002) 59.

CHAPTER 3

# *"Nibbling on Greek learning":*
# *the Christian predicament*

The encounter between ancient Hellenism and Christianity in all of their forms has been one of the main coordinates of the evolution of "western" culture, and Byzantium was perhaps the most quintessentially western culture in this regard. The complexity and philosophical scope of this theme preemptively defeat any attempt to offer a comprehensive or theoretically innovative analysis. Beyond the difficulty of defining the two protagonists, the theme involves a vast amount of material, requires expertise in many disciplines, and raises philosophical issues that transcend historical inquiry. Many studies, for instance, have discussed the social backgrounds of the new faith, which necessarily drew its adherents from among those of the old; the common ground, exchange, and dialogue between pagans and Christians in late antiquity; the contributions of philosophy to the development of the doctrines of the Church; and the inevitable, albeit qualified, appropriation by Christians of the ideal of cultural Hellenism associated with the Second Sophistic.

Fewer studies have explored the urgent ethical tension underlying that cultural appropriation, a tension that has been articulated in uncompromising terms by modern philosophers such as Hegel and Nietzsche: how did a religion of humility and spiritual transcendence come to terms with an aristocratic and agonistic culture that never fully renounced bodily beauty and delight? This challenge is compounded by the heterophony of our sources. There never was a single Hellenism or Christianity, even among their chief exponents. Within the former, for instance, Plato's legacy was ever at odds with the tradition of ancient rhetoric, while, on the other side, the bodily mortification and obscurantism of the desert anchorites was admired but not necessarily imitated by the more urbane and learned Church Fathers. In late antiquity, despite various fruitful encounters among these different strains, movements, and individuals, conflict created confusion and inner torment, leading, in Byzantium, to a deep-seated bad conscience. No one whose faith was truly orthodox shared our belief that a comfortable symbiosis was possible between the ethical demands of Christianity and the charms of the Greek legacy. Hellenism was always an "outsider" and its history in Byzantium was determined by the degree to which learned men could overcome, ignore, or embrace its otherness.

The present chapter will differ from existing treatments of the Hellenic heritage of early Christianity by asking a prior question that has tended to receive less attention, namely why Hellenism was problematic to begin with. The first section explores the challenges posed by Hellenism to the first Christians, focusing more on their reception of classical texts than the social and religious context of the Greek world under Rome. What was it about Greek culture that made it so problematic to the leaders of the new faith *beyond* the mere fact of its paganism? The second section discusses in detail the challenge posed by the emperor Julian to the Christian appropriation of the classics, because the strident and *plausible* way in which he posed the dilemma facing Christians resulted in a permanent state of unease among Byzantine Hellenists. The third section looks at the response by some of the Church Fathers to Julian's challenge and the long-term solutions that emerged before the eleventh century. The overall aim of the chapter is to delimit the cognitive, cultural, and authoritative space that Greek *paideia* was allowed to occupy in a Christian society permanently fractured by zones of contestation, complementing the discussion in the previous chapter that situated Hellenism within the gradual acceptance of a dominant Roman identity. These complementary relations (Hellenic and Roman / Hellenic and Christian) were asymmetrical and evolved along different axes, especially when crisis called for reconfiguration: when Hellenism was revived as a quasi-autonomous cultural and philosophical tradition in the eleventh and twelfth centuries, it challenged Christian values and beliefs, whereas when it was revived as a quasi-national label in the thirteenth it was accommodated within the Roman identity of Byzantium. It was not until the end of the Byzantine millennium, in the belated Platonism and Hellenic nationalism of Georgios Gemistos Plethon, that these two strands merged in a proposal for a new philosophical, religious, and national outlook.

## BETWEEN GREEKS AND BARBARIANS, WITHIN HELLENISM

From the classical age to the Second Sophistic, Hellenism was defined by those who took themselves to be Hellenes of the highest order and who contrasted their ideals to "barbarism," whether ethnic or linguistic. Starting with the early Christians, however, and for the next thousand years, the meaning of Hellenism would be contested and then defined by men who self-consciously opposed it and who saw themselves as the defenders of a "barbarian wisdom" who used Greek culture at most as a means and not an end. This was the most significant rupture in the otherwise gradual evolution of Hellenism as an ideal in antiquity, leading to bizarre results. Many Christians came to believe that the entirety of Greek culture was tainted by its religious side, and so the whole was identified with the part; this part was, in turn, amalgamated with all non-Christian cults, regardless of whether they were culturally "Greek." Theologically, the Fathers decreed that "anyone who says that there are two gods is Hellenizing,"[1] though the exact number of gods varied: "when I say God, I mean the Father, the Son, and the Holy Spirit . . . [neither more nor less] lest we Judaize on account of the unicity of [divine] rule or Hellenize on account of its superfluity."[2] For the Byzantines, "Hellenism" could simply mean "polytheism."[3] Accordingly, and violating any perspective from within Hellenism, Persian Zoroastrians, Arabs who practiced human sacrifice, native north Africans, the early Rus', and the Chinese were all Hellenes, i.e., they were not Christians. In late antiquity, the word was also borrowed by Coptic to designate pagan Egyptians.[4] "Greeks," then, now included exactly those who had previously been barbarians. Given the canonical status of the classical polarity, this must count as one of the most startling semantic reversals in history, and is partly attributable to the fact that it was the first time in history when what it meant to be Greek was being (re)defined by people who rejected the Hellenic ideal. The word acquired a derogatory sense, to which legislation gave its official stamp, referring to the "impious and loathsome Hellenes."[5]

This transformation, which would taint all later efforts by the Byzantines to engage with the classical legacy, requires some explanation. Despite intense recent interest in the cultural history of early Christianity and the origins of the Latin Christian term *paganus*, scholars have been reluctant to ask *why* Greek-speaking Christians decided to refer to pagans as Hellenes. The fact is noted but put aside as an oddity (and possibly an embarrassment), for we generally do not call the pagans of late antiquity Hellenes, for all that some of them, like Julian, accepted the label. One of the reasons for this lack of interest is that many want to believe in the essential compatibility of

---

[1] Pseudo-Athanasios, *Against the Arians* 4.10.   [2] Gregorios of Nazianzos, *Or.* 45.4 (*Easter Oration*).
[3] Demetrios Tornikes, *Letter* 32 (p. 196), relying on the passage of Gregorios quoted above.
[4] Prokopios, *Buildings* 6.4.12; Euagrios, *Ecclesiastical History* 6.21–22; Theophylaktos Simokattes, *History* 5.14.3; Ioannes Moschos, *Spiritual Meadow* 133, 138; Coptic: Frankfurter (1998) 77–79. See Lechner (1954) 42–43.
[5] *Cod. Just.* 1.11.10. In general, see Lechner (1954) 10–46, and 41 for legislation in Greek.

Christianity and classical culture and assume that the religious side of Hellenism can easily be separated from the "cultural," by which what is generally meant here is the philosophical. Indeed, the Church Fathers who fashioned ideals of Christian humanism engaged fruitfully with ancient philosophy, but "philosophy" here stands largely for doctrines about God and the soul, making it easy for us to see where they and, say, the Platonists "agreed" or "disagreed." Hence many discussions of the relationship between Christianity and Hellenism become treatments of the role of "natural reason" in theology.[6]

Yet philosophy was only one part of Greek culture and its metaphysical side was not the dominant voice in the polyphony of Hellenic *paideia*, which was also shaped by the ideals of the orators and poets as well as by a wide range of cultural practices including gymnasia, games, and political assemblies, which many Christians rejected not because of their metaphysical doctrines but because their values were too worldly; they were "pagan" in a broader sense than merely involving cult. Philosophers had in fact challenged those other (often competing) Hellenic ideals for centuries before the Church appropriated their strictures for its own purposes. Thus, the scholarly division of Hellenism into paganism and metaphysics manages to leave out precisely the extensive middle ground that was the main point at issue, namely the underlying values of the mainstream of the Greek tradition. It was those values that made Hellenic culture problematic and not only the pollutions of pagan "cult." The current model which holds that "paganism" can easily be separated from the rest of Hellenism cannot explain why the Byzantines distrusted Greek texts and the culture that produced them more than they distrusted tangible survivals of pagan cult. For example, Photios (in the ninth century) reacted far more negatively to the indecent eroticism of the ancient romance novels than he did to a contemporary report of some men who had broken into a "Hellenic tomb" in search of coins and, finding none, sacrificed and ate a dog to

[6] E.g., Jaeger (1961) 10–11, where programmatic statements about culture and *paideia* are reduced to philosophy on the (false) premise that it "was the most representative part of that which was alive in Greek culture at the time." The remainder follows accordingly, as do Chadwick (1966) 11, 38 ff., 82 ff., 104; Pelikan (1993) *passim*; see Rowe (1994) and Henaut (1994) on A. Harnack. The "Hellenization of Christianity" has traditionally been discussed on the narrow ground of metaphysics: see Lutz-Bachmann (1992). For a survey of *Hellenes* in early Christian thought, see Jüthner (1923) 87–103. Modern Greek scholars, on the other hand, have national reasons for endorsing continuity between the classical and the Christian traditions (statements to that effect routinely appear in Greek newspapers). Yet *pace*, e.g., Constantelos (1998) x, Christianity was hardly a "clarification" of ancient Greek culture and the "Hellenic-Christian tradition" was never recognized as such before the nationalist revivals of the late Ottoman period. Most Byzantines would have regarded it as a contradiction in terms. National bias here has gotten the better of Christian bias.

compel Earth to yield up her treasures. With detachment and clinical precision, and possibly boredom too, Photios calculated how many days of penance were appropriate (show leniency if they are otherwise good men, he tells the bishop).[7] In short, Hellenism was dangerous less because it might lead one to believe in the eternity of the world or to sacrifice and eat dogs but because it promoted un-Christian notions about the good life, such as could be found in erotic literature.

"Hellene" became a Christian concept only gradually. By looking at the origin of its usage, we will better understand the permanent tension that lay at the heart of Byzantine classicism. A passage in Mark (7.26) seems to use the word to mean gentile: a woman healed by Jesus is labeled "*Hellenis*" even though she is also noted as being Syro-Phoenician by *genos*; on the other hand, it may mean only that she spoke Greek. In general, the first Christians followed Hellenistic Jewish tradition and called non-believers *ethnikoi*.[8] The Greeks were only one among the foreign and non-believing nations, as we see in Tatianos' *Address to the Greeks* of the mid-second century. Greeks are there differentiated from Karians and others (1.1–2), and their antiquities are compared to those of the Chaldaeans and Egyptians (36–38). But, as we can see in the very title of the work, Tatianos apparently believed that it was the Greeks and not any other nation that he had to "address." He targeted all aspects of their culture, certainly their philosophy, theology, and religion, but also their festivals, drama, rhetoric, poetry, sports, and laws (22–28). His attack was not limited to religion, for he also drew attention to their agonistic and worldly values: "I have no desire to rule, I do not wish to be rich; I do not seek command, I hate fornication, I am not driven by greed to go on voyages; I am not in competition for athletes' garlands, or tormented by ambition" (11.1). All this Tatianos apparently regarded as quintessentially Greek. In short, for him "the Greeks" were as much a (misguided) ethical model as they were a national community whose ambitions and values had to be rejected along with their religion because all of it stemmed from the same theological sin.[9]

"Born in the land of the Assyrians," Tatianos vaunted the "barbarian wisdom" of Christianity (12.5, 29.1, 35.1, 42.1). But we should not see in all this a simple opposition between Hellenism and Christianity. Like his contemporary Lucian, Tatianos was a "Syrian" and so an outsider's view of the "Greeks" came naturally to him. In contrast to Lucian, however, his

[7] Novels: Lauxtermann (1999); dog: Photios, *Letter* 293. Consider what their fate would have been in late medieval and early modern Europe.
[8] See p. 87 above.    [9] Gaca (1999) 181–183.

acquisition of *paideia* (such as it was) magnified rather than diminished his alienation. He wrote a treatise in Greek about the Greeks, which means that despite his ostensible renunciation of Hellenism he continued to stake a claim in ancient and ongoing debates within it, as a philosophical purveyor of barbarian wisdom. There was a growing market for this within the Greek world in the period of the Antonines, when thinkers such as Noumenios turned to a variety of exotic and barbarian sources of knowledge. The polemical amelioration of "barbarism," after all, could only make sense if it were directed at a Greek audience; moreover, Tatianos and other exponents of the new "barbarian wisdom" had no interest in the culture and religions of *actual* barbarians. They were not ethnographers, but rather aimed to make Christianity attractive to prospective converts within the Greek world. If they occasionally praised barbarians (other than the Jews) for their virtues and inventions, they did so only to attack the Greeks, their pretensions, and their cultural dominion.[10] As a rhetorical strategy, moreover, this was a move that had solid precedents within the Greek tradition of self-criticism, from Herodotos onward, even though here it was taken to a different level of hostility.

As we will see at the end of this chapter, some Platonist philosophers were at the same time likewise staking a position somewhere between Hellenism and barbarian wisdom, and they too were addressing a Greek market with a craving for the exotic. The novelist Iamblichos, a contemporary of Tatianos, wrote a romantic tale called *The Babylonian Story* claiming "that he was Syrian on both sides, not in the sense that he was among those Greeks who settled in Syria but a true native, knowing the language and raised with their customs." This may well have been an authorial persona devised to promote the book among readers who sought barbarian authenticity.[11] So too Heliodoros, the author of the *Aithiopika*, claimed at the end of his novel that he was "a Phoenician from Emessa." Perhaps the author was in some vague sense a Phoenician, like the jurist Ulpianus and the philosopher Porphyrios, but there is nothing really "Phoenician" about his book, whose horizons of intelligibility are circum-scribed well within the Greek literary tradition. Heliodoros was basically exploiting the persona of the outsider to cast himself as a "literary inter-loper in the Greek world," to complicate his literary "genealogy." His goal

---

[10] E.g., Gregorios of Nazianzos, *First Invective against Julian*; and Theodoretos of Kyrrhos, *A Cure for the Hellenic Disease.*
[11] Photios, *Bibliotheke* 94 (v. II, p. 40 n. 1). For barbarian wisdom, see pp. 168–171 below.

was "to review traditional material from an alien angle," an act of harmless if "transgressive effrontery."[12]

Tatianos too, then, was both an outsider and a specialized performer of "otherness" *within* Hellenism, situated in margins that were gradually becoming the mainstream, through both philosophy and fiction. "It is not clear whether converts to Christianity were 'defecting' from Hellenism ... or participating in a cultural shift in which some individuals revised sources of Greek culture in order to embrace diversity and antiquity of traditions."[13] However, this could not be done without fundamental contradictions. To attack the Greeks, Tatianos had to depict them as a distinct and identifiable nation with specific cultural traditions; on the other hand, to appropriate all that he needed for the construction of his new Christian persona and its propagation within the Greek world, he had to fall back on the fiction invented by Hellenistic Judaism that the Greeks had stolen all that was good in their culture from the Old Testament. This exercise dismantled Hellenism into a series of acts of larceny, making it amenable to exploitation: "I am not even sure who I should be calling Greek," Tatianos announces (1.3). Thus the same thing was by turns both good (albeit stolen) and bad. So too, Eusebios of Kaisareia (ca. 310) could appropriate all that he liked of Plato's philosophy (a fair deal, in fact) so long as he argued that Plato had copied Moses. An acceptable site of Hellenic culture was thus reinstated within the Christian order, only reinscribed as barbarian wisdom. Eusebios was clever enough to notice the passage in the *Republic* where Sokrates wonders whether the ideal city that he has just proposed might already be founded among some barbarian nation "far outside our field of vision."[14] This clearly had to refer to Moses. The authority of canonical Greeks was being simultaneously undermined and used to buttress new arguments.

Resources, therefore, existed in Greek for the articulation of anti-Hellenic identities. The Christian apologists also based their attacks on Greek history on the works of the Egyptian Manethon, of the Chaldaean Berossos, and of the Jew Josephos, for whom the Greeks were literally a foreign nation.[15] The Christians, then, though they constituted a religious and not a national community, began to formulate their collective history by borrowing the perspectives of non-Hellenic nations. Of course, it was the Jewish background that proved the most influential here (had Rome

---

[12] Whitmarsh (1998) 96–97, 124; for Heliodoros' literary "Phoenician games," see Bowie (1998).
[13] Lyman (2003) 40–41, on Justin; cf. Swain (1999); Stroumsa (1999).
[14] Eusebios, *Evangelical Preparation* 12.26 citing Plato, *Republic* 499c–d; see Schott (2003) 522–526. For the Plato passage, see p. 20 above.
[15] Grant (1988) 11–18, 90–91.

converted to an Egyptian religion, "Hellenism" would have had a different history, one worth pondering). In the Old Testament and in Josephos, the main sources for Jewish history, the Greeks are a nation of polluted religious practices who oppress the Jews. As we saw in the first chapter, the literature of the Maccabean revolt offered a virulently anti-Hellenic impetus for Christian martyr literature, while at the same time Alexandrian Judaism had formulated arguments in the opposite direction, by which Hellenism was made into a more congenial environment for barbarian wisdom.

Tatianos' holistic and outsider's view of Greek culture was shared by the other early apologists, such as his teacher Justin, Apollinarios, and Miltiades. Regardless of whether they had Greek backgrounds or not, as Christians they adopted the polemical Jewish perspective. In their books *Against the Greeks*, the Greeks are considered as one among many other foreign nations.[16] Clement of Alexandria (ca. 200), the teacher of the Christian Platonist Origenes, contrasted Greeks and barbarians in his *Exhortation to the Greeks*, which took aim at Greek philosophy, myth, and cult, though it also devoted a few words to the ridicule of the religion of other nations, for example the Egyptians. Gregorios "the Wonder-worker" remarked that his teacher Origenes encouraged the study of both Greek and barbarian wisdom.[17] Still, for all that the Greeks were being treated as one opponent among many others, they were clearly also the most important, which was only to be expected, as anyone who divides the world into Greeks and barbarians reveals a Greek education and outlook. We see again that the rejection of Hellenism was premised on an acceptance of its basic terms, and this is the key for explaining why it was eventually identified as *the* enemy. Christian discourse was operating within the semantic margins of Hellenism from the very start, drawing upon the resources that were available there but reversing its basic polarities.

Moreover, the apologists clearly did not identify Hellenism narrowly with "paganism" (this belief has propped up modern European attempts to salvage the compatibility of Greek "culture" with modern versions of Christianity). They scrutinized and criticized all aspects of the culture. Certainly, their outlook was fundamentally theological, but they were interested in far more than belief and cult. Greek religion had to be totally rejected, but most early Christian writers believed that countless sites of the

---

[16] For these works, see Eusebios, *Ecclesiastical History* 4.18.1–4, 4.27.1, 5.17.5. In the fourth century, Ephraim the Syrian attacked "the poison of the wisdom of the Greeks," using the Syriac word for the Greek nation, not that for paganism: Bowersock (1990) 34, with 11 on Syriac terms.

[17] Clement of Alexandria, *Exhortation to the Greeks* 12.93; see Gaca (1999) 183–185; barbarian wisdom: Hartog (2001) 9. Gregorios Thaumatourgos, *An Address and Panegyric to Origenes* 13.

culture that we consider secular and "safe" were products of the same underlying theological pollution. Tatianos rejected Greek social values as too worldly. Clement detected idolatry in drama, music, statues, and athletic games. His Latin contemporary Tertullianus believed that most social customs and traditions in the empire were contaminated by idolatry. Where then did the boundaries between secular and sacred lie, between what we may call cultural and religious Hellenism? "It might be suggested that it is only his previous *religion*, not his manner of life, that the convert would need to renounce. But where does that religion end, and his manner of life, his 'secular' customs or 'culture' begin?"[18]

Hellenism was a comprehensive problem for the early Christians because, whatever its precise form, it was a comprehensive ideal for non-Christians. We cannot reduce it to "paganism," if by that we mean only ritual acts and beliefs about the gods. By the time Greek thinkers noticed the new faith, Christianity had already engaged with their cultural traditions and philosophy on multiple levels. The apologists were men who possessed Greek *paideia* but were loyal to a faith and ethics that they brazenly called barbarian. Under the guise of cultural and national outsiders, they exploited the subversive aspects of the philosophical Greek tradition and turned them against the mainstays of the Hellenic cultural order. It was for this apostasy, for their attempt to fracture the culture and reveal its contradictions, that they were attacked by critics such as Kelsos. In the past, those who had labored to acquire *paideia* were ranked as Greeks and expected to conform to the consensus of elite opinion and to the social and divine order of the empire regardless of what they privately thought about the gods.[19] But Christians were hard to classify. Witness the terminological uncertainty in the attack by the Platonist philosopher Porphyrios against the Christian philosopher Origenes: Porphyrios claims that he was not a Christian originally but rather "a Greek with a Greek *paideia*, who drove headlong toward a barbarian audacity," yet after this barbarization he still "Hellenized with respect to his beliefs about God," for instance by "consorting" with Plato.[20] It would be a shallow view of this passage that made "paganism" its chief concern: the entire Hellenic legacy was being renegotiated in relation to "barbarian" alternatives that were just then clamoring for attention and allegiance (and which cut close to Porphyrios'

---

[18] Markus (1990) 6; see 1–17, for an excellent discussion. Clement of Alexandria, *Exhortation to the Greeks* 2.29, 3.36, 4.50–53, *passim*. For Tertullianus, see, e.g., his treatise *On Idolatry*.
[19] For Kelsos, see Wilken (1984) 94–125; for philosophers and religion, Kaldellis (1999a) 123–126.
[20] Porphyrios in Eusebios, *Ecclesiastical History* 6.19.7–8; see Schott (2005) 308–309 and *passim*.

own researches). The logic steps in the direction of later Christian usage by refiguring the polarity of Greeks and barbarians into one of Greeks and Christians.

By the second century most Christian writers and most new Christians came from Greek cultural backgrounds. Ironically, that segment of the early Church mentioned in the Acts of the Apostles which was to become dominant in the Roman world represented the "Hellenists" as opposed to the "Hebrews" in one of the first splits in the community. Jerome claims that in Rome Christians were reviled as *Graikoi* (a word that lacked religious significance in the West), presumably because of their predominantly Greek origin.[21] They were too Greek to be Jews in the East and too Greek to be Romans at Rome, and even the most philosophical among them were too barbarian to be Greek, at least in the eyes of Porphyrios. He would have accepted Origenes were it not for his barbaric faith. Thus, as former Hellenes who wished to spread the message and live up to its demands, they had to contend personally and politically with a culture whose dominant element was Greek. They had to externalize their own Hellenism and adopt a "barbarian" stance. That is why, in the end, the apologists who set the tone of Christian polemic directed their attacks against the Greeks and not, say, the Egyptians. The latter were only a regional problem. Most cults in the eastern empire had already been considerably Hellenized and could be subsumed under the Hellenic target. One stone could kill all the birds.[22]

That Greeks would bear the brunt of Christian polemic was presaged already in Paul's epistles. Shaped at least to this degree by his *paideia*, Paul combined the Jewish polarity of Jews versus gentiles with the Greek one of Greeks versus barbarians by subdividing gentiles into Greeks and barbarians. And his attacks on the gentiles often suggest "that he had the Greeks exclusively or chiefly in mind. No other culture beside the Greeks so well fits the cluster of traits toward which the Apostle directs his ire: anthropomorphic icons, the prominence of 'wise' men whose knowledge stems from dialectical reasoning, and openly homoerotic practices."[23] It was therefore fitting that Athens, the heart of Hellenic culture and "a city filled with idols," should pose the greatest intellectual challenge to Paul and hosted what must be the strangest episode in the New Testament. It is only there, at any rate, that the verb *chleuazein* (i.e., to ridicule) occurs in the

---

[21] Acts of the Apostles 6.1; Jerome, *Letter* 54.5. For the religious connotations of *Graecus* in the medieval period and later, see Goldhill (2002) 4, 26, 30; Christou (2003) 114–117. See p. 337 below.
[22] Sartre (2005) 318.     [23] Gaca (1999) 175; cf. Romans 1.14–16.

text: Paul boldly climbed the Areopagos but was laughed off the stage at the very moment when he reached the most barbaric part of his message, the resurrection of the dead.[24]

Hellenism thus gradually came to stand for the totality of the gentiles, for all that had to be reformed or abolished; in other words, it lent its name to all that was un-Christian. In the writings of Eusebios (ca. 310) it is not always clear whether Hellenes are Greeks, Greeks *qua* pagans, or pagans who might not be Greek in any other way; in a parallel usage, both he and other early Christian writers casually used "Greeks and barbarians" to mean "everyone."[25] This was a habit of thought that they did not try to harmonize with the way they were now dividing up the world. The "Greeks" were not so much one kind of pagan group as they were now becoming representative of all pagans. In a treatise against paganism (ca. 330), Athanasios of Alexandria explicitly addresses an audience of Hellenes and yet attacks the beliefs and cults of other "nations" too. As the bishop of the chief city of Egypt he naturally attacks Egyptian paganism as well, but by then the Greeks had clearly become the archetypal gentiles who had led the others into apostasy from God.[26] By the mid-fourth century, as we saw at the beginning of this section, Hellenism had become equivalent to being anything but a Christian or a Jew. In the 370s, the heresiologist Epiphanios of Salamis (on Cyprus) placed the origin of Hellenism around the time of the Tower of Babel; it was introduced to the Greeks later, he says, through the worship of dead kings like Kronos and Zeus. Here we observe the complete separation of the concept of Hellenism from the Greeks themselves: having been defined as idolatry, it had to be given an origin sufficiently ancient and Biblical to account for all instances of it. Occasionally we still get attacks on the Greeks as a more narrowly construed cultural or national group, but the onset of Romanization was just then making the "nations" of the ancient Mediterranean obsolete.[27]

The Greek world constituted the audience against which Christians had to define themselves in order to fully be represented, as the Greek tradition became (and still is) the main arbiter of identity in the ancient world. Both Romans and Christians had entered that world as a *tertium quid* of sorts

---

[24] Acts of the Apostles 17.16–34. See Rubenson (2006); Kaldellis (2008).

[25] Hellenism and paganism are equated in Eusebios' late *Life of Constantine* 2.44. "Everyone": Lechner (1954) 12 and n. 10.

[26] Unfortunately, we do not know whether the original title was *Against the Idols* or *Against the Greeks*: see Thomson's introduction, xx–xxii. In section 6, Athanasios attacks Gnostics or Manichaeans but calls them Hellenes. For attacks on other nations, see sections 22–26; cf. Lechner (1954) 33–34; Gaca (1999) 189–192.

[27] Epiphanios, *Panarion* 3. See Gaca (1999) 192–195 on a passage in Ioannes Chrysostomos.

between Greeks and barbarians on the one hand and between pagans and Jews on the other. They both had to explain themselves in Greek terms, but still retain a self-consciously foreign or barbarian identity. To complicate matters, the signs of Hellenism lacked stability, making them helpfully malleable and accommodating but also inconclusive and frustrating. Were the Christians Greeks or barbarians? It is probably best to study them either as both or as neither. Like the Romans, they had to engage in various rescriptive maneuvers from within the margins of Hellenism, casting themselves both inside and out. Old polarities were retained, but radically renegotiated. "For in the first place," asked Eusebios,

anyone might naturally want to know who we are that have come forward to write: are we Greeks or barbarians? Or what can be intermediate to these? And what do we claim to be – not in regard to the name, because this is manifest to all – but in the manner and purpose of our life? For they would see that we agree neither with the opinions of the Greeks nor with the customs of the barbarians.[28]

The result was a spectrum of opinion, ranging from Christians who placed themselves firmly within the Hellenic tradition (if a bit off to the side) to those who postulated a radical difference (but failed to reflect on their irreversible entanglements). Yet, as we will see when we turn to the aftermath of Julian's challenge, most Christian thinkers did not have a fixed identity in this matter; rather, they modulated their stance based on their circumstances. That is what made Christian Hellenism so flexible and controversial and, in Byzantium, so adaptable and renewable.

### THE CHALLENGE OF HELLENISM

To judge from their writings, which probably paint a misleading picture, the early Christians were profoundly alienated from the Greek cities in which they lived. As late as the late fifth century, many felt that they had to avoid all public spectacles, the hippodrome, the theater, the games, as well as prostitutes, oracles, temples, sacrifices, and magicians. Dangers more subtle and pernicious than the wrath of merely human persecutors lurked everywhere as the banalities of daily life acquired a sinister and even Satanic subtext. Social customs and ambitions could be traced back to the same apostasy from God that had given rise to paganism: one had to renounce all "secular life."[29] Even Clement of Alexandria, regarded today as the most

---

[28] Eusebios of Kaisareia, *Evangelical Preparation* 1.2.1. *triton genos*: Jüthner (1923) 92–95; Inglebert (2001) 110–111 n. 8.

[29] Trombley (2001) v. II, 31, on Zacharias of Mytilene.

liberal of the early teachers, advised abstinence from political and social life.[30] In the long run, of course, the culture of the Greek polis did not survive the end of antiquity and its more offensive pagan aspects were gradually eliminated through local initiative and imperial decree. By the Byzantine period, society had been sufficiently sanitized; at any rate, the "triumph" of the Church had rendered the survival of ancient habits innocuous. The enduring challenge of Hellenism, in any case, did not come from this direction and was not limited to cult.

Most of the scholarship on the question of "Hellenism and Christianity" focuses on metaphysics, that is the degree to which Christian doctrine absorbed late Platonism, and on the struggle against paganism narrowly defined, which is reduced in practice to a historical narrative of the end of pagan worship. It is argued here, by contrast, that the main challenge posed by Hellenism were the ethical and philosophical alternatives that it offered through its *paideia*, which survived the fall of the Greek polis and always attracted the elite. The Byzantines never ceased in their labor of trying to reconcile their faith with the high culture that they had inherited from antiquity, trying (in vain) to define the proper and most anodyne place of a *paideia* purified of paganism in a Christian society.

That was easier said than done, for the problems posed by classical *paideia* were more insidious than its links to pagan cult, which were weak. Difficult as it was to separate "religion" from "culture," Christians faced a greater challenge in that the virtues preached by the New Testament constituted a direct rejection of many of the qualities that made Greek literature valuable in the first place. Much of the New Testament was indeed "folly" to the Greeks. Drawing on aspects of the Jewish tradition, Scripture blessed the meek, the poor, the humble, the weak, the foolish, those who were despised and outcasts and who lacked sophistication and refinement; it condemned ambition and intellectual pride and enjoined pity and compassion, forgiveness and even love for one's enemies, patience, childlike innocence, groundless hope, and total abstinence where before there was only moderation. Paul's message was addressed to those who counted for nothing in a world ruled by emulators of Achilles and Plato.

Not many of you are wise by human standards, not many influential, not many from noble families. No, God chose those who by human standards are fools to shame the wise; he chose those who by human standards are weak to shame the strong, those who by human standards are common and contemptible – indeed

---

[30] E.g., Clement of Alexandria, *Stromateis* 3.15; cf. Edwards (2004b) 227.

those who count for nothing – to reduce to nothing all those who do count for something. (1 Corinthians 1.26–28)

The apologists and the Fathers knew exactly what this meant in terms of their surrounding culture and so they proceeded to condemn every aspect of Greek literature that we listed above. What came to power here may have had faint parallels in the Greek tradition, but its roots were understood to be un-Hellenic, "barbarian." As a result, any people who converted to the new faith and yet still consumed Greek culture were bound to harbor deep antinomies. This ethical rift paradoxically turned back on itself and affected the reception of other aspects of the Jewish tradition. The fifth-century ecclesiastical historian Philostorgios claimed that Ulfila, the translator of the Gothic Bible, omitted the Book of Kings "containing the history of the wars in order to dampen the battle lust of a people who delighted in warfare," a decision that may explain the absence of important military terms from the extant Gothic Bible.[31]

That the problem of Hellenism had more to do with ethics than either cult or metaphysics is shown in Basileios of Kaisareia's famous *Address to young men on how they might profit from Greek literature*, written in about 370 and destined to became a standard discussion of the issue in Byzantium (and beyond). We will discuss this text in more detail below; for now let us note how Basileios prefaces his discussion right after he has stated that he is going to explain how Christians may select the good and discard the bad from among all that ancient authors say. "We, my children" (he means "we Christians")

do not believe that this human life has any worth, nor do we consider or call anything wholly good that is useful to us only for that. Not pride in ancestors, or strength of body, beauty, greatness, honors given by all of mankind, not even kingship itself, nor any great thing that one should happen to mention, if it were human, for we do not judge it to be even worth praying for; we do not admire those who possess these things, but our hopes extend much further and we do everything in preparation for another life.[32]

That is the problem of Greek literature for Basileios, not paganism, which he mentions only once and parenthetically (in the discussion of poetry). This is all the more significant in that Basileios wrote his treatise soon after the Hellenic-pagan assault of Julian, who had restored the cults and tried to

---

[31] Wolfram (1988) 75.
[32] Basileios of Kaisareia, *Address to young men on how they might profit from Greek literature* 2.1–2; cf. 5 for turning the other cheek and praying for our enemies, 7–8 for bodily distractions.

link them to the Greek literary tradition. Basileios ignored this passing cloud because he knew what the real challenges would be in the future.

On a superficial reading, Basileios' treatise advises Christians to select the good from Greek literature and ignore the bad (we will consider a closer reading below). This strategy became a commonplace in later centuries, and the premise remained that the primary danger was ethical rather than religious. In the early seventh century, Georgios of Alexandria included in his *Life of Ioannes Chrysostomos* a largely fictitious episode in which the saint travels to Athens for postgraduate work with the intention of keeping the good and discarding the bad aspects of Greek *paideia* (an allusion to Basileios' thesis). Georgios then has the prefect of Athens state as a challenge to Ioannes that *paideia* and Christianity are "incompatible (*asymphonos*)" as the former incites love of rule and arrogance while the latter inculcates humility, poverty, and continence. We are made to expect a justification for why a Christian should go to Athens. Unfortunately, in his typecast response Ioannes attacks Greek myth and does not touch upon the more serious underlying issues.[33] It was easier to pose the problem than to offer a satisfactory solution.

The scope for Hellenism in Byzantium was limited by the fact that many of the early Christians felt profoundly alienated from the Greek tradition. What did the latter look like from their point of view? Read superficially – and most reading is superficial – epic celebrated the heroes' martial skill, noble ancestry, and fleeting enjoyment of material life. Lyric poetry and romance novels reveled in physical beauty and exposed in too much detail the workings of an all-too-human *eros*. The orators craved distinction, made philology a performative art, and fought for their clients and cities rather than for the truth or God. They lied too much. Historiography documented wars of ambition and celebrated bloody generals. In political life, worldly honor was sought and bestowed for success or virtue. The desire for revenge, wealth, glory, and power was held to be natural. Aristotle ranked justified pride in one's own achievements among the virtues. Philosophy eschewed the authority of gods, sacred texts, priests, and religious communities; it valorized pure reason and led to teachings such as Skepticism and Epicureanism. Platonism set a higher moral standard, but tried to make the cosmos intelligible to the mind without seeking divine assistance, condemning itself to a merely human level of cognition. All this and more was said about the Greek tradition by the Church

[33] Georgios of Alexandria, *Life of Ioannes Chrysostomos* 4 (pp. 81–82); for the historicity of the episode, Trombley (2001) v. I, 295–303, 333–341; Kaldellis (2008).

Fathers. It was a stance lodged at a deep level in the Byzantines' ideology, though that did not make it automatically dominant.

When asked what effect the conversion to Christianity had on the empire, A. H. M. Jones replied "none at all." This counterintuitive answer was meant to draw attention to the topics that Jones himself studied, mostly legal, economic, and administrative, which were the least affected by the new faith. But beyond those fields, Christianity – or those deeper changes in ancient society of which Christianity was the most powerful manifestation – caused key aspects of Greek culture to go extinct; interestingly, these corresponded closely with the aspects of Hellenism singled out by the Maccabean reactionaries in the 160s BC. The culture of the gymnasium and admiration for the naked body gradually disappeared as did the images, rituals, artifacts, and beliefs of ancient religion; if not destroyed, at any rate they were ideologically neutralized and retained as museum pieces. Sexuality was now regulated by a new set of values and the public and literary performance of homoeroticism gradually terminated. "Virginity until death had been considered the ultimate tragedy for a woman," but "now it was the highest spiritual status ... A half-starved body, de-sexed and disfigured by fasting, could be presented as having a special beauty, a new female heroism."[34] No one who compares the robed and invariably unsmiling figures of Byzantium to the statues of the ancient gods and heroes can say that Christianity had no visible effect.

The greatest effects were perhaps not visible. No philosophy was tenable that did not rest on divine revelation and that drew the mind away from God's Word; the faculties of unaided human reason came under intense attack. More basically, the way in which people represented themselves and their desires to themselves and to others – what we may call their ideology – also experienced fundamental changes. In an ancient papyrus we find a prayer for "sustenance, health, safety, wealth, the blessing of children, knowledge, a good name, goodwill on the part of other men, sound judgment, honor, memory, grace, shapeliness, beauty in the eyes of all men who see me." Most Byzantines, who were only human, certainly desired these things, but the record of prayers that they left behind testifies overwhelmingly to their overriding need for salvation. As an ideal of private and public goods, the papyrus list was no longer tenable both because it openly represented desires that were ideologically suppressed in Byzantium and because it did not address spiritual anxieties that were equally powerful. To still wish for those qualities would have required extreme clarity and honesty

[34] Clark (2001) 276; for sexual values, Gaca (2003).

about one's nature or, and this is crucial for our theme, familiarity with ancient literature.[35]

These lost cultural practices were associated with Hellenism in one way or another by the early Christians. "Lost" is perhaps too strong and premature, for whenever Byzantine society evolved in a way that made it possible to again desire such things openly, its thinkers and writers turned back to the Hellenic tradition for help in representing them to themselves again. This was especially the case with the revival of philosophy in the eleventh century and with the more worldly and anthropocentric ethics of the twelfth. The Christian tradition lacked a vocabulary with which to discuss certain things in a positive way, for example bodily beauty and unguided human rationality, because it had set itself against them from the beginning. But the fact that it tended to associate what were often natural human desires with Hellenism had a paradoxical effect, for what had at first represented only "paganism" and the distinct cultural forms of the Greeks came by extension to encompass within its semantic range all those areas of natural life that did not conform to Christian stricture. According to a broader logic, Hellenism included everything that was un-Christian, at least in the eyes of a given preacher. Given, moreover, that most Christian preaching encoded an extreme moral idealism, the pragmatic, immoral, or indifferent lives of most Christians tended to fall into the category of Hellenism, again according to the visionaries. Ioannes Chrysostomos wished to transform the world into a vast monastery under episcopal authority. When his flock, as was natural, failed to attain this ideal and lived "according to the world," he reminded them again and again of the fundamental differences between Christian and Hellenic ethics. In this way, and by implication, he made his own flock into Hellenes, not in the sense that they were pagans of course; rather, they fell into the trap that Christian moralism had set for itself. The paradox of this ideological elaboration was that when Christians had to make concessions to reality they had to become more like Greeks. To paraphrase Horace, when you expel Hellenism with a pitchfork, it still comes back.

This was not a great problem for the majority of Christians, who did not worry overmuch about such abstractions and took their preachers in stride. But we are here concerned with those who did leave a record of their anxieties, who, for better or for worse, took it upon themselves to represent the culture to us. We can trace in our sources the "Hellenic"

---

[35] Papyrus: Graf (1997) 158–159; also Fowden (1986) 25–26; cf. Lucian, *Anacharsis* 15 on the benefits of athletics; distrust of the mind: MacMullen (1990) ch. 11.

concessions that had to be made when reality blatantly failed to gratify pious hopes. For example, Eusebios had called for a radical revaluation of Greek historiography.

Other writers of historical works have confined themselves to the written tradition of victories in wars, of triumphs over enemies, of the exploits of generals and the valor of soldiers, men stained in blood and with countless murders for the sake of children and country and other possessions; but it is wars most peaceful, waged for the very peace of the soul, and men who therein have been valiant for truth rather than for country, and for piety rather than for their dear ones, that our record . . . will inscribe on everlasting monuments.[36]

But Christian history turned out to be less peaceful than Eusebios had anticipated. A century later, his continuator Sokrates apologetically asked his readers (in the exactly corresponding passage of *his* history) to forgive him for mingling so many accounts of wars with ecclesiastical events. He confessed his fear that readers might become weary of the incessant and contentious disputes among the bishops and also because the history of the Church was now fused with that of the empire. By the end of antiquity, the separation of sacred and secular history was impossible to maintain. In the late sixth century, the last ecclesiastical historian, Euagrios, listed Ephoros, Theopompos, and Polybios among his predecessors, along with Eusebios.[37] We see here how the Greek tradition stepped in to bridge the gap when reality could no longer be described in purely Christian terms. This would be a recurring theme in the revival of Hellenism in later centuries. For example, Hellenists of the twelfth century such as Eustathios of Thessalonike seemed to side with the Hellenes of late antiquity such as Julian and Libanios in their struggle against boorish and hypocritical Christian monks. Extreme asceticism had created grotesque paradoxes: opposites met when zealotry, pursuing abasement, lapsed into a pride more superb than that of Aristotle's gentleman, as moderate Christian observers warned.[38] These debates opened ruptures into which dormant alternatives could flow. Hellenism in Christian Byzantium constituted a set of nominally suppressed paradigms that could be used to expand the field of ethical and aesthetic representation.

"Hellenism and Christianity" was a constructed opposition, constantly negotiated and variously represented in early Christian and Byzantine culture. Its terms could be modulated to suit different rhetorical contexts.

---

[36] Euseblos, *Ecclesiastical History* 5 pr.
[37] Sokrates, *Ecclesiastical History* 5 pr.; Euagrios, *Ecclesiastical History* 5.24.
[38] E.g., Euagrios Pontikos, *Praktikos* 13–14, 31; *Chapters on Prayer* 7; for Libanios, Wilken (1983) 27; for Julian, see below; for Eustathios, see p. 254 below.

As we saw, a bishop could hail the superiority and triumph of Christianity over Hellenism one day and the next lament that his flock were no better than Hellenes. There was no contradiction here and no attempt to create consistency regarding key terms. Hellenism and Christianity were not monoliths with fixed natures that could be precisely defined and contrasted. What we face in our sources is a matrix of fertile tensions generated by a dynamic interaction of a range of attitudes, needs, and beliefs. Hellenism was alternately Satanic or only regrettable, resourceful and beautiful or tempting and dangerous, depending on need, opportunity, and context. Witness the fifth-century bishop and theologian Theodoretos of Kyrrhos: he sent his young charges to study under the notorious pagan teacher Isokasios, enjoining him in one letter to teach them the "tongue of Hellas," Attic eloquence, and good morals.[39] Yet the same man also wrote *A Cure for the Hellenic Disease*, i.e., paganism. Unfortunately, no one ever pressed Theodoretos to clarify where he stood exactly on "the question" of Hellenism.

The main battleground for Hellenism in Byzantium was *paideia*, that is the education of a small (albeit hardly negligible) part of the population. To repeat, the majority of Byzantines did not worry about Hellenism one way or the other, but those who did engage with it were acutely aware of the underlying tensions because engagement implied conditional acceptance, which inevitably created a bad conscience. Many early Christians, having defined themselves against "the Greeks," became defensive when they then had to go back "outside" to acquire goods that they had disowned, for example philosophical notions that one could not find in Scripture. Following the lead of Origenes (himself of dubious repute in later times), this was called "spoiling the Egyptians," a reference to the gold plundered by the Israelites from Egypt and used to build the Ark (this idea too had been pioneered in Hellenistic Judaism).[40] Clement of Alexandria was the most "liberal" of the early teachers in holding that Greek *paideia* originated in God and so could be known by Christians. But to defend this he had to argue that when Paul declared that the wisdom of this world is folly to God what he really meant was *only* that one should not take *pride* in human wisdom; likewise, when Paul had warned against the philosophies of this world, in reality he meant only Epicureanism.[41]

[39] Theodoretos, *Letter* 44.
[40] Famously in Augustine, *On Christian Doctrine* 2.39–42, but commonplace: Jastram (1994) 192 and 201–202 n. 11; Frizzell (1994).
[41] Clement of Alexandria, *Stromateis* 1.11 on 1 Corinthians 3.19–20 and Colossians 2.8; cf. Edwards (2004b) 227–228.

Not surprisingly, it was the most learned Christians who were the most conflicted about the value of Greek *paideia*. On the Latin side, Tertullianus, one of the most educated men of his times, believed that literature was fundamentally contaminated by idolatry and should not be *taught* by Christians even if it could be *known* by them safely, a subtle distinction that well reflected his clever mind. "What does Athens have to do with Jerusalem?" he famously asked regarding Greek philosophy, echoing Paul's stark questions, "What do righteousness and wickedness have in common? What fellowship can light have with darkness? What harmony is there between Christ and Belial?" (2 Corinthians 6.14–16). The implied answer was, of course, "nothing." Elsewhere Tertullianus again asked rhetorically, "What do the philosopher and the Christian have in common, the one a disciple of Greece, the other of Heaven?"[42] Scholars have tried to blunt the edge of these sharp questions and present a more open-minded Tertullianus, but the case is weak. If he did not "wish to reject philosophy as such, but to indicate the superiority of Christianity,"[43] he could easily have said so. At the very least he was irresponsible, "ready to burn up the whole tradition in his rhetorical pyromania."[44]

The paradox remained, and two centuries later it would trouble the self-tortured Jerome, who asked rhetorically in one of his letters, "What has Virgil to do with the Gospels and Cicero with Paul? . . . We ought not to drink the cup of Christ and the cup of devils at the same time." He recounts a nightmare in which Christ accused him, "You are a Ciceronian, not a Christian!" Yet Jerome was a colossus of erudition and would remain so despite his promise to Christ in the dream never to read secular books again. His letter is certainly "didactic," but that does not absolve him of the basic contradiction. Years later, though before lesser judges, he still had to defend himself against the charge of citing secular literature excessively.[45]

The same tensions were operative in the Greek world. For one thing, the stylistic mediocrity of Scripture challenged the linguistic codes of Atticism; it also strained the faith and the pride of educated Christians. Jerome frankly admitted that sometimes the uncouth language of the Prophets repulsed him.[46] The relatively unadorned prose of the Bible was regarded as "barbaric" and therefore un-Hellenic both by believers such as Basileios of Kaisareia and by Hellenes such as Porphyrios. But this seeming

[42] Tertullianus, *On Idolatry* 10.5 6; *On the Interdiction of Heretics* 7; *Apology* 46.
[43] Helleman (1994b) 368 discussing J.-D. Fredouille; cf. Sider (1980).    [44] Edwards (2004a) 189.
[45] Jerome, *Letters* 22.29–30 and 70; for contests over Jerome's mixed signals, Goldhill (2002) 20–24.
[46] Jerome, *Letter* 22.30.

agreement reflected opposing valorizations. We see again how the same cultural code could be inverted to produce diametrically opposed meanings. In the face of scorn, Christians brazenly acknowledged and thereby ameliorated the barbarian provenance of their Gospels. The low quality of the prose became a guarantee of their "outsider" authenticity.[47] Compared to the ornate Attic style of the philosophers and orators, the language of Scripture could be cast as "the plain truth." Accordingly, the monastic founder Hypatios (in the mid-fifth century) faulted lawyers who joined his monastery and yet continued to "philosophize in conversation through the arts of their *paideia*." He urged them to use "correct speech," probably Biblical *koine*.[48] "It was subtle of God to learn Greek when he wished to become an author," quipped Nietzsche, "and not to learn it better."[49]

But Atticism exerted a powerful pull of its own. Even Luke had already tried to improve the language of Mark, and many of the Fathers, trained by the best sophists, aimed at pure Attic style and did not use the language of Scripture, even paraphrasing it into more elegant Greek when they quoted it. This was not necessarily done only for strategic reasons, to convert pagans; high culture, after all, has intrinsic attractions. Gregorios of Nyssa mailed his treatise against the heretic Eunomios to students of Libanios hoping that their master would praise its style. St. Thekla posthumously healed a grammarian "because he was a lover of beautiful speech (*philologos*) and culture (*philomousos*) and was always pleased when she was praised with eloquence." The grammarian had begun his prayer with a Homeric quotation, which especially "charmed the martyr."[50]

There were fundamental disagreements about the value of Greek *paideia*, which remained unresolved. Was it good, many wondered, merely insufficient without faith; was it useless, neither good nor bad; or was it dangerous? In late antiquity, debates on this question between Hellenes and Christians and among Christians themselves began with the career of

[47] For Tatianos, see above. Meliton of Sardeis in Grant (1988) 95; Clement of Alexandria, *Stromateis* 1.20 ("a divine and barbarous philosophy"); Basileios of Kaisareia, *Letter* 339 (addressed to Libanios, a significant fact). For the authors of the Old Testament as barbarians, see Eusebios, *Evangelical Preparation* 11.5, on which Schott (2003). Dionysios of Alexandria claimed that the author of Revelation "did not Hellenize well, but uses barbarian idioms" (in Eusebios, ibid. 7.25.26). On the other side, see Porphyrios in ibid. 6.19.7; Julian, *Against the Galilaians* 202a, 221e; unnamed pagans in Theodoretos, *A Cure for the Hellenic Disease*, preface 1; and in Isidoros of Pelousion, *Letter* 4.28. For Christians as barbarians, see Julian in Barnes (1989) 321. For similar claims from the fourteenth century, see Ševčenko (1981) 299; in the early modern period, Goldhill (2002) 35.
[48] Kallinikos, *Life of Hypatios* 29.3; cf. Trombley (2001) v. II, 76.
[49] Nietzsche, *Beyond Good and Evil* 121.
[50] Gregorios of Nyssa, *Letter* 15; *The Miracles of St. Thekla* 38. In general, see Kustas (1973) 35; Ševčenko (1981) 298–300; Browning (1983) 47–50; Alexiou (2002) 45–52. Paraphrasis: Ševčenko (1980) 58, 61.

the Christian Platonist Origenes. We saw above that Porphyrios recognized Origenes' *paideia* but faulted him for lapsing into religious barbarism. Eusebios by contrast, who inherited Origenes' vast library, praised him for transcending *paideia* by giving away his books and living "a more philosophical life." *Paideia* was esteemed in learned circles, but the rise of anti-intellectual monasticism soon challenged all urbane ideals, leaving all cultured Christians trapped in a marginalized middle ground. The fifth-century ecclesiastical historian Sozomenos, a lawyer in the capital, was compelled by an unsynthesized system of values to praise *both* the eloquence of heretics *and* the monks' willful disregard of all learning. The intense hostility that many monks felt toward intellectual life – amply attested in hagiographic sources and part of the general "distrust of the mind" that rose to power in this period – further problematized Hellenism, at least for those Christians who believed that ascetics held the moral high ground. In 376 the fundamentalist bishop and heretic-hunter Epiphanios of Salamis (on Cyprus) accused Origenes of having been blinded by his Greek *paideia*, breaking from the suspect tradition of Eusebios.[51] Epiphanios' extremism was but the insecurity of a mediocre mind in a world of well-educated bishops, and it would have a powerful following in Byzantium.

To conclude, Greek literature was problematic to some degree because of the pagan culture it reflected. The *Apostolic Constitutions*, regarded as canonical in the fourth century, proposed the institution of an all-Christian curriculum and commanded the faithful to "Stay away from gentile books ... For what is lacking in the law of God that you turn to those *ethnomyths*? If you want to read about history, you have the books of Kings; if you want something wise and poetic, you have the Prophets, Job, and the author of Proverbs" (1.6). Such proposals were echoed in early modern times, when the revival of Hellenic studies again threatened the purity of the faith.[52]

Yet such proposals were unworkable because they did not address the deeper problem, which was that Hellenism was complicit with the ordering of Christian rhetoric and identity in so many ways that it could not be cut away without extreme and self-destructive violence. At the same time, however, it embodied permanent alternatives to all Christian positions. No society can be monolithically Christian, for its ideological margins are

[51] Porphyrios and Eusebios in Eusebios, *Ecclesiastical History* 6.19. For Sozomenos and others, see Allen (1987). Epiphanios, *Panarion* 64.72.9; cf. Markellos of Ankyra in Eusebios, *Against Markellos* 1.24 (pp. 22–23); for distrust of the mind, MacMullen (1990) ch. 11; for Epiphanios' ignorance, Ševčenko (1980) 67 n. 31.
[52] Goldhill (2002) 39–40.

too crowded and too easy to reach. We should not accept the monoliths that our sources insistently and inconsistently attempt to construct, but at the same time we should not minimize the differences. "Essence" is beyond our reach, perhaps, but general trends and attitudes are not. For example, even the late Platonists, who were closest to the Fathers among ancient philosophers, criticized the substitution of faith for reason and dismissed the reliance on prayer in matters that called for practical virtue.[53]

Certainly, it is easy to downplay the gap between the ethical demands of the new faith and the "philosophical standard" that prevailed under the Roman empire, for the two did have much in common. This approach has been urged by historians who argue that Christian debates over the content and value of *paideia* were merely extensions of those of antiquity. But this approach, while correct in one sense, fails to account for that "new" message which Christians believed they were propagating, that message which created all that anguish over the proper place of Greek culture.[54] It tends to focus on Christianity's least novel aspects, for example on love of neighbors, which, viewed as universal benevolence and linked to *imitatio Dei*, can easily be documented in the philosophical tradition, and especially Platonism. But each step in the argument takes us away from the New Testament – say, the Sermon on the Mount – and onto the common ground of philosophical debate among pagans and Christians, which was conducted in fairly conventional terms. It results in such bizarre conclusions as that Ioannes Chrysostomos "was incapable of comprehending the intentions of Matthew in any other *cadre* than that of the popular Platonism of late antiquity."[55]

That Ioannes was deeply influenced by popular Platonism and could express the Christian message in its terms cannot be denied, but he was not incapable of doing otherwise nor was his message basically one of Platonism. Elsewhere he revealed himself a sublime exponent of the new table of values: when he claimed that a humble sinner is greater than a just man who thinks well of himself he knew that this made little sense to the Greeks. Witness the Platonist Kelsos, two centuries earlier, who wondered why "God will receive the unjust man if, conscious of his wickedness, he humbles himself; but as for the just man, though he may look up to Him with virtue from the start, God will not receive him." This was not "mere malice" on Kelsos' part, as Origenes unfairly claimed; rather, he did not regard pride as such a terrible sin, if a sin

---

[53] Kelsos in Origenes, *Against Kelsos* 1.9; Porphyrios (?) in Eusebios, *Evangelical Preparation* 1.3; cf. Kaldellis (2003) 313–314.
[54] E.g., Rappe (2001).    [55] Whittaker (1979) 220.

at all, and could ask with genuine incomprehension, "what evil is it not to have sinned?"[56] Ioannes Chrysostomos knew how to deal with such men:

Do you see the Prophet, how he considers it a great harm, no less than Hell itself, for the common enemy to be cheerful, to see him strong and regard himself as sublime ... Let us then aim and struggle for this, that we not allow the enemy to become elevated, that we not reveal him to be strong, and that we not become the cause of his cheerfulness, but, to the contrary, let us labor to make him humble, an object of contempt, sick, downcast, sullen.[57]

This is pure Nietzsche, only turned on his head.[58]

## THE LEGACY OF JULIAN

As it happened, chance prevented the leaders of the Christian community from meeting the challenge of Hellenism on their own terms. Into a world less than half converted and before a Church rent by heresy and still unsure of its own identity, stepped a young philosopher-emperor who forcefully and eloquently asserted the independence of Hellenism as a comprehensive cultural system, postulating the unity of its ethical, philosophical, literary, and religious aspects.

Julian reigned as sole emperor for under two years, in 361–363. Yet in the past century he has generated a far larger bibliography than any other emperor, excepting perhaps only Augustus and Constantine, including historical novels and admiring poems. At first this seems strange, since his reactionary policies were immediately reversed by his successors when he died in battle against the Persians. At least one historian has complained that this stream of publications has drawn attention away from others who reigned longer and had a greater historical impact.[59] The point is valid, but a defense may be made. In his effort to divert the evolution of Roman society, this "thorn in the side of Constantine's pious family" (as he was called by a Byzantine historian)[60] exposed the inner workings of the nascent imperial-Christian system as well as the contradictions that rent the Christian appropriation of the classics. He stirred up trouble, forcing men to take stands on policies and attitudes that they would have preferred to establish more quietly at the centers of power. His reign therefore

---

[56] Ioannes Chrysostomos, *Homily on Psalm* 4.3. Kelsos in Origenes, *Against Kelsos* 3.62; cf. Porphyrios (?), *Against the Christians* fr. 87. For Julian, see below. Against the equation of Platonism and Christianity: Edwards (2004b) 212–216, 223, on theological and religious grounds.
[57] Ioannes Chrysostomos, *Homily on Psalm* 12.2.     [58] Cf. Nietzsche, *The Anti-Christ* 5, 24.
[59] Treadgold (1998) 345–346.     [60] Psellos, *Historia Syntomos* 57.

generated both heat and light. Besides, our fascination with his reign and personality merely continues that of his own contemporaries. We possess more works about Julian, both for and against, than any other ancient ruler. In addition, the psychological candor of his writings makes him one of the few ancient men whose inner world we can glimpse. These facts justify the attention he has received.

The Byzantines also never forgot Julian. His legacy was a constant reminder that Hellenism was not, as many wanted to believe, merely a docile handmaiden of the faith but rather could be activated as a powerful alternative to it. Julian's writings, preserved as a model of style by Christians drawn to his engaging personality, remained available to the curious.[61] Around 440, Kyrillos, bishop of Alexandria, wrote a long refutation of his treatise *Against the Galilaians* (what the Apostate called Christians to belittle them), explaining in the preface that the work's eloquence and arguments were widely believed to be irrefutable and were still instilling doubts in the faithful.[62] Julian was again refuted in the early tenth century by the acerbic Arethas of Kaisareia, who also accused his own enemy Leon Choirosphaktes of admiring the impious emperor and siding with him against the Fathers. In fact, Leon is not above suspicion of unorthodoxy and even Arethas has been suspected of playing a part in the transmission of Julian's works.[63] In 1083 the humanist bishop Ioannes Mauropous concluded an oration on the "hierarchs" of the Church (Basileios of Kaisareia, Gregorios of Nazianzos, and Ioannes Chrysostomos) by again attacking Julian's argument for the unity of Hellenic *paideia* and religion and condemning all who agreed with him. In sum, the "*pontifex maximus* of Hellenism" was a permanent fixture of the Byzantine imagination, whose relevance was paradoxically reaffirmed every time he was denounced.[64] What had provoked all this?

Under the influence of philosophers, Julian had renounced Christ in favor of Neoplatonic paganism and had loudly affirmed an indissoluble link between Hellenic *paideia* and un-Christian beliefs and values. Yet

---

[61] Athanassiadi (2001) 148 n. 17, and below. For the memory of Julian, see Athanassiadi (1977); Braun and Richer (1978) part 2; for his personality, Armstrong (1984) 5–7 and Smith (1995) esp. 10 (a good study of Julian's religion in thought and in practice); for his *paideia*, Bouffartigue (1992) esp. ch. 12.

[62] Kyrillos of Alexandria, *Address to Theodosios II* 405 (*Against Julian* 508c–d).

[63] Arethas of Kaisareia, *Antirrhetikos regarding Marriage* 21 (*op.* 14, v. I, pp. 167–168); *To Thomas Patrikios* (*op.* 15, p. 180); *Choirosphaktes, or the Wizard-Hater* (*op.* 21, p. 212); and esp. *Refutation of Julian* (*op.* 24, pp. 221–225); cf. Lemerle (1986) 262–263. For Leon, see Magdalino (1997).

[64] Ioannes Mauropous, *Oration in Praise of the Three Holy Fathers, the Great Basileios, Gregorios the Theologian, and Ioannes Chrysostomos* (*op.* 178, pp. 116–117); see Agapitos (1998a) 189–190. Quotation: Athanassiadi (2006) 57.

those were not the only grounds for anxiety. His austere and irreproachable private life, sincere devotion to justice and concern for the welfare of his subjects, military vigor, hatred of despotism, and aversion to legal brutality, did not fit the mold of a tyrant, which further irritated his ideological opponents. Beyond the outpouring of affection from his pagan subjects, even many ordinary Christians admired him despite his violent condemnation by their own leaders. In the vicious invectives that he delivered upon Julian's death, Gregorios of Nazianzos asked: "Must our ears be filled with the praise of his good administration of the public post, relaxation of taxes, good choice of magistrates, and punishment of robbery?" All this was nullified, Gregorios believed, by the religious controversy that Julian had stirred up. But the praise rankled all the more because it probably originated within the saint's own congregation. This is more telling than all the eulogies of his friends – Platonists in the late fifth century still dated events from Julian's accession – as is the grudging admission by Ambrosius of Milan that the provinces were still praising Julian as late as 392.[65] A Byzantine historian noted that Julian "alone governed the Roman empire well," heaping praise on him and comparing him to Marcus Aurelius. The only flaw that he notes is that Julian rejected Christ, but this too is placed in a brief sentence at the end.[66] It was likewise Christians who moved Julian's body from Tarsos to Constantinople, where it was interred along with the rest of his family in the church of the Holy Apostles. His tomb could still be seen (and smelled) in the twelfth century. He was joined there by, among all people, Justinian and ... Gregorios of Nazianzos! We see here how in some ways the logic of the Roman state was unaffected by Christianity: a good emperor was worth all honors.[67]

Moreover, the fact that we still possess virtually all of Julian's works proves that he was admired as a stylist in Byzantium.[68] In a didactic work for the emperor Michael VII Doukas (1071–1078) containing brief imperial portraits, the philosopher Michael Psellos drew attention to Julian's

---

[65] Gregorios of Nazianzos, *Or.* 4.75 (*First Invective against Julian*); Ambrosius, *Consolation for the Death of Valentinianus III* 21 (cf. Prudentius, *Apotheosis* 449 ff.); Marinos, *Life of Proklos* 36. In the early fifth century, the usurper Constantinus III renamed his sons Constans and Julian, "cashing in on the reputation of Constantine the Great": Snyder (2003) 79.

[66] Ioannes of Antioch fr. 272. For this author, see Karpozilos (1997) 574–582. W. Treadgold (pers. comm.) believes that Ioannes paraphrased Eustathios of Epiphaneia (ca. 500).

[67] Konstantinos VII, *Book of Ceremonies* 2.42 (v. I, p. 646); cf. Grierson (1962) 40–41: Theodosius I "was most active in turning the church of the Holy Apostles into an imperial mausoleum, and the paganism of Julian could easily be overlooked in view of the imperial office he had held"; also Kelly (2003) 594 and n. 33. For the role of Eunomios in the transfer, see Van Dam (2003) 31 with 198 n. 34; for Gregorios, Flusin (1998). Twelfth century: Ciggaar (1973) 340, 350–351.

[68] Bidez and Cumont (1898) esp. 25–26.

superstition but also noted that "he begged his own gods to set him free
from the compulsion of sleep and greedy desire for luxuries and to make his
love (*eros*) of knowledge (*gnôsis*) intense and uninterrupted." In his many
writings, Psellos attributed an *eros* for *gnôsis* to only one other person:
himself.[69] In short, not all Byzantines shared Gregorios' bitter hatred for
the last pagan emperor. Be that as it may, it matters more that Julian was
*heard* than that he was admired. He successfully claimed a place for himself
in the ongoing Byzantine debate regarding the authority and meaning of
Hellenic *paideia*. What, then, did he have to say? We are fortunate in the
case of Julian to be able to study his philosophical view of Hellenism and
Christianity in conjunction with the practical measures that he sought to
implement as emperor; in fact we must do so because the relationship
between the two has often been misunderstood.

On 17 June 362, Julian issued an edict requiring all candidates for
municipal teaching posts to conform to high moral standards in addition
to strictly professional standards of eloquence. Appointments had to be
approved by Julian himself or by other imperial officials (depending on
who "we" are in the edict). By itself this sparked no controversy and even
continued to apply under later Christian emperors. It was part of the broader
effort by the later Roman state to bring municipal affairs under imperial
supervision.[70] This edict would not have affected the majority of teachers in
the empire, who taught privately and were supported by student fees.

Around the same time Julian issued another edict – or perhaps this was
only a letter clarifying his intent – arguing on moral and religious grounds
that Christians should not teach Greek literature. Since its main concern is
the *ethical* dimension of teaching in relation to the subject matter of
Hellenic literature and religion, it is not unreasonable to link it to the
edict of June 362, though they may have been separate measures in a
broader program of reform.[71]

We hold that upright culture is not luxurious elegance with words and language
but the healthy disposition of an intelligent mind and true beliefs about the good

---

[69] Cf. Michael Psellos, *Historia Syntomos* 57, with *Encomium in Honor of His Mother* 29 (p. 148) and *On Incredible Reports* 101–103 (*Phil. Min. I* 32). The editor of the *Historia Syntomos* notes that Psellos' portrait of Julian "is much less unfavorable for Julian than in most of the Byzantine presentations" (132); also Ljubarskij (1993) 219. For Julian's bibliomania, Bouffartigue (1992) 605–606.

[70] *Cod. Theod.* 13.3.5 = *Cod. Just.* 10.53.7; for the immediate and long-term context, Athanassiadi (1994) 12; Germino (2004) chs. 1 and 5.

[71] Julian, *Letter* 61c (Bidez and Cumont)/36 (Wright). Banchich (1993) views the two texts as independent but does not consider that they use the same moral argument; for a survey of sources and scholarship (mostly Italian), see Germino (2004), who does not think this text was strictly speaking a law (ch. 4).

and the bad, the beautiful and the shameful. Whoever believes one thing and teaches another to his students seems to lack *paideia* to the degree that he is not an honest man ... So it is necessary for all who wish to teach anything to be equitable in their manner and not to carry within their souls beliefs that they combat in public; much more so than all others, I think, should be those who associate with the youth and teach them letters, who are interpreters of ancient texts, whether rhetors, grammarians, or, even more so, sophists. For they desire to teach not only letters but morals and say that their proper field is political philosophy ... What then? Did the gods not grant *paideia* to Homer and Hesiod, Demosthenes, Herodotos and Thucydides, Isokrates and Lysias? Did some of them not believe themselves to be consecrated to Hermes, while others to the Muses? It is out of place, I believe, for those who interpret their works to dishonor the gods whom they honored ... I give them the choice not to teach those things which they do not consider worthy; yet should they be willing to teach, let them do so first by deed, by convincing their students that neither Homer nor Hesiod nor any of the others whom they teach were guilty of impiety, folly, or deceit with respect to the gods. Since they receive their wages and live off the writings of those authors, they reveal themselves to be shamefully greedy and show that they would endure anything for the sake of a few drachmas ... But if they think that those men were wise whose works they teach and whose prophets, so to speak, they are, then let them first zealously imitate them in their piety to the gods. If, however, they think that those authors were mistaken with respect to the most honorable gods, let them walk over to the churches of the Galilaians and expound Matthew and Luke ... For initiators and teachers let there be a common law: no student wishing to learn shall be excluded ... For it is not reasonable to take children who do not yet know which way to turn and to lead them unwillingly and by fear to our ancestral beliefs ... I think that we must educate idiots, not chastise them.

Granting the premises that *paideia* was as much about moral instruction as it was about learning the technical aspects of eloquence and that the Greek authors were linked to Greek religion (neither of which was controversial in late antiquity), the argument is clear and watertight. Yet it is also bound to irk all who wish to partake of classical culture but who do not believe in the gods of Homer, including Christians and modern historians. Thus, where Julian basically wanted to protect the authors and gods whom he revered from Christian abuse and to promote Hellenic piety, many who have written about this edict from Julian's time onward have misrepresented it as an act of tyranny aimed against the Christians, which occludes the philosophical issues that it raises. Gregorios himself began this by claiming that Julian wanted to deprive Christians of *paideia*. Christians in the fifth century then added that Julian excluded Christian children from the schools, in accordance with their gradual transformation of their own fears and insinuations into confirmed historical facts. Even though their claim is refuted by the explicit language of the text itself, it is repeated in many modern discussions, almost all of which claim that the intent of the edict was to deprive Christians of classical culture.[72]

What for Julian was an argument about the foundations of his own faith has been recast as anti-Christian legislation. This distortion is then written back into the provisions of the edict, in defiance of the text itself. But Julian very precisely did *not* want to deprive Christians of all access to Greek *paideia* because he believed that exposure to it might cure their "idiocy." In *Against the Galilaians*, he opined that any Christian with a noble nature who is exposed to Greek *paideia* will reject his faith (229c–d). Whether this is true is here irrelevant. Julian himself is actually the only person we know who apostatized under the influence of his teachers. Almost all Christians before Constantine and most of the Fathers of the fourth century studied under pagan masters with no adverse effect on their faith and no bitter memory of the experience. Some then referred friends and students to those teachers, even to Libanios, a man who believed that "these two things, the worship of the gods and the study of letters, are akin to each other."[73] Few or no "Christians ever suggested that children should be brought up differently, away from the pagan schools,"[74] and Julian explicitly stated in his law that unwilling children should not be led by fear to accept ancestral beliefs. Thus even if all teachers had henceforth been required to be pagans, as most of them were anyway, that would not have advanced his cause much.

Furthermore, it is wrong from a legal point of view to say that Julian banned all Christians from teaching. It is likely that in pursuance of the edict of June 362 this law applied only to holders of municipal chairs and not to the vast majority of teachers, who taught privately and were paid by their students. There were no laws regarding private teachers, nor could they easily have been enforced. The only men we know who were affected by the law were Marius Victorinus of Rome and Prohairesios of Athens, both of whom are noted as holding municipal chairs. Julian even granted

---

[72] Gregorios of Nazianzos, *Ors.* 4.5–6, 101 ff., 5.39 (*First* and *Second Invectives against Julian*); cf. the ecclesiastical historians Rufinus 10.33, Sokrates 3.12, Sozomenos 5.18, and Theodoretos 3.8; Augustine, *City of God against the Pagans* 18.52; cf. *Confessions* 8.5.10. Many modern discussions echo the Christian interpretation; it would be pointless to cite them. For the amplification of abuse against Julian in the fifth century, see Penella (1993).
[73] Libanios, *Or.* 62.8 (*To those who jeered at his* paideia). For pagan teachers, see Tertullianus, *On Idolatry* 10.7; Basileios of Kaisareia, *Letters* 335, 337, 346; Gregorios of Nazianzos, *Or.* 43.21 (*Funeral Oration for Basileios*), and see McLynn (2006) 219; Augustine, *Confessions* 2.3.8. Hypatia taught both pagans and Christians: Dzielska (1996) 42–46; for Theodoretos, see p. 138 above.
[74] Marrou (1956) 321. For some fictitious attempts, see Nimmo Smith (2001) xvii.

Prohairesios an exception, which was refused; the old sophist was still teaching, albeit privately, when the pagan Eunapios became his adoring student.[75] Such, then, was the net practical effect of the law as far as we know regarding this well-documented period. Broader claims about *all* teaching being affected are products of rhetorical exaggeration.[76]

Julian's law caused an uproar not because a handful of Christian teachers were fired but because it implied more broadly that Christians could not in good conscience study Greek literature or appreciate Greek art, inspired as they were by the gods and contaminated, in Julian's own words, by beliefs regarding "the good and the bad, the beautiful and the shameful" that were antithetical to those of the Gospels. Julian was in effect siding with Christian hard-liners who wanted nothing to do with Hellenism; he put his finger on a problem that others did not want to face with such clarity. This explains why the most bitter reaction came not from the hard-liners but from men such as Gregorios, who took pride in his *paideia*, was genuinely in love with its aesthetic and moral qualities, and was torn by its conflict with his faith. If we can trust our sources, this was not the only time that Julian forced Christians to live up to their own principles. There were complaints that he excluded them from imperial service on the "pretext" that their religion barred them from judging others and from using violence. That this was greeted with more outrage than logic reveals an appreciation of Julian's cynicism.[77] It is possible that we are dealing here with theoretical arguments that Julian made against the Christians with a polemical rather than a strictly legal intention but which his enemies later treated speciously as a specific enactment. Something similar, I suspect, has happened in the case of the law on teachers. A polemical point was taken by Christian polemicists as a legal enactment (even in violation of the law's explicit wording) and then written into history as its actual effect.[78] But Julian developed a similar position in his *Against the Galilaians*, which surely did not have the force of law.

---

[75] Banchich (1993). For doubts about Prohairesios and the date of Eunapios' arrival, see Goulet (2000).

[76] Or abbreviation, in the case of Ammianus Marcellinus 25.4.20. Ironically, the historian has just stated that "the laws that Julian enacted stated exactly what was to be done or left undone."

[77] Julian, *Epistulae et Leges* 50 (pp. 57–59); cf. Tertullianus, *On Idolatry* 17–18: the exercise of power is incompatible with humility. The response of Gregorios of Nazianzos, *Or.* 4.99 (*First Invective against Julian*), is typically weak; cf. Photios, *Letter* 187. Julian confiscated the property of feuding Christians in Edessa to help them attain the kingdom of heaven: *Letter* 40/115 (Wright/Bidez and Cumont); cf. Matthew 19.23 26.

[78] See Pricoco (1980), with Criscuolo (1987) 166–167 n. 6. Julian argued on religious grounds against eating fish: *Or.* 5.176b–177b (*Hymn to the Mother of the Gods*). Obviously, this did not have the force of law.

If the reading of your own Scriptures is sufficient for you, why do you nibble at the learning of the Hellenes? ... But this learning of ours has caused every noble person that nature has produced among you to abandon atheism [i.e., Christianity] ... When a man is good by nature and moreover partakes of our *paideia* he becomes a gift of the gods to men, either by kindling the light of knowledge, or by founding some political constitution, or by routing numbers of his country's foes, or even by traveling far over the earth and sea, and thus proving himself a man of heroic mold ... Now this would be a clear proof: choose out children from among you all and train and educate them in your Scriptures and if, when they come to manhood, they prove to have nobler qualities than slaves, then you may believe that I am talking nonsense ... Yet writings by whose aid men can acquire courage, wisdom, and justice, these you ascribe to Satan and to those who worship Satan![79]

To us, of course, Julian's vision of Hellenic *paideia* seems monolithic and implausible. Thucydides, to name only one, was not inspired by the gods and did not write religious literature; he was an atheist. Nor is it likely that Plato "worshipped idols," which Julian mentions with relish to chastise Christians for relying on his theology.[80] Furthermore, the texts of the Greek canon obviously do not speak with one voice on ethical matters. The Hellenic legacy did not have this level of coherence – Achilles and Sokrates, Homer and Plato, did not stand for the same things – but on the other hand it is equally true that the theoretical problems facing the Christian appropriation of the classics were deeper than polemicists like Gregorios of Nazianzos were willing to admit. If classical texts "did not transmit a Julianist Hellenic Orthodoxy which they did not contain ... they have transmitted a whole complex of ways of thinking, feeling and imagining which are not compatible with Biblicist and ecclesiastical Christianity."[81] At any rate, all sides could agree that the Gospels were not about promoting science, founding states, routing enemies, and traveling the seas, all of which receive extensive attention in Greek literature. It was not by the detestable teaching of the Galilaians, Julian reminded the people of Alexandria, that king Ptolemaios had made their city great and prosperous.[82] The emperor thereby claimed for the Hellenic tradition all human achievements that had shaped the history and improved the lot of mankind, Christians included. The Gospels could

---

[79] Julian, *Against the Galilaians* 229c–230a. For Julian's Hellenic, and specifically Platonic, virtues, see Huart (1978); for the Neoplatonic dimension, Curta (1995) 193–208.

[80] Julian, *Against the Galilaians* 49a. Many Christian writers openly admitted that Plato was an idolater and condemned him for it: Gaca (1999) 188, 191, 194–195.

[81] Armstrong (1984) 8, who adds: "The Muses and Lady Philosophy are not to be recommended as priests' housekeepers."

[82] Julian, *Letter* 47/III.433d (Wright/Bidez and Cumont).

not take credit for these works, but Christians wanted to continue to benefit from them while casting aspersion on their divine sources.

In linking literature, history, and religion in this way, Julian was not "out of touch" with his time as is often claimed, and probably represented what most pagans believed about the foundations of Greek culture. His belief that classical authors were divinely inspired was widespread. Homer and Hesiod were widely regarded as theologians. The literary critic Dionysios of Halikarnassos had written that many regarded even Thucydides as divinely inspired. In his *Defense of Rhetoric*, Aristeides labored to prove that the poets and orators were in fact inspired by the Muses.[83] It was a commonplace to believe that one's progress in *paideia* was due to divine assistance and "an idea of sacredness attached to the institution [of the grammarian] and to its texts."[84] Recent studies have likewise explored the religious aspect of the ancient romances, subtle and yet pervasive.[85] Evidence of this kind can easily be multiplied. Tertullianus did not imagine that "idolatry" was everywhere.

Julian's idea of Hellenism, however, did not have a strictly religious *as opposed to* a cultural meaning, as is often supposed; his outlook was more holistic than the equation of Hellenism and paganism. Let us look again at his references to Greeks and Greek things. The vast majority of them are "national," referring at once to the people, history, religion, and literature of the ancient Greeks, who are contrasted in this sense to Celts, Egyptians, etc. There is something "scholarly" about this usage; one would be hard-pressed to prove from Julian's writings that the Greek nation still exists, as almost all of his references are to classical antiquity. Moreover, it is not easy to find *strictly* cultural or *strictly* religious instances of the word, given that for Julian the two formed "an indivisible whole."[86] The same was probably true for all educated pagans who accepted the label of Hellene. Julian's admirer, the historian Zosimos (ca. 500), called the Goth Fravitta "a barbarian by *genos*, but otherwise a Greek, not only with respect to his

---

[83] Homer: Lamberton (1986); Dionysios, *On Thucydides* 34; Ailios Aristeides, *Or.* 2.47–59, 75, 84–113, 391; cf. Dion Chrysostomos, *Or.* 18.3, 33.12, 36.32–35.

[84] Divine assistance: Fronto, *Letter* 2.2.4; Kassios Dion 73.23.3–5 (about his own work); and many passages in Libanios. For Himerios, see below n. 109. Grammarians: Kaster (1988) 15–16. Julian's writings are full of references to the divine inspiration of the canonical authors, esp. Homer and philosophers such as Plato and Iamblichos.

[85] Chalk (1960) on Longos.

[86] Athanassiadi-Fowden (1977) 347. For the divine origin of nations, see Julian, *Against the Galilaians*; for Julian's Hellenism as equal to paganism, Cameron and Long (1993) 66–68 and Cameron (1993), who rely on the small unrepresentative sample in the index of the Bidez and Cumont edition of *Epistulae et Leges*, which glosses many instances as "paganus" without discussion. Cameron does not discuss in detail any individual uses of the word by Julian.

manner and lifestyle, but also his religion" (5.20). Attempts to impose strict consistency on Julian's concept of Hellenism fail because he frequently modulates the word to refer to either the whole or a part of the inherited conglomerate of Hellenic identity, whether ethnicity, culture, or religion. For example, in an early oration he praised the Christian empress Eusebia for the purity of her Greek descent (*genos*).[87] So here is a strictly ethnic sense. Yet, as we saw in the previous chapter, Julian believed that he himself was at once an ethnic Thrakian, a Roman national, and, like his "Gallic" friend Saloustios, a Greek by *paideia*.[88] Of strictly religious uses of "Hellen" in his works there are few or none. In the few instances when he refers to someone as "a true Greek" in connection with his religion, it hardly means that the rest of that person's culture is being excluded.[89] Julian never equates Hellenes and pagans; in fact, after his conversion he probably had no concept for "pagan." His emphasis in *Against the Galilaians* on Hellenes, Jews, and Christians does not replicate the standard Christian tripartition, because he also discusses there (pagan) Celts, Germans, and Egyptians as distinct from the other three groups (e.g., 116a ff.). By his own admission his religious-philosophical beliefs were not purely "Greek" anyway. For example, in his *Hymn to King Helios* he pauses to note that the Chaldaean wisdom of Iamblichos is not familiar to Greeks (147a).

Freed from the Christian outlook of his childhood, Julian reverted to the pluralistic outlook of an earlier age. Romania for him encompassed a diversity of "national" traditions each of which had distinctive religious and cultural aspects. Hellenism was only one among them, if most important for Julian personally; it encompassed literary, ethical, and historical traditions. Yet from the standpoint of a Roman of the fourth century, this Hellenism was a unified inheritance that emerged from the monuments of the *ancient* Greeks rather than from any Greeks who may still have been

---

[87] Julian, *Or.* 3.110b (*Panegyric for the Empress Eusebia*).

[88] Julian, *Letter* 53/97 (Wright/Bidez and Cumont) claims that Libanios' "speeches are admired by all true Hellenes," but the letter begins by praising the sophist's piety. *Letter* 69/201.413d (possibly spurious) praises a certain Himerios for being "a Greek man, possessing true *paideia*."

[89] Julian, *Letter* 35/78: "show me [by sacrificing] a man who is a pure Greek among the Kappadokians," implies that other Kappadokians are Greek in *other* respects. In *Letter* 58/98.400c, Julian tells Libanios that Batnai has a barbaric name but is a Hellenic place, "above all" because of the sacrifices performed there. This means that it was Hellenic in other respects too (Ammianus 14.3.3 says that it was founded by Makedonians, and note the contrast between barbarism and Hellenism in Julian's letter). The same ambiguity characterizes the famous letter to the priest Arsakios (22/84a): the opening line may refer to Hellenism *qua* paganism, but this cannot be said about the "Hellenic villages" mentioned later (he does not mean "pagan villages"). *Pace* Bouffartigue (1991) 252–254 these are not "strict references to paganism." In general, see Bouffartigue (1992) 658–669; Van Dam (2002) 101; Curta (2002) 5–6, citing previous bibliography.

around. Julian was a Roman who looked back to ancient Greece, the culture and thought of which he supplemented with what he took to be the "barbarian" wisdom of the Chaldaeans. His view of the world, in other words, and his articulation of a unified pagan Hellenism within it, challenged the outlook of his Christian opponents by dividing the world in a very different way, and that is in part why he made them so uncomfortable. *Paideia*, he argued, could not be separated from the belief in the gods and the performance of cult.

Julian's Hellenism had a richness and vitality that would not be possible in any subsequent age. There are few ancient and Byzantine writers who exhibit a comparable personal fascination with, and knowledge of, so many aspects of ancient Greek culture. In fact, Julian's very perception of the present was filtered through the lens of Hellenism; his trained gaze automatically elicited the classical associations of words, cities, and landscapes. All occasions, whether dire, playful, or polemical, brought to mind tags and comparisons from ancient literature. He became a living performance of his own *paideia*, assuming in turn the personae of Odysseus, Alexander the Great, or Marcus Aurelius. His "capacity for linking his philosophical ideas with his life was boundless, and he often seemed to be living in a fantasy landscape of mythological heroes and historical legends."[90] To his friend Saloustios he noted – fully in accordance with what he would later say to Christians – that "it is not right to praise and not to imitate the Homeric heroes." Before the walls of Ktesiphon, after defeating a Persian army, he offered horse-races and athletic games. His tutor had in any case convinced him that the world of Homer was more real than the physical one around him: "Have you a passion for horse races? There is one in Homer, very cleverly described. Take the book and study it."[91] This was not the theologized Homer of the Platonists; it was a literary world valued for its richness of detail and not as an allegorical rendition of abstract signs and imperceptible realities.[92]

It fell upon Julian to defend this fantasy world, the living heart of ancient Hellenism, from Christian attack in the grim realities of the later Roman empire. "These two things are the peak of their theology," he snapped, "to

---

[90] Van Dam (2002) 159–160; for Alexander, Germino (2004) 4–6 n. 7.
[91] Heroes: Julian, *Or.* 8.250a (*Consolation to himself upon the departure of the most excellent Saloustios*). Races: Libanios, *Or.* 1.133 (*My Life, or Regarding His Own Fortune*), 18.253–255 (*Funeral Oration for Julian*); Eunapios fr. 27.3–4. Teacher: Julian, *Misopogon* 351d.
[92] For Julian's Homeric *paideia*, see Athanassiadi (1992) ch. 1; Curta (1995) 185–188; cf. Athanassiadi (2001) 52 and Lamberton (1986) 134–139 for his Homer.

hiss at the demons and make the sign of the cross on their foreheads."[93] We know from Christian sources that some did in fact "spit on outer (ἔξωθεν) learning as false and treacherous." Some Christian teachers were specifically instructed to "reveal at all times to those whom they teach that what the gentiles call gods are really demons."[94] Why should those who believed this be allowed to make a living by teaching the poets at public expense? No sinister "strategy" need be ascribed to Julian's law on education beyond the spirited defense of his sacred traditions. "On May 22, 1836, the Smyrna Ecclesiastical Committee ... [proclaimed] that education and religion were inextricably bound and that a teacher of a different faith could not teach their children 'what he neither believes nor has been taught to believe.'" So too, over a century later the philosopher Bertrand Russell was not allowed to teach logic and mathematics in New York because, as the Board of Education of the State put it, "the public schools encourage the belief in God, recognizing the simple fact that ours is a religious nation ... [and] one of the prerequisites of a teacher is a good moral character."[95]

OURS OR THEIRS? THE UNEASY PATRISTIC SETTLEMENT

Julian's challenge was no trivial matter for learned Christians. His was certainly an idiosyncratic personality, but he was also emperor of the Roman world and could use every medium available to that office to broadcast and promote his vision of Hellenism. That vision, moreover, could not easily be denounced as a fraud or error, for Julian's literary and philosophical credentials were impeccable by the high standards of that age. By driving a wedge between Greek *paideia* and the Christian faith, Julian soured their ongoing rapprochement, with potentially serious social consequences, for the ambitions of the ruling class had not changed upon its conversion to Christianity. Classical culture was a traditional pursuit of the elite and a badge of gentlemanly refinement. Many no doubt loved it

---

[93] Julian, *Letter* 19/79 (Wright/Bidez and Cumont). These practices are attested: Bolton (1968), also Caecilius (the pagan) in Minucius Felix, *Octavius* 8.4; Kelsos in Origenes, *Against Kelsos* 8.38; Eusebios, *Ecclesiastical History* 10.4.16; Valentinianus in Sozomenos, *Ecclesiastical History* 6.6 (not a true story).

[94] Gregorios of Nazianzos, *Or.* 43.11 (*Funeral Oration on Basileios*). Teachers: *Canons of Hippolytos* 12 (possibly a fourth-century text); Lactantius, *Divine Institutes* 5.1–2.

[95] Smyrna: Augustinos (1992) 117; cf. Matalas (2002) 56, 66–67. Russell: P. Edwards in Russell (1957) xiii, 229. In September 2005, Italian media reported that Caterina Bonci, a teacher of religion in a Catholic school, had been fired because Church authorities considered her to be "too sexy" and her dress too provocative. Church officials claimed it was because she was divorced and no one could teach religion in a Catholic school who did not practice the tenets of the faith (Ms. Bonci was divorced in 2000).

for its own sake, but it was often a requirement for high office. Julian and Constantius had jointly decreed in 360 that "no person shall obtain a post of the first rank unless it shall be proved that he excels in long practice of liberal studies and that he is so polished in literary matters that words flow from his pen faultlessly."[96] This was yet another way in which Romania was unaffected by its conversion.

The notables of the late fourth-century empire, many of whom had been born into Christian families and had not faced the painful choices of an earlier age, now required a classical culture purified of paganism and controversy. We should not forget that there were always Christians who were ready to basically agree with Julian and refuse to even "nibble on the learning of the Greeks." The popularity of this option throughout the Byzantine period (and beyond) should not be underestimated, nor was it associated exclusively with the most rigorous exponents of the ascetic movements. The fervent anti-intellectualism of these circles, which has not received due attention in the recent interest in late-antique "holiness," was enshrined in canonical hagiographic texts such as Athanasios' *Life of Antonios* and the popular hymns of Romanos the Melodos (sixth century). These authorities promoted the notion among a large part of the population that the more correct Christian choice was the wholesale rejection of Hellenism.[97] Even Ioannes Chrysostomos admitted that the Hellenic thinkers were pleasant to behold on the outside but inside were only "ashes and dust and nothing healthy, 'their throats an open grave' full of filth and rot."[98] Any Christian appropriation of the classics always had to contend with this.

Julian could not easily be refuted, and because his challenge continued to lurk in the margins even after the fervor of his reign had passed, any settlement of the issue would always require a great deal of "forgetting." Christians had to pretend – to the point that it became a natural response – that the ancient texts were *not really* linked to beliefs about the gods and that even the temples which they admired had *not really* been places of demon-worship. Herein lay the origin of our own notion of "the classics": a corpus defined aesthetically that puts us in touch with "the tradition," whose values intrigue us but which we are not likely to emulate, and whose religion we

---

[96] *Cod. Theod.* 14.1.1, tr. and discussed in Wilson (1983) 2; cf. 50–51 for imperial initiatives relating to classical culture; for the social role of *paideia* in the fourth century, Brown (1992) ch. 1; Van Dam (2002) 80–94.
[97] For Romanos, see Alexiou (2002) 54 and 463 n. 26; see also Browning (1975b) 18–19; Garzya (1992) 39–40; Saradi (1995) 12–13.
[98] Ioannes Chysostomos, *Homily on the Gospel of John* 66.3 citing Psalm 5.10.

hardly understand. What Julian regarded as hymns and theology was for the Byzantines only poetry and eloquence; what he regarded as the statues and temples of the gods was for them – after the craze for their destruction had subsided – mere art and landmarks. As early as 382 the emperor Theodosius I had decreed regarding a specific temple in the East that

> it shall continually be open ... in which images are reported to have been placed which must be measured by the value of their art rather than by their divinity ... You shall permit the temple to be open, but in such a way that the performance of sacrifices forbidden therein may not be supposed to be permitted under the pretext of such access.[99]

Even pagan art could be put on display in Christian Constantinople. For such Hellenism to be displayed, all that had once challenged and even terrified had to be first neutralized. The gods now became art and Homer mere verse. "Classical Studies," the study of ancient culture in a Christian society, is inevitably trivial compared to Julian's Hellenism, which was alive and had claws and real gods. It was codified in late antiquity and Byzantium as a discipline and passed into the West after 1204. One of the breakthroughs of modern research has been to recover the original religious function and character of so much of Greek art and literature. What we are looking at in the period of late antiquity is the process by which those things were "forgotten" in the interest of creating a Christian world.

Among the first who hastened to meet Christian demand for sanitized classics was the philosopher and court orator Themistios, whom we discussed in the previous chapter. Criticized by Julian, Libanios, and Palladas for selling out his philosophical independence in exchange for lucrative imperial service, Themistios was one of the pioneers of a new "neutral" *paideia* that highlighted affinities between Hellenism and Christianity by offering up the teachings of the latter in the guise of the former. For example, in an oration before the emperor Valens he asserted that it was Sokrates who had first commanded men not to harm their enemies. Themistios was promoted and honored by all the Christian emperors of his time, in exchange for which he graced their regimes with the legitimacy of rhetoric and political philosophy.[100]

---

[99] *Cod. Theod.* 16.10.8; but cf. Arcadius and Honorius in 16.10.16: "If there should be any temples in the country districts, they shall be torn down without disturbance or tumult. For when they are torn down and removed, the material basis for all superstition will be destroyed." For the new attitudes, see Saradi-Mendelovici (1990); Lepelley (1994); Saradi (1995) 24–28; Bassett (2004) 111–120.

[100] Themistios, *Or.* 7.95a–b (*Concerning those who have suffered misfortune*). See Heather and Moncur (2001) 57, 60–68, 97–101; and p. 72 above. Another pagan sophist catering to Christians was Bemarchios, according to his rival Libanios: *Or.* 1.39 ff. (*My Life, or Regarding His Own Fortune*).

The patristic settlement of the question emerged from the various short- and long-term reactions to Julian's argument regarding Christian teachers. The first recorded reaction is described by the fifth-century ecclesiastical historians. The two Apollinarioi, the father a grammarian and the son a rhetorician (and later a heretical bishop), decided to produce a Christian equivalent of Greek *paideia*, including a Christian grammar; an epic version of the Pentateuch; poems in all meters, comedies, and tragedies based on the Old Testament; and Platonic dialogues based on the Gospels. These curious works do not survive, though they were not without precedent or sequel. Hellenistic Jews had written epic and tragic versions of their sacred stories in imitation of Greek forms. A version of the Gospel of John in epic verse was later attributed to Nonnos of Panopolis (late fifth century), while the empress Eudokia in the early fifth century and a certain Patrikios fashioned Homeric centones of the Christian message (these are verses of Homer rearranged to tell a new story).[101]

The Apollinarioi reproduced the forms of Greek literature but supplied them with a Christian content. Yet there is some discomfort in this enterprise. Why did Scripture need a classicizing supplement? Its stylistic revision invited comparison with the original and implied improvement, while at the same time the quality of the revision was unlikely to have matched the standards of Homer and Plato. Requiring Scripture to compete with pagan works on the latter's terms was a bad idea. Had the Holy Spirit intended for the story of Moses to be told in Homeric verse it would have been so told. In the end, few Byzantines had any interest in this sort of thing; they kept their classics separate from Scripture, as "outer" and "inner." The Apollinarioi received the attention of the ecclesiastical historians probably because the empress Eudokia was producing similar works while they were writing.[102] Besides, the allure of classical culture rests in part on the prestigious traditions that evolve around it and the diachronic reception that establishes its authority. Being educated means being in touch with those specific traditions; it is not purely a question of meter or genre in the abstract. Christians *wanted* to know (if at a "theoretical" distance) about the gods and ancient Athens because their own language

---

[101] Apollinarioi: see the *Ecclesiastical Histories* of Sokrates 2.46, 3.16, and Sozomenos 5.18. Sokrates' views, which presuppose the post-Julianic settlement, will be discussed below. For the fifth-century Homeric Psalter wrongly ascribed to Apollinarios, see Ševčenko (1980) 65–66 n. 10. Jews: Gruen (1998). Nonnos and Eudokia: Hunger (1978) v, II, 100 ff.; Cameron (1982) 281–285; Johnson (2006) 99–104. Patrikios: *Greek Anthology* 1.119. For a Euripidean Biblical drama ascribed to Ioannes of Damaskos, see Lauxtermann (2003) 134.

[102] Urbainczyk (1997) 33–34.

and literature were deeply enmeshed in the ongoing dialogue on their meaning and worth. More importantly – though this could not easily be admitted – many Christians wanted to read genuine heroic literature and Hellenic philosophy because it made them think and imagine in ways that the Bible could not. This was the challenge and the temptation of Hellenism in Byzantium.

One highly self-conscious Christian thinker who engaged on a personal level with Greek literature and who wrote the most famous response to Julian was Gregorios of Nazianzos. He had recently been forcibly ordained a priest by his father, the bishop of Nazianzos, and may have been teaching there as a rhetor, which deepened his stake in the education law. Gregorios' response is often hailed as a definitive refutation of the Apostate, though it is nothing of the kind. Many historians simply intuit that Julian was wrong because in their mind classical culture is "not really" pagan, so they acclaim any loud denunciation of that position. But the sheer hysteria of Gregorios' *Invectives* is embarrassing even to his admirers.[103] The diabolical emperor who emerges from these pages – a beastly creature of pure evil, possessed by demons (4.56), who condoned the eating of Christian virgins (4.87), and himself sacrificed children and maidens (4.92) – is unreal. Gregorios relies on rumor, insinuation, and conjecture about what Julian would have done had he returned a victor from Persia (4.96, 4.111–112, 5.39), and on tortured logic (Julian persecuted Christians by not persecuting them: 4.27, 4.58). He gloats over the misfortune of the emperor's friends, the prospect of their everlasting damnation, and the tortures that Julian will personally suffer in the afterlife (5.37–38).

Gregorios was one of the most fascinating and intellectually troubled men of his age; we should say a few words about him before examining his response to Julian. His personal ideal was aristocratic leisure devoted to literature and philosophy, but he also acknowledged the spiritual value of personal asceticism. He vacillated between the two and failed to combine them, fleeing erratically from the responsibilities of his episcopal appointments (Sasima, Nazianzos, and Constantinople) and practicing moderate asceticism, though without devoting himself wholeheartedly to contemplative withdrawal or even to a life without servants. He never overcame the conceits of his class (pride, honor, and loyalty to family and friends) or renounced its privileges. He was critical of both worldly bishops and

---

[103] See the opinions in Coulie (1982) 138 n. 1; Hanson (1988) 707 and n. 12; Van Dam (2002) 195. The best introduction is Bernardi (1978); also Criscuolo (1987). The commentary by Kurmann (1988) is useful, but not interpretive. For Gregorios as rhetor, see McLynn (2006).

uneducated monks and was regarded in return as "arrogant."[104] This left him in an awkward position, lacking a clear niche in the evolving articulation of the Christian world in the fourth century. He was moreover a bad judge of character, eager to love and idolize anyone who shared his theology and *paideia*, such as Maximos the Cynic and Basileios of Kaisareia. But his fulsome praise turned to bitter abuse when they both betrayed him. His sensitivities are reflected in his many orations, letters, and poems, which the Byzantines regarded (rightly) as models of literary style equal to the best ancient writers. His strong passions, however, and turbulent career made it difficult for him to reflect calmly and measure his responses.

The decade that Gregorios spent in Athens as a student was the happiest of his life. It was then that he consummated his "passionate *eros* for all *logoi*." Naturally, this *eros* was highly exclusive. Gregorios disdained those who lacked culture, both Christians and pagans, especially when they sought power, and he helped young men of good family to acquire an education. But he made sure to always remind them that *paideia* was only a preparation for the worship of God. He consecrated his own *logos* to the service of his faith and discouraged Basileios' brother Gregorios (later the bishop of Nyssa) from following a career in rhetoric, suggesting that this amounted to a rejection of Christ. What he probably meant was that such a career fell short of the level of devotion that men of quality owed to God, though he believed that it was possible to serve God in ways that sublimated the skills of orators and philosophers. Gregorios' provocative effort to combine Christian ideals with those of the Second Sophistic can be seen as a chapter in the traditional struggle between rhetoric and philosophy, or between the active and the contemplative lives.[105] But complicating his efforts was the fact that Athens – "the golden city, the home of letters" – was a pagan city that also attracted the likes of Julian. Gregorios never forgot this. In his *Funeral Oration for Basileios*, he would offer a striking account of how pious young Christians acquired their classical education while avoiding the contamination of the city's pervasive idolatry. It was not easy. Gregorios was trying to do intellectually what he proudly noted that his mother had done socially: never had she touched pagan women, no matter how closely related or honorable, nor had she ever eaten at the same

[104] Gregorios of Nazianzos, *A Complaint for His Sufferings* 74 (*Poem* 2.1.19).
[105] *Eros*: Gregorios of Nazianzos, *Poem on His Own Life* 112–113; for Gregorios at Athens, see McGuckin (2001) 16 n. 54, 53–83. Young men: *Poem* 2.2.4 (*Nikoboulos to His Father*), esp. 77 ff., and 2.2.8 (*To Seleukos*), esp. 24–64, 181–319. Nyssa: *Letter* 11. Gregorios' ideals: Ruether (1969).

table with pagans.[106] What Julian did in 362 was effectively to burst into Gregorios' house of learning and demand the tastiest food for himself.

The premise of Julian's argument was that *paideia* primarily consists not in technical instruction in the use of language but in "beliefs about the good and the bad" and beliefs about the gods. Gregorios *never* addresses this core issue in his *Invectives against Julian*. The position he does attack – that the Greek language itself and its technical use belong exclusively to "Greeks" and that Christians should therefore not use them (4.4–6, 4.100–110, 5.39) – entirely avoids Julian's point. Through some painful puns on *logos*, Gregorios waxes indignant about the attempt to deprive Christians of *logoi*, including the alphabet, the Attic dialect, and poetic meter, arguing that those who have invented something do not have exclusive rights to it; besides, he argues, the Greeks did not invent much of all this but rather stole them from eastern peoples. But an interest in mere language is precisely what Julian disclaims in the first sentence of the surviving text of his "law." It is possible that Gregorios, writing during or soon after Julian's reign, knew little about what the emperor had actually said and was reacting instead to second-hand accounts of those sections of Julian's *Against the Galilaians* that listed all the inventions of the ancient Greeks (178a ff.).[107] He also seizes the chance to ridicule figures of Greek myth, legend, and history, including Solon and Plato, and contrast them to the superior virtue of contemporary Christians (4.70–73). Later, he ridicules the chief values of the Greek city and the immorality of the gods (4.113–121) – typical stuff. But this polemic only reinforces Julian's point that Christians should stay away from Greek culture and fails to address the key question, namely why Gregorios himself had spent ten years studying authors who promoted a morality and religion so antithetical to his own ("counterfeit learning," he calls it in 5.29). Contrary to what many scholars assert, Gregorios' "Hellenism" here does not signify Greek culture as a whole but only the Greek language.[108] He charges Julian with disingenuously changing the meaning of Hellene from language to religion, but this complaint is itself disingenuous (4.5), for elsewhere in his extensive corpus Gregorios almost always uses Hellene to mean pagan, evincing little or no interest in the linguistic sense that he plays up here. Julian, by contrast, was

[106] Athens: Gregorios of Nazianzos, *Or.* 43.14–24 (*Funeral Oration for Basileios*). Mother: *Or.* 18.10 (*Funeral Oration for His Father*).
[107] Cf. Germino (2004) 75–76.
[108] E.g., Dostálová (1983), esp. 8–10, who uses evidence from other texts and authors to find "cultural Hellenism" in Gregorios' response to Julian. Many others can be cited.

consistent in his usage and knew that culture and religion cannot so easily be separated.[109]

Gregorios had no adequate philosophical solution for the quagmire of his own Hellenism. The violence of his reaction was due to his insecurity. Julian's challenge effectively outflanked him in his own struggle against fundamentalist Christians who "spat on that outer (ἔξωθεν) learning as false and treacherous and leading us away from God." In other works, Gregorios confessed that *paideia* was "the chief of all good things that human beings possess," but failed to articulate a cogent theoretical defense of it on Christian grounds; it was not enough to say that it occasionally offered some advantage to the aims of piety.[110] Consequently, his *Invectives* did not lead to a stable Byzantine resolution, though they did shape the perception of Julian himself and inspired a range of works about him. It has been proposed that the famous last Delphic oracle "Tell the king . . . ," which was supposedly delivered to Julian by his friend Oribasios, was in fact modeled on Gregorios' polemical account of the silence that had befallen the ancient oracles (5.32).[111] As late as ca. 1200, the rhetorician Nikephoros Chrysoberges was still refuting Julian, this time in an *ethopoeia* on "What response (*logoi*) a Christian philologist would give when Julian the Apostate tried to stop him from reading Hellenic books." Chrysoberges followed Gregorios in placing emphasis on the Greek language itself rather than on what Julian had actually argued.[112] Such refutations had the paradoxical effect of renewing Julian's challenge to the Byzantines' various attempts at Hellenism and keeping it always before their eyes.

A solid refutation of Julian would in any case have accomplished little. Had Gregorios rigorously argued that Homer and Thucydides were neither inspired by nor believed in the gods, that would not have been of much use to Christians, who would still have had to negotiate between their faith and an alien culture (and it would have put atheism at the heart of their curriculum). By contrast, where Gregorios succeeded brilliantly was in producing a *practical demonstration* of what it meant for a Christian to be both classically educated and strong in the faith, even if the theoretical problems remained unresolved. His orations, letters, and poems demonstrated how

---

[109] McGuckin (2001) 75 suggests that Gregorios Christianized the argument of his pagan professor at Athens, Himerios, that a rhetorician's speeches are offerings to the gods. Himerios visited Julian at Constantinople and endorsed his program. For the controversy in general, see Criscuolo (1987); Van Dam (2002) ch. 11.

[110] Gregorios of Nazianzos, *Or.* 43.11 (*Funeral Oration for Basileios*). For his failure, see also Ruether (1969) 164; Curta (2002) 4, 9–10.

[111] Athanassiadi (1977) 107; for other possibilities, Smith (1995) 285 n. 31.

[112] In Asmus (1906); Widmann (1935–1936) 22–23, 275–280.

Atticism, rhetoric, and verse; allusion, philosophy, and irony; wit, eloquence, and learning, could serve the faith, at least as the latter was understood by this aristocratic philosopher-rhetor. In one poem, he declared his intention to use poetry to lead men to God: why should only those "outside" use it for their vain babbling? This was not the Apollinarian project of converting Christian texts into a classical form, but of endowing classical forms with a new and personal Christian purpose. Gregorios deliberately "arranged a collection of orations which effectively covered the major needs of preaching . . .: encomia, consolations, doctrinal instructions, [etc.] . . . The whole corpus of his work, therefore, was in a real sense shaped and focused by Julian's brief but portentous challenge."[113] That is why he chose classical genres in which to deliver his message rather than those that had been developed for Christian use, such as Biblical commentaries, apologetic treatises, and sermons.[114] We may imagine Gregorios as a Christian Cicero, "translating" the culture and literature of the Greeks for the benefit of his own people, in this case the Greek-speaking Christian world. Some of his programmatic statements definitely remind us of Cicero: "I wanted to make sure that those 'outside' don't get the best of us in literature."[115]

The result was an "alternative" corpus of Christian classical literature, and the idea seems to have caught on, even if in practice Christian pedagogues could create their own curriculum from among the works of all the Church Fathers and not only Gregorios.[116] At any rate, if Julian's challenge remained unanswered, Gregorios effectively performed a counter-challenge. *Paideia*, he agreed, *was* more than technique, but could proclaim a different God and serve new virtues, for example charity and abstinence (humility was not really within his purview). The Greeks were not to be superseded: they could remain as an enduring source of instruction and inspiration. "Like a judge, bid the *logoi* of the Hellenes to serve the proclamation of true doctrine," Gregorios advised a young notable.[117] He made it so that his own works, including the five theological orations that defined the faith for all posterity, could not be understood by anyone who lacked a proper education. Christian philosophy was thereby linked to the classics at its very foundations. The two would exist in a perpetual counterpoint, the one enslaved to the other as if by court order. It was calculated irony – and arrogance – that led Gregorios to pack his *Invectives against Julian* densely with classical

---

[113] Gregorios of Nazianzos, *Poem* 2.1.39; and McGuckin (2001) 118, and (2006) for the poems.
[114] Wilken (1983) 102.    [115] Gregorios of Nazianzos, *Poem* 2.1.39 (*On Matters of Measure*).
[116] See Zacharias of Mytilene in Trombley (2001) v. II, 32–33.
[117] Gregorios of Nazianzos, *Poem* 2.2.8 (*To Seleukos*) 240–243.

*exempla* and deploy Attic as well as Biblical insults to denigrate the last pagan emperor. Byzantine readers required special commentaries to grasp these references. What a place to learn the myths and rituals of ancient Greece![118] *Paideia* was flamboyantly mastered and redirected, made to repudiate and even attack its own past. Elsewhere, Gregorios lifted Libanios' phrases in praise of Julian and used them to praise monks.[119] On the architectural side, he wrote an epigram (30) commemorating his rededication of a pagan temple as a Christian church.

Yet the deeper problem remained. As Julian noted at the beginning of his treatise *Against the Galilaians*, counter-charges should not be brought before the original indictments have been answered. The works and persona of Gregorios provided a positive model of Christian *paideia* that was imitated by many, but did not explain the precise value that classical literature held for Christians or ameliorate its troubling aspects. Gregorios himself alternated between praising "outer" learning as the best thing in the world (when defending himself against obscurantist Christians) and damning its vanity and babbling (against pagan critics). Theology and philosophical ethics could perhaps be of use to Christians along with the techniques of rhetoric, but what of the aesthetic and poetic aspects of Greek culture, its chief attractions? What possible value could Homer have? Sokrates, an ecclesiastical historian writing in the 430s, exemplifies this dilemma. Enjoying a good education himself, he argued that the work of the Apollinarioi, designed to replace the corpus of Greek literature with Christian counterparts, was unnecessary because Greek learning can be beneficial to Christians as it is. Philosophy approximated the truth of the Gospels and, besides, how else could Christians master the logical tools by which to refute pagan errors?[120] A literature studied only to refute itself! We, at any rate, should not be deceived: that was *not* why Christians read it. But Sokrates could not admit the truth to himself without making serious concessions and eliciting unwelcome insights. Perhaps the Bible did not adequately satisfy all legitimate spiritual needs.

Gregorios' brilliant performance offered a way for Christians to continue to participate in the core tensions of the Greek tradition and

---

[118] See Nimmo Smith (2001) for the *Commentaries* of pseudo-Nonnos; also Coulie (1982). Mixed abuse: Schmitz (1993); for Gregorios' classical imagery, Ševčenko (1980) 57–60, and 63 for the commentators his works attracted; for the *exempla* in his corpus, Demoen (1996). For a Byzantine author (Ignatios the Deacon, early ninth century), who may have learned his classical allusions from Gregorios or pseudo-Nonnos, see Lambakis (2001) 116 117, 122 123.

[119] Wilken (1983) 112.

[120] Sokrates, *Ecclesiastical History* 3.16; for similar views, Wilson (1983) 8–9. Sokrates' other argument (also in Jerome, *Letter* 70), that Paul cited pagan texts, only shifts the burden.

overshadowed many anxieties but did not dispel unease or disarm temptation. Julian was not merely imagining things when he said that anyone who
was thoroughly educated in Greek literature and thought would not turn
out a good Christian. All Gregorios could do in this regard was advise
young Christians to pick the good from Greek literature and leave the bad,
as bees do with flowers, or, viewing the classics "as a single plant, to avoid
the thorns but pluck the rose."[121] He probably lifted these images from
Basileios' *Address to young men on how they might profit from Greek literature*, which we mentioned briefly above. It is worth taking another look at
this work because it became a classic and guided the studies of many
Christians in Byzantium and modern Europe.[122] Basileios' thesis seems
simple, almost too simplistic. Like Odysseus who blocked his ears with wax
against the beautiful but deadly song of the Sirens (4.2), Christians are to
take in the good and reject the bad when reading Greek literature. Basileios'
chief concern, as we saw, is with ethics, not paganism. Accordingly – and
without ever mentioning Julian – he cites many positive Greek *exempla* and
shows how they approximate Truth. Through a study of these "decaffei-
nated" classics,[123] Christians may prepare for higher things.

If only it were that simple! Odysseus, the reader may recall, did *not* block
his ears against the Sirens; rather, he blocked the ears of his companions
while exposing himself safely to the beauty of their deadly song. Basileios'
"mistake" is fatal to the conventional reading of his treatise. In fact, many
of the *exempla* that he cites are likewise distorted in order to yield up
positive models for Christians. He deliberately ignores context, smoothes
over nuances, or changes the meaning of texts.[124] Unlike Gregorios,
Basileios does not denounce the negative side of Greek literature; rather,
he suppresses it in the hope that students will not find in Greek literature
what they have not been told that they will find. The song of the Sirens is
made less deadly by being made less beautiful and tempting. That this was
a deliberate attempt to rarefy and ameliorate is proven by the fact that, in a
treatise ostensibly designed to teach Christians how to choose the good and
reject the bad, Basileios cites *no* negative *exempla*, limiting himself to some
vague warnings in the introduction (4.3–6). He suppresses Julian's

---

[121] Gregorios of Nazianzos, *Poem* 2.2.8 (*To Seleukos*) 38–44, 60–61.
[122] Bees and thorns: Basileios of Kaisareia, *Address to young men on how they might profit from Greek
    literature* 4.7–8. For other metaphors (banking; taking up with another man's wife!), see Wilson
    (1983) 8–9; for the influence of Basileios' treatise, Schucan (1973) esp. ch. 2 on Byzantium; Van Dam
    (2002) 186 with 246 n. 10.
[123] Armstrong (1984) 8.
[124] Though slightly overstated, the thesis of Fortin (1996) is the best way forward.

challenge because he knew that speaking about it would merely draw more attention to the Apostate's arguments.

Unlike Gregorios, Basileios regarded "Athens" largely as "a waste of time" and, in the guidelines that he wrote for the education of orphans, he made no provision for classical culture alongside the study of Scripture.[125] Still, he knew that most upper-class Christians would be reading classical literature whether he wanted them to or not. Through a brilliant pedagogical insight, he realized that the best way to protect those who were not yet strong in the faith from the dangers of Hellenism was not to denounce it, but to preempt it by assimilating it to Christianity and so making it bland; in other words, by blocking the ears of young Christians before they heard the song in its pristine beauty. "What they could not overcome by their own judgment," wrote Cassiodorus of Odysseus' followers, "they conquered instead by insensibility."[126] Basileios' strategy suggests that mature Christians such as himself and Gregorios could hear the song of the Sirens in its fullness without danger, lashed as they were (like the real Odysseus) to the mast of faith (this was, in fact, a common image among the early Christians).[127] But for other Christians it was best that their ears be made dull and insensitive to that deadly song.

To conclude, what Christian Byzantium inherited from Hellenic antiquity was a set of tensions rather than a resolution. There could be no easy resolution, as the issues were too complicated, and after Julian no one wanted to tackle them seriously. Moreover, with the Neoplatonic turn toward barbarian revelation (see below), no one remained to advocate Hellenism's autonomous values. Still, they were always there, if only in the margins or as an implied supplement, whenever they were denounced or held to be merely "useful." But before the emergence of new Byzantine Hellenisms, there was a will to forget. Christianity had, after all, "triumphed" over Hellenism and made it a maidservant of the faith. "The letter of divine wisdom is flat," said the learned monk Isidoros of Pelousion

---

[125] Athens: Basileios of Kaisareia, *Letter* 223.2 (to Eustathios of Sebasteia), alluding to 1 Corinthians 1.20 on the vanity of worldly wisdom. Considering its addressee, this letter is not necessarily unqualified testimony, but cf. Gregorios of Nazianzos, *Or.* 43.18 (*Funeral Oration for Basileios*). Orphanages: *The Long Rules: Question* 15.

[126] Cassiodorus, *Variae* 2.40.10 (Theoderic to Boethius).

[127] Ševčenko (1980) 57 with 67–68 n. 36. The Sirens were a commonplace; e.g., Clement of Alexandria, *Exhortation to the Greeks* 12.91; Zacharias of Mytilene, *Ammonios, Or the World is not as Old as God*, in *PG* LXXXV (1864) 1037a; in general, see Rahner (1963) ch. 7. Personal experience confirms the wisdom of Basileios' approach. The aim of state-issued textbooks for "Religion" classes in Greek schools is to prove that Orthodoxy is superior to all other religions and philosophies, but their violent denunciation of Nietzsche's ideas proved the only spur to lively discussion and further reading.

(ca. 410), "but the sense is sublime. Of the outer wisdom, on the other hand, the expression is brilliant, but the deed is lowly. Whoever manages to combine the sense of the former with the expression of the latter would justly be deemed most wise."[128] This methodology, postulating distinctions between content ("ours") and form ("theirs"), imposed hermeneutical priorities that did not bode well for the study of classical literature. On the other hand, it meant that form could be invoked to justify the preservation of otherwise indefensible content. In preparing an edition of the pederastic epigrams of Straton of Sardeis, Konstantinos Kephalas (ca. 900) argued defensively that the reader should "take personal delight in the diction of the epigrams, not in their meaning." But what delights he and his circle of fellow Hellenists took is unknown to us.[129]

## CONCLUSION: THE END OF ANCIENT HELLENISM

Even before the end of late antiquity – let us say by AD 400 – it becomes difficult to find anyone claiming to be a *Hellen*. This is a sure sign that a massive cultural shift had taken place. Most of the elements of unity and continuity that had been cited by the Athenians during the Persian Wars recounted by Herodotos had failed and ceased to generate Hellenic identities: "we are one in blood and one in language; those shrines of the gods belong to us all in common, and the sacrifices in common, and there are our habits, bred of a common upbringing" (8.144.2). Blood had been diluted by the vast expansion of Hellenic culture and eventually ceased to matter in the new Roman polity. Along with almost everyone else, Greeks became Romans and lost any sense of being a distinct nation among others more quickly and thoroughly than has yet been realized. After Libanios, we no longer hear any echoes of Plutarch or Pausanias, who accepted the Roman empire while maintaining the historical, cultural, and ethnic boundaries between Greeks and Romans. At most, now, a *Hellen* was a man from Greece, a notion too trivial to merit controversy in our sources.

In a parallel movement, as the Greeks converted to Christianity they lost the bond of continuity secured by their "shrines" and "sacrifices," and severed their communal ties to that ancient religious nexus of images, stories, beliefs, and gods that had formerly made Greek culture so distinctive. As Christians, they now grafted themselves onto another history, that of God's Chosen People, in which there was no difference between Greek and Jew. Origins were now traced to different places, peoples, Scriptures,

[128] Isidoros of Pelousion, *Letter* 5.281; cf. Kustas (1973) 34–35.   [129] See Lauxtermann (2003) 96–97.

and institutions, which further reinforced the transnational enterprise of the Roman empire and pointed away from the land of Greece. Granted, paganism persisted in some places and circles until the sixth century, and some of its adherents (such as Julian) happily accepted the polemical Christian label *Hellen*. But few followed him in this after ca. 400. This kind of "Hellenism" had been invented by Christians for polemical purposes and did not reflect the outlook of most pagans around the empire. Even Julian, as we saw, meant both more and less by it than did his Christian enemies: *more*, as it was not limited to religion, and *less*, as he believed in a plurality of religious and national traditions, of which Hellenism was only one. The Christian notion of the *Hellen* did not stimulate the creation of new Hellenic identities (unlike the polemic against "the Jews," which consolidated that which it denounced).[130]

To take another element mentioned by the Athenians in Herodotos, the Greek language has had a continuous history over the past 3,000 years and has changed less than any other language in a comparable amount of time (in fact, less than other languages have changed in far shorter amounts of time). But linguistics by itself is insufficient. For language to form the basis of a group identity it must be so constituted in a specific cultural context. There were people before Homer who spoke Greek, but they did not call it that; more importantly, to the degree that language contributed to whatever ethnic, cultural, or political identities existed in the Bronze Age, it did so in accordance with other historical coordinates, contributing, for instance, to an "Achaian" identity, however that was understood. This was *before* the historical construction of Greek identity in the Archaic age.[131] So too *after* the demise of ancient Hellenism: the Byzantines knew that they spoke "Greek" but did not for that reason consider themselves *to be* Greek, except in that specific sense, parallel to the geographical one mentioned above. In fact, we have seen that they often called their language "the language of the Romans," or "Roman," since they were Romans and that was the language that they spoke. In his *Invectives against Julian*, Gregorios of Nazianzos likewise broke the link between the language and whatever broader identities sought to make use of it, whether religious or national. In this sense, language was neutral for him and could just as easily serve the Christian community as Julian's pagan Hellenism.[132]

There is no doubt: Hellenism failed in late antiquity, it "fell" to outside forces. The "barbarians" – Romans and Christians – had won, yet, to be sure, these barbarians had always defined themselves in relation to Hellenism, in

[130] Schwartz (2001).    [131] For which, see Hall (2002).    [132] For Greek as Roman, see pp. 113–114 above.

both apposition and opposition. They had developed discursive identities within the broader world of Greek culture and so various sites of Hellenism later survived inside them; all these systems of knowledge, power, and culture interpenetrated each other by the end. Still, historians have not explained what caused Hellenism to collapse in the face of "barbarism," when it had made such a strong showing as late as the Second Sophistic. The exuberance of Greek identity in that period is shown, from a Byzantine perspective, to have been somewhat hollow, too shrill a protest perhaps.[133] Already the market of ideas was saturated by self-professed barbaric alternatives to classical Hellenism, which our Atticist sources tried to disguise or recast into their idiom. Many of these alternatives were frauds, in the sense that they were either forgeries or projected by Greek writers onto foreign nations to give them mystical authenticity, while those that had an authentic foreign origin or element had been worked out in a Greek context and served up to a Greek audience.[134] A decisive shift had occurred. In the fourth century BC a Platonist could state that "whatever the Greeks have taken from the barbarians they have perfected and made more beautiful," and in the Hellenistic period a representative of eastern wisdom could be praised for being "a Hellene not only in his speech but in his soul."[135] But during the high imperial era Greeks were gradually taken in by oriental fictions of their own making.

Not all of these orientalisms were fictitious. We discussed Christianity as one "barbarian" contender among the empire's many religions and many of its roots were authentically foreign, though we must remember that the version of Christianity that finally came to power had been pioneered by the "Hellenists" of the early community (Acts 6.1). We find the same insider-outsider stance among the late Platonists, whom we might otherwise have expected to be the champions of Hellenism against its enemies. Yet with few exceptions like Julian, they were not, as they too were trying to graft "barbarian" supplements onto the Hellenic tradition. Both Christians and Platonists in late antiquity praised their teachers for knowing the theology of "both Greeks and barbarians."[136] Each now had a specialized allure.

Consider the progression from Plotinos to Proklos.[137] Plotinos (AD 205–270) knew himself to belong to the mainstream of Hellenic philosophy. In fact, he equated "the Greeks" with Plato, a narrowly philosophical sense

---

[133] Cf. Ando (2004) 98.     [134] Momigliano (1971); Fowden (1986) 214–215; Hartog (2001) 73–74.

[135] Pseudo-Plato (Philippos of Opous?), *Epinomis* 987d; Klearchos in Josephos, *Against Apion* 1.180.

[136] Cf. Gregorios Thaumatourgos, *An Address and Panegyric to Origenes* 13, with Marinos, *Proklos, or on Happiness* 22.

[137] I am indebted to Athanassiadi (2006) esp. 129–132.

of Hellenism that implied a defensive awareness of competing "national" schools of thought (this sense would be revived by Michael Psellos eight centuries later). Plotinos attacked the Gnostics: what was good in them was not new (it had already been said by the Greeks, i.e., Plato) and what was new in them was not good. Plotinos therefore cast himself as a defender of the Greeks against Gnostic misuse and assigned to his students the task of debunking other texts of "alien wisdom." Porphyrios (232–ca. 305), who proved that certain books attributed to Zoroaster were recent forgeries, was actually a scholar with very wide-ranging interests. He combed through the religions and traditions of many of the nations of the East in order to construct a single and universal true philosophy, but in this he still positioned himself as a Greek looking out. His sources for foreign customs were Greek and he operated intellectually an entirely Greek framework. He even consented to change his own name from its Semitic original Malchos.[138]

After Porphyrios Greek philosophy – what we call Neoplatonism – became increasingly seduced by the "barbarian" allure. This was complemented on the ethical side by the exaltation of religious, mystical, and priestly virtues at the expense of the civic and even the intellectual virtues of the classical tradition, and on the epistemological side by the acceptance of divine revelation over rational thought, for instance of barbarian oracles over logical argumentation. Certainly, Greek thinkers had always experimented in these directions, but around AD 300 we can document a shift in the dominant paradigm, as hieratic and anti-Greek elements came to the fore. The confluence of these changes, complementing the "distrust of the mind" prominent in Christian circles,[139] has not been explained and is difficult to define in the anti-rationalist climate of much recent scholarship (historians of philosophy just pass the torch at this point to scholars of religion). These trends matured in Iamblichos of Chalkis (d. ca. 325), who insisted on the divine power of untranslated barbarian names and championed the mystical practice of theurgy, capping philosophy with pious magic. Of course, his entire system is unthinkable outside the Greek philosophical tradition, but it is set here in the *service* of mysticism, divination, prayer, ritual, and theurgy, whose highest perfections he understood to be non-Greek. It is not yet clear whether Iamblichos – like the *Chaldaean Oracles* and Hermetic texts he liked to read – represented a lurch essentially within Greek circles toward a "barbarian" self-presentation or

---

[138] Plotinos, *Enneads* 2.9.6. Porphyrios, *On the Life of Plotinos and the Order of his Books* 16; see Millar (1997); Schott (2005) 279, 288–294.
[139] MacMullen (1990) ch. 11; cf. Inglebert (2001) 204–209, 274–278.

whether we are witnessing here genuine non-Greek elements breaking out of the margins and expressing themselves in the language of later Greek philosophy. The author of one of the Hermetica – those quasi-philosophical revelations put in the mouth of Hermes Trismegistos, a.k.a. the Egyptian Thoth – admitted that translating Egyptian produces distortion "for Greek philosophy is only the noise of words."[140]

Unlike Plotinos, Iamblichos did not situate himself primarily within the Greek tradition, claiming inspiration from "Egyptian" and "Chaldaean" sources, though what this meant is unclear. Certainly, no Egyptian who was unfamiliar with the subtleties of Greek metaphysics could have understood his writings. A wealthy scion of a Syrian priestly-princely family, Iamblichos attacked "the Greeks" for translating foreign names, which neutralized the mystic power of their original forms. Complementing the anti-Hellenic rhetoric of contemporary Christians, he asserted often that whatever was good in Greek philosophy was actually learned by Pythagoras and Plato from oriental masters. Iamblichos was searching for barbarian "authenticity." Yet even though he takes on the authorial persona of an Egyptian priest in one work, at one point he slips and refers to "all the Greeks and barbarians." And one of his contemporary followers (in the early fourth century) saw him as "the savior of Hellenism (τὸ ἑλληνικόν)" – whatever that could have meant in an age when many words were quickly changing their meanings. Iamblichos' anti-Hellenism, moreover, did little to dampen Julian's enthusiasm for Greece, and Julian was probably his most passionate disciple.[141]

The late Platonists, then, whom Christian teachers regarded as their most dangerous philosophical foes, were not primarily interested in defending any ideal of Hellenism. After Plotinos, their allegiance was to "multi-ethnic" systems of divine knowledge of which Hellenism was only one component; the language, terminology, modes, and doctrines of what we call ancient Greek philosophy were now easily subsumed under various barbarian labels based on the thesis that Pythagoras and Plato had learned all in the East. This Hellenistic Jewish idea had in fact been challenged in the early third century by the sophist Philostratos of Athens and the scholarly compiler Diogenes Laertios, both of whom belonged more to the waning world of the Second

---

[140] *Corpus Hermeticum* 16.1–2; see Fowden (1986) 37–38; for the Hermetica between Greece and Egypt, ibid. 72–74; Hengel (1974) v. I, 212–214. For the provenance of the *Chaldaean Oracles*, see Kingsley (1995) 304 n. 48; Athanassiadi (1999) and (2006) 39–47, and 157–158 for the Hermetica.

[141] Iamblichos, *On the Mysteries* 1.1, 7.5, 4.6; see Athanassiadi (2006) 155–162; in general, Shaw (1995); for his follower, ibid. 151, 169, 187, citing previous treatments; Fowden (1986) 131–141.

Sophistic than to the innovations of Neoplatonism. Diogenes devoted his preface to the refutation of all who claim that philosophy began among barbarians (whether Egyptians, Chaldaeans, or Zoroastrians). Not only philosophy, he counters, but the human race itself began with the Greeks (1.1–12) – whatever that means. And in his highly Atticizing life of the Pythagorean sage Apollonios, Philostratos, who was "Greek to the point of vanity,"[142] affirmed the superiority of Hellenic philosophy and ways of life in order to neutralize and even subsume barbarian "encroachments."[143]

The later Platonists, by contrast, viewed barbarian wisdom as superior to Hellenic philosophy in decisive respects. Moreover, they neglected cultural sites that could have supported alternative, non-philosophical, versions of Hellenism, such as history and rhetoric. Most were not great stylists and despised rhetoric, seeing themselves as mere "technicians" of metaphysics.[144] Proklos (AD 410–485) exemplifies this simultaneous narrowing of Hellenism and expansion into alien wisdom. According to his biographer Marinos, Proklos used to say that he would abolish all ancient writings except the *Chaldaean Oracles* and Plato's *Timaios* if he could, because too many people read them unintelligently. This sits oddly beside his own wide reading; at any rate, it sounds like something one says in the safety of knowing that it cannot happen, a dramatic way of highlighting what is really important.[145] But all this made the Platonists unfit and unwilling to defend any ideal of Hellenism as comprehensively as Julian had attempted. Julian, however, was trained in rhetoric, modeled his political and military career on the heroes of old, and enjoyed Homer for the real world that Homer brought into being.

By AD 405 Hellenism has come to such a pass that Synesios of Kyrene, who was a true philosopher and a skilled rhetor, could declare that "a philosopher should not be evil in any way or boorish, but should be initiated in the mysteries of the Graces and be a Hellene in a most precise sense, namely that he should be able to hold converse with humanity through his familiarity with every work of literature." This was the most that he could offer in defense of his Hellenism against obscurantist monks and Platonists who despised eloquence: good manners, literary refinement, and being in touch with the tradition. It was not nothing, to be sure, and it would be a real accomplishment when Byzantines could later admit even that. "Hellenism as he understood it was a view of the world necessary and basic to the sanity of

[142] Edwards (2004b) 219.     [143] Swain (1999).     [144] E.g., Athanassiadi (2006) 192–194, 203, 207.
[145] Marinos, *Proklos, or on Happiness* 38.

any religion, even Christianity."[146] But we should not lose sight of his liminal and, in Byzantium, increasingly untenable position: a Platonist student of Hypatia; a married bishop who did not accept the Resurrection except, at most, as a useful myth; a descendant of the Herakleidai who wrote hymns in Doric; an aristocrat who enjoyed hunting, chasing bandits across the desert, and high politics in Constantinople; such a man had more room in his soul than most.

[146] Synesios, *Dion, or on My Way of Life* 4.42b and *passim*; cf. Bregman (1982) 127–137 (quotation from 136); Cameron and Long (1993) 62 ff.

# Hellenism in limbo: the middle years (400–1040)

Between Synesios and Psellos, so for a period of six centuries, Hellenic identity went into abeyance. It had only a hypothetical existence, being a relic of the past that could be glimpsed in ancient texts; or the antithesis of Christianity, something that could both negate and complement but whose power was never actualized; or fragmented markers that signified little, for example the mere fact of language or geography. Not all of its elements even survived the end of antiquity. Having described the storms of late antiquity, it is useful to take stock of Hellenism and see what was jettisoned, what retained, and what washed up on the shores of Byzantium, to be salvaged in later times. The religions of the ancient Greeks, for example, were more or less ended by the end of antiquity. Some of their elements were absorbed into Christianity, but not in a way that threatened or could spark a revival. It was not until the very end of Byzantium, with Georgios Gemistos Plethon, that a revival was even imagined, and it too led nowhere. The end of paganism entailed the obsolescence of certain ancient centers of Greek identity, chiefly Delphi and Olympia. During the early Roman empire, when Hellenism spread throughout the East, those places had served to draw attention to the Greek homeland. Now a de-Hellenized Greece found itself with hardly any Christian credentials and no imperial capital.

Along with the religions of antiquity, many of the social customs and cultural practices that defined ancient Hellenism, such as gymnastics, were also abolished. Christianity had likewise created a new art and architecture to serve its rituals and project its ideology, and whatever traces of the civic mentality of the polis remained yet in the time of Julian were gradually lost during the course of late antiquity through a combination of heavy-handed imperial control and the damage wrought by a turbulent history. The land of Greece itself remained and was still called Hellas, but its inhabitants no longer took pride in this. They too were now just Romans and Christians, not really different from Byzantines elsewhere. As local inhabitants of Greece they were now often called Helladikoi ("those who lived in Greece") and not Hellenes ("Greeks"), to avoid confusing them with pagans.[1] The Greek language also remained, but it too could just as well be called "the language of the Romans" and, before the period that will be examined in the second part of this study, few took pride in the fact that their language was Greek anyway. Defining elements of ancient Hellenism that did survive, then, were relabeled to serve new ideologies and could not compete with the Roman and Christian outlook of Byzantium.

The aspect of ancient Hellenism that could potentially carve a space out for itself within the basic modes and orders of orthodox Romania was classical literature – Hellenism as the *paideia* of the elite – which was mostly preserved for its intrinsic intellectual and aesthetical worth despite the radical heteronomies that it encoded. As we will see, it was the philosophy, science, poetry, rhetoric, and literature of the ancient Greeks, the equal of which no other ancient people had produced, that stimulated new Byzantine Hellenicities. But the reinvention of Hellenic identities through *paideia* was not a necessary historical development; it was activated by eccentric individuals under special circumstances, and not until the eleventh century. We see this if we consider the literary culture of the fifth and sixth centuries AD, when Christianity enjoyed a comfortable supremacy and feared "paganism" far less than it had in the fourth century, which had been an era of both open and simmering religious polemics.

In those last two centuries of antiquity, we witness the emergence of what we may call a Christian classical culture, though, as mentioned, it did not result in any new transformations of Greek identity such as proliferated in the period AD 100–400. This development has not yet been studied as a distinct literary and cultural phenomenon. Until the fourth century, Christian literature – or the texts that Christians wrote – were exclusively *about* what it meant to be Christian, to explain the new doctrines, polemicize against paganism, fashion new moralities and social identities, and recast classical culture to serve new interests. But in the fifth and sixth centuries we have works written by (or for) Christians that cover a fuller range of human experience in forms that imitated and built upon classical literature. We also find a closer engagement with the classics in works of a more narrowly Christian nature, including the use of quasi-pagan personifications and images that would have been unthinkable in earlier Christian centuries. We may imagine this development in two ways, depending on our view of agency: first, as a turn within Christian culture to the classics, facilitated by the waning of the anxiety over paganism; or, second, as a

[1] Jüthner (1923) 114.

continuation of classical culture, only by Christians. Classical *paideia* had a dynamic history and attractions of its own, and it is not surprising that it found followers among the Christians. Future studies will show whether these were Christians who turned to the classics or whether we now have rhetors and scholars who only happened to be Christians, perhaps only on Sunday. It becomes difficult in this period to tell the difference between them and non-Christians who were addressing the same educated audience.

Already in the fourth century, Christians are attested as public professors of philosophy (e.g., Marius Victorinus at Rome) and rhetoric (e.g., Prohairesios at Athens, possibly a Christian). The politician and teacher Ausonius of Bordeaux penned a Christian prayer, but his corpus consists mostly of playful, witty, and erotic poems. Gregorios of Nazianzos made room for the "joy of literature" in his project for a new Christian *paideia*, though it is unclear how much independence he was willing to grant to its aesthetics.[2] By the end of the fifth century, we can speak of a Christian classical literature, in both Latin and Greek. Dracontius in Vandal North Africa wrote Christian and secular – in fact mythological – poems. Boethius in Rome produced technical philosophical works that owed nothing to his faith, and even his more famous *Consolation of Philosophy* was neutral in this respect. In the East, the traditions of rhetoric, episto-lography, and *ekphrasis* were continued by writers who happened to be Christians and who occasionally wrote on Christian topics. Most of their works, however, have no religious content and are concerned with style and the traditions of Greek rhetoric.

The orators of Gaza around the turn of the fifth century exemplify this fusion, or rather juxtaposition, of cultural and religious loyalties. Prokopios wrote Biblical commentaries and polemicized against the philosopher Proklos but also produced a panegyric for the emperor Anastasios and wrote rhetorical exercises including a description of scenes painted from a tragedy of Euripides and a character-sketch (*ethopoeia*) of Aphrodite mourn-ing for Adonis and another of Phoenix (of the *Iliad*) mourning for Achilles. His student Chorikios wrote an experimental *Defense of Mimes* in one moment (mimes performed lascivious ancient myths) and described the churches of his native city in another. Aineias of Gaza wrote a dialogue, the *Theophrastos*, which advocated Christian points without giving offense to non-Christians and avoiding technical Christian vocabulary. The work is a display of rhetorical tact and skill and has been contrasted to the *Ammonios*

---

[2] McGuckin (2006) 209–210. Only specific points will be referenced in this survey. In general, see also Inglebert (2001) 561, 570.

by Aineias' contemporary Zacharias, also a rhetor and later a bishop. This dialogue is more aggressively Christian, and does not flaunt mythological allusions.[3] The difference between them is indicative of the range of attitudes that could be expected of Christian writers and audiences.

Imitation of the classics – a term that should be understood as subtle adaptation and variation and not as unimaginative and slavish copying – was now practiced within Christian genres. As we saw, the ecclesiastical historians of the fifth century admitted secular history into their narratives and even situated themselves within the tradition of classical historiography, which Eusebios of Kaisareia had explicitly disavowed. Even the author of the *Life and Miracles of Saint Thekla* (mid-fifth century) intelligently modeled important aspects of his work on Herodotos. By the end of the sixth century, the rhetor and church lawyer Euagrios was devising quasi-mythological personifications of concepts such as "opportunity" (*kairos*) for his *Ecclesiastical History*, a literary choice that, again, Eusebios had deliberately avoided. In short, it had become possible for Christian authors and artists to use casually images from ancient mythology "for ornament, entertainment, or instruction."[4]

This climate seems to have even produced a poet, Nonnos of Panopolis in Egypt, who wrote an epic religious poem on Dionysos in India (the *Dionysiaka*) as well as a verse paraphrase of the Gospel of John. Debates over whether it really was one man who wrote both works tend to reveal more about our assumptions than about his time, but the strangeness of it cannot be denied. A parallel fusion may be seen in the exactly contemporary conversion of the Parthenon in Athens into a church of the Mother of God – the Christian Parthenos. This was done in such a way that it preserved much of the Parthenon's architecture, its pagan and Hellenic associations, and civic role. The conversion was not necessarily made by "Christians," at least as we are used to imagining them (i.e., as not being "pagans"). Throughout Byzantium, Athens would remain a curious laboratory for the synthesis of classical and Christian cultural and religious elements.[5] We must also recognize that many of the writers in the sixth-century East – e.g., the jurist Tribonianus, the chronicler and prosopographer Hesychios, the

[3] Watts (2005) 216–218.
[4] Liebeschuetz (1995) 196 and (2001) 225–231; ecclesiastical historians: see p. 137 above; Thekla: Johnson (2006) 19–21, 114, 120; Euagrios: Chesnut (1986) 191, 219–220; also Bowersock (1990) 65, 66. Dioskoros of Aphrodito (in Egypt), a sixth-century lawyer and poet, well reflects this synthesis of mythology and Christianity: MacCoull (1988) ch. 3, with commentary. For examples from art and daily objects, Kalavrezou (2003) *passim*; for architecture, Saradi (1997).
[5] Nonnos: Johnson (2006) 95–99. Parthenon: Kaldellis (2008).

professor of Latin and antiquarian Ioannes Lydos, the historians Prokopios and Agathias, and the philosophers Simplikios, Olympiodoros, and others – were probably (in some cases certainly) not Christians, though most of them knowingly and very carefully wrote for a mostly Christian audience. That audience was interested now not so much in religious controversy (which at this late hour was largely confined to philosophical disputations) but rather in jurisprudence, scholarship, logic, rhetoric, history, and poetry for their own sake. In other words, a secular Christian culture had appeared.[6]

Some fictitious erotic letters were written in the early sixth century by a certain Aristainetos, revealing an extensive first-hand command of the classics. Toward the end of the century the lawyer, poet, and historian Agathias and his friends in Constantinople exchanged and collected erotic (and even homoerotic) epigrams as well as Christian and pagan poems. Apparently, there was nothing incongruous in writing a description of Hagia Sophia one day and an epigram about feeling up a woman's soft breasts on the next. We should not assume that any of this was a faithful reflection of contemporary life.[7] Such works were both less and more than historical sources: they were literature. Christian classicism flourished into the seventh century. Stephanos of Alexandria (a native of Athens) was appointed by the emperor Herakleios (AD 610–642) to teach philosophy in Constantinople; the poet Georgios of Pisidia combined Biblical and epic images in praising the emperor's campaigns; and the lawyer Theophylaktos Simokattes wrote a classicizing, though openly Christian, history of the reign of the emperor Maurikios (AD 582–602) as well as a collection of letters that included erotic and other traditional rhetorical themes.

The Christian classicism of the fifth through the early seventh centuries produced authors such as Synesios, Prokopios, and Georgios of Pisidia who wrote in different genres and whom the Byzantines would regard as established classics alongside their Second Sophistic, Hellenistic, and Attic predecessors. This literary movement has not yet been studied in its own right and tends to be viewed through the distorting lens of the pagan–Christian polemic of the fourth century. As can be seen from the above survey, its expressions went beyond the facile combination of Hellenic style with Christian content, the resolution that some early theorists of Christian literature had called for. Ancient genres, which corresponded to basic ways of viewing the world, simply continued to be written and consumed, only now by Christians, with no alteration in their fundamental modes or moral outlook.

---

[6] For these figures, see Kaldellis (1999b), (2003), (2004a), (2005a), and (2005c).
[7] Cf. McCail (1971); Trombley (2001) v. II, 48–49; Lauxterman (2003) 131–132.

It is not clear, on the other hand, to what degree we may talk of fusion here, since in most respects the Christian and the classical sat side by side and were not integrated on a deeper level. Different codes were devised for different circumstances. For example, classical *exempla* are rarer in letters to churchmen and monks than to secular addressees or one's own school friends, and rarer in theological or exegetical than in rhetorical or poetic works. Somehow they were deemed less appropriate in those contexts, limiting the stage on which classicism could be performed.[8] A bishop who fulminated against the "Hellenic disease" in one treatise could politely write the next day to a pagan rhetorician and recommend Christian students to be educated in the "Hellenic eloquence." A professor could mock the Greek gods in a Christian oration and then describe the luxurious beauty of Aphrodite to show off his skill in an *ekphrasis*.

Still, if we exclude Synesios, who was truly ambiguous, the flame of a "Christian Hellenism" seems not to have been ignited by the creative sparks of this period. And hard-line Christian attitudes continued to flourish alongside it all. Some continued to reject Greek *paideia*, insisting that Scripture could satisfy all needs. A more subtle response was to use poetry and rhetoric to proclaim the Christian message and even to denounce "Athens." The great liturgical poet of the sixth century, Romanos Melodos, proclaimed the triumph of the "Galilaians" over the Athenians, sarcastically using Julian's derogatory term for Christians. In another poem (of a kind known as *kontakia*), he sneered at all pagan philosophers and writers.[9] The presumed defeat of the cultural ideal associated with Athens was literally being celebrated from the pulpit of Hagia Sophia in Constantinople. It was at this time (late fifth to early seventh centuries) that the most famous hymn in the orthodox canon was composed. It is called the Akathistos, because the congregation stands while it is being sung, and it is in honor of the Mother of God. In the Salutations of the Theotokos, it gloats over the defeat of Athens.

> Hail, vessel of God's wisdom,
> Hail, repository of his providence,
> Hail, you who reveal the philosophers as unwise,
> Hail, you who refute the vain weavers of words,
> Hail, for the bickerers are now feebleminded,

[8] Littlewood (1988) 149 and (1999) 32–33; Demoen (1996) 128–141, 204–206; Lambakis (2001) 126; Ljubarskij (2004a) 118 n. 62; for other considerations, Mullett (1997) 160.
[9] Romanos Melodos, *Kontakion* 31: *On the Mission of the Apostles* 16.2; cf. *Kontakion* 33: *On Pentecost* 17 (pp. 247, 265); in general, see Hunger (1984).

Hail, for the poets of myths have wasted away,
Hail, you who sliced through the Athenians' twisting.[10]

Beautiful though these poems may be, they are also hostile to the life of the mind and the world of letters. But most educated Christians believed that there were ways other than denunciation for engaging with the classical tradition, ways that could serve the worship of God. Besides, they did not want years of training and all their skills and thoughts corralled into a series of "Hails." The moment of Christian classicism that we have surveyed is proof of this. Unfortunately, we cannot say what that moment would have led to in the long run had it not been violently destroyed along with the world of which it was a part.

The great war between Byzantium and Persia in the early seventh century, which lasted for almost three decades and witnessed the long occupation of the East by Persian armies, left the empire in ruins and financially exhausted. Victory proved transient as Arab armies swept through the Near East and North Africa, seizing and then annexing about three fourths of Rome's territory. Within the empire all efforts were directed to military defense, as regular invasions depopulated both towns and country. High culture came to an abrupt end. The next century and a half, from the mid-seventh to the late eighth century, were the bleakest in Roman history in almost all ways, certainly in terms of literature, art, architecture, and social life. The moment of Christian classicism we have been describing ended, and was only very slowly recaptured.

Most of the writing that survives from what has been called Byzantium's "Dark Age" consists of hymns, theology, saints' lives, and canonical regulations. The controversy over icons that erupted in the early eighth century occupied the attention of the empire's learned men for over a century and diverted it away from literature and into polemical disputation. From the start, then, the textual culture of middle Byzantium was more ecclesiastical, Biblical, and theological, as well as more sparse, than that of late antiquity. The origins of this shift have been placed as early as the late sixth century,[11] and in any case it was intensified by the conditions of the Dark Age. But already at the end of the eighth century we begin to again encounter learned figures such as Tarasios (imperial administrator and then patriarch in 784–806); his student and biographer Ignatios the deacon;

---

[10] *Akathistos Hymnos* 16.6–12 (p. 36).    [11] Cameron (1981); Liebeschuetz (2001) 239–248.

and Methodios, who also become patriarch toward the end of his life (843–847); all of whom clearly had a good classical education and could "imitate" ancient literature in the subtle and innovative way of Byzantine *mimesis*. Ignatios, for example, fashioned a Platonic dialogue on the question of icons in his *Life of the Patriarch Nikephoros*, a clever fusion of Christian and classical literary methods, and his writings are otherwise full of classical *exempla*. He and Methodios wrote works in many genres, both prose and verse, indicating the existence of an audience for literature.[12] The greatest monument of middle Byzantine classicism was certainly the corpus of hundreds of reviews of ancient texts written by the future patriarch Photios in the mid-ninth century, known as the *Bibliotheke*. This collection reveals that scholars of this period were again interested in reading ancient literature, had access to many more books of it than survive today, and, more importantly, that they were willing and able to appreciate them on purely stylistic grounds, even in defiance of their religious affiliation.[13]

There is no reason to rehearse here the story of how Byzantium received the classical tradition in the period of revival between the "gap" of 640–780 and the later gap of almost a century that the philosopher Michael Psellos claimed had existed before he came onto the scene in the eleventh century. The story of manuscripts, libraries, schools, encyclopedias, and lexica has been outlined by others.[14] By the tenth century, Byzantium had again invested its resources into creating a highly sophisticated if unsystematic forum for classical education. The state sponsored faculties of higher education in the capital which drew students from all the provinces, and maintained libraries and archives. The quality and complexity of prose and verse steadily increased until near-perfect imitations (even forgeries) of ancient authors could be produced. Attic rhetoric soared far above spoken everyday Greek to heights of obscurity and convolution; literary reputations now had to be defended against accusations of excess. The Byzantine scholar seems to have had fairly easy access to ancient texts (no long journeys were required to locate manuscripts), and to more of it than survives today. He (rarely she) was assisted by a wide range of lexicographical, prosopographical, anthological, and encyclopedic reference works, the direct ancestors of those in use today. Ancient texts were emended and improved just as they were

---

[12] Ignatios the deacon, *Life of the Patriarch Nikephoros* 172–185; for Nikephoros' education, 148–151; for multiple genres, see Mango's introduction to Ignatios' correspondence, 7–18; Lauxtermann (2003) 111–113, 141–142.
[13] In general, see Treadgold (1980) and (1984).    [14] Wilson (1983); Lemerle (1986).

being copied anew into minuscule script. This scholarly activity and the rhetorical training that formed the base of all higher education contributed directly to the revival of letters. Histories, biographies, saints' lives, sermons, and other genres became increasingly more sophisticated in their literary ambitions and nuanced in their presentation of human issues.[15] Ancient models were imitated with greater originality.

What is important for our theme, however, is that, with one exception, this so-called Byzantine Humanism did not lead to any experiments in the fashioning of new Hellenic identities. Also, little was produced by way of Christian literary mythography and mythological art.[16] Photios was puzzled by the pagan myths that he encountered in Christian writers of late antiquity and disapproved of the eroticism of the ancient novels.[17]

There were less friendly readers than Photios. Fundamentalist attitudes were more to the fore than they had been among the Christian philosophers and sophists of late antiquity. Many voices in Byzantium between the sixth and the tenth centuries called for the rejection of Greek *paideia* and proclaimed again the triumph of Paul over Plato and of Christian New Rome over pagan Athens.[18] In the early tenth century, Ioannes Kaminiates, who wrote a first-hand account of the capture of Thessalonike by the Arabs in 904, noted that Orpheus, the Muse of Homer, and the babbling of the Sirens were as nothing next to the hymns sung in the church of St. Demetrios. They stood for falsehood, deceit, and the vanity of the Greeks.[19] In his will, the tenth-century diplomat and bishop of Synada Leon, a witty and attractive personality, confessed among his sins that "I didn't pray at all, but spent the whole day loafing instead; or I didn't devote my attention to religious texts; or I spent more time than I should reading 'outer' literature."[20] This could be Jerome in his dream, "Ciceronian" rather than Christian.

The persistence of such anxieties proves that "outer" literature was always on probation; it posed a standing temptation and so its use had to be continually renegotiated, qualified, atoned for. And it harbored more serious dangers than merely taking time away from prayer. One hymn

---

[15] See, e.g., Ljubarskij (1992a); for poetry, Lauxtermann (2003) ch. 4. This revival used to be called the Macedonian Renaissance after the dynasty that ruled from 867, but the revival preceded it and was not stimulated by imperial patronage in quite this way.

[16] Hunger (1969–1970) 19; Weitzmann (1981) 50.

[17] E.g., Photios, *Bibliotheke* 160; cf. Lauxtermann (1999).

[18] Cited by Browning (1975b) 18–19; Garzya (1992) 39–40; Saradi (1995) 12–13.

[19] Ioannes Kaminiates, *The Capture of Thessalonike* 11. There is a controversy about the date of this work, but the tenth century is probable. For Christian views on the Sirens, see Rahner (1963) ch. 7.

[20] Leon of Synada, *Letter* 31 (his will).

condemned the early ninth-century iconoclast patriarch Ioannes the Grammarian as "equal to the Hellenes, who boasted of their texts, which the voices of the just have justly scattered."[21] The truth of the accusation is not relevant here, only the acknowledgment by many Byzantines of its likelihood. Ioannes' (and Photios') contemporary Leon the Philosopher is a better-known case. An inventor, mathematician, archbishop of Thessalonike (briefly), classical scholar and editor of Plato, poet and professor of "outer" philosophy at Constantinople, and one of the first Byzantine authors in whom we can safely detect the influence of Lucian, he was denounced as a Hellene after his death by a rather hysterical student. Leon, we are told, lost his soul in a sea of impiety and was deceived by the philosophers he so loved. Leon had in fact called himself a Hellene in his own lifetime, at any rate according to the title of one of his epigrams: "Leon the Philosopher, the so-called Hellene, to Himself." Certainly Leon was no "pagan," nor was he claiming to be such. His defensiveness in the title, however, implies an effort to ameliorate a preexisting stigma. What others had intended as an accusation, probably of heterodoxy – and we must not forget that "a charge of Hellenism was no laughing matter"[22] – he was now turning around and presenting as a badge of philosophy and *paideia*. This ambitious and even deliberately shocking amelioration of the terrible word prefigures the experiments of later centuries, which we will examine below. In the epigram itself, Leon thanks Fortune for giving him a quiet life in accordance with Epicurean teachings as well as freedom from lust.[23] Whatever the relation between the poem's authorial persona and Leon himself, we know that he and his circle were involved in the promotion and production of erotic literature, which seems to have elicited condemnation from contemporaries and which would not be continued before the twelfth century. Byzantium was not yet ready for Leon's brazenly Hellenic version of classical scholarship and philosophy.[24] When, toward the end of the ninth century, Konstantinos Kephalas prepared an early version of the *Greek Anthology*, he made sure to place Christian epigrams first "even if it displeases the Hellenes," as he put it rather defensively.[25]

---

[21] Lemerle (1986) 164.
[22] Cameron (1997) 7; cf. Cameron (1982) 268–270 for the first such accusations (against the prefect Kyros of Panopolis); in general, Rochow (1991).
[23] See Lemerle (1986) ch. 6, esp. 198–204 for Konstantinos the Sicilian and Leon's poem (= *Greek Anthology* 15.12); also Westerink (1986) 199–200; Katsaros (1993); for Lucian, Robinson (1979) 68–69.
[24] Lauxtermann (1999) 169–170; (2003) 96–107; for the problem of voice, ibid. 37–38.
[25] *Greek Anthology*, pr. to book 1; cf. Lauxtermann (2003) 97.

It is no proof of Leon's orthodoxy that he was praised by the philosopher and diplomat Leon Choirosphaktes (ca. 900). This Leon was himself accused of Hellenism in turn and has recently been exposed as unortho-dox.[26] The eleventh-century philosopher Psellos was also accused of hete-rodoxy by contemporaries who suspected that his involvement with Hellenic philosophy had gone too far, a charge that, as we will see, was quite plausible. At the end of Byzantine history, Georgios Gemistos Plethon more or less openly broke with Christianity in favor of a revived Hellenism that he conceived in such universal terms that he reminds us of Julian. In fact, Plethon, like Choirosphaktes and other dissident intellectuals in Byzantium, was compared to Julian.[27] The following chapters will bridge part of the gap between Psellos and Plethon, though it will not support K. N. Sathas' eccentric belief in a continuous chain of pagan-philosophical Hellenism running throughout Byzantine history.[28] Hellenism was not always philosophy, nor was philosophy the same as paganism even when it broke with Christian doctrines. Nor will the following chapters validate Julian's belief that *any* noble mind who receives a Greek education will invariably reject Christianity. Still, despite the undeniable fact that many Byzantines managed to successfully combine both worlds, Greek and Christian, all believed that the two were ultimately distinct and that Hellenism was potentially subversive of both doctrine and good morals.

Between the defeat of Julian and his friends in the fourth century and the revival of philosophy and classicizing literature in the eleventh and twelfth centuries, Hellenism – the discursive construction of Greek identity – lay in a kind of limbo. It had always been flexible and adaptable, but, with the exception of a few bold men such as Synesios and Leon the Philosopher, no one had any interest in ameliorating a term whose real or imaginary adherents were angrily denounced and persecuted by the religious and political authorities. The hard-liners' loud attack on Hellenism-as-paganism discouraged cultural investment and pride in other configurations of the Greek tradition, even those that were inno-cuous to the faith. It was only when Psellos attempted to revive ancient philosophy in the eleventh century that Hellenism became a permanent contributor to the ongoing negotiation about the articulation of Byzantine

---

[26] Magdalino (1997); for his praise of Leon, Lemerle (1986) 203–204.
[27] Gennadios Scholarios, *Letter to the Empress regarding Gemistos' Book* (p. 152).
[28] Sathas (1888) i–lxiii.

culture. It was a philosopher who pioneered the reaction, but it need not have happened that way.

Hellenism, as we have seen throughout, was a complex sign. Even in antiquity it was a zone of permanent contestation, referring to a wide range of existential attributes that remained always potential until they were creatively selected, valorized, and recombined at the instigation of specific circumstances and men. The Panhellenist anti-Persian ideology of the Athenians in Herodotos was as much a political act as the national reform instigated by the Hellenizers in pre-Maccabean Jerusalem; as the imagination of the antiquarian Pausanias, who dreamt the freedom of a conquered nation; as the Gallic philosopher Favorinus, who wanted his statue in Corinth to be reinstated; as the professor of rhetoric Libanios, who canvassed the late Roman aristocracy for students; and as the Roman emperor Julian with his Hellenic-Chaldaean infatuations. In the middle Byzantine period, until it began to be reassembled for new purposes, Hellenism lay dormant, dispersed into marginal or banal settings. It meant many things, though there was rarely any confusion or polemic about them. All these different senses could be used in the same text without trouble, for they were banal and did not destabilize the consensus of Christian Romania. When we begin to see them used in ways that we do not immediately understand, in ways for which prior usage has not prepared us, as happens in Psellos and Ioannes Tzetzes, then we will know that something new was afoot.

Before moving on to those innovative developments, let us enumerate the senses of Hellenism that would have been familiar to Byzantine writers before Psellos changed the intellectual scene.

First, something could be called Hellenic in connection with the geographical region of mainland Greece or, more specifically, with the Byzantine "theme" (province) of Hellas. This usage never conveyed a national sense, unless we understand nationality in the loose Roman manner, i.e., geographically, in which case Greeks were on a par with Paphlagonians and Thrakians. The term "Helladikos" was often used instead to avoid confusion with the pagan Greeks ("Hellenes").[29] Moreover, when Byzantines did begin to refer to themselves as Greeks in a national sense, in the thirteenth century, they were not expanding upon this territorial meaning. Unlike its modern version, national Hellenism in Byzantium was not a

[29] Charanis (1972) XVII with XXI 3–5; pace XVII 619 on nationality. For a bishop "from the land of the Hellenes," see Constantelos (1998) 168; Curta (2004) 528 n. 46. For Byzantine Hellas, see Koder and Hild (1976) esp. 37–40. For a "judge of the Hellenes," i.e., of the theme of Hellas, see Ioannes Skylitzes, *Historical Synopsis: Konstantinos IX Monomachos* 1 (p. 423). Garzya (1992) 30–31 confuses geography and ethnicity.

function of landscape, territory, or "place" in general,[30] at any rate not before the protonationalism of Georgios Gemistos Plethon, who identified the Peloponnese as the ancestral homeland of the Greeks.[31] The only instance of local "Hellenic" pride known to me occurs in the *Life of Loukas of Steiris* (tenth century), where the glory of the theme of Hellas is contrasted to that of the adjacent theme of the Peloponnese, which also had a claim on the saint's legacy. This had to do with regional pride sparked by a dispute over a saint; it was incidental that his monastery was in Greece. Though the text never refers to the theme's inhabitants as Hellenes, it does call pagans "the *ethnê*," probably to avoid confusion.[32]

Second, by Hellenes the Byzantines could also mean the ancient Greeks in the same way as do modern historians. These Greeks were an ancient, pagan, and foreign people like the Egyptians and the Persians, only they were better known through their history, literature, and monuments; also, they happened to speak the same language as the Byzantines. But before the thirteenth century there was no clear sense among the Byzantines that any of these ancient Greeks had survived into modern times and, apart from the ambiguous and indirect Arabic testimony that we discussed earlier, no speculation or interest regarding the historical fate of the ancient Greek nation.[33]

Third – and most prominently – pagans of any kind were called Hellenes, including both the ancient Greeks and certain barbarians beyond the empire's current frontiers. Given that the ancient Greeks were pagans, this sense and the previous one were often fused whenever a Byzantine denounced the folly of the "Greeks" who, say, believed in the gods of Homer. Both meanings were perhaps reflected in Michael Attaleiates' report of an earthquake that leveled a "Hellenic temple" in Kyzikos that had become a local attraction.[34] This was both a pagan temple as opposed to a church (the same word could be used for churches), and it was also a Greek temple in the more historical sense.

Fourth, a Greek (Ἕλλην ἀνὴρ) could be anyone who (simply) spoke Greek. This usage, encountered frequently, was utterly neutral with respect to religion, ethnicity, or social status.[35] When it referred to the mere fact of

---

[30] Cf. Peckham (2001).

[31] Georgios Gemistos Plethon, *Letter to Manuel Palaiologos regarding the Affairs of the Peloponnese* (pp. 248 ff.).

[32] E.g., *The Life of Loukas of Steiris* 50.   [33] See p. 118 above.

[34] Michael Attaleiates, *History* 90. For the ruins of Kyzikos in other writers, see Saradi-Mendelovici (1990) 59. For Hellenes as pagans, see Lechner (1954) 16–46; Rochow (1991).

[35] E.g., Anna Komnene, *Alexiad* 7.3.4: the Greek name of a place (as opposed to Slavic); *hellênizôn* or *Hellên anêr* means to speak Greek rather than another language: Theophylaktos Hephaistos, *Letter* 96 (p. 489); Ioannes Kinnamos, *History* 4.4; many more references exist: see Lechner (1954) 11.

one's language, in other words when it did not denote elite *paideia*, this kind of Hellenism rarely excited interest or pride. It was only the language spoken by most Romans and could therefore also be called "the language of the Romans" instead of "Greek." As we saw earlier, "to Romanize" and "to Hellenize" could mean the same thing in this context. But Byzantine writers knew that Latin was the ancestral language of the Romans, so in other contexts they called their language "Hellenic" or even "Greek": ἐξελληνίσαι could refer to the translation of a text from Latin (or another language) into Greek, and *Graikos* differentiated a Greek-speaking Roman from a Latin-speaker.[36] These labels did not necessarily carry ideological weight, but sometimes they did, as in the exchange of insults between Michael III and pope Nicolaus I in the 860s that we noted above (ch. 2). In the twelfth and thirteenth centuries, the "mere fact" of language acquired a special importance, but that was because the Byzantines were trying to define themselves as "Greek Romans" in the face of conflict, conquest, and persecution by Latin Romans. What had formerly been taken mostly for granted now became a matter of urgent concern.

Fifth – and this was to a degree an extension of the previous sense – Hellenism could denote the possession of classical *paideia*, including facility with rhetorical Greek, a knowledge of philosophy, and even the urbane qualities associated with the Second Sophistic. The young Symeon (and future saint), we are told, decided *not* to perfect his studies by "Hellenizing his tongue with that outside learning (ἐξελληνισθῆναι τὴν γλῶτταν τῇ ἀναλήψει παιδείας τῆς θύραθεν . . . τῆς ἔξωθεν)," i.e., to become a scholar of Attic Greek.[37] The homely writer Kekaumenos likewise confessed that "I did not receive a Hellenic *paideia* and so cannot turn a phrase" (76). Texts that contained useful information but lacked "the Hellenic Muse" or "Hellenic *paideia*" were liable to be rewritten in accordance with higher stylistic standards, as Konstantinos VII Porphyrogennetos did with a treatise on imperial expeditions. Yet in another of his works, the same emperor claims that he will avoid an "Atticized" style in order to communicate more directly.[38] So it seems that Hellenism-as-Atticism offered both advantages and disadvantages.

[36] E.g., Photios, *Bibliotheke* 252 (v. VII, p. 209); Georgios Pachymeres, *History* 13.14 (v. IV, p. 649); "romanize": see p. 114 above; Graikos: see p. 68 above.

[37] Niketas Stethatos, *Life of Symeon the New Theologian* 2; for a tenth-century reference to Hellenic *paideia*, Lemerle (1986) 217. Liudprand of Cremona, *Antapodosis* 3.29, claims that the Bulgarian king Symeon was called a "demi-Greek" because of his progress with Aristotle and Demosthenes as a child (he was educated in Constantinople).

[38] Cf. Konstantinos VII, *What should be done when the emperor goes on campaign* 30–39 (p. 96) with his *De administrando imperio* 1. These modulations were strategic: see Psellos, *Letter KD* 135.

Elite Hellenism was a skill and required training. In a technical rhetorical sense, *Hellenismos* denoted the purity of one's vocabulary according to
a putative classical standard. The debate over what the latter was exactly
had raged since Hellenistic times and continued in Byzantine scholarly
circles.[39] But highbrow Hellenism was not limited to rhetorical conventions. Anna Komnene boasted in the preface of the *Alexiad* that "I have
eagerly studied how to Hellenize to the highest degree, so I am not ignorant
of rhetoric and I am versed in the arts of Aristotle and the dialogues of Plato"
(1.2). Accordingly, Anna tried to write the purest Attic and avoid "barbarisms."[40] Yet her ideal of Hellenism included both rhetoric and philosophy,
and philosophy carried with it a whole range of powers and associations that
could not always be neutralized. It did not necessarily compromise one's
religion, but it was not entirely harmless either. Educated Byzantines
believed that one could acquire *paideia* without ceasing to be a good
Christian, yet they never forgot that Greek culture as a whole was pagan
and worldly and so dangerous and alien. It was θύραθεν or ἔξωθεν, it came
"from outside," and so was strictly speaking not "ours." It *could*, if taken to
extremes or taken on its own terms, imperil one's soul. This is certainly what
happened to Michael Psellos, with whom our story begins anew.

---

[39] Antiquity: Jüthner (1923) 39–43; Athanassiadi-Fowden (1977) 334–335; Swain (1996) 22, 55, 62; Blank
(1998) xxxiv–xl. Byzantium: Kustas (1973) 86, 94; e.g., Ioannes Tzetzes, *Histories* 11.139, 12.576–584
(pp. 436, 492–493), responding to Aphthonios.
[40] See Hunger (1978) v. I, 407–408.

# PART II

# Hellenic revivals in Byzantium

At the turn of the first millennium the empire of New Rome was the oldest and most dynamic state in the world and comprised the most civilized portions of the Christian world. Its borders, long defended by native frontier troops, were being expanded by the most disciplined and techno-logically advanced army of its time. The unity of Byzantine society was grounded in the equality of Roman law and a deep sense of a common and ancient Roman identity; cemented by the efficiency of a complex bureau-cracy; nourished and strengthened by the institutions and principles of the Christian Church; sublimated by Greek rhetoric; and confirmed by the passage of ten centuries. At the end of the reign of Basileios II (976–1025), the longest in Roman history, its territory included Asia Minor and Armenia, the Balkan peninsula south of the Danube, and the southern regions of both Italy and the Crimea. Serbia, Croatia, Georgia, and some Arab emirates in Syria and Mesopotamia had accepted a dependent status.

The empire was never again to be as powerful in the five centuries that yet remained to it, though its decline was neither steady nor inexorable. Crisis invigorated the sources of Roman strength and catastrophe was usually followed by decades of resurgence. The Komnenoi (1081–1185) largely reversed the decline of the late eleventh century and the Laskarids founded a resilient and even expansionist state at Nikaia that managed to reclaim the capital from the aggressors of 1204. Yet much was lost each time the empire was forced to reconstitute itself. By the fourteenth century, the emperors' sway hardly extended beyond the walls of their City and a few dependent lands and islands. Yet, perhaps paradoxically, these four cen-turies of political and military decline witnessed vigorous intellectual growth and progress. Rhetoric and historiography flourished; fiction and philosophy were revived; and the skills of classical scholarship attained a level of perfection not matched in Europe before the later Italian Renaissance. Intellectuals and humanists experimented in new directions, questioning the religion, values, and ideology that had sustained the empire and shaped its cultural development since the triumph of Christianity and the foundation of New Rome in late antiquity.

The second part of this study will examine how these developments resulted in a revival of Hellenism in Byzantium, including the preoccupation with the body of literature that the Byzantines had inherited from the ancient Greeks and the concept itself of being Greek. What place could Hellenism occupy in this society? What could it mean to be Greek and to whom? How and why did these concepts change during this period? The answers to these questions should be of interest not only to students of Byzantium, for, on the one hand, this revival shaped the discipline of classical scholarship that the Byzantines handed over to the West after 1204, a gift whose effects can still be perceived even if its origins are rarely acknowledged; while, on the other hand, the reconstitution of Greek identity in the empire's twilight years foreshadowed one of the first national Revolutions of the modern era.

The change began after AD 1000, in three movements that recovered different aspects of the Hellenic legacy. In the eleventh century, Michael Psellos attempted to revive an autonomous Greek philosophy. When this experiment was checked, a class of humanists emerged in the twelfth century who explored the literary and ethical aspects of ancient Hellenism. When Byzantium collapsed again at the end of that century, some scholars in the thirteenth century began to explore the notion of a national continuity with ancient Greece, which gave them an advantage in confronting an expanding West. These three movements, each of which was separated from its successor by violent political disruptions, are discussed in the following three chapters. Ancient Hellenism was never entirely rebuilt, but the excavations were methodical and the restorations beautiful and often original.

# CHAPTER 4

# Michael Psellos and the instauration of philosophy

Where to start with Psellos? The word "unique" is often used lightly by historians but in this case it is no idle epithet. Psellos' radical philosophical proposals, his manifold and innovative writings on all subjects, his prestigious and historically impactive career at the court, his importance as a source for the eleventh century, and his decisive influence on Byzantine intellectual life, make him the most amazing figure in Byzantine history. He cannot be "explained," at least not yet. Psellos appeared almost out of nowhere and very self-consciously revolutionized intellectual life without regard for our categories and narratives. He is especially important for the revival of Byzantine Hellenism, which sprung from him like Athena from the head of Zeus, disrupting any notion of a gradual development. In fact, it took his intellectual and literary heirs long to absorb his thought, and few would go as far as he did in replacing the Christian component of Byzantine culture with Greek philosophical alternatives.

Psellos cannot easily be "summarized," even if only under one aspect, as will be attempted here. To begin with, we lack the basic groundwork. There is still no biography or secure chronology for his manifold writings. Though most of them have been published, few have received careful individual study. This makes matters difficult because depending on the audience, circumstance, and philosophical or political goals of each work, Psellos has something different to say, often modulating or entirely contradicting what he says elsewhere. Much of this, I believe, especially regarding the restoration of philosophy, resulted from his effort to propagate his ideas while appeasing those who (rightly) doubted the sincerity of his faith. That is only one of the challenges that face us. Psellos was in addition a subtle, allusive, and playful writer, and he also tended to convert texts about others, even their funeral orations, into platforms for his own ideas, which usually led him to his favorite topic, himself. He was addicted to autobiography, yet the persona that emerges from his works is extremely complex and difficult of access, never transparently sincere though always profound, in an inimitable rhetorical way.[1] This reflected the complexity and entanglements of his broader project as well as what for lack of a better term we may label his psychological flexibility. In a letter to his friend Ioannes Xiphilinos he says that "I have still not understood myself, whether I am some divine treasure or a beast more complex than Typhon." Sokrates, in the passage from which this line is quoted, offers a slightly different alternative to Typhon: "a more gentle and simpler animal, partaking in its nature of some divine and tame portion."[2] It was one of Psellos' central ideas that we are both animal and divine and should not deny either part of our nature.

For these reasons it is risky to systematize Psellos' thought, especially given that his works have not yet been studied individually.[3] It must therefore be acknowledged at the outset here that the conclusions of the following survey are tentative and that the selection of material in it is necessarily partial. Still, Psellos cannot be removed from the history of Hellenism in Byzantium. Future studies will hopefully add more detail and accuracy to his startling role in that process as well as explain the gap that separates him from the more timid Hellenists who followed him in the twelfth century. Put into this broader perspective, Psellos is even more amazing than he appears in comparison to his own bleak age.

A brief biography is necessary first, because the meaning and mode of expression of Psellos' works were often a function of his political circumstances.[4] In the subsequent sections we will discuss the importance of Hellenism for his revolutionary ideas about philosophy, science, and ethics, and then examine how his preoccupation with Hellenism affected the way he talked about the empire and its culture as a whole.

Konstantinos Psellos was born in 1018 in Constantinople to a middle-class family, at a time when the empire was at the peak of its power. He acquired a superb education and began to serve as a secretary for high officials, eventually acquiring a post at the court. His rhetorical skill and personal charm brought him to the attention of Konstantinos IX Monomachos (1042–1055), who employed him as an official spokesman (as would all emperors thereafter). At the same time, he was privately teaching philosophy, science, and rhetoric, while his friend Ioannes Xiphilinos taught law. Monomachos was soon persuaded to reform

---

[1] See, e.g., Papaioannou (2000).     [2] Psellos, *Letter KD* 191; Plato, *Phaidros* 230a.
[3] See Kaldellis (1999a) 13–16; for a list of his works and bibliography, Moore (2005).
[4] A slightly fuller narrative is now in Kaldellis (2006) 3–10.

education in the capital, founding two new departments, one of law under Xiphilinos and one of philosophy under Psellos, who took the title of "Consul of the Philosophers."

By the early 1050s Psellos' circle was losing power at the court. His friends were fleeing the capital, some of them becoming monks. He himself was accused of harboring non-Christian beliefs and was required to produce a confession of orthodoxy. With the ascendancy of the ambitious patriarch Keroularios, Psellos decided to leave and become a monk in Bithynia (under the name Michael). But Monomachos soon died and Psellos hated the monastic life, so this retreat lasted less than a year. In 1056 he was back in Constantinople, teaching, writing, and still playing politics. He was soon allied to the Doukas family, which came to the throne in 1059. Psellos advised the emperor Konstantinos X and tutored his son, who later reigned as Michael VII (1071–1078). But first Psellos had to weather the years of Romanos IV Diogenes (1067–1071), who tried to reverse years of military decline, and finally suffered a disastrous defeat at Manzikert (1071). Psellos was among those who supported Romanos' vicious blinding, but the regime of his protégé Michael VII proved disastrous, bringing Byzantium to the verge of total defeat. Even Psellos lost favor at the court during the 1070s, and must have died at some point during that decade. While brilliant as an orator, historian, scholar, and teacher, Psellos' political activity has been characterized as unscrupulous and he has been personally accused of contributing to the decline of Byzantium during the eleventh century.

## "UNBLOCKING THE STREAMS OF PHILOSOPHY"

Whatever historical role scholars eventually assign to Psellos in the decline of Byzantium in the eleventh century, there is no question that his philosophical, literary, and pedagogical career revolutionized intellectual culture. We will study the reception of his work in the twelfth century in the next chapter. Here we will examine the contours, and some of the details, of his project of philosophical revival, which he announced boldly in the central section of his court history / auto-philosophical memoirs, a literary masterpiece known as the *Chronographia*.

You who are reading my book today will confirm that I found philosophy only after it had breathed its last, at least as far as its own exponents were concerned, and I alone revived it with my own powers, having found no worthwhile teachers, nor even a seed of wisdom in Greece or the barbarian lands, though I searched everywhere (6.37).

Psellos goes on to explain that the superficiality of contemporary teachers led him to search for the truth in the thought of Plato and Aristotle, and from there in Plotinos, Porphyrios, Iamblichos, and especially the great Proklos, from the last of whom he learned "conceptual precision" (6.37–38).[5] He then began a systematic exploration of knowledge, subordinating all disciplines, including rhetoric, to philosophy (6.38–41). He makes a brief allusion to his knowledge of Christian philosophy in 6.42 but goes on to emphasize that

> if I gathered a small part of wisdom, it came from no living fount; finding the sources choked up, I had to open them and clean them out myself, drawing out with great effort the pure stream (*nama*) which had lain in the depths. For at the present time neither Athens, nor Nikomedeia, nor Alexandria (the one that faces Egypt), nor Phoenicia, not even both Romes, whether the first and lesser one [Rome] or the later and greater one [Constantinople], nor any other city is flourishing with regard to *logoi* (6.42–43).

We must not underestimate the revolutionary nature of Psellos' claims here, which we may be tempted to do by parallels from the history of modern philosophy, when such boasts became commonplace (in Machiavelli, Bacon, Descartes, and others). What Psellos was proposing had no precedents in the conservative mentality of Byzantine intellectual culture. When emperors were praised for reviving learning, only the endowment of its institutions was meant; and when scholars were so praised, it meant that they had reinvigorated the traditional disciplines of rhetoric and theology.[6] Innovation and intellectual change there certainly were, if muted, but they were always understood as a reaffirmation of the tradition. There are no parallels for Psellos' boast in the first person.

Psellos' philosophy, moreover, is evidently something different from the Christianity that currently prevails in "Greece" and the "barbarian lands." What he has in mind once flourished in cities such as Athens and Alexandria, he tells us, but apparently does so no longer. Its "living fount" and "pure stream (*nama*)" have been "choked up" – for how long, one wonders? And who blocked them up? Its sources are Plato, Aristotle, and Proklos. These thinkers form the basis of Psellos' philosophical revolution. "Plato and Aristotle's 'birth-throes,' by which I am both born and formed," he once told his students, "suffice for me to bring forth mental

---

[5] Jenkins (2006) is an excellent account of Psellos and Proklos.
[6] Browning (1975a) 6; Magdalino (1993) 324; Radošević (1993).

offspring" (i.e., in you).[7] His praise for these non-Christian thinkers was extraordinary: "The length of a single letter," he wrote elsewhere, "cannot contain the secrets of Plato's boundless thought any more than a bucket can fit the Atlantic ocean. But we must love him, even if we can spy out only a tiny bit of his innermost sanctuary."[8] This enthusiasm often got Psellos into trouble, to which we will turn below. But we note already that he was thinking along the lines of "Greeks and barbarians" when contemplating the intellectual scene of his times, and his Greeks were all philosophers; by contrast, when writing about imperial affairs he would refer to "Romans and barbarians." So there is implied here a modern Greece of sorts, i.e., a place where Greek is still spoken, and then there is old Greece, whose wisdom some unnamed persons "choked up."

Psellos' philosophical ambitions and pedagogical responsibilities were not limited to metaphysics, as the autobiographical digression of the *Chronographia* might suggest. Even there he admits the key contribution made by rhetoric to the propagation of his project and notes that it is possible for a specialist in one field (in his case, "philosophy") to acquire a solid grounding in others.[9] In his lectures he frequently encourages his students to acquire all kinds of knowledge, for "a philosopher ought to be multifarious" – *pantodapos* was one of his favorite words. For instance, they should study history, geography, and music.[10] A treatise on a popular women's festival begins by stating that "philosophy pays attention not only to great matters, but also to those that seem to the many to be childish and of no interest."[11] Accordingly, in the thousands of pages that Psellos wrote, we find that every genre is represented and every field of knowledge surveyed, bar none. His literary versatility is unparalleled among ancient and medieval writers and his epistemological scope as a teacher surpasses even that of Aristotle. His revolution in knowledge was, then, both radical and comprehensive.

The longest list that Psellos produced of his own intellectual interests, many pages' worth, occurs at the end of the encomium that he wrote in 1054 for his mother as he was trying to abandon Monomachos' court. This was also a time when his faith was being questioned by both enemies

---

[7] Psellos, *To students left behind by the interpretation of Aristotle's* On Interpretation 28–30 (*Or. Min.* 36).

[8] Psellos, *A different interpretation of Platonic thought based on the* Timaios (*Phil. Min. II* 5; p. 9, 7–10).

[9] Psellos, *Chronographia* 6.40–41; for rhetoric, Kaldellis (1999a) chs. 19–22.

[10] Psellos, *Theol. I* 114.1–5; *pantodapos*: Duffy and Papaioannou (2003) 225–226.

[11] Psellos, *On the women's festival of Agathê in Byzantium* (*Misc.* p. 527); on this see Kaldellis (2006) 179–186. For the universal scope of philosophy, see also *On Philosophy* (*Phil. Min. I* 1).

(probably Keroularios) and friends (Xiphilinos). The purpose of the enco-mium, which was probably written long after her death, was to present her as a saint so as to invest his philosophy with her as a mantle (in fact, he states repeatedly that it was she who encouraged and nourished his studies, even as he admits that his own bookish philosophy was different from her saintly asceticism). He offers here three justifications for his interest in esoteric and suspect fields such as astrology and the Chaldaean oracles. The first is that he must know them to refute them (28c), a standard (and rather lame) defense; also, "the unquenchable love for every kind of knowledge of the soul and the demands of my students have induced me to indulge in all those fields ... But if I observed anything that lay outside of our doctrines, even if it were supported by the most rigorous arguments and saturated with every wisdom and grace, I despised it as a completely meaningless piece of utter nonsense" (29a; cf. 30a).[12] The only part of this that we may safely accept is "the insatiable desire" that he claims to have had "for all manner of studies; I would not want anything to escape my notice, but would love it all even if it means knowing the things beneath the earth" – an allusion to the atheist scientist Sokrates in Aristophanes' *Clouds*. We should note that an "insatiable desire for learning" was postulated by Plato as a distinctive trait of philosophers.[13]

Psellos makes it clear that his chief guides in this ambitious project were ancient philosophers: Plato, Aristotle, and Proklos. From a Byzantine point of view they were Greek in at least two senses: they were pagan, or at any rate not Christian, and they belonged to the ancient nation of the Greeks. They were not, in either case, "ours." Did Psellos conceive his philosophical project as Hellenic? The multifarious lectures that he deliv-ered as Consul of the Philosophers in 1047–1054 are a good starting-point for this problem, but we must first note some factors that constrained the freedom of his expositions. Most of Psellos' students would have come from the wealthier sectors of society. We do not know whether he taught different topics to different "classes," or used different approaches, but his

---

[12] Knowledge *regarding* the soul or knowledge *possessed* by the soul? See Psellos, *Encomium for his Mother* 24d and *passim*; for a study, Kaldellis (2006) ch. 1. For astrology, cf. Anna Komnene, *Alexiad* 6.7.3 with Magdalino (2003b) esp. 24.

[13] Psellos, *On Incredible Reports* 100–106 (*Phil. Min. I* 32), with the usual excuses and denials (cf. *Chronographia* 5.19, 6.65–67, 6A.11–12); cf. Plato, *Republic* 475c. For things beneath the earth, see Aristophanes, *Clouds* 187–194; Plato, *Apology of Sokrates* 18b, 19b, 23d. Psellos responds to Aristophanes in *When he resigned from the rank of* protasêkrêtis 100 ff. (*Or. Min.* 8), and accepts for himself the role of the comic poet's Sokrates in *Regarding the Golden Chain in Homer* 2–3 (*Phil. Min. I* 46). He there offers another list of his philosophical interests, focusing on practical and scientific fields.

so-called "theological" lectures in particular (in reality, they are "exeget-ical") were probably addressed to current or future churchmen.[14] So what-ever radical philosophical ideas he may have wanted to instill in his students would, for the most part, have to be insinuated under the cover of traditional notions rather than proclaimed for what they were. Psellos knew that he was being watched and even so he often roused the suspicions of the enforcers of Orthodoxy. As we will see, the subversive effects of his teachings led, at the end of the century, to the reactionary establishment of an official educational system designed to teach roughly the same topics, only under the immediate control of the emperor and the patriarch. All this makes Psellos' strategy for exposing his students to Greek wisdom that much more fascinating.

At first sight, in Psellos' lectures the Greeks are one among many ancient nations that had a distinctive national wisdom. A lecture on these nations was prompted one day when Psellos went to class prepared to talk about the Psalms but his students wanted him to talk instead about the varieties of philosophy.[15] These, he responded impromptu, were five, corresponding to the Chaldaeans, Egyptians, Greeks, Jews, and "our *genos*," i.e., Christians. Greek philosophy may be further divided into sects, e.g., Epicurean, Stoic, etc., but here Psellos treats it as unified (elsewhere he emphasizes that different opinions prevailed among the Greeks).[16] He admits that little is known of Egyptian philosophy,[17] but, drawing on ancient writers about Egypt, he surveys the symbolism of zoomorphic gods. Chaldaean thought was mostly astrological for him; Psellos summa-rizes in this connection the so-called *Chaldaean Oracles*, but admits that this topic was esoteric, pernicious, and off-limits (yet he wrote treatises on their interpretation, quoting fragments that would otherwise have been lost and boasting that he was the only one of his contemporaries who could give an accurate account of them).[18] Psellos next cites elements of Jewish history, belief, and practice, some filtered through Christian exegesis.[19] Finally, "we" reject the Egyptians and the Chaldaeans but eclectically accept aspects of Greek thought, especially of their science of nature. "We" also reject many Jewish practices but accept their books and every-thing in their beliefs that points toward Jesus. Psellos concludes with a

---

[14] Kaldellis (2005b).
[15] Psellos, *To those who asked about the number of philosophical discourses* (*Phil. Min. I* 3).
[16] Cf. Psellos, *Theol. I* 23.28–32    [17] Cf. Psellos, *Theol. I* 23.56.
[18] Boast: Psellos, *Theol. I* 23.53–54. His main discussions are *Phil. Min. II* 38–41 and *Theol. I* 23A; for his role in their preservation, Majercik (1989) 3; Athanassiadi (1999) 149–151 and (2002).
[19] For Jewish "philosophy" in antiquity, see Hengel (1974) 255–261.

formulation of Christian doctrine but then notes that his voice has given out and most of his audience is tired of taking notes anyway.

For Psellos' students, in short, the Greeks are as foreign as the Egyptians, except insofar as "we" accept some of their teachings. Of course, what Psellos took to be Egyptian and Chaldaean wisdom was in some respects Greek wisdom in disguise or at any rate belonged to the broad theological *koine* of late antiquity. Psellos, like some of the later Platonists, was probably unaware of this and so he took Chairemon as an authentic authority on Egyptian philosophy and Ioulianos the theurgist as a Chaldaean whose verses were "discovered" by "our Greeks," namely Iamblichos and "that truly divine man, Proklos," who "abandoned Greek things in their rush toward those others."[20] But this problem should not detain us here. Psellos actually says little about Egyptians and Jews, and his discussions of the *Chaldaean Oracles* are few and circumscribed. Our focus should be fixed on the relationship between "us" and "the Greeks." Like Plotinos, when Psellos says "the Greeks" he does not mean all of ancient culture; he usually has a specific Platonist in mind.[21] And the question of who "we" really are is complicated, for instance, by Psellos' assumption of the first-person voice of Aristotle in writing paraphrases of his work.[22] In the next century this authorial fiction would broaden to include a plurality of assumed Hellenic, even pagan, narrative voices, but for Psellos the problem of Hellenism was that of philosophy in a Christian world.

Here we run into a serious hermeneutical problem. It is hard to identify Psellos' own beliefs in the hundreds of pages of commentaries and lectures that he devoted to philosophical, theological, and scientific topics. It is safe to say that he wanted to *disseminate* a knowledge of ancient philosophy and establish it at the core of Byzantine education; to inject philosophical references into the public discourse of Byzantium, especially in rhetoric and epistolography, and naturalize them there; and to revive a rational, scientific understanding of the world, even if adjusted to a rarefied pietism. Some have realized that his persistent attempts to present Hellenic notions about God and the soul in Christian terms and, conversely, to explicate Christian doctrines in terms of Hellenic thought bespeak an attempt to "reconcile" the two: "Psellos is trying to do for Neoplatonism and Proklos what Aquinas was later to do for Aristotle."[23] We could cite here such

---

[20] Psellos, *Theol. I* 23.48–51. For barbarian wisdom, see pp. 168–171 above.
[21] Many citations can be offered: see, e.g., *Theol. I* 22.38–39 where Proklos is called "the chief of the most theological of the Greeks," or *Theol. I* 32.119–122, where "the Greeks" are Porphyrios. For Plotinos, see pp. 168–169 above.
[22] Ierodiakonou (2004) 108.    [23] Munitiz (1991) 230.

statements that Psellos made as that "we do not traduce *all* Greek opinions, for some of them support our own doctrine," though "I know that some of them conflict with it."[24]

But "reconciliation" is ambiguous. For example, may certain Christian doctrines be sacrificed in this compromise with "the exceedingly wise Greeks" and the "divine Proklos"?[25] More importantly, might such mediation require a philosophical standard that is independent of the two sides, creating a neutral ground where doctrine must submit to the arbitration of philosophy? And what may that ground be if not an autonomous philosophy? Consider, for example, the gradually unfolding logic of one of Psellos' lectures:

I want you ... to know that Hellenic wisdom may go wrong in its opinion about divinity and have a not-flawless theological component, but still it understood nature just as the Maker made it. It is necessary for us to take theories from there about those matters and, with regard to our own wisdom, recognize its form and its truth but break through its letter as though it were a wrapper, pulling up the hidden spirit as though it were pearl. Don't think that what Moses said was the last word of truth, nor regard his formulations about the supreme Being as self-sufficient but bring them into conjunction with those [i.e., Greek notions] and bring those to a new resolution. Nor should you entirely dismiss the texts of the Greeks from which men set out to theologize.[26]

"Reconciliation" does not get us very far here. Psellos is basically deconstructing the polarity between Greeks and Christians by superimposing on them the more basic philosophical polarity of truth and error, which is unexpectedly found to cut across rather than between them. First, by distinguishing between the inner truth and the outer wrapping of Scripture and Christian doctrine, Psellos calls into question "common" notions about them. What if Christianity is not what "we" have thought it was all along? How do we know what it is? In his oration for his mother, he notes that Scripture and the terminology of Christian worship are "full of mystery and ineffable initiation ... in brief, every single passage of the Gospels is imbued with an implanted significance which the many cannot easily grasp."[27] So much then for the faith of the average Byzantine! And what if to extract the inner pearl of Christianity we need Greek wisdom? For example, Psellos begins one treatise by conceding that "our doctrine of

---

[24] Psellos, *That ousia is self-subsisting* 53–54, 119 (*Phil. Min. I* 7).
[25] Psellos, *Solutions to problems of physics* 50–51 (*Phil. Min. I* 16), *Theol. I* 23.48–51.
[26] Psellos, *He reproaches his students for laziness* 70–82 (*Or. Min.* 24). "These" and "those" at the end are probably the teachings of Moses and of the Greeks, though other combinations are possible.
[27] Psellos, *Encomium for his Mother* 29c–d.

the Trinity" is self-sufficient, but the Greeks can help us to demonstrate and better understand it; and this leads to a discussion of Proklos![28] Elsewhere Psellos claims that prior interpreters of the theology of Gregorios of Nazianzos failed because they did not approach his thought from the standpoint of "Sokratic *epistêmê*," and ended up following the letter rather than the "deeper theories." The first witness whom Psellos calls in his new explication of the Theologian is "the wise Iamblichos," and he concludes by noting, "so you see, O students, how one approaches theological formulations on the basis of *epistêmê*. We find the wise Plato doing the same in many places."[29]

One could think that Psellos is merely trying to justify the study of Greek philosophy by showing how it elucidates Christian wisdom, even if the Fathers themselves would not have liked what he was doing. But it is not quite so simple as that, for it is not entirely clear whose truth is being promulgated here under whose name (the faith of the average Byzantine is being rejected in favor of a Neoplatonic system). Matters are even more complicated than that, for Psellos often points out that the texts of the Greeks too have inner and outer meanings. Plato and Aristotle both had "hidden" teachings while "Hellenic mysteries and initiatory rites concealed the truth under the most common garb." Psellos' friend Niketas, a fellow teacher in Constantinople,

removed their covering and revealed the teaching that was hidden within ... In such a way did he admire Homer: he did not cling to the letter of the text, as did many, neither were his ears charmed by the meter, nor did he devote himself to appearances, but he searched after the hidden beauty, cutting through matter with reason and contemplation, finally penetrating into the inner sanctum.[30]

Pagan myths are not just stories that Christians should dismiss as false religion; for Psellos, they too point to secret inner truths, as do Christian texts. So where can we start our quest for Truth? It seems that Christian texts and doctrines are as opaque as Homer was for the Neoplatonists. Emblematic of this confusion is Psellos' allusion in a chapter of the *Chronographia* to certain "theological verses," which seems to be a conflation of one line from Numbers and another from the *Odyssey*.[31] *What*, we need to ask, are we supposed to reconcile *with what*? Psellos has

---

[28] Psellos, *On theology and the distinctions among Greek doctrines* (*Phil. Min. II* 35).
[29] Psellos, *Theol. I* 90; for preliminary assessments of the lectures, Maltese (1994); O'Meara (1998); Duffy (2002) 147.
[30] Plato: Psellos, *Chronographia* 3.3 (cf. 3.13). Niketas: *Funeral Oration for Niketas* 10; on the latter, Cesaretti (1991) 29–43. References to Plato's hidden doctrines abound, esp. in the *Phil. Min. II.*
[31] Kaldellis (1999a) 46.

destabilized our frame of reference. Christianity is not what we thought it was, and neither is Greek wisdom. We are in an epistemological free-fall of esoteric signs and the only person who can point the way out is Psellos.

Yet all roads in Psellos' world ultimately lead back to Plato and Proklos. Consider his allegories on Greek myth. In one he shows how a verse in Homer about the gods can be made to yield a Christian sense, "thereby transforming falsehood into truth ... and making salty water drinkable," but the discussion relies on Platonic terms and points to Platonic doctrines.[32] Elsewhere he admits that "you do not want me to allegorize these Greek things in a Greek way alone, but also to transpose their secret meanings into our beliefs." So he interprets the Golden Chain in a Platonic way and then in an equivalent Christian way, though the only authority that he cites even in the second is Plato.[33] There is reason to think that Psellos was consciously imposing (rather than discovering) allegorical meaning when dealing with Greek topics; we should then be especially careful in reading his Christian exegesis, which also bears signs of cynical manipulation.[34]

If Plato "mystically reveals our theology" and Proklos can be quoted in the exegesis of Christian doctrine, Christian texts and symbols can conversely be "translated" into a Platonic idiom. "Sinai – that I may philosophize to you about this as well," Psellos wrote to Xiphilinos, "did not, like some physical mountain, lead Moses up and God down, but rather symbolizes the rise of the soul up from matter."[35] With few exceptions, Psellos' theological lectures are a vast exercise of this sort. Not that this kind of exegesis was foreign to the Christian tradition, but here it is practiced on an unparalleled scale and in the absence of credible signs of the exegete's Christian piety. We need detailed studies of these lectures. Based on a preliminary reading, I suspect that the outcome will be startling. Psellos is not trying to "buttress" Christian doctrine with philosophy or "enrich" it with Greek eloquence. He is abolishing its autonomy by fusing it with Platonic thought and making the two interpenetrate each other. Despite programmatic statements that ascribe primacy to Christian doctrine, in practice Psellos treats both it and Greek myth as coded versions of the same Platonic doctrines. He is effectively trying to make it impossible for

---

[32] Psellos, *Allegory on "The gods were assembled, sitting at the side of Zeus"* esp. 9–18, 138–141 (*Phil. Min. I* 42); for levels of analysis in the allegories, Cesaretti (1991) 29–123, though without comparing Psellos' treatment of Christian myths; for prior Christian use of pagan myths, see the studies cited by Podskalsky (2003) 328–329 n. 47. See Schott (2005) 296–299 on Porphyrios and eastern traditions.
[33] Psellos, *Regarding the Golden Chain in Homer (Phil. Min. I* 46).     [34] Roilos (2005) 121–124.
[35] Plato: Psellos, *Theol. I* 78.108; Proklos: Duffy (2002) 151 n. 45; Sinai: *Letter to Ioannes Xiphilinos* 5d.

Christians – at least those Christians taught by him – to expound their beliefs without first talking about Proklos. This is subversion, not reconciliation, and it is very cleverly done at that.

That Psellos' project was controversial in his own time is suggested by an oration in praise of the Fathers of the Church delivered from the pulpit of Hagia Sophia after Psellos' death by his then octogenarian former teacher Ioannes Mauropous. Toward the end of his oration Mauropous attacks an anonymous opponent who "is wise according to the flesh," boasts of logic and science, and dares to admire the poets' gods. Mauropous may have meant Julian (who was always, in the Byzantine imagination, the Fathers' chief foe), but his strictures could just as well apply to Psellos. Was this indirect criticism, in the Byzantine manner?[36] If these were the attitudes that Psellos found in his closest colleagues and friends, it is no wonder that he boasted of being the only true philosopher among them, a boast whose correlate was the lament that "I philosophize alone in unphilosophical times."[37] A full reckoning may one day prove that Psellos was lying to his students when he denied "that my goal is for you to exchange our doctrines for Hellenic beliefs – I would be mad to do that." But *mania*, we should remember, is given a positive philosophical valuation by Sokrates in the *Phaidros*: "the best things we have come from madness."[38] Be that as it may, Psellos' denial shows that one *could have thought* this mad thing of him and probably that some *did think* this. And Psellos' denials and disclaimers have little value, as we will see.

## SCIENCE AND DISSIMULATION

Psellos' interest in Greek science was a central component of his philosophical project and his use of it complements what we have seen already of his deeper objectives. We cited a passage above according to which the Greeks were wrong about God but still they understood nature as God made it. This does not imply that all of their scientific theories were correct, only that their approach to nature, namely (as we will see) their search for physical causes, was superior to Christian ignorance and indifference about such matters. In many treatises and lectures, Psellos defines nature as an

---

[36] Ioannes Mauropous, *Oration in Praise of the Three Holy Fathers, the Great Basileios, Gregorios the Theologian, and Ioannes Chrysostomos* (*op.* 178, p. 116); cf. Agapitos (1998a) 189–190; Ljubarskij (2004a) 222.

[37] Boast: Psellos, *Chronographia* 6.192. Lament: *To those who think that the philosopher loves material rewards* 52–53 (*Or. Min.* 6).

[38] Psellos, *That ousia is self-subsisting* 118–121 (*Phil. Min. I* 7); cf. Plato, *Phaidros* 244a–245b, 265a–b.

intermediary between the physical world and God. Ultimately God is the cause of everything, as he is the maker of nature, but if we wish to under-stand any particular aspect of the world we first have to look for its proximate, physical causes. Now, to modern ears all this may sound pietistic and typical of Byzantium. However, by far the dominant attitude among writers in Byzantium was to ascribe everything directly to God and bother no further. From this point of view, the effect of Psellos' project was to push God out of the world as far as prudence allowed and create space for autonomous scientific inquiry based on Greek notions. This repre-sented a rejection of the popular Christian attitude that ridiculed any kind of learning that did not lead directly to God, an attitude that Psellos' friend Xiphilinos adopted when he reproached him in 1055 for pointlessly spend-ing too much time with "your Plato" and other Greeks.[39] It was for good reason that many suspected the sincerity of Psellos' faith, and asked him to produce a confession of faith.[40]

"Know this too," Psellos wrote in a treatise on physical questions, "that our *logos* [i.e., Christianity] does not make a great fuss about the causes of these things, but ascribes the governance of all things to divine decrees … The Greek does not differ, but he also inquires regarding the proximate nature of events." To be sure, the Greek's theories may be wrong, "yet I have gone over them with you not so that you may worship them but only that you know them" – a typical ploy. When it comes, then, to physics, "our" writers do not enjoy a presumptive (or rhetorical) advantage, as they do at first sight regarding matters of divinity.[41] In a lecture reproaching his students for laziness – where he complains that for their sake he stays up late at night reading books and writing lectures – Psellos shames them by accusing them "of living in accordance with common notions" and of not caring why chasms open in the earth or why sea-water is salty. One asks, "what good is all that for making a living?" while another contents himself with saying that God causes earthquakes and "pays no regard to inter-mediate nature." Psellos now has to deny defensively that he denies providence, but adds that God does not have such a hands-on approach to the world and, besides, one still has to explain why he causes certain things at some times and not at others.[42]

---

[39] Christian attitudes: MacMullen (1997) 87–89; Psellos, *Letter to Ioannes Xiphilinos passim*; for the contours of Byzantine science, Pontikos (1992) ch. 2.

[40] Psellos, *Theol. II* 35, with Garzya (1967); cf. Psellos, *Encomium for the Blessed Patriarch Michael Keroularios* (*Hist. Byz. et alia* p. 355), for a possible allusion to this.

[41] Psellos, *Solutions to problems of physics* 73–83 (*Phil. Min. I* 16); cf. ibid. 4 ff.

[42] Psellos, *He reproaches his students for laziness* 45–69 (*Or. Min.* 24).

"Nothing happens without a cause."[43] Psellos accordingly set out to teach his contemporaries and his future readers about the physical causes of all things in the world, even the most trivial and bizarre things, drawing freely from (and often simplifying) Aristotle, Aristotle's Neoplatonic commentators, and ancient medical writers. His *Multifarious Instruction*, dedicated first to Konstantinos IX and then to Michael VII, begins with chapters on theology and metaphysics and concludes with the cause of twins, the size of the sun and moon, and why the tears of wild boars are not salty. No topic was off-limits. There is no fundamental difference between the genitals of men and women, he explains, except that the former are made to protrude. "Remain calm," he instructs his possibly shocked Byzantine reader, until you have heard the argument. Why does sex seem more pleasant to those who dream about it than to those who actually have it, he wonders elsewhere.[44] Nor did Psellos confine himself to theory: he performed classroom experiments in hydraulics and optics based on the manuals of Heron and Archimedes.[45]

Psellos' belief in a relatively autonomous natural realm inevitably led him to debunk alleged miracles and marvels. He wrote a treatise on an echo-chamber in Nikomedeia that many believed produced sound "from no cause whatever," while others believed it was a *teras* or a fraud produced by hidden pipes. Psellos gives a physical explanation for the occurrence and adds, significantly, that the experimental evidence that many demanded of him could not be conclusive as conditions in the room could not be properly controlled. To support this he cites the parallel of some of Archimedes' experiments.[46] In a poem, he argues that *selêniasmos* (probably epilepsy) was caused neither by demonic possession nor the Moon, but could be explained by *physikoi logoi*. In this, then, he followed the Hippokratics.[47] He also attributes to psychosomatic states some psychological disturbances that were popularly attributed to demonic activity.[48] I have argued elsewhere that in the *Chronographia* he effectively denies that God plays any role in political history or that prayers and religious healings can cure diseases or reverse the decrees of nature. His analysis of imperial decline is couched entirely in terms of political factors and the court; he does not suggest that God was punishing the Romans for their sins, as many of his contemporaries believed. Also, in one chapter of that work he

---

[43] Psellos, *Solutions to problems of physics* 268 (*Phil. Min. I* 16).
[44] Psellos, *Solutions to problems of physics* 84–88, 159 (*Phil. Min. I* 16).
[45] Psellos, *When he resigned from the rank of* protasêkrêtis 168–175 (*Or. Min.* 8).
[46] Psellos, *On the echo-chamber in Nikomedeia* (*Phil. Min. I* 31).
[47] Psellos, *Poem* 11. See Volk (1990) 116–120.   [48] O'Meara (1998) 439.

argued that a certain growth on the tomb of the empress Zoe was in accordance with "natural law" and not, as her widower Monomachos wanted to believe, a miracle; yet, at the time, Psellos the courtier had endorsed the alleged miracle in a panegyrical speech. His account of the event in the *Chronographia* sets the record straight and, in line with the ulterior purposes of the work, exposes the mendacity of politically motivated rhetoric, including his own.[49]

This brings us to a basic problem in the understanding of Psellos' works that we have so far only hinted at, namely the degree to which he had to lie or at any rate dissimulate to protect himself when speaking publicly, especially when he was addressing imperial and ecclesiastical audiences. Psellos needed to maintain a degree of credibility, which meant that occasionally he had to endorse conventional beliefs, even if only in a qualified way, while finding subtle ways of communicating the results of his own researches. One of his main purposes in the *Chronographia* was to expose both the mendacity and the utility of rhetoric in this regard: it allowed him to speak out of both sides of his mouth. This places us in a torturous maze of denials, confessions, qualifications, excuses, and outright contradictions. A good general rule for dealing with this problem is this: "when an author living in an age when people are persecuted for heterodoxy expresses contradictory sentiments regarding religion, the burden of proof . . . lies with those who would uphold his piety."[50]

For example, beyond the general idea that all of nature can be ascribed to God, earthquakes are the *only specific* phenomenon that Psellos ascribes to God. Considering that he would not accept such an explanation from his students for any other physical event, he evidently went out of his way in this case to uphold a conventional belief. *He* had no reason to treat them differently from other natural events, except that they had a special place in Byzantine piety, eliciting religious anxieties and commemoration, including liturgies.[51] This was a delicate topic and required careful treatment, but for political rather than philosophical reasons. We are fortunate to have a speech that Psellos delivered to an audience of monks or priests regarding the earthquake of 23 September 1063, probably on the day itself. Its lucid and especially beautiful prose constitutes a masterpiece of discreet and

---

[49] Psellos, *Chronographia* 6.183; cf. Kaldellis (1999a) 95–97; no providence: ibid. chs. 13–15; nature over faith: ch. 12.

[50] Schaefer (1990) 42 n. 5. Cf. Kaldellis (1999a) 161 for dissimulation, ibid. ch. 4, also Psellos, *Letter KD* 212; *Praise of Italos* 9 ff. (*Or. Min.* 19).

[51] Croke (1981); Dagron (1981); Vercleyen (1988); but cf. Kaldellis (1999b) 211–213; for the unique treatment of earthquakes in eleventh-century thought, Telelis (2003) 440.

respectful instruction. Psellos endorses the view throughout that the earth-quake was caused by God because of "our" sins, but he gradually builds up a thesis for a semi-autonomous Nature. God works through physical causes (147–149); whereas some who are outside "our *logos*" ascribe events to nature without invoking God [i.e., the Greeks], we believe in God, whether he acts through intermediary causes or not (165–176). Psellos says that this is not the place to give an account of those intermediary causes (176–177), but he does so anyway and then claims that "the many," those who believe that God personally takes a hand in directing the universe, are irrational, "for divine nature is entirely outside of the universe" (203–206). After drawing this astonishing conclusion, he returns to the audience's pious beliefs, though not without failing to note – mischievously, I suspect – that churches offered no protection during the earthquake that just occurred, indeed they seemed to draw a greater measure of divine wrath! (250–252). Psellos of course knew perfectly well that "the many" hoped that churches could protect them during natural disasters.[52]

Psellos was a master of the art of deliberate contradiction; of saying one thing and meaning another; of saying one thing and then doing another; and of saying different things to different people. Nor can we rely on what he says *most often* – hermeneutics is not democratic – especially if it reflects common notions. His pervasive dissimulation should qualify our under-standing of his Hellenism in particular. It is possible that he never felt safe enough to reveal the depth of his heterodoxy and had none to whom he could open his mind. "I philosophize alone in unphilosophical times."[53] Let us consider his modulations of one image in particular. Psellos fre-quently juxtaposes the "briny" or "salty" waters of Greek philosophy with the *nama* (the pure drinkable water) of Christian doctrine, but, as we saw, in the *Chronographia* the *nama* that he found in the depths sprang from the ancient philosophers.[54] He expresses contradictory opinions regarding the worth of the *Chaldaean Oracles* and goes on at length about topics that he then abruptly dismisses as nonsense, which has been seen as a possibly

---

[52] Psellos, *Regarding the earthquake that occurred on 23 September* (*Phil. Min. I* 30). *On earthquakes and motions of the earth* (*Phil. Min. I* 29) begins and ends by endorsing a pietistic view and offers a list of possible "proximate causes" in the middle. *On earthquakes* (*Phil. Min. I* 26) does not mention God (but is only a paragraph long). Churches: Kaldellis (2004a) 211. For the earthquake of 1063, see Michael Attaleiates, *History* 87–91, who is responding to Psellos' lecture in some way.

[53] Psellos, *To those who think that the philosopher loves material rewards* 52–53 (*Or. Min. 6*).

[54] Cf. Duffy (2001) with Kaldellis (1999a) 15–16, 130–131. For Platonic *nama*, see also *A different interpretation of Platonic thought based on the* Timaios (*Phil. Min. II* 5; p. 6, 19–20). Cf. Erasmus in Goldhill (2002) 27.

"hypocritical compliance with the tenets of Christianity."[55] In a discussion of the myth in the *Phaidros*, he argues that one should interpret the dialogue by following Plato and the Greeks and not by imposing on it what "we" want to find there. Having done so in a dispassionate way, he concludes: "a Platonic approach, then, for Platonic things. This is the same as to say, an absurd approach for absurd things." Did it grieve him, we must wonder, to have to say such stupid things?[56]

Psellos developed strategies for deflecting unwanted attention. He could tailor his message to his audience, as in the speech regarding the earthquake of 1063. In a letter addressed to Aimilianos, patriarch of Antioch, he admits with regard to their respective literary styles that "I, perhaps, am a Platonist, but you practice evangelical simplicity. Yet even though I happen to have become a wise man, I do not choose to Atticize always or to everyone. When I wish to address divine men in particular, I pour my speech from their jugs."[57] This was one way by which he managed to be all things to all people. In the Fathers he found a repertoire of arguments to justify his interest in pagan thought. When Xiphilinos accused him of abandoning Christianity to take up with Plato, Psellos responded indignantly. Did not Gregorios and Basileios also study and admire Plato? Must not Plato, a mixture of clear and salty waters, be studied if he is to be refuted? – as if eleventh-century Constantinople were crawling with Platonists who had to be refuted by Psellos! He even takes the offensive, accusing Xiphilinos, with an allusion to Plato, of being a Plato-hater, a misologist, and a hater of philosophy, for denying that any but Christian learning has value. Xiphilinos has mistaken his monastic abode and his arrogant rejection of scholarship for a superior way of life, whereas it is really Psellos, "the city-dweller," who is closer to the truth.[58]

In a letter to a learned monk, Psellos claimed that for him that "outside wisdom" was merely a useful tool for the study of "our wisdom."[59] But he does not say this in the central section of the *Chronographia* where he announces his project of philosophical revival, where what is being revived is precisely Greek wisdom and where he gives "our wisdom" short shrift. Why did he give such contradictory impressions? Moreover, his professed

---

[55] Oracles: Duffy (1995) 86; compliance: Athanassiadi (2002) 246.
[56] Psellos, *Explanation of the chariot-racing of the souls and the march of the gods in Plato's* Phaidros (*Phil. Min. II* 7). It is possible that some texts in this collection were not by Psellos: Pontikos (1992) viii, xxxii.
[57] Psellos, *Letter KD* 135.
[58] Psellos, *Letter to Ioannes Xiphilinos passim*. Cf. Plato, *Phaidon* 89c ff.; Eunapios, *Lives of the Philosophers and the Sophists* 481.
[59] Psellos, *Letter KD* 267.

admiration for Gregorios of Nazianzos was cynical to a degree and has been misunderstood in the scholarship. To be sure, Gregorios provided a Christian model for the combination of philosophy and rhetoric and was, of the Church Fathers, the most open to Greek *paideia*. He therefore offered a good starting-point and cover for Psellos' project (as did another of his favorites, Synesios). Yet there are grounds for caution, though they can only be stated generally here. First, the treatises that Psellos devoted to Gregorios and the other Church Fathers discuss and praise their *style* rather than the *substance* of their thought.[60] Second, as we will see, Psellos had a distinctly different conception of ethical life than Gregorios, in many crucial ways a directly antithetical one. In a passage of the *Chronographia* he even quotes one of the saint's lines in order to reveal his utter opposition to the values of the monastic life.[61]

Third, Gregorios shared the early Christian disdain for natural science. His *Second Theological Oration* contains a lyrical evocation of the beauty of the world, but his purpose is to make human wisdom seem pale and insignificant compared to the majesty of God.

> Do your naturalists and vain wise men have anything to say? . . . Or shall I once and for all philosophize about this on the basis of Scripture? . . . What can you possibly say that is philosophical about thunder and lightning, O you who thunder from the earth? . . . Let faith lead us rather than reason . . . I will not tolerate Him being praised with words other than my own [presumably Scripture].[62]

Gregorios fits exactly the profile of Psellos' "irrational" people who want to skip past nature and go directly to God. His stance toward science is as different from Psellos' as his mystical view of nature is undermined by Psellos' mechanistic and worldly approach. This entails crucial theological differences. Psellos, as we saw, pointedly pushes God "outside" the universe to make room for nature and was ready to make this argument before an assembly of bishops or monks. Gregorios, on the other hand, declared that he would not pronounce on this question for any answer would compromise the incomprehensibility of God. But he considers only the

---

[60] Psellos, *On the styles of Gregorios the Theologian, Basileios the Great, Chrysostomos, and Gregorios of Nyssa* (*De oper. daem.* pp. 124–131); *To the vestarchês Pothos, who asked him to write about the theological style*; and *On Ioannes Chrysostomos*. In another work, *On the style of some texts* (*De oper. daem.* pp. 48–52), Gregorios is one among many literary models; see Kriaras (1972) 68–70; Karpozilos (1982) 163–164; Wilson (1983) 166–172; Hörandner (1996); for Psellos' defensive use of Gregorios and Synesios, Criscuolo (1981) 1–14, 19–20.

[61] Kaldellis (1999a) 83.

[62] Gregorios of Nazianzos, *Or.* 28.27–29 (*The Second Theological Oration*). For Psellos on thunder and lightning, cf. *Phil. Min. I* 22, 27–28.

possibilities that God is *en* or *hyper* the universe (rejecting both), whereas Psellos places him *exô*, a crucial difference in terminology.[63]

We will see in connection with his ethics and "humanism" that Psellos knowingly reversed the basic polarities of Patristic thought in those spheres of thought as well. His playful and self-deprecating comments mask profound and far-reaching commitments. In a letter sent possibly to Aimilianos, the patriarch of Antioch, he divides Truth into two philosophies and claims for himself the "earthly" one that gushes up salty water from below, while assigning to his correspondent the "heavenly" one that rains down drinkable water.[64] If this was light-hearted or in jest, it was not thereby also idle. Were Psellos a true follower of Gregorios or of any Church Father, he would have let pagan oracles and the salty waters of Hellenic theology and "earth-bound" philosophy lie where the Fathers had buried them at the end of antiquity. He would not have tried to bring them up from the depths.

Psellos' professions of innocence and confessions of faith should carry little weight with us as they were probably involuntary. Unlike Sokrates, he had no interest in dying for his beliefs – or rather his lack of beliefs – and martyrdom he would have considered the result of an inflexible, arrogant, and self-righteous mentality. Lying, at any rate, he took to be a necessary skill for serious political men, but it also had a playful side. In a letter, he confessed to often stealing icons from churches "because they depict the art (*technê*) of the painter." But, "when I came under suspicion, I immediately swore that I had not done it." The purely aesthetic appreciation of religious art is interesting enough; but what especially commands attention is "the inner freedom that a Christian scholar must have had ... to boast that he steals from churches!"[65]

## BETWEEN BODY AND SOUL: A NEW HUMANISM

Psellos' "humanism" has received some attention by scholars in part because he stated its goals more explicitly. He aimed to reunite body and soul, the physical and the intellectual, male and female, even heaven and earth, all of which he believed had been sundered by those who practiced

---

[63] Gregorios of Nazianzos, *Or.* 28.10–11 (*The Second Theological Oration*). Psellos' lecture on this passage of Gregorios (*Theol. I* 52.100–143) is exegetical, with no independent commentary.
[64] Psellos, *Letter G* 12; for the recipient, Papaioannou (1998) 83 (I find Aimilianos more likely than Ioannes Doukas).
[65] Psellos, *Letter KD* 129; cf. Oikonomides (1991a) 36 (who translates "I swore that I would not do it again"); Cutler and Browning (1992) 28–29. Quotation: Ljubarskij (2004a) 355.

asceticism and renunciation to an extreme; in his mind, however, these "extremists" *were* the mainstream of Byzantine monasticism and Christian ethics. In many works, including letters, orations, and the *Chronographia*, he projected a compelling and consistent view of integrated humanity as against the radical polarization and self-alienation that were invented and demanded by ascetic Christianity. This effort complemented the rehabilitation of natural science. In both fields, Psellos' aim was to enable people to see themselves for what they really were rather than for what they ought to be according to the ascetics who had seized power along with the moral high ground. Without losing sight of the inherent superiority of the philosophical life as explicated by Plato, Psellos set out to rescue the material body from the epistemological and moral margin to which it had been relegated. This partly explains the paradox that he, the most philosophical and elitist of all Byzantines, wrote so many detailed descriptions of the passions, weaknesses, temptations, and daily habits and follies of his contemporaries, including himself. It was in this sphere that he would revolutionize intellectual life in Byzantium, as we will see when we turn to his humanist heirs of the following century.

In an effort to move Byzantine culture in this direction, which could only result in a closer engagement with the more anthropological pluralism of ancient literature, Psellos produced over half a dozen systematic formulations of views that could have shocked some of his readers. Yet he indulged, in his usual half-jesting half-serious manner, in confounding their expectations.

For I am a man, a soul attached to a body. Therefore I take pleasure in both thoughts and sensations. Should someone else manage to establish his soul above his body, he will be happy and blessed. But I, even though I only half-live in the body, must still love it.

As far as I am concerned, philosophy is divided into two parts. One part of it seems free from emotion (*apathes*) and harsh, and only the mind can imagine it, while the other seems sociable and philanthropic. Of these, I praised the first one, but did not love it; the second one, however, although I admire it less, I emulate more. It is because of this that I cared for my parents in their old age, showed affection to my brothers, and give what is due to my friends.[66]

The freedom from temptation and emotion and detachment from material life that was demanded by the ascetic life and glorified in hagiography suppresses the tender feelings that people who are not saints experience with their families and friends. Psellos tried to fashion a discourse that

[66] Psellos, *Letter KD* 160; *Letter S* 17.

would enable his readers to talk meaningfully about the things that they loved without having to subsume them under denaturing abstractions, just as his scientific project would enable them to talk about nature without having to invoke God at every juncture; and both would lead them to talk more about the Greeks. We see here the serious intent behind Psellos' light-hearted admission that he stood for an "earthly" philosophy in contrast to patriarch Aimilianos' "heavenly" one.

We saw that Psellos recognized the historical existence of five national philosophies, though only two of them, the Greek and "ours," held his attention for long. In a different sense philosophy was divided into two parts, namely into its earthly and heavenly varieties, and here Psellos presented himself openly as a partisan of the former. He sometimes did this gently, as in the encomium for his mother, where he contrasts her extreme ascetic regime ("your philosophy") to his more bookish and worldly life ("my philosophy"). He was here, as elsewhere, hiding behind the Christian cliché of unworthiness and exploiting it for his own defensive purposes.

This was for her the chief object of meditation and philosophy: to cut her hair to the very root, to make her body rough, her knees hard with calluses, to harden her fingers, and to live purely in the presence of the pure God ... Yet, O mother, though I admire and regard you with amazement, I am not entirely capable of emulating you. To the contrary ... my devotion to philosophy [i.e., his current monastic state] is limited to its cloak ... As though I were resisting your righteous advice and bending against the rule, I do not entirely philosophize according to that philosophy which is so dear to you, and I do not know what fate took hold of me from the very beginning and fixated me onto the study of books, from which I cannot break away.[67]

Psellos could project this contrast more firmly, respectfully or polemi-cally depending on the addressee and context. Yet in all cases the target of his attack was the Christian ideal that denigrated the body and called for total devotion to God and a state of *apatheia*. This ideal, in his view, tended to produce thoroughly unlikeable self-righteous men who could not func-tion well socially, much less govern a state as sometimes happened in Byzantium. Their attitude, he explains at length in a digression in the *Chronographia*, is "more suitable to eternity than to our times, to the afterlife than to the present life ... For the life of the body, being more political in nature, harmonizes more easily with our present circumstances. I would even go so far as to say that the affections of the soul are adapted to

[67] Psellos, *Encomium for his Mother* 2c–d, 11b, 26a.

our bodily life" (6A.7). Psellos went out of his way elsewhere to suggest that body and soul may be organically linked.[68] As for those who try to sever them,

if some man should manage to surpass the body and take his stand at an extreme of the intellectual life, what will he have in common with the affairs of men? ... Let him go up to a high and lofty mountain and stand in the company of angels, so that he may shine with a heavenly light. He will have thus separated himself from men and renounced human society. But no one has ever entirely triumphed over nature and if such a person happened to be entrusted with the direction of political affairs, he should take care to handle matters in a political manner and not pretend that he possessed the straightness of a yardstick. For not everyone has been made perfect to such a degree. (6A.8)

Psellos goes on to advocate a middle position between the rejection of the body, which he sarcastically calls "perfection," and indulgence in its pleasures.[69]

If the soul chooses the middle path, even though it experiences many and powerful passions, as though it had chosen the exact center of a circle, then it creates the political man. This soul is neither entirely divine nor intellectual, but neither is it in love with material pleasures and ruled by passion. (6A.8; cf. *Letters S* 154, 157)

Psellos went well beyond the rehabilitation of the body: he revalued the fundamental modes and orders of ethical life, countering the otherworldly bias of the official faith and restoring the political orientation of Greek thought. His new villains were fundamentalists like Keroularios or, at any rate, the image of them that he created in polemical texts. Possessing absolute standards of truth gained through mystical experience, such men were unyielding, narrow-minded, and imposed their inflexible notions of justice on a complex world. In a bitter *Letter to Michael Keroularios*, probably meant to be circulated, Psellos attacked the patriarch on precisely these grounds and defended his own worldly stance, embracing his bodily side and admitting that on occasion he would even give in to some of its temptations. "Like some of the stars," he wrote on another occasion to a priest or monk, "I am too much in motion ... My nature is not simple but composed of contrary elements."[70]

---

[68] Psellos, *Encomium for his Mother* 3a, 4a. This deserves more extensive study; for the *Chronographia* passages, Criscuolo (1982a) 155–161; Kaldellis (1999a) ch. 23, which considers Psellos' relation to orthodox Platonism. Cf. Synesios' similar polemics in Bregman (1982) 132.

[69] For how Psellos conceptualized middle positions and mixed states, see Jenkins (2006).

[70] Psellos, *Letter to Michael Keroularios* 2a; see Ljubarskij (1992b) 176–177. Cf. *Letter A* 1. For Keroularios, see Tinnefeld (1989); Ljubarskij (2004a) 125–140.

It comes as no surprise, then, that like the outspoken Hellenes of late antiquity such as Julian, Libanios, and Synesios, Psellos opposed monasticism, rejecting its ideals and suggesting that monks were in fact unable to renounce their bodies, despite their efforts and claims. His comment that whole whales pulled up from the ocean could not satisfy their hunger echoes Libanios' vicious description of the "black-robed tribe that eats more then elephants." Still, their failure resulted not in a more balanced attitude toward their own humanity but in a hypocritical and suppressed sensuality that was, moreover, costly to the state. Both Psellos and his contemporary the historian Michael Attaleiates cynically proposed that monastic wealth be confiscated to "assist" the monks in their quest to renounce the world; it would also benefit the state that both men governed.[71] His own experience of life in the habit, which began when he fled to a monastery on Mt. Olympos in Bithynia in 1054–1055, was miserable. He had composed a witty parody of the liturgy exposing one of the holy mountain's heavy drinkers, and later exchanged acerbic letters and poems with the monks. "Father Zeus," one of them mocked him, "you could not endure Olympos even briefly, your goddesses weren't there with you," to which Psellos responded with a torrent of abuse.[72]

Psellos' revaluation of material life had a positive political component. Because of his theoretical interest and personal involvement in politics, Psellos elaborated the political aspects of his anthropology. He developed the concept of the "political man," a man educated enough to adorn the state with culture but discerning and morally flexible enough to do what the times demanded. Psellos associated this ideal with his friend, the statesman and patriarch Konstantinos Leichoudes (but not exclusively with him). Another friend, the teacher Niketas, was deemed worthy of office, Psellos wrote, because

he was so agreeable to all that he seemed similar to that statue which has been celebrated by so many, upon which some technique known to sculptors had so arranged the eyes on either side that they seemed to be both still and in movement, and thus the statue seemed to cast its gaze equally among onlookers who stood on either side of it.[73]

---

[71] For monasticism, see esp. Psellos, *Chronographia* 3.16 (whales), 6A.18, 7.59, with Kaldellis (1999a) ch. 10; Ljubarskij (2004a) 149–154. Libanios, *Or.* 30.8 (*To the Emperor Theodosios, On Behalf of the Temples*). Michael Attaleiates, *History* 61–62.

[72] Parody: Psellos, *Poem* 22. Exchanges: *Poem* 21 and *Letters S* 35, 166–167, 185, with de Vries-van der Velden (1996) 119. In the 1040s he had opposed Mauropous' decision to be tonsured: Karpozilos (1982) 27–28.

[73] Leichoudes: Criscuolo (1981) 20–22; (1982a) 138–139, 160–162; (1982b) 207–214; and (1983) 15–16, 60–72; Ljubarskij (2004a) 92–95. Niketas: Psellos, *Funeral Oration for Niketas* 12–13.

The political man is a work of art, carefully crafted to combine opposites. A different type is represented for Psellos by military men like Basileios II, who lacked the refinement of the perfect political type and who practiced a form of asceticism in their effort to master themselves and others on campaigns and in battle; such men Psellos seems to have deemed necessary for the survival of the state and he gave much thought to the problem of reconciling them to his own political and philosophical ideals.[74]

Psellos was the first Byzantine since late antiquity who can be said to have had a *political philosophy*, a distinction owed to the exigencies of his career. On one occasion he went so far as to admit that *praxis* comes before *theôria* and the practical man before the theoretical one – but he said this in a tent full of angry generals![75] I have argued that in the *Chronographia* Psellos advocates a thoroughly secular conception of the state, thereby creating a congenial theoretical home for himself, given that he spent so much of his life in the palace and had to present himself as a court philosopher. In his *Letter to Michael Keroularios*, he praised the emperor Isaakios for "harmonizing political philosophy with rule over subjects" by "reintroducing philosophy into imperial affairs," i.e., by agreeing to sponsor Psellos himself. Psellos offered, as precedents for his own position, *exempla* lifted from the fourth-century philosopher-statesman Themistios, who, as we saw in Chapter 2, was himself eager to promote philosophy at the court and also had to defend himself, like Psellos, with an *Oration in reply to those who found fault with him for accepting public office.*[76] Psellos too faced resistance, for "philosophy" in Byzantine tradition stood mostly for monasticism and speculative theology. Such "philosophers" were not expected to get their hands dirty (or their pockets lined) in politics. Like Themistios, Psellos defended himself against the charge that he had betrayed his higher calling and, on occasion, had to surrender some of his offices. But he did not concede any theoretical ground. He argued that philosophy confers practical benefits, for instance through military technology. He cited the ancient philosophical ideal of political engagement, offering Plato and Aristotle as his models. In this way, Psellos' political *praxis* and *theôria* were likewise bound up with his general revival of ancient thought.[77]

---

[74] Kaldellis (1999a) ch. 6, 22–25.    [75] Psellos, *Chronographia* 7.28.

[76] Psellos, *Letter to Michael Keroularios* 4b, citing Themistios, *Or.* 34.8, on whom see pp. 72–73 above; secular state: Kaldellis (1999a) chs. 5–9.

[77] Psellos, *When he resigned from the rank of* protasêkrêtis esp. 121–134 (*Or. Min.* 8). Greek precedents are cited throughout, also in *To the slanderer who posted his accusations in writing* (*Or. Min.* 7), another defensive tract.

A word must be said at this point on the term "humanism," because it is used in different senses. Byzantinists have often meant by it nothing more than classical scholarship or, say, the use of Plato in resolving a theological debate.[78] But such things do not constitute humanism, even if they are often a part of it. Few scholars or Platonists in Byzantium (or elsewhere) were humanists, though of course few pure types will be found to fit any definition. Still, a constellation of general characteristics may be charted to make the concept meaningful and applicable. Humanism involves an interest in the manifold expressions of human life that transgresses the normative constraints of traditional or official truths. It also tends to seek standards for human behavior within the realm of experience. We saw above that Psellos based his ideas on how he should live on an inclusive understanding of what it means to be human (*anthrôpos*). "It is quite necessary," he wrote to a friend, "that one not live according to other people's notions; so don't weigh me by foreign measures: each should be understood by his own rule and standard."[79] According to his own testimony in many works, Psellos' own epistemology was based only on books and personally lived experience. He was therefore scornful of claims to divine or supernatural inspiration made by certain authorities.

Moreover, Psellos was interested precisely in those dark, aberrant, and earthy aspects of human behavior that had been excluded by the moralizing polarities of Byzantine rhetoric, and he devised ways to represent them anew. Consistent with this rehabilitation of the fullness of humanity, he was eager (like Montaigne) to divulge his own petty sins and weaknesses and even took pride in them, albeit playfully so as to ironize his ultimate commitments. In a letter to his friend Ioannes Doukas, who had also been forced to become a monk for political reasons but seems to have fallen in love with a girl, Psellos jokingly casts aside their common "monastic garb and life" and admits to an infatuation in his youth with a pair of "slanted eyes and skin that was off-white ... For you too are made of earth just as I am."[80] Psellos fashioned a new subjectivity that did not exclude weakness and transgression, but expanded its depth by promoting an ideal more suitable to human beings than to angels. In a letter to some monks, he

---

[78] Lemerle (1986) and Stephanou (1949) respectively. Basilikopoulou-Ioannidou (1971–1972) 170 is promising, but ultimately disappointing; see rather Magdalino (1993) 398; Garzya (1992) 46. Byzantine humanism is a different matter from the Byzantine contribution to the Renaissance.

[79] Psellos, *Letter S* 1; cf. Ljubarskij (2004a) 298–299, 326.

[80] Psellos, *Letter G* 4; cf. *Chronographia* 6.150: "my narrative has passed over in silence many absurd events, which would bring shame upon the author." To say this is not the same as to silence those events.

admitted that if he compared his sins against God to the knowledge he has
gathered from books, the former would overwhelm the latter. Yet "I rejoice
more in the latter, however little it may be, than I am depressed by the
former, however many they may be."[81] Humanists, then, to complete our
definition, are fascinated by the ambiguities of experience and are ready to
accept indeterminacy. Their inquiries are often aporetic, whence their
preferred mode of expression is often rhetorical (literary or artistic).
Humanism draws heavily on the classical tradition, finding there models
of beauty and virtue that are free of the rigid doctrines of later ages. Yet
because it represents a *reaction* to the reductionism of official truths and the
psychological crudities of dogmatism, monasticism, and scholasticism, as
well as (in modern times) of science, nationalism, and corporatism, that is
fascism and capitalism, it rarely makes sense to speak of humanism in
antiquity itself.

As we will see in the next chapter, the humanists of the Komnenian era
cultivated an ideal of refinement that was largely independent of their faith
and sought to revive aspects of Greece in their persons and works, occasionally even rehabilitating "the Greeks" collectively on aesthetic grounds
and in spite of their paganism. Those scholars' belief that beauty and virtue
transcended religion was typically humanist, even if it was expressed more
often in practice than in theory. Yet I have found no aspect of the humanist
enterprise of the twelfth century that is not already developed in Psellos.
The implications of this fact are staggering, and it certainly complicates any
notion of a linear and gradual development that we might propose for the
period as a whole. Moreover, for reasons that we will discuss but which are
not fully clear, Psellos was philosophically more advanced than his twelfth-
century successors in that he was prepared to follow his axioms to their
logical conclusions. For example, his teacher and friend Mauropous was
closer to the spirit of twelfth-century humanism when he wrote a poem
pleading that Christ save Plato and Plutarch for, of all "outsiders," they
came the closest to the divine *logos*.[82] It is extremely unlikely, however, that
Psellos believed in Hell in the first place. His lack of interest in the
afterlife in the thousands of pages he wrote is powerful testimony to the
unimportance of such notions. For him, Plato needed rehabilitation, not
personal salvation.

---

[81] Psellos, *Letter KD* 36.
[82] Ioannes Mauropous, *Epigram* 43 (p. 24); cf. Karpozilos (1982) 103–104, for Mauropous' slight
engagement with the classics (despite the credit these verses have earned him).

What Psellos bequeathed to posterity, besides a philosophy that was partially emancipated from Christian oversight, was a psychology whose scope and nuance were almost without precedent. To be sure, Byzantine intellectual culture had moved in that direction already,[83] but nothing quite prepares us for, say, the *Chronographia*. The psychological sensitivity that Psellos deployed there has received little attention, though an outline may be given of its major features here. First, we observe an interest in eroticism, a topic muted in Byzantium prior to this. The *Chronographia* also pays detailed attention to the physical appearance of its protagonists and makes physiognostic diagnoses of their characters. Psellos highlights sensual qualities and plays up erotic passions. As a result, his account of the affair of Zoe and Michael in Book 3 and the various affairs of Konstantinos IX Monomachos in Book 6 make his text read at times like a part-bawdy part-*noir* romance novel. Psellos knew the ancient novels well, two of which he reviewed in an essay from a literary standpoint, praising the one for "breathing the grace of Aphrodite" and criticizing the other for "neglecting the lovers' relations." In another essay he revealed that he had studied and used techniques from the ancient novels in his own writing.[84]

Psellos' interest in "physical appearances" and beauty was not innocent. It too was a self-conscious correction of Christian attitudes. In a funeral oration for a student named Ioannes, Psellos defensively requests that he not be criticized for praising Ioannes' beauty and tries to explain away why Scripture so often disparages that quality. Following this renegotiation of cultural patrimonies, it makes sense that he then goes on to compare Ioannes with classical statues and heroes. The humanists of the next century would also turn to classical models when they wanted to say things that were not treated favorably (or at all) in Scripture. To give another example, Psellos' encomium for his mother, which includes sections on his father and sister, alludes throughout to Gregorios of Nazianzos' funeral orations for his father and sister, which often praise the saint's mother as well. Yet whereas Gregorios paid little attention to the physical appearance of his loved ones – and Psellos too concedes that as a "philosopher" he should not do so either – nevertheless he goes on, in typical violation of his promises, to give detailed descriptions of his family's physical beauty,

---

[83] For one aspect, see Ljubarskij (1992a).
[84] Psellos, *What is the difference between the novels that deal with Charikleia and Leukippe?* 32 (p. 92); cf. *On the style of some texts (De oper. daem.* pp. 48–52); cf. Ljubarskij (2004a) 333.

including his own! He did the same for his daughter Styliane who died young.[85]

Psellos was fascinated by the nooks and crannies of social life. In a series of playful letters he introduced the ribald wandering monk Elias to provincial magistrates. This man could tell tales, perform music and dance, and knew all about the prostitutes in the capital. The details of his life that Psellos recounts are curious, but more interesting is the fact that Psellos must have seen something of himself in this man who was neither (or both) Greek and barbarian, earthly and heavenly, a monk and frequenter of taverns, devoted to both God and Mammon, suspended always between extremes.[86] Psellos peered into the corners of his own soul too. He was, he admits, in touch with his feminine side and willing to acknowledge it to others in moments of emotional weakness or joy, associating it with his soft, gentle, and delicate self; in his capacity as Sokratic educator he was, of course, a midwife as well.[87] For all that, he was not immune to the charms of the heroic life. A partisan of military rule, he often compared the generals who appear in the *Chronographia* to the heroes of Homer, fashioning martial images of "blood, sweat, and dust." Ioannes Batatzes, for example, "in the physique of his body and the strength of his arms was equal to the celebrated heroes of old." Psellos was possibly echoing the rising popularity of heroic family chronicles that would contribute to the explosion of martial literature under the Komnenoi; yet, again, he was ahead of the curve and stimulated the trend, in historiography at any rate.[88]

To conclude, Psellos was entirely comfortable in the day-to-day world of orthodox piety, whose air he breathed all his life. Always a mixture of elements, he could be moved by love, compassion, and pity, if perhaps not by humility. He could undermine Christian doctrine in his morning lectures and spend the night with his mother in a convent. He rarely allowed philosophy to disrupt personal relationships. He engaged, even theoretically, with folk traditions and was well aware of the kind of world he inhabited: he never deceived himself into thinking that eleventh-century Byzantium was anything like classical Greece. And yet his philosophy had ruptured the veil of that world. He saw the sensuality harbored by

---

[85] Psellos, *Monodia for his student Ioannes the* patrikios (pp. 149–150); *Encomium for his Mother* esp. 2c–d for the disclaimer; *Regarding his daughter Styliane, who died before the age of marriage* (*Misc.* esp. pp. 68–77). In general, see Ljubarskij (2004a) ch. 7; Kaldellis (2006) 38–39.

[86] Dennis (2003) for introduction and translation.

[87] Psellos, *Letters S* 72, 157, 180; see Littlewood (1981) 140–142; Papaioannou (2000).

[88] Chronicles: Roueché (1988) 127–129; martial bias and imagery: Psellos, *Chronographia* 6.122 with Kaldellis (1999a) 181–183.

monasticism and understood the heroic qualities and Machiavellian skills that sustained the empire. He knew that un-Christian values would persist despite not being acknowledged by the dominant orthodox discourse, for nature cannot be tossed out. His sensitivity to these aspects of life was perhaps first stimulated and then enhanced by his serious engagement with ancient literature, especially poetic and erotic. Just as his philosophical and scientific inquiries were rooted in Greek thought, the distinctive features of his humanism represented a separate if parallel rehabilitation of Hellenism. In his multifarious writings, Psellos invented a persona that could touch Orthodoxy when necessary and wear its garb but that could also veer sharply toward classical values and images. He created a middle ground distinctively his own, answerable only to his own Typhonic personality, for all that it would guide the steps of many others yet to come.

HELLENES IN THE ELEVENTH CENTURY?

Psellos' engagement with Hellenism entailed philosophical, scientific, ethical, and literary innovations, but did it result in any closer identification with the Greeks themselves? Did his Hellenocentric outlook affect the way he talked about his fellow Romans and their culture?

Whatever innovations we find in this regard, we will have to read them against a persistently Roman background. Psellos calls the empire Roman (more accurately, "of the Romans") throughout the *Chronographia*. Both there and in the didactic *Historia Syntomos* that he wrote for Michael VII, he traces the institutions and history of the state to ancient Rome. In many works, he cites Romulus as an *exemplum* and on two occasions emphatically asserts his own patriotism – which some may have had reason to doubt – as a *philoromaios*, *philopatris*, and *philopolis*.[89] We must remember that Psellos spent much of his life at the Byzantine court, where the laws, symbols, terminology, and ideology of Roman rule were pervasive and powerful. In his day-to-day affairs he would have been dealing constantly with "Roman" matters. Still, he was aware of the composite nature of the culture, in particular of its three main originative elements: Roman, Greek, and Hebrew.[90]

The Christian dimension of imperial ideology was something to which Psellos paid little attention, especially when he was not constrained to do so by circumstance. But was he ever tempted to paint his patriotism with the

---

[89] Romulus: Fisher (1994); patriotism: Psellos, *Chronographia* 6.154, 6.190.     [90] See p. 3 above.

brush of Hellenism? We have already seen that when Psellos announces his philosophical project in the *Chronographia* he boasts that he could previously not find "even a seed of wisdom in Greece or the barbarian lands, though I searched everywhere" (6.37). "Greece" here refers to the empire of his own time and not merely to the Greek mainland. So Psellos' overriding interest in philosophy led him in this one instance to replace the political polarity of Romans and barbarians with the cultural one of Greeks and barbarians. "Greece" here is Romania, only viewed from the standpoint of its higher culture and philosophy. Rome proper Psellos seems to have associated with the arts of government and war. In a short work rebuking the impetuousness of his student Ioannes Italos, he notes that the Roman tradition was not famed for science; its glories were rather men such as Brutus, Cato, and Lucullus, "who did nothing other than worship Ares."[91]

If there is a Hellenic bias here, it is less a personal identification as a Greek than a preference for the contribution of the Greeks to Byzantine culture over that of the ancient Romans. It resulted in a tendency to describe the state of the Byzantine world in Greek rather than Roman terms. This is shown in a defense that Psellos once had to offer of his student Italos, who had come from Italy to study in Constantinople. Italos had maintained in a debate among the students that "Greece and its colonies in Ionia" had been stripped of their wisdom which had now passed to "Assyrians, Medes, and Egyptians ... Greeks now barbarize while barbarians Hellenize." A Greek today, finding himself at the "palace of Dareios," would hear things he had never heard before despite his knowledge of Greek, while an arrogant barbarian would feel contempt for the superficiality of the philosophy taught in "Greece and our entire territory." Italos was probably referring here to the Arab mastery of Greek science and philosophy.[92] Psellos unfortunately does not discuss his pupil's theory, though he would probably have endorsed it on the "Greek" side – at least for the period before *he* began to teach! Instead, in defense of Italos he goes on to appraise his style, damning it with faint and ambiguous praise.

Still, we have evidence here that Italos, a student in Psellos' school, was talking about the present from a Hellenocentric standpoint, even if to condemn the current state of "Greece." We may be tempted to dismiss this terminology as mere classical affectation. Byzantium and the Islamic world

---

[91] Psellos, *To Ioannes the Lombard who was forcing him to accelerate his instruction* 97–100 (*Or. Min.* 18).
[92] Psellos, *Praise of Italos* 2, 30–55 (*Or. Min.* 19); cf. *Letter S* 169; see Magdalino (1996c) 23–24 and (2003b) 26–28; for Arab Hellenism, Gutas (1998) 84–95.

are reconfigured as "Greece" and "Assyria" and endowed with obsolete items such as "Ionia" and the "palaces of Dareios." And yet there is innovation here, for we have seen that the Byzantines did not typically figure *themselves* in classicizing terms as Greeks but as Ausones. Interestingly, at the beginning of this speech it is Italos whom Psellos calls a "Latinos and Auson," because he actually did hail from Italy. What we are observing here is the beginning of a deep shift in classicizing terminology, certainly fostered by the Hellenocentric outlook of Psellos' philosophy and soon to be reinforced by the rise of the West. Among intellectuals, Romania was being refigured as Hellas while Latin and Ausonian associations were being displaced to actual westerners. (In the next chapter, we will examine the acceleration of this trend in the Komnenian period.)

Psellos could call himself and other Byzantines "Greeks," though only in limited respects that are immediately specified, e.g., with regard to language or *paideia*.[93] What he was not interested in doing was postulating a linear national continuity between himself and the ancient Greeks; so there are no "modern Greeks" in his view of the world. As we saw, in the overwhelming majority of his lectures the Greeks are basically a foreign nation, separated from "us" by a gulf of time and religious difference. It only happens that their science is based on nature and is therefore accessible to all who know Greek regardless of their religion and culture. Italos, after all, argued that even the barbarians today are well versed in Greek wisdom.

Still, Psellos' program required that he rehabilitate those ancient Greeks from "our" suspicions and highlight their affinities with "us." The fact that the land of Greece was part of the territory of the empire may have been accidental as far as he was concerned, but it allowed him to create rhetorical "passages" that linked modern Romans and ancient Greeks. For example, in quoting Sokrates' advice to his students that they find teachers in the cities of Greece, Psellos adds coyly in a parenthesis, "And why not in Byzantion?" Byzantion was of course an ancient city, but in its modern incarnation as Constantinople it points to Psellos' school as the heir of Sokratic philosophy.[94] Such parallels, however, were the conceits of rhetorical ingenuity and do not point to any revived Hellenic national identity.

More consequential for the future of Hellenism in Byzantium would be the revival of the polarity of Greeks and barbarians, which tended by

---

[93] E.g., Psellos, *Letter KD* 190.
[94] Psellos, *To his students regarding philosophy and rhetoric* 26 (*Or. Min.* 25).

default to cast "us" implicitly as Greeks, for, whatever else we may be (Christians, Romans, etc.), we are assuredly not barbarians. In looking for ancient *exempla* to make a point in one treatise, Psellos opts to "pass by the barbarians and those who dwell apart from us in both land and custom" and turns instead to "the most wise Greeks – and by Greeks I mean those whose honorable name delimits that land opposite of ours."[95] In this comparison, "we" live in Constantinople and not in Greece, but Greeks are proper models for us because they are wise, civilized (by definition), and lived nearby. It is but a small step for us to actually be called Greeks, even if only rhetorically. We are Greeks, after all, insofar as we are not barbarians. But what kinds of barbarians could stimulate such a reaction? In Byzantium there were basically two kinds: foreign enemies and internal groups that were still being assimilated. Foreigners were often infidels and always un-Roman, and so did not threaten Byzantine identities, but internal barbarians had claims that could not be ignored: against them, Byzantine intellectuals required additional modalities of distinction. This is how Hellenism, in the form of *paideia*, came into the picture in the twelfth century. The process, we see, was underway with Psellos in the eleventh. In the *Chronographia*, he complains about internal "barbarians" who had attained positions of power. Note the alternative to which they are contrasted: "we are governed all too often by men we bought as slaves from the barbarians; great commands are entrusted not to men like Perikles or Themistokles but to the lowliest Spartakos."[96] Roman slaves are denigrated here by comparison to Greek heroes. The link to Greece was reinforced by the fact that modern-day Romans spoke Greek, though, still, no national continuity was posited on this linguistic basis.[97]

Psellos had no particular interest in the land of Greece itself, apart from the rhetorical passages already noted. Two letters reveal that its decrepitude depressed the magistrates who were sent to govern it. He tried to console them by pointing to its ancient glory: "Was all that in vain?"[98] But as far as we know he made no effort to visit Greece himself. His interest in Hellenism was almost completely philosophical, not territorial or national. His treatises on Athenian topography and legal terminology were probably intended as study aids for his students, who had to master the orators and

---

[95] Psellos, *To his private secretary* 33–35 (*Or. Min.* 17).
[96] Psellos, *Chronographia* 6.134. In the *Letter to Michael Keroularios* 9b, Psellos seems to label his own realm "Greece" while that governed by the patriarch as "a barbarian land." The Greek–barbarian polarity is here deployed in purely intra-Roman cultural polemic.
[97] Cf. Psellos, *Letter S* 169.   [98] Psellos, *Letters S* 26, 33.

historians, and are explicable in terms of his manifold corpus of writings.[99] Still, in one letter he apparently asks an official in Greece to send him some statues, which indicates that he may have had a collection; moreover, he wrote descriptions of ancient artworks and tried to interpret them in minor essays.[100] We may therefore add aesthetic appreciation to his mostly philosophical and humanistic engagement with Hellenism. Still, he never called himself a Greek. He recommended an Athenian acquaintance in a letter, noting that we must love children on account of their fathers, in this case the ancient Athenian heroes. But this is a standard rhetorical device, by which one's "ancestors" are always the most famous ancient inhabitants of one's town. No idea of Greek continuity can be based on such conventional statements.[101]

Let us close with an episode that illustrates the ambiguity that attends all notions of Hellenic identity in the eleventh century and the conceptual obstacles that the Byzantines had to overcome before they could reassert any notion of ethnic or national Hellenism. In his dramatic account of the fall of Michael V in 1042, Psellos notes that the urban mob marched to secure Theodora, the sister of the empress Zoe, after having chosen as its leader "one of the top men who had served her father [Konstantinos VIII] . . . a man who was not a Greek by *genos* but whose character was still of the noblest birth, his stature heroic, and the respect that he inspired rooted in ancestral pride" (5.36). This unprecedented attestation of Greek *genos* in Byzantium hardly proves that the Byzantines believed that they were ethnic Greeks.[102] But what did Psellos mean? He could not have meant that this man was not from the region of Greece, for why would he bother to note that? Most Byzantines were not. In fact, we happen to know who he was: he was the *patrikios* Konstantinos Kabasilas, from a family that had already produced a *doux* of Thessalonike in 1022 and that would have an illustrious future in high office.[103] Whatever Kabasilas' precise ethnic ancestry, Psellos goes out of his way to praise his ancient nobility, which means that he wanted his readers to believe that he was a native Roman of noble descent. What did it mean, then, that he was not a Greek by *genos?* I believe that Psellos is making an ethical comparison here: *even though*

---

[99] Psellos, *On Athenian places and names* (*De. oper. daem.* pp. 44–48); *To his students regarding legal terminology* (ibid. 95–110); cf. Magdalino (1993) 400.

[100] Papamastorakis (2004) 119.     [101] Psellos, *Letter S* 20. See p. 330 below.

[102] *Pace,* e.g., Vryonis (1978) 232; Charanis (1978) 89; Angelov (2005) 301. Nor does it have to do with their alleged "international" outlook: Pitsakis (1991) 106; (1995) 32.

[103] Konstantinos: Ioannes Skylitzes, *Historical Synopsis: Michael V* 1 (p. 418); *doux:* ibid.: *Basileios II and Konstantinos VII* 46 (p. 368). For the family, see Angelopoulos (1977).

Kabasilas was not one of the (ancient) Greeks (a standard for heroic nobility), still he possessed the noble qualities that we associate with them. This is consistent with Psellos' high estimation of the moral qualities of the Greeks in the *Chronographia* and elsewhere and prefigures their elevation to the pinnacle of natural virtue by the humanists of the twelfth century.

# CHAPTER 5

# The Third Sophistic: the performance of Hellenism under the Komnenoi

## ANATHEMA UPON PHILOSOPHY

A lone philosopher in an age of opportunity, Psellos opened up many fronts in his struggle to establish Hellenism at the heart of Byzantine intellectual life. His revolutionary project aimed to set metaphysics, science, ethics, and literature on a new basis whose foundations had been laid by the ancient Greeks. Though he had allies, students, and friends, as well as enemies, his contemporary impact cannot be gauged. It seems to have been limited, to judge from the silence that surrounds him. Modern references to "the eleventh-century revival of letters" should be treated with caution: without Psellos, the eleventh century would be one of the bleakest in Byzantine secular literature. The previous chapter took the form of an exposition of his ideas because he was the sole prophet of Hellenism in his age.

The revolutionary philosophy of one century is often the common sense of the next. This chapter is about Psellos' twelfth-century heirs, whose Hellenisms were blocked in some respects and facilitated in others. Through well-publicized prosecutions, the Komnenian regime discouraged the pursuit of a key aspect of Psellos' project, metaphysics, even while in other ways it was encouraging the development of the Hellenic sites of the culture. Komnenian society happened to evolve in a way that made the cultivation of Hellenism into a powerful trend. Psellos' heirs, a few dozen men and one woman, participated in this enterprise without necessarily sharing his philosophy or even knowing its revolutionary objectives. But ultimately they served his aims nonetheless, just as in a different way they served those of their political masters. Because they moved in the same circles and were exponents of the same general trends, a thematic exposition that draws on them all simultaneously is more appropriate here, though an effort will be made to preserve the quirky personalities of these poets, orators, scholars, and humanists.

Many historians today look to the Komnenian period for the origin of the "national" Hellenism that properly emerged in the thirteenth century and later in Byzantium. But it is the wrong place to look. Komnenian Hellenism was largely a matter of high culture, differentiating a segment of the elite from the majority of Byzantines; it was a class, not a national, identity. In this form, Hellenism was incapable of replacing the ingrained habits of Roman identity and had no interest in doing so, even when its rhetoric was experimentally extended into the sphere of national discourse (as it was by Psellos, albeit only haphazardly). Nor was it yet a reaction to the rise of the West, though it contained within it the seeds of that reaction. Rather, it represented a step in the gradual development of classical studies in Byzantium, which Psellos had elevated to a new level. It is unlikely, as we will see, that there was a strong link or even much continuity between the Hellenism of the Komnenian empire and that which emerged in the aftermath of 1204, though the two converged in certain rhetorical ways.

The role in this process ascribed here to Psellos requires justification, for in some studies he is misleadingly cited as merely one exemplar of a broad trend in Byzantine culture that spanned the eleventh and twelfth centuries and whose origins were social and economic.[1] But Psellos precedes all other instances of this trend by almost a century and should not be assimilated to them; moreover, his project, which exerted an enormous influence on later writers, certainly did not have social or economic "causes." The following fact merits attention: Psellos is the only secular Byzantine author who is repeatedly mentioned and praised by later writers. Such posthumous standing in Byzantium was unprecedented and began immediately upon his death. Theophylaktos Hephaistos, later bishop of Bulgaria, had studied under Psellos and praised him in two letters, a consolation for his death to Psellos' brother and a recommendation for his grandson.[2] "The most wise Psellos" is also the only post-sixth-century author cited as a model of style in a treatise on composition ascribed to Gregorios Pardos, bishop of Corinth in the early twelfth century and author of philological treatises (including one on the dialects of ancient Greek). Gregorios ranks Psellos' encomium for his mother among the four best orations ever written (with

---

[1] Notably Kazhdan and Epstein (1985). In its aims and methods this is an admirable and rare book, but its treatment of Psellos exemplifies its conflation of (at least) two different periods. The "populism" of the eleventh century (which receives virtually no attention) was unlike the regime of the Komnenoi. For a careful presentation that minds the gap between Psellos and his heirs, see Magdalino (1993) esp. 382–406, esp. 393 ff.

[2] Theophylaktos Hephaistos, *Letters* 27, 132. See Mullett (1997) 136, 138–139, 143; E. Papaioannou in Kaldellis (2006) 176–178.

Demosthenes, Aristeides, and Gregorios of Nazianzos).[3] The historian Anna Komnene, daughter of the new dynasty's founder, idolized Psellos for "attaining the peak of all knowledge" and "becoming famous for his wisdom," ambitions that she shared.[4] The classical scholar Eustathios, in a short work on the phrase *kyrie eleêson* written probably before he became bishop of Thessalonike, concludes by comparing his own "dark and shadowy" treatment of the question to the "shining and cloudless sun" of the "all-great" Psellos.[5] Psellos, again, is the only Byzantine author cited as a model orator by the otherwise sour scholar Ioannes Tzetzes, who notes that "he flourished a hundred years before us." Tzetzes also wrote a poem praising one of Psellos' commentaries on Aristotle by elaborating the image of a diver bringing pearls to the surface – and praise from Tzetzes was rare. Psellos' philosophical commentaries were among the very few that were written after the sixth century and still treated as standard by later Byzantines.[6] Michael Choniates, bishop of Athens in the late twelfth century and a student of Eustathios, ranked Psellos – "who lived shortly before us" – with Cato, Cicero, Arrianos, and Themistios, all men who attained perfection in philosophy yet did not neglect politics. Psellos is again the only Byzantine in that list and was also the direct source of Choniates' opinions regarding the relationship between philosophy and politics.[7] Finally, Psellos' summary of Roman law was being cited as authoritative in the early thirteenth century (by men who were educated in the twelfth). Our witness to these debates, Demetrios Chomatenos, the bishop of Ochrid, calls him "the most wise Psellos" and concedes that even if his opinion does not prevail "we are still dealing with the opinion of a wise man with much experience in the law."[8]

We should add to this list the many subsequent Byzantine historians who consulted, copied, or imitated his *Chronographia* with or without acknowledgment (e.g., Nikephoros Bryennios, Anna, and Ioannes Zonaras); the dozens of mostly philosophical works falsely attributed to him (a sure measure of an author's authority); and all those who read him

[3] Gregorios Pardos, *[On Composition]* 31–33, 36, 38 (pp. 320–322; see 110–111 in general). The point is emphasized by Walker (2004) 54–55 (independently). For Gregorios, see Wilson (1983) 184–190.

[4] Anna Komnene, *Alexiad* 5.8.3.

[5] Eustathios, *Exercise on the "Kyrie eleêson"* (*Or.* 5, Wirth p. 76), referring to Psellos, *Theol. I* 13. For a possible allusion, see Cesaretti (1991) 141 n. 11. See p. 297 below.

[6] Ioannes Tzetzes, *Histories* 11.712–713 (p. 457); poem: Duffy (1998); commentaries: ibid. 444 and (2002) 154. For Tzetzes' rejection of Psellos' reading of Homer, see Cesaretti (1991) ch. 4.

[7] Michael Choniates, *Letter* 28; see Kolovou (1999) 268–270. For Michael Glykas' "high regard" for Psellos, see Magdalino (1993) 405.

[8] Demetrios Chomatenos, *Various Works* 26 (pp. 104–105), quoting Psellos, *Poem* 8.

without recording their debt.[9] No other secular Byzantine author attained such canonical status. "Most Byzantine texts did not belong to the literary canon of the Byzantines." It was the classics and the Fathers who were rather "awarded the sort of institutionalized literary prestige the average Byzantine author could only hope for in his wildest dreams."[10] Psellos was not an average author, and his dreams changed a culture. What is important for our purposes – and not coincidental – is that most of the writers mentioned above who admired Psellos were also among the key figures in the revival of Hellenism in the twelfth century.

Our story begins in the years following Psellos' death, which saw the rise of Alexios I Komnenos (1081–1118) and the fall of Psellos' student Ioannes Italos, who had succeeded him as Consul of the Philosophers. Italos' condemnation and the prosecutions that followed would decisively limit the scope of philosophical Hellenism in the Komnenian empire. In March 1082 and at the instigation of Alexios, Italos, who had an analytical mind but a combative personality lacking charm, was formally charged before an ecclesiastical-imperial tribunal with an assortment of heresies and the crime of using Hellenic philosophy to interpret Christianity. Italos was forced to recant and confined to a monastery. Scholars who have examined the documents associated with this event have concluded that the tribunal twisted Italos' words at every turn to produce the desired result. Cynical motives have been ascribed to the prime mover, Alexios himself, who staged events that gave his shaky regime the appeal of religious traditionalism. The emperor's own piety had been called into question by his confiscation of Church wealth and Italos was connected to the Doukai and the Normans of Italy, a convenient victim. "It was a show trial, influenced in part by both narrow and broad political motives but certainly also by intellectual prejudice."[11] Bishops who questioned the proceedings were intimidated. The trial was therefore as much about the relationship between the new emperor and the Church as that between the orthodox establishment and the philosophers. Alexios followed it up with a strongly worded and even violent order to the patriarch "to condemn," according to one historian, "any and all individuals who may be found guilty of the

---

[9] For the twelfth-century philosopher and medical professor Michael Italikos, see Criscuolo (1971) 59–61; for the *maïstor* of the philosophers Manuel Karantenos, Criscuolo (1977) 107, 112; for Anna, Linnér (1983); Trapp (2003) 139; and Connor (2004) 249–254; for Psellos' philosophical legacy, Pontikos (1992); for his appearance in the *Timarion*, see p. 281 below. For the extent of his manuscript corpus, Moore (2005).

[10] Lauxtermann (2003) 75.

[11] Clucas (1981) 55. Clucas chronicles the trial; for the documents, Gouillard (1985). The main narrative source is Anna Komnene, *Alexiad* 5.8–9; for views of Italos, Magdalino (2002) 172.

'crime' of practicing philosophy in any independent fashion which appeared dangerously tangential to Christian dogma."[12] An appendix was rammed onto the *Synodikon of Orthodoxy* – a liturgical text recited on the Feast of Orthodoxy, originally meant to celebrate the defeat of iconoclasm. It would henceforth sport a forceful and rather incoherent condemnation of the Hellenic errors of Italos.

(ii) Anathema upon those who claim to be pious but shamelessly or rather impiously introduce the ungodly teaching of the Hellenes into the Orthodox Catholic Church concerning human souls and heaven and earth and other created objects . . .
(vii) Anathema upon those who go through a course of Hellenic studies and are taught not simply for the sake of education but follow these empty notions and believe in them as the truth, upholding them as a firm foundation to such an extent that they lead others to them, sometimes secretly, sometimes openly, and then without hesitation.
(viii) Anathema upon those who of their own accord invent an account of our Creation along with other myths, who accept the Platonic Forms as true, who say that matter possesses independent substance and is shaped by the Forms, who openly question the power of the Creator to bring all things from non-existence to existence, and as their Creator to impose a beginning and end on all things in the manner of their Lord and Master.[13]

We will never know the degree to which Psellos and his intellectual legacy rather than Italos were preoccupying whoever drafted these anathemas. At any rate, we must not downplay the issues raised at the trial. Modern historians who have retried the case and acquitted Italos have relied uncritically upon what the accused said "openly" rather than on what he probably was teaching "secretly" (to use the terms of the anathema). Ioannes Italos' student Eustratios, bishop of Nikaia, was condemned in 1117 by the Church for employing reason to clarify the faith, a method that allegedly led him into heresy. In fact, in a doctrinal letter against the Armenian Monophysites, Eustratios cited as authorities "the wise thinkers among the Greeks" along with "those who dogmatize about God on our side." Certainly, Eustratios protested his innocence. But his accuser Niketas, bishop of Herakleia, countered that when Eustratios protested that he had never believed such things as were imputed to him, he was only trying to deceive his listeners, "for it is obvious that he has believed these very things for a long time now." All this inhibited philosophical speculation in Byzantium and would be confirmed by the continued repression

---

[12] Clucas (1981) 58.     [13] *Synodikon of Orthodoxy* 184–249 (pp. 56–61); tr. from Wilson (1983) 154.

of philosophers. About twenty-five trials are attested. Like a reverse Bill of Rights, the *Synodikon* duly expanded to proscribe the heresies and Hellenisms of all who implied that philosophy could operate independently of doctrine. Though certainly lenient in comparison with the West (medieval or modern), this repression was unparalleled in Byzantium since the tyranny of Justinian. As under Justinian, it was instigated and executed largely by the imperial authorities, not the Church, and was often viewed with suspicion by the clergy, who had other grounds to oppose the involvement of the Komnenoi in ecclesiastical affairs. However, young men who aspired to a career in education, the Church, or the court voluntarily abstained from pursuits that were officially indexed. Self-censorship is easily induced by a minimal show of force and disapproval.[14]

Higher education in the capital was reorganized and placed under the supervision of imperial and ecclesiastical authorities. A series of "chairs" was established for rhetoric, philosophy, theology, and Scripture, and are collectively known today as the "Patriarchal Academy," though whether this resembled a western university is debated. At any rate, a "college" of professors were now employed to cover the subjects that Psellos had single-handedly taught in the eleventh century.[15] But these men were not cast in his mold. Their job was to ensure the conformity of higher education to traditional and even reactionary religious standards. This change is nicely reflected in the "inaugural" imperial oration of Michael, recently appointed Consul of Philosophers in 1166 (the office may in fact have been vacant for decades before this). Alluding to some of the condemned teachings of Italos, Michael promised to subordinate philosophy to theology, combat heresy, and institute a curriculum based mostly on Aristotle.[16] In 1170 he was elevated to the patriarchal throne. But overall it seems that few of these professors were actively hunting down heresy. Most were careerists who occasionally engaged in contentious disputes with each other over issues of little general interest.

To be sure, the *ideal* of philosophy and the writings of Plato lost little of their appeal. Theodoros Prodromos, a versatile author we will discuss below, wrote a satire defending Plato against the petty criticisms of a fellow

[14] For repression, see Browning (1975a) 15–19, 22–23 (estimate on 19); Clucas (1981) 3–8, 67–73; Magdalino (1991c); for additions to the *Synodikon*, Gouillard (1967) 183–237; for Eustratios, Joannou (1954) esp. 373, with Eustratios of Nikaia, *Refutation of the Monophysites* (pp. 163–164) and Niketas of Herakleia, *Apologia and Accusation: Why he does not accept the bishop of Nikaia* (pp. 302–304); for Alexios and the Church, Magdalino (1993) 268–274.
[15] Kaldellis (2005b).
[16] Michael ὁ τοῦ Ἀγχιάλου, *Oration to emperor Manuel, written when he was Consul of Philosophers* 69–119, 197–214 (pp. 189–190, 192–193).

professor (*The friend of Plato, or the tanner*). But this hardly entered dangerous territory. Still, Prodromos was accused of heresy, a charge we know about only because he tried to repulse it in a poem. Unfortunately we cannot reconstruct the details of the case, but the doctrine of the Trinity was involved and, unsurprisingly, too much Plato. Like Psellos, Prodromos hid behind Basileios and Gregorios, the protective amulets of Byzantine Hellenism.[17]

Scientific inquiry did not stop and commentaries were again written on Aristotle. However, metaphysics, and Platonism in particular, were out of favor, despite one manuscript that indicates a continued interest in Psellos' manner of philosophical speculation. Nikolaos, bishop of Methone and one of the emperor Manuel I Komnenos' theological advisors, wrote a refutation of Proklos in the 1150s which begins by dismissing the worldly wisdom of the Greeks that Christ had nullified. In orations of the period, even the names of the Neoplatonists are sometimes treated as emblems of heresy.[18] Gone were the days when Psellos could casually refer to the "divine Proklos." The most that could be managed – and this only by a Komnenian prince, possibly Alexios' son Isaakios – was a bowdlerization of Proklos' treatise on the nature of evil to make it conform to Christian doctrine; this was basically Psellos in reverse. In a commentary on book 6 of Aristotle's *Nikomachean Ethics*, Eustratios of Nikaia relied heavily on Proklos, but did not admit the debt openly. It has also been argued that Makrembolites' romantic novel, which will be discussed below, relied on a Proklan view of Eros, but such implicit usage could not challenge official beliefs on a doctrinal level.[19] Platonism had gone underground, in this sense at least.

Yet the setback to philosophy did not terminate the revival of Hellenism in other respects. Whereas in the eleventh century it was limited to one man, it now became a broad literary movement. Many of the limbs of Psellos' Typhonic project lived on even after the trunk was slain; in fact

---

[17] Theodoros Prodromos, *Poem* 59 (with Hörandner's commentary); see Magdalino (1993) 390–391; and Messis (2004) 317–318 for political motivations.

[18] Nikolaos of Methone, *Refutation of Proklos'* Elements of Theology. Angelou, the editor, provides an introduction; see lvii–lviii on Proklos in the twelfth century; also Magdalino (1993) 332–334; for Proklos in Byzantium, Parry (2006); for the manuscript, Pontikos (1992).

[19] Isaakios Komnenos, *On the* Hypostasis *of Evil*. For the Christian editing, see Rizzo's introduction, iii–xxiv; for authorship, Kindstrand's introduction to Isaakios' *Preface to Homer*, 18–20. For scholarly, philosophical, and scientific interests under Alexios I, see Wilson (1983) 180–184. Eustratios' debts to Proklos were discussed by M. Trizio at The Second Bi-Annual Workshop in Byzantine Intellectual History: The Medieval Greek Commentaries on the *Nicomachean Ethics* (University of Notre Dame, 2006). Makrembolites: Roilos (2005) 175–183, 196–203.

they were invigorated by other aspects of the Komnenian environment. Scholars and humanists diverted their energies to rhetoric, classical studies, poetry, fiction, satire, and a romantic idealization of antiquity. In these sites they experimented with new Hellenic identities, though no integrated collective Hellenic identity emerged from these unsystematic trials. With few exceptions, Hellenism remained a persona that was enacted in specific contexts and projected in performance. It was an aspect of professional display, a sign of social status, and a means of promotion; for very few did it acquire a deeper existential meaning. For all that they tried to imagine themselves into the world of the Second Sophistic, the demotic and orthodox aspects of their lives exerted a pull that their classicism overcame only partially. Hellenism in the twelfth century, as we will see, was in many ways a fantasy and its chief expressions were works of fiction.

Moreover, these new performative identities generally coexisted with Orthodoxy on all levels – whether personal, social, or philosophical – though sometimes they uneasily had to make room for each other or even clashed. Anna Komnene, for instance, desperately envied Psellos' learning and reputation and praised her own "perfect Hellenism" in the first lines of her *Alexiad* (pr. 1.2). In this she flouted the will of her parents, who, according to her eulogist,

believed that grammar, based as it is on poetry, is characterized by polytheism, or rather atheism, the qualities of myths, which tell of the love affairs of infatuated gods, the rape of maidens, and the abductions of boys, and which contain other such splendid things that are indecent in both word and speech; all this they deemed dangerous enough for men, but for women and maidens they rightly deemed it utterly pernicious.[20]

As we will see, Alexios failed to impose his fundamentalist principles on his own family, much less on the rest of the empire, just as the austere and monastic style of his court was gradually transformed by his heirs into its very opposite. Anna's brother Isaakios wrote two short treatises on Homer, of an introductory nature to be sure, yet they praise the poet's skill and exhibit no Christian odium.[21] Ironically, it was precisely the needs of the

---

[20] Georgios Tornikes, *Funeral Oration for Anna Komnene* (pp. 243–245). They were not alone: Jeffreys (1984) 205 for the monk Iakobos; for a survey of the period, Reinsch (2000) here 87; for an earlier example, Gregorios of Nyssa, *Life of Makrina* 3. In the *Preface* to her *Diataxis* 16 (p. 99), Anna says that her parents did not debar her from learning, but her testimony on family issues is not necessarily preferable to that of Tornikes, and is suspiciously defensive. For the authorship of this text, see Buckler (1929) 9–10.

[21] Isaakios Komnenos, *Preface to Homer* and *On the Events Omitted by Homer and on the Quality and Character of the Greeks and Trojans at Troy* (see Kindstrand's introduction, 11–20).

regime that fueled a renewed interest in the heroic world of antiquity and created a style of literature that was almost neopagan in its obsession with mythological allusions and its fascination with ancient Greece. Love affairs, the abduction of maidens, and all that had worried Anna's parents, became the order of the day in imperial and sophistic circles.

## EMPERORS AND SOPHISTS

The state seized by Alexios Komnenos was in shambles, territorially reduced, financially crippled, and almost defenseless. To restore stability and deal with new invasions from west, north, and east, Alexios lurched from one stop-gap measure to another; expediency triumphed over principle and precedent; and temporary policies were allowed to became permanent as he was forced to turn attention to the next crisis. Turks were hired in the thousands to fight Normans, and Franks to fight Turks. The army ceased to be a national Roman institution.[22] The powerful civil administration of the earlier part of the eleventh century was subordinated to the military and aristocratic magnates of the Komnenian regime. Alexios effectively turned his family into a system of government as he entrusted departments of state, entire regions, and army units to relatives and in-laws. By the time of his grandson Manuel I (1143–1180), the state was as much an interlocking system of impersonal offices as an extended family business; the emperor was both *pater familias* and chief magistrate; and the empire was almost as Komnenian as it was Roman. Through marriage alliances and a prodigious birth-rate, the clan and its affiliates – the "Komnenodoukikon," one early wit dubbed it – became a new aristocracy for Byzantium, monopolizing offices and titles, indeed claiming them on the basis of birth. The family name was used as a title. Toward the end, it even seems to have become a crime for commoners to marry above their station into the new aristocracy.[23]

Naturally, there were reactions from those who stood to lose, especially the civil bureaucracy. The historians Ioannes Zonaras (d. after 1159) and Niketas Choniates (d. 1217) were effectively excluded from real power in the new system even though they rose to high positions in the

---

[22] Treadgold (1995) 7; for Alexios' "policies," Angold (1997) 150–151.

[23] Komnenodoukikon: Theodoros Prodromos, *Nuptial Oration for the Sons of the Kaisar* (p. 347): the sons of Nikephoros Bryennios and Anna Komnene were Alexios Komnenos and Ioannes Doukas. It later became an actual name. For the Komnenian system, see Magdalino (1993) ch. 3 (the indispensable starting-point for the study of the period) and (1996a) 147–152; Neville (2004) 31–34, 63; for its origin, Krsmanović (2003) esp. 105–106. Crime: Magdalino (1984) 64; Angold (1995) 413.

administration. Zonaras noted the virtues of Alexios at the end of his universal chronicle but condemned him for desiring to change the *politeia*: Alexios, he claims, did not consider himself the steward of public affairs but their master (*despotês*). He believed that the palace was his house and ruled through his family, not the Senate (18.29). Choniates accused Manuel of treating his subjects not as free men but as slaves that came to him through inheritance (60, 143, 209).[24] In his long and detailed *History*, one of the most subtle of Byzantine texts, we find less the terminology of Roman offices than a complex and sophisticated vocabulary for designating family relations. Even Anna admitted that her father had wrongly appointed incompetent men to critical posts on the basis of lineage rather than merit. That had not been a major problem in Byzantium before.[25]

Family rule had short-term advantages and long-term disadvantages. Initially, it provided Alexios with a reliable and close-knit group that could govern a reduced state, but as the empire expanded again power began to slip from the ruler's hands and was dispersed among his increasingly independent satellites. It became difficult to control the family through the mechanisms of personal loyalty, while the mentality of impersonal office-holding had eroded. Dozens of princes, princelings, imperial cousins, and ambitious in-laws felt entitled to seize power whenever opportunity beckoned. They began to deal with foreign powers, which would have been virtually unthinkable in the past. Policy and loyalty were devolved and dissipated, and, toward the end of the century, Byzantium witnessed its first break-away principalities. The state came apart at the seams as the center could not control the periphery. The unity of the Roman nation was broken through family quarrels. The Middle Ages had finally caught up to Byzantium, at the worst possible moment.

The empire's political troubles will form the backdrop of the next chapter of this study. Here we will concentrate on the apogee of Komnenian power, for, catastrophic though the system was in the end, it was undoubtedly glorious at its peak, under Manuel I Komnenos. Few monarchs have so glamorously cultivated their martial splendor and aristocratic finesse. The new elite, despite its religious conservatism, began to reject the gravity and stolidity of the Byzantine tradition and even broke with what many regarded as its core Christian values. These men took the

---

[24] See Magdalino (1983); (1993) 188–189.
[25] Anna Komnene, *Alexiad* 12.2.6; cf. Eustathios, *The Capture of Thessalonike* 32 (pp. 36–37), who notes that the masses were deceived by Andronikos, being "*agathoi* Christians." Does the word have its modern sense of "naive"? For previous attitudes toward noble birth, see Kazhdan (1984a) 43–45.

world seriously and lived for its pleasures. A new language was required for this new style and in many respects traditional Christian forms were inadequate compared to what Greek literature had to offer. What has been called the "aristocratization" of Byzantine culture facilitated the Hellenic entanglements of the twelfth-century sophists.

With the exception of the historians Nikephoros Bryennios and his wife Anna Komnene,[26] these sophists were not members of the Komnenian elite, though they were linked to it through ties of patronage and acknowledged their dependence on its munificence. After acquiring a higher education that stressed rhetoric, our sophists hoped for administrative posts or chairs in the "Patriarchal Academy." They supplemented whatever income they made there by teaching privately, delivering orations for the imperial family, and by fees and honoraria for commissioned works. Many were appointed bishops in the provinces, where they complained bitterly about the lack of culture and boorish locals.[27] But not all ended up in the Church. Theodoros Prodromos and Ioannes Tzetzes remained teachers and writers in Constantinople, seeking aristocratic patronage and lamenting their miserable conditions when they failed to obtain it.

These men knew each other fairly well for they all participated in, indeed constituted, the exclusive world of highbrow literary culture. Unfortunately, we lack the detailed information that would allow us to reconstruct their individual biographies and their history as a group. Some connections can be established through letters and mutual ties of patronage, but the social mechanisms of their world are unclear, in particular the role of patrons in inspiring and shaping their works. Our texts conceal an undercurrent of personal relations. Rhetorical skill, at any rate, had to be performed, whether in the classroom, before the emperor (sometimes in formal debates), or in gatherings of the sophists themselves and their patrons. The term *theatron*, whose exact meaning is controversial, generally designated the forum where such displays occurred and where new works were read or recited. Performance, after all, requires an audience of peers and patrons. Our sources point to an active and engaged intellectual community, exemplified by the bustling academic activity at the school

---

[26] Jeffreys (2003b).

[27] E.g., Theophylaktos Hephaistos (Ochrid), Georgios Tornikes (Ephesos), Michael Italikos (Philippoupolis), Basileios Pediadites (Kerkyra), Michael Choniates (Athens), and Eustathios (Thessalonike). For the literature and rhetoric of exile, see Mullett (1995) and (1997) 247–260. Some scholars accuse them of elitism, but they too complain about the low level of culture in the towns that host their own colleges, if these are not major metropolitan centers.

of the church of the Holy Apostles described by Nikolaos Mesarites (ca. 1200).[28]

Let us be more precise about the skills required for these performances, and offer a composite picture of these scholars' education (though few would have reached the level of a Prodromos or Eustathios). The bedrock of Komnenian Hellenism was a knowledge of Attic and *koine* Greek, by now an artificial idiom in comparison to the spoken language (which was close to modern Greek). Years were spent mastering the ability to declaim in the language of Plato, Libanios, or Gregorios, studying conventions that were codified in manuals of grammatical and rhetorical theory, and reading and memorizing ancient texts. We should strongly resist the current prejudice that Byzantine writers had their classics from handy anthologies. The evidence for florilegia is meager; manuscripts of ancient authors usually contain complete texts; and the close reading of quotations and allusions reveals a knowledge and even intertextual dependence on the original context.[29]

Byzantine scholars strove to cleanse their language of "barbarism," including foreign and demotic Greek words and images.[30] The scholarly aids available to them – handbooks, dictionaries, critical editions, commentaries, and encyclopedias – were comparable to those used today; in fact, our tradition of classical scholarship is descended from that of Byzantium and specifically from the commentaries and lexika produced in these centuries. Of course, Komnenian scholars had a far superior command and appreciation of the Greek language than we do, even of its Attic form, and were masters of its nuances, wordplay, tropes, "humor, figures of speech, puns, riddles, and allegories."[31] The long cadences of their prose could be as magnificent as the euphonic balance of their aphorisms. They also had a comprehensive and generally sound knowledge of the history and literature of antiquity from Homer to Georgios Pisides (seventh century AD). Their lives were spent in this world of professional classicism, which was imagined and reconstructed by scholarship and which they entered whenever they switched stylistic registers.

A high standard of refinement, sophistication, and wit fueled competition, innovation, and experimentation; it also led, unsurprisingly, to bitter complaints about the low level of learning in others.

---

[28] Nikolaos Mesarites, *Description of the Church of the Holy Apostles* 8–11. The basic studies are Mullett (1984); Jeffreys (1984) 204–207; Magdalino (1993) ch. 5, esp. 316–356.
[29] Cf. Littlewood (1988) 152–153.    [30] E.g., Basilikopoulou-Ioannidou (1971–1972) 77–78.
[31] Grigoriadis (1998) 3.

Performers and teachers of rhetoric and grammar often adopted a conceited attitude toward what they called "barbarism," a term encompassing all kinds of literary incompetence . . . It was a society with a public yearning for linguistic eccentricities, demonstrations of witty puns and other forms of wordplay, and narratives bulging from mythological garnish as well as references and quotations from the classics or the Bible.[32]

The performative aspect of Byzantine classicism has been underestimated in modern accounts. To exaggerate slightly, our silent and sluggish *reading* of Komnenian literature yields as paltry an image of its performance by one of these trained orators as reading the score of a symphony compares to the experience of its actual sound. The reason we have been slow to appreciate the virtues of this culture – beyond differences in taste, which stem in part from the fact that we have forgotten the sound even of our own languages spoken with artistry – is to be found in our inferior grasp of the nuances of the language and our alienation from its literary tradition, the two pillars of Byzantine classicism. For Komnenian scholars that tradition was not some dead thing to be dissected but a living font of eloquence and wisdom, the basis of personal worth and cultural refinement. This also enabled them to operate on a philological level beyond our reach. They made a game of writing in complex structures that require decoding: the inner meaning was often the opposite of the surface sense of the words. Indeed, they boasted of this skill and challenged readers (or listeners) to decipher the code.[33]

In part this was a game, but it also allowed the sophists to say things that were not safe to say openly. This was a *standard* skill, despite its absence from modern surveys. Nikolaos Mesarites, whose account of the school attached to the Holy Apostles we noted above, states regarding students of rhetoric that "those who have achieved the higher and more complete stages, weave webs of phrases and transform the written sense into riddles, saying one thing with their tongues, but hiding something else in their minds" – a statement that itself alludes to the *Iliad*. The rhetorical tradition from Isokrates to the Byzantine manuals and on to Psellos was full of advice for how to criticize while appearing to praise and how to satirize under the disguise of glorifying. No one with an education could be taken at face value. Michael, addressing Manuel I after being appointed Consul of the Philosophers, had to reassure his audience that his (excessive) praise was not false flattery or secret irony – which hardly proves that it was not! Any

---

[32] Grigoriadis (1998) 110–111. This is an insightful, if unsystematic, study by a promising scholar whose life was cut short. For philological polemics, see Garzya (1973); for praise, Lauxtermann (2003) 46.
[33] For the live performance of Byzantine texts, see Lauxterman (2003) 55–57.

sentence could contain a subtle allusion to a canonical text, supplying a hidden qualification or reversal.[34] "In Byzantium especially it seems to have been a definite principle always to look below the surface, never to take anything at its face value."[35]

The linguistic basis of Komnenian Hellenism, what I am calling the Third Sophistic of Greek literature, has scarcely been studied. We do not know exactly what the standards of linguistic purity were, or whether any precise standards were accepted by the entire sophistic community. We are probably dealing with various levels of style, from purist Attic to a respectable _koine_, which would have often blended together in various combinations based on personal preference, genre, and circumstance.[36] We must also consider the (inevitable) gap between theory and practice, which made everyone vulnerable to the charge of barbarism, and the competition to establish a personal style. Nikephoros Basilakes claimed to have invented _basilakizein_, which he posited as "analogous to what _gorgiazein_ was among the ancient sophists."[37] What is important is that performance took place in an idiom sufficiently removed from spoken Greek to act as a marker of identity for the sophists, the only people for whom "Hellenism" had any positive value in this period. Anna's need to paraphrase in _koine_ a popular song about her father is well known (2.4.9).

Despite the hegemony of elevated Greek, from a linguistic point of view this period has also gained attention because of its experiments in demoticizing verse, including four poems by Ptochoprodromos (i.e., "poor" or "wretched" Prodromos, probably Theodoros himself) and one by Michael Glykas, both of whom were capable of writing in elevated Greek. These poems have received extensive commentary, yet we do not know what prompted them nor how they were received.[38] Some have been tempted to see in them an authentic expression of national Hellenism – the voice of the people – but it must be stressed, first, that they were not written by the

---

[34] Nikolaos Mesarites, _Description of the Church of the Holy Apostles_ 8.3 (citing Homer, _Iliad_ 9.313); Michael ὁ τοῦ Ἀγχιάλου, _Oration to emperor Manuel, written when he was Consul of Philosophers_ 240–244 (pp. 193–194). I have dealt with esoteric writing in other publications.

[35] Buckler (1929) 88; cf. Macrides and Magdalino (1992) 119: "the problem in reading Byzantine authors is knowing when, and how, they are having you on." Also Ljubarskij (2004a) 130.

[36] The basic study remains Ševčenko (1981).

[37] Nikephoros Basilakes, _Preface to the book containing his works_ 4 (_Or. et ep._ p. 3). See Trapp (2003) 138.

[38] See Beck (1971) 101–109; Beaton (1987); Grigoriadis (1998) 10–12, citing previous discussions. There were also mixed texts, e.g., _Digenes Akrites_ (see below), and poems that occasionally break out "in what is nearly Modern Greek": Jeffreys (2003c) 98. Ptochoprodromos' editor, Eideneier, does not believe that an author of the caliber of Prodromos could or would write like this (24–40), but that hardly seems ruled out. Beaton (1987) and Alexiou (1986) and (2002) 127–148 (tentatively) accept Prodromic authorship. The idea of a vernacular poet imitating Prodromos collapses in on itself.

people but by self-conscious intellectuals and, second, that there was no such thing as national Hellenism at this time, only the highbrow Hellenism of the sophists, which is accordingly our chief concern in this chapter. Whatever demoticizing poems may have meant to contemporaries, they played no discernible role in the evolution of Hellenic identities. In fact, by implicitly acknowledging the gap between spoken and Attic Greek, they may have served to highlight the exclusivity of elite *paideia*.

When viewed positively in the twelfth century, Hellenism designated an exclusive cultural refinement of restricted social scope. Its artificial and highbrow qualities made it very precisely an *anti*-national phenomenon, given that it enforced a distinction between more and less educated Romans. "Artificiality," however, must not taint our appreciation of its literary products, as happens all too often. It has never been proven that good literature must be written in the language "of the people," if not necessarily *by* the people – that conceit stems from modern nationalism. Nor should one translate nationalist rhetoric into an aesthetic criterion. "Artificiality," after all, has always been part of the Greek tradition. Homer's epics were written in a dialect corresponding to no spoken form of Greek; Pindar did not use his native Boiotian Aiolic but an artificial Doric; Herodotos, from Dorian-Karian Halikarnassos, wrote in Ionian, as did Hellanikos, from Aiolic Lesbos, and Alexander's Cretan admiral Nearchos. The speeches in Thucydides would probably have been as incomprehensible to the average Athenian of his time as those of the Second Sophistic would be later. Moreover, Byzantine orators can meet their predecessors halfway, for perhaps they spoke *koine* Greek on a daily basis more often than is realized. We just do not know how Anna – a hugely conceited woman – spoke in informal settings. Why must we assume that performance was limited to texts? Juvenal testified that pretentious Roman women would cry out in Greek during sex.[39] All the formal occasions attended by this philological elite would probably have been conducted in *koine*, which is not to say that everyone in the *theatron* understood everything that was being said. But the rhythms of their prose reveal a subtle appreciation for the *sound* of the language. Reading a few thousand of Tzetzes' verses persuades that the man thought that way. With these men we are at any rate beyond the level of our belabored "Attic prose comp."

---

[39] Juvenal, *Satires* 6.185 ff., on which Kaimio (1979) 189–194. According to an eyewitness, Attic was spoken at the late Palaiologan court: Wilson (1983) 5; for the school at Kydonies before the Revolution, Augustinos (1994) 249.

Obviously, there were degrees of linguistic attainment that corresponded roughly to the level of engagement with classical literature. The men who form the subject matter of this chapter were a minority. To put their literary activities into perspective one should consider that perhaps the majority of texts written in the period were Scriptural exegesis and theological polemic against the Latins and against real or imagined heresies within Byzantium.[40] There is no reason why these works, many of which are still unpublished, should be regarded as less typical of Komnenian literary culture than the innovations of the Hellenists. They too responded to current developments, though with less originality. We should, then, think more in terms of a spectrum ranging from creative sophists obsessed with Greek things (Prodromos and Tzetzes); bishop-scholars who combined Hellenic nobility with Christian ethics (Eustathios and Michael Choniates); professional philosophers with ecclesiastical ambitions (Michael III); professors of Scripture interested in the classical tradition (Nikephoros Basilakes); officials with varying levels of interest in Hellenism (e.g., Ioannes Zonaras, Gregorios Antiochos, and Niketas Choniates); controversial analytical philosophers (Eustratios of Nikaia); philosophical and anti-Hellenic religious polemicists (Nikolaos of Methone); and, finally, those who used rhetoric to attack theological opponents but who had no interest in classical literature. What these men shared was the ability to participate in public debates and to praise the emperor on public formal occasions in elevated Greek.

Moreover, even though the Hellenists performed original experiments in humanist revaluation, they were not isolated from the surrounding culture. Their engagement with the classics occupied an existential space whose scope varied by author but was never a comprehensive identity. Prodromos wrote – probably on commission, and *for* commission – popular commentaries on church hymns and poems on the books of the Bible and for saints and feast-days. Like some of his colleagues, he lived in a monastery for a time. Eustathios showed a constant concern for both the spiritual and material welfare of his flock, tried to reform the monks of his city, and exhibited greater solicitude for the poor than for pretentious aristocrats. He composed many religious and ecclesiastical works and illustrated his commentaries on Homer with evidence drawn from

---

[40] See, e.g., the works of Nikolaos of Methone listed in the introduction to Angelou's edition of his *Refutation of Proklos'* Elements of Theology (xxv–xlvi); of the professor Ioannes Kastamonites, in Katsaros (1988); and of his colleagues in Browning (1962–1963). In general, see Beck (1959) 609–663; Magdalino (1993) 366–370.

demotic speech and local customs.[41] The aesthetics of everyday life in Constantinople, its sounds and sights, were different from those of any classical city in antiquity, excepting only the multitude of ancient statues that offered a glimpse into the lost alternatives of the body. It was this personal engagement with the demotic beliefs and practices of a non-classical world, which were so unwelcome in the fantasies of Hellenist literature, that set Komnenian scholars apart from their Second Sophistic models. Their world was more complex, requiring different cultural codes for lay, ecclesiastical, monastic, royal, and scholarly audiences. And yet, as we will see, at one end of this communicative spectrum these men did possess distinctive traits that differentiated them from the mainstream of their society and that make it possible today to speak of Byzantine Hellenism.

## HELLENISM AS AN EXPANSION OF MORAL AND AESTHETIC CATEGORIES

Our focus will remain on that part of the literary spectrum that preoccu-pied itself with classical culture beyond what had been customary in Byzantium since the sixth century, for it was in those circles that new Hellenisms were performed. The question has rarely been posed why so many writers suddenly developed such an unprecedented level of interest in ancient Greece.[42] Psellos' pioneering intellectual career and literary legacy contributed to this development, though what we need to know is why so many were prepared to receive him, given that they had incentives to avoid a major component of his philosophical project. Certainly, the economic and demographic expansion of the empire under the Komnenoi enabled more young men to acquire a higher education, while the emergence of an aristocracy with intellectual and artistic pretensions created a larger market for their skills. Such theories cannot be proven on the basis of the current evidence, yet there does seem to have been a broader and more diverse market for new literature in the twelfth century as opposed to the eleventh and a concomitantly larger production – *hugely* larger, if we remove the works of one man, Psellos, from the comparison. Part of the answer may lie in the nature of the new aristocracy and the attempts by a handful of

---

[41] Prodromos: Hörandner (1974) 37–56, here 44–48; Miller (2003) 221. Eustathios: Browning (1964) 15–16; Kazhdan and Constable (1982) 114. Concern for the poor: Magdalino (1984) 67.

[42] Cf. Kazhdan and Epstein (1985) 138–139, for unsatisfactory anwers.

second- and third-tier princes to act as mini-emperors by cultivating the traditional imperial image of artistic and literary patronage.

Despite a possible rise in the popularity of military saints at this time,[43] the Christian tradition proved unable to cater to the military-heroic *êthos* of the Komnenoi, at least as that was expressed in the history of the 1070s written by Nikephoros Bryennios, the son-in-law of Alexios, in ca. 1120. It celebrates the glorious deeds of martial nobles and is "Homeric" in that it accepts the values of Homer's heroes as opposed to those of the poet himself (who kept a critical distance from the wrathful honor of Achilles). Martial exploits are emphasized throughout. Bryennios gives detailed descriptions of arms and armor, of the physical appearance and noble demeanor of great men, and of the impressions that they made on awestruck soldiers or commoners. In an astonishing break with the Byzantine tradition, he praises almost all noble warriors regardless of whether they were fighting for or against the legitimate government in Constantinople. As with Achilles, their nobility is independent of legality. Bryennios' own family history would have predisposed him to such a view, as he was himself part of the Komnenian system, yet his grandfather had been defeated by Alexios (fighting on behalf of Nikephoros III Botaneiates) and blinded. He presents that war as one between two equivalent contestants, going so far as to state that his ancestor's visage was so noble as to be "worthy of *tyrannis*," (4.15), an amazing statement, given that in Byzantium *tyrannis*, or rebellion, had long been considered one of the worst offenses. The phrase is in fact lifted from a play of Euripides and recurs in two of Prodromos' imperial poems as well.[44] We observe here the origins of the ultimate dissolution of the Komnenian system, as the princes believed their own Achillean rhetoric and drew swords against their rulers.

Bryennios also says that it would require "another *Iliad* to recount the achievements" of his ancestor – as though the *Iliad*'s point is to praise Achilles. Indeed, he and his wife Anna collaborated in writing an *Iliad* for Alexios, the *Alexiad*, which reflects that outlook.[45] The emphasis that Michael Attaleiates, a historian of eleventh-century Byzantium, had placed

---

[43] Kazhdan and Constable (1982) 111–112; Holmes (2005) 219.

[44] Euripides fr. 15.2; and Theodoros Prodromos, *Poems* 43.14, 54.41. Cf. Theophanes Continuatus, Book 4: *Life of Michael III* 44 (p. 208), used in a scandalous context. This development had been brewing since Leon the Deacon in the tenth century and Psellos in the eleventh: Roueché (1988); Kaldellis (1999a) 182–184; Holmes (2005) 202–239.

[45] For Anna and epic, see Buckler (1929) 51–61; Katičić (1957); Macrides (2000) 67–70; and Connor (2004) 245–249, 257, 260–261; for the aristocratization of culture and militarization of the emperor, Kazhdan (1984a); (1984b) 38–40, 146; Kazhdan and Epstein (1985) 99, 106–113; Magdalino (1993) 418–423, 448–449, and ch. 6 *passim*.

on administration and the armies is here replaced by emotive heroism, a change that corresponds to the transformation of the regime itself. In a poem for the warlike Ioannes II (1118–1143), Prodromos boasted that to praise the emperor properly Homer would have to be brought back from Hades and given ten mouths. By the beginning of the thirteenth century, even bishops were being compared to the ancient heroes and "whole new *Iliads*" were deemed necessary for their praises.[46] The twelfth was in other ways a *Homeric* century. Beyond the ethos that pervades these texts, we witness at the same time the production of Homeric scholia, lexika, summaries, prolegomena, and commentaries; the use of many Homeric themes in rhetorical exercises; allegorical interpretations; and the constant citation of epic verses in works of all kind. This Homeric obsession was complemented by the revival of ancient skepticism regarding "the poet" and the historicity of his tales.[47] But anti-Homeric skepticism had been part of the Homeric game since antiquity. In this case, it did nothing to undermine Homer; rather, it made the sophists feel that they were as sophisticated as the ancient thinkers and orators whom they were imitating.

The aristocratization of culture promoted the heroization of the emperor. The image of a divinely static Christian monarch practicing the virtues of piety, humility, justice, and generosity gave way to the restless warrior wielding a spear like Achilles and rushing into battle covered in blood and sweat. These images had been pioneered by Psellos, but now they became commonplace. Prodromos revived Homeric hexameters to celebrate imperial triumphs, making "the military ethos of the Komnenian aristocracy acceptable to the literary antiquarianism of the predominantly non-Komnenian intellectual elite."[48] The need to also Christianize these images led to peculiar conjunctions. Nikephoros Basilakes praised Ioannes II Komnenos for wading through oceans of barbarian blood spilled by his sword, and then notes that the cities were calling him the heir of Christ. In his funeral oration for Manuel, right after praising the emperor for imitating Christ Eustathios goes on to praise him for being a perfect knight, foot-soldier, and hand-to-hand warrior (*hippotês*, *pezomachos*, and *monomachos*). It was odd enough to talk about the emperor in this way, to say nothing about doing so in church. Eustathios concludes his Lent homily of

---

[46] Theodoros Prodromos, *Poem* 4 251–257; cf. 11.18–19. Attaleiates: Krallis (2006). Bishops: Anonymous, *Monodia for Michael Choniates* 2 (p. 237).
[47] Basilikopoulou-Ioannidou (1971–1972); de Boel (2003) 169; Lasithiotakis (2005) 54–55.
[48] Magdalino (1993) 431.

1176, an otherwise Christian sermon, with an epic account of Manuel's exploits in Asia Minor that is full of blood, the din of battle, and flash of weapons. Prodromos put it well in another comparison of Christ to Manuel: the former was baptized in water for our sake while the latter was cleansed of sweat; the former crushed serpents' heads while the latter bent the heads of barbarians.[49] So much for Eusebios of Kaisareia's boast that the peaceful wars of the Christian spirit would triumph over the bloody wars of pagan men.

These images transgressed the Christian sensitivities of the past. In the preface to his history (10), Bryennios ignored Biblical prohibitions in offering a defense and even praise of just revenge (*ekdikêsis*), linking it to aristocratic rights. Similar attitudes were found among the sophists. In a letter Ioannes Tzetzes praised the bishop of Dristra for suffering like Christ when he was assaulted by a foreign gang. But, Tzetzes continues, he should not imitate Christ in asking God to forgive them; rather, he should curse them and beg God for their destruction. If he won't do this because he is a priest, "then *I* will."[50] To be sure, this is glib and specious, an exaggerated condolence, but it cannot simply be dismissed for all that. It reveals a readiness to accept explicitly non-Christian values, which, in other texts, were linked to Hellenic precedents and teachings. Nikephoros Basilakes wrote a rhetorical exercise extolling just revenge and swift punishment as the savior and guardian of all communities, following what he took to be the moral lessons of Sophokles. And in an essay on what a man must do when two friends quarrel, Eustathios concedes that it is incumbent on us to hate those whom our friends hate, citing as proof Patroklos, who hated Agamemnon for the sake of Achilles, and Sthenelos, who stood with Diomedes. Eustathios' exploration of the requirements of friendship is interesting enough by itself, but what draws our attention is that he tries to reconcile Aristotle with the Christian demand for universal love and for love of God.[51]

In short, the classical turn of the twelfth century was partly due to the need of the Komnenian aristocracy to exalt virtues that the Fathers had either neglected or condemned and to which the Byzantine tradition had

---

[49] Nikephoros Basilakes, *Oration for the Emperor Ioannes Komnenos* 1 (*Or. et ep.* pp. 49–50). Eustathios, *Funeral Oration for the Emperor Manuel Komnenos* 61–62 (*Or.* 23, Tafel p. 210); *Preparatory Oration for Lent* (*Or.* 2, Wirth pp. 41–45). Theodoros Prodromos, *Poem* 33.2–5.

[50] Ioannes Tzetzes, *Letter* 66. See Shepard (1979) 206–210, 235–237.

[51] Nikephoros Basilakes, *Progymnasma* 26 (*On Sophokles*, Elektra *1505–1507: Prog. e mon.* pp. 110–115); see pp. 258–260 below, for *progymnasmata*. Eustathios, *That it is not possible for one to deal with friends who differ in character* (*Or.* 3, Wirth pp. 46–54).

paid scant attention. The sophists, for their part, in representing the behavior of the nobility and even the competitive ethos of their own class, found inspiration and models in classical literature. All this in turn contributed to the return with a vengeance of neopagan imagery, which, as we saw in an earlier chapter, had gained some acceptance in Christian circles of the sixth century before being banished from the repertoire of literary symbolism. The pagan gods were now back in fashion, just as one could turn to Sophokles and Aristotle to resolve ethical problems. For example, Anna calls warriors the "lovers" or "henchmen of Ares." Alluding to the *Iliad*, she compares her husband to Herakles and his bow to that of Apollo. In connection with her mother's beauty, she affects to wonder whether that Athena who was described by the poets had ever existed; well, *now* she was revealed among mortals! Was this flirtation with myth her way of repaying her parents for trying to bar her from learning about the gods?[52] But she was not alone. We can speak of a literary cult of Greek mythology in the Komnenian empire, with Ares, Herakles, and the Graces being invoked most frequently. One poem, addressed to a noblewoman and describing a work of art, mentions Graces, Cupids, and their like in virtually every line, with an almost suffocating effect.[53] It is almost as though pent-up energy was being released. The gods were now invoked without pious Christian disclaimers. To the contrary, in an oration for Anna and Bryennios' sons, Prodromos suggested that "the Greeks" may have been stating the truth about the Graces and the Muses after all.[54] Of course, no one mistook the intent of such statements. As one orator put it, Greek myth is "transfigured into a true symbol" of the subject at hand: the Cyclops' loss of his eye stands for the Senate's loss of the oration's deceased honorand.[55]

These literary citations bespeak a comfortable acquaintance with pagan myth and, more importantly, an acceptance of it as a symbolic and comparative language by which to describe and interpret the world. In effect, the sophists were constructing a discursive space into which they could step and, for a brief performative moment, become Greeks, even

---

[52] Ares: Anna Komnene, *Alexiad* 2.7.2, 5.4.4, 7.9.7; bow: 10.9.8; Athena: 3.3.4. For more, see, e.g., Basilikopoulou-Ioannidou (1971–1972) 122–125; Kazhdan and Epstein (1985) 86, 109. Countless more can be cited; for the gap in mythological allusions between ca. 650 and Psellos, ibid. 136–138; Hunger (1969–1970) 25 ff.; Anagnostakis and Papamastorakis (2004) 222–224.

[53] Anderson and Jeffreys (1994) 11–13.

[54] Theodoros Prodromos, *Nuptial Oration for the Sons of the Kaisar* (p. 347); cf. Michael Attaleiates, *History* 133: events showed that Hesiod was right and rumor, *Phêmê*, is a goddess.

[55] Niketas Eugenianos (?), *Funeral Oration for his Son* (pp. 209–210). Cf. Niketas Choniates, *Letter* 1 (*Or. et ep.* pp. 201–202) on the "meaning" of a myth.

"pagans." They did this because they needed a language with which to discuss things like heroic warfare and physical beauty for which Christian literary culture was unsuited, as well as to satirize their society and its rulers. In this symbolic space, they joined company with the likes of Julian, who had defended myth's symbolic significance: "poetry deprived of myth is merely versification," he had claimed.[56] But myth was now purely literary; there was no religion behind it as had been the case with Julian. Komnenian mythology prefigured that of early modern Europe: "in a milieu of social affability where the cultivation of wit and subtlety was accompanied by a search for pleasurable diversions, paganism found a new appeal." It was safe because it was perfectly understood on all sides that in rhetorical contexts this mythologizing was purely rhetorical.[57] In other contexts one could go further. We will see below that Eustathios and Tzetzes allegorized the gods in various ways, but they did so in order to save Homer's reputation from Christian odium and not because they wanted to develop new mythological philosophies of their own. In his commentaries on Homer and Hesiod, Ioannes Galenos, scholar and deacon, went so far as to interpret the Greek gods as figurations of Christian equivalents, for example Zeus as God and the Titans as evil, and Herakles as Jesus, alongside the ancient modes of scientific and historical allegorization (according to which, as he puts it, the Greeks mistook *Physiogonia* for *Theogonia*). His aim was to "transubstantiate" myth "into a more divine form," to beautify "the ugliness of Greek myths" by making it look more like "our Truth."[58]

Such experiments were rare and, unlike Psellos' Platonic transmutations of myth, were more rhetorical than philosophical. The place of mytho-logical classicism was literary, and in some texts it attained baroque proportions. In Eustathios' account of the *Capture of Thessalonike* (1185), we find far more Greek gods and creatures of mythology mentioned by name than actual Byzantines or Normans. Yet we should not dismiss this as uniformly affected and artificial. The language of mythology does not communicate only through symbols with fixed values (e.g., Ares = war). These symbols activate a shared world of stories that encode a vast array of specific situations. Depending on their usage, the names of heroes and gods (as of Old Testament figures) allude to parallels and models by which readers could better understand or judge their present-day counterparts. At first sight it may seem that Eustathios loses no chance to drop a proverb or a

---

[56] Julian, *Or.* 7.207b (*To the Cynic Herakleios*).  [57] Augustinos (1994) 14.
[58] Ioannes Galenos, *Allegories on Hesiod's* Theogony (pp. 295–296, 336); see Roilos (2005) 128–130.

piece of ancient lore or wisdom, allude to Homer, or generally make a classical or Biblical comparison. In reality, he is deliberately manipulating these allusions to create a pseudo-epic satirizing his anti-heroes Andronikos I Komnenos (1182–1185) and David Komnenos (the useless governor of the city). The effect is lost on those who lack Eustathios' classical and specifically Homeric education, for allusions have to be referred back to their original context to be appreciated, but is seen to be brilliant when its mechanisms are revealed. Eustathios accepted Greek heroism, so long as it was coupled with virtue, but was perfectly capable of turning the tables on it when heroes turned tail and fled.[59] Allusions could praise and satirize simultaneously.[60]

The study of Komnenian mythology has barely begun. We cannot fully explain the explosion of interest in it nor systematize the idiosyncrasies of its use. I suspect, however, that there are general patterns to be found here, which will reveal how the sophists carefully adapted the language of myth to their present concerns. This was not a purely *verbal* imitation of antiquity. Without having any statistics, I think that the emphasis on Ares in writings of this period, far greater than in antiquity, reflects the warlike ethos of the Komnenoi. By contrast, though he was popular in antiquity, Zeus was now relatively absent, probably because his stature cut too close for comfort. The frequent invocations of Hermes, the Muses, and the Graces reveal the self-conscious awareness by the sophists of their own status as professional producers of elite culture. And the vocabulary of Eros highlights the sexual rhetoric of the new literature as well as the excesses of the regime itself in this direction. Hellenic mythology, therefore, may yet unlock the structural semantics of the culture of the age.[61]

The militarism, follies, and excesses of the Komnenian regime, especially under Manuel, gave the sophists ground to further Psellos' exploration of sexual life. As with Eustathios, the panegyrist of Manuel and critic of Andronikos, engagement with classical literature was Janus-like, serving both to exalt the extravagance of the princes and to satirize them, sometimes simultaneously. The classical turn was facilitated by the new moral context. Manuel and his men flaunted their wealth and spent their time making love and war. They rushed into battle, hunted, and then adorned their palaces with scenes of hunting and war. The canon lawyer and titular bishop of Antioch Theodoros Balsamon was offended that the houses of

[59] Sarris (1995–1997); for Niketas Choniates, Nardi (2002) 125–128.   [60] E.g., Alexiou (1983) 40–43.
[61] Dionysos: Anagnostakis and Papamastorakis (2004) 233–249; Eros: Magdalino (1992); Hermes: Roilos (2005) 50–53.

the rich – "erotomaniacs," he called them – were full of erotic literature and artwork. But even he included in his canon commentaries a digression on cunnilingus adorned with many showy classical references – to explain how a priest might defile his lips![62] Nor did the later Komnenoi conceal the pleasure they took in these activities, which they regarded as essential to the good life. The Christian tradition, by contrast, interested Manuel mostly as a function of his office and as propaganda, namely to the extent that it exalted him personally, magnified the glory of his throne, and legitimated his claims on Italy; his interest in theology, in his mind at least, elevated him to the ranks of the great theologians of the past, though most found it an annoying hobby. Beyond that, he flagrantly violated Christian mores, for instance by competing with his cousin Andronikos in the seduction of their nieces. These "were not simple infidelities . . . This public flouting of both moral codes and canon strictures on incest reveals the social tenden-cies of the era even more than do the acts themselves."[63] The historian Niketas Choniates would look back on this world after the disaster of 1204 and expose its degeneration with unparalleled sarcastic wit, thus revealing himself its product as well as its critic.

What Psellos had called the "earthly" life was pursued and celebrated. It was probably around 1100 that the tales of Digenes Akrites became popular in Constantinople. The hero of an epic romance that has survived in later versions, Digenes was a frontiersman who spent his brief life hunting, fighting (often for no reason), seducing maidens, raping other women, and building palaces, with God or the saints always on his lips though he never once went to church or met a priest. In his world, men are praised almost exclusively for physical strength, noble birth, and wealth, and women for beauty. The origins of this poem, written in a linguistic register between *koine* and spoken Greek, are controversial. Suffice it to say that despite a few allusions to "high" literature it does not stem from the classicists' milieu and reflects a formal orthodoxy unconcerned with the ancient world. "Stop copying Homer and the myths of Achilles," the poet admon-ishes in fundamentalist fashion, "all those lies of the Hellenes." His outlook is thoroughly Christian and Roman, the only exceptions being the person-ification of Eros in the amorous life of Digenes and the folk-hero Alexander the Great, who conquered the world with the help of God and is presented

[62] Theodoros Balsamon, *Commentary on Canon 100 of the Council in Troullo*, in *PG* CXXXVII (1865) 861; cunnilingus: Viscuso (2005) 323–326. For a palace mosaic depicting the Earth as a voluptuous woman, see Konstantinos Manasses, *Ekphrasis of the Earth in the Form of a Woman*.
[63] Kazhdan and Epstein (1985) 102; Magdalino (1993) 453–454. Hunting: Koukoules (1932); for palaces, including literary and archaeological evidence, Hunt (1984).

here as a model for Digenes. What is important about this poem for us is that it reflects from a demotic point of view the same world that the classicists were also struggling to represent (only they were doing so via the Greek tradition). Most of the Komnenoi "probably felt more at home in the philistine fantasy world of Digenes Akrites, a man's man who lived in the country, never met an intellectual, and devoted himself to sex and violence."[64]

Anna did not hide her admiration for Bohemond's physical appearance, her father's Norman nemesis and a man she despised morally. But she gives a detailed description of his entire body nonetheless (13.10.4–5). Here we have an aesthetic judgment independent of the moral sphere: the beautiful is not the same as the good and may be openly carnal. Interest in sexuality peaked as polite society accepted a mode of discourse about the body – and bodily parts and functions – that had little precedent outside of specialized medical writings. In fact, medicine may have played a role here. In his account of Anna's education, her eulogist Georgios Tornikes interjects a comparison to medical dissections of human bodies, which were practiced in Byzantium, though it is unclear whether he means that Anna had witnessed them. In any case, Aristotelian studies may have enhanced her literary descriptions of living bodies. Literary categories were again being expanded with the assistance of Hellenic science; Tornikes is explicit that Anna's predecessors in wisdom were Greek.[65] Anna's attitude to gender could also be blunt. According to Choniates, she complained that nature had given her a hole while the protrusion had gone to her indecisive husband; had it been the other way around, *she* would have been emperor instead of her brother Ioannes, whom she hated. Princesses had come a long way since the bridal show in 830 of the emperor Theophilos, who discussed gender roles with the learned contestant Kassia through polite and subtle Biblical allusions.[66]

Entire works were now devoted to secular themes that had so far received little or no attention in Byzantine literature, certainly not at the court. Apart from the romantic novels, which we will discuss in the next section in connection with their ancient settings, the Ptochoprodromic vernacular

---

[64] Magdalino (1984) 69; for Manuel and Digenes, Magdalino (1993) 1–2, 127, 421, 449; Ljubarskij (2000) 169–170. Homer and Alexander: *Digenes Akrites* G 4.27–30, E 709–721. For social values, Magdalino (1989); for religion, Angold (1989a).

[65] Dissections: Georgios Tornikes, *Funeral Oration for Anna Komnene* (p. 225); predecessors: see p. 290 below. For autopsies, see, e.g., Michael Choniates, *Letter* 102.12–13; and Miller (1997) 187–189; for the *Pantokratôr* hospital founded by Anna's brother, see ibid. ch. 2; for her medical knowledge, Buckler (1929) 215–221; cf. Magdalino (1993) 361–366.

[66] Niketas Choniates, *History* 10; cf. Treadgold (1988) 269.

poems combined popular slang and low humor with allusions to Homer and Aristophanes to inject sexual innuendo into homely situations. These poems, which include the occasional blasphemy, have been rightly labeled subversive, though this does not mean that readers in high places would not have enjoyed them.[67] It is appropriate again to speak of humanism, namely an interest in previously neglected, despised, and proscribed aspects of human behavior. Using the traditional tools of Byzantine philology and classicism, authors now tried to explore the psychology and daily lives of both average and extraordinary human beings simply for their own sake and not in order to subject them to the polarities of moralizing rhetoric.[68] This development peaked in such works as the romance of Eustathios Makrembolites, *Hysmine and Hysminias*, which explores, without any overt Christian prejudice, the subjective psychology of erotic passion from a pagan standpoint. What makes this work especially relevant here is that it represented the revival of a long-defunct ancient genre. Not only, then, did the sophists imitate the masters of the Second Sophistic, they attempted to place their readers in the imaginary position of ancient Greeks and so set their stories in classical times with only the most allusive hints of the passage of time and the very existence of Christianity.

A sophisticated, cynical, and pleasure-seeking society was fertile ground for the reemergence of satire, which subverted authorship along with authority in its attempt to represent the world comically through the eyes of its target. The corollary of its reemergence was the rise of the author in Byzantium, by which I mean not merely someone whose professional and personal life is invested in writing and who experiments with different genres, but who also regards or at least presents himself primarily as an author, a "struggling writer." The author emerged along with the discovery and subversion of his subject matter, which was usually lifted from daily habits and customs that had long lain beneath the notice of more official literature; this was also a function of the stratification of Komnenian society, which separated the sophists from the ruling class in a much starker way than had formerly been the case. Theodoros Prodromos, chief among the Komnenian satirists, comes across to us as someone who writes for a living, who turns his hand to philosophy, courtly panegyric, scholarly annotation, and satire, and who depends on Komnenian beneficence to

---

[67] Alexiou (1986) and (2002) 127–148 (their antecedents were not exactly literature: 81–86). For eroticism in Manganeios, see Magdalino (1992); Jeffreys (2003b) 96.

[68] For humanism, see pp. 215–216 above; for this period, Kazhdan and Epstein (1985) 210–225; Magdalino (1993) 398–412.

survive. Whereas Ioannes Tzetzes maintained a rather coherent authorial persona by intruding his grating name and annoying personality into all his works, and even Psellos projects a fairly consistent and identifiable image of himself despite the variety of genres in which he wrote, Prodromos experimented widely with voice, genre, and style (the Ptochoprodromic demotic poems may well be his). At this stage, it is still difficult to talk about him as "an author," given that the extent of his corpus is uncertain along with the dates, circumstances, and audiences of his works. There have been few sustained literary analyses. A very preliminary assessment has identified certain key recurring themes, including introspection, psychological sensitivity to the point of tragedy, and an interest in physical appearance.[69] He is a literary goldmine waiting to be tapped.

Prodromos' interests ranged from the sublime to the most homely, and here we again run into the problem of Byzantine ideological versatility and the layering of meaning. His poems praising the ruling family promote military heroism, noble birth, and wealth.[70] But praise could easily turn to satire with a shift in circumstance and language, as we saw with Eustathios. Prodromos also wrote a mock play, the *Katomyomachia* ("Cat-and-Mouse Battle"), that plunders Homer (for the mock epic content) and parodies the tragedians (in the genre) to savage Komnenian society. The speech of the lead mouse, Kreillos, echoes the military rhetoric of Prodromos' imperial verses; the poem probably contains specific allusions that we can no longer recover.[71] Likewise, the conventional piety of his commissioned works must be set alongside the merciless satire of monks in the Ptochoprodromic poems and other comic works.[72] Prodromos, then, was the Lucian of this Third Sophistic, and Lucian clearly inspired such pieces as *Against a dirty old hag; The ignorant man, or the grammarian on his own terms*; and *The executioner, or the doctor*. Not only are they Lucianic in style and language, they rarely betray that they were written in and about a Christian society. All the allusions are classical. To ridicule his own age, then, Prodromos assumed a Hellenic mode and pretended to be living a thousand years in the past. Other works blurred historical boundaries and so created bridges between the Greek past and the Byzantine present.

---

[69] Kazhdan (1984b) ch. 3, esp. 112–114. For his life, see Hörandner (1974) 21–32; Messis (2004) 317–319; for struggling poets, Beaton (1987); Magdalino (1993) 340–343; Lauxtermann (2003) 36, 46.

[70] Kazhdan (1984b) 106–108.

[71] Theodoros Prodromos, *Katomyomachia* esp. 145 ff. See Hunger's introduction, 40–61; Hunger (1969–1970) 36–37, Cresci (2001).

[72] See Hunger's introduction to Prodromos' *Katomyomachia*, 59–60; Alexiou (2002) 132–133, 139–142. Papadopoulos (1935) 7 conjectured that Prodromos wrote the *Life of Meletios* to please the monks who put him up; cf. Angold (1995) 373. See below for the subversive aspects of this text.

Prodromos' brief philosophical dialogue *Xenedemos, or Voices*, reflects the social and linguistic ambiance of Sokrates' Athens but is clearly set in Constantinople.[73] Such works were "classics for our times."

In short, the classical inheritance provided the vehicle and the inspiration for the moral, aesthetic, and literary expansion of Byzantine literature. This may strike us as atavistic and artificial, as we expect societies experiencing cultural growth to develop on their own terms, which we then call creative, original, etc. But this is to impose the western experience on Byzantium. The Byzantines had never been cut off from the classical tradition in the first place and so, when circumstance favored literary development, it was only natural that they should reactivate the quasi-dormant texts of their schooling rather than invent their own (though Ptochoprodromos did that too). The different course taken by literature in the West was due to the loss and then rediscovery of the classical tradition, and the emergence of the vernacular languages. Byzantine authors were fated to imitate, though as we have seen they did so with creativity, taste, and subversive wit.[74]

Scholars have noted the reemergence of satire in the form of poems, plays, and dialogues, where the debt to Aristophanes and Lucian was direct and often obvious. But we should probably be thinking less in terms of genre and more of a general satirical spirit that contaminated other genres, including historiography (e.g., in Eustathios and Niketas Choniates), epistolography (e.g., in Tzetzes), poetry, and almost certainly, albeit covertly, imperial panegyric as well.[75] The line between straight-faced and tongue-in-cheek became very fine. Satire became something of a cultural habit. The canonist Balsamon (in ca. 1180) railed against actors who were staging satirical shows about monks and the clergy, and toward the end of the century the grammarian Basileios Pediadites was fired for writing blasphemous verses (but was later made bishop of Kerkyra).[76]

All this entailed a deep shift in moral values. Discussions of humor in Byzantium invariably concede that laughter was frowned upon in the orthodox tradition.[77] Not one Byzantine icon so much as cracks a smile. But new attitudes emerged here too among the Hellenists. Nikephoros Basilakes was professor "of the Apostle," i.e., St. Paul, before being exiled

---

[73] Charalampopoulos (2005).    [74] Cf. Littlewood (2006) 13–14.

[75] Genre: Hunger (1978) v. II, 149–158 (high-style) and Baldwin (1982) (unsystematic); Lucian in Byzantium: Robinson (1979) 68–81; satirical spirit: Grigoriadis (1998) 8–10, limited to genre; and Roilos (2005) 231–238, recognizing "genre flexibility."

[76] Balsamon: Browning (1989a) 424; Pediadites: Browning (1962–1963) 21–22.

[77] Kazhdan and Constable (1982) 62; Garland (1990a) 3; Haldon (2002) 60–62.

from the capital in 1157 for taking the wrong side in a theological wrangle. In the preface to his collected works, he noted that as a student he had daily taken in ancient wisdom (indeed, his orations are overloaded with classical allusions) "but did not neglect our indoor Muse either." He then lists four verse satires among his early works and admits that young men today love to laugh and play jokes. Yet when he later "peeped into the meadow of our theosophy," he realized that "Christians ought to weep, not laugh," and so he burned those juvenilia to escape the unquenchable fires of Hell. But, he adds, possibly with regret, not all praised this action.[78] Among them may have been his colleague Eustathios, a professor of rhetoric and later the bishop of Thessalonike. In a sarcastic address to his detractors – and he had many in his new city – Eustathios confessed that between the tears of Herakleitos and the laughter of Demokritos "I incline most toward Demokritos, as to human nature itself, for it is by nature that humor is a human quality." Tears, on the other hand, "distort our human nature." A massive shift in psychology can be glimpsed behind these statements, whose Hellenic source is evident in the very *exempla* that this classical scholar chose to cast them in. In his *Inquiry into monastic life for the correction of its abuses* (early 1180s), he was willing to allow monks to smile and even laugh from time to time, stating explicitly that "I am no friend of those who want to banish laughter altogether."[79]

Eustathios' treatise brings us to another factor that certainly contributed to the classical turn of twelfth-century literary culture, namely a noticeable decline in the authority and appeal of traditional Christian ideals, though it is impossible to say now which was cause and which effect. The exaltation of classical Greece, mediated through Psellos' soul-*and*-body humanism, may have led to a reaction against the ideological excesses that were built into the orthodox conception of the perfect life, founded as it had been originally on the rejection of the worldly virtues of the Greek city. Alternatively, Hellenism may have stepped in to fill the void that was created by a retreating system of beliefs. Be that as it may, monasticism and fundamentalism lost their credibility in intellectual circles, especially among Hellenists, though the degree to which this extended beyond their ranks is unclear. A broader cultural shift is indicated perhaps by the general decline in hagiography. Few saints' lives were written in the twelfth

---

[78] Nikephoros Basilakes, *Preface to the book containing his works* 2, 5–6 (*Or. et ep.* pp. 2, 4–5); for his fall, Magdalino (1993) 279–281; Angold (1995) 82–83; for the preface, Angold (1999) 42.

[79] Eustathios, *To those who accuse him of bearing a grudge if he should ever remember that he was once wronged* 93 (*Or.* 14, Tafel p. 120); *Inquiry into monastic life for the correction of its abuses* 29 (*Or.* 24, Tafel p. 221).

century and those that were were often unconventional literary experiments penned by the Hellenists. The *Life of Philotheos* by Eustathios, for example, essentially "contained a negation of the ascetic way of life."[80]

The reaction against the monks had begun in the eleventh century and is already fully developed in the histories of Psellos and Michael Attaleiates. For Psellos, hagiography was another opportunity for mischief. When he rewrote the life of Auxentios he altered certain details to make the saint's career mirror his own![81] Prodromos seems to have used his *Life of Saint Meletios the Younger* as a covert vehicle for a sarcastic caricature of his contemporaries, as an exposé of the excesses, conceits, and "social pathologies" of the new elite.[82] Many authors of the age, including Prodromos, Ptochoprodromos, Tzetzes, Balsamon, Eustathios, Euthymios Malakes (bishop of New Patras and friend of Eustathios), and Niketas Choniates, polemically depicted monks and would-be holy men as morally undisciplined, as cynical exploiters of popular superstitions, and as "fraudulent, greedy, or superfluous."[83] Their invectives and calls for reform should probably not be seen as a reaction to any sudden and drastic deterioration in the standards of monastic life, though perhaps that happened to a degree (as evidenced by the rising wealth and social ambitions of individual monks and communities). In his *Inquiry into monastic life*, Eustathios paints an interesting picture of monks fully assimilated to the secular and aristocratic values of society, including business ventures, horse-riding, and hunting with dogs and falcons. In his commentary on the *Odyssey*, he sarcastically compares the Cyclopes to the hermits of his own age who receive goods without having to work for them.[84]

It is more likely that the behavior that was now being condemned and ridiculed was no different from what had gone on in Byzantium for centuries, only it was now being seen through the lens of a new moral

[80] Kazhdan (1984a) 50; Kazhdan and Epstein (1985) 94.

[81] Kazhdan (1983a); Kazhdan and Epstein (1985) 223–224; see now Fisher (2006). For Psellos and Attaleiates on monks, see p. 213 above and Kaldellis (2007b).

[82] Messis (2004) esp. 320–339 (unpersuasive in some parts). For Tzetzes' *Life of St. Loukia*, see p. 305 below.

[83] Magdalino (1981) 54; also (1993) 388–389; Kazhdan and Epstein (1985) 93–95; Kazhdan (1985) esp. 482–487; and Angold (1995) 289–291, 348–359. For Christophoros Mytilenaios (eleventh century), see Roilos (2005) 274–275; for Tzetzes, see p. 306 below; for Malakes, Bonis' introduction to his works, 21; for Eustathios, Kazhdan (1984b) 150–153, 162; Roilos (2005) 281–282; for Niketas Choniates, Magdalino (1983) 329; Garland (1990a) 19. This was accompanied by a decline in hymnography: Grigoriadis (1998) 7, citing relevant bibliography.

[84] Eustathios, *Inquiry into monastic life for the correction of its abuses passim*, esp. 168–169 (*Or.* 24, Tafel p. 255); for the context, Metzler (2006). For monastic wealth, see Laiou (1991b) 291 ff. (on Eustathios); in general, Morris (1995). Cyclopes: Kazhdan (1983b) 377.

outlook. A culture of satire emerges more when authors change their outlook than when their targets change their habits for the worse, for all societies always include the worst. The exploration of the soul and the reconfiguration of human psychology that Psellos had pioneered encouraged the discovery of less flattering motives for traditional behavior. The very premises of monastic life were called into question by men who had now come to share not merely the rhetorical skill but the social values and contempt for monks displayed by ancient Hellenists like Libanios.[85] Eustathios condemned the monks' anti-intellectualism and wished to transform them into scholars like himself who did not despise pagan learning. The ancient institutional tension between bishops and unruly monks may have contributed to this flare-up, as well as the competition for patrons between scholars and holy men. It is striking how often the frustration of the former centers on the ease with which monks secured aristocratic and even imperial favor. No years of training or parsing archaic forms for them: sometimes even utter silence could be offered as proof of holiness!

To conclude, the new empire of the Komnenoi blocked the advancement of philosophy but offered the Hellenists other opportunities to experiment in new fields. We have outlined the role of this small group of intellectuals in the moral developments of the age. These developments, however, placed them in an awkward position with respect to the Christian tradition and forced them to acknowledge its limitations, even if only rhetorically. As imperial panegyrists they turned to antiquity to find models for the worldly splendor of their princes to complement those of the Old Testament. As professionals whose status and self-esteem were based on secular learning, they were gradually led to idealize Greece as a place of perfect culture, its religion notwithstanding. From that standpoint they could not but satirize their society and traditions. Hellenism was a stance that evolved out of traditional scholarly occupations. Presently, we will examine the sophists' halting steps toward the fashioning of a new Hellenic identity. The first steps in that direction were acts of the imagination. Scholarship enabled the recreation of a Hellenic fantasy, an alternative vision of the world that expressed secret yearnings but deflected criticism by avoiding serious commitment. Komnenian Hellenism began as a vocation, became a habit of thought, and finally, through a series of elaborate rhetorical acts, generated an alternative world of its own. In the process, it laid the groundwork for the revival of new Hellenic identities.

---

[85] For Libanios against the monks, see Wilken (1983) 27.

HELLENIC FANTASY WORLDS: THE NEW ROMANCE NOVELS

The Hellenic habit infiltrated most sites of literate culture, even legal, diplomatic, theological, and ecclesiastical texts. The testimony of witnesses in court was rewritten to accord with Attic usage, and a judge of the twelfth century wrote a tragic poem adapting classical drama to a case of murder and cannibalism that he had heard: "it was through this learning that he . . . was able to do justice to a human being whose experience and situation were so far removed from his own. Was this not humanism in the fullest sense of the word?"[86] Ioannes Apokaukos, bishop of Naupaktos in the early thirteenth century (but educationally a product of the Komnenian empire), quoted Aristophanes and Homer in a case of divorce to present the comic condition of the plaintiffs. In the spirit of *philanthrôpia*, he set strict canons aside and granted a divorce.[87] But not all classicism advanced understanding. In 1199, the emperor Alexios III Angelos sent an official letter to the city of Genoa which began as follows: "The sayings and opinions of the wise men among the Greeks are not false, rather they often hit the mark. Their wise poet Hesiod declared that the whole city suffers because of a bad man."[88] The imperial chancery was clearly staffed with sophists, but what would the Genoese have made of this?

Though rhetorical, this endorsement of pagan veracity, issuing from the highest authority, posed starkly the question of the ancients' epistemological status. Were they true absolutely albeit only in part (their paganism had to be rejected), or merely in a qualified sense, for example within the boundaries of a specific rhetorical act that required the suspension of ordinary rules governing the reception of pagan notions? Our evidence is mixed. One incident suggests that *pagan* Greece could be cited as a source of legitimacy even in ecclesiastical matters. According to Anna, when Alexios tried to justify his seizure of Church property before an assembly of officers and bishops, his arguments were based on necessity, on the canons, and the example of David; in passing, however, he also alluded to the precedent of Perikles and the treasury of Athena, whose gold was likewise used to meet military emergencies! This was not strictly speaking a valid legal argument and Alexios would probably not have pressed it had he been challenged. Still, it is fascinating to see how Perikles' reputation as a leader could allow the practices of pagan temples to be cited in a Christian dispute. The authority of the *exemplum* lies somewhere between mere

---

[86] Macrides (1985) 163, 168, with text, translation, and discussion.
[87] Fögen (1982) for text, translation, and discussion.     [88] Wilson (1983) 3, who is unsympathetic.

classical elaboration and serious legal argument. The Greeks were pushing their way to the top.[89]

Of course, it is also possible that we are dealing with a literary elaboration by Anna, our source, in which case the value of the episode greatly diminishes: an assembly of officers and bishops was not quite the same as the readership of the *Alexiad*. But this is only a possibility. When Alexios' chief opponent in the matter, Leon, bishop of Chalkedon, wrote a treatise against the confiscation, his first argument of precedent was drawn from the legal status of the property of pagan temples in antiquity. To be sure, Leon goes on to claim that the same provisions that obtained for temples obtain also for churches, and all his other arguments are strictly within the faith. Still, it is fascinating that he should find pagan practice to be at all relevant. Perhaps he was carried away by a legal train of thought, as even Justinian's *Corpus* preserved older opinions on the property rights of temples. But whatever we call it, it amounted to a formal recognition of at least the legal authority of pagan antiquity and its relevance to current affairs. This was not a case of merely copying the ancients when their ideas were useful albeit without acknowledgment and so with a bad conscience (as, for instance, iconophiles did in the struggle over icons); here, Greek precedent is explicitly cited as a source of legitimacy in the present.[90]

For the most part in Komnenian literature the authority of Greek religion was dependent on the rhetorical conventions and literary aims of the particular work. When the sophists cited Greek beliefs and teachings they did not intend them to be taken at face value but only in the qualified sense that rhetoric can establish between author and audience: a realm is fashioned where Christian strictures may harmlessly (and temporarily) be suspended for the sake of style, illustration, showing-off, and edification. In a letter to a friend, Theophylaktos quotes Homer on Zeus in order to illustrate how he is buffeted by the Devil and succored by God. He does not mean to suggest that Zeus exists or that he is to be identified with either God or the Devil. This is only a manner of speaking, self-consciously addressed by a bishop to a fellow classicist ("your poets"). Still, this "translation" of a Christian existential predicament into the language and gods of Homer reveals a need to operate simultaneously on two registers.[91] Trained for years in classical literature and appointed bishops in the provinces, the

---

[89] Anna Komnene, *Alexiad* 6.3.

[90] Glavinas (1972) 89 for Alexios and 110–111 for Leon (whose treatise remains unpublished, though the relevant portions are quoted here). Cf. Theodoros Balsamon in Stolte (1991) 207; Dagron (2003) 262–263.

[91] Theophylaktos Hephaistos, *Letter* 31.

sophists had to believe that their two thought-systems were compatible, perhaps even that they converged deep down or on a level that only philology could discover. Granted, the Christian element was understood to be ontologically primary and the pagan existed in the ambiguous space between literary affectation and make-believe, but a considerable will-to-believe can be detected in this negotiated reconciliation. The gap, as we will see when we discuss the *Timarion*, could easily close, and then the pagan view unexpectedly turned out to be the dominant one. For more orthodox writers than the author of that text, Greece was like a caged beast admired for its beauty, strength, and exotic allure, and, despite the anathemas of the *Synodikon* (or even because of them), its appeal was paradoxically enhanced by the chance that some "maniac" might set it free.

Beside illustration, there was apposition. In a funeral oration Konstantinos Manasses adduces a "Greek" apophthegm about God as equivalent to one from the Psalms.[92] There is nothing especially pagan about this saying, but Manasses is very self-conscious about what he is doing and draws attention to it, alerting us that the juxtaposition is offered in a specific mode: our religious inhibitions, he is telling us, should be disengaged for the effect is supposed to operate on a rhetorical level. Thus did Hellenizing rhetoric create imaginary spaces into which the sophists and their audiences could enter and, for a while, play at being Greek and take their *paideia* at face value. How, then, did they imagine Greek spaces?

The primary instrument of Hellenist imagination was naturally language. The effort to compose and declaim in a purified Attic or *koine* was itself a creative act of linguistic anachronism that activated the classicist fiction and guaranteed the conditional reception of its content (much like our "once upon a time"). The contemporary world was made to disappear as author and audience temporarily entered a skillfully reconstructed illusion of antiquity where Basilakes could play at being a new Demosthenes, Anna a new Homer or Thucydides, and Prodromos a Lucian.[93] A Byzantine genre usually given little attention, the *progymnasmata*, is crucial here because it was an important forum for this kind of literary practice and reveals the underlying mentality. *Progymnasmata* were exercises in various categories of rhetoric that mostly took their themes from Greek myth and history, though a few were Christian. We have over fifty by Basilakes and about half a dozen by Nikephoros Chrysoberges from the end of the century. But it is likely that most educated Byzantines

---

[92] Konstantinos Manasses, *Funeral Oration for Nikephoros Komnenos* 124–128 (p. 306).
[93] For Basilakes and Demosthenes, see pp. 286–287 below.

composed them during their training. Some take the form of what so-and-so would say in an unforeseen or plausible circumstance and required that the orator put himself in the position of a Greek god, hero, or historical figure and declaim accordingly. We have eleven such by Basilakes on Greek themes, eleven on Biblical themes, as well as the curious "what would Hades say upon the resurrection of Lazaros." The pagan ones are of interest here, because the sophist had to immerse himself completely in the role, remove all anachronisms from his language and thinking, and render a convincing account of how Zeus gazed amorously at Io (the cow) or how Pasiphae fell passionately in love with the bull (these had to titillate too).[94]

The paganism of these pieces is luxuriant and unapologetic. We here find Byzantine writers frowning upon lack of respect to the *gods*; acclaiming Zeus as the supreme god ("he who watches over all"); and finding just revenge to be in accord with a true moral order. In playful encomia (e.g., of dogs), one could talk about the gods in the guise of a contemporary of Xenophon.[95] Of special interest are hortatory *progymnasmata*, for these concerned moral themes and could not entirely occlude Christianity. Discussing a verse of Sophokles, Basilakes praises the poet for avoiding all the disgraceful immorality of the myths – *phlyaria* is a technical derogatory Christian term. Obviously, the Hellenist illusion does not fully take over here. But Basilakes then offers a moral defense of the pagan poet. Sophokles wrote edifying stories and, by using pious language, avoided abusing the gods, which would have encouraged the young to be licentious! Is this an exercise? If so, it is not one in which we must pretend not to be Christians, for Sophokles is defended here explicitly in the face of Christian objections. Basilakes translates "our" pietistic assumptions directly into classical terms with the result that the difference between "us" and "them" effectively vanishes. By arguing that true morality can be promoted in a pagan context by virtuous poets, the text relativizes religion; it suggests that piety is a constant and that the ancient gods could be, in their time and in their way, guarantors of morality. By assuming a universal moral standard, the exercise blurs its theological commitments.

---

[94] Biblical themes: Nikephoros Basilakes, *Progymnasmata* 30–37, 40–42 (*Prog. e mon.* pp. 139–160, 166–183); Greek: 43–54 (ibid. pp. 183–224); Hades: 39 (pp. 163–166); Pasiphae: 19 (pp. 94–95); cf. 16 (pp. 99–100) for a tale of incestuous *eros*. For Chrysoberges, see p. 161 above. For *progymnasmata* in general, Hunger (1969–1970) 19–21; (1978) v. I, 92 120; Roilos (2005) 32 40; for their artistry, Littlewood (1980).

[95] Respect for gods: Nikephoros Basilakes, *Progymnasmata* 8 and 26 (*Prog. e mon.* pp. 79 and 113); Zeus: 5 (ibid. p. 85); revenge: 10 (pp. 92–93) and 26 (pp. 110–115); encomia: 29 (p. 133).

The illusion is convincing and I doubt that our classicists could easily tell that these were twelfth-century compositions, if they were put to the test. To be sure, it was less the case that the Byzantine sophists were imitating antiquity itself as that they were following the instructions and example of their ancient models, such as Hermogenes, Aphthonios, and Libanios. But this only displaces, and does not neutralize, the argument. We should not underrate the significance of these pieces because their imitation of Hellenism was a formal requirement of the genre, for we still have to explain why they were written at all. It seems that they were composed precisely *because* they enabled the sophists to engage in this role-playing; they liked pretending to be pagan masters of rhetoric. It has also been suggested that literary formalism was a pretext for the covert indulgence in erotic pleasures that were ordinarily suppressed; after all, *eros*, in various forms and perversions, is the main theme of Basilakes' *progymnasmata*, along with the conquest of nature by skill (*technē*).[96] Both of these themes also dominate the romance novels of the period.

Isolated texts of this kind can possibly be found in most periods of Byzantine literature. What makes these significant is their sheer frequency in the twelfth century and their proximity to the apogee of Hellenic fantasy-writing in Byzantium, the romance novels of the middle years of the century composed by Prodromos, Eustathios (or Eumathios) Makrembolites, Niketas Eugenianos, and Konstantinos Manasses (only fragments survive of the latter). There are, in fact, close textual and generic links between Basilakes' *progymnasmata* and the novel of Makrembolites; both, after all, were products of the same Hellenizing milieu and its rhetorical background.[97] The novels are between nine and eleven books long (about 120 pages each); they are told in the third person and in verse, except for Makrembolites', which is in first-person prose; and all have the same basic plot, which is that of the ancient romance novels that they all imitate: a young couple in love run away and are separated by pirates, barbarians, shipwrecks, or wars, preserving their virginity remarkably through it all; on the way they make friends (whose stories are similar), reunite, and marry. Despite this similarity in outline, in practice the novels are highly varied and idiosyncratic; conceptually they are worlds apart. Eugenianos focuses on the elaboration of the plot; Makrembolites on the

---

[96] Beck (1982) 144–147; cf. Pignani's introduction to Basilakes, p. 34.

[97] See Pignani's introduction to Basilakes' *Progymnasmata*, pp. 41–42, and the *index locorum*, p. 405; Beaton (1996) 25–26, 80–81, 88, 212. The titles are: Theodoros Prodromos, *Rhodanthe and Dosikles*; Eustathios Makrembolites, *Hysmine and Hysminias*; Niketas Eugenianos, *Drosilla and Charikles*; and Konstantinos Manasses, *Aristandros and Kallithea*.

subjective experience of *eros*, though his underlying theme is the second-order relationship among *eros*, nature, and art (*technê*), especially the *technê* of the novelist himself; while Prodromos takes war and religion as his chief themes. While Makrembolites is more "artistic," in both treatment and subject matter, Prodromos is philosophical and weaves interesting perspectives into his narrative, which we will examine separately below.[98]

Long despised and neglected, the novels are now slowly eliciting studies of their generic complexity; their frequent allusions to classical literature and intertextual use of the ancient novels and, very likely, of each other; and their literary motifs and strategies. We will not discuss these aspects here, except to the degree required by our chief theme. Moreover, the writing of these books cannot really be *explained* at present, though it can be contextualized and made less strange. For instance, their interest in *eros* suits the literary experiments of the age, as does their imitation of ancient genres and evocation of a pagan Greece where, as a rule, no contemporary or Christian references disrupt the Hellenist illusion. Their simultaneous appearance with the vernacular French romances has generated more questions than answers, but the problem of who influenced whom places an unrealistic burden on the word "influence." Literature cannot be "explained" by establishing tenuous chronological or prosopographical links. Byzantine literary culture amply met the preconditions for the reinvention of the novel. Beyond the Hellenist experiments discussed above, many of the motifs of the novel had survived in saints' lives and legal petitions.[99] Similar arguments can be made for the autonomy of the western developments.

The key feature of the Byzantine novels is that they are learned, meaning that they are imitations of an ancient genre (albeit in verse, except for Makrembolites). Written in classical Greek, their execution depended on a high level of scholarship, literary and historical, such as existed only in Byzantium. It is important to emphasize the degree of self-consciousness in this enterprise. The novelists do not admit the chronological and religious gap that lies between them and their models, a strategy that enables – or requires – their readers to imagine themselves among the (pagan and

---

[98] For an introduction, see Beaton (1996) chs. 4–5; for their relative and absolute chronology, ibid. 79–81, 211–212; Agapitos (2000) 181, 184–185. Chronology does not affect this discussion.

[99] Saints' lives: Hägg (1983) 154–165; Garland (1990b) 63 n. 5. Petitions: Neville (2004) 170. The western romances are linked to the later vernacular Byzantine romances, but probably have little to do with the twelfth-century novels. For the shift from "influence" to native developments, see Magdalino (1992). Agapitos (1998b) 145 proposes that the novels reflect a deepening interest in the theory of drama.

Greek) audience of the original ancient novels. The Third Sophistic thus assimilates itself to the Second, pretending that nothing has changed in the meantime. Of course, we, and the Byzantine reader, know well that much has happened in a thousand years and so we look for hints. The novels oblige, albeit never obviously; contemporary allusions are deliberate and executed with skill. (We will look below at possible references to Christianity and contemporary history.) Indirect references in the texts to the authors themselves emphasize the distance between the Hellenic fiction and its Byzantine creator. For instance, Eugenianos has one of his characters claim as his models heroes from the ancient novels (6.386–390, 440–451), saying that they lived "long ago."[100] But how long ago can they have lived in this timeless Hellenic world? Spoken by one of the *characters* about the *author's* models, the statement alludes to the gap separating Eugenianos from *his* Second Sophistic predecessors. Also, at the end of Makrembolites' novel, the first-person narrator assumes a more detached perspective and wonders who might possess such a perfect "Atticizing" style as could faithfully reflect the wondrous nature of his adventures (11.19). He then expresses the hope that even if the other gods do not establish eternal memorials to his love, the arts of Hermes will enable "one who is born much later" to immortalize them through rhetoric (11.22). The narrator thus alludes to the author, and specifically to his rhetorical skill, which is in many other ways the subject of the novel in the first place.[101]

As literary artifacts the novels must be read against the intense cultivation of rhetoric in the twelfth century and its experiments in both old and new forms. As with the popularity of the novel in the Second Sophistic, the genre enabled the sophists to perform their skills in new and challenging ways. For example, "Prodromos planned the novel to include one rhetorical tour de force in each book."[102] Moreover, the novelists, and Makrembolites in particular, made the complex relation of *eros*, nature, and art a matter for conscious reflection and infused their stories with a metanarrative developing those themes. Beyond the themes of its main narrative, then, *Hysmine and Hysminias* is also *about* the art of writing itself, the interplay of nature and representation, whose nexus is *eros*. This may sound complex and "modernist," yet it was perhaps a standard feature of

---

[100] Jouanno (1989) 350–353; Burton (2003) 257–259.
[101] Beaton (1996) 86–87; Agapitos (2000) 183–184.
[102] Jeffreys (1998) 193; cf. 194: "Prodromos' prime motivation in writing the [novel] was arguably to produce a superlative act of mimesis." For the variety of styles and genres, see Meunier (1991) 199–206, 226; for the performative aspect, Roilos (2000) 110–113; in general, see now Roilos (2005). Second Sophistic: Reardon (1974); twelfth century: Harder (2003).

Byzantine rhetoric, whose playful reflexivity we are now beginning to understand. When reading the novels, we must ask what each episode suggests about the author himself, his enterprise, and his relation to us, his readers, just as Hysminias attempts to "decode the Delphic riddles" of the painter (*technitês*) in the garden of Sosthenes (2.8).[103]

This aspect of the works has not been studied systematically. To do so would require expertise in literary criticism, engagement with the philosophical concerns of the text – Makrembolites himself calls them that – as well as *enjoying* the work in the first place, all of which have traditionally been rare qualities in Byzantine Studies. Our concern here, however, is not in what the novelists had to say about *technê* itself, but in their relationship to the Greek past in which they conducted their experiments. We will limit the discussion to the recreation of a pagan Hellenic fantasy, the setting where the novelists chose to develop their broader themes regarding *eros* and *logos*. What they did was to recreate an image of antiquity free of anachronism, chiefly of reference to Christianity and to the authors' own world. This was the rule, which, on occasion, was broken, though this was done deliberately, from a position of strength and not by mistake. To achieve this effect, the novelists had to deploy all of their scholarly skills and their knowledge of antiquity, put themselves in a classical frame of mind, and produce an illusion that could convince discerning peers and exacting patrons. To be sure, *some* features of the novels' setting, such as the vague temporal frame and the indifference to the political life of the ancient cities, can be explained by the direct imitation of the ancient novels; obviously, this is a "literary Greece."[104] But the effect could not be pulled off without a developed historical sense, for the setting of the ancient novels could not be simulated merely through imitation. The illusions were a crowning achievement of literary Hellenism and a testament to Byzantine scholarship.[105]

What did historicism entail in practice? First, the novels are thoroughly and even obsessively pagan. Not only do the protagonists, with whom we

---

[103] The reflexive aspect has been glimpsed but not studied systematically: Beaton (1996) 65–67, 87–88; Jouanno (2000) 93 and (2005) 26–27; Roilos (2000) 113 and (2005) 50–61, 103–112, and *passim*; Burton (2003) 255: "The character is testing the gardener in the same way that Eugenianos is testing his readers" (also 261–262, 265–267). In arguing against specific aspects of Beaton's reading, Agapitos and Smith (1992) 42–44 go too far in denying reflexivity. For analysis of the narratives, see Alexiou (2002) 111–114, citing previous discussions. I am unpersuaded by allegorical readings. For Byzantine rhetoric as postmodern, see Roilos (2000) 109; Walker (2004) 57–58; for authorial reflexivity in the ancient novels, Whitmarsh (2001) 81, citing previous discussions.

[104] Jouanno (2005) emphasizes imitation of the ancient novels.

[105] Historical sense: Kaldellis (2007a). Aspects of the present discussion have been taken from there.

are meant to sympathize, believe in the gods, they are constantly talking about them, praying to them, holding festivals in their honor, and, yes, even sacrificing to them. It is likely that this religiosity exceeds that in the ancient novels, and goes well beyond the day-to-day piety of the ancient world itself. But, on the whole, the novelists get the details right.[106] It is important that they do not apologize or ever comment on their characters' religion (as did, say, the poet of *Beowulf*, who likewise wrote about pagan heroes for a Christian society). Furthermore, as we saw with Basilakes' exercises, taking this world at face value requires accepting its religion as *virtuous*. Cities and individuals are praised for their piety. There is no sign that the narrators do not themselves believe in the gods, which places their Christian readers in the position of having to suspend, not their disbelief, but precisely their *belief* in order to enjoy the fiction. By speaking in the first person, Makrembolites compounds the illusion by making us view the world through the eyes of Hysminias and partake directly of the paganism in which he is steeped (he is a sacred herald). What Prodromos does is perhaps still bolder, as he speaks in the third person but makes many comments throughout that imply the narrator's belief in the gods and their benevolence (e.g., 1.65–67: it was not unreasonable that a goddess should help Rhodes; 6.84–88: one cannot escape fate, for the gods are everywhere). This disjoins the actual author from his authorial persona; it presents us with an author who *chooses* to act pagan, even if only for the purposes of one work, a choice that Makrembolites' narrator does not have. (This authorial strategy may be traced to Psellos' assumption of the first-person voice of Aristotle in writing paraphrases of his works.[107]) Finally, both characters and narrators in the novels believe that the gods actively intervene in their lives, and sometimes they do just that, albeit indirectly, in dreams, omens, oracles, and miracles.[108]

Timeless fictions that do not reflect contemporary realities or mentalities make modern historians uncomfortable. Efforts have accordingly been made to historicize them by discovering allusions to Christian and Byzantine realities. The results are generally plausible, but we must be careful in evaluating them. First we must accept that in its essentials the

[106] Macrides and Magdalino (1992) 151; Harder (2000) 69–72 (perhaps too strict); Jouanno (2005) 21–26. One wonders how modern historical novels would fare under such scrutiny.
[107] Ierodiakonou (2004) 108.
[108] A dream by Dionysos: Niketas Eugenianos, *Drosilla and Charikles* 6.664–668; the miracle of Artemis' statue: Eustathios Makrembolites, *Hysmine and Hysminias* 8.7, 11.17; an (apparent) omen by Zeus: 6.10, 10.11; an oracle of Apollo: ibid. 10.13; a dolphin sent by Hermes (?): ibid. 11.14; Selene saves Kratandros in the fire: Theodoros Prodromos, *Rhodanthe and Dosikles* 1.386–393; a Delphic oracle: ibid. 9.190–233.

setting is utterly unlike the authors' world, being Greek rather than Roman; pagan rather than Christian; and based on city-states, not empires (except for Prodromos' novel). The polarities of their moral universe are those of the ancient novels: chance vs. providence, slavery vs. freedom, city vs. country, Hellenes vs. barbarians, nature vs. *technê*. Everyday life, social relations, and manners of speech also do not correspond to the experience of any Byzantine. For example, the characters use ancient expressions that only the sophists themselves would have used in a Byzantine setting.[109] These enhanced the illusion of authenticity.

Setting Prodromos aside for now, what purpose do the Christian allusions serve in the novels? In the case of Makrembolites, they are faint, consisting of the practice of foot-washing (which is not exclusively Christian) and some language that possibly echoes the sufferings of the martyrs. Their purpose, in any case, is literary, that is they are either illustrative or subordinated to the development of the novel's own themes; it does not seem that they are meant to inspire deeper or subversive thoughts about Christian practices or beliefs.[110] The case of Eugenianos is more complex. We have there, for instance, erotic language that seems to echo the Song of Songs; a character declaring that a god had brought the couple together and then asking "who can separate those whom a god has united?" (3.12, 7.264; alluding to Matthew 19.6); and a marriage at the end that, contrary to ancient practice, takes place inside a temple with the priest presiding (this occurs in Prodromos as well). These allusions are too few and ambiguous to establish "a Christian context . . . despite the ostensibly antique settings."[111] Quite the contrary, the context is thoroughly pagan. No reader would have concluded that these characters were Christians at heart when they constantly say things like "I give thanks to you, son of Zeus, the greatest of the gods" (8.73–74). Their polytheism is too explicit for "Zeus" to be taken as a classicizing name for the Christian God (by contrast, the poet of *Beowulf*, after acknowledging that his heroes are pagan, has them talk about "God" thereafter as though they were not). No, Eugenianos was not trying to make his readers feel more "comfortable" with this material. Drosilla refers to the god in question, Dionysos, as *anax*, not *kyrie* as a Christian would (7.210). The thoroughly pagan context denatures and subverts any Christian references that may be worked into

---

[109] Basilikopoulou-Ioannidou (1971–1972) 85; for the world of the novels, Beaton (2000) esp. 183.

[110] Burton (1998) 208–213.

[111] Jeffreys (2004) 83. Roilos (2005) 210–233 has recently argued for extensive use of the Song of Songs in Eugeneianos.

it. For example, one scholar has suggested that Eugenianos was interpreting "the Song of Solomon sexually and literally . . . against orthodox opinion."[112] Jesus' words about marriage are likewise used in connection with an erotic infatuation inspired by Dionysos that leads to elopement; the line is used again later, only now it has become "those whom the *gods* have joined" (9.186). In Eugenianos' fiction, the gods prevail in the end.

The study of the novels is in its infancy and so we do not know whether they were meant to offer serious arguments about pagan and Christian practices or beliefs. Additional study will be required before we can interpret the temple marriages.[113] But even a casual reading reveals what the novelists believed that the fiction was good for. It offered a venue for the rhetorical performance of *eros*, an aspect of the humanism of the period that, as we saw, was seeking outlets, given the traditional aversion of the culture to such topics. In the imaginary Greece of the sophists, inhibitions could be relaxed as part of a harmless fantasy. So we get detailed descriptions of the bodily graces of young men and women.[114] In Makrembolites, we read powerful and explicit first-person accounts of erotic infatuation and arousal (3.7, 3.10; see 5.1 for a wet dream). There is also clever genital innuendo. When Eugenianos introduces his couple, he describes the lush vegetation around them, including "the roses' calyxes, that being closed or rather a little opened, shut the flower within like a maiden in her chamber"; and, "in the middle of the spring stood a pillar, skillfully hollowed within, like a long pipe, through which the flowing water rose" (1.83–85, 93–96). Or, on approaching a maiden: "Greetings, gardener of so many flowers, why don't you open your door also for me?" (4.246–247; see her response at 270–288). Much in these novels is written in explicit recognition that "*eros* often does not know shame" (7.61), in other words their subject matter is expected to violate social mores and decorum (virginity, however, must be preserved for marriage). The authors do not shirk this shamelessness, though they are generally more discreet than their ancient counterparts in raising topics banned by Christianity, such as homoeroticism.[115] Hysmine and Hysminias certainly flirt with incest; besides their names, they pretend to be siblings in the story even as they get it on. Be that as it

[112] Burton (1998) 203.
[113] Cf. Burton (2000) 405–408: marriage in a temple resolves the problems caused by Rhodanthe's abduction and situates the novel in contemporary Byzantine debates. Is it possible that this was a genuine anachronism? The classical texts read by Byzantine scholars do not specify the institutions of ancient marriage.
[114] Theodoros Prodromos, *Rhodanthe and Dosikles* 1.39–60, 2.206–220, 7.213–238; Eustathios Makrembolites, *Hysmine and Hysminias* 3.6; Niketas Eugenianos, *Drosilla and Charikles* 1.120–158.
[115] Burton (2003) 267–272.

may, the shameless way in which she flirts with him at the beginning totally violates the rules of feminine decorum. Her behavior, and that of some of the other women, is often exactly that which the Bible ascribes to whores.[116]

In short, it was to the Greeks that educated Byzantines inevitably turned when they wanted a world of laughter, drinking, and rejoicing, of delight in the body and physical beauty, *eros*, and of Bacchic dances. Much of this behavior had been condemned by the Church. Eugenianos' protagonists are even advised to prefer joy over sorrow, if both should fall upon them.[117] It is impossible that the novelists meant to condemn this kind of behavior, given that they describe it with such artistry, grace, and evident sympathy. They may have viewed it with irony (especially Prodromos), but this is not the same as condemnation. Nor could they have been unaware that their literary priorities violated orthodox strictures. We are dealing, then, with a Hellenism that supplements the official culture, that provides outlets for expression in marginalized areas. But to what extent did the creators and audience identify with the fantasy? Opposite extremes have been proposed: on the one hand, they would have regarded the Greek protagonists as their own; on the other, they would have viewed them as alien, with no collective or moral links to their own Roman and Christian world.[118]

In terms of both authors and audience, we are dealing here exclusively with the empire's intellectual elite. Later in the chapter, we will examine the steps taken by this elite toward fashioning a new Greek identity. Those steps, albeit tentative and inconclusive, corresponded in many ways to the modalities of Hellenism in the novels, in particular the rejection of barbarism. In other words, the polarity of Greeks vs. barbarians is important in the novels and was likewise fundamental to the revival of Greek identity in the twelfth century. To be sure, Byzantium was unlike the novels' world of small city-states. But the action of the novels does not take place in the cities, whose political life and wars are absent. Instead, the protagonists adventure in barbarian lands and rarely interact with other Greeks (except in Makrembolites, though most of his drama is domestic rather than civic). So too, in the social world of twelfth-century Byzantium the sophists' attempt to fashion new Hellenic identities was driven by their need to differentiate themselves from the barbarians who were assaulting the

---

[116] Gaca (2003) 167, on the ancient novels; Garland (1990b) 72 for Hysmine, and 70–81 for the novels' sexual morality (a survey).
[117] Niketas Eugenianos, *Drosilla and Charikles* 9.108–143; cf. 7.270–308 for dancing. Cf. Eustathios on p. 253 above.
[118] National Greek solidarity: Jouanno (1992) 300; Beaton (1996) 73; cf. 13–14; *contra*: Agapitos (1993) 110 (the Greek setting was as foreign as a Latin one).

empire militarily from outside and from those who were advancing within it socially and politically. Under those circumstances, anyone who was not a barbarian was one of "us," and the classical tradition predisposed these scholars to regard non-barbarians as Greeks.

The contrast between Greeks and barbarians in the novels is expressed in moral, religious, and linguistic terms. The narrator in Makrembolites laments his enslavement to barbarians and wonders whether he should take up arms against them "in the Greek way." But his captors are defeated by other Greeks, and so now he laments being enslaved "to Greeks, who speak the same language" (8.9). This is the novel in which the adventure is most contracted, as Makrembolites is more interested in the theme of slavery than in that of Hellenism vs. barbarism (his characters are enslaved to Eros, to barbarians, and then to Greeks, allowing the theme to be explored from many perspectives). Still, if being Greek means fighting barbarians and speaking Greek, then Byzantine readers would have identified with these fictitious Greeks. Granted, they are pagans even in their Hellenism; for instance, they cremate their dead "in the Greek manner." But one does not sympathize with the barbarians on this count, for they are worse; e.g., they practice human sacrifice.[119] Generally, then, the Greeks of the novels are presented as civilized in ways that Byzantines would appreciate, even when that civilization is ironized, regardless of the fact that they are pagans. Hence there is no Christian editorializing against sacrifices and such. By contrast, in the novels a "barbarian by nature delights in drunkenness . . . especially if he's easily carried off an abundance of property belonging to others."[120] Byzantine readers would have thought of Latins or Turks at this point. In short, the focus on barbarians compensates for the relative absence of the Greek city. Hellenism, i.e., the reader in his capacity as make-believe Greek, is defined negatively as that which is not barbarous. That is perhaps why the barbarians are more imprecisely named and undifferentiated in the Byzantine novel in comparison to its ancient counterpart.[121] "Barbarian" is a generic category that defines "us" by inversion.

We should not take this identification too far. We are still far from being able to plot the range of reactions of the Byzantine audience, but certainly

[119] Cremation: Niketas Eugenianos, *Drosilla and Charikles* 9.4; sacrifices: ibid. 4.93–95; see below for Prodromos.
[120] Niketas Eugenianos, *Drosilla and Charikles* 1.160–165; cf. Theodoros Prodromos, *Rhodanthe and Dosikles* 1.110–111; Eustathios Makrembolites, *Hysmine and Hysminias* 11.15; Konstantinos Manasses, *Aristandros and Kallithea* fr. 7.
[121] Jouanno (1992) 265, 271; for the ancient novels, Bowie (1991) 186–194.

no one was advocating a return to such a Greece. It is improbable that the protagonists of these works were upheld as ethical ideals, even beyond their "passivity" that alienates modern readers (though this is a feature of the ancient novels as well). Hysminias and Dosikles have little to say to anyone facing the challenges of the twelfth century, especially a Komnenian warlord.[122] This is mostly because they are not complete people, but vehicles for the exploration of the power of *eros* and *logos* (it is tragic pathos that produces the effect of passivity). We identify with the characters largely for the purpose of enjoying a rhetorical demonstration that flatters our critical skills.

Still, as we have seen, the values of the sophists and the warlords did not coincide. The Hellenist fantasy may have done more than just provide an outlet for its authors' rhetorical ambitions; it may have encoded their anxieties, just as the very different world of the violent and boorish Digenes Akrites pleased their Komnenian lords. To be sure, no character in the novels appears to be a sophist. But what had to be a *profession* in Byzantium might appear in more natural ways in its original classical setting. We are perhaps missing what the novels take for granted, for its protagonists naturally possess many of the skills on which the sophists staked their social position in Komnenian high society. They speak an Attic Greek that is complex enough, know and cite their literature, and command the mythological code by which they embellish experience. By contrast, the love-letter that Chrysilla, the wife of the barbarian chief, sends to Charikles is written by Eugenianos in a simplistic style to indicate her exclusion from the charmed circle of Hellenism (5.197–237).[123] But what chiefly differentiates protagonists from barbarians is that the former are not warlike and do not try to impose their will on others (except through *eros*, and here they restrain themselves); even in their own cities they are apolitical. It could well be, then, that the novels were revived in part because they expressed the insecurity of a cultural elite in the face of the warlords and barbarians who were governing the Byzantine empire.[124] This is strikingly illustrated by a scene in Prodromos. When barbarians seize the town, massacre its people, and capture the protagonists, Dosikles dares to speak up as they are being marched to the ships. But a "rude" barbarian "giant" who was near him strikes him full in the face and shuts him up (6.172–185). The *eros* of the protagonists is a private affair that must

---

[122] Kazhdan (1967) 115–117, has a point. Passivity: Beaton (1996) 63 with Agapitos and Smith (1992) 38–40.
[123] Jouanno (1992) 296–297.     [124] Macrides and Magdalino (1992) 151–152, 155.

survive in a hostile world. Perhaps the sophists felt likewise about their *logos* and the fragility of their Hellenism in the unclassical world of the twelfth century. Many of them, including Prodromos, complained of poverty, of the indifference of high society to their *paideia*, and, in a half-playful way, of slavery to their masters' whims. However rhetorical, these themes were never so popular before the sophists' emergence in middle Byzantium.[125] Still, as Bryaxes, Dosikles' new barbarian captor, explains as he is about to sacrifice him to the gods, "good order" (*eutaxia*, a key virtue of the Byzantine *politeia*) requires slaves to obey their masters (7.355–370).

Ares was no friend of the Muses, causing the interests of the sophists and the Komnenoi to diverge. Prodromos expressed this strongly in an oration to Isaakios Komnenos, the youngest son of Alexios I, who had philosophical and literary interests. This rare conjunction of power and learning allows Philosophy herself to step into the speech and take the floor against Ares. That beastly god, she says, has taken all the kings and the better portion of mankind for himself, leaving private citizens and day-laborers to me. One might object, she says, by citing Alexander, Cato, and Marcus Aurelius, who philosophized while leading armies, but they were few and all lived in the past. Isaakios is now alone in again uniting war and philosophy.[126] We see here again how Greek mythology was used to represent contemporary concerns; the passage also reveals how the Komnenian system may have appeared to the most philosophical of its flatterers. We can now turn to the political philosophy of Prodromos' novel. Whereas the other novels focus on Hermes, Dionysos, Eros, and the Graces – the gods of the sophists themselves as well as of their characters – Prodromos devotes a long section to Ares – the chief god of the Komnenoi and of the barbarians of his fantasy world. When the latter burst into the captured town and destroy its people, "a multitude of evil Erinnyes were dancing . . . Pallas was playing, Ares was lustful" (6.119–123), and the "Greeks" were dying.

## A PHILOSOPHER'S NOVEL: PRODROMOS ON
## RELIGION AND WAR

It should already be evident that the twelfth-century novels were highly original and thoughtful compositions and that this was largely because of, not despite, their imitation of ancient prototypes. Hellenism, reactivated at

[125] Beaton (1987); Magdalino (1993) 340–343.
[126] Theodoros Prodromos, *Oration for Isaakios Komnenos* 146–158, 194–200 (pp. 116–117).

an opportune moment, provided Byzantine writers with a forum of the imagination in which to discuss topics that had been neglected and, within the protective framework of fantasy, to develop original perspectives on them. These topics could be timeless, such as *eros* and *technê*. In the case of Prodromos, imitation of antiquity disguised satire of Christian Romania. Hellenism created a detour to the present. *Rhodanthe and Dosikles* shares the qualities of the Byzantine novels discussed above, but in it the satirical spirit prevails. Prodromos is again revealed as the Platonic Lucian of his age: though he satirizes, he does not offer any "answers," in fact he ironizes his own position as the defender of *logos* in a barbarous society.

First, a caveat. *Rhodanthe and Dosikles* has received virtually no studies as a work of literature. The following reading can hardly do justice to the complexity of its allusions or its dizzying spiral of reflexive irony. What is offered here is only a basic survey of its main themes. This work requires a commentary and discussion of the kind that is normally reserved for prestigious classical texts.[127]

From a narrative point of view, the most striking aspect of *Rhodanthe and Dosikles* is the barbarian "digression" of the three central books (4–6). We there lose sight of the protagonists, sometimes entirely, and the main plot is displaced in favor of the war between the two barbarian kings, Mistylos and Bryaxes. How is this to be explained? No doubt, this war offered Prodromos the opportunity to indulge in elaborate set-pieces, such as the banquet at which Mistylos' lieutenant Gobryas impresses Bryaxes' envoy Artaxanes with the marvels of his master's power (book 4); Bryaxes' long speech to his men before battle (book 5); and the war and laments of book 6. Moreover, scholars have detected traces of Byzantine ceremonial in the descriptions of the banquet and warfare (involving frogmen that sink ships from below). But even if these are contemporary allusions, what exactly do they mean? Detecting them does not explain why they are there in the first place. Likewise, calling the middle books, or the entire novel for that matter, an exercise in *mimesis*, implies that the work is thematically incoherent, frivolous, and not about anything in particular *as literature*.

We should demand more of Prodromos, and what we expect is satire. To begin with, he is vague regarding the identity of these barbarians. The kingdom and ethnicity of Mistylos are not specified. Bryaxes governs from the city of Pissa, though where this is we never learn (it may allude to Italian

---

[127] One day, when the classical bias in hiring abates, it will be possible for Hellenists to write fewer unread dissertations on Homer and more on buried gems like Prodromos.

Pisa, but is hardly the same).[128] The barbarians are not anchored in space, which allows the reader to imagine various associations. Specifically, they are no mere bandits or thugs, as in the other novels. Like the emperors and kings of the twelfth century, Mistylos and Bryaxes govern large realms with navies, armies, and cavalry. They exchange envoys and correspondence, have a developed protocol and ceremony for receiving guests, and go to war with each other over cities whose ownership is contested. This, in a nutshell, is the world of the twelfth century. Moreover, the dramatic date of the story is destabilized by a peculiar incident. When Kratandros, a Cypriot who becomes Dosikles' companion, is recounting his own story in book 1, he narrates how his father Kraton, in defending him against the charge of murder, proposed that he endure a trial by fire, in which the goddess Selene vindicated him (1.374–404). The anachronism is blatant, as Prodromos and his audience certainly would have known. (In the next century, some Byzantines recognized this practice as firmly western.[129]) Prodromos thereby disrupts the historicist illusion, signaling that the time frame may not be as it seems. These Greeks are a fiction, and the fiction is ultimately under the power of the author. Perhaps, then, its system of signs is different from what we may have assumed at the beginning; the novel might be "history." This makes us think about who these people really are (just as, conversely, in the preface to the *Education of Kyros* Xenophon tells us that his hero conquered Egypt, signaling the quasi-fictional nature of a work that at first sight appears to be historical).

What are the defining characteristics of these barbarians? On the first page of the novel we are introduced to their aggression and injustice, as Mistylos' men attack and sack the city of Rhodes, butchering its people. We have no reason to think that the attack was provoked. The subsequent war with Bryaxes concerns the fictional city of Rhamnon: Bryaxes claims it indignantly as his own (4.58–60), but Mistylos responds that he stole it fair and square from another king, Mitranes (4.452–504), who is ominously out of the picture. The narrator gives no indication about who was in the right, as though it did not matter. And in fact the question of justice is relevant to these warlords only in their correspondence; in practice, it is violence that determines who holds what. Bryaxes' capture of Mistylos' city is accompanied by such carnage and atrocities that the narrator is moved to tragic

---

[128] Jouanno (1992) 265. Pisa: Hunger (1978) v. II, 132.

[129] Cupane (1974), looking for "influences." For the ordeal in thirteenth-century Byzantium, see ibid. 167–168; Lock (1995) 273. Ioannes Tzetzes, *Allegories on the* Iliad, prol. 820, snuck Bulgarians into the Trojan War.

pathos (6.114–191). Still, despite their aggression these barbarians are very pious, in their own twisted way. After taking Rhodes, Mistylos sacrifices some captives to his gods in sincere gratitude for their protection (1.454–461). But the temporal signs are again disrupted when one of the victims, Nausikrates, faces execution in a way that reminds us of the Christian martyrs (1.485–501).[130] Who are these kings? Who are their victims?

Mistylos is so fearful of the gods that he will not surrender Rhodanthe to his lieutenant Gobryas because he has dedicated her to sacred service. It would be impious as well as unjust to offend the gods, he says, because they protect us when we commit injustices against others! (3.182–264) Apparently it does not matter to him that he has attacked people who were performing religious rituals for the dead (3.104–118). In a work that is about to become openly Platonic, it is reasonable to cite in this connection the hypothetical argument for injustice made by Glaukon and Adeimantos in book 2 of the *Republic*: unjust men can effectively bribe the gods for protection, or at least deflect their anger. The most unjust man may be the one who appears to be the most pious. At the beginning of book 4 of Prodromos' novel, Mistylos assumes the guise of a priest, though we are not told that he actually was a priest (just as Byzantine writers came short of saying that their emperor actually was a priest).[131] Bryaxes, however, is equally pious, and in his speech before the battle he expects that the gods will grant him victory because he has suffered an injustice (esp. 5.206–208, 228–229, 313–315). But his gods are the same as those of Mistylos. And when his soldiers take the city they too show no respect for religion, plundering temples and destroying statues (6.114–116). So we have two barbarian *basileis* waging bloody wars in the name of justice and worshiping the same gods. In reality, both are unjust and superstitious. The parallels with the world of the twelfth century thicken.

It is at this point that Prodromos flirts with blasphemy. Before the war, in order to impress Artaxanes, Bryaxes' lieutenant, Gobryas serves him a banquet that includes a cooked lamb that gives birth to a flock of birds and a performer who fakes his own bloody suicide, only to be "resurrected" by Gobryas in the name of his *despotês* Mistylos. Some have seen this as an allusion to Byzantine imperial receptions, which tried to impress visitors with such devices. If so, it is a grotesque parody not merely of the

---

[130] Burton (2000) 196–197. For the moral equivalence of Mistylos and Bryaxes, see Meunier (1991) 222–223.

[131] See Dagron (2003), esp. ch. 8 for the Komnenian period.

ceremonial in question but of the rhetorical forms that Prodromos is imitating here;[132] moreover, the fake miracles cut even closer to home. Artaxanes is fooled by them and persuaded by the argument of Gobryas that Zeus gave birth to Dionysos and Athena from his thigh and head (4.134–313). We may think that the purpose of the scene is to expose pagan deceit and credulity by mocking the myths, but what interest could Prodromos have had in that? What wit was there to be had in that? In fact, the miracles are ambiguous: pagan and ridiculous on the surface, but Christian and subversive if we look more closely. For Gobryas presents the first miracle as proof that his lord has power over "the nature of beings" and the second as proof that he can raise the dead. And that is how Artaxanes presents them later to his master Bryaxes (5.51–88), who is not fooled. But they correspond precisely to the first and to the most famous of the miracles of Jesus, namely the changing of water into wine at the banquet of Cana and Lazarus' resurrection. Bryaxes' response is worth quoting: "I will find out for myself whether this wonder-worker can raise the dead and change natures, if he falls down dead by my sword and then raises himself up again" (5.81–88).[133] Benighted pagan barbarian or indirect and hence safe vehicle of Christian satire?

Prodromos is the only one of our four novelists who poses religion as a philosophical problem. Only his characters question the existence of providence and they do so constantly in the face of misfortune, causing us to wonder too. Dosikles comments sarcastically on how Zeus Xenios must have been sleeping when he let Glaukon, the pair's host, die in the barbarian attack (3.125–131). He wonders why Zeus does not punish the offenders (3.478–486). Later, believing that Rhodanthe is dead, he wonders what good her father's prayers had done (6.385–386). Rhodanthe has similar doubts (7.129–137). But if the gods are asleep, what causes misfortune? The blame is persistently laid on Tyche, "chance," by both Greeks and barbarians, reflecting the conceptual coherence of Prodromos' intention. His satirical talents would have been wasted if they were aimed at long-extinct gods. Chance steps in whenever faith wavers. At one point, Dosikles calls Hermes a liar for predicting his marriage to Rhodanthe; better to believe in nothing (6.394–403). Rhodanthe also suspects that the gods lied (7.91). But of course the marriage does take place, and faith is restored. At any rate, the narrator asks rhetorically, "Who was there who

---

[132] Macrides and Magdalino (1992) 150–152; Beaton (1996) 73–75. Parody: Roilos (2000) 113–120.
[133] Burton (2000) 194–195. For the rhetorical and satirical aspects of this banquet, see now Roilos (2005) 253–288.

did not thank the gods?" (8.414) Perhaps one who realizes that the protagonists are reunited only because Tyche made Rhodanthe the slave of
Kraton, the father of Dosikles' fellow prisoner (e.g., 7.8, among many
passages to that effect), and because the fire on which Bryaxes intended to
immolate Dosikles was put out by a sudden rain-storm (8.120–124). The
barbarians view this as divine intervention, but the text does not say so; for
all we know that too could have been Tyche.[134]

The characters' faith may be restored, even that of the narrator, but not
necessarily ours or the author's. In addition to the matter of agency – Tyche
vs. the gods – religion is subjected to a Platonic revision in *Rhodanthe and
Dosikles*, though always within the limits of the novel's satirical intention.
In book 7, Prodromos, like Xenophon in the *Education of Kyros*, introduces
a mock Platonic dialogue into his mock historical narrative when Bryaxes
persuades Dosikles to accept being sacrificed to the gods (for they receive
only the best offerings); then, as Bryaxes is torn between piety and pity,
Kratandros, Dosikles' friend, persuades him that the gods really desire
animal, not human, offerings – after all, shouldn't the king himself be
sacrificed according to his own logic, as he is the best of all? A Christian
might read these pages as a refutation of pagan error, and such a reading is
hinted at in the metanarrative when Bryaxes prefaces his philosophical
discussion by saying that he was going to ask his captives about their
religion (*thrêskeia*) but now sees that it is obvious (7.394–399). The question makes sense only if there are "Christians" in this world. Prodromos
artfully hints at religious difference, without having to specify its source.
The virtuous captives are "Christians," while Bryaxes is the worst kind of
barbarian. But this has the unexpected effect of ameliorating Kratandros'
advocacy of *animal* sacrifice, the main form of sacrifice that Christianity
had condemned. Surely, it is better than human sacrifice. Bryaxes is now
not sure what to do, when Kraton, Kratandros' father, appears and pleads
for the life of his son. In a pitiful speech using Scriptural language, he
argues that the gods want only salvation, not flesh and blood (8.50–68). But
this transcendence of animal sacrifice comes at a cost. Kraton's speech is
linked to the novel's persistent allusions to the Eucharist (cf. Mistylos'

---

[134] The concluding affirmation of providence is peculiar, linked to the healing of Rhodanthe's paralysis
(caused by a rival's drugs). The narrator (who is not the same as the author) says that the gods
intervened because they hate evil (8.460–463) and Dosikles praises the gods for healing her
(8.512–515). But this is the most inappropriate place for such a reaction, as her paralysis was cured
by an herb that a bear used to heal itself when being hunted and observed by Dosikles. The
benefactor was nature and art, which Prodromos calls *physikê technitis* (8.477). For the primary role
of Tyche in another Byzantine narrative, see Kaldellis (2004a) ch. 5.

ability to change the nature of things), which consisted symbolically of the eating of Christ's flesh. Throughout the novel, Prodromos refers to the eating of human flesh and blood in "disturbing" and disgusting ways. His interest in this question has been linked to contemporary debates over whether the Eucharist should be understood literally or symbolically.[135]

To conclude, we note again what Hellenic fantasy was good for in the twelfth century. Far from "reconfirming existing prejudices . . . the novelists seem to be raising questions about their contemporary world by highlighting possible parallels between Christian and pagan practices." The genre "offered a 'safe' medium . . . for raising questions about the Resurrection and the Eucharist."[136] It also enabled trenchant criticism of the kings and emperors of the period. But for Prodromos, these questions remain at the level of satire. There are no answers. Even his own independently attested Platonic standpoint is ironized: it is Bryaxes who leads the philosophical dialogue, not his intended victims, and the *logos* of Kraton fails to persuade him. Only the sudden rain did that.

HELLENIC AFTERWORLDS: THE *TIMARION*

In American public life, only comedians may hint at the truth. They are allowed this by the guardians of opinion because their apparent lack of seriousness places them outside the realm of consequential political discourse; it also transmutes our indignation into laughter, neutralizing it. So too with "Hellenic" satire in Byzantium. The fiction of rhetorical imitation and satire's conciliatory foolishness diffused the implied challenge to Orthodoxy and the court. The satirist contorts and thereby neutralizes the dissident within himself. It seems that Prodromos dedicated *Rhodanthe and Dosikles* to the Kaisar Nikephoros Bryennios.[137] Nikephoros, then, was either incapable of grasping the esoteric allusions of the satire (the laugh was on him); or was capable of laughing at his faith and empire (why not?); or believed that indignation at the laughter of others was inappropriate for a patron of art and *paideia* ("who cares?"). But play could go "too far" and "cross the line," just as it still can now. Instead of being harmless fantasy and role-playing – or being able to hide behind those guises – Hellenic satire experimented with radical alternatives in a way that was *not foolish enough*.

---

[135] Burton (1998) 182–190. Less plausibly, Harder (2000) 75–76, 79, sees an uncomplicated Christian standpoint.
[136] Burton (1998) 214–215.  [137] Agapitos (2000).

It is notoriously difficult to know the mind of a satirist, but easy enough to know that of the man he has offended, and the latter may tell us more about the precarious status and limits of Hellenism in Byzantine society than the former. In the case of the *Timarion*, a work relating a journey to the fair of Thessalonike and thence to Hades, we are lucky to know the reaction of Konstantinos Akropolites, a statesman and writer of the early fourteenth century, expressing his mind to an unnamed friend. Akropolites concludes that the author had set out to ridicule the Christian faith and restore Greek mythology. "He was shrewd enough to assume the veneer of a Christian refuting open error and commending true belief . . . whilst all the time his intention was to string together pagan nonsense . . . and to make light of things that should properly induce awe." Akropolites would have burned the book were he not restrained by a friend in high regard. So Christian opinion, at any rate, was not unanimous.[138]

The author of the *Timarion* (the name of the protagonist) is anonymous. Various possibilities have been proposed (including Prodromos himself) but all are guesses.[139] Timarion's barrister in Hades is Theodoros of Smyrne, Ioannes Italos' successor to Psellos' old chair of Consul of the Philosophers. Theodoros was still alive in 1112, but it is not necessary to date the work after his death.[140] He is satirized, as is (almost) everything else in the work, but in good fun. In any case, many of those encountered in Hades lived in the late eleventh century, for instance Psellos and Italos, so the work must have been written soon after. The narrator claims Kappadokian origin (5) and has a special interest in people from Asia Minor. Unfortunately, there are too many local and contemporary references in his tale that we can no longer grasp. Certainly, the work is associated with the circle of Theodoros and takes aim at his interest in rhetoric, philosophy, and medicine.

The *Timarion* mixes genres. It is certainly a satire and is preserved among the works of Lucian, whom it quotes often (along with other authors, chiefly Homer and Euripides). On the surface it is a dialogue between Timarion and his friend Kydion. Timarion narrates his journey to the fair in Thessalonike in honor of St. Demetrios, which allows him to offer *ekphraseis* of the river Axios, of the fair itself, and the governor of the city. He then narrates his journey to Hades, which begins when two soul-gathering demons misdiagnose his condition. This leads to their trial by a

[138] Akropolites' letter is in Treu (1892) 364–365 and Romano's ed. of the *Timarion*, pp. 43–45; tr. from Baldwin (1984) 24–26.
[139] See Alexiou (2002) 100–101.     [140] Tsolakis (1990) 117; *contra*: Alexiou (2002) 104.

panel of judges and Greek doctors in Hades, who return Timarion back to his body. The prose is a simple Attic, but the contents are so diverse and bewildering that one does not know where to begin. What "angle" grants access to the world of this forty-page fantasy? There is, for instance, the dialogic format; the *ekphraseis* of Thessalonike; the medical debates; the interest in philosophers; the journey to Hades; the satire of Byzantine society; and the obscure contemporary references. Moreover, there has been only *one* modern attempt to interpret the *Timarion* as literature, and it focuses on a small part of the text, the sarcastic description of the governor of Thessalonike.[141]

We will not dwell here on Timarion's satire of Byzantine society, which focuses on gluttony and class-divisions, except to note that this satire, operating as a metadialogic theme, explains the presence of the *ekphraseis* of Thessalonike, which are otherwise irrelevant to the main story. Timarion's intention is to tell Kydion the "tragic" part of his tale only (2), but Kydion insists on an elaborate account. Timarion now accuses him of "avarice" and an "insatiability" for tales (*akousmata*: 3–4) – terms that link Kydion to the vices of Byzantine society. Though useful to economic historians, the *ekphraseis* are present only in this part of the text and are characterized by "the inflated style of Byzantine diction, from which the author has the merit of being usually free."[142] They are parodies of the genre and satirize the Byzantines' love of rhetorical display, likening it to their physical gluttony. (Yet doesn't Timarion effectively perform what he ridicules? Such are the complications of satire.) When he turns to his underworld journey, he signals that he is returning to his original tragic theme (10), from which he was diverted by Kydion's greedy desire for rhetorical displays.

Timarion falls sick and is visited by two demons who escort his soul to Hades. That is when things begin to go wrong for his Christian world-view. We know that he is a Christian because his purpose in traveling to Thessalonike was "pious" (2) and because he paid respect to the saint while there (10). To be sure, he tends to garb his faith in classical dress: he calls the festival of St. Demetrios the Demetria, comparing it to the Panathenaia among the ancient Athenians and the Panionia among the Milesians (5). At first sight, this is innocuous classicism, unless one remembers that the

---

[141] Alexiou (1983); (2002) 106–107.
[142] Tozer (1881) 246. The standard view treats Kydion as a clumsy dramatic device, i.e., it cannot explain him. Alexiou (2002) 103 is an exception, but wrongly sees Thessalonike as "the center of the dialogue" (105).

Athenians did actually have a Demetria of their own, which, Plutarch says, was a servile invention honoring king Demetrios, among other disgusting things they did to flatter him.[143] Moreover, the equation of pagan and Christian festivals will take on a different light once we uncover (in Hades) what relation actually obtains among religions. This is hinted at already when the demons come to his bed: speaking with hindsight, Timarion explains to Kydion that the souls of the dead are judged according to the "customs and laws of the dead" (13), which do not appear to be the same as God's laws. Later we discover that the Laws of the Dead that govern Hades may be called divine but are in fact the laws of nature that govern the body (32, 34). At the moment, we may infer that the demons are not obeying the Christian God from the fact that they are obeying a tablet in Hades inscribed with the opinions of Asklepios and Hippokrates (13), i.e., with opinions about the health of the body expressed by a Hellenic god and a medical writer. We have begun to cross a threshold into a world where the "errors of the Greeks" are in fact truths. Are the demons merely classicizing about death by talking about Greek doctors or do pagans actually rule in Hades? Is classicism merely a way of speaking, or is it in fact the way things are?

The journey to Hades confirms that pagans had it right after all. "Hades" is not the Christian afterlife, consisting of Heaven and Hell, but the dreary and unitary realm of the dead known from Greek sources. It has gates made of iron, guarded by "the god whom the Hellenes call Kerberos" (14–15). But this is not the realm of Hades known from Greek sources, for *everyone* ends up here, pagan and Christian alike, rich and poor, good and bad. We move from a Christian world to a Greek afterworld. Hades merely replicates the social divisions of the world of the living, so Timarion can extend his satire of Byzantine society to the afterworld. Some souls appear to be punished for their sins, and the demons inform Timarion that the life of each is carefully examined by judges so that he may be given what he deserves (22). Presently, Timarion encounters his old teacher Theodoros of Smyrne, who appears much better than he did in life and calls upon the "dear gods" when he recognizes his former pupil (23). Theodoros explains that in the world above his art was subject to popular tastes and so inclined to sophistry, whereas here it has become true philosophy and *paideia* in the proper sense (25). "I have said this," he adds, "to remove *planê* from your soul and revive our old ways (*archaia synêtheia*)," which on the surface refers to Timarion's lack of recognition and the renewal of his teacher's acquaintance. But *planê*

---

[143] Plutarch, *Demetrios* 12.

was also a technical Christian term for religious error; is the *planê* that will be "removed" Timarion's Christian faith? The statement is ambiguous. Hades is ruled by pagans and their gods: Greek *paideia*, he is basically saying, becomes true philosophy when it is freed from the constraints of a Christian society. Hellenism is activated in a world that has Greek gods; however, this is now a dead world.

In any case, Theodoros, a trained speaker, promises to defend Timarion in court, the purpose of which will not be to examine the worth of his life but the validity of his death, "so that you may go back to a second life and obtain the revival that you so desire" (26), another ambiguous statement in a Christian context. Timarion admits that this all appears as a "riddle" to him (27: *ainigma*). He has certainly realized by now that Hades is not at all as he had been taught to believe. How can you be so confident regarding the trial, he asks his old teacher, when the judges are "Hellenes" and hate us "Galilaians"? You too, after all, are a follower of Christ (27). We note that in Hades Christians are so far under the power of Greeks that they are referred to by the term preferred by the emperor Julian, their nemesis. The affected rhetorical classicism of the *ekphraseis* of Thessalonike has now become a grim reality. Theodoros, however, believes that he can handle these "medical gods of the Greeks" (27–29). He respects Galenos the most, then Hippokrates. But his contempt for Asklepios seems to result not from Christian bias against the only one among the doctors who was actually a god but from a preference for science over oracular mysticism.

At any rate, Theodoros tells Timarion that "you should not fear judges who are Greeks in faith (*hellênothrêskoi*)" because they honor justice. This is why they were chosen to be judges in the first place. We wonder immediately why Christians were not chosen. Theodoros continues. These judges are completely impartial toward religion and do not allow it to interfere with their verdicts. All here may freely practice their own *hairesis*, i.e., worship (cf. also 39). This, we realize, would certainly not be the case in any Christian version of the afterlife. But here, in the world of the Greeks, Christians are viewed as a mere *hairesis*, a "heresy" in their own parlance – though the Greeks don't hold it against them! Theodoros adds that when the fame of the "Galilaians" spread to the entire world, "providence" allowed *one* of them to be a judge, and chose the emperor Theophilos. Theodoros explains that Theophilos was among the most just emperors, so Timarion ought not worry. What Theodoros does not say, though we all know it, is that Theophilos was a notorious iconoclast, condemned as a heretic in the Byzantine tradition. Again, religious impartiality flouts the wishes of the orthodox: the pagans treat even Christians more impartially than the Christians themselves do. Besides, it is fitting that the *hairesis* of the Christians have a heretic appointed to the court. And what is this "providence"? Surely it cannot be Christ. It is some pagan god who must, in his fairness, accommodate the rise of Christianity. The pagans were right after all.

The specific aspect of the *Timarion* that most angered Akropolites, in fact the only one that he mentions in his letter, was the setting of pagan judges over the souls of those for whom Christ had died. His reaction is perfectly intelligible. Christian doctrine made no provision for the salvation of pagans. Rarely was the notion even entertained that the most virtuous among them, say, Plato, might be saved.[144] And even then they would humbly take a place among the choirs of Heaven. The *Timarion* does not merely abolish the distinction between Heaven and Hell, throwing all the dead together, it grants supreme authority to Greek judges and postulates a non-Christian supreme deity. Moreover, it suggests that Greeks are more just than Christians because of their religious impartiality. At this point, for many Christian readers the work would probably have ceased to be amusing. It mocked matters that called for the most reverent awe, and this is to say nothing of its more subtle blasphemies.[145]

The judges find for Timarion, and now things get really interesting for us. Our search for Byzantine Hellenism may have led us into the world of the dead but it is in for a pleasant surprise, for the clerk of the court is none other than . . . Psellos, the stuttering (*hypopsellizôn*) sophist of Byzantium (41), who joins the group. On its way back through the dark parts of Hades (the court convened in the Elysian Fields, which are full of light and gardens), the party arrives at the dwellings of the sophists and the philosophers (42). Here our author shows his hand: he is seized by an *eros* for knowledge, one of Psellos' favorite phrases.[146] His underlying interest in philosophy and rhetoric is revealed. He is not interested in meeting Christian saints, for the sake of whom he ostensibly went to Thessalonike in the first

[144] See Chadwick (1966) 45 (Clement and Justin); for later views, see Ioannes Lydos, *On the Months* 4.47 (Homer), on which Kaldellis (2003) 308–309; Anastasios Sinaïtes, *Questions and Answers* III, in *PG* LXXXIX (1865) 764; Photios, *Bibliotheke* 170; Kekaumenos, *Strategikon* 36 (an interesting take on the centurion Cornelius in Acts, here called a Hellen); Ioannes Mauropous, *Epigram* 43: Plato and Plutarch (p. 24); Nikephoros Blemmydes, *Basilikos Andrias* 61–64 (Trajan). For later (post-Byzantine) iconographic "salvation," see Saradi (1995) 33–39 and (1997) 419; Constantelos (1998) 167–168; Athanassiadi (2001) 189 n. 8.

[145] Why is the trial in recess for two days and two nights? (36) Besides the joke about days and nights passing in Hades, is it so that Timarion may rise again on the third day? Why, then, the reference to vegetables? Cf. 46 on how long it has been since someone was brought back to life.

[146] See p. 146 above.

place.[147] The guiding lights of his mind, the people he most wants to meet, are the ancient philosophers. We now meet the leaders of the pre-Sokratic sects (*haireseis*) sitting together and quietly discussing their doctrines (43). They are the only residents of Hades who appear to be happy, i.e., their chosen way of life is not hampered by their being dead. But when Ioannes Italos draws near, he is repulsed by Pythagoras: "you have dared to put on that garment of the Galilaians, O vile man, which they call divine and heavenly – I mean baptism – and yet you want to sit with us, who lived with science and syllogistic wisdom? Either take off this new thing or get away from us" (43). This is a bold statement of what a Byzantine must do if he is to practice ancient philosophy. Italos, presented here very unfavorably, refuses, but Diogenes reminds him that he is hated by the Galilaians as well (referring to his trial under Alexios). When he goes over to the orators, they throw stones at him, so unworthy of their company do they regard him (44).[148]

Italos is thoroughly castigated in the *Timarion*, whose author belonged to the circle of his successor Theodoros. Not so Psellos, who now occasions one of the most fascinating scenes in the work. The philosophers embrace and welcome him – which is the author's way of saying that Psellos was not a Christian, and rightly so, as we saw in the previous chapter – but they do not exactly treat him as an equal nor does he regard himself as their equal. When he goes over to the orators, however, he is honored beyond measure. Timarion praises the virtues of Psellos' prose style at length (45). In all, this is the most penetrating assessment of the two philosophers of the eleventh century that has been written. Whoever wrote the *Timarion* knew exactly what he was about, and the fact that we have so often had to read between the lines means that his work was more than a satire. Akropolites had good reason to suspect it. Despite its playfulness on the surface, the *Timarion* is dead serious in its view of Hellenes and Galilaians. Which leaves only the most crucial question: Where is Plato in this Hades?

Viewed as a commentary on Byzantine intellectual life, the *Timarion* suggests that the Greeks were superior in philosophy, rhetoric, medicine, and justice. Their legal approach to religious difference is more just than that of the Christians, though their philosophers are more strict: to join their circle one has to renounce Christianity. This Psellos had done, and

---

[147] In *Timarion* 3 the "going down" to Thessalonike for the festival alludes to the first line of Plato's *Republic*, where Sokrates says that he went down to the Peiraieus for the festival of Bendis: Baldwin (1984) 84 n. 21. This physical descent, in both texts, is transcended by a philosophical ascent (for the significance of going down, and into what, see book 7 of the *Republic*).

[148] For Italos, see p. 228 above.

quite possibly the author of the *Timarion* too. But this confrontation between Greeks and Christians, in which the former prevail, occurs on carefully selected ground. The work is structured by dialogue, satire, *ekphrasis*, forensic oratory, medical theory, and philosophy, in other words by precisely those genres and fields in which the Greeks excelled. "God" is absent. At the end of the narrative, Kydion asks how the orators treated Theodoros. Timarion replies that Theodoros did not have much to do with them, except with Polemon, Herodes (Attikos), and (Ailios) Aristeides, with whom he regularly discussed rhetoric. This image nicely captures the direct conversation between the Second and Third Sophistic. So perhaps in Byzantium, as in Hades, religious difference was irrelevant when the common ground was Greek *paideia*.

### TOWARD A NEW HELLENIC IDENTITY

It was not the conscious intention of the twelfth-century orators and scholars to create a new Hellenic identity, in other words to attach the name to a set of ideals and rally around them, as Julian and Synesios had done in late antiquity, each in his own way. Nor did they ever unequivocally identify themselves as Greeks in any sense that transcended the mere fact of their native language. Their usage of the word was circuitous, if not defensive, and in text after text it was limited to its adjectival and verbal forms: they "Hellenized" rather than outright called themselves Greeks. And yet the internal logic of their devotion to the classical past contained within it the seeds of such an identification. They revised basic polarities – Greek vs. barbarian replaced Christian vs. pagan and Roman vs. barbarian. The ineradicable Christian suspicion of Hellenism was concealed in some circles by a series of rhetorical acts in which the ancient Greeks played positive and leading roles. This section discusses the mechanisms of this process and offers additional explanations for the Hellenic turn of literary culture.

Of course, few of the developments of twelfth-century Hellenism were without precedent in Byzantium. What we are dealing with is an unparalleled investment by a broad sector of the learned elite in one of the cultural "options" that had always been available but had so far lain relatively dormant. Scholars now began to unfold the logic of their Hellenic heritage and relate it to their own lives in a way that verged asymptotically on the creation of a Hellenic identity.

Classical *exempla*, for instance, had always been part of the Byzantine literary tradition. Some had entered the language early on and provided

*Hellenic revivals in Byzantium*

enduring reminders of the greatness of individual pagans. The legacy of Alexander the Great in particular was not owned by scholars, as he was a hero in folk tales throughout Europe and the Near and Far East, having been Christianized as a godly hero in the popular imagination of Byzantium.[149] Among the intellectuals, with whom we are chiefly concerned, the authority of the classical past as a body of specialized knowledge had fluctuated over the centuries and its cultural significance was at times minimal. The twelfth century, by contrast, witnessed the culmination of a process by which *antiquity as a whole* came to represent the peak of natural human achievement, with profound consequences for intellectual life in a Christian society (as the West would discover some three centuries later). This process led to the establishment of an ethical sphere independent of religion and defined by pagan paradigms, parallel to the one that Psellos had tried to create for philosophy and natural science. How did this come about and what were its consequences?

The use of classical comparisons carries important implications. To say that Ioannes II surpassed the ancients as a soldier and statesman automatically valorizes the latter as standards of greatness. It implies that they are generally superior to us, but that the truly exceptional among us may surpass them. The classical legacy may, then, even come to be perceived as oppressive. In praising the emperor, Eustathios once complained that it is unreasonable to think that good men lived only yesterday and the day before; room must be made for greatness in the present. This means, however, that many were thinking just that.[150] Even when the ancients were (rhetorically) surpassed, their authority did not diminish. To the contrary, it was reaffirmed, just as Julian's challenge to the Fathers was renewed every time he was refuted by an anxious Byzantine. For example, to exalt the ancestry of Nikephoros Komnenos (grandson of Anna and Bryennios), Konstantinos Manasses disparages Pelops and Kekrops by saying that they were in truth foreign interlopers and not true Greeks, thereby implying that Nikephoros' ancestry was more pure than that of the house of Atreus and of the Athenians, the most famous Greeks of old. But in doing this, he affirms the Greeks as the best standard of illustrious descent and postulates "pure Greek" ancestry as something desirable – though still without outright stating that any Byzantine of his time actually possessed it.[151]

[149] E.g., in *Digenes*: Lasithiotakis (2005) 51–56.
[150] Eustathios, *Oration to the Patriarch Michael* (*Or.* 8, Wirth pp. 113–114), tr. and discussion in Magdalino (1993) 484–485.
[151] Konstantinos Manasses, *Funeral Oration for Nikephoros Komnenos* 90–93 (p. 305).

The sophists now did not merely use stock classical *exempla* as a routine part of their rhetorical arsenal, they did so enthusiastically, often to the complete exclusion of Christian models, and competed to expand the repertoire of episodes and heroes that could be used as models or insightful parallels for current events and persons. This pervasive and even obsessive citation of ancient history complemented the acceptance of Greek mythology as a new symbolic language and revealed an eagerness to draw comparisons between the present and the (pagan) past, to figure Byzantium, in other words, as ᵕ new Greece. For instance, praising Ioannes II for his victories over the "Persians," i.e., the Seljuk Turks of Asia Minor, Prodromos expressed his admiration through a figured classical paradigm: a new Xerxes demanded, but did not receive, earth and water "from our Greece" (ἐκ τῆς καθ' ἡμᾶς Ἑλλάδος). This trope does not quite identify the empire with Greece; rather, in it the Seljuk "plays Xerxes to our Greece." It was perhaps only coincidental that the geography of the classical paradigm so closely corresponded to that of the current conflict, though this may have encouraged the leap from figure to precise identification in the long run.[152]

It is a small step from *exemplum* that may be surpassed to model that must be imitated. In the speech delivered in 1166 before Manuel by Michael, Consul of the Philosophers, we view in condensed form the history of Byzantine engagement with Greece. Michael has just finished attacking Hellenic error about the gods when he goes on to praise the emperor for surpassing, among others, Alexander the Great. Michael grants that Alexander was valorous and a great conqueror, but he proved incapable of taming his anger and baser instincts. "He was derided as a barbarian instead of being a true Greek."[153] Michael does not come right out and say that *Manuel* proved to be a true Greek (just as Prodromos did not say that the empire that defeated the Seljuk "Xerxes" was in fact Greece). Yet by contrasting Hellenism to barbarism he switches codes from his previous condemnation of Hellenism as paganism. This new Hellenism stands for positive qualities, and, if Alexander himself did not live up to them, Manuel presumably did. Michael does not specify

---

[152] Theodoros Prodromos, *Poem* 5.71–73; cf. 11.111–113. Cf. (also with Xerxes) Euthymios Tornikes, *Oration for Alexios III Angelos* 11 (p. 65): τὴν ἐμὴν Ἑλλάδα (the editor notes that this may be a reference to the family's Theban origin, i.e., "my native Greece"). For estimates of classical vs. Biblical *exempla*, see Basilikopoulou-Ioannidou (1971–1972) 96–97.

[153] Michael ὁ τοῦ Ἀγχιάλου, *Oration to emperor Manuel I, written when he was Consul of Philosophers* 199 (p. 192: Greek theology), 270–289 (pp. 194–195: Alexander ἀντὶ Ἕλληνος διεγελᾶτο ὡς βάρβαρος). Manuel was often compared to Alexander: Stone (2001b) 233 for prose; Jeffreys (2003c) 96 for poetry.

these qualities, but they represent the opposite of barbarism, and Manuel is, presumably, no barbarian. That makes him a Greek, but only by implication.

Michael's speech nicely condenses the broad shift that occurred in Byzantine attitudes toward the ancient Greeks during the eleventh and twelfth centuries. The Greeks went from being regarded as deceived and deceitful pagans to paragons of natural virtue. We catch glimpses of a more reverential attitude even in writers who had no great interest in Hellenism as such but who had professional reasons to admire ancient achievements. Psellos' contemporary Kekaumenos, author of a book of dour maxims, warns his readers not to be discouraged into thinking that the ancients had discovered *all* strategies and tricks for winning in war, "for they were only human beings, as are you; so invent your own." It was unsurprising that those who were interested in military theory should hold the ancient captains in high regard and even imagine that they were superhuman,[154] which confirms Eustathios' testimony that reverence for Greece could be perceived as oppressive, as enervating action and pride in the present. An interest in military affairs, moreover, was only one possible source of admiration. Specialists in other fields likewise situated themselves within the ancient tradition. Twelfth-century doctors boasted of having Galenos as their master.[155]

Given their cultural preoccupations and social interests, the sophists of the twelfth century admired other aspects of ancient Greek culture than warfare and medicine. To praise the official Alexios Aristenos in ca. 1140, the professor Nikephoros Basilakes highlights his Hellenic and Attic speech and avoidance of all barbarisms, comparing him as an orator to Cicero and to "the Paianian" (i.e., Demosthenes). Again, Hellenism is introduced as the opposite of barbarism – linguistic this time – though it is also given positive models in the form of great statesmen. Basilakes emphasizes how Aristenos "strove to emulate, admired, and was amazed" by those ancient men who had combined politics with rhetoric, as though this were the peak of human perfection. The ancient orators, therefore, were admired not only for their rhetorical perfection but also ethically, as citizens and men. In an oration praising the patriarch Nikolaos Mouzalon (in ca. 1150), Basilakes offers a theoretical framework for his admiration of the Greeks. He begins by comparing himself to the Paianian facing a wise *theatron*

---

[154] Kekaumenos, *Strategikon* 15; cf. 18. For classicism in a military treatise dating from the middle period, see Kaldellis (2004b).
[155] Miller (1997) 30 and *passim*; Pontikos (1992) xxxvi–xxxvii.

whose collective soul was "hyper-reverent" and whose tongue was "hyper-attic." The balanced combination of spiritual and Hellenic qualities alerts us to the fact that this was an ecclesiastical audience. Indeed, our new Demosthenes admits that the man of the hour was not Phokion or Cato, "men who were austere . . . but mortal, whose mortal virtue came from the earth, given that they did not draw the good down from heaven." The patriarch, by contrast, is like a new Moses, but Basilakes confesses that he cannot do justice to his inner deity and so will praise him as a man and in a human way.[156] The ancient statesmen, therefore, represent the earthly and mortal virtue that Psellos had proclaimed and that Basilakes now would *rather* talk about.

Precisely because they valorized secular eloquence and refinement, the Komnenian scholars admired the ancients – and the Greeks in particular – as paragons of cultural perfection and natural virtue. In so doing they appropriated the Greeks' own modalities and view of the world. Prodromos, in a short work attacking the proverb that poverty begets wisdom, situated the Greeks, who were philosophers and lovers of learning but not too wealthy, midway between the Phoenicians, who were wealthy but unwise, and the Skythians, who were neither wealthy nor wise. His analysis is framed by Plato's thesis regarding the three parts of the soul, with the Greeks corresponding to the rational part. "But," adds Prodromos the struggling poet-scholar, "if one turns to look at our own times" he will find that wisdom begets poverty instead. Greece is not cited here as a high standard to which Komnenian society aspires and surpasses but as a superior in contrast to which it is criticized. As Byzantine intellectuals became less disturbed by the paganism of the ancient authors and heroes and turned to them as models of natural virtue in an ethical field increasingly independent of Christian strictures, Hellenism was gradually redefined from being the negative opposite of Christianity to being the positive opposite of barbarism. Yet it is not clear where Prodromos situates his own contemporaries between Hellenism and barbarism. "We" are worse than the Greeks and so obviously not the same as them. Perhaps, however, we *should* be more like them.[157] We may, then, venture to say that those who were pleased with their lot, i.e., emperors, prelates, and rich patrons, were happy to be told that they surpassed the ancients; but those who were not

---

[156] Nikephoros Basilakes, *Oration for Alexios Aristenos* 18, 20 (*Or. et ep.* pp. 17–18); *Oration for the Patriarch Nikolaos Mouzalon* 1–2 (ibid. pp. 75–76). These orations are drenched in classical references. For the latter's circumstances, see Angold (1995) 81.

[157] Theodoros Prodromos, *Refutation of the notion that wisdom accompanies poverty* 1317b–1318a; cf. Plato, *Republic* 435e–436a.

so fortunate, namely the sophists themselves, liked to imagine a world where learning and scholarship were respected and a time when orators like Demosthenes and Cato were statesmen and heroes by virtue of the fact that they were orators. The myth of virtuous antiquity served the social interests of its caretakers.

Over time, the logic of these newly revived classical polarities tended to promote identification with the Greek label. This is most evident in Eustathios, whom we will discuss separately below. Before the twelfth century, most Byzantines viewed the world through the polarities of Roman vs. barbarian and Greek vs. Christian. Psellos complained that the borders were no longer keeping "Romanity and barbarity" separate. To convey the extraordinary nature of an event, Attaleiates said that it was unparalleled among the "Romans, Persians, and the other *ethnê*," which was his way of saying "everyone."[158] But when, a century later, Anna wanted to highlight an extraordinary event, she said that it was unparalleled among either "the Greeks or the barbarians." This usage is found in Eustathios and others, even those who generally felt more comfortable with Christian rather than Hellenic paradigms. This expression *implied* that "we" are the Greeks, since the world is divided into Greeks and barbarians and we are not barbarians.[159] So whereas in antiquity "the barbarian" was invented to stand for everything that was un-Hellenic (or specifically un-Athenian), the logic of antonymy now operated in reverse: we must be Greeks or like Greeks (even if we do not call ourselves that) because we are certainly not Franks or Turks. Barbarism was the starting-point this time around.

In describing the arrival of the First Crusade, Anna apologizes for having to sully her text with barbarian terms, noting apologetically that Homer did so as well for the sake of accuracy (10.8.1). On the next page she describes a weapon used by the Crusaders called a *tzagra*, "a barbarian bow entirely unknown to the Greeks" (10.8.6). Who are these Greeks? Obviously, they must include present-day Romans, but that is only an inference. It may refer to the ancients, from whom "we" know about weapons. What Anna means is that the *tzagra* is not mentioned in any

---

[158] Psellos, *Letter KD* 207; Michael Attaleiates, *History* 42.
[159] Anna Komnene, *Alexiad* 11.12.3, 13.10.4; Eustathios, *The Capture of Thessalonike* 67 (p. 86); Georgios Tornikes, *Funeral Oration for Anna Komnene* (p. 297; for his religious preferences, p. 29). For Romans and barbarians in Anna, see Impellizzeri (1984); Reinsch (1996); for barbarians in twelfth-century texts, Jouanno (1992) 278–286. Here I differ from Macrides and Magdalino (1992) 155: "The division of the world into Hellenes and barbarians implied that the Romans were among the latter and that the empire was a barbarian state." Rome reverted back to a *tertium quid*.

Greek text, which includes those of the empire of New Rome. This usage is vague, but it does imply that "we" are Greek, if only because of our language and literature. The long-term consequences of all this can be observed in the fourteenth century, when the pro-western statesman and scholar Demetrios Kydones complained that the division of the world into Greeks and barbarians led Byzantine intellectuals into the complacent belief that Latin theology had no merits and that they themselves were the heirs of Plato while the Latins had only weapons and trades.[160] However, much had changed by his time for him to call this into question. We are now studying its initial recovery.

By valorizing cultural over religious identity, the revival of the Greek–barbarian polarity resolved the latent ideological asymmetry created by the superimposition in Byzantine thought of two different heterologies, one classical, in which *we* are the Greeks, and the other Christian, in which *they* are the Greeks. In the late tenth century, for example, the general and high official Nikephoros Ouranos wrote that Christians are supposed to be as morally superior to Greeks as Greeks are to barbarians.[161] The combination here of different polarities is incongruous, for can barbarians not be Christians? Under the Komnenoi, being Roman and Christian was apparently not enough. Romans, especially educated Romans, were refigured as Greeks, and Hellenism became their exclusive cultural preserve, which differentiated them from, say, Christian barbarians. Consider, by contrast, the treaty of Diabolis (1108), in which the Norman Bohemond surrendered to Alexios and became his liege (*lizios*). The text reflects a western outlook and terminology, but is preserved by Anna in Greek. The circumlocution by which it indicates that Bohemond will oppose "anyone" who attacks Alexios is "whether they belong to the Christian *genos* or are foreign to our faith, those whom we call *paganoi*."[162] Whereas Anna divided the world into Greeks and barbarians, Latin Christians (still) divided it by faith.

Did these developments result in a Hellenic identity? It has been claimed that around 1150 the ethnonym Hellene "surfaces as an unmistakable national usage."[163] When looked at closely, however, most of the passages on which this claim is based do not construct a national Hellenism and do

---

[160] Demetrios Kydones, *Apologia for his Faith* (p. 365).
[161] Nikephoros Ouranos, *Letter* 35 (pp. 234–235); cf. Romans 1.14–16.
[162] Anna Komnene, *Alexiad* 13.12.2, 13.12.11. Bohemond promises that regions in Syria would be subject to the emperor, including "Sezer, which the Greeks call Larissa" (13.12.18). This is a western way of referring to the Byzantines and reveals nothing about how the latter viewed themselves, though it may have reinforced latent tendencies to identify with Hellenism (see below).
[163] Magdalino (1991a) 10; (1993) 400.

not even promote a straightforward identification with any manner of Hellenism, only a qualified, asymptotic approach to it. It is often claimed, for instance, that, when Tornikes praises Anna for her wisdom – human and secular in addition to "ours" – he claims that "her ancestors (*propatores*) were Greek." But the pronoun "her" refers to "wisdom," not to Anna: Tornikes is conceding that even though God revealed truth to "us" through St. Paul, still the forefathers of Anna's wisdom were Greeks (I say "conceding" because on the first page of the oration he had called the Greeks pagans with no hope of salvation). This does create a link of sorts between Anna and the Greeks, but not one that involves ethnicity. In fact, the latter would not necessarily be the case even if the pronoun did refer to Anna rather than to her wisdom: her *propatores* would then most likely be her cultural models, not her biological ancestors. Aineias, orator of Gaza in ca. 500, had one of the interlocutors in his dialogue *Theophrastos* refer to Plato as his "ancestor" (*progonos*).[164] Hippokrates was likewise considered the "ancestor" of all doctors. And in terms of actual biological descent, the orators of the twelfth century kept their genealogical options open and did not limit themselves to an exclusively Greek model.[165] In fact, what Tornikes says is even more qualified than we have suggested: "even if" the ancestors of Anna's wisdom regarding nature were Greeks, God later revealed to us the deeper truth about the world (ταύτης [sc. σοφίας] γὰρ εἰ καὶ προπάτορες γεγόνασιν Ἕλληνες, ἀλλ᾿ ὁ Θεὸς κατὰ τὸν τοῦ μακαρίου Παύλου λόγον ἡμῖν ἀπεκάλυψε . . .).

There were avenues other than biological descent by which to fashion a collective Greek identity of sorts. One was language. Cultural chauvinism divided the world into "Greeks and barbarians," which were ideal rhetorical types that could be invoked regardless of whether one side actually was or even spoke Greek. But the fact that most Byzantines did speak Greek facilitated the acceptance of this polarity and, by extension, of the Hellenism that it entailed. The most interesting passage in this connection is Anna's account of her father's restoration of the Orphanotropheion in Constantinople. The school attached to this charitable institution had students of all *genê*: "you could see the Latin being educated, the

---

[164] Georgios Tornikes, *Funeral Oration for Anna Komnene* (p. 231; cf. 221, 279 for Greeks as pagans). Anna is similarly compared to Greek women by Konstantinos Manasses, *Funeral Oration for Nikephoros Komnenos* 145–164 (pp. 307–308), with no imputation of ethnicity. Aineias, *Theophrastos: A Dialogue on the Immortality of the Soul and the Resurrection of Bodies*, in PG LXXXV (1864) 880a.

[165] Magdalino (1984) 61, 69; Jeffreys (1984) 206; Kazhdan (1984a) 50; Kazhdan and Epstein (1985) 103, for various options. See p. 89 above.

Skythian Hellenizing, the Roman studying the writings of the Greeks, and the illiterate Greek Hellenizing properly."[166] The last category does not imply that Anna regarded the Byzantines as basically Greek. These "Greeks" are almost certainly a subcategory of the general Roman population, referring to Byzantines who spoke Greek but were uneducated; it merely means the average "Greek-speaker." They are also mentioned in a speech to Alexios by Manuel Straboromanos, who praises the emperor's kindness to poor peasants "who did not Hellenize much in their speech, in fact one might say that they barbarized in Greek." These terms had a linguistic sense, and the rhetoric that surrounds them here reflected the values of the sophists. Referring to the Orphanotropheion at the same time as Anna in his funeral oration for Stephanos Skylitzes (bishop of Trebizond), Prodromos says that Skylitzes' students at the Orphanotropheion had included "barbarians along with Greeks."[167] Again, this is a linguistic distinction, though it is not innocent of the broader implications of dividing the world into those two camps: Romans have become Greeks in that they are not barbarians.

In referring to Romans as Greeks based on their language, these authors anticipate the developments of the thirteenth century. But such references were rare in the twelfth century. Moreover, Anna certainly had no national sense of Hellenism in mind when she mentioned the presence of Greeks at the school. She meant only to designate Romans in their capacity as speakers of Greek and could just as easily have split them into educated and uneducated; it would have amounted to the same thing. As we saw, for her *hellenizein* and *romaïzein* meant the same: to speak Greek, or "Roman."[168] Merely speaking Greek was banal for her and the sophists. The more interesting meaning of the word was not merely speaking the language but knowing it properly as a philologist, the way Anna boasted in her preface, citing Plato and Aristotle. Few attained such perfection. In this sense, Hellenism was precisely *not* a national quality but one limited to the educated elite. Komnenian "Greece" was an exclusive realm populated by a select few. In a panegyric, Nikephoros Basilakes equated Greece with the ability to declaim in the proper rhetorical manner and to rule over civilized people with justice and refinement, as Perikles had done.[169] Few Romans

---

[166] Anna Komnene, *Alexiad* 15.7.9. For the school, see Miller (2003) ch. 8.
[167] Manuel Straboromanos, *Oration to Alexios Komnenos* (p. 183). Theodoros Prodromos, *Funeral Oration for Stephanos Skylitzes, Bishop of Trebizond* 42–43 (p. 7). Koder (2003) 308 opines that Anna is differentiating between the "Romans" of Constantinople and the "Greeks" of Greece.
[168] Anna Komnene, *Alexiad* 7.3.4 and 7.8.3; see p. 114 above.
[169] Nikephoros Basilakes, *Oration for Alexios Aristenos* 29–30 (*Or. et ep.* pp. 22–23).

could do either, which was why such praise was used in panegyrics for the ruling elite. "Greece" was sometimes a rhetorical standard used to exclude *Romans* who could not do such things.

Consider a letter addressed by Georgios Tornikes to the official Ioannes Kamateros (1153–1155), which has also been adduced as proof of the emerging national Hellenism of the Byzantines. Tornikes begins by invoking Hermes as the mediator of *logos* and requests a favor on behalf of his maternal uncle, the nephew of Theophylaktos, bishop of Bulgaria. "It seems to me that a philhellene and liberal man," he tells Kamateros, "does not equally rank a Greek among barbarians nor a free man among those who are slaves by nature." Tornikes finds it unacceptable that men "who have a barbarous tongue, to say nothing of the mentality that goes with it, and who are the servants of Ares" should be preferred over one "who is beyond even a Greek in his mentality and speech and a hero as well, and a lover of the Muses and Hermes."[170] What is going on here? Evidently, a "barbarian" was trying to secure the same favor from Kamateros, but we cannot be sure that he was an actual barbarian from beyond the frontier; all we can really say about him is that his Attic Greek was not up to standard and that he had a military career. Perhaps he was among the barbarians who took up Roman service under the Komnenoi, in which case we have here an example of how the rhetoric of barbarism could discriminate against new Romans. Tornikes' uncle may have even been facing competition from an uncouth provincial who was Roman in every respect. We have seen how the sophists could label even each other as barbarians based on perceived linguistic flaws. The meaning of *Hellen* and philhellene here is given away by the praise of *logos* and the allusion to "the secret sense of the myth of Hermes." Philhellenes belong to an exclusive club defined by high culture: they are not Greeks as such, but are compared to Greeks in their *paideia*. Hence, Tornikes' uncle "is beyond even a Greek." This exclusive sense was also implied when authors used the adjective *panhellenion*, commonly to designate a *theatron*. It does not refer to a representative assembly of the Greek people (there being no such thing in anyone's mind at the time); what it meant, alluding to the literary conventions of late antiquity, was that those present were more culturally refined than other Romans and could grasp subtle compositions in Attic style. "Sublimely Hellenic" is a better translation than

---

[170] Georgios Tornikes, *Letter* 10 (p. 129). Previous surveys have found no *philhellenes* between the fourth and the fifteenth centuries: Irmscher (1967). More will surely be found, e.g., from 1247, Iakobos of Bulgaria, *Monodia for Andronikos Palaiologos* (p. 71).

"pan-Hellenic" for this stock phrase, the equivalent of Basilakes' "hyper-attic *theatron*."[171]

The social exclusivity of Hellenism, especially as it is deployed in Tornikes' letter, suggests an additional historical explanation for the Hellenic turn of the period. Many historians have asserted that the military disasters of the eleventh century reduced the empire to its more Hellenic regions, making the empire into an ethnic Greek state that naturally would take a greater interest in all things Greek.[172] However, there are many problems with this theory and it is more likely that the exact opposite happened. The crisis of the eleventh century ushered in a period of intense instability, characterized by the frequent passage of foreign armies through Byzantine territory, by increased contact in the capital and the provinces with foreigners of all kinds, by a pervasive military, commercial, theological, and ideological contest with the Latin West, by a greater reliance on ethnic mercenaries, and by the rise of an aristocracy that took in new members faster than they could learn how to set aside their ethnic backgrounds. In these circumstances, the emphasis on Hellenism may have represented the reaction of the cultural elite to a perceived *increase* in ethnic diversity rather than the natural product of cultural, ethnic, or linguistic, homogeneity. This is born out by the terms of Tornikes' letter.

The imperial army, alone among Roman institutions, had always included "ethnic" regiments, but under the Komnenoi it came to consist of them.[173] Anna's narrative of her father's reign reveals a sharp awareness of this development: she draws attention to Alexios' recruitment among barbarians of all kinds (including Turks, Arabs, Skythians, Italians, Franks, Germans, and Scandinavians) and she admits that he could not trust his army precisely because of its diversity. Modern attempts to defend this practice notwithstanding, ethnic armies were perceived as unreliable and

---

[171] E.g., Psellos, *Letter KD* 190; Georgios Tornikes, *Letter* 24 (p. 165); Nikephoros Basilakes, *Oration for Alexios Aristenos* 4 (*Or. et ep.* p. 11); *Oration for the Patriarch Nikolaos Mouzalon* 1 (ibid. p. 75); Nikolaos Mesarites, *Funeral Oration for his Brother Ioannes* 29 (p. 42). With Browning, I find the Panhellenion in Michael ὁ τοῦ Ἀγχιάλου, *Oration to emperor Manuel I, written when he was Consul of Philosophers* 360–361, inexplicable (p. 197, with note on 210), perhaps corrupt. For late antiquity, see, e.g., the *theatron hellenikon* and *panhellenion* in Synesios, *Letter* 101, on which Cameron and Long (1993) 79–80.

[172] E.g., Magdalino (1993) 312; Beaton (1996) 9–10; Reinsch (1996) 258; also many modern Greek publications, e.g., Svoronos (2004) 66–67. Moles (1969) 102, Stephenson (2003) 97–98, and others, place the end of the "multi-ethnic empire" and the origin of the Greek state after 1204. Laiou (1991a) 81 is better here.

[173] Basileios II: Cheynet (2003b) 87; the Komnenoi: Magdalino (1993) 231–232; Haldon (1999) 226–228.

were often disloyal.[174] Moreover, the military nature of the regime meant that barbarian officers rose to positions of power at the court and eclipsed the sophists and intellectuals; this makes the "Hellenic" reaction more intelligible. Manuel especially acquired a reputation for promoting Latins to high offices, relying on them to the exclusion of native Roman subjects and adopting Latin habits such as jousting. It is often difficult to identify imperial officials of western origin in the sources and understand how their "westernness" opened or closed opportunities for them at the court, the capital, and the provinces.[175] In addition, a more complicated and dangerous international context led to intense diplomatic activity and a greater prominence for foreign dignitaries at the court. In an oration for Manuel (of 1173 or 1174), Eustathios commented on the sheer variety of odd languages and strange national dress that gathered at the court from the ends of the earth, including Skythian, Dalmatian, Arab, Armenian, Ethiopian, German, and Italian. As an epilogue to a commissioned poem on the *Theogony*, Tzetzes appended some verses on his ability to greet all the residents of Constantinople in their native tongues, including Skythians, Persians, Latins, Alans, Arabs, Rus', and Jews.[176]

Far from approximating a homogeneous Hellenic nation-state, in the twelfth century Byzantium came closer to being a genuine "multi-ethnic empire" than it ever had since the consolidation of Romania in late antiquity, at least insofar as the intellectuals were concerned (the only ones for whom Hellenism mattered). To be sure, linguistic Hellenism had long been valorized in response to internal minorities, e.g., by Psellos against "barbarians" who attained high office (though they were probably only Byzantines who had not passed through his school) and by Theophylaktos against the Bulgarians.[177] Moreover, there is no way now to quantify ethnic diversity. But what counts is the *perception* of diversity on the part of the sophists. In this period they may have feared that absorption was taking place faster than assimilation. By insisting on Hellenism, they retreated into an exclusive world of high culture that defined proper society narrowly by excluding "barbaric" arrivals or by compelling them through the reciprocal obligations of patronage to acknowledge the cultural

---

[174] Anna Komnene, *Alexiad* 3.2.2, 8.3.4, 14.3.8; Ioannes Kinnamos, *History* 4.13, 4.24; Eustathios, *The Capture of Thessalonike* 69, 73–74 (pp. 88, 92–95).

[175] Western influence: Magdalino (1993) 91, 106–108, 221–223, 226; westerners: (2003a) 49–56.

[176] Eustathios, *Oration for the Emperor Manuel Komnenos* (*Or.* 16, Wirth pp. 263–264); Ioannes Tzetzes, *Epilogue to the Theogony* and *Histories* 13.356–363 (p. 528). For foreigners in the Komnenian empire, see Magdalino (1981) 59 and n. 44; Kazhdan and Epstein (1985) 172–185.

[177] Psellos: p. 222 above; Theophylaktos Hephaistos, *Letters* 48, 110.

superiority of the (politically subordinate) class of orators and poets. The sophists definitely knew that their world was fragile and vulnerable, that the warlords and "barbarians" did not completely share their values. Hellenism throve only within the highly protected environment of the Constantinopolitan *theatra*. When its students were forced to leave the capital they panicked: would they now become barbarians? This was a common lament in their letters "from exile," whether from Bulgaria, Kilikia, or even Athens (a special cause for irony in the case of Michael Choniates, as we will see). Would they lose their "Hellenism"?[178] In those conditions, they risked never speaking Attic again, of becoming like the average Romans in their flocks, like barbarians.

## ANTI-LATIN HELLENISM

The barbarians who caused the orators such anxiety were not the same in the twelfth century as they had been in the eleventh. It was the Turkish conquest of Asia Minor that elicited Attaleiates' *Roman* response to imperial crisis in the late eleventh century.[179] In the twelfth century, by contrast, the Turks occasioned less worry than the armies of the Crusaders and the ambitions of western warlords. The Turks, moreover, were a purely military problem, whereas the Latins posed a major ideological challenge to Byzantine society, for they too were Christian and claimed the Roman legacy for themselves as well. This is not the place to review all the grounds for tension that existed between the two halves of the former Roman empire, whether cultural, political, linguistic, theological, or ecclesiastical. These are outlined in many publications. What is important for us is that unlike the nomads of East and North, the Latins articulated an ideological challenge to Byzantium on the basis of principles that the Byzantines themselves accepted, such as their shared religion and "Roman" history. Accordingly, the twelfth century witnessed a surge in anti-Latin attitudes directed against the West itself, against westerners who entered Byzantine society, and against even the temptations of the Byzantines themselves, what has been called the "internal West."[180] The sophists were as caught up in this struggle as were, on a different plane, the theologians who were busy refuting Latin errors. To what degree was Hellenism reinforced by these ideological wars? As we have seen, it is probably an exaggeration to "wonder whether Byzantines would ever have been moved to rehabilitate

[178] See Mullett (1995) esp. 42, 44–47.    [179] Kaldellis (2007b).    [180] Magdalino (1993) 387.

Hellenism if they had no need to label Latin Christians as barbarians."[181] But how were these developments linked?

For as long as the West was weak and the empire preoccupied with Muslim and pagan foes, the Byzantines unproblematically regarded themselves as *the* Roman and Christian nation. But when the West began to press against them, they could no longer claim exclusive possession of that dual identity. Inevitably, language was used as a differentiating marker between the Latin West and the Greek East. This linguistic break perfectly suited the antiquarian tendencies of the sophists, who could easily cast themselves in classical garb as ancient Greeks facing western Romans. The professor Nikephoros Basilakes tells us that his brother Konstantinos, who knew Latin, was sent as an ambassador to the West and proved himself "a Greek among the Romans and a Roman among the Greeks." On one level, these terms have a linguistic meaning, as Konstantinos could not have been a "Roman among the Greeks," i.e., among the Byzantines, in any sense other than that he knew Latin (the Byzantines are Greeks here insofar as they are Greek-speakers). But note that Nikephoros also contrasts his brother's western embassy (favorably) to that of the philosopher Karneades, infusing this linguistic distinction between East and West with the historical and national distinction between ancient Greeks and Romans.[182] Some Byzantines were now playing Greece to the Latins' Rome, just as others imagined that the Turks were playing Persia to their Greece. Would a "modern Greece" emerge in Byzantium from these classicizing figurations?

The mid-1150s, when Konstantinos Basilakes died on campaign in Italy, was a period of heightened tension between East and West. Such times were bound to elicit polemic or, at least, lack of courtesy, which fell into predictable patterns. Westerners called the Byzantines *Graeci*, a term that could neutrally signify language but could also be imbued with pejorative connotations; we will discuss it in the next chapter. For their part, the Byzantines could, without prejudice to their Roman identity, muster Hellenic cultural chauvinism against Latin impudence. This could involve putting down the Latin language as vastly inferior to Greek, as in the infamous letter by Michael III to pope Nicolaus I in the ninth century. Ordinarily, then, it was insufficient that one merely spoke the language to be labeled a Greek (though this could happen, as we saw in Anna's passage

[181] Magdalino (1993) 407; (1991a) 12; Macrides and Magdalino (1992) 155–156.
[182] Nikephoros Basilakes, *Monodia for his brother Konstantinos who died in the Sicilian War* 160–166 (*Prog. e mon.* p. 242).

about the school founded by her father); but when that language came under attack by westerners, the Byzantines rallied to its defense and accepted the label. This, then, was a reactive Hellenism, based on language and adopted for defensive purposes against the West.

An illuminating example comes from the 1150s. An exercise survives by Eustathios regarding a papal embassy of 1154 that led to a disputation between Anselm of Havelberg and Basileios, bishop of Thessalonike, on the issues that divided the Churches. Anselm began on a conciliatory note, by repudiating both the arrogance of the Latin race and the excessive verbal inventiveness of the Greek. But when one of those who were "most combative" deplored that very quality of Greek and spoke up in favor of the Latin Fathers, he had to be put in his place. The response took the form of a dazzling explication of the manifold nuances of the phrase *kyrie eleêson*, which demonstrated the subtle power of Greek in contrast to "Roman quibbling." Here "we" are "Hellenes," though only insofar as we speak Greek (but note that elsewhere in the piece Eustathios also refers to pagans – who only dimly perceived the truth – as Hellenes, without explaining that he is switching senses; as in so many Byzantine texts that mix different senses of *Hellên*, context is crucial). Interestingly, when the demonstration was over, someone recalled that another who was "altogether great and truly *hypertimos* among the wise, whose speech may have faltered (*psella*) but whose philosophy was piercing and thunderous," had also discoursed on the phrase *kyrie eleêson*. Psellos' lecture was duly brought out and read; all then knew that their own exposition had been like a gloomy night compared to his cloudless and bright sun. Still, Eustathios hopes in conclusion that his exercise demonstrates "the profundity of the language of Greece and its resourcefulness in writing."[183]

Anti-western Hellenism is expressed also in a letter sent by Georgios Tornikes, at the time a secretary of the patriarchate, to Georgios Bourtzes, bishop of Athens, in 1154, the very year of the debate between Anselm and Basileios (in fact, Eustathios was a colleague of Tornikes in Constantinople and is mentioned in the letter as an informant). Most of the text concerns ecclesiastical matters, but its preface is of great interest. Bourtzes has returned from Dyrrachion, where he had spent time while on a mission to Italy (which seems to have been canceled). "And now," writes Tornikes, "instead of telling us all about the Capitolium, the Forum of Appius, and

---

[183] Eustathios, *Exercise on the "Kyrie eleêson"* (*Or.* 5, Wirth esp. pp. 61, 66, and 76–77, alluding to Psellos, *Theol. I* 13). Psellos' name was evidently mistaken as a speech impediment. For the debate, see Russell (1979–1980) 22–23.

the Three Taverns, which you would have, had you returned out of Italy, indulge in Hellenic sights (*theamata*); instead of that barbarian and arrogant tongue take your fill of elegant Attic." This confirms that Greek monuments were indeed tourist "sights" for the Byzantines, for Bourtzes has returned to Athens, where there were plenty to see and where the language was, according to the code of classicizing affectation, "Attic." And yet, Tornikes continues, his laughter should be mixed with tears, for Athens is now lacking in wisdom, freedom, noble speech, and grace; instead of Sokrateses and Platos, one finds only bronze-workers plying their trade. In one paragraph, then, we witness the triumph of things Greek over things Italian followed by the lament for the decline of the Byzantine present compared to sage antiquity: ancient Greece prevails. Unlike most Byzantines, Tornikes evidently did not regard Italy and Latin as part of his cultural ancestry and exhibited nostalgia rather for the Greek past: the monuments and language may remain, but Athens now lacks the *people* that made it great.

Still, Tornikes is hardly disconsolate. He goes on to exhort Bourtzes to set aside the old protector of his city, Athena Pallas, that *undignified* virgin, in favor of its new patron, the Mother of God, who is not vouched for by *myths*. St. Paul's visit made Athens a greater city than it had been before. Tornikes' final word in this complex arbitration of cultural heritage is a strident affirmation of Christian superiority. This does not mean, however, that his deployment of the rhetoric of Hellenism and his previous estimation of the relative worth of languages and cultures are discarded, as they reflect both the sophists' nostalgia for antiquity and their polemic against the Latins. Those subordinate negotiations (Greek vs. Latin; past vs. present) could, under different circumstances, come to the fore and eclipse the supremacy even of the Christian faith. We will see something like this happen to Michael Choniates, bishop of Athens in the period of imperial collapse (1182–1204). His faith in the Virgin at times failed to console him for the loss of ancient virtue and the ruin of Athens.[184]

These two texts are the extent of anti-Latin Hellenism in twelfth-century Byzantium. Comparatively, it is small. As we will see, it was in the thirteenth century, after the conquest of most of the empire by western forces, that Hellenic labels and associations were used primarily in order to

---

[184] Georgios Tornikes, *Letter* 7 (pp. 205–209; see p. 213 for Eustathios and p. 14 for Tornikes' office). For the ecclesiastical context, see Angold (1995) 81–82; for Tornikes' colleagues, Browning (1962–1963) 34–37; for monuments as "sights," Saradi-Mendelovici (1990) 58–60; Kaldellis (2008). The Forum of Appius and the Three Taverns are from Acts of the Apostles 28.15.

set Byzantines off from Catholics. This happened quickly after 1204, with a sense of shock and a rupture in the continuity of the themes we have been discussing. In the sophistic circles of the Komnenian empire, by contrast, Hellenism for the most part evolved gradually according to the inner logic of Byzantine literature and society (whose precise mechanisms still largely elude us). Only a preliminary sketch has been offered here: the new regime required a new art of representation; fewer plugged their ears against the Siren voices of classical literature; Psellos had shown the way and had tempted many; for their part, the sophists defended and promoted their class interests; and Roman chauvinism sought a means to elevate "insiders" and the cultured elite against new arrivals from both East and West. Hellenism played into all these developments.

Despite its fixation on the past, Byzantine classicism was never insulated from the present. The very language that seemed to deny the present and exalt the ideals of the past was highly sensitive to contemporary developments. For instance, the rise of the West and its infiltration of Byzantine society displaced the signifiers of the classical code. Just as the Turks were now Persians and Byzantium was refigured as Greece – though in a qualified way, as "our version of Greece" (ἡ καθ᾽ ἡμᾶς Ἑλλάς) – the code of Roman antiquity was schematically reallocated to those of western extraction. For example, the Normans could now be referred to as Ausones, a term that the Byzantines usually reserved for themselves. In court poetry, brides from Hungary and Germany were designated as descendants of "Julius Caesar," which only means that they were descended from a western king. But when someone was called a scion of Aeneas, did that automatically mean that he was a Latin? Not in all cases, as long-established Byzantine families such as the Doukai were also said to descend from him. Yet even a few cases signify a significant surrender of part of the classical code to accommodate western claims. Such a shift would have pushed the Byzantines further in the direction of embracing the specifically Greek component of their cultural history. This component was highly prestigious and had the advantage of being owned exclusively by Byzantium (especially after the decline of Arab Hellenism).[185] In the next chapter, we will see how this trend was accelerated by the conquest of

---

[185] Normans: Stone (2001b) 233. Caesar: Hörandner (1993) 164–165; Jeffreys and Jeffreys (1994) 55; also Theodoros Prodromos, *Poem* 7.6, and the sources cited in Hörandner's commentary, pp. 231–232. Caesar and Augustus as ancestors of a Hungarian princess: Niketas Choniates, *Nuptial Oration for Isaakios II Angelos* (*Or.* 5 in *Or. et ep.* pp. 36, 40). Aeneas: Jeffreys (1984) 206; for more descendants, Nikephoros Basilakes, *Oration for Alexios Aristenos* 9 (*Or. et ep.* p. 13); and Konstantinos Manasses, *Funeral Oration for Nikephoros Komnenos* 164–169 (p. 308), referring probably to Michael

Byzantium at the hands of these western descendants of Aeneas. That event alienated the Byzantines from aspects of the Roman tradition.

Still, our focus here on the revival of Hellenism should not overshadow the basic continuity of the Byzantines' sense of Roman identity. No Byzantine in this or any other period renounced it, even if some, like Tornikes, seem to have given up its specifically Italian or Latin background. The enthusiasm for ancient Greece among the sophists was matched by the parallel acceptance of Roman paradigms and *exempla*. Without being able to provide exact statistics, I estimate that over a third of the *exempla* in twelfth-century texts are Roman rather than Greek. Given the advantage that Greek antiquity enjoyed in Byzantium in terms of scholarly access, and its acknowledged superiority in precisely those cultural sites developed by the sophists, this testifies powerfully to our writers' Roman identity, which was serious precisely because it was casual and unselfconscious. Yet, being scholars they tended to follow their sources. Frankly, they knew a lot more about Perikles than about Cato. Even so, it is amazing how often they cite Cato, a figure whose huge popularity in the twelfth century has not been studied. In many circles, there was even enthusiasm for Rome. We may cite the interest in Roman law, "the art of the Italians"; the emperor Manuel's extravagant revival of imperial Roman titles, ideology, and claims to Italy; Tzetzes' admiration of Cato; and Zonaras' theoretical interest in the history of the Republic.[186]

We should think of Komnenian Hellenism as the dominant partner in a broader Byzantine interest in Graeco-Roman antiquity. It was dominant because certain cultural sites were Greek to begin with, such as philosophy and medicine, and also because the Byzantines had access to antiquity only through Greek texts, which made poetry, drama, and rhetoric basically Greek for them too. But they learned about Roman heroes and Roman wars (mostly from Plutarch) and never forgot that many of their Roman "ancestors" were writers and orators as well. Even though they could not read ancient Latin texts, they often *pretended* that these were generally available, for the *ideal* of the cultured statesman was more important than what, say, Cicero or Caesar had actually said. In an oration for the sons of Nikephoros Bryennios, Prodromos likened their father generally to the

Hagiotheodorites, whose family was probably not of western origin: Barzos (1984) v. I, 319 n. 12. *Timarion* 8 links descent from Aeneas to Italian origin. For the difficulty in identifying westerners, see Kazhdan (2001) 91–99; Magdalino (2003a).

[186] Law: Oikonomides (1991b), but Magdalino (1985) 176–177 for its decline. Manuel: Macrides and Magdalino (1992) 121–122; cf. Magdalino (1993) 106 noting the irony that it was during the reign of this westernizing and Romanizing emperor that "Byzantine intellectuals began to call themselves Hellenes." For Zonaras, see p. 62 above. For Tzetzes, see below.

ancient Greeks and Romans, saying that none of them combined political and literary activity quite as perfectly as he. Elsewhere he praised Ioannes II for a triumph unlike any that had occurred "in elder Rome or Greece."[187] We have here a notion akin to our "Graeco-Roman antiquity." But most Byzantines still identified with the Roman part of it.

### IOANNES TZETZES: PROFESSIONAL CLASSICISM

Two writers of the twelfth century stand out in the revival of Byzantine Hellenism. Ioannes Tzetzes was possibly the first Byzantine to claim Greek ancestry, while Eustathios of Thessalonike often presents the Greeks as paragons of natural virtue, an attitude he imparted to his students, including Michael Choniates. They were exact contemporaries, living from about 1110 to after the emperor Manuel's death in 1180, and were both what we may call professional Hellenists, in that they made their living teaching the classics and commenting on ancient texts (though their careers were quite different). Their scholia and commentaries are major sources for ancient literature and criticism, though they themselves have received virtually no attention as men and authors in their own right. Works by each remain unpublished.[188]

Tzetzes lived by teaching and writing on commission. Many of his poems basically summarize and explain ancient literature to members of the extended imperial family: "classics for dummies."[189] His facility with verse was amazing; hundreds of lines may have flowed from his pen on a given day. He remained a "struggling scholar" and never obtained high office in the court or the Church. He was arrogant, petty, and acerbic, and made nasty comments about everything from monks to the style of Thucydides, in other words about anyone honored above him. His didactic attitude is so condescending as to almost be a parody. Still, his puns can be witty,[190] and his rapid style is unmistakable. Both he and Eustathios were careful observers of daily life, the latter to deepen his understanding of philology and life in antiquity, the former to find material to denounce (satire is too mild a word here). Both men exemplify the Hellenists' social

---

[187] Theodoros Prodromos, *Nuptial Oration for the Sons of the Kaisar* (p. 349); *Poem* 16.181–182; *Oration for Isaakios Komnenos* 194–200 (p. 117).

[188] For their scholarship, see Hunger (1978) v. II, 59–67; Wilson (1983) 190–204 (unfairly dismissive); Budelmann (2002). For Tzetzes, see Wendel (1948).

[189] Cf. Jeffreys (1974) 143 and 148–162.

[190] Thucydides: Ioannes Tzetzes, *Epilogue to Thucydides*. Monks: see below. Wit: Grigoriadis (1998) 86–94.

opportunities in this period, freelance scholar and teacher on the one hand, salaried professor, court orator, and bishop on the other. As we will see, each in his own way both reflected and advanced Byzantium's ideological entanglement with ancient Greece.

In a letter to a certain Isaakios Komnenos (6), Tzetzes claims that his descent on his mother's side was from Georgian nobility ("Iberians") while on his father's it was "purely Greek." What does this extraordinary statement mean? Is Tzetzes using these terms in the standard geographical sense that prevailed in Byzantium? For instance, the narrator of the *Timarion* says that there were Greeks present at the fair of St. Demetrios in Thessalonike, by which he means people "from Greece" to be set alongside those from other parts of the empire, such as Makedonians and Kappadokians (5; cf. 28). Or is Tzetzes implying that the empire consisted of various ethnicities, the Greeks being one among them? Fortunately, in another text he clarifies his genealogy. This is the *Histories* (or *Chiliades*), a massive commentary on his own letters: it is over 12,000 verses long (and accompanied by scholia of its own!). The exact relationship between these two texts has not yet been worked out. The *Histories* consists of hundreds of sections that explain the classical allusions in the *Letters*; the whole thing was meant as a pedagogical aid for those whose education was not up to par. In fact, it is likely that the letters, or at any rate the published edition of them that Tzetzes himself probably compiled, were designed to contain as many *exempla* and references as could be crammed into them for the purposes of pedagogy. It is not certain, then, which of these two texts is "primary." We are dealing with an odd exercise here and it would not be surprising if many of the letters were written (or rewritten) with the *Histories* in mind.[191]

In the section of the *Histories* that comments on letter 6, Tzetzes traces his genealogy on both sides. His great-grandmother on his mother's side was a relative of Maria of Alania, the empress of Michael VII Doukas and Nikephoros III Botaneiates (he correctly notes that Maria was from Georgia, not Alania, and that malicious rumor had it that his own ancestor was her servant, not a relative). This woman married a certain famous Konstantinos, who, it has now been shown, was none other than the nephew of the patriarch Michael Keroularios, the close friend of Psellos.[192] They produced a daughter (Tzetzes' maternal grandmother), who married a certain *exaktôr* Georgios. Tzetzes' father's side, on the other

---

[191] Shepard (1979) 202 suspects, on different grounds, that some letters were not sent.
[192] Ioannes Tzetzes, *Histories* 5.585–630 (pp. 190–191). See Gautier (1970).

hand, which in the letter he calls "purely Greek," was less illustrious. His father Michael had personally educated Tzetzes in letters and practical affairs, as Cato the elder had educated his own son. This Michael was the son of another Ioannes Tzetzes, who was illiterate but wealthy. The latter's father, in turn, was a native of the capital. The conclusion, then, is that Tzetzes himself is Iberian on his mother's side and "purely Greek" both on his father's as well as on his mother's paternal father's, i.e., the *exaktôr* Georgios. In short, we are not dealing here with natives of the Greek mainland, but with Byzantines in general, especially from the capital, i.e., with what other writers would call "Romans." But why doesn't he just call them that?

Let us reconsider the letter to Isaakios Komnenos.[193] Its purpose is to denounce to Isaakios his own secretary, a man with the improbable name of Lepreas (possibly a code-name). Assuming an improbably haughty tone to a social superior, Tzetzes tells Isaakios that he has warned him already about this fellow and says that he does not now wish to appear to be more barbaric than "the Italians, I mean the Ausonian Romans" (alluding to Rome under the kings and the early Republic). Although these Romans were aggressive and barbaric, their custom was to throw a spear into enemy territory as a warning before going to war. "And if this custom continues to this day, you would know it better than I, given that you occupy yourself with wars and know about them." This claim echoes the twelfth-century Hellenists' representation of the Komnenoi as men of war. How much more, therefore, Tzetzes continues, should *I* respect this custom (i.e., of warning enemies before war), seeing as I am descended from Iberian nobility on my mother's side and am also purely Greek on my father's? In short, Tzetzes is not chiefly interested in presenting himself as Greek, or half-Greek; he is interested in presenting himself as *noble*. On his mother's side, then, he has this covered through royal ancestry; he calls his father's side Greek to ennoble it in contrast to Isaakios' Roman-Ausonian way of life. The possibility of the survival of "Ausonian" customs shows that Tzetzes was aware of the continuity between the Republic and Byzantium, but we observe an interesting realignment: some Byzantines, especially the warlike Komnenoi, are more Roman (and presumably more barbarous) than others. For his part, and for the rhetorical purposes of this letter, Tzetzes presents himself as belonging to the more Greek and presumably more civilized side of Byzantine culture. This is a moral or

---

[193] For Isaakios, see Grünbart (1996) 179–180.

vocational distinction cast in terms of ethnicity. "Greece" and "Rome" are cultural options within the same society.

Tzetzes' idiosyncratic character prevents us from assuming that his views reflected those of his contemporaries. It is possible that his audience would not have understood what he meant by "Greek descent." Were there Greeks in the empire, then? Who had heard of such a thing since antiquity? There is no solid evidence that Tzetzes "believed" this either beyond the rhetorical purposes of one letter. Elsewhere in his writings the Greeks are an ancient nation or "babbling" pagans. And he himself has given us reason to doubt the sincerity of his genealogical pronouncements. In a letter to the high official Nikephoros Serblias, Tzetzes praises Nikephoros' descent from the Roman Servilii, but in the commentary section of the *Histories* he reveals the "ambidextrous" power of rhetoric: one could just as easily derive Serblias from a Serb named Elias.[194]

It is not surprising that Tzetzes, a Hellenist through and through, believed that Greek descent was a matter for pride. His entire intellectual and professional life was devoted to the preservation and correct under-standing of the classical legacy, and his social status and authority (such as it was) depended on his philology. He could imitate Homeric verse fairly well,[195] and his knowledge of ancient history and literature clearly sur-passed that of most modern classicists. His mistakes are due to quoting from memory, which testifies in his favor: "My library is in my head," he wrote once, "I own no books due to dire poverty."[196] As we saw, his letters are essentially exercises in classical allusion. Any topic, person, or action could bring forth from him whole lists of classical precedents, which he then had to explain in the *Histories*. Any person in his letters may take on the guise of Agamemnon or Sokrates: Tzetzes always wrote of the present in terms of the language and heroes of antiquity. In another improbable letter (50), he warns the bishop of Ephesos not to bring his attendant Ioannes, whom he considers lacking in *paideia*. "Just as it is said that above the entrance to Plato's school was inscribed the phrase 'let no one enter who lacks geometry,' so too an unwritten epigram is inscribed above mine

[194] Ioannes Tzetzes, *Letter* 18; *Histories* 7.295–301 (p. 267); cf. Magdalino (1984) 61. For another instance of rhetorical dissimulation, see Macrides and Magdalino (1992) 119–120, which also suggests continuity between Byzantium and the Republic. A problematic passage must be cited here. The scholia to Lykophron's *Alexandra* ascribed to Tzetzes' brother (but certainly by Tzetzes himself) offer various explanations for the name Auson and add that "some call us Graikoi Hellenes Ausones" (p. 34). It is not clear *who* is being called *what* here; also, is Tzetzes alluding to contemporary usage or to ancient commentators?
[195] Basilikopoulou-Ioannidou (1971–1972) 121–122.
[196] Ioannes Tzetzes, *Allegories on the* Iliad 15.87–88 (p. 183).

that silently says, 'let no one pass Tzetzes' threshold who lacks *paideia*.'" It is not surprising that such a man should boast of pure Hellenic descent when the occasion called for it.

What is surprising, rather, is Tzetzes' view of the Roman component of Byzantine culture. In the letter to Isaakios, we saw, he calls the ancient Romans barbarians and implies that their legacy survives in the modern Byzantine army. A similarly negative view of Roman power is found in his sole hagiographic exercise, the short *Life of Saint Loukia* of Syracuse, martyred under Diocletian. Loukia, Tzetzes claims, was a descendant of Archimedes (Syracuse's famous mathematician). Before her execution by the beastly governor, she compares herself at length to her *propatôr*. "Tzetzes uses a standard Christian genre in order to imagine an alliance of Christian faith and Hellenic wisdom against the brute power and ignorance of Rome . . . we are reminded of *Rhodanthe and Dosikles*, with its contrast between the non-political culture of the Hellenes and the imposing courts and armies of the barbarians."[197] We can understand why a professional Hellenist would adopt such a stance, especially one whose opportunity for employment and advancement was in the hands of warlords and who, moreover, seems to have been excluded from the lucrative performance of imperial rhetoric. (Eustathios, no less a Hellenist as we will see, thoroughly identified with the Roman order, but his career was more closely tied to its fortunes.)

We should not ascribe to Tzetzes a coherent ideology in this matter (or, probably, in any other). His *Letters* and *Histories* are full of Roman stories, and he displays there no greater bias than he does elsewhere against every-one else. He too viewed antiquity as "Graeco-Roman," with Greece in the lead probably only because it was more accessible. When at one point poverty reduced him to selling his books, he was in the end left with some fragmentary mathematical works, which probably no one wanted, and Plutarch's *Lives*, which he would probably not give up.[198] In all likelihood, it was mostly from Plutarch that he knew about the figure whom he admired above all others, the irascible and boastful Cato (the censor). Interestingly, he suppresses Cato's prejudice against Hellenic culture and emphasizes instead the fact that he took a personal interest in educating his son in all things, spiritual and practical, Hellenic and Roman. This struck a personal chord in Tzetzes, whose own father had done the same, teaching him, like Cato, to despise riches and power (a skill that certainly came in handy later). This made Tzetzes himself "a living portrait of Cato." The

[197] Macrides and Magdalino (1992) 154–155; Magdalino (1991a) 11.    [198] See Wilson (1983) 190.

comparison is developed at length, with Tzetzes concluding that his own passion for justice was more similar to that of the younger Cato. Just as the latter wanted to rid his country of tyrants with his own sword, so too Tzetzes wants to . . . kill corrupt priests! This seems to have been another obsession of his. His letters are full of abuse against monks and unworthy priests, which is surely not unrelated to the fact that he may have lived in a monastery.[199]

Whatever we make of this outrageous comparison between a poor Byzantine Hellenist and a Republican statesman, it shows that Tzetzes was as capable of emulating ancient Romans, even notorious anti-Hellenists, as he was of claiming Greek descent. His admiration for Cato, moreover, was linked to his dislike of the ecclesiastical establishment and, beyond that, his literary interests were thoroughly secular. We find the occasional Scriptural reference, especially in letters to churchmen. But even those are basically showpieces of classicism. In a curious "letter" of consolation (38) to a deacon whose mother had died, Tzetzes rebukes grief as a sign of weak faith. Surely, he says, you don't believe Homer's view of the afterlife (which he quotes) or that of Aischylos (another quotation), for you know "our" doctrines. But, he continues, *I* would rather not cite "our" witnesses but those "outside," because they are more persuasive, i.e., when they agree with "our" doctrines. So he now moves on to discuss Sokrates' view of death. All roads lead to Greece.

Professional Hellenists like Tzetzes (and Eustathios) had an interest in downplaying the Greeks' paganism. In the *Life of Saint Loukia* Tzetzes does not call pagans "Hellenes" but "idol-worshipers." In his commentaries on Homer, he explicitly ascribes "*all*" wisdom" and profundity to the poet, whose "champion" he claimed to be. Consequently, he denies that Homer had believed in "demons" and deploys a range of explanations for the presence of the gods in the poems. For instance, they were Homer's concession to the need to entertain the youth, or they were really meant allegorically: the gods stand for natural elements, psychic properties, stars and planets, or fate and providence.[200] In the *Histories*, Tzetzes also

---

[199] Cato: the chief passage is Ioannes Tzetzes, *Histories* 3.105–234 (pp. 88–92); see also 4.564–598 (pp. 149–150), 5.615–616 (p. 191), 6.303–319 (p. 220); cf. 10.624–674 with 11.13–39 (pp. 430–431); *Letter* 77; *Allegories on the* Iliad, prol. 724–739. For Cato and son, see Plutarch, *Marcus Cato* 20. For abuse against false monks, etc., see *Letters* 14, 41, 57, 84, 104, 106, and *Histories* 9.241–270 (pp. 354–355), 9.314–325 (pp. 357–358). Monastery: *Letter* 79.

[200] See Cesaretti (1991) 154–158, 178–179, 184; for Tzetzes' Homer-worship, see 181–183 and *passim*; briefly: Hunger (1954) 46–52; Wilson (1983) 193; Kazhdan and Epstein (1985) 134; Budelmann (2002) 156–157; Roilos (2005) 124–127. Tzetzes uses this mode of interpretation often; see esp. his *Allegories from the Verse-Chronicle*.

adopted a euhemerist approach: "Zeus" was what they used to call kings and Hades was king of the Molossians.[201] Dionysos he even rehabilitated by equating with none other than Noah, who was, it seems, a historical king. But there was no consistent hermeneutical policy at work here. In a different work, Tzetzes scoffed at attempts to equate Homer's gods with the Cherubim and Seraphim, apparently a dig at Psellos' metaphysical allegories.[202]

In general, Tzetzes avoided stories about the gods in the *Histories* as he did stories from the Bible, sticking with classical history. Beyond these implicit concessions, he was not especially defensive about his career, which required him to talk constantly about pagan gods and heroes, probably because by the mid-twelfth century he no longer had to be. He did not have to defend the value of classical scholarship and his fights were about purely philological and personal matters. Tzetzes evinces virtually no interest in Christian perspectives and writers. He tried to understand ancient writers on what he took to be their own terms. Byzantine Hellenism had matured. It had come a long way from the demonization of Hellenism that prevailed in past centuries. A shift in values among the political and intellectual elites, and the rise of professional classicism, had conveyed scholars almost to the opposite extreme. Homer was idolized and one could have a mental life immersed in the classics. Hellenism was, if not yet a way of life or an identity, at least a vocation.

### EUSTATHIOS OF THESSALONIKE: SCHOLAR, BISHOP, HUMANIST

Like Tzetzes, Eustathios too was combative, sarcastic, and could be vulgar and shocking. But there is an ethical and conceptual grandeur in his scholarship and orations that is missing from Tzetzes. He was revered as a teacher and admired as an orator at Manuel's court, and was eventually appointed to the see of Thessalonike, where he fought in vain against powerful monastic and other interests and tried to reform various social habits. He was there when the Normans sacked the city in 1185, an event of which he wrote a moving and heavily classicizing account. Though no philosopher, he was a man of principle. He came to view slavery as wrong

---

[201] Zeus: Ioannes Tzetzes, *Histories* 1.477 (p. 22), 2.163 (p. 49), 2.749 (p. 73), 5.453–454 (pp. 184–185), 7.28 (p. 253), Hades. 2.409 (p. 58), 2.751 (p. 73). For Assyrian and Persian euhemerism, see 7.353 ff. (pp. 269–270); for Hermes and Osiris, *Letter* 6.

[202] Dionysos: Anagnostakis and Papamastorakis (2004) 237–238. Cherubim: Tzetzes, *Allegories on the Odyssey*, preface 52 (p. 254); cf. Cesaretti (1991) 138–139.

and freed his slaves in his will. He was outraged by monastic hypocrisy, and, though he spoke often on the emperor's behalf, he could criticize imperial power when conscience called. Eustathios led the ecclesiastical opposition when Manuel proposed relaxing the oath required of Muslim converts. He was also an original thinker. He was the first to view Venice as an example of the mixed constitution, a notion that became popular in Renaissance political thought. He contrasted the performance (*hypokrisis*) of ancient drama favorably to its Byzantine counterpart, which was for him merely social "hypocrisy."[203] Moreover, he had profound respect for the ancient Greeks and found a place for them in his view of all that was good.

If Eustathios' Hellenism represented a break from patristic attitudes, as it clearly did, his contemporaries were ready to accept it without comment, and so he passed by the underlying difficulties without comment. In a sense, he merely deepened what many already thought and practiced implicitly. His rehabilitation of Hellenism did not, as with Psellos, aim at a fundamental ethical and cultural reform; rather, it was an attitude born of broad scholarship and admiration for men who could be known only through ancient books. Had he actually seen them in person, he might have been more critical or sarcastic, as he was with his own contemporaries. But too much was being invested in this Hellenism by the sophists and too many expectations were being placed on the moral benefits of Hellenic *philologia* for the Greeks themselves to be subjected to critical scrutiny. There was a considerable will to believe in all this. If not a philosophy, then, Eustathios at least had an ideal, which he probably performed in the classroom and lecture-hall more often than he advocated in print.

Unfortunately, the promise of this deeper engagement with the Greeks was cut short when the Crusaders ruined Eustathios' world soon after his death. His style of humanistic and scholarly Hellenism found few imitators after 1204, partly because the political and social world of Komnenian scholarship had been destroyed and partly because the parameters of identity were defined differently, engaging "Hellenism" in new struggles. It is tempting to wonder how Byzantine intellectual culture would have evolved had it not been murdered by western colonialism; Eustathios

---

[203] Slavery: Eustathios, *Letter* 26 (Tafel p. 334), on which Kazhdan (1984b) 164–167. Monks: see p. 254 above. Criticizes power: Sarris (1995–1997). Oath: Niketas Choniates, *History* 216–219, on which see the studies cited by Reinert (1998) 149 n. 76. Venice: Kazhdan (1984b) 161; Magdalino (1983) 334–335. Drama: *On Hypokrisis (Or.* 12; Tafel pp. 88–98), on which Wilson (1983) 200–201; Sarris (1995–1997) 22. As a teacher, Browning (1962–1963) 190–193; for his effect, Michael Choniates, *Monodia for Eustathios of Thessalonike* 8 ff. (Lambros v. I, pp. 286 ff.). Angold (1995) ch. 8 paints his episcopacy negatively, but the evidence can be read otherwise. For Eustathios' point of view, see Magdalino (1996b).

might well have set its tone. We may catch glimpses of this alternative future in his students, especially Michael Choniates, but even his turn to the past was indelibly shaped by the collapse of Byzantium in the years before 1204.

Eustathios' extant works, mostly imperial orations, sermons, and scholarly commentaries, run into the thousands of pages. To understand his rehabilitation of the ancient Greeks we will have to bring together passages from a variety of texts. In principle, this is risky because it effaces the immediate context of each. In Eustathios' case the risk is diminished by the fact that he offers his views on the Greeks frankly and consistently, without requiring us to read far between the lines. The difficulty is rather in reading and actually comprehending his vast and rhetorically complex corpus. One of his orations can take days to figure out.

For Eustathios, then, *Hellen* does on occasion mean pagan and can be used in standard pejorative expressions such as "the nonsense of the Greeks" refuted by the martyrs.[204] But these occur chiefly in ecclesiastical works; moreover, it is remarkable how rarely they occur even there. Even in sermons on the martyrs, Eustathios prefers, like Tzetzes in the *Life of Saint Loukia*, to call pagans "idol-worshipers."[205] In this regard the classical scholar got the better of the orthodox preacher. In fact, on occasion Eustathios views the Greeks kindly even *as* pagans. Trying to persuade his flock not to steal or appropriate Church property, he cites the Greeks as models of piety, for *they* did not lay hands on property that they had consecrated to temples. Their conduct was reverent (*eulabôs*) and even, "in the manner of their way of thinking, beseeming a sacred matter (*hieroprepôs*)."[206] We must, of course, take this with a grain of salt. Eustathios is trying to shame his flock, and a standard way of doing this was to compare "us" unfavorably to outsiders, whether Greek pagans, barbarians, heretics, or barbarian Christians. Still, he takes the topos a step further, as he seems to relativize piety and admit that the Greeks were, in their own way, pious. We may be tempted to dismiss this too as rhetorical, and the speciousness of the argument would have been apparent to many in the audience. But even an argument that was weak and suspect on theological grounds could

---

[204] E.g., Eustathios, *Encomium for the Great Martyr Demetrios* 14 (*Or.* 21, Tafel p. 170); *Inquiry into monastic life for the correction of its abuses* 74 (*Or.* 24, Tafel p. 232); *Exercise on the "Kyrie eleêson"* (*Or.* 5, Wirth p. 66).

[205] E.g., Eustathios, *Oration on the Martyrdom of Alpheios, Zosimos, Alexandros, and Markos* (*Or.* 4, Tafel pp. 30–35).

[206] Eustathios, *Preparatory Oration for Lent* 50 (*Or.* 11, Tafel p. 72); cf. *Memorandum on a Case* (*Or.* 18, Wirth p. 307).

establish itself in the repertoire of truth if it was spoken with authority, accepted without protest, and then confirmed by repetition. Eustathios, for his part, had a fairly consistent position on the matter as he admired the Hellenes and was inclined to rehabilitate, if not their religion (which was theologically impossible), then at least their piety (which reflected only on their virtue). Here too we observe his will to believe, for he could have found many episodes from Greek history where temple property was stolen or plundered. But the ideal of the Greeks was too important to be sullied by such critical scholarship.

In the preface to his commentary on Pindar, Eustathios notes the poet's reputation for piety and explains all the ways how he honored the pagan gods. Of course, he is following his scholarly sources here, but the lack of Christian editorializing in a handbook that must reflect lectures delivered over the course of many years is indicative.[207] The seriousness of the passage quoted above (on the piety of the pagans) is therefore enhanced by its place in an overall scheme of acceptance of the Greeks despite their paganism. Interestingly, there is a similar passage in his student Michael Choniates' *Oration to Saint Leonides*, who praises the ancient Athenians for honoring their dead with public burials and speeches. Are "we," then, going to ignore the martyrs who lie here? Will we fall short of the zeal for virtue shown by the Greeks?[208]

After all, it was these very Greeks who wrote the literature that Eustathios spent a significant part of his life studying and whose language he strove so hard to master. The scholar-bishop of the twelfth century was closely linked to those idolaters through that language. A reference to Greeks as Greek-speakers, then, could slip into a discussion of Greeks as pagans, and the context predisposed him to regard them favorably even with respect to their false religion. In a work where this happens, he says that in their worship of Zeus and establishment of an altar to pity or mercy (*eleos*), the Greeks dimly apprehended what Christians would know more clearly.[209] This, then, was a man who could have made room in Heaven for many Greeks, not just for Plato and Plutarch, but for actual idol-worshiping pagans.

Eustathios is prepared to countenance Hellenic religion because for him the Greeks were paragons of natural virtue. Let us, then, consider virtues other than piety. At the close of his treatise on monastic reform, he refers to

---

[207] Eustathios, *Preface to the Commentary on Pindar* 27 (pp. 46–53).

[208] Michael Choniates, *Regarding the Holy Martyr Leonides* 1–2 (Lambros v. I, p. 150).

[209] Eustathios, *Exercise on the "Kyrie eleêson"* (*Or.* 5, Wirth p. 68). For the altar, see Kaldellis (2008).

an ancient war between Greeks and Skythians in which the Greeks, who trusted in sworn oaths, were tricked by the treacherous Skythians but finally drove them back on account of their "Hellenic manliness (*andrikon*)." Elsewhere, in a letter praising a friend, Eustathios claims to see in him "a spark of that ancient Greek nobility (*eugeneia*)," an allusion to his *paideia*. And, arguing in a Lenten sermon that a Christian ought to judge others with compassion and wisdom, he adds that he should "Hellenize with respect to having a benevolent disposition (*kaloêtheia*)" and not give in to barbaric savagery.[210] This ethical alliance of Hellenic decency and Christian pity represented an advance over previous views that posited a hierarchy (in descending order) of Christians, Greeks, and barbarians. It also anticipated Hellenic ideals that emerged in the late eighteenth century, before the creation of Greek nationalism.[211] In another letter, he compares the "Kimmerian" lands of Makedonia to the "sunny and clear land of Greece." The aestheticization of Greece itself by a classical scholar who had probably never visited it was also another feature of modern philhellenism.[212]

Still, this preoccupation with Hellenism, which in Eustathios' case was not only professional but ethical, did not result in any clear notions regarding Greek identity *in the present*. The parameters of Eustathios' world remained Roman and Christian. To be sure, he conjoins these two terms most powerfully in imperial orations,[213] but there is no reason to doubt that he identified with them; he was not merely projecting them for the occasion. Besides, at this stage Hellenism was not ready to replace either element, as its religion was problematic at best and its national sense submerged under the universal ideals of *paideia*, or rather exalted by them out of reach of the majority. There was simply no reason for Hellenism to usurp the place of national Roman consciousness in Byzantium; they were not in competition with each other.

---

[210] Manliness: Eustathios, *Inquiry into monastic life for the correction of its abuses* 204 (*Or.* 24, Tafel pp. 266–267); cf. Nikephoros Basilakes, *Monodia for his brother Konstantinos who died in the Sicilian War* 260–270 (*Prog. e mon.* p. 247). The war has not been identified. Nobility: *Letter* 31 (Tafel p. 339). Benevolence: *Preparatory Oration for Lent* 25 (*Or.* 11, Tafel p. 66), on which Magdalino (1993) 410–411.

[211] Hierarchy: Nikephoros Ouranos, *Letter* 35 (pp. 234–235); see p. 289 above. Modern views: Rigas Velestinlis in Woodhouse (1995) 26.

[212] Eustathios, *Letter* 45 (Tafel p. 349). Cf. Marchand (1996) 108.

[213] E.g., Eustathios, *Oration to the emperor Manuel Komnenos, given when he was still a candidate for the Church of Myra* (*Or.* 13, Wirth p. 207); *Funeral Oration for the Emperor Manuel Komnenos* 45 (*Or.* 23, Tafel p. 207): *Romaïkon stratopedon* and *phylon Christianikon*.

What we find instead in Eustathios is consistent with the "asymptotic" approach to Hellenic identity that characterizes the Komnenian period as a whole, that is, we find a series of rhetorical acts that place the speaker or the audience in the position of Greeks for the purpose of a specific comparison or insight. These acts are not logically related to each other and often refer to different parts of human experience; moreover, there is no expectation that one will continue to inhabit those imaginary spaces when the exercise is over. The mere fact of the Greek language, for instance, enabled Eustathios to refer to his fellow Byzantines as Greeks in a qualified way. So, on the basis of language people could be divided into Greeks and barbarians, and at one point Eustathios speaks of "the Greek of our time (ὁ καθ᾽ ἡμᾶς ῞Ελλην)." We might translate this as "he who is Greek among us *in this sense*," in contrast, that is, to "the barbarian." Though he says that this "broad" distinction between Greeks and barbarians correlates to differences in *ethnos*, we have seen that this word in Byzantium did not usually refer to ethnicity or nationality, and in fact Eustathios then clarifies that the distinction is in fact linguistic (*glôssa*).[214] Nevertheless, it is still important that Byzantines could now be called Greeks, even if only in this qualified way. In an age when foreigners, especially Latins, flooded the court, the capital, and the provinces, the occasions for this usage must have multiplied and unintentionally played into unrelated and emerging controversies. In a debate about the relative worth of the Greek and Latin languages, Eustathios again calls his fellow Byzantines "Hellenes," which for him was positive, as he regarded Greek as an ennobling language.[215] But this linguistic chauvinism may have played into the hands of Latin *political* ambitions by reinforcing the western attack against the Roman identity of Byzantium, according to which the Byzantines were not true Romans but only Greeklings. We will see in the next chapter how Byzantines subject to Latin rule in the thirteenth century coped with the mixed positive and negative qualities that were associated with *Hellen* and *Graikos*.

There were other contexts in which the Byzantines could be presented as Greeks, some of them contradictory to others. As we saw, classicizing rhetoric cast the battles in Asia Minor between Byzantines and Turks in the guise of the ancient wars between "Greeks" and "Persians." In Eustathios' version, the Greek element is called noble (*eugenes*) and the

[214] Eustathios, *Preparatory Oration for Lent* 37 (*Or.* 15, Tafel pp. 134–135); cf. *Oration to the emperor Manuel Komnenos, given when he was still a candidate for the Church of Myra* (*Or.* 13, Wirth p. 219).
[215] Eustathios, *Exercise on the "Kyrie eleêson"* (*Or.* 5, Wirth pp. 61, 76); *Letter* 41 (Tafel p. 344). See p. 297 above.

barbarian ignoble (*dysgenes*).[216] We are led to imagine, for only a moment, that the Byzantines are a race of noble Greeks. Yet, as we have seen, the main thrust of Komnenian Hellenism was precisely to differentiate common Byzantines from classically educated "philhellenes." There was a tension between collective and exclusive notions of Hellenism here. In one of his catechetical orations, Michael Choniates says that his teacher Eustathios' tomb had become the site of healing miracles. But this, he adds playfully, is not amazing. Eustathios' *true* miracles were in fact performed while he was alive, when he opened people's eyes and ears to science and cured tongues of their barbarism by teaching them how to Atticize![217] But few would have been cured in this way. There are also moments when Eustathios the orator cast himself as a Greek, slipping into a Hellenic persona that belonged to the repertoire of Attic performance. In an amusing account of a lavish imperial banquet, he describes how the stables had been turned into kitchens: one sees there mules carrying food rather than – "as a Greek might put it" – teams ready for the sacred games. This hypothetical Greek, whose perspective we must briefly adopt to follow the image, is also clearly an ancient pagan.[218]

In short, there were various ways in which the Byzantines could be *like* Greeks, even if they were not all compatible, but no one was willing to say that they *were* Greeks. It was easier to imply that there was something Greek "going on here" than to specify what it was. In a letter, Eustathios refers to "the ancient Greeks," which implies that there are modern Greeks, but he never specifies who they might be.[219] In his commentary on the verses of the *Iliad* where the terms Hellas and Hellenes first appear (*Iliad* 2.683–684), Eustathios restricts himself to the myth of Hellen and an explanation of Homeric usage. His only contemporary reference is to say that Hellas did not originally have the same geographical scope as it does "with us."[220]

For Eustathios, Hellenic *paideia* was above all an ethical and intellectual ideal; philology ultimately ennobled practical and even episcopal activity. And yet, for all that he was a man of principle, he avoided the hard choices entailed by this stance. We find in him no systematic exposition of the basic

---

[216] Eustathios, *Oration to the emperor Manuel Komnenos* (*Or.* 14, Wirth p. 235).
[217] Michael Choniates, *Catechetical Oration* 19 (p. 361). For Eustathios' Atticism, see Stone (2001a) 329–332.
[218] Eustathios, *Oration on the magnificent public banquets on the occasion of the weddings of the imperial princes* (*Or.* 10, Wirth pp. 171–173).
[219] Eustathios, *Letter* 7 (Tafel p. 316).
[220] Eustathios, *Commentaries on Homer's* Iliad 2.683–684 (v. I, pp. 498–500).

principles of his Hellenism and no resolution of its long-recognized conflicts with the truth of the Gospels. He did not pretend that they did not
exist, but felt safe in ignoring them as though they did not matter, almost as
though they were ludicrous. Here is how the preface of his commentary on
the *Iliad* begins: "Perhaps it would be good if one were to abstain from
Homer's Sirens right from the beginning, or block his ears with wax, or
take another path, to avoid being bewitched by them." Referring to
classical texts as Sirens was a commonplace in Byzantium. The Sirens
lured men to their deaths: in Christian terms, one jeopardized one's
immortality by listening to Homer, and Eustathios almost certainly had
in mind here Basileios of Kaisareia's famous *Address to young men on how
they might profit from Greek literature*, which advised Christians to block
their ears with wax against all that is bad in classical texts.[221] But what does
his optative mean here? It appears to be heavily ironic, especially if we read
it in context. The reader of this commentary is already no novice: in order
to read it (a huge and hugely expensive production), he must already have
mastered Homeric and Attic Greek, he must know how to read a commentary (which entails accomplishment in classical scholarship), and must
have an interest in Homer to begin with (and may have known long
stretches of the poem by heart). If this sentence was how Eustathios
began his lectures, well, we must then imagine the foremost Homerist of
his day beginning his class on the *Iliad* by telling his students – all of them
adults, all of them able Hellenists – that one might opt instead to adhere to
the most fundamentalist strain of Christian thought. In such a context,
when the ears had already heard the dangerous song, this could only have
been a joke. It probably provoked laughter, which is the best way of eliding
hard choices.

Eustathios' ensuing defense of the study of Homer in the preface of his
commentary reinforces the suspicion that he did not take the fundamentalist position seriously at all. He says that he is not aware that any of the
ancient sages did not taste of Homer's poetry, especially those of the
"outside" wisdom, whom he goes on to list by categories, including even
the Pythia. This is an aggressive defense of secular wisdom. The study of
Homer is justified by its importance for understanding other *pagan* writers,
and not on Christian terms. The classics had apparently become by then an
autonomous standard of excellence so that their very existence refuted the
fundamentalist position. More importantly, he goes on, one should study

---

[221] Eustathios, *Commentaries on Homer's* Iliad, preface (v. I, p. 1), partly translated in Herington (1969).
For Eustathios on the Sirens, see Cesaretti (1991) 225. See p. 164 above for Basileios' treatise.

the *Iliad* in order to learn from it a "myriad" of good things: ethics, philosophy, rhetoric, strategy, arts, and sciences. Only then is the problem of myth raised: "one might say that for *this* Homer risks losing our admiration." Eustathios answers this challenge with the same confidence as had Tzetzes, whom he followed: the myths are allegorical and the poet devised them to charm those who would otherwise be deaf to his sublime philosophy.[222] Far from protecting students against the Sirens' song, this Christian exegete has become their mouthpiece. In a lament over Eustathios' tomb a few days after his death, his former colleague in Constantinople Euthymios Malakes noted that the master's eloquence and wisdom were so great that all lovers of the Muses would hang from his speech requiring no wax in their ears, like those who sailed past the Sirens, for they were willing to die right there for the sake of that sweet discourse.[223]

In his *Inquiry into monastic life for the correction of its abuses*, Eustathios attacked Christian obscurantism, arguing that monks should read in all fields, beyond ecclesiastical and theological literature.[224] This proposal, however, along with his deep admiration for Homer, was not based on any carefully worked-out philosophy of "reconciliation" between Hellenism and Christianity that reached the fundamentals of the issue. In another admonitory work, Eustathios notes, in a passage on how good and bad things come together, that "of the words of Hellenic wisdom, some lead to ultimate destruction (*olethros*), but others led many to the opposite."[225] Is the "opposite" Christian salvation? But that is all that Eustathios tells us, leaving us to wonder how Hellenic wisdom can lead to "the opposite of ultimate destruction." In his lament for Eustathios' death, Michael Choniates notes how his teacher was being acclaimed in Heaven by the Fathers for using Greek philosophy in the service of Christian theosophy.[226] It is one thing to *justify* your interest in the Greeks by arguing that you are subordinating them to Christian theology, but it is another to claim that you will be rewarded in Heaven for doing so. In the past, those who were signaled out for special attention in Heaven were ascetics; now, in an age of declining hagiography and skepticism about monastic values, it is Hellenism that earns you a choir of saints.

---

[222] Cesaretti (1991) chs. 8–9; briefly: Roilos (2005) 127–128.
[223] Euthymios Malakes, *Monodia for Eustathios, read upon his grave a few days after his death* 4 (p. 80).
[224] Eustathios, *Inquiry into monastic life for the correction of its abuses* 143, 146 (*Or.* 24, Tafel pp. 249–250). For Eustathios and monasticism, see p. 254 above.
[225] Eustathios, *Against an Overachieving Stylite in Thessalonike* 74 (*Or.* 22, Tafel p. 195).
[226] Michael Choniates, *Monodia for Eustathios of Thessalonike* 50 (Lambros v. I, p. 304).

In the end, however, these hopes were backed only by the self-serving assumptions prevailing among the hundred or so Hellenists in the Komnenian empire. It was all premised on a constant avoidance of the deeper questions and made possible by the rhetorical illusion of harmony. This stance was similar to that of many of the humanists of the early Renaissance. Their love of Greece was literary and aesthetic, and secured against Christian suspicion not by philosophy but by performative acts that established a consensus of implicit agreement, as though the question had finally been resolved somewhere else, by someone else. A broad shift in society brought many Hellenists to power in the Church, the bureaucracy, and the circles of aristocratic patronage. But there was no reason for them to fear the challenges that Psellos had faced: he had brought those challenges upon himself precisely by working through the philosophical issues. By avoiding philosophy, in the twelfth century Hellenism protected itself against theology. Under these circumstances, to question or condemn Greek tastes would have merely amounted to bad taste, and that was one thing even the Komnenoi were anxious to avoid. So, like the classicists of the eighteenth century, scholars and warlords conspired to pretend that the writers and "the great actors of antiquity were somehow also their contemporaries, a mirror for their own selves, a font of morals, a template for virtuous statecraft and peerless expression."[227]

---

[227] Winterer (2002) 138.

# CHAPTER 6

# Imperial failure and the emergence of national Hellenism

## MICHAEL CHONIATES AND THE "BLESSED" GREEKS

Rome, Greece, Scripture, and the history of the Church provided the Byzantines with a diverse source of ideals and potential identities awaiting (re)activation at the right moment, to be excerpted, recombined, and infused with new meaning. In times of crisis, Byzantine writers could turn to aspects of that past for comfort, answers, or models for the future. Some looked to the Bible or the Fathers, others to Greece or Rome. The history of these choices reflects both personal decisions and broad cultural changes that are otherwise difficult to identify in Byzantium, given the relative stability of its representational modes. In the eleventh century, for example, the historian Michael Attaleiates, who had spent his life in law and administration, turned to the pagan Romans of the Republic for explanations and solutions to the empire's decline. Attaleiates had to admit that the pagans had triumphed in their wars despite the fact that they knew nothing of God's word and did not practice Christian virtues. Attaleiates lost his faith in the link between empire and Orthodoxy, and marveled at the magnificence of the ancient Romans. Why could his own countrymen not emulate their virtue?[1]

Attaleiates' Romanocentric response to imperial decline in the eleventh century forms a nice contrast to the Hellenocentric responses to the crisis that terminated the age of the Komnenoi. Soon after the death of Manuel, Byzantium entered another spiral of decline and dissolution. But the Roman model proved less attractive to those who coped with this phase of decline and reinvention, especially given the "Roman" origin of the new enemy, the Christian Crusaders of the Latin West (by contrast, Attaleiates had to deal with Turks). Moreover, this time the empire's spokesmen were trained Hellenists. The jurist and historian of the eleventh century was

[1] Kaldellis (2007b).

effectively the product of a different culture. Here we see how far-reaching the Hellenist revolution of the twelfth century had been.

In particular, we will attempt to explain the reaction of Michael Choniates to the late twelfth-century round of imperial decline. Our discussion will revolve around a letter that he sent to a high official in Constantinople in a moment of frustration. A single moment, perhaps, but one in which the main themes of the Hellenist revival and the themes of Michael's life intersect most dynamically. It also prefigures the shift that Byzantine identity underwent in the next century toward a more explicit identification with ancient Greece. Michael's outburst moved Hellenism from the realm of *paideia* to an expression of personal and national anguish and insecurity, parallel to that of Attaleiates a century earlier, only with a new referent. Greece displaced Rome, and this time it was Greece's ancient glories that undermined imperial Christian conceit. Faith alone failed when it could no longer guarantee supremacy or even safety. To be sure, the reaction we will be studying here belonged to one man and was the product of unique circumstances, but those circumstances were ideally suited to expose the underlying tensions and subterranean developments of Komnenian Hellenism. To understand it, we must take account of Michael's first years as the bishop of Athens as well as of the state of the empire in the generation before its collapse.

Michael Choniates was a student and friend of Eustathios of Thessalonike. He arrived in Athens as its new bishop in 1182.[2] By the mid-1180s, the situation there as in other parts of the empire had deteriorated so far that he wrote a bitter letter to the *prôtoasêkrêtis* Demetrios Drimys in Constantinople castigating official inactivity and pleading for relief. Drimys knew local conditions, for in ca. 1183–1185 he had been *praitôr* (governor) of Hellas and the Peloponnese. Michael had then honored him with an address that, in typical Byzantine fashion, combined praise for the official himself and the emperor (Andronikos I) with a desperate appeal for help. In this it conformed to type; still, the *Address to the* praitôr *Demetrios Drimys* revolved around themes that would pre-occupy Michael during the two decades that he held the see of Athens.

Michael begins the *Address* by hoping that Drimys will prove to be another Theseus for Athens, a founder devoted to justice. This city, he explains, used to be great but is now old and decrepit. If it preserves a trace of its former excellence in rhetoric embodied in its current spokesman

---

[2] The basic studies are Stadtmüller (1934), who established the framework; Setton (1944); Angold (1995) ch. 9; and Kolovou (1999).

(Michael himself), it has lost the greatness that it owed to the philosophers and statesmen of old (1–2). Michael is not a happy shepherd, tending such a diminished and miserable flock. He sings to himself on "this rock" (the Akropolis), but his only answer is an echo. He is in danger of reverting to savagery, here, of all places, in "wise" Athens (3). Drimys must respect the signs of the city's ancient greatness (4) and weep for the broken walls, the fallen homes over which farmers now till. Time has been more cruel to the city than even the Persians were; no trace remains of the Lykeion and only a fragment of the Poikile Stoa (5). And yet "Greece and the Peloponnese will revert to their ancient happiness" now that Drimys has arrived, for he may be compared to Solon and Aristeides in his concern for justice and knowledge of the legislative art. Besides, "Hellenic uprightness" is nothing compared to that of Christ, as a child is to a man (7–12). So Michael here sets the classical past beneath the Christian present. An obligatory and mostly insincere praise of the reigning emperor takes up the remainder of the *Address* (13–39). The conclusion is devoted to the plight of the cities and to a plea for tax-relief and better governance (40–50). The ideal he promotes here is the ancient Athenian statesman Aristeides the Just, who restored foreign cities without asking or taking anything for himself (41).[3] The address, then, vacillates between Greek justice and Christian virtue, trying vaguely to combine them.

Though no Aristeides, Drimys was a good governor, and so Michael was upset when he departed for Constantinople. The swift deterioration of provincial conditions prompted the bitter *Letter* 50 that the bishop sent to the former *praitôr* sometime after 1185. Taking up the themes of his *Address*, Michael reevaluates the relation between antiquity and the present, or between paganism and Christianity. He now reconsiders how far faith alone, the sole advantage that the Byzantines enjoy over the Greeks, can make up for the lack of virtue in this age of decline. He rebukes Drimys for not returning to Greece to restore the rule of justice, comparing the land to a sinking ship and an ailing patient. He accuses him of shirking his duty so that he may live at ease with his wife and children in Constantinople and avoid the hassle and danger of the journey. Michael hints that he is not speaking now purely as a rhetor but as a bishop too – and God is watching. "O those blessed men," he exclaims suddenly, turning to the ancient Greeks. "I do not reproach them for their distorted religion but call them

---

[3] Michael Choniates, *Address to the* praitôr *Demetrios Drimys* (Lambros v. I, pp. 157–179). For Drimys, see Herrin (1975) 268; for Michael and the emperors, Kolovou (1999) 228–232; for Greece and Athens, see below. Cf. the parallel *Address to the* praitôr *Nikephoros Prosouchos* (Lambros v. I, pp. 142–149).

*blessed* because, even though they worshiped thusly, they practiced virtue and knew beauty, daring the sea and long journeys to put human life in order." He cites examples of ancient heroes, including Aristeides, Plato, and Herakles, who labored to make human life better. But *you*, you delicate residents of the capital, do not set foot outside the walls and leave us to the mercy of cruel tax-collectors. *We* make the wealth, but *you* gather it to yourselves, sitting comfortably in your homes.[4]

The letter is rhetorical, in both style and argument. For example, it was typical to try and shame Christians by lamenting that pagans took the prize for virtue.[5] But this does not mean that Michael's outburst was "merely" rhetorical, that it does not reflect frustration and painful realizations. After all, he explicitly draws attention to the fact that he is speaking in this instance "more as a bishop than a rhetor," in other words from a higher moral standpoint, and he concludes by acknowledging that "I have slightly transgressed the limits of the conventions of epistolography." He is explicitly signaling his intention of saying something that goes beyond rhetorical conventions. He praises Drimys as a just governor and then accuses him of shirking his duty. Surely the man was moved by the spectacle of a bishop doubting the worth of his own faith and "blessing" pagans for their virtue in spite of their paganism. It is here, at the point where Michael felt that he had to break the rules of rhetoric, that we glimpse his turmoil better than we do in the more controlled public speeches. He momentarily doubts what he had previously proclaimed on many occasions, namely that Christians can be better than the most virtuous pagans by the very fact that they are Christians. In a moment of frustration, his *paideia* told him a painful truth about his own time. Faith alone could not fully bridge the gap.

Michael's letter illuminates many important themes in Byzantine history, including the unequal relationship between Constantinople and the provinces; the tension between "rhetoric" and the frank-speaking that the bishops inherited from ancient philosophers; and the leading role that late twelfth-century bishops played in promoting the interests of their cities. But here we are chiefly interested in Michael's invocation of Hellenism at the nexus of all these concerns, with its pathetic mixture of stridency and

---

[4] Michael Choniates, *Letter* 50; for the dates, see Kolovou's introduction, pp. 78*–79*, and (1999) 145; for the economic complaints, Setton (1944) 192–195; Herrin (1970) 196–199; for praise of Herakles and others, Michael Choniates, *Address to the Emperor's Brother-in-Law, the* Logothetes *Basileios Kamateros* 1–3 (Lambros v. I, pp. 312–313). For the flow of goods to the capital, cf. Ailios Aristeides, *Or.* 26.11–12 (*Roman Oration*).

[5] Kaldellis (2007b) 13 n. 24.

regret. How, we should ask, had the Greeks come to constitute a standing *reproach* against the Byzantines, where before those in power had been praised for surpassing them? And why the Greeks rather than the ancient Romans? What made Michael's letter, its tone and choices, possible?

The answer should partly be located in the shift of cultural values effected by twelfth-century Hellenism. With the exception of Psellos, the eleventh century was not greatly concerned with things Greek, far less obsessed with them. Its chief historian, Michael Attaleiates, specialized in law and governance, which gave his outlook a thoroughly Roman slant. His *History* classicizes on occasion, but does not perform Attic learning. Choniates, for all that we associate him with a period of decline and the aftermath of 1204 (when he spent two decades in exile), was a product of the bloom of Komnenian scholarship. He was a student of Eustathios, the greatest Hellenist of the age; reading their works in sequence confirms the influence of Eustathian style on his prose and mind. In contrast to Attaleiates, then, Michael's training was more philological and Greek than it was administrative and Roman. But philology signified far more than mere linguistic expertise. *Paideia* shaped one's character and outlook. It pointed toward a certain kind of wisdom about the greatest things and was not limited to style, unless by style we understand something very serious. In exile after the conquest of Athens by the Crusaders, Michael collected his orations into one volume and gave them an idiosyncratic preface whose first word is *philologos*: "the author of this book is a *philologos* and a lover of both forms of wisdom, ours and the one outside." *Logos* comprised both discourse and reason and, on a higher level, culminated in God's Logos. So a *philologos* was not only a "philologist" in our sense but the opposite of Sokrates' *misologos* in Plato's *Phaedo* (89d), who resents reason and hates the philosophical life. Michael knew that classical culture, like Christianity, makes claims on the way we live and is far more than an adornment of speech. His understanding and practice of friendship, for instance, were deeply influenced by Aristotle, who was for him more a guide to life than a theoretician. Even access to philosophy, after all, was mediated by *philologia*, and *logos* was of the Greeks, just as Attaleiates had known that *praxis* was of the Romans.[6]

---

[6] *Philologos*: Michael Choniates, Protheôria *to the Present Book* 1 (Lambros v. I, p. 3); Michael defends *philologia* in a mildly ironic work *To those who accused him of not liking to promote himself* (Lambros v. I, pp. 7–23); on this, Magdalino (1993) 337–339. For friendship, Kolovou (1999) 237–253; for *philologia*, ibid. 255–258; for *philologos* in antiquity, Kuch (1965); for Eustathios' influence on Michael, Lambros v. I, p. ιδ´ and λζ (confirmed by the present author).

However, the ideological realignment that occurs in the letter to Drimys required more than the shift in cultural priorities from Rome to Greece. Twelfth-century Hellenism was, after all, largely complicit in the ideology, the policies, and the self-promotion of the Komnenoi, or at least of the Constantinopolitan elite that Michael indicts in the letter. Despite the strange directions that it could follow (e.g., in the *Timarion*), Komnenian Hellenism was fueled by the needs of panegyric and high-style entertainment. The Greeks were paragons of virtue to be surpassed or models of culture to be emulated. Michael belonged to precisely that class of men who left their own hometowns – in his case Chonai (ancient Kolossai) in Asia Minor – to acquire a classical *paideia* in the capital, which then enabled them to perform Greek *logoi* before their Komnenoi patrons. Regardless of their origin, the sophists considered themselves to be Constantinopolitans and bemoaned the low standards of culture in the cities to which they were posted as bishops. The letter to Drimys represents a rupture with panegyrical Hellenism as well as a break with the outlook of Michael's peers in the capital.

Of course, Michael never fully broke with his class; almost all his friends belonged to it. But provincial life in an age of decline gave him new perspectives. Though he complained about the conditions and the backwardness of the locals compared to proper Hellenized Constantinopolitans, he took his duties seriously. He worked hard at his catechetical orations and spoke passionately on behalf of his city before the governors, trying to secure justice and tax-relief (both activities fell under the purview of *philology*). Within five years he had begun to refer to "my Athens" and "my Marathon-fighters,"[7] and before the Crusaders arrived he led the city's defense against the rebel Leon Sgouros, mounting catapults on the walls of the Akropolis and driving him away. His devotion to the material and spiritual well-being of his flock earned him a place among the city's saints, as attested by two haloed images in local chapels.[8] Duty and love, then, put him at odds with what he now perceived to be the indifferent and exploitative elites of Constantinople. At that point his Hellenism began to serve the interests of Athens rather than of the imperial center.

Michael's adoption of a provincial outlook was part of a broader trend in this period. Despite its political and military decline, the empire continued to expand economically and demographically. Regional centers evolved into small political, economic, and cultural alternatives to Constantinople.

---

[7] Michael Choniates, *Encomium to Isaakios II Angelos* 45 and 85 (Lambros v. I, pp. 234 and 256).
[8] Kolovou (1999) 22. For Sgouros, see pp. 364–365 below.

Networks of correspondence sprung up that were not focused on the capital, chiefly among Michael and other bishops in Greece. This period also witnessed the rise of local patriotism, fueled in some cases by a strong anti-Constantinopolitan sentiment. Michael's letter to Drimys reflects those developments, which contributed to the empire's fragmentation on the eve of the Fourth Crusade. Ironically, they also contributed to its reconstitution in the next century by provincial centers such as Nikaia that resisted the new *Latin* masters of Constantinople.[9] It is appropriate, then, that our sources for the period were written by Hellenists who were trained in Constantinople and who either were then posted to the provinces (Eustathios and Michael) or took refuge there after 1204 (like the author of our main *History*, Michael's brother Niketas). The perspective of our information is thus dispersed to regional centers along with the empire's Hellenizing elite.

Michael represents the first case of self-conscious provincial Hellenism in Byzantium. It does not matter that he himself was thoroughly of the capital in his training and tastes. In fact, that may have been one of the requirements for the evolution of his thinking in this direction, which brings us to the most crucial point. That Michael had a Hellenic *paideia*, in contrast to Attaleiates' devotion to the Roman traditions of law and governance, does not by itself suffice to explain his outburst in the letter to Drimys; nor was it enough that he was posted to a provincial city, given that many other Hellenists who became bishops did not evolve in the same direction. The catalyst for Michael's "blessing" of the Greeks was, it seems, the fact that he was posted specifically to *Athens*.

## ATHENS: A CHRISTIAN CITY AND ITS CLASSICIST BISHOP

To judge from Michael's letters and speeches, the impact of the city of Athens on him was profound, if not always happy. He there had to confront the physical reality of a place that had been central to his *paideia* but which had existed for him only as an abstract label for an ideal of language and thought. Komnenian Hellenists boasted the "Attic" refinement of their speech and fancied themselves "sons of Athens," but none related this ideal to the city itself, certainly not in its present state. Their Atticism served the regime in the capital and was performed in its *theatra*.

[9] Towns: Harvey (1989) ch. 6 (also for economic expansion); for Athens, see below; for local patriotism, Ahrweiler (1975a) 87–102; Magdalino (1993) 153–154 and (2000) 160–161; for exploitation by the center, Neratzi-Varmazi (1997).

They seem to have mostly forgotten that the place was *real*, that it existed apart from their literary circles, and that if it were allowed to speak for itself it might not praise the emperors. By a chance episcopal appointment, the Attic ideal, embodied in Michael, returned and had to face the physical remains of its origin over a thousand years after the two had taken divergent paths. For Michael it was a homecoming of sorts, as Athens was where he "belonged" in a sense, and it eventually caused him to reevaluate his prior loyalties, especially to Constantinople.

He was not in an altogether foreign place. Byzantine classicists, after all, knew intimately the history, great men, anecdotes, religion, social and political institutions, topography, monuments, language, idioms, and literature of ancient Athens, as well or better than do their modern counterparts. For the benefit of a friend who "loved not merely Athens but Athenian place-names," Psellos had already excerpted Strabon's account of its topography into a separate treatise. There is no indication that Psellos had ever been to Athens himself, but for once we would like to know more about his friend: was his interest sparked by a first-hand experience of the city or did he merely want to know more about the names that came up in his reading of classical literature? In the twelfth century, Athens comes to our attention rather more often. In an unpublished letter, the professor of rhetoric Nikolaos Kataphloron (perhaps Eustathios' uncle) asks his friend, the governor of Greece, to compare the famous sights of Athens with the way he had imagined them as a student. "Do the Athenians still have an Areiopagos? Or has it crumbled away?" This was a rare moment, a Byzantine professor thinking to bring his *paideia* into relation with the city's physical state. A generation later, in writing to his former teacher, the bishop of Athens Nikolaos Hagiotheodorites (d. 1175), Gregorios Antiochos could not resist showing off his familiarity with Athenian topography; nor could Eustathios when he delivered a funeral oration for the same bishop. Those men all knew the city intimately, if from a distance of time and space. In a letter to an official in Constantinople, Choniates mentioned "that plague that fell upon Attica, having its origin in Ethiopia – you know the one, for how not? Surely you have it by heart."[10] Athens was not a place for which Byzantine writers had to dredge up obscure mythological links in order to present it in classical garb. Its ruins came alive in

[10] Psellos: Rhoby (2001). Nikolaos Kataphloron: Magdalino (1991a) 14; for his career, Browning (1962–1963) 18–19. Gregorios Antiochos, *Letter to Nikolaos Hagiotheodorites* 10, 22–23 (pp. 403–404, 407); for the recipient, Darrouzès (1962) 70–71. Eustathios, *Funeral Oration for Nikolaos Hagiotheodorites, Bishop of Athens (Or.* 1, Wirth p. 4). Michael Choniates, *Letter* 32.5. Thucydides' plague account was popular: Kaldellis (2004a) 26–27.

their rhetorical imagination by activating so much knowledge they had absorbed along with their *paideia*.

Athens was a meaningful cultural sign, but the centuries had deposited so many layers upon its ruins that its precise meaning was ambiguous and open to negotiation. To summarize a complex but fascinating story, the ideal of Athens had been contested in the "culture wars" of late antiquity. Julian enlisted it in his program of pagan-Hellenic revival, whereas Christian hard-liners such as the popular liturgical poet Romanos Melodos (sixth century) gloated at the triumph over the Athenians by the "Galilaians," alluding to Julian's dismissive term for Christians and, possibly, to Justinian's expulsion of the Platonists from Athens in 529. The conflicted middle-ground of Byzantine Hellenism was staked out, as we saw, by Gregorios of Nazianzos, who loved Athens "the golden" for its *logos* but reviled its deeply ingrained paganism, which persisted into later antiquity.[11] Echoes of Romanos' triumphalism reverberated in later times, for instance in the satisfaction expressed by the poet Ioannes Geometres (tenth century) regarding the dominion of "heavenly" New Rome over "earthly" Athens.[12] But the days of such attitudes were numbered, as something extraordinary had happened in Athens, which has, amazingly, escaped the notice of modern scholarship. The Parthenon, rededicated as a church in honor of the Mother of God, became one of the most important centers of pilgrimage in the Byzantine world, revered far beyond the small circle of Hellenists. And while our texts claim (or defensively insist) that the pilgrimage was made to honor Christ's Mother, there is reason to think that there was much more going on beneath the surface. It was specious to claim that the Parthenon was just like any other church; it seems, instead, that a potent classical monument managed to insinuate itself into the field of Byzantine piety, destabilizing the normal signs of its orthodoxy. Pagan Greece here became constitutive of a form of Christian piety, with curious consequences that cannot be discussed now. As for Geometres' triumphal boast, it seems that Athens had the last laugh after all, for the most powerful emperor of the poet's time traveled to Athens to pay his respects upon the Akropolis.[13]

The Mother of God had joined forces with the Hellenists to protect Athens from the likes of Romanos and Geometres. Besides, most references

---

[11] For Julian and Gregorios, see p. 59 and p. 159 above. Romanos Melodos, *Kontakion* 31: *On the Mission of the Apostles* 16.2; cf. 331 *On Pentecost* 17 for the nonsense of the philosophers (pp. 247 and 265). For Justinian, see Agathias, *Histories* 2.30–31, with Kaldellis (1999b) 240–242.

[12] Ioannes Geometres, *Poems* 109–110, in *PG* CVI (1863) 950–951; see Hunger (1990) 51–52.

[13] For all this, see Kaldellis (2008).

to Athens in our period are in letters addressed to its bishops, where a hard-line approach to ancient Greece would have been inappropriate. In the twelfth century, the mere name of Athens was a pretext for classical allusions and showmanship; in fact, clichés evolved for writing to and about its bishops. The authors of these texts typically lament the city's ruin and praise its past excellence in *logoi* and wisdom, which, they proudly declare, their addressee has now restored to pristine glory; in fact, he has surpassed the ancient philosophers and orators in their respective disciplines and in their hometown to boot. In his funeral oration for Nikolaos Hagiotheodorites, Eustathios calls the city "blessed" on account of both its past greatness and its good fortune in having Nikolaos as bishop. This is the same word with which Michael would "bless" the Greeks only a few years later in his letter to Drimys. Eustathios adds that as a man of affairs Nikolaos surpassed Aristeides and Solon, who, as we saw, were Michael's favorite statesmen from antiquity.[14]

While on the subject of Eustathios' influence, let us note also an address that he delivered to his flock in Thessalonike, reproaching them in ca. 1177 for not coming to church in sufficient numbers. Eustathios was greatly embarrassed, as two friends were present, one from Constantinople and another from Athens, who compared the paltry attendance in Thessalonike to that in their own cities, where no one stayed home. Are we going to take this, Eustathios asks? How can Athens, "so old and now only a shadow of its ancient blessedness," rival our city, now in the flower of its bloom?[15] Far from being stained with paganism, Athens here appeared as pious in comparison to a Christian city such as Thessalonike. Of course, there was an element of "mere" rhetoric here, as preachers habitually compared their flocks unfavorably to outsiders – other Christians, heretics, or pagans – to exhort them to pay attention. Ironically, Michael would do the same in Athens, despite the boasts of Eustathios' Athenian friend. He too complained that his flock did not come to church but proffered inventive excuses, nor did they pay attention to his sermons. But these were problems

---

[14] Eustathios, *Funeral Oration for Nikolaos Hagiotheodorites, Bishop of Athens* (*Or.* 1, Wirth pp. 4, 11, 13); for an analysis, Agapitos (1999), esp. 140 n. 85 for Athens. For the clichés, see also Alexandros of Nikaia, *Letter* 18 (tenth century) (p. 96); Georgios Tornikes, *Letter* 5 to Georgios Bourtzes (p. 113); Euthymios Malakes, *Funeral Oration for Nikolaos Hagiotheodorites* 1, 7 (pp. 154, 160), for whose authorship, see Darrouzès (1965) 158. An eloquent example is Euthymios Malakes, *Letter* 1 to Michael Choniates (pp. 38–40), a reply to the latter's *Letter* 20. See also the *Monodia for Michael Choniates* 5 (pp. 240–241), by the bishop's (anonymous) nephew.

[15] Eustathios, *He is aggrieved that the people did not come to prayer* (*Or.* 4, Wirth pp. 57–58); see Magdalino (1996b) 229–230.

that bishops faced everywhere, and most, even Michael, sought to shame their congregations by praising the good habits of others.[16]

Athens, then, was a prestigious post in the mid-twelfth century, at least among the classically educated. Michael says that when his appointment was announced many congratulated him for gaining "most renown and golden Athens," though he had mixed feelings about leaving Constantinople. Their reaction reveals how classicism differentially valorized the empire's geography but, ironically, it also shows how *Roman* Michael's world still was. A thousand years before, Plinius had congratulated a friend for obtaining Greece as his province: "revere its ancient glory and current old age . . . It is Athens you are approaching."[17] Perceptions of the city in both periods, among those who were sent out to govern it from Rome (whether Old or New), were shaped by romantic nostalgia and admiration for classical culture. The niche that Athens occupied in the rhetorical repertoire of the twelfth century was, then, quite analogous to that of Hellenic *paideia* in the overall articulation of Komnenian culture. Its infamous paganism was avoided in polite conversation, being subsumed under the enthusiasm for all things classical. At most, the Virgin was said to have washed away that ancient stain and raised the city to an even greater glory.[18] The Akropolis, once the peak of impurity, had, over the centuries and by a bizarre transformation, made the city into a major site of Christian devotion.

Michael was not at all troubled by the ancient demons of his new city. His episcopal residence was in the Propylaia and his cathedral in the Parthenon.[19] Like Eustathios, he refrains from calling pagans generally *Hellenes* (though he sometimes has to admit that his "blessed" Hellenes were in fact pagans). Even in his catechetical orations, which are more Scriptural in tone and content than his other works, he prefers the term "idol-worshipers." Greek and Christian elements coexist comfortably in his work. We saw that in the first line of the preface to his collected works he cites "inner" and "outer" wisdom as parallel and, it seems, even complementary components of *philologia*. In another work, he cites "Xenophon and Herodotos, those good men," along with "the most wise Paul," as

---

[16] Michael Choniates, *Catechetical Oration* 1.26–29 (Lambros v. I, p. 117); Protheôria *to the Present Book* 4 (p. 4); *Regarding the Holy Martyr Leonides* 1–2 (p. 150); *Oration given when he was at the Euboian Euripos* 10 (p. 183); *Homily on why man is a composite being* 21 (p. 195); and *Catechetical Oration* 14 (pp. 24–25). See also Kaldellis (2007b) 13 n. 24.
[17] Cf. Michael Choniates, *Inaugural Address at Athens* 8, 11–12 (Lambros v. I, pp. 95, 97), with Plinius, *Letter* 8.24, on which Swain (1996) 66–67.
[18] See the letter of Georgios Tornikes to Georgios Bourtzes, p. 298 above.
[19] Parthenon: Kaldellis (2008). Propylaia: Tanoulas (1997) 20.

authorities on his hometown Chonai. In a letter "asking" for news, he explains that "ask" can be taken either "evangelically" as "humbly entreat" (*parakalô*) or in a "Hellenic way" as "inquire in order to learn" (*pynthanomai*). This distinction nicely captures his own awareness of the philological and moral duality of his education. Occasionally he notes (or takes it for granted) that Christianity was superior, but this confidence was not solid, as we see in the letter to Drimys, and we must ask why.[20]

Something had fractured the comfortable symbiosis of Greek and Christian culture, which Komnenian Hellenists had taken for granted. Michael had carried the logic of classicism to the point where he had to compare ancient virtues to Christian vices. Putting things so starkly shocked him and led him to a series of reassessments between past and present, between ancient Greece and modern Rome, and between paganism and Christianity. To track the evolution of his thoughts, let us look closely at his *Inaugural Address at Athens*, which he began to compose while still in Constantinople, because it shows what was on his mind when he arrived and deploys many of the rhetorical clichés that we have already seen, though in a highly original synthesis. It will then be easier to understand his disillusionment with the Christian "containment" of what Athens had once meant, culminating in the letter to Drimys. In that letter it was as much ancient Athens speaking out against the ideology imposed on it by Christian Byzantium as it was Byzantine Athens rebelling against its exploitation by Constantinople.

The *Inaugural Address* is a beautiful expression of classical rhetoric serving pastoral concerns. Michael wins the Athenians over by praising their history and ancestors; he then abstracts from the *place* to the virtue of its men; and he finally elevates virtue to Christian perfection, implying that the classical past, for all its virtues, should not distract from the goal of salvation. In other words, he builds up to Christian themes from within the classical tradition, manipulating the latter throughout to gain a favorable reception from his Athenian audience and signal his episcopal priorities. It is a thoughtful and successful performance of Christian classicism, enhanced by the unique setting (in or in front of the Parthenon).[21]

It is not right, Michael declares, to "observe silence in such a *philologos polis*, the mother of all wisdom." You are "Athenians, descended from

---

[20] For intermingling of Greek and Christian elements, see Kolovou (1999) 201–276. Chonai: Michael Choniates, *Encomium for Niketas, Bishop of Chonai* 39 (Lambros v. I, p. 36); "ask": *Letter* 145.4.

[21] Michael Choniates, *Inaugural Address at Athens* (Lambros v. I, pp. 93–106); for philological commentary, Rhoby (2002); for a summary, Setton (1944) 187–190.

native Athenians who would rather do nothing other than say or hear something new" (2). Through this allusion Michael assimilates himself to St. Paul speaking before the Areopagos.[22] His speech, he says, will be painted in Attic colors, so that it is most familiar to you and appropriate (3). He describes a religious festival of the ancient Athenians that involved a torch relay and transforms it into a symbol of the "more holy" Christian faith, which is passed down through the generations, a race in which he hopes that "we" will not lag (4–7). Many congratulated me, he continues, for receiving "most renown and golden Athens," but I had reservations, knowing my own weaknesses and those of human nature; I know what it means to govern people in Christ's name (8–13). Besides, is Athens today the same as it once was? Even if one were to show me the ancient landmarks – it seems that Michael had already been given a tour – I would still not believe that I was beholding the ancient Athenians. In any case, the ancients were not great because of their place but because of their virtue and wisdom (14–15). My task is to instill evangelical truth and be a pastor, while yours is to obey me in this. Your ancestors' love of beauty would be shamed if you do not now turn it to a pious purpose. Time cannot have eliminated all trace of their noble qualities (16–20). I have learned from books that the founders of your city were kind and accepting to strangers – this reveals Michael's own insecurity – and, in addition, that they listened to reason. It was not so much Perikles who tamed them as it was their own nature that led them to be tamed – another plea disguised in classical garb (21–24). If, then, you descend from those wise, great-hearted, and rational men, time will prove your Attic blood to me (25). But I expect you to surpass them, as they were in the thrall of distorted and false beliefs about God (26). Even so, they did not neglect virtue and proved to be better than their gods on account of "the greatness of their nature and the unshackled disposition of their minds" (27). But you who know God, or rather who are known by God, must surpass them to the same degree that our faith surpasses theirs, as truth surpasses falsehood or light darkness (28–29). How shameful it would be if they prove to have been more virtuous (30–31). Awaken, Christians! "This Akropolis is freed of the tyranny of the pseudo-virgin Athena" and casts the light of the eternal virgin, the Mother of God, not merely over the city or the whole of Attica, but wherever the sun shines (32–33). Michael concludes by asking his flock to look past the Akropolis to the divine light (34–38).

---

[22] Acts of the Apostles 17.21; see Kaldellis (2008). Michael repeats the allusion at 22.

Michael composed his *Inaugural Address* with care, turning the formal-
ities of the genre to his advantage. The occasion required that he praise the
city for its past before exhorting its citizens to emulate their ancestors,
based on the rhetorical convention that moral qualities were inherited
biologically. In our investigation of the unfolding logic of Hellenism in
Byzantium, we should, then, not make too much of Michael's assertion
that his Athenians were descended from their ancient namesakes. He had
no good reason to think otherwise, and did not mean by it to make them
any less Roman. It was a standard rhetorical trope, and easy to use with
Athenians. In fact, other cities were supposed to be compared to ancient
Athens, which set the standard for glory and culture.[23] But the *Address*
reflects a recurring anxiety as to whether modern Christians could be as
virtuous as the idealized Greeks of Michael's *paideia*. There are moments
when he downplays the comparison and praises his flock on their own
terms rather than on the impossible terms set by their ancestors. Ultimately
it came down to the question of whether Christianity could suffice in the
absence of the rest of all virtue. Michael does not confront that possibility
in his *Address*, but the gamble of his comparison was imprudent. He had set
the stakes too high and the rhetorical argument was destabilized by the turn
of historical events.

The empire began to fall apart immediately after Manuel's death in 1180.
We need not investigate here the causes of this decline, only list its
symptoms, especially as they would have appeared to the bishop of
Athens. The Komnenoi dynasty was replaced by a weaker offshoot, the
Angeloi. The new regime could not dominate the sprawling aristocracy,
whose members behaved increasingly as independent lords, demanding
concessions and striking deals with the enemies of Romania. The consensus that held Roman society together was evaporating at the highest levels.
The army gradually disintegrated, which allowed many local magnates to
seize power at the provincial level. The empire, for the first time in history,
fell apart into essentially autonomous principalities on the periphery that
preferred independence and whose leaders did not seek the throne, which
would at least have signaled a commitment to unity. Imperial defenses were
weakened and inroads made by both land and sea, from every direction.
Piracy made life in the Aegean unstable and, often, short. The regions
controlled by Constantinople, including Attica, were squeezed by ruthless

---

[23] See Julian's *Letter to the Senate and People of the Athenians* 268a ff.; *Misopogon* 348b–d; for the empress
Eudokia, Cameron (1982) 278; for the theory, Foss (1996) 125, 157, with a statement by Theodoros
Metochites at 167; for the comparison used by bishops in the twelfth century, Magdalino (1993) 154.

tax-collectors and warlords, without receiving protection in return. When the Crusaders arrived at Constantinople in 1203, they faced a demoralized and disorganized city, not a state.[24]

Against this background, the letter to Drimys makes more sense. In 1182, when he arrived at Athens, Michael had no idea that he would witness the two worst decades in Byzantine history. A few years later his hope that Christianity could make people better than the ancient Greeks had been shaken. Perhaps he realized now how much that hope assumed in terms of the "natural" virtues that sustained civil life, to say nothing of the imperial greatness that he himself had known for forty years under Manuel. The Athens that he lived in, full of ruins and populated by artisans rather than orators and philosophers, could not compete with the city of Perikles. This comparison, which must have frequently intruded itself upon his thoughts, led to more general comparisons between the twelfth-century Roman empire and his idealized image of antiquity. Each day would have tilted the balance in favor of the latter. The pastoral and theological tone of the letter to Drimys, where the argument of the *Inaugural* is effectively reversed, reveals that Michael recognized the inefficacy of his faith to make up the balance. That is why in the letter he emphasizes the Greeks' love of beauty and the good and turns from divine law to political wisdom.[25] Can't we have some, just *some*, ancient virtue? We witness here the marriage of Attaleiates' turn to a more virtuous past in explicit recognition of its paganism, and the idealized Hellenism of the sophists.

Michael did not lose his faith. We are not dealing with anything quite so radical. Rather, he had to confront the deep and permanent tension between the requirements of the Christian faith and the attraction of the Hellenic virtues. His oration in honor of the Athenian martyr Leonides highlights this disjunction. The ancient Athenians, he begins, honored those who fell in battle with public funerals and speeches; are we, then, he asks rhetorically, going to fall so short of their zeal for virtue that we will fail to honor the martyrs who lie buried among us? To make the contrast poignant, he adds that the Greeks were honoring mere "lovers of danger" who died well in battle for their city, whereas "we" honor "martyrs for the truth . . . who fought battles not of flesh and blood and who did not die for an earthly city, but fought against the fleshless powers of darkness and for

---

[24] For the decline, see Angold (1997) ch. 16 for a narrative; Cheynet (1990) 110–156 for a list of revolts and 427–458 for an interpretation, Lilie (1984) for the failure of the center; Savvides (1987) for separatist states; and Herrin (1975) for the view from Greece. The seeds of these developments were sown during the 1070s, but their growth was arrested by the three Komnenoi.

[25] Michael Choniates, *Letter* 50.6 and 11.

the City of God."[26] The comparison is meant to favor the Christian side, which is appropriate in a laudation of martyrs. At the end of the speech, Michael predictably compares the martyr to Leonidas at Thermopylai, again finding for the Christian. This illustrates that for him, as for the Church Fathers, the tension between Greece and Christ was not purely theological but fundamentally moral, a battle of competing ideas of the good. Conflicting values jostled for the loyalty of educated Byzantines, and perhaps of all Christians. Which prevailed at any moment was probably determined only by circumstance; few had the audacity, like Psellos, to work through the underlying problems. Michael's speech in praise of the martyrs is "rhetorical" in this way, as it conforms to the occasion, but it also reveals the polarities between which he himself wavered.

Later in life (he was nearly eighty) Michael admitted to an abbot that he had no share of monastic philosophy and had spent his years politicking in the turmoil of secular life.[27] There is an element of exaggerated humility here and deference to his correspondent, but the claim was basically true. Michael was a very political bishop, and there must have been times at Athens when he wished that the empire had more such "lovers of danger" as those ancient Athenians and Spartans, men more like Leonidas than Leonides. What compels our attention in the letter to Drimys is Michael's praise of the Greeks for "daring the sea and long journeys" to make life better. This was not banal praise, as Christian writers had *attacked* the Greeks for doing just that: "daring the sea" revealed only their greed, ambition, and worldliness. Even Eustathios condemned the "unnatural art of seafaring." Julian, by contrast, had praised the pagans for "traveling far over the earth and sea and proving themselves heroes."[28] Michael, the political bishop, was trapped between these two views.

Soon after the programmatic statements and guarded encomium of the *Inaugural Address*, Michael realized that this Byzantine town was no Athens, at least according to his lofty standards. In his first catechetical oration, he admitted that his hopes of finding true descendants of the Athenians has been frustrated and that his brushing-up of Attic performance for the delivery of the speech had been in vain. His flock could not

---

[26] Michael Choniates, *Oration for the Martyr Leonides and his Companions* 1–2, 14–15 (Lambros v. I, pp. 150, 154–155). The date is unknown: Kolovou (1999) 34.

[27] Michael Choniates, *Letter* 161; for his views on political life, Kolovou (1999) 265–270.

[28] Tatianos, *Address to the Greeks* 11.1: "I am not driven by greed to go on voyages." Eustathios: Magdalino (1996b) 233. Julian, *Against the Galilaians* 229e. For Eustathios on the Athenian fleet, see Macrides and Magdalino (1992) 147; for Theodoros Metochites on Greeks and the sea, Garzya (1992) 34–35; for Byzantine fear of the sea, Kazhdan and Constable (1982) 42; Mpazaiou-Barabas (1993); for images of sea-travel, see Mullett (2002).

follow his philology. In truth, Athenians were now just ignorant barbarians. "Living in Athens, I see Athens nowhere," one of his poems lamented. Where were the famous courts, the laws, the generals, the orators? Where had they all gone? The city that had once defeated the Persians on both land and sea was now oppressed by a handful of pirate ships. Granted, the grace of the land remained and the clarity of the air, the honey of Hymettos and especially "the Akropolis itself, upon which I feel as though I am standing at the edge of heaven. But that *philologos* generation that was so full of wisdom has passed away and an uncultured one has taken its place, poor in mind and poor in body." Even his prose was likely to degrade, in *Athens* of all places.[29] That last complaint was written early in his tenure. He admitted that the ancient paradox had come true for him: "this Atticist has now become a barbarist . . . being for so long in Greece, I have become a barbarian." This line from Euripides' *Orestes* (485) was a favorite among Byzantine scholars, especially those of the twelfth century, and revealed the insecurity and fragility of their *paideia*, their Hellenism, amidst a world that was basically unclassical.[30] This, more than anything, shows up Michael's praise of the Athenians' ancestry in his *Inaugural Address* as largely rhetorical. His view of Hellenism was basically that of the sophists, cultural rather than ethnic, which is why he could present himself as the only Hellene among the Athenians, albeit one who was gradually going "native," i.e., barbarian.

In the twelfth century Athens was a large and prosperous town, whose economic and demographic growth was not terribly affected by the decline of Byzantium. Its alleged squalor in the late twelfth century has been postulated solely on the basis of Michael's testimony.[31] But that testimony might not be reliable on this point, as Michael saw what he expected to see,

[29] "Ignorant barbarians": Michael Choniates, *Catechetical Oration* 1.49–51 (Lambros v. I, 124); "living": *Verses on Athens* 17 (v. II, p. 397), on which see Livanos (2006); "Persians": *Address to the* praitôr *Nikephoros Prosouchos* 16 (v. I, p. 147) (Persians and pirates are among his favorite contrasts); "Akropolis," etc.: *Letters* 8 and 20. Later letters critical of conditions in Athens include 60–62, 132. For Athens in Michael's works, Hunger (1990) 55–58; Kolovou (1999) 233–235; Kaldellis (2008); for his disillusionment, Setton (1944) 190–192.

[30] Michael Choniates, *Letters* 52 and 28; cited also in the *Encomium to Isaakios II Angelos* 18 (Lambros v. I, p. 218), in connection with Andronikos I. For other authors, see Mullett (1997) 275–276, to which these may be added: Julian, *Letter* 3/8.441b–c (Wright/Bidez and Cumont); Ioannes Geometres, *Poem* 33, in *PG* CVI (1863) 922; Nikephoros Basilakes, *Letter* 2 (a striking instance, in *Or. et ep.* p. 113); Ioannes Tzetzes, *Letter* 13 with *Histories* 6.945–948, which explains the origin and context. Cf. also Libanios, *Letter* 369.9; Eustathios, *Letter* 18 (Tafel pp. 327–328), for similar worries. For ancient notions of barbarization, see p. 25 above; for Byzantine anxieties, Lechner (1954) 84–92. For the *Orestes* passage, see Saïd (2002) esp. 81–83, 100.

[31] Relative prosperity of the empire: Harvey (1989) ch. 6; Greece: Herrin (1976); Angold (1997) 280–286; Athens: Travlos (1993) 151, 160–162; Kazanaki-Lappa (2002).

namely ruin, or rather he did not see what he wanted to see, namely a living vestige of ancient Athens.[32] The ruins of Athens can trigger pride in the past and encode ambitions for the future, as for example for many in modern Greece.[33] On the other hand, they may also instill a sense of inferiority and reinforce the anxiety of decline, as they did for Michael and for others even in modern times. Imagined Greece can be an awesome burden. Nietzsche described its effects on German philosophers: "One is no longer at home anywhere; at last one longs for that place in which alone one can be at home, because it is the only place in which one would want to be at home: the *Greek* world!" A Greek aphorist in Nietzsche's tradition has written, in an essay on *The Misery of Being Greek*, that "any people descended from the ancient Greeks are automatically unhappy – unless they can forget them or surpass them."[34] Michael could do neither, as he watched his world fall apart. The ruins of Athens were not an occasion for him to gloat as a Christian,[35] but rather to lament as a Roman Hellenist. True Athens remained for him fixed in eternal glory but trapped in his imagination. An expression in one of his poems suggests that he may have commissioned a painting of the city in all its classical splendor, a work that we dearly wish we possessed. The poem begins by declaring Michael's *eros* for ancient Athens, his "embracing of an idol" that has "vanished, hidden in the depths of forgetfulness."[36] In his mind the ruins about him stood for all that was good about ancient Greece and all that was wrong with his fellow Romans, a symbol of decline and a standing reproach of their inadequacies. And worse was to come. In late 1204 or early 1205 Michael had to surrender his city to Bonifatius, the marquis of Montferrat, and go into exile.

EAST AND WEST: NEGOTIATING LABELS IN 1204

In April 1204 the fourth wave of European colonialism in the Levant seized the capital of Romania. The Crusaders then dismembered the empire's territories to exploit them on the feudal model and attempted to impose the Latin Church on its people. But greed, arrogance, incompetence, and faction botched the takeover. Fragments of Byzantium regrouped in Asia

---

[32] Cf. Tomadakis (1956–1957) 103.
[33] Skopetea (1988) 198–199; Bastéa (2000); Peckham (2001) 16, 27, 34, 41, 117–118, 120, 122 (archaeology becomes a metaphor for a range of enterprises constitutive of the nation).
[34] Nietzsche, *The Will to Power* 419; Dimou (1975) 49; for the belief in nineteenth-century Greece that the ancients were better, Skopetea (1988) 236.
[35] Magdalino (1991a) 13.
[36] Michael Choniates, *Verses on Athens* (Lambros v. II, p. 397); see Speck (1975); for the poem, Livanos (2006); for epigrams and Byzantine art, Lauxtermann (2003) ch. 5.

Minor and Greece and swiftly regained territory; the subject people rejected the Latin Church and, in many areas, rebelled against their new overlords; and even the West itself lost interest in the tiny colonial princi-palities of Greece and the dysfunctional regime of Constantinople that was an empire in name only. Yet the damage was done: the Roman *politeia* was shattered, and the Byzantines' Roman identity was defined and sustained by the laws, customs, and institutions of their *politeia*. Romania had been the historical expression of their shared political, social, cultural, and religious values. How could it survive foreign rule, especially hierarchical, racial, and feudal orders? In the splinter states, the *politeia* was reconsti-tuted, but the splintering of the empire was not the only challenge facing the Byzantines' sense of Roman unity.

The usurpers in Constantinople had claims of their own to the Roman legacy. The center of their Church was at Rome; their formal language was Latin; their laws were increasingly influenced by the Roman tradition; and many had claimed the greatness and legitimacy of the Roman empire for their own nations and kingdoms. Conquerors and subjects had enough in common that they could imagine themselves as one, but in the end this proximity only highlighted their ineradicable and deep differences. The alignments were all wrong. For example, some Byzantines may have considered Latin their "ancestral tongue," but now they could no longer understand it and even despised it. The different customs of the two halves of Constantine's former empire, their religious worship, social forms, art, architecture, clothing, food, facial hair, in short virtually all the *indicia* of identity, erected barriers that ideological rapprochement operating in the abstract could not overcome. The inefficacy of universal ideals made the failure of union all the more painful and frustrating. Conquest had brought the two halves of Christendom too close for comfort, but siblings made for more bitter enemies as they contested a theoretically indivisible patrimony.

Some grievances were ideological and old. The Byzantine *basileis*, the direct heirs of Augustus, had since the ninth century AD denied the imperial title to the successors of Charlemagne, calling them mere kings of the Franks; the latter, in turn, often denied that their eastern counter-parts were Romans, calling them instead kings of the Greeks. A common faith promised unity, but in reality even small divergences in ritual and doctrine had become causes or pretexts for separation, and heretics, even schismatics, were regarded as worse than pagans. The Church of New Rome also rejected the arrogant and uncanonical assertions of supremacy newly advanced by its metropolis. But other grievances were more recent and material. The Byzantines never forgot Norman aggression, and 1204 confirmed their suspicion that the Latins had desired to conquer Constantinople from the outset. Crusades indeed! The sack of the City was especially bloody, as had been the sack of Thessalonike in 1185. The Latins, for their part, never forgot the arrests and confiscations of 1171 and the massacre of 1182. "Between us and them," wrote Niketas Choniates soon after 1204, "the greatest gulf of disagreement has been fixed and we are separated in purpose and diametrically opposed, even though we are closely associated and frequently share the same dwelling" (301). For the Byzantines, Latins were boorish, violent, arrogant, and greedy; for the Latins, the Byzantines were effeminate, duplicitous, quibblers, and greedy.[37] From these terms alone one can tell who was more dangerous for the survival of the other.

All this has been often discussed. What is most important for our theme is that the Latins, now masters of Romania, refused to call the Byzantines Romans, preferring the ethnonym *Graeci*, which the Byzantines rendered as Γραικοί rather than translating it as *Hellenes* (they had no reason to believe that they were being called *pagans*). A variety of motives promoted this western usage. Sometimes the ethnonym was used to avoid confusing the Byzantines with the ancient Romans, with the contemporary Romans of Rome, or with anyone in the West who may have been claiming the name at any time. For example, the Carolingians had at first called their own realm Romania, then only the Italian provinces, and finally only the region of Ravenna (which still bears that name).[38] Moreover, western authors, like the Byzantines themselves (though not to the same degree), liked to classicize by using ancient labels, in whose terms the Byzantines naturally appeared as Greeks. A poem celebrating the gift of an organ by Constantinople to the western court in the ninth century reached even further back and called them "Pelasgians." In a diplomatic letter of the thirteenth century, they are called *Achivi* (Achaians),[39] a term that had pejorative connotations in Virgil. Also, the Byzantines did speak Greek and it was not unreasonable to call a people by their language.

All this, however, glosses over the effective truth of the matter, which is that by the twelfth century western usage was politically motivated. *Graecus* was meant as a rejection of the Byzantines' claim to the imperial Roman legacy and thereby undercut their authority to rule first in the West and, after 1204, in their own lands as well. In short, to a great extent westerners

---

[37] Hunger (1987); for Byzantine terms for westerners, Kazhdan (2001); for the Byzantine usage of *Latinos*, Koder (2002); for the widening gulf between East and West, Ahrweiler (1975a) 75–87.
[38] Wolff (1976) II 2–3.    [39] Pelasgians: Williams (1980) 31. *Achivi*: Martin (2002) 477.

called Byzantines Greeks *because they did not want to call them Romans.* Of course, the practice had become conventional and did not evince odium on every occasion. For example, in translating official documents, the Venetians rendered *Romaios* as *Graecus.*[40] Yet this substitution was not ideologically neutral and sometimes was deliberately disparaging (like calling modern Germans Goths or Huns). In 871, Louis II wrote to Basileios I that "the Greeks" had ceased to be emperors of the Romans because of their heresies and because they had abandoned Rome, its people, and its language.[41] This bias is also well illustrated in Liudprand of Cremona's famous *Embassy to Constantinople* (AD 968), whose "Greeks" are loaded with stereotypes from classical Rome (e.g., faithless, greedy, and obsequious) and late antiquity (e.g., prone to heresy).[42] Moreover, by calling the Byzantines what the ancient Romans had called their eastern neighbors, western medieval writers further reinforced their own links to ancient Rome. In the twelfth century, the Byzantines could even be cast as the weak descendants of the Greeks whose strength was broken at Troy and who thereafter hated all foreigners as new Trojans. Thus, the Franks were again linked to the ancient Romans, as both peoples were imagined to be scions of Troy. The Trojan myth was even used after 1204 to justify the conquest of Constantinople.[43]

The City's conquest complicated western perceptions. The Venetians, the papacy, and others were now happy to call the land that they jointly owned "Romania," where before they had not been willing to do so. The Genoese, to spite the Venetians, recognized the polity of Nikaia as Romania. The new Latin emperors of Romania tried to invest their rule with the forms and ceremonies of the Byzantine regime. Ironically, they too experienced western condescension, as the West still did not consider the "emperor of Constantinople" a real emperor of the Romans, especially when it became apparent that his regime was among the weakest in the region. It is unlikely that anyone, in either East or West, believed in the Latin emperors' continuity with the Byzantine *basileis*, much less with the ancient Roman ones. Unfortunately, we have no sources that illuminate

---

[40] E.g., Laiou (1998) 175.  [41] See Fögen (1998) 21 n. 40; Wickham (1998) 253–254.

[42] Liudprand of Cremona, *Embassy to Constantinople* 22, 28, 30. For what popes and emperors called the Byzantine ruler before 1204, see Dölger (1953) 79–80; Wolff (1976) II 14–18; for *Graecus* in the twelfth century, Magdalino (1993) 84, 105, 246, 311; Ciggaar (1996) 235; in late antiquity and before, see p. 115 above; for *Graecus* as "heretic" in the medieval West, Christou (2003) 114–117. If a Byzantine were given the chance to respond to the hypocrisy and mendacity of western usage on this point, he might sound like Romanides (2002) 270–295.

[43] Ciggaar (1996) 26, 95, 97–98; Shawcross (2003) 125 and *passim.*

the attitude of the Byzantine subjects of the Latin empire. Certainly, they recognized the authority of the Latin "emperor" when he could enforce it but turned against him repeatedly when he could not and sided with almost every rival power.[44]

In one respect, however, westerners were united, namely in calling the Greek-speaking orthodox population of the former empire "Greeks." Our sources come largely from the Catholic hierarchy, which was trying to impose its authority in Greece; from Italian archives, which focus on economic and administrative matters and pay no attention to the attitudes and possible identity crisis of the subject people; and from western chronicles that tell us much about the activities of kings and barons and their relations with the West but little or nothing about how their subjects viewed them (or how these subjects viewed themselves). The so-called Greek voice can be heard only in the splinter states of Epeiros and Nikaia, and, as the discussion will show, what they had to say there was complex and even conflicted. Modern historians have preferred to follow the western sources and simply call the Byzantines "Greeks" after 1204. Ideologically, however, this is not a neutral choice. It reflects the western bias that the Roman legacy is "essentially" western. It also conforms to the belief of many modern Greeks since the nineteenth century that Byzantium was "essentially" Greek and that medieval observers, otherwise reviled as colonial occupiers, saw more clearly what the Byzantines had denied to themselves for centuries. Greek interest in Byzantium, measured in publications, peaks for the period after 1204, a date that is often taken as the origin of "modern" Greek history. Here we will follow neither of these traditions uncritically. The Byzantines had every right to the Roman name and legacy, more so in some ways than any of their neighbors and rivals; moreover, we will not make the mistake of assuming that the terminology of colonial rule faithfully reflects the identities and concerns of its victims.

As we will see, neither the Byzantines of the free successor states nor those under Latin rule lost their sense of Roman identity. However, they had to make concessions and adjust their terms to suit the new circumstances. Ambiguities regarding *romanitas* that had previously been relegated to the margins of the Byzantine outlook, such as western claims to

---

[44] Wolff (1976) I 192–193 (subjects of Latin Romania), II 7–9 (Venetians), 9–11 (Genoese); Lock (1995) 162–173 for the Latin empire. The term Romania could be used geographically, referring to the whole or some part (not always the same part) of the former empire.

Rome, now came to the fore, while trends that had not matured, such as the elite infatuation with Hellenism under the Komnenoi, were pressed into different forms of ideological service. We saw in the previous chapter how some distinctively Roman aspects of the language of classicism (e.g., descent from Julius Caesar) had been reserved in Komnenian rhetoric for westerners, whose presence had dramatically increased in the age of the Crusades and had to be accommodated rhetorically.[45] Conversely, the fact that the aggressors and beneficiaries of 1204 were identified predominantly as Italians would have made the classicizing label "Ausones" (referring to ancient Italians) less attractive. The Byzantines had not forgotten that the city after which they were named lay in the West, and many of them probably knew from contact with westerners that since the eighth century "Roman" could mean specifically the Roman Church. Even before the twelfth century Byzantine theologians had used the term Roman in ecclesiastical polemic to refer to the Latin Church: the errors of the Latins could be called the errors of the "Romans."[46] Naturally, the inhabitants of the city of Rome were also called Romans. In the days of Justinian, the historian Prokopios had to use the same label for them as for the Byzantine army under Belisarios occupying their city, two groups that did not always get along. In that century, monasteries "of the Romans" existed in Constantinople, meaning of Latin-speakers from the West.[47]

Many Byzantines would have been aware of these potentially disruptive senses of the word before 1204, but the reality of Byzantine power and the thoroughness of its Roman identity would have relegated them comfortably to the margins. Yet the onset of Latin rule brought them to the center. The term Roman was destabilized, partly on grounds that the Byzantines had always known and were now forced to confront, and partly because at that very time a Roman revival was under way in the West itself, reinforcing its claim to the name. If the Byzantines did not stop referring to themselves as Romans, others in the East did. For example, in the age of the Crusades the Armenians began to refer to the Franks in their midst, rather than to the Byzantines, as Romans. And in the long term, some Byzantines would become inventive in their efforts to preserve both western and eastern claims to the Roman legacy. In a commentary on Dionysios of

---

[45] See p. 299 above.
[46] Roman as Catholic: Burns (2003) 379. Keroularios: Kolbaba (2000) 23–25; Stephenson (2003) 76.
[47] Prokopios, *Wars* 5.20 ff. (it could also refer to "ancient Romans," sometimes a distinct category for Prokopios). Monasteries: Janin (1969) 446–447.

Halikarnassos (the historian of early Rome) dedicated to the Latin prince of Samothrake, the fifteenth-century scholar Ioannes Kanaboutzes referred to the Romans in Dionysios as "Romanoi" (a transliteration of the Latin name) rather than "Romaioi" (the Greek version).[48]

Conversely, the Hellenic label had become more attractive to Byzantine intellectuals already from the age of the Komnenoi, for reasons that were, at first, only indirectly related to western expansion. But by the late twelfth century, i.e., *before* 1204, we begin to find references to the Byzantines as Greeks that have a broader collective sense and are not limited to mere language or *paideia*. It is interesting that in both instances the Byzantines are being contrasted explicitly to the Latins. In a homily delivered in Euboia, Michael Choniates exhorted his flock to behave decorously in church. In ancient times, he argues, it was the barbarians who were unruly and the Greeks who were silent, even when marching into battle, "but now this has been reversed. One sees the Celts and the Germans and the Italians going to church in an orderly fashion . . . but the Hellenes, who are governed by *paideusis* down to their last utterance and very gait," misbehave.[49] We observe here the familiar features of Komnenian Hellenism: the present is discussed in the figured language of classical "equivalents" and Homeric allusions, and the Byzantines are categorized as Greeks by inversion, namely because they are not barbarians. But this passage goes further in postulating a continuity between ancient and modern Greeks that is not based on language alone, suggesting that there are in fact Greeks present here and now, not merely people who are "like" them in a conditional sense. Crucially, it does so in an ecclesiastical context. The Hellenes are the orthodox, as opposed to the Celts, Germans, and Italians, who are . . . what? Latin? Roman? A year after 1204, Michael was already comparing the situation of his fellow Byzantines to "the barbarization of the Hellenes that they used to talk about in ancient times."[50]

Likewise, according to one scholar's report, a still unpublished oration of Nikephoros Chrysoberges praises the empress Euphrosyne, the wife of Alexios III Angelos (1195–1203), "for being a Hellene of the Hellenes,

---

[48] Roman revival: Magdalino (1983) 344. Armenians: Bartikian (1993) 733. Ioannes Kanaboutzes, *Commentary on Dionysios of Halikarnassos*, *passim*, esp. p. 12: Justinian was one of "our" emperors. "Romaioi" is used for Byzantium: p. 26, but cf. 33. His argument regarding Roman–Hellenic relations in antiquity bears curiously on Byzantine–Latin relations in his own time.

[49] Michael Choniates, *Homily when he visited the Euboian Euripos* 9–10 (Lambros v. I, p. 183). The allusion is to Homer, *Iliad* 3.1–9. Kolovou (1999) 28 dates this to 1185–1195.

[50] Michael Choniates, *Letter* 145; for examples of what he means, see p. 25 above.

without a drop of Latin blood."[51] Discussion of this passage must of course await its publication, but at first sight it too follows the rising tide of anti-Latin Hellenism. As we would expect, hostility to the Latins and a freer acceptance of the Greek label were promoted by the events of 1204, indeed the two developments were closely linked. This can be documented in the works of Niketas Choniates and Ioannes Apokaukos, men born in the middle years of the twelfth century who enjoyed an excellent Hellenic education and had to cope with the ruin of Romania at Nikaia and Naupaktos respectively. Their testimony is crucial because in different ways they were official spokesmen for the successor states of Nikaia and Epeiros.

Niketas Choniates, Michael's younger brother and student, had a career in the civil administration and belonged to the class of men who delivered imperial orations. He also wrote a monumental history of Byzantium from 1118 to 1206, our most important source. It is also a literary masterpiece whose subtleties and ironies-within-ironies we are only now beginning to grasp. Niketas is one of the most deconstructive of Byzantine writers. Historiography enabled him, as it had Psellos, to undermine the panegyrical boasts of his own speeches. He blames the imperial system itself for contributing to the decline of the empire and parades the flaws of almost every person who appears in his work, even those he seems to admire. In his estimation, Latin greed and aggression were complemented on the Byzantine side by torpor and incompetence. Niketas' subtle psychology and vivid images are constructed carefully by a complex and seemingly redundant prose. The *History* is a literary goldmine waiting to be tapped.[52]

It seems that Niketas began writing the *History* in 1185 and continued to expand and revise it until after 1206 (he died in 1217), publishing at least two versions, one before and another after 1204. He calls his fellow Byzantines "Romans" throughout the work, except on some occasions when he is speaking from the point of view of German emperors (who, for him, are "kings"), where the Byzantines are contemptuously but correctly called Graikoi (411, 477; cf. 595). But there are other passages where Niketas,

[51] Browning (1971) 214 (wrongly called the wife of Isaakios II). Browning does not specify the oration. If he means the *Oration for the Patriarch Ioannes X Kamateros* 5 (p. 51; cf. p. 38 for a list of Chrysoberges' works), then the passage has been distorted in the summary quoted above. For Euphrosyne, see Polemis (1968) 131. Nothing else is known about her ancestry.

[52] For a conventional introduction, see Hunger (1978) v. I, 429–441; for his politics, Magdalino (1983); as a source on Manuel, Magdalino (1993) 477–483 and *passim*; for his life and letters, van Dieten (1971). Kazhdan proposed a literary reading of the *History*: Kazhdan (1984b) ch. 7. He studied Niketas' terminology for the body and warfare. Much more must be done. For his irony, see Ljubarskij (2004b), a preliminary look.

probably for the first time in all of Byzantine literature, unambiguously refers to the Byzantines as Hellenes, in a sense that seems to go beyond the mere fact of language and is equivalent to the ethnonym Romans. In his account of the sack of Thessalonike by the Normans in 1185, he says that Latins are "Roman-haters" who loathe "Hellenic men" (301), a statement that is not found in Eustathios' *Capture of Thessalonike*, Niketas' main source here (Eustathios calls them only "Roman-haters").[53] In his subsequent lament over the sack of Constantinople in 1204, Niketas considers that perhaps he should not be glorifying the victories of barbarians over Hellenes, given that historiography was the Hellenes' most beautiful invention and should not be used against them in this way (580). This implies that the Byzantines are just as Hellenic as were the ancient historians themselves.

Finally, in his account of the Crusaders' conquest of Greece after 1204, Niketas describes their "achievements against the Hellenes" (610), referring either to the Byzantines as a whole or to the inhabitants of Greece. Either way, we have a collective and even potentially national use of the ethnonym such as we failed to find in the writings of the Komnenian period. It has been noted that the narrative about the Crusaders in Greece "is replete with classical cultural references," making "the 'Romans' the descendants of the Hellenes. What is paramount in this self-definition is the Greek language and classical culture."[54] Granted, but what separates Niketas in this instance from the Hellenists of the previous century, who also valorized language and culture, is his readiness to extend the Hellenic label to all Greek-speaking Romans and not merely to those who possessed Greek *paideia*, however much he flaunts his own here. Moreover – and this is crucial – he is not calling his fellow Romans Greeks only *because* they spoke Greek: the Crusaders were not here conquering Greek-speakers, they were conquering *Greeks*.

In Niketas' *History*, the Byzantines are also cast as Greeks in ways that, by Komnenian standards, were more conventional. For instance, Niketas says that after 1204 it was hateful to his people to serve the Latins, whose speech differed from that of the Hellenes and who were brutal and arrogant (602). Niketas refers to the Roman language as Greek throughout the *History*, so we should not make too much of this passage (though it partially reveals the grounds for resistance to Latin rule later: subjects and masters spoke different languages). Referring to the events of 1199, he claims that the empire had been governed so badly, while the behavior of

---

[53] Eustathios, *The Capture of Thessalonike* 116 (p. 128).    [54] Laiou (1991a) 80–81.

a Turkish chief in Asia Minor was so merciful, that many abandoned their fatherland (*patris*) and its "Hellenic cities" to settle among the barbarians (495–496). By itself this passage too may reflect only the standard division of the world into (nomadic) barbarians and (urban) Greeks. But when viewed against his explicit identifications of the Byzantines as Hellenes in the passages that we examined above, these more conventional senses of Hellenism acquire a deeper significance. Niketas was prepared to view the Byzantines as a Greek nation, though unfortunately he nowhere provides the historical argumentation that would explain and justify this view.

It is interesting, moreover, that the passages in which Niketas makes the broader identification between Byzantines and Hellenes occur only toward the end of his work, especially in reaction to Latin aggression. Most or all of these passages were written after 1204. It may, then, have been the experience of the Latin conquest that drove him to embrace the Hellenic label more explicitly and more broadly than he would have otherwise. In earlier sections of the *History*, by contrast, Hellenes even appear as pagans (444). And the imperial orations that Niketas delivered before 1204 make use of the standard repertoire of classical comparisons, but never call the Byzantines Hellenes. Yet an oration written for Theodoros I Laskaris, the first independent ruler of Nikaia, begins pointedly by invoking Alexander and the wars in which Greeks prevailed over barbarians; Niketas then explains how the new emperor "Alexandrizes" in his own right.[55] So even in the case of this one author – our first witness to the aftermath of 1204 – the Latin presence seems to have precipitated a closer identification with the idea of a transhistorical Greek experience.

Niketas knew what the Latins themselves thought of the Byzantines. In his lament for Constantinople, he refers sarcastically to how much more pious the Latins were than "we Graikoi" (575). But the conquered now had to adjust their identities to the prejudices of their victors. It is likely that Niketas' belated Hellenism was an attempt to ameliorate the western perception of the Graikoi, a term that, after 1204, came to encapsulate every western prejudice against the Byzantines and was foisted upon them by the Latins. If we must be Graikoi, we may as well be Hellenes and take pride in it. It is possible, then, that Niketas, like other Byzantines, was pushed into embracing Hellenism. On the other hand, there may also be a satirical element in this new terminology. Niketas calls the Byzantines

---

[55] Niketas Choniates, *Oration for Theodoros I Laskaris* (*Or.* 14 in *Or. et ep.* pp. 129, 141: ἀλεξανδρίζειν). Similar images are in *Or.* 16 to Theodoros I, when he killed the sultan of Ikonion in battle in 1211 (esp. *Or. et ep.* pp. 170–172).

Hellenes only in the midst of their defeat by the Latins, whether at Thessalonike or Constantinople. Is this meant to contrast the glorious victories of the ancient Greeks to the ignominious defeats of their modern descendants? "Our affairs are not at all like those of the time of Solon," he notes as his narrative continues past 1204 (585). Is he mocking his people, who should have been victorious Romans, as defeated Greeks? We have seen that Niketas was embarrassed to be writing a work of Greek historiography in order to record Greek defeats. Unfortunately, we will not be able to answer these questions before we know much more about the levels of irony in the *History*.

Ioannes Apokaukos was appointed bishop of Naupaktos around 1200 and so found himself in the realm of Epeiros after the fall of Constantinople. For the next thirty years he was one of the leading prelates of the Orthodox Church and played a key role in the negotiations between Nikaia and Epeiros regarding the apportionment of the rights and titles of Romania, political and ecclesiastical. He recognized the patriarch at Nikaia but was loyal to the rulers of Epeiros, though he was openly critical of both when he thought them unjust or unreasonable. His official correspondence is unsurprisingly concerned with matters of ecclesiastical administration and reflects an orthodox outlook (as well as a fascination with the troubles of everyday life). Apokaukos was conscious of living amidst the ruins of Romania and believed that Nikaia and Epeiros – designated by most Byzantines of the period in neutral terms as the "East" and "West" – were trying to restore it to unity. He wanted them to join together against the Latin enemy and refused to serve on an embassy to Rome. He hated the Latins and believed that there was no point in negotiating with terrorists of a different race, language, and distorted faith.[56]

Apokaukos rarely refers to things Greek, but those few passages are interesting because they reveal that he was thinking along the same lines as Niketas Choniates. The most famous instance is found in a letter to the emperor Theodoros Doukas Komnenos of Epeiros. Apokaukos compares him favorably to emperors of the past who lost their empire through indolence. Before coming to the business at hand (a personal request), he praises Theodoros' labors and hopes that he will conquer the world. Rid us of these wild beasts, he pleads, "who have ground me the *Hellen*, the

---

[56] For Apokaukos as bishop, see Angold (1995) ch. 10; for his correspondence, Lambropoulos (1988). For East, West, and the Latins, see *Letter V* 15; for claiming territory back from the Latins, *Letter V* 17 (p. 275); for unity of East and West, *Letter V* 27 (p. 294). Apokaukos expressed hatred for the Latins often.

*Graikos*, between their teeth."[57] The beasts are clearly the Latins, which gives these terms a bitter and sarcastic sense: this is what *they* call me. Or is that true only of the second term, which refracts Apokaukos' own identity through a western lens? It is not clear to what degree he accepts either ethnonym for himself, though *Hellen* is probably his attempt to ameliorate the pejorative *Graikos* (i.e., what they call Graikos, I will call a Hellen.)

Another part of the bishop's correspondence sheds some light on this ambiguity. Apokaukos had invited Georgios Bardanes, an Athenian student of Michael Choniates, to take up the see of Bonditza. Bardanes politely refused and Apokaukos later helped him become bishop of Kerkyra (1219). In their exchange regarding Bonditza, Apokaukos and Bardanes express a preference for posts in Greek-speaking lands. The former noted that the advantage of Bonditza was that it was "entirely Hellenic [i.e., in language] and lay in the midst of the Graikoi."[58] Given that the Latin presence does not interfere with the terms of the discussion, we have here proof that the two men could refer to themselves as Hellenes and Graikoi *in contrast to the other orthodox peoples of the Balkans* rather than merely in contrast to the Latins. It is understandable that they should wish to govern those who spoke their own language. But does their stance imply a fracturing of the Byzantine Church along linguistic or ethnic lines? And how did they conceive the ideological relationship between Graikoi-Hellenes and Romans at large?[59] Unfortunately, the letters do not clarify these fine but important points. When we turn to evidence from other Byzantines in those dark times, we find that their Roman patriotism, nationalism even, was strengthened and not diminished by the conquest.

## *MODERNI GRAECI* OR ROMANS? BYZANTINES UNDER LATIN OCCUPATION

In tracing the connection between imperial decline and the emergence of a collective Hellenic identity, we have so far considered men who had all acquired Hellenic *paideia* in Constantinople before 1204 (except for

---

[57] Ioannes Apokaukos, *Letter PK* 13 (p. 273).

[58] The dossier is Ioannes Apokaukos, *Letters V* 5, 6, 11 (esp. pp. 249, 252, 257). The exchange is fascinating because it reveals what such men looked for in a see. Georgios Tornikes also hints why he turned down Corinth in the mid-eleventh century: *Letter* 9 (pp. 124–125).

[59] "Graikos" was used in the nineteenth century to refer to the Greek-speaking subjects of the Patriarchate as opposed to Greek nationals, who were called Hellenes and were subject to the Church of Greece. But the gloss scarcely disguised the fact that the former often served the interests of the latter to the detriment of other Balkan nationalities, whose existence they did not acknowledge until it was too late: Matalas (2002) 33, 169–172, 214.

Georgios Bardanes, who acquired it in Athens); who became provincial bishops (except for Niketas Choniates); and who took sides in the ideological struggle between Nikaia and Epeiros (except for Michael Choniates, who remained neutral). They also knew each other well. Michael and Niketas were brothers, while Apokaukos, Michael, and Bardanes were friends. They shared the same cultural outlook. Michael was the student of Eustathios and the teacher of Niketas and Bardanes.[60] But what about the majority of Byzantines? How did those who were not predisposed by their *paideia* to see themselves as Greeks (of some sort) respond to the ideological challenge of the Latin conquest?

Our suspicion that their attitudes were probably different in at least some respects from that of the Hellenists is confirmed by a famous passage in Niketas' *History*. As he fled with fellow refugees to Selymbria, "the rustic peasants greatly mocked us who came from Constantinople, and foolishly called our current state of poverty and nakedness a true equality of status (*isopoliteia*)." In such moments, class division and the gap between arrogant Constantinopolitans and oppressed provincials disrupted Roman unity; Niketas' reciprocal contempt for commoners is evident in his *History*. We could, then, conclude that high officials such as he were more hurt by the destruction of the Roman *politeia* than were the peasants in the fields, who might have benefited from a change of masters. But Niketas' view, shared by all other Byzantines who spoke on the issue, was that the Latins hated Romans regardless of their social status. This partly explains why Niketas' newly found Hellenism was not limited to the cultured elite but had a "national" scope, and why, in the passage just quoted, the historian goes on to explain why the peasants' mockery of his party and of the Byzantine ideal of civic equality was misguided, "because they had not yet been educated (*paideuomenoi*) by their neighbors' misfortunes" (593). Fun as it was to watch the mighty brought low, soon those peasants would understand the importance of the former *isopoliteia*, when they too were enslaved by a racist feudal order. Then they would realize what they had lost and what they had mocked, and the Latin yoke would again spur Roman unity.

Given the nature of our sources, we will never have access to the views of the majority of the population during this phase of Byzantine history, especially as they would have been more torn by contradiction and in rapid flux than at any other time. The most stable evidence comes from Nikaia,

---

[60] Lampsidis (1988) questions the identification of Apokaukos' uncle with the author Manasses as well as the latter's appointment to the see of Naupaktos.

where the *politeia* was reconstituted. Based on the testimony of its writers, as well as on that state's strength and expansion, it has often been argued that its ideology enjoyed broad popular support. We will therefore examine Nikaia separately below. From there came the writers who tell us the most about this period and about the state that restored the empire in 1261. Let us, then, first examine the fragments of Romania that came under Latin rule. How did they respond to their new circumstances? The question is relevant to the Graeco-Roman identity of Nikaia, for that state was not isolated from the rest of Romania. The Byzantines of Nikaia knew well what was going on beyond their narrow borders.

The image of the lands surrounding the Aegean in the thirteenth century was a miniature of that which medieval Europe had presented only a few years earlier: a relatively stable and centralized state of the Romans in the East facing a medley of social and political systems in the West. Latin Romania, like western Europe, featured an emperor with little control over subjects and resources, who was barely recognized by his peers; semi-independent lords imposing different versions of feudal law on subject populations; an independent papacy dreaming of universal rule; the Venetian non-feudal commercial republic and its branch-offices; and adventurers exploiting every weakness to carve out lands to rule by their will. Such was the medieval West; such was now Romania. There was no uniformity in administration, taxation, economy, law, social differentiation, or religious worship. In some cases, feudal, Venetian, and Byzantine elements were stitched together in the hope that the golem would live.[61] There was, however, one thing that remained constant from Crete to Constantinople and that contributed to the failure of the experiment: "Greeks" and "Latins" were almost totally segregated communities. In the thirteenth century, there were few mixed marriages and conversions, even where the Roman Church was not allowed to persecute. The Greeks were despised by their new masters and legally defined as subjects with fewer rights. Lands were confiscated on a huge scale to support western lords and settlers. Many fled to Epeiros and Nikaia or helped their armies against the Latins. On Crete they rebelled often against the Venetian colonial regime.[62]

---

[61] For the case of Lampsakos, for example, see Jacoby (1993); for the variety of systems, (1989) 2–3, and 18–19 for the continuation of some Byzantine practices.

[62] See Wolff (1957); Jacoby (1989) 5–9; Lock (1995) ch. 11. For Crete, see below; for refugees to the free states, see pp. 367–368 below.

Crusaders marching south after 1204 were welcomed in some cities, but such receptions revealed more fear than joy, and hope quickly turned to hatred. Fair and able lords could muster some local support and troops, but few met that description (e.g., Henri, Latin emperor of Constantinople in 1206–1216). The one region where a symbiosis of sorts was achieved was the Peloponnese (or Morea), where a few local magnates were allowed into the lower echelons of the feudal order. But even they enjoyed fewer rights; their "integration" was a legal fiction invented to meet practical difficulties. If the bulk of the population was quiet that was only because its rulers were mild and not because they were recognized as legitimate. Cultural fusion was restricted to a thin layer that disappeared quickly after the Byzantine reconquest. Besides, by accepting positions in a feudal order, Greek magnates had to abandon the ideology of the Roman *isopoliteia* mocked by Niketas' peasants before they too were subjected to vastly less egalitarian orders. Collaborators were probably drawn from precisely those provincial elements that had defied the *politeia* in the years prior to 1204 and had sought to establish themselves as independent lords.[63]

Most Byzantines would have hated their new rulers not only because they were oppressive – economically and socially the *isopoliteia* had been oppressive too – but also because they were of a different race, had different customs, spoke a different language, and practiced a different faith. Historians warn against the homogenizing terms "Frank" and "Latin" that masked the westerners' diverse origins, but it is quite significant that the Byzantines had no interest in making finer distinctions. As in the twelfth century, hatred against the Latins at the popular level was probably deeper than among the intellectuals, whose *paideia* and cosmopolitan experience allowed for nuance and admiration in individual cases. The pope saw this hatred in Michael Doukas of Epeiros beheading Latin priests left and right in 1212 and in Greeks scrubbing altars clean after they had been used in Latin rites.[64] In the (temporary) absence of Romania, it was now the Church that "acted as a cultural focus," though it is at first sight less clear how it "played a major role in the crystallization of a new Greek collective identity,"[65] as some historians have asserted. The Venetian Marin

[63] For cultural fusion in the Morea and its limits, see Topping (1977) 5–10, 22; for the magnates, Jacoby (1967), an analysis of their economic and legal status (see esp. 477); also Ferluga (1972); Kordoses (1987) 45–57. For the contrast between feudal society and the Roman impersonal *politeia*, see Jacoby (1973).
[64] Lock (1995) 211, 220, 275; cf. Gill (1979) 104 for Cyprus; for popular "Latinophobia" under the Komnenoi, Angold (1995) 507–508, 513–514; Simpson (1999). Cf. *Chronicle of the Morea* 758–768.
[65] Jacoby (1989) 25.

Sanudo Torsello famously noted that "on Cyprus, Crete, Euboia, Rhodes, and on other islands as well as in the principate of the Morea, despite the fact that these regions are ruled by the Franks and are subject to the Roman Church, still, almost their entire population is Greek: they cleave to this heresy and their hearts are devoted to Greek things and, when they will be able to express it freely, they will do so."[66] But again we must ask, what does "Greek" mean in all of this, and to whom?

Sanudo was rare if not unique among western writers in noting – if not exactly trying to understand – the outlook of the Byzantine subjects of Latin Romania. But we must be more careful than he in identifying the foundation of the difference they perceived between themselves and their oppressors, whether that difference translated into active resistance or only subsisted under relatively peaceful symbiosis. Western sources for Latin Romania refer often to the *Graeci*, but almost never specify whether they mean Greek-speakers, former or current subjects of the Byzantine emperors, or members of the Orthodox Church. Rarely did the West acknowledge that they did not in fact use western labels. In 1246, pope Innocentius IV appointed a legate to protect "the Greeks of those parts, by whatsoever name they go."[67] Modern scholars have universally followed western usage. Amazingly, *no one* has tried to ascertain what these "Greeks" called themselves and why. Below we will consider sources relating to the ecclesiastical debates of the early thirteenth century, and in the next section we will examine the evidence for the Roman state of Nikaia. But it is worth noting first that we are occasionally able to peak behind the veil of western distortion and into the territories under Latin rule, and what we see there agrees with what we will find when we turn to the Church and Nikaia: the *Graeci* of our sources (the "Greeks" of modern accounts) continued to regard themselves primarily as *Romans*, that is as members of the *politeia* of (Byzantine) Romania, even if they were cut off from their rightful rulers. Their loyalty to the Orthodox Church, it turns out, was strong but only an aspect of their loyalty to the particular national community of Romania that encompassed it.

Venetian Crete is probably the only region under Latin rule where we are in a position to document the persistence of Roman national sentiment despite the bias in our sources. Of course, to speak of "Venetian Crete" is premature, as the Republic faced serious and widespread revolts in the thirteenth century. This must indicate something by itself, but it is not immediately apparent *what*, as we have little evidence regarding the rebels'

---

[66] Marin Sanudo Torsello, *History of Romania* 15 (pp. 166–169).  [67] Cited in Gill (1977) 82.

ideology. Certainly, a combination of family, local, economic, religious, and opportunistic motives may be ascribed to them, but this is true for all wars. "Nationality" is never a pure agent, not even in the most nationalist and anti-colonial modern conflicts. Rather, we should ask whether the rebels declared *any* ideological commitment to Romania, for that would indicate the broader community to which they felt they belonged. In fact, many of them did more than merely declare themselves for Romania. It seems that they wished to rejoin it, as their rebellions were often aided or fomented by the emperors at Nikaia and, after 1261, Constantinople. To be sure, personal rivalries sometimes undermined these rebellions, and many mistrusted the Byzantine government, especially after 1261, and decided more pragmatically among their options. In addition, the fragmentation of Romania that begun in the late twelfth century may have been exacerbated by foreign rule, but we don't know that. What is certain is that many Cretans felt an affinity with Byzantines elsewhere. By 1296 some had left the island to serve the emperor Andronikos II Palaiologos "because they could not bear Italian rule."[68] In 1299 Venice concluded a treaty with the most successful rebel, Alexios Kallerges, which is crucial here because the text of it survives in both languages. In it, wherever the Latin refers to Greeks, the Greek refers to *Romans*.[69] The survival of the name almost a century after the conquest is all the more remarkable in that the subjects of the Latin states certainly had to refer to themselves as Graikoi when they addressed their new masters. Yet we see here that when they were strong enough to declare for themselves, they presented themselves as Roman "minorities" separated from their larger *politeia*. They continued to refer to the Byzantine emperor as "our emperor" until

---

[68] Georgios Pachymeres, *History* 9.8 (v. III, p. 235); Marin Sanudo Torsello, *History of Romania* 16 (pp. 170–171). For thirteenth-century Crete, see now Gasparis (2005) esp. 236–237; for the rebellions, Xanthoudides (1939), influenced by Greek nationalism, but rightly doubting the motives ascribed to the rebels in the Venetian sources; Borsari (1963) ch. 2, esp. 30–31, 40–41 (and *passim* for thirteenth-century Crete); Topping (1977) 14–15; Svoronos (1989); Maltezou (1990) 23–40; cf. 47–52 for a discussion of possible motives (wrongly equating *autokratoria* with *orthodoxia*); (1999) 110–112 recognizes the importance of "customs." Thiriet (1959) 117–118 denies that Byzantium was a nation (mistaking the *basileus* for the essence of the *politeia*), but defines it as basically a nation: a single state, religion, language, and common customs and way of life eight centuries old. Later he refers to the motive of "la libération nationale" from the Venetians, but is unsure of its importance (134–135). Then he asks: "Résistance nationale? Perhaps not in the exact modern sense of the word" (143) – the shibboleth of anachronism, as no other credible sense is proposed. The same phrase – nationalism, but "not exactly in the modern sense" – occurs in most studies quoted above.

[69] Xanthoudides (1902); Mertzios (1949). I have been unable to locate a document of protest sent by the Cretans to the doge in the first decades of Venetian rule: for summary and citations, see Xanthoudides (1939) 21–23. For revolts and pro-imperial sentiment on Cyprus, see Kyrris (1992).

the fall of Constantinople to the Turks in 1453, and raised revolts in his name.[70]

Our vision beyond Crete is darkened by the paucity of contemporary sources. The evidence of later sources, however, proves that former Byzantines now under western rule continued to call themselves Romans and did not take to either version of the Greek ethnonym (Graikos or Hellen). This is especially true of the "vernacular" Greek chronicles, which were composed in various regions of Latin Greece. The fourteenth-century Greek version of the verse *Chronicle of the Morea*, though reflecting the hostility of the French aristocracy against Byzantium and its Church, calls both the Greek-speaking population of the Morea and the Byzantines of the Constantinopolitan empire *Romans*. It is the only "western" source to do so – western in outlook, if Greek in language – but this oddity has been overlooked in the scholarship. If the Greek version of this verse chronicle was based on the French prose version, its poet oddly changed *Grex* to *Romaioi* throughout (the reverse substitution is easier to explain, which suggests another argument for the priority of the Greek version). One of the two Greek versions digresses to explain that these arrogant Romans used to be called Hellenes but had changed their name and taken that of Rome before becoming schismatics. This surprising claim does not occur in any other version of the work and the milieu that gave rise to it cannot be determined precisely.[71]

The early fifteenth-century *Chronicle of the Tocco*, celebrating the rule of that Italian family in Epeiros, was written from a local Gianniot point of view. It too testifies that the "native" population of that region was as Roman as that of Constantinople and all other Byzantine lands, differentiating them from Franks, Serbs, Albanians, and others. The chronicler calls their language "the tongue of the Romans" and not Greek or Hellenic.[72] The *Chronicle of Cyprus*, written by Leontios Machairas in the early fifteenth century from an orthodox point of view, also calls the Greek-speaking inhabitants of the island, as well as the Byzantines of the empire, Romans; their language too he calls Roman, not Greek. "Hellenes"

---

[70] Xanthoudides (1939) 100, 111; Maltezou (1999) 106–108. Tsougarakis (2001) 52–53, 59 rightly rejects a recent attempt to fuse "Greeks and Latins" on fourteenth-century Crete, but in (1995) he questionably highlights language to yield a *Greek* identity.

[71] *Chronicle of the Morea* 795–797; elsewhere Hellenes are the ancient Greeks: 1557, 1774; for various problems, and this passage in particular, see Aerts (1990) 140. The priority of the Greek version was strongly argued by M. Jeffreys (1975). For the idea that the ancient Greeks became Romans, see Georgios Akropolites in p. 382 below.

[72] *Chronicle of the Tocco* 3431 (see the index, p. 538). Preka (1992) 305 glosses Roman as Greek.

in this work are only the abominable pagans.[73] Roman, we should add, was not a mere label; as on Crete, it expressed national aspirations. The Orthodox Church of Cyprus recognized the emperor and patriarch at Nikaia and often sought their approval and confirmation.[74] Likewise, some Romans in Constantinople assisted the Nikaian general Alexios Strategopoulos to retake the City in 1261, though it is risky to generalize from this one act. "We have almost no information about the state of mind of the Greeks still under Latin jurisdiction during this period, but we do know enough to lead us to conjecture that they were aware of the deterioration of the Latin position, and were awaiting only a favorable moment to act."[75] That this outlook was shared by many explains how Ioannes III Doukas Batatzes of Nikaia had, in the decades leading up to 1261, regained so much territory with so little effort, as the historian Georgios Akropolites noted with amazement.[76]

Ultimately, it is to ecclesiastical debates that we must turn if we wish to hear the Byzantine voice in the convulsions of the first decades of the thirteenth century and evaluate how it responded to the western pressure to be "Greek." Here we must be especially cautious, because the sources in question primarily regard ecclesiastical matters and, if read superficially, may give the impression that the Byzantines understood themselves as a religious community, in other words that the *politeia* was only an *ekklesia*. In fact, they point to a very different conclusion, and they also reinforce the thesis that the *politeia* in question was still firmly understood to be Roman and not panorthodox.

We saw that in the twelfth century Hellenic identity was generated largely by enthusiasm for secular *paideia*, but in the thirteenth century the context had totally changed. The world of Constantinopolitan *theatra* had vanished and the last Hellenists had become bishops and refugees in the provinces, where they had to cope with imperial fragmentation and Latin aggression. A very different sense of Greek identity was now forced by an ascendant West upon a reluctant East. This Hellenism – such as it was – no longer aimed to define the sophists against "barbarians" by using the criterion of high culture, but rather to define the Byzantines' place in the broader Christian world. Who were the survivors of Romania now that

---

[73] Leontios Machairas, *Chronicle* 31, 73 for Hellenes; *passim* for Romans; Moschonas (1993b) 136 for language. For these terms in the chronicles, see Maltezou (1999) 107, 112–113.

[74] Angold (1972) 3–4, 6; Gill (1977) 74, 78–79, 81. This came at the price of interference by Nikaia.

[75] Wolff (1957) 332. For the collaborators, see Georgios Akropolites, *History* 85; Marin Sanudo Torsello, *History of Romania* 5 (p. 123).

[76] Georgios Akropolites, *History* 44.

their centralizing institutions had been destroyed and the labels of their national identity usurped? As noted, we do not know how average Byzantines reacted to this challenge, but we do have some access to the views of clergy and monks, who bridged the cultural and social gap between them and the sophists. Orthodox resistance to the aggressors emerged swiftly after 1204 and so the first attempts to come to terms with the new situation are reflected in ecclesiastical texts. The majority of texts generated by the ecclesiastical disputes of the early thirteenth century are in Latin and uniformly label the Byzantines as *Graeci*. In the few texts that have survived from the Greek side we observe a quite diverse terminology that reflects nothing less than a crisis of identity. The Latin presence disrupted a functional ideological system by driving wedges deep into its previously ignored fissures.

For example, a letter sent by the orthodox clergy of Constantinople to pope Innocentius III during the reign of Henri (1206–1216) refers to the two sides as Latins and Romans. But in a letter of the early 1230s to pope Gregorius IX, the patriarch-in-exile at Nikaia Germanos II refers to them as the Roman Church and the Graikoi, exhibiting no irony or detachment when using the latter term.[77] So who were the "true" Romans and what should one call the orthodox/Byzantine community? For not only do the two systems employed in these letters conflict, the internal consistency of each is illusory. To begin with Germanos, he had just sent a series of letters to the Cypriot Church referring not to Romans and Graikoi but to Latins and Romans, the latter being the Byzantines. One might be tempted here to translate "Roman" as "orthodox," but he also divides Cyprus' orthodox community into Romans and Syrians, revealing, again, the national significance of "Roman" for the Byzantines. In these letters, Germanos uses the term Graikos only with reference to the Latin view of the eastern Church.[78] In another letter to some Roman cardinals, he notes that Ethiopians, Syrians, Georgians, Bulgarians, and other orthodox

---

[77] *Letter of the Constantinopolitan Clergy to pope Innocentius*, in *PG* CXL (1887) 293–298, here 293b, 296b, 297a. Germanos, *Letter to pope Gregorios passim*. See van Dieten (1990) 113 n. 11; Angelov (2005) 301.

[78] Germanos, *Letters to the Cypriot Church* 2 (pp. 14, 19; for Romans, see also pp. 9, 13, 30; for Graikoi, pp. 17, 38). For the context, see Angold (1989b) 72–73; for Cyprus, Efthimiou (1987) on religious issues; Kyrris (1992); Moschonas (1993b) for the different communities; and Nicolaou-Konnari, (2005) esp. 14–15 for minorities and 59–61 for "Romans" (their identity wrongly reduced to orthodoxy and language). In a letter of 1263, pope Urbanus IV also recognized "both Greeks and Syrians" on Cyprus: ibid. 49; Gill (1979) 104 and (1977) 90, 92. Germanos' contemporary Demetrios Chomatenos, bishop of Ochrid, once uses Graikos to differentiate Greek-speakers from Georgians: *Various Works* 54.1 (p. 198, on whether communion with Latins is permitted), and in a Latin context: Dimou (1992) 283–284; Angelov (2005) 300 n. 44. See above for Apokaukos.

peoples – all of them evidently non-Romans – fell under the authority of his office.[79] Therefore, while on some occasions he employs Graikos to mean orthodox, his use of it in the letter to Gregorius IX cited above can be viewed as a diplomatic choice of wording, designed to avoid confusion. The orthodox clergy of Cyprus likewise referred to their own people as "Romans."[80]

As for the Constantinopolitan clergy in the early years after the conquest (when they sent the letter to Innocentius III cited above), their inner conflicts are revealed in the dossier assembled by Nikolaos Mesarites regarding the debates in Constantinople between them and the Latins (including the papal legates and the new Venetian patriarch). Mesarites, like the Choniates brothers, belonged to the class of late Komnenian sophists. After the death of his brother Ioannes in 1207, he left for Nikaia and became bishop of Ephesos in 1211. In his funeral oration for Ioannes as well as in separate documentary collections, he preserved edited transcripts of negotiations between the representatives of the two Churches in which Nikolaos and Ioannes themselves were present (in fact, they were leading spokesmen on the Byzantine side). These collections are important because they preserve the record of many voices. They also do not classicize, and so record the very terms that priests and monks were using to define themselves to the Latins. We should certainly be cautious in using them as sources for the theological side of the debates, as they are partisan; also, it seems that Nikolaos copied into them anti-papal treatises verbatim.[81] But we are not interested here in the theological arguments proper, and, as we will see, it is unlikely that Mesarites invented the ethnonyms and labels used in these texts.

We notice quickly in these documents how ambiguous the term "Roman" had become. It could refer to the Byzantines themselves (though rarely), to their realm (or former realm), and to their emperor (after 1205 Theodoros I Laskaris of Nikaia); or to the Church of Rome and its representatives. It is usually clear from the context whether "we" or "they" are the Romans in each case. A Byzantine could therefore speak of "Roman arrogance" or "Roman ignorance" and expect not to be misunderstood by his own side.[82] Still, a certain degree of ideological destabilization,

---

[79] See Angelov (2005) 307.     [80] Magoulias (1964) 80.

[81] Spiteris (1977) is probably right, but goes too far in labelling them "fictional." See also van Dieten (1990) 104–109, who highlights the originality of the Mesarites brothers' use of traditional arguments. For Nikolaos' literary pretensions, see Kazhdan (1984b) ch. 6.

[82] Nikolaos Mesarites, *The Disputation with the Latin Patriarch Thomas* 8 (II, p. 24); *Sermon on the Events of 1214* 14, 16 (III, pp. 21–22). Roman Church: e.g., *Disputation* 8 (II, p. 24); *Sermon* 34 (III, pp. 34–35).

from the Byzantine point of view, is undeniable. A letter sent by the Constantinopolitan clergy to Theodoros I in 1207 (written and delivered by Nikolaos) praised him for restoring the power of the Romans (i.e., the Byzantines) and declared his enemies to be the Aineiadai (the descendants of Aeneas, i.e., the Latins) and those born of Agar, i.e., the Muslims. Again we see how the classical labels of ancient Italy were now being used to label the Latin enemies instead of the Byzantines themselves, as had been the custom. Likewise, whereas before 1204 Byzantines could refer to their own laws as "the Italian science" and to its students as "Italikoi," after 1204 those names were reserved for the "tyranny" and "arrogance" of foreign aggressors. The shift can easily be documented in the letters of Michael Choniates, who lived in exile for two decades after 1204.[83] And while some were carving up the classical tradition along the battle lines of the age, others were doing the same to the Christian tradition. Mesarites notes that during one of his meetings with cardinal Pelagius in 1214 the Latins celebrated the feast of St. Cecilia, "who was a Roman by *genos*" (she was a martyr born in third-century Rome to a patrician family).[84] Still, there was no consistency in the use of these labels in the thirteenth century. The patriarch-in-exile Germanos II referred to the Byzantines as Ausones and to the Constantinopolitan patriarchate (which he claimed) as the Roman one.[85]

The term used most commonly in Mesarites' dossier to refer to the Greek-speaking clergy is in fact *Graikos*. As we have seen, in the past this term could be used without prejudice to refer to the Byzantines as Greek-rather than Latin-speaking Romans, especially in ecclesiastical assemblies including both western and eastern churchmen. Its usage in these debates continued this tradition, only the word was now imbued with the sting of defeat and humiliation at the hands of the Latins, of prejudice, contempt, and an ideological denial of the Byzantines' Roman identity. It was now clearly displeasing to Mesarites' side and in need of replacement or ideological amelioration. Usually it is employed only by Latins or when events are presented from their perspective. When used by the Byzantines themselves we should probably imagine it in quotation marks. They consent, for

---

[83] Aineiadai: Nikolaos Mesarites, *Letter of the Clergy of Constantinople to the Emperor Theodoros* 2, 4 (II, pp. 27–28). For the context, see Gill (1979) 35. In the eleventh century, Ioannes Mauropous called Ioannes Xiphilinos "Italikos" for his legal knowledge: *Letter* 28 (p. 113, and the commentary on p. 224). For the shift after 1204, see the index to the *Letters* of Michael Choniates (p. 305).

[84] Nikolaos Mesarites, *Sermon on the Events of 1214* 23 (III, p. 27). For the debate with Pelagius, see Hoeck and Loenertz (1965) 54–62; Gill (1979) 40–42.

[85] Germanos II, *Response to the Archbishop of Bulgaria* 19–20, 33–34 (pp. 34–35).

the sake of argument, to a linguistic division between Graikoi and Italians.[86] A number of passages reveal Byzantine anxiety about a term that obviously reflects a Latin bias, and Nikolaos tries in various ways to counter the disadvantage at which it puts his side. In the disputation of 1206 he asserts that Morosini, Latin patriarch of Constantinople, has been appointed over his *ethnos* and not over "us, whom you call *Graikoi*, though properly it should be *grammatikoi*, for a true knowledge of the nature of beings has always been found among those who speak Greek." Graikos is here feebly ameliorated as "speaker of Greek," a desirable quality.[87] The cardinal Pelagius, whom Nikolaos addresses in the debates of 1214 as "you Roman," is made to praise the power and divine inspiration of Greek, though he is unpersuaded by the Greeks' theological arguments. When Nikolaos returned to Nikaia from this meeting, the patriarch Theodoros Eirenikos was angry that Pelagius had not addressed him as bishop of the Constantinopolitans but rather "of the Graikoi." Nikolaos protests that this happened against his objections, but puts a good face on it by saying that the patriarch should not be angry because the title bestowed on him by the cardinal in fact extended his authority to the whole world, for where is Greek not spoken?[88]

No one in these documents is called a Hellen, and *hellenizein* signifies only that one can understand Greek.[89] The sense of a crisis of identity is powerful, as stateless Byzantines seem to have lost their confidence in the Roman name and had to adjust to a derogatory label. They labored to turn it to their advantage by highlighting its linguistic side, but the stigma remained. The patriarch Theodoros knew that he was being insulted when he was addressed as the archpriest "of the Graikoi." Others coined neutral labels. Addressing the Latins as "Romans" at a meeting in Hagia Sophia at the end of 1204, Ioannes Mesarites referred to his side as the "Byzantioi" – what archaizing Byzantines sometimes called the residents of Constantinople – declaring that they would not submit to the pope: regardless of who ruled their physical bodies, their souls were loyal to the

---

[86] Graikos from a Latin perspective: Nikolaos Mesarites, *Funeral Oration for his Brother Ioannes* 36 (I, p. 47); *The Disputation with the Latin Patriarch Thomas* 3 (II, p. 17). Graikoi and Italoi: ibid. 3 (II, p. 18). Later Byzantines reluctantly acknowledged that Latins called them Graikoi: Mauromatis (1987) 185, 188–189.

[87] Nikolaos Mesarites, *The Disputation with the Latin Patriarch Thomas* 5 (II, p. 21). For the debates of 1206, see Hoeck and Loenertz (1965) 30–54; Gill (1979) 33.

[88] "You, the Roman": Nikolaos Mesarites, *Sermon on the Events of 1214* 24 (III, p. 28); praise of Greek: 31 (p. 33); the patriarch's reaction: 51 (p. 47). Cf. Gounaridis (1986) 249–250.

[89] E.g., Nikolaos Mesarites, *The Disputation with the Latin Patriarch Thomas* 2 (II, p. 16), said of the Venetians.

patriarch Ioannes X Kamateros (who had fled to Didymoteichon and would die in 1206).[90] Byzantioi, or "Byzantines," is probably still the best term for us to use. Even though it meant only "Constantinopolitan" at that time, it avoids the ambiguities of *Romaios*, *Hellen*, and *Graikos* that compromise modern narratives.

We should not, however, conclude that Ioannes could not see past Constantinople, that the memory and ideological power of Romania were abolished and replaced by a purely orthodox outlook, or that he was genuinely indifferent to the worldly authority ruling over his nation's former capital. Rather, he chose to focus on his orthodox identity to the exclusion of any political one because in the bleak days of late 1204 he had no other point of reference and because the point of the debates specifically concerned his spiritual allegiance. In Georgios Akropolites' account of the legation of Pelagius, the monks and clergy of Constantinople declare to the Latin emperor Henri that "we are of a different *genos* and obey a different high priest. We will submit to your authority so that you may rule our bodies, but we will not submit in our spirits and souls."[91] The traditional repertoire of defensive orthodox stances included the renunciation of worldly power in favor of the City of God. Normally, this stance was asserted in the face of tyrannical or heretical emperors. Now it was being invoked in response to the lack of an emperor.

Yet despite the monks' and clergy's (strategic) pose of indifference to secular power, we saw above that they quickly acknowledged Theodoros I Laskaris as their emperor and begged him to restore the unity of Romania. And when, in the debates of October 1206, the cardinal Benedictus accused them of being unruly, they replied that it would have been easy for them to flee to Laskaris or to "the lands of barbarians who share our faith," but instead "we remain here enduring a myriad of woes at the hands of your *ethnos*."[92] In other words, the difference between them and the Latins was not purely religious, as is shown by the use throughout Mesarites' accounts of the terms *allophyloi* and *alloglossoi* – men of different race and different language. The Byzantine clergy recognized that there were "barbarians" who shared their faith, in other words that orthodoxy did not make one a Roman. It is crucial that such national considerations shaped debates that aspired to be "purely" ecclesiastical. Precisely when it was being violently

---

[90] Nikolaos Mesarites, *Funeral Oration for his Brother Ioannes* 38 (I, p. 49). For this meeting, see Gill (1979) 32.

[91] Georgios Akropolites, *History* 17.

[92] Nikolaos Mesarites, *Funeral Oration for his Brother Ioannes* 49 (I, p. 62). For the embassy of Benedictus, see Hoeck and Loenertz (1965) 30–54; Gill (1979) 32–34.

destroyed, Romania revealed itself as a national community that encompassed *only part* of the orthodox world, and every effort was bent toward its
reconstitution. The Byzantines failed (or rather never tried) to define
themselves in purely religious terms against the Latins. Their outlook
was shaped by the memory of their once and future *politeia*, which
regrouped at Nikaia and was eventually reconstituted in Constantinople.

Every day of Latin rule deepened "Greek" hatred of the new "Romans."
Soon after 1204, Konstantinos Stilbes, formerly a professor in
Constantinople and bishop of Kyzikos before witnessing the atrocities of
1204, produced a new list of western "errors." In contrast to his other
(unpublished) works, which are highly sophistic, this one is written in
straightforward prose, probably because it was intended for wide circula-
tion. Among familiar items, we find this: the Latins do not honor saints of a
foreign race (*phylon*); moreover, despite the fact that the emperor
Constantine belonged to their own *genos* and championed Orthodoxy
among them, the Graikoi, and every other *ethnos*, they hate him for
establishing the empire of New Rome because they feel that it belongs to
them. Again we see the "ethnic" fragmentation of Christendom that we
observed above in Mesarites' comment on the *genos* of St. Cecilia. It is not
clear, however, how Stilbes defined these *ethnê* and *genê*. Certainly more
was involved than a purely ecclesiastical division, for instance language,
customs, and various notions of ethnicity. In his defense of Constantine,
Stilbes divides mankind into Latins, Graikoi, and others. The Byzantines
apparently belong to the *ethnos* of the Graikoi. However, on the few other
occasions when he refers to the orthodox as Graikoi, it is only from the
Latin point of view.[93]

According to Stilbes, the Latins also do not fully trust St. Paul, ostensibly
because he was not an eyewitness of Christ's life but in reality because of the
indictments contained in his epistle to the Romans, "namely against
themselves." This postulates a continuity between ancient Romans and
modern Latins. But this is contradicted by the final "error," according to
which the West is full of heresy because the ancient Romans were destroyed
by the Vandals, who then spread their heresies. This breaks the link
between the ancient Romans and the modern Latins. Some of the latter,
he says, do not differ in their impiety from "the ancient Hellenes." At this
point, Stilbes was copying an anti-Latin treatise formerly ascribed to

---

[93] Konstantinos Stilbes, *Errors of the Latin Church* 49 for saints and Constantine (p. 73), and 57, 59 for
the Byzantines as Graikoi (p. 76). For Latin "errors," see Kolbaba (2000) and 185–186 for Stilbes; for
the context of his list, Angold (1989b) 67–69 and (1995) 516–518.

Photios but now known to belong probably to the twelfth century.[94] As with other Komnenian writers we have discussed, Stilbes (or his source) does not specify who the "modern Hellenes" are to which the ancient ones, namely the "pagans," are to be contrasted. We might deem this omission unfortunate, as it would tell us much about the evolution of Byzantine notions of Hellenic identity, but we must recognize that the vagueness of the formulation lies precisely at the heart of our subject. It was in the very nature of Byzantine Hellenism that Stilbes could not simply state what he seems to imply, especially in a religious work such as this. The "modern Hellenes" were an implication, a logical corollary that could not yet be admitted as an existing reality.

Stilbes' failure to identify the modern Hellenes is curiously rectified in a *Treatise Against the Errors of the Greeks (Graecorum)* by Dominican missionaries in Constantinople in 1252. After marshaling the authority of *all* the Fathers – *patres antiqui, tam Graeci, quam Latini* – to demonstrate that truth lay with the *Ecclesia Romana*, it concludes that the modern Greeks – *moderni Graeci* – have deviated from tradition. So while Stilbes would probably have placed the break between ancient and modern Greeks with Constantine, who converted the Graikoi along with all other *ethnê*, the Dominicans, for their own polemical reasons, date it to sometime after the patristic age, probably in the seventh century. Of course, the criterion here was not a coherent view of national Greek history but a contestation over a theological patrimony. Moreover, the modern Greeks did not come into being with Constantine or at some later point in the early Middle Ages, but rather, ironically, in these very debates between the likes of Stilbes and the Dominicans, who were creating that which they were attacking. The *Tractatus* in fact became the basis for future Dominican polemics against "the Greeks."[95]

Though the existence of "modern" Hellenes was implied in much rhetoric of the Komnenian period, their emergence properly belongs to the next century, when the idea of a modern Greek *ethnos* was raised in debates that even monks and churchmen could not pretend were strictly ecclesiastical. No one believed that if the questions of the *filioque*, papal primacy, and leavened or unleavened bread were resolved, Graikoi and Latins would finally effect union. The format of theological debate may

[94] Konstantinos Stilbes, *Errors of the Latin Church* 47 for Paul (p. 73), 104 for the Vandals (pp. 90–91). For the text Stilbes was copying (the *Opusculum contra Francos*), see Kolder (2002) 29–30; Kolbaba (2000) *passim*, esp. 178.

[95] *Tractatus contra errores Graecorum*, in *PG* CXX (1887) 483–574, here 526a. See Gill (1979) 143; Angold (1989b) 76–77; Delacroix-Besnier (1997) 201–212, and *passim* for Dominican activities.

have rested on that theoretical notion, but in reality everyone knew that there was more at stake, evinced in the constant references to *glossa, ethnos, genos,* and *phylon.* Ecclesiastical union was undermined by deep national sentiments that the monks and priests at Constantinople could only hint at in the first years of the occupation. The Byzantines did not accept the western label of Graikos, but in the free empire of Nikaia they fashioned a new Hellenic identity to complement their Roman identity. Before examining their response, it is worth pausing to wonder what the Dominicans' *moderni Graeci* would have looked like in Greek, if it is true that the *Tractatus* was originally written in that language and then translated into Latin. Would they have been oἱ νῦν Γραικοί? Οἱ καθ' ἡμᾶς? Or perhaps oἱ νέοι? Surely not Ἕλληνες.

## ROMAN NATIONALISM IN THE SUCCESSOR STATES

It is well known that the thirteenth century witnessed a resurgence of Byzantine interest in Hellenism, though its contours and aims were different from those of its twelfth-century predecessor. Under the Komnenoi, Hellenism was the elite culture of a small group of trained scholars and expressed their insecurity in a society governed by warlords who were sometimes of foreign origin. In the thirteenth century, and especially at Nikaia, the interest in Hellenism was still confined to a few but was meant by them in a national sense that theoretically encompassed all Byzantines. Accordingly, many modern Greek historians have dated the origin of the Neohellenic nation to this period,[96] although this view has not gained wide acceptance outside Greece. Critics see merely a continuation of the "medieval universalist Christian empire."[97] This response, at any rate, is certainly wrong, for Byzantium was never a "medieval universalist Christian empire," only the state of the Romans. But the Greek position must not be accepted without qualification either, as the aftermath of 1204 did not alter the *Roman* basis of Byzantine national identity. The criteria for being regarded as a Roman remained the same. What changed was the fragmentation of the state. This temporarily forced Byzantine writers to talk about the nation *independently of the state,* revealing the particular national assumptions that had previously been subsumed under imperial unity

---

[96] Vakalopoulos (1974) 61–91 (for whom any reference to Greece, even geographic, implies a national identity); Moles (1969); Ahrweiler (1975a) 110–111.

[97] Mango (1965), whose view is an apocalyptic fantasy; Irmscher (1970) and (1972), whose exact target is not clear: *Greek* patriotism? *Nikaian* patriotism? Nikaian *patriotism*? Angold (1975b) 51–53 attempts to mediate.

and therefore taken for granted. Plotting the continuity of Roman nationalism reveals that the new rhetoric of Hellenism did not postulate a new Greek
nation but was rather intended to buttress the Roman claims of Nikaia
against the Latins. The Byzantines used their Hellenism to explain what
kind of Romans they were in opposition to their new enemies, who were
also Romans albeit of a different sort. Still, this development certainly did
foreshadow the emergence of a Greek national identity in later times and
there was a continuity between the two, at least at the level of the intellectuals.

Romania was broken. It was divided, in the language of the time,
between the "eastern" and "western Roman lands" that we misleadingly
call "the empire of Nikaia" and "the Despotate of Epeiros." There was in
addition "the empire of Trebizond," which seems, at least initially, to have
had the same objectives and ideology as its two rivals, but it must be
excluded from this discussion for lack of texts from the thirteenth century.[98] Nikaia and Epeiros were mostly concerned with each other anyway.
Their leaders and spokesmen knew that they were dealing with two fragments of a former whole. What both had lost, in addition to each other,
was Constantinople. Thus complaints regarding division were complemented by the lament of exile. In a speech written by Niketas Choniates
around 1208, the first emperor at Nikaia Theodoros I Laskaris declared his
intention to become "one shepherd for one flock" and reclaim "our father-
lands," especially the capital.[99] At about the same time, the first patriarch-
in-exile at Nikaia, Michael Autoreianos (a friend of Eustathios and Michael
Choniates), was told in a speech by the deacon Sergios that his destiny was
to reunite the dismembered Church.[100]

Both speeches, in their hatred of the Latin aggressors, allude to the fall
of the Temple and the Babylonian Captivity, which became prominent
themes in the rhetoric of the period. Summarizing events, the fourteenth-
century historian Nikephoros Gregoras wrote that "the state of the Romans
was broken into many pieces, like a large ship caught in a tempest." The
same image had been used by Michael Choniates, who praised Laskaris,
"the emperor of the East," for "saving the fragments of the Roman *politeia*
in Asia."[101] In letters to the Nikaian patriarchs written slightly over a decade

[98] See Eastmond (2004) for what the monuments say.
[99] Niketas Choniates, *Selention on behalf of Theodoros I Laskaris* (*Or.* 13 in *Or. et ep.* p. 128; the full title
refers to the "western" and "eastern" Roman lands); for the date, van Dieten (1971) 141–142. For the
visual rhetoric of exile at Trebizond, see Eastmond (2004) 73, 104.
[100] Sergios the deacon, *First* Didaskalia *(Encomium for the Patriarch Michael Autoreianos) passim.*
[101] Nikephoros Gregoras, *Roman History* 1.2; cf. Georgios Akropolites, *History* 7. Michael Choniates,
*Letter* 94. For Biblical imagery and irredentist ideology, see Angelov (2005) 296–299.

later, the bishop of Naupaktos Ioannes Apokaukos praised his own ruler of Epeiros for reclaiming lands from the Latins and restoring them to Roman authority. He wished that "western" and "eastern" forces would unite and scatter the common foe. Choniates' student Bardanes, the bishop of Kerkyra, expressed the same wish to the patriarch Germanos II (ca. 1226), only regarding the Church: "who will put its ruins back together?"[102] Almost everyone wanted union, and the bishops of the West were generally willing to accept the Nikaian patriarch. The real obstacle to political union was that each of their secular rulers wanted to be the one to effect it, by taking Constantinople. Neither side wanted union on the other's terms, which even led to the formulation of theoretical arguments in favor of temporary political separation, something that had been unthinkable in the past.[103]

To speak of fracture and reunion as all these men did implied a conception of the whole. It was precisely now, when Romania was in peril of being permanently lost, that the Byzantines most strongly affirmed what they had always believed their state to have been. Not coincidentally, it is now that modern historians, who otherwise deny that Byzantium was a national state, concede that the states that came into being after 1204 were national – or "protonational" – in conception. But the proponents of union in the first decades after 1204 were old or middle-aged and their conception of Roman unity had been shaped long before the experience of exile. They were not innovating about the fundamentals. So what was it exactly that they wanted to put back together?

The unity that the Byzantines preoccupied themselves with after 1204 was not primarily that of Orthodoxy, as is often asserted.[104] As we saw, they had no wish to unite with *barbarian* orthodox peoples. Orthodoxy, after all, is a matter of shared religious belief and practice; the orthodox are united (in communion) so long as they mutually regard each other as orthodox. There was never any need to "unite" them politically and the Byzantines never made an effort to do so in all their history. Demetrios Chomatenos, bishop of Ochrid (1216–1236), argued that the "eastern" and

---

[102] Ioannes Apokaukos, *Letter V* 17 (p. 275); *V* 27 (p. 294). Georgios Bardanes, *Letter to the Patriarch Germanos II* 14 (p. 113).

[103] Angold (1995) 538–539. For the debates, see Stavridou-Zaphraka (1990) for politics; Karpozilos (1973) for the Church; also Angold (1995) ch. 25. For the two states, see Angold (1975a) and Nicol (1957); Chrysos (1992).

[104] *pace* Angold (1995) 538; (1972) offers a better, albeit still preliminary, definition of unity after 1204; (1975b) 62, 67–68 almost grasps its national basis ("not just religion . . . rather by race and language"); so too Ahrweiler (1975b) 36–38, but calls the experiment Greek and sees a rupture with Byzantium. I have found no systematic attempt to address this question.

"western Roman lands" were already united in their faith even if they were politically divided (though he was unique among contemporaries in attempting to justify provisional political separation).[105] What was really at stake was the unity of Romania. Even negotiations regarding Church union concerned not the whole of "Orthodoxy" but only the "western" and the "eastern" Roman lands, namely the fragments of Romania – so, at any rate, believed the bishops of Epeiros in a letter sent after 1225 to the patriarch Germanos II. They went on to praise their own new emperor Theodoros Komnenos for defeating "the enemies of Romania," "restoring the cities to the authority of the Romans," and purifying the churches of "Latin filth." The bishops made it clear that the "unified *politeia*" that Theodoros was restoring included neither the (heretical or schismatic) Latins nor the (orthodox) "Skythians" (i.e., Bulgarians). In Thessalonike, Apokaukos claims in another letter, Theodoros was supported by the orthodox Greek-speaking populace – he means by the Romans.[106] At this level, Church union was only an aspect of national reconstruction (albeit a necessary aspect).

The desire for political union, on the other hand, was not motivated by sheer devotion to the "monarchical ideal," which, some believe, "was ingrained in the mind of the Byzantine Man."[107] The Byzantines did not want union *because* they held to monarchy or because this ideal mirrored the One God in heaven, as churchmen occasionally reminded them. Each of the two successor states was monarchical to begin with; the imperative to merge was generated by the desire for national unity, for otherwise we cannot explain why they were interested in merging only with other Romans. Romans, we have seen, were not defined arbitrarily as the collectivity of the subjects of the emperor. The nation was prior to the emperor, who was only its chief executive and collective expression: he was the emperor because there were Romans *of whom he could be* the emperor. The roots of both monarchy and national unity were older than the idea that the one emperor mirrored the One God in heaven and they were not theological to begin with. We see this clearly when we consider that the theological parallel by itself could never legitimate a ruler whose position

---

[105] Demetrios Chomatenos, *Various Works* 112, 114 (pp. 368–378). For provisional separation, see Angold (1995) 538–539.

[106] Ioannes Apokaukos, *Letter V* 26 (p. 290: East and West; p. 292: Theodoros and Romania). The letter was written on behalf of the "western" bishops. Thessalonike: *Letter V* 4 (p. 248).

[107] Brezeanu (1978) esp. 57, 59. Once he has examined the evidence, he seems to realize that he is dealing with a nation founded on religion, language, and culture, but buries this at the end of a long footnote: 63 and n. 29.

was disputed by a rival. Any emperor then had to demonstrate, usually through a spokesman, that he had been chosen by the entire nation, including the Senate, Church, and army. That is exactly what Demetrios Chomatenos argued on behalf of Theodoros of Epeiros. What legitimated his position was not some rhetorical comparison to the One God, or an allusion to the line in Homer's *Iliad* about the need to have one king (another commonplace in this rhetoric), but rather, as he put it, the "consensus of all" – *consensus omnium*, Ciceronian ideology in thirteenth-century Epeiros! The purpose of the emperor's office was "to benefit the nation (*laos*)" and to fight "on behalf of his *patris* and *homophyloi*" (those of the same race). These notions regarding the actual basis and purpose of imperial power were quite standard. Ioannes III Doukas Batatzes of Nikaia insisted that his authority was based on "common consent" and that its sole purpose was to benefit its subjects.[108] This was the Byzantine conception of the state; the emperor as God's vice-regent on earth was theological-rhetorical dressing, useless in a crisis.

National unity was at stake. A synod of bishops proclaimed in 1226 that it would never do for people of the same *genos* to have two emperors.[109] The same idea can be found in the letters written by Michael Choniates after 1204, when he was in exile on the island of Keos refusing to take sides between East and West. He too called for campaigns to liberate Constantinople from the cruel and rapacious Latins, who spoke a barbarian tongue, were of a different *ethnos* or *genos*, and had corrupted the worship of Christ by the worship of gold. In a long letter of ca. 1207 castigating the violent ambitions of the provincial warlord Leon Sgouros, Michael laments "that we were not only oppressed by those men of a different *phylon*" – meaning the Latins – "but this man who is allegedly of the same *ethnos* as us added to our woes . . . The *heterogeneis* are now milder to the Romans in comparison to this *homogenês*." Here *genos*, *ethnos*, *phylon*, refer to the Romans, of whom Leon Sgouros was one, despite his aggressive behavior. We note again how interchangeable these terms were, so that we should not insist on a strong "ethnic" reading. In Michael's usage they point to what we call a nation. He did not see being a Roman merely in terms of political allegiance or Orthodoxy, as do modern historians of Byzantium. For Michael Romania was the nexus of language, religion,

---

[108] Election: Demetrios Chomatenos, *Various Works* 114.3–4 (p. 372, to Germanos II); office: 110 *passim* (pp. 363–367, to Theodoros Komnenos of Epeiros); see Stavridou-Zaphraka (1990) 128, 167; Angelov (2005) 308. For *consensus*, see Ando (2000) *passim*. Batatzes: Nikephoros Gregoras, *Roman History* 3.1.

[109] Nikephoros Blemmydes, *A Partial Account* 1.23.

customs, and perhaps ethnicity too (though this is hard to discern in the denatured terminology).[110] It was only a national logic, not some "multi-ethnic universal Christian empire," that could compel Michael to regard Sgouros, a man he loathed and a political rebel to boot, as one of his "own kind."

In recounting Sgouros' siege of Athens in his *History*, Michael's brother Niketas reveals how clearly he and Michael understood the difference between being Christian and being Roman. Addressing the rebel, Michael "said that it was not fitting for one who was called a Christian and reckoned among the Romans to wage war against the Romans, unless he were paying mere lip service to Christ's name and was, in his heart, far removed from those who are named after Him, while, as for being Roman, he was like them only with respect to his dress and speech" (606). Being Christian is a matter of ethics and faith, but being Roman is to belong to a nationally defined political community.

Unfortunately, separatists like Sgouros have left no account of themselves. Clearly their actions, both before and after 1204, tended to the dismemberment of Romania, but we do not know how they presented themselves in relation to the ideology of national unity. It is unlikely that they projected any ideology beyond what opportunism might invent, in other words they probably found it difficult to *persuade* anyone to join them on non-pragmatic grounds. Most of these rebels, it seems, returned to the fold when the successor states became powerful again, but we still do not fully understand the unraveling of Romania before 1204, and neither did Niketas. He lamented in his *History* that the *homogeneia* had been ripped apart by factions, which the Latins picked off one by one (625). At the same time, Nikolaos Mesarites complained that "when our *patris* was conquered" some members of the imperial family seized portions of "the Roman land" and preferred to submit to the Latins rather "than to their own blood (*aima*) and race (*phylē*)."[111]

Bulgarians and Serbs, even those living near or within the territories of the western lands, were certainly not considered Romans, despite being orthodox.[112] The basis for the differentiation was again national, though the easiest criterion to use on a daily basis was language. Chomatenos, Apokaukos, and Bardanes valorized the "Greek" or "Roman" language as

---

[110] Michael Choniates, *Letter* 148.4 and 100.29–30; for Sgouros, see now Blachopoulou (2002), whose interpretation is filtered through the lens of *Greek* nationalism. For the terminology, see p. 87 above.
[111] Nikolaos Mesarites, *Sermon on the Events of 1214* 20 (III, p. 25).
[112] Dimou (1992) 290–295 for references.

superior to any other and clearly used it as a differentiating marker of Roman identity.[113] There were other such markers. To persuade the *Bulgarian* residents of his own city of Melenikon to submit to Ioannes III Doukas Batatzes of Nikaia, the leading citizen Nikolaos Manglabites argued that Batatzes' son and heir Theodoros was married to the daughter of the Bulgarian king and was therefore their legitimate ruler, while to his *Roman* fellow citizens he argued that their land had once belonged to the Roman authority and they themselves were Romans by *genos*. Conversely, it made sense to Georgios Akropolites that (other) Bulgarians under Nikaian authority wanted to cast off the "yoke of the *alloglossoi*" – namely of the Romans – and join their own *homophyloi*.[114]

"Nationalism" – beyond just national identity – was not far from all this. Bishop Chomatenos was proud to be a Roman and considered both Latins and Bulgarians to be enemies of the Romans. He instructed his own ruler Theodoros of Epeiros to fight "for his *patris* and *homophyloi*." Batatzes of Nikaia was praised by his own son for waging wars "on behalf of the *genos*."[115] More interestingly, in an official act addressed to "the subjects of the emperor and all the soldiers" and written in simple Greek so that it could be disseminated widely, the patriarch at Nikaia Michael IV Autoreianos forgave the sins of all who died "fighting for God and country on behalf of the common salvation and liberation of the nation (*laos*)." The act begins with a stirring piece of nationalist trumpetry: "Roman Men! – for this name by itself suffices to recall your ancient valor. You who are born of a great *genos* and take pride in your ancestors . . . It is time now for you to show us your virtue . . . on behalf of both your faith and the liberty of our *genos*." The patriarch exhorts them to fight for their *patris* against the *ethnê* and against "everyone who is opposed to you," so presumably against orthodox enemies as well. The *laos* he is addressing are the Romans, not the Christians (though they certainly were understood to be Christians too). In a different act recognizing Theodoros I Laskaris as emperor, the patriarch swears allegiance on behalf of all the subjects and promises that none will betray Laskaris to "any enemy, whether Roman or *ethnikos*, crowned or

---

[113] Dimou (1992) 282–283, 284–285, for references. For minorities in northern Epeiros (as perceived by Apokaukos and Chomatenos), see Kiousopoulou (1990) 22–23.

[114] Georgios Akropolites, *History* 44 (Manglabites) and 54 (Bulgarians). For the former, see Gounarides (1986) 255–256; Macrides (2003) 204–205.

[115] Enemies: Dimou (1992) 280–283; *homophyloi*: Demetrios Chomatenos, *Various Works* 110.2 (p. 364, to Theodoros Komnenos of Epeiros). Theodoros II Laskaris, *Encomium for Ioannes III Doukas Batatzes* 6 (*op. rh.* p. 32).

not, not even against the grandsons of sir Andronikos" (who founded the principality of Trebizond).[116]

We cannot dismiss these charged words as "aberrant."[117] Autoreianos' background lay in the bureaucracy of the capital before 1204, and he was a friend of Eustathios and Michael Choniates. What was new in his address was the remission of sins, not the nationalism. Even *if* the army he was addressing included many foreign mercenaries, as had always been the case in Byzantium, we should not conclude that there was nothing to being Roman beyond the mere fact of serving an emperor.[118] To the contrary, the effacement of foreign elements from the national rhetoric shows that official spokesmen did not want to allow minorities to disrupt the illusion of national homogeneity and sought to Romanize them, by subsuming them rhetorically to the collectivity. That is consistent with the practice of modern nations. The army included foreigners, but that was probably the only institution in which their presence was felt. Overall their numbers in the Nikaian empire were small and it seems that even in the army they were assimilated.[119]

This discussion was deemed necessary as a backdrop for the evaluation of the evidence for "Hellenism" in thirteenth-century Byzantium. That evidence is often lifted out of its thoroughly Roman context and used to proclaim the birth of a *Greek* nationalism that complemented an alleged "withering of Roman traditions."[120] As we see, no such withering occurred. The subjects and rulers of both the "western" and "eastern" Roman lands were as Roman as the Byzantines had ever been, and we do not *explain* anything about them by calling them Greeks. The founders of the empire of Nikaia were refugees from the capital and all their efforts were bent on its recapture. Their sons born at Nikaia continued to regard themselves as Constantinopolitans. But during the exile, Nikaia was the center of Roman power and they treated it as a surrogate for Constantinople, replicating its institutions and even making it look physically like the city they had lost. The move was not unlike that from Rome to New Rome, only it was involuntary and expected to be temporary. A mass exodus of refugees from

---

[116] For text, translation, and commentary, see Oikonomides (1967) esp. 117–119, 123, and 131 ff.; for the rivalry of Nikaia and Trebizond, Lampsidis (1980).

[117] As would, e.g., Obolensky (1972) 1.

[118] Oikonomides (1967) 131 draws extreme conclusions about Byzantine non-identity from these groups. For readings of this text as "internationalist" despite its acknowledged "national element," see Pitsakis (1991) 103–106 and (1995) 29 (based on *a priori* notions).

[119] Ahrweiler (1965) 22–28; Angold (1975a) 105–106 (ch. 9 for the army in general); and Bartusis (1992) ch. 1, esp. 26–29. Compare Trebizond: Eastmond (2004) 21–22, 95–96, 150.

[120] Moles (1969) 99.

the capital and other areas under Latin rule to the "free" western and eastern lands, an event without precedent in Byzantium, reinforced this sense of collective exile.[121] The rhetoric that issued from this unique calamity was stridently Roman.

## IMPERIAL HELLENISM: IOANNES III BATATZES AND THEODOROS II LASKARIS

We examined earlier the Hellenism of the leading intellectual figures of the first decades after 1204, who had matured in the Komnenian age and viewed their victimization by the Latins through the lens of Hellenic *paideia*. When we turn to the generation that matured after 1204, we find that the evidence for Hellenism is more scattered, fragmented, and later in date than is usually assumed. Crucially, it no longer revolves around high culture but has moved down the social scale. Linguistically, "Hellenes" are now no longer those who have mastered Attic rhetoric but those whose language is Greek. This shift accompanies catastrophic changes in the institutions of cultural life. Gone were the capital's *theatra*, the extensive personal and public libraries, the gold with which to reward and the official posts with which to maintain a regiment of trained orators and literati. The humanism, literary experiments, and classical scholarship that sustained Komnenian Hellenism came to an end with the final version of the *History* of Niketas Choniates. The greatest scholar of the following era, Nikephoros Blemmydes, had to travel throughout Greece and the Aegean to locate manuscripts. This was not an exciting moment of rediscovery, comparable to the manuscript-hunts of the Renaissance, but an inconvenience imposed by cultural collapse. Blemmydes was trying to put some of the pieces back together; as he put it, "our vast culture has been extinguished." Apokaukos too was nostalgic for the starry world of philosophers and orators that was lost when the capital was sacked. A late

---

[121] For refugees, see Robert de Clari, *The Conquest of Constantinople* 80 (p. 80); Michael Choniates, *Monodia for his Brother, Niketas Choniates* 26 (Lambros v. I, p. 354), and *Letters* 94, 129, and 136; Nikolaos Mesarites, *Funeral Oration for his Brother Ioannes* 49 (I, p. 62), and *Letter of the Clergy of Constantinople to the Emperor Theodoros* 1 (II, p. 26); Michael II of Epeiros, Chrysoboullon *for the Monastery of Hilarion* p. 345; Demetrios Chomatenos, *Various Works* 22.5, 50.4 (pp. 87, 186); Nikephoros Blemmydes, *A Partial Account* 2.7, 2.25; Theodoros II Laskaris, *Satire on his Pedagogue* 7 (*op. rh.* p. 160); for the western sources, see Talbot (1993) 244–245; in general, Ahrweiler (1975b) 29; Kordoses (1987) 29–36; also Dendias (1953) and Maltezou (1999) 114–115 for Epeiros. They included or produced leading men, including the future patriarch Germanos II, Nikephoros Blemmydes, Georgios Akropolites, and Georgios Pachymeres, for whose attitude see Lambakis (2004) 22. Architectural imitation: Foss (1996) 95; at Trebizond: Eastmond (2004) 113–114.

thirteenth-century continuator of the *History* of Georgios Akropolites (possibly Theodoros Skoutariotes) claims that Batatzes created libraries in all the cities and that his son, Theodoros II Laskaris, a philosopher in his own right, collected books and scholars with the result that learning, "which had been reduced to nothing after the destruction of the Queen of Cities, now began to revive." Yet with the possible exception of Laskaris himself these schools failed to produce any Hellenists, or "Hellenes," of the kind that had once frequented the Komnenian courts, nor a general culture of satire, eroticism, and heresy.[122]

Looking at Niketas Choniates and Apokaukos, we found that the terms *Graikos* and *Hellen* were now increasingly being used to differentiate the Byzantines from the Latins based on religion and speech, two key components and signifiers of Roman identity. Thus, in some circles, a Hellenism of sorts had already grafted itself upon Byzantine national identity. But there was no systematic reworking of Roman ideology or consensus among the national spokesmen regarding this new development.

The most important text in this connection is a polemical letter sent by the emperor of Nikaia Batatzes to pope Gregorius IX in 1237 in response to a papal missive. The pope had appealed to "the wisdom of the Greeks" – just when his armies had ruined their culture – and, threatening another Crusade, demanded that Batatzes submit to the Roman Church, whose authority was heavenly and not of this earth. He also demanded that Batatzes cease his war against Jean de Brienne, the Latin ruler of Constantinople (1231–1237). To appreciate Batatzes' response we have to remember that he was among the most capable Byzantine emperors. He had driven both rivals and enemies from the field, extended the borders of his realm, was recognized in most of the former lands of Romania as the legitimate emperor of the Romans, and was beloved by his subjects for his justice and his efforts to increase their prosperity through careful administration. He was later revered as a saint in Asia Minor. Such a man had no patience for papal effrontery, and his response, made from a position of strength, reveals the scorn and sarcasm with which most Byzantines must

---

[122] Manuscripts: Nikephoros Blemmydes, *A Partial Account* 1.58, 1.63–64, 2.22, 2.44; extinguished: *Basilikos Andrias* 166; Ioannes Apokaukos, *Letter S* 7 (p. 248); on the context, see Lambropoulos (1988) 155–156. Theodoros Skoutariotes, *Additions to the* History *of Georgios Akropolites* 33, 52 (pp. 286, 297–298); and the letter by Theodoros II Laskaris to the teachers in the school he established: *Letter* 217 (pp. 271–276). Total decline of education (exaggerated): Gregorios of Cyprus, *Encomium for Michael VIII Palaiologos,* in *PG* CXLII (1885) 345–386, here 380–381 (excepting his teacher Akropolites). For education, see Wilson (1983) 218–225; Browning (1983) 71–72; Foss (1996) 67–71; and Constantinides (1982) 5–27 and (2003) 41–44; for science and metaphysics, Pontikos (1992) xv–xvi; for manuscripts and libraries, Katsaros (1980) 377–384.

have treated the claims of the West upon their lands and loyalties, at least when they were not compelled by force and fear to dissemble. It is worth quoting the bulk of this text, which has never been published in English.

Ioannes Doukas, faithful-in-Christ *basileus* and *autokratôr* of the Romans, to the Most Holy pope of elder Rome, Gregorios . . .

When those who were sent by your Holiness approached my Imperial Majesty they gave me a letter, which they claimed was yours and insisted that it was addressed to me. Yet I, seeing that its contents were absurd, could not believe that it was yours and thought that it was by someone who is extremely irrational, whose soul is full of delusion and arrogance . . . This letter says that wisdom reigns in our Hellenic race and streams of it flowed out to all other places as from a spring; also that it is necessary for us, who are so distinguished by this wisdom, not to forget the antiquity of your throne, as though this were a great theorem that requires much wisdom to be understood. But what need is there of wisdom to understand what your throne is? If it stood upon the clouds or was airborne somewhere, perhaps we would need meteorological wisdom to understand it, along with thunderbolts and lightning and other such things . . . But since it is planted firmly on earth, and differs in no way from other episcopal thrones, how is knowledge of it not readily at hand for everyone?

That wisdom springs from our *genos* and that it blossomed first among us before being transmitted to others . . . is said truly. But how did you forget, or, rather, if you did not forget, how did you suppress the fact that, in addition to our reigning wisdom, imperial authority in this world was also bestowed upon our *genos* by Constantine the Great? . . . For who does not know that the rights of his succession passed to our *genos* and that we are his legal heirs and successors? You demand that we not neglect your throne and its authority. Shall we, then, not counter-demand that you observe and recognize our just rights to the authority and power of Constantinople, which rights originated in the days of Constantine the Great and, passing from him through a long series of rulers of our *genos* that extended for about a millennium, has come to us? Indeed, it came to my own progenitors, those of the *genos* of the Doukai and Komnenoi (there is no need to mention others), whose families were Hellenic. These men of my *genos* held sway in Constantinople for hundreds of years, and the Church of Rome as well as its high priests pro-claimed them emperors of the Romans. How, then, does it seem right to you that we do not reign, that you have crowned Ioannes of Pretouna [Jean de Brienne] emperor? What right does he have to the imperial position of the pious Constantine the Great? Whose rights have prevailed in this instance? How is it that you approve unjust and grasping attitudes and hands, and regard as a matter of law that thieving and murderous takeover by which the Latins installed themselves in the city of Constantine? . . . Even though we have been forced to change our location, regarding our rights to that authority we remain unmoved and unchanging, by the grace of God. For he who is emperor rules over a nation (*ethnos*) and a people (*laos*) and a multitude, not over rocks and wooden beams, which make the walls and towers.

This letter also said the following, that your heralds had traversed the entire world preaching the message of the Cross; and that a large number of warriors had assembled for the liberation of the Holy Land . . . When we heard this, our hearts were gladdened and our hopes raised, thinking, as was only reasonable, that these avengers of the Holy Lands would start their work of vengeance with our own country, and impose upon those who have enslaved it the just penalty that they deserve for violating sacred churches, profaning sacred vessels, and perpetrating every kind of unholy deed against Christians. But then your letter went on to call Ioannes "the emperor of Constantinople" and "the dear son" of Your Honor . . . And so we laugh, considering the irony of "Holy Lands" and the jokes at the expense of the Cross. These notions they [i.e., the Crusaders] devised to further their own ambitions and are merely a noble disguise for their love of power and gold.

Batatzes declares that he will never stop in his efforts to reclaim Constantinople, for he does not recognize the jurisdiction and authority of Jean de Brienne. And should more Crusaders come, "we have the means to defend ourselves."

We must be careful in interpreting this sarcastic and amusing document. Batatzes' principal concern is not to announce his Hellenic ancestry but to assert his rights to the Roman imperial legacy. It was in fact Gregorius' letter that put him in the "Greek" position, by praising the wisdom that originated among the Greeks and spread out from them to other nations. Batatzes acknowledges the compliment, but immediately asserts that his *genos*, meaning presumably the Greeks, had also inherited the imperial mantle of Constantine. It is the latter that he cares about chiefly, not his ethnic ancestry. Even when he refers to the families from which he was descended, the Doukai and Komnenoi, and admits that they were Greek, still the point that he emphasizes is that they were the legitimate heirs of Constantine and had been recognized as such by the Church of Rome. In other words, he rejects the position into which the pope apparently wanted to situate him in accordance with western interests, namely of being Greek rather than Roman. There is no question that the latter means infinitely more to him, though this did not mean that he had to renounce the former, given that the Byzantines did not think that having an "ethnic" ancestry had much to do with being Roman. But there is no Greek nationalism here. "Hellenism" is pushed onto Batatzes by the West; he does not "emphasize" it of his own volition, as has been claimed, and he would probably not have mentioned it at all had it not been presupposed by the pope. Nor is it even clear that he takes pride in it, as opposed to it being something that he is forced to acknowledge and argue around. Still, he does not try to refute it, by arguing for instance, as others had in the past, that the Doukai were descended from a

*Roman* family that had moved to the East with Constantine. Perhaps he was unaware of those rhetorical exercises.[123]

Batatzes' letter is significant for the history of Byzantine Hellenism because it is the first instance of a Byzantine accepting that his ethnic origins were Greek in a way that linked him to the "wise" ancients. In other words, Greek ethnicity is valorized by the pope and the emperor because it establishes links to classical culture. In this way the Byzantine Hellenism of the thirteenth century presupposes that of the twelfth.

If Batatzes wanted to further annoy Gregorius, he could not have done much better than to marry the daughter of the German emperor Frederick II Hohenstaufen (in ca. 1244). This anti-papal alliance generated official letters written in Greek at the western court in 1250. Frederick, "emperor of the Romans, Augustus by the grace of God," addresses Batatzes as "*basileus* of the Graikoi,*" but in one of the letters he refers to Batatzes' subjects as Romans and praises their Orthodoxy (yet in a parallel letter to Michael II of Epeiros, Frederick refers to *his* subjects as Graikoi). Where Gregorius had praised the Greeks for spreading their wisdom to other nations, Frederick praises Batatzes' subjects – whoever he thought they were – for spreading Orthodoxy.[124] These documents reveal that Batatzes did not call himself a *Hellen* in diplomatic correspondence and did not expect others to so call him, for it would have cost Frederick no more to do so than it had the pope. Nor does it seems that the ethnonym was employed for internal purposes. In 1252, Iakobos, the former bishop of Ochrid, delivered an address to Batatzes which makes no reference to Greeks, only to Romans; Greece appears here only as a region of the empire. Under Batatzes, then, there was no imperial program to "emphasize" Hellenic descent or anything else Hellenic.[125]

In contrast to his father, the emperor Theodoros II Laskaris (1254–1258) took a personal interest in a more "national" idea of Hellenism, whose terms we can now put into perspective. Laskaris was groomed for the

---

[123] My interpretation of the letter is the opposite of Christou (2003) 134 and takes issue with Vakalopoulos (1974) 76; Angold (1975b) 56; Gounaridis (1986) 251; Garzya (1992) 32; and Angelov (2005) 302 n. 51, according to whom Batatzes "emphasized" or "boasted of his Hellenic descent." See Grumel (1930) for the letter of Gregorius and a French translation of that of Batatzes, whose authenticity is established. For Batatzes' reign, see Angold (1975a) *passim*; for his canonization, Macrides (1981) 69–71; Polemis (1983); and Dagron (2003) 152; for the Doukai's ancestry, see p. 89 above.

[124] Frederick II, *Greek Letters* 1.20 (Michael II of Epeiros); 2.1, 2.19–21 and 4.1–2 (Batatzes) (pp. 320, 323). For the diplomacy of the period, citing previous bibliography, see Merendino (1975); Martin (2002) esp. 479–480, 482 for the titles.

[125] Greece: Iakobos of Bulgaria, *Address to Ioannes III Doukas Batatzes* (pp. 86, 89); for the context, Angelov (2003) 68.

throne and studied under the most learned scholars of his age, Blemmydes and Akropolites, though both later became his enemies. He was an able ruler but grew suspicious of the aristocracy and was cruel toward the end of his reign. He was an accomplished writer and left a large collection of letters and many rhetorical, philosophical, theological, and satirical works. Some of these were not published until very recently; none have benefited from literary analysis. Laskaris' style is difficult and uses many words that he coined himself. His personality is engaging though often comes across as pessimistic, morose, and distracted by his weaknesses (he suffered bad health and epilepsy). He was serious in the pursuit of wisdom and despised worldly glory, probably genuinely. He took his duties as a Christian monarch very seriously, but his works show a preference for classical *exempla*, modes, and genres.[126]

In many passages, Laskaris casually refers to Hellenes where others would have referred to Romans. In an *Encomium* to his father he refers to the "Hellenic breasts" of the imperial soldiers, those "sons of the Hellenes." In the same text, Alexander the Great is mentioned as a former king of the Hellenes, implying that Batatzes rules the same nation (except that his subjects are Christian).[127] In two letters Laskaris, now emperor, refers to Byzantine soldiers simply as Hellenes. "The nations move against us," he says in another letter to Blemmydes, naming Persians, Italians, Bulgarians, and Serbs. "The Hellenes (τὸ Ἑλληνικὸν) must help themselves, alone, looking to their own resources." To his close friend Georgios Mouzalon he wrote that God placed many Persians under the authority of the Hellenic race (*phylon*) for the good of Romaïs (Romania). In another letter, he awaits the return of his ambassador, the bishop of Sardeis, "from Europe to Greece (τὸ Ἑλληνικὸν)." This *Greece* does not necessarily refer only to Asia Minor, as is supposed, because the bishop was in Rome and so the reference may be more general; it may refer to all the lands inhabited by Greeks. In a parallel letter to that bishop, Laskaris asks directly when he will return from Europe to Greece, specifying that he will have to pass through Thrake before reaching "inner Asia." So his conception of "Greece" was probably not limited to Asia Minor.[128] This is a crucial reversal of prior

---

[126] For an introduction, see Krikonis' edition of *On Christian Theology*, 15–40; Georgiopoulou (1990) 1–67; for the letters, Heisenberg (1900); for his vocabulary, Trapp (2003) 142–143; for his political thought, Angelov (2004) 511–516.

[127] Theodoros II Laskaris, *Encomium for Ioannes III Doukas Batatzes* 6, 14 (*op. rh.* pp. 34, 53, 54).

[128] Hellenic soldiers: Theodoros II Laskaris, *Letters* 202 and 204 (pp. 250, 253); help themselves: 44 (p. 58); Persians: 214 (p. 266); Sardeis: 118 (p. 165) and 125 (pp. 174–176). In general, see Angold (1975b) 64–65; Koder (1996) 5 and (2003) 310–312; for the embassy to Rome, Gill (1979) 91–92;

Byzantine usage. In the past, "Greeks" had been those who lived in Greece; now "Greece" was wherever Greeks lived.

This last letter also reveals that Laskaris' use of the Hellenic ethnonym was still polysemic. He recounts there a philosophical debate at the court with a German margrave (Berthold of Hohenburg), whom he praises for his manners and for being educated in both the Italian and the Hellenic *paideia*. The latter, of course, was common to both ancient and "modern" Hellenes and, as we will see, is clearly understood by Laskaris as a link between them. But when Laskaris says that the debate included "the theology of the Hellenes," he is clearly referring to the ancients only. He then boasts that the debate reflected glory on the Hellenes: "a victory of the Hellenes over the Italians." These now must be his own people, who presumably do not share "the theology of the [ancient] Hellenes." Yet a few lines later he calls them Ausones (and casually calls them Romans in his various works). In short, *Hellen* was for him a way of saying *Roman* – these are Romans *as* Greeks – though it does not always mean that. Conventional meanings could supervene. In a liturgical oration he dismissed "Hellenic speculation on nature" as "impious." But we should not make too much of this typecast expression that was virtually required by the context.[129]

The Greeks had typically been perceived as foreigners by the Byzantines, even by Psellos. Laskaris was the first who was willing to identify with them as their direct intellectual *and* ethnic heir. In a letter to Hagiotheodorites he admits that, while his correspondent was well versed in the Gospels, he himself was unworthy of them and, anyway, preferred "the Hellenic dialect, which I love more than breathing itself" (i.e., Attic over Biblical Greek). Elsewhere he rehabilitates the teachings of "the most philosophical Hellenes, that *genos* which thought so well and so powerfully." Of course, the need to rehabilitate implies a certain distance between "us" and "them." But in his accounts of the debate with the margrave, Laskaris is clearly proud of his own Hellenes, who possess Hellenic wisdom and can defeat the Latins with it. "The whole company of the margrave was routed by Hellenic philosophy," he boasts.[130] In an anti-Latin treatise ostensibly on

there is no question that the first letter cited here refers to some kind of military reform, but it is not clear that it spells out a plan to dismiss foreign mercenaries and recruit only native Greeks, as Angold (1975a) 185 and others assert.

[129] Debate: Theodoros II Laskaris, *Letters* 125, 40 (pp. 174–176, 51–52), on which see Angold (1995) 527–528; impious: *Oration on Our Surpassingly Holy Mistress, the Theotokos* 12–13. Berthold IV, margrave of Hohenburg (in the Bavarian Nordgau), was married to the sister (or niece) of Frederick II Hohenstaufen's favorite mistress, the mother of his illegitimate children, including Constanze, who, renamed Anna, married Laskaris' father Batatzes (his second wife).

[130] Hellenic dialect: Theodoros II Laskaris, *Letter* 216 (p. 268); philosophical *genos*: *Letter* 109 (p. 152); margrave: *Letters* 40 and 125 (pp. 51–52, 174–176).

the problem of the procession of the Holy Spirit, he digresses at length to prove that because Greece is in the geographical middle of the earth – he even furnishes a diagram – "the Hellenic *genos* is superior to all others on account of its position and good climate and therefore in cleverness and science." He offers the ancient writers themselves as proof of this superiority (those from whom he took the argument in the first place), and makes his polemical intent clear: "every kind of philosophy and knowledge was either an invention of the Hellenes or was improved by them . . . But you, O Italian, in whom do you boast?" If Hellenic *logos* has been quiet, he explains, that is because of circumstance and Latin aggression. The *panhellenion* is now free, at Nikaia at any rate, "and Nikaia is comparable to Athens . . . Go to school, if you will, and learn that philosophizing is of the Hellenes." Laskaris follows this with a provocative and evocative assertion of Hellenic continuity: "the same air that was then, is now ours too; the Hellenic language is ours; and we are drawn from their blood . . . But what wisdom ever came from *you* to *us*?"[131]

That, at any rate, was how Laskaris presented his case to "the Italian." It was a biological, geographical, linguistic, and cultural argument for continuity and was made ostensibly in support of a theological position, even though the digression takes on a life of its own. In a letter to Blemmydes, however, Laskaris sees matters more pessimistically, though the premise of continuity remains the same: he there expresses a fear that philosophy will flee "from us – for it started with the Hellenes, who despise it now as foreign – and go to the barbarians." The same continuity is implied as in the anti-Latin treatise, but it gives less comfort; the modern Greeks are not elevated by their ancient patrimony but are rather unfavorably compared to their ancestors. This passage, moreover, is the first known instance of Byzantine intellectual insecurity toward the West, and it is no accident that it is expressed by the first Byzantine author who believed in continuity from ancient Greece.[132]

A stronger argument for continuity had never been made in Byzantium. Laskaris presents himself and his subjects as the biological and intellectual heirs of the Greeks. He believes that their bravery in battle, their language, philosophy, theology, and climate were superior to those of anyone else. But if we prioritize the elements of continuity, we find that the most

---

[131] Theodoros II Laskaris, *On Christian Theology* 7.1–10 (pp. 137–143). For Nikaia as Athens, see his *Praise of Nikaia* 3 (*op. rh.* pp. 71–73). For Greece in the middle, see, e.g., Hippokrates, *Airs, Waters, Places* 12; pseudo-Plato, *Epinomis* 987d; Aristotle, *Politics* 1327b18 ff.; Ailios Aristeides, *Panathenaic Oration* 15–16. Cf. Theodoros Metochites in Garzya (1992) 33.
[132] Theodoros II Laskaris, *Letter* 5 (p. 8); see Clucas (1981) 243.

important one for Laskaris was philosophical. In other words, he did not begin with a holistic belief in continuity which then happened to entail that he had a claim to ancient philosophy; rather, it seems that he identified with ancient philosophy through his studies – "I am an Athenian," he declared in the anti-Latin treatise – to such an extent that he claimed it as a national prerogative, explaining the persistence of philosophy in the land of Greece through the argument from continuity. That argument was not hard to make, for language, climate, history, and even blood were all there if one cared to see things that way. What is remarkable, perhaps, is that no other Byzantine, especially in the Komnenian period, had yet to make the connection in that way. It was now advocated in response to unique circumstances and from an idiosyncratic point of view that fused philosophical, historical, and national concerns; Laskaris was very much a philosopher-king. Hellenic continuity was, then, yet another argument in his arsenal of theological and cultural polemic.

In short, Laskaris finally fused the two meanings of Hellenism whose complex interwoven history we have been tracking throughout this study: *paideia* and collective "national" identity. Classical culture did not for him define the Roman *elite* against other Romans but had for the first time become a defining *national* quality and a matter for collective pride. But the nation in question was the Roman one: we should make no mistake about this. Laskaris was no less a Roman than any other Byzantine; he did not replace Romania with Hellas. What he did do was, first, accept the Greek ethnic origin of his nation, as had his father in 1237 (though without any particular enthusiasm), and, second, stake national pride on Greek *paideia* in the face of the Latin colonial and theological challenge. What enabled this transformation of elite culture into a national quality was the fact that Laskaris was *both* an emperor in an age of increased national anxiety *and* a trained Hellenist in the tradition of the twelfth-century humanists. Whereas the latter had used their Hellenism as an exclusive badge of class, Laskaris fused it with Roman national pride. This combination, ironically, had not been possible under the aristocratic and militaristic Komnenoi. It is interesting, moreover, that Laskaris seems to have been unaware that he was innovating. In all likelihood, he did not know the history of Byzantine Hellenism as we do now.

Interestingly, Laskaris' "holistic" Hellenism seems to have included an archaeological aspect as well, which postulated distinctions between ancient glory and modern worthlessness in a way that foreshadowed the moodier aspects of Hellenism in our era. Now, the Byzantines had always been interested in ancient ruins – Athens seems to have supported a tourist infrastructure – but here ruins were for the first time entangled in broader debates about identity.[133] Here is what Laskaris wrote to Akropolites about the city of Pergamos.

It received us, though it is difficult to gain a view of the whole of it and no less difficult to climb to the top. It is full of sights, but these have aged and withered with time, showing us, as if in a mirror, the splendor and magnificence of those who built them. They are full of Hellenic genius and represent its wisdom. The city displays these things and reproaches us, as their descendants, with the majesty of ancestral glory. For these things are awe-inspiring compared to modern restorations . . . In the midst of the buildings you can see decrepit huts and the ruins of abandoned houses, a sight that causes much grief. What mouse-holes are to our houses one might say that the latter are compared to these buildings that have passed away. And if the analogy holds with regard to their residents, O woe for the misfortune of those who live today! How unequal, how inferior! On either side of the walls of the great theater there are circular towers made of regular stonework and encircled by friezes. These were neither made nor conceived by anyone alive today. It is amazing even to look upon them . . . The foot of the hill is more beautiful than the peak, as is the city of the dead than that of the living. Beholding this city, then, how depressed we were, how skittish; we were joyously glad and weeping and laughing at the same time.[134]

We see here the misery of the "modern" Greek, fated to exult in those very works that prove to him his own worthlessness. "It is a terrible thing not only to be unable to surpass the works of your father, but to be unable to understand them."[135] Speaking of fathers and forefathers, Laskaris was always aware that as an emperor he ruled in the shadow of his father, a far greater man than he whom he praised and idolized in many works. He also knew that he would never rival his teacher Blemmydes in philosophy. The insecurities of ancestor-worship were a part of his life from the beginning. By accepting the Greeks as his ancestors he could at least hold his head up high when talking to westerners, despite the fact that he ruled a corner of southeastern Europe surrounded by Bulgarians and Turks. But that pride came at a high price, for as a Greek he was doomed to be inferior (again) in his own eyes.

This is a turning point in the evolution of Hellenism, for the ruins of the ancient cities had not elicited such reactions before, at least not before Michael Choniates arrived in Athens. Both Choniates and Laskaris vacillated between a depressive admiration of antiquity and the official position of their faith that no matter how great the ancients appeared to be, Christians were superior.[136] Both were trained Hellenists, which made

---

[133] Kaldellis (2008).   [134] Theodoros II Laskaris, *Letter* 80 (pp. 107–108).   [135] Dimou (1975) 54.
[136] For Choniates, see above; Theodoros II Laskaris, *Praise of Nikaia* 3 (*op. rh.* pp. 71–73).

them more sensitive to what the world had lost when ancient Greek culture was extinguished (though they did not specify when exactly that happened). In reading Laskaris' description of Pergamos, "one is reminded of Petrarch's similar experience when he visited Rome a hundred years later. But there is a difference: the significance of Laskaris' attitude is that he contrasts the wretchedness of his age, not with the good old days of Justinian, but with the time of the Hellenes."[137] We may speak of Romantic Hellenism. In fact, we could even go further and postulate a Hellenic nationalism. After all, Laskaris calls his nation and its soldiers Greeks; believes that they are descended from the ancient Greeks, whose *paideia*, language, and blood they all share; calls their land Greece and admires his ancestors' monuments. Only religion had fundamentally changed, but Laskaris is generally silent about that. In short, none of the foundations on which the Greek nation was (re)imagined in modern times was lacking in his conception; he even had some of the same emotional reactions and archaeological fantasies.[138]

Still, there is something unsatisfying about this interpretation. We expect the birth of a new nation – or the rebirth of an old one – to be accompanied by more self-consciousness and ideological turmoil. Laskaris never confronts head-on the crucial problems that would be addressed in the fifteenth century by Neo-Hellenist thinkers (Georgios Gemistos Plethon and Laonikos Chalkokondyles), and later by the founders of modern Greece. In scattered texts and letters, he took advantage of cultural attributes that lay near at hand (the land, the language, the philosophy); he did not systematically set out to prove anything or explain what exactly it meant to be a Greek beyond possessing those attributes which happened to come to the Byzantines through the depths of time. Where had the Greeks been for the past two millennia? What was their relation to the Romans? Laskaris does not tell us. It was enough for him to proudly or polemically cite this or that, here and there. His references to Greeks – modern and ancient – are sporadic and casual, as though he is not saying anything new. In a sense, he is not. His national Hellenism rides comfortably because it is carried by the existing nation: Romania. Laskaris has merely shifted his focus toward the Hellenic end of the spectrum of Byzantium's cultural background, but this is perhaps more flavor than substance. He scatters references but does not, in the end, build up

[137] Mango (1963) 69.
[138] Cf. in Politis (1998) 4: "I wondered at them [ancient ruins] and bewailed / our race of today and was full of tears."

anything solid or independent out of them. His Hellenism is only an expression of his Roman nationalism, which has been modulated, as so often before, to meet new challenges.

Besides, Laskaris was probably alone in all this. We do not know whether he was the only one crying and laughing at Pergamos (or what his companions thought of that). In all likelihood, they could accommodate to his moods, for that is what his Hellenism was, ultimately. Yet none of the writers who came out of the empire of Nikaia went as far as he did in identifying Greece and Rome. It is worth looking at three of them, briefly, even though they wrote after the end of the Nikaian period (1261). The comparison reveals that we are not dealing with a general trend but separate and idiosyncratic formulations, as each writer came to grips in a different way with the complex ideological tensions of the thirteenth century.

### THE INTELLECTUALS OF NIKAIA

Nikephoros Blemmydes, Laskaris' mentor in philosophy and later his bitter enemy, was born in Constantinople before the fall and became the leading scholar of his age (1197–ca. 1269). He was an able logician, a pious monk, and even went on a pilgrimage to Jerusalem. He was less of a humanist, in the manner of Psellos and the twelfth-century sophists, and more interested in theology, logic, and natural science. He was also narrow-minded, arrogant, self-righteous, insubordinate, and ill-at-ease with human company.[139] He was harried by charges of homosexuality and boasted in his autobiography of the favors done him by those in high places, especially God. He recounts four assassination attempts made against him and carefully narrates the deaths of his enemies. He probably believed that he was a saint and hoped he would be revered after his death. He wrote the autobiography partly to promote this claim.[140]

Blemmydes' technical works have received very little attention and some have not been properly published. We will limit our discussion to the *Basilikos Andrias* (*Imperial Statue*), a 'mirror of princes' consisting of 219 short aphorisms addressed to Laskaris, and the autobiography, because these are the works in which he mentions, respectively, pagan Hellenes and modern Greeks. Neither work has so far been the object of much discussion.

---

[139] Cf. Nikephoros Blemmydes, *A Partial Account* 1.36, 1.38, 2.41.
[140] Deaths: Agapitos (1998c); self-canonization: Munitiz (1981); in general, Angold (1995) 554–560; for his education, Constantinides (1982) 7–27.

Probably in conformity with Laskaris' tastes, there are no Christian *exempla* in the *Andrias*. Blemmydes uses classical models to illustrate secular virtues along with a few Old Testament figures for religious ones. His model of kingship is Trajan (whom he calls Nerva). Trajan was so serene, compassionate, and merciful that he was forgiven his ignorance and "impiety" (i.e., paganism) by the intercession of pope Gregorius I.[141] "Compassion," Blemmydes declares, "outweighs impiety if it is supported by the prayers of a righteous man" (61–64). Is this a plea for Laskaris to curb his suspicion and cruelty? And is the "righteous man" who can pray on his behalf Blemmydes himself? Blemmydes also praises Kyros and Alexander the Great (86) and "the Athenians of old, who divided their activities between the exercise of letters and law, and that of land and naval warfare" (136–139). This reminds us of Choniates' frustrated praise of the Greeks in the letter to Drimys, and we find that Blemmydes' classical turn is inspired by the same event, the decline of Byzantium in the years before 1204. "If people of this kind are difficult to find today, it is because they are ignored, while the wicked are preferred . . . Why else has our vast culture been extinguished . . . except because we dismissed people of this kind and selected their opposites to hold both secular and spiritual offices?" (165–166). Greek virtue was apparently good enough for the Church now.

The valorization of antiquity in the *Basilikos Andrias* may have been designed to appeal to its addressee, who loved its language, philosophy, and monuments. Oddly, there is little evidence that Blemmydes himself was inspired by the ancients. Yet in his autobiography, which he wrote after the recapture of Constantinople in 1261, he calls the Romans of the state of Nikaia "Hellenes" on one occasion (and never calls them Romans) and once refers to the Asian lands of Nikaia as "this *here* Hellas," i.e., as opposed to the Greek mainland.[142] As with Laskaris, we have here a region being called Greece because Greeks lived in it, rather than the reverse, which had been the rule for centuries in Byzantium. But it would be a mistake to conclude from these passages that Blemmydes shared Laskaris' Hellenic interpretation of the Roman nation. The explanation for his usage lies in a completely different direction. Blemmydes spent much of his life in theological controversy against the Latins. It was they who were the real "Romans" for him, being members of the Roman Church.[143] Blemmydes

---

[141] For this tale, see pseudo-Ioannes of Damaskos (Michael Synkellos?), *On those who have been laid to rest in the faith* 16, in *PG* XCV (1864) 247–278, here 261–264. For an introduction to the *Statue*, see Christou (1996).

[142] Nikephoros Blemmydes, *A Partial Account* 1.6, 2.25.

[143] Nikephoros Blemmydes, *A Partial Account* 1.47, 2.25 ff., 2.50 f., 2.61.

was not emotionally attached to the ethnonym Hellen, as was Laskaris, given that he uses it only once in a contemporary sense and probably only to avoid confusing the Byzantines of Nikaia with the Romans of (Elder) Rome, against whom he was engaged in bitter polemic; he probably meant nothing more by "Hellen" than "Greek-speaker." Nor does he seem to have cared much for the Roman label either, given how casually he surrendered it to his foes. Religious identity was more important to him than to Laskaris. Blemmydes was, moreover, unique in respecting the independence of the states of Rhodes and Epeiros and believed that they should not have been absorbed by Nikaia against their will.[144] "Hellen" in a national sense meant as little to him as "Roman." To a casual observer, then, Blemmydes and Laskaris seem to belong to a "Hellenic" movement, but this is true only in the sense that their Hellenism was a response to Latin colonialism. When we look closer, their positions appear to have been as different as their personalities.

The statesman Georgios Akropolites (1217–1282) was the student of Blemmydes and a teacher of Laskaris. Yet his outlook on these problems was different from either of theirs. In his *History* of the years 1204–1261, Akropolites never calls anyone a Greek. His Romans are fully Roman and proud of it. When Michael Palaiologos (the future Michael VIII) was asked to submit to an ordeal to prove his innocence in a plot, Akropolites has him respond that ordeals do not accord with Roman or ecclesiastical law. "If I were born of barbarians and raised with barbarian customs, then I would submit to a trial in the barbarian way. But as I am a Roman born of Romans, I expect to be tried in accordance with Roman law" (50).[145] "Greek" in Akropolites is used only in connection with language (76) and geography (80), a usage that conforms to ancient Byzantine convention and bypasses the developments of the twelfth or thirteenth century.

Akropolites' indifference to the name Hellen may be linked to the fact that he was one of those few Byzantines who actually was inspired by an ecumenical Roman vision. At least, he invoked it for rhetorical purposes in a treatise *Against the Latins* that he wrote while imprisoned in Epeiros in the late 1250s. He begins by addressing the Latins as "Romans, you who come from elder Rome; I wish to call you brothers because we *think* and *believe* the same way (*homognômones* and *homophrones*)." In other words, the transnational "Roman" identity evoked here excludes precisely the elements

---

[144] Nikephoros Blemmydes, *A Partial Account* 1.81, 2.23, called "highly idiosyncratic" by Angold (1975b) 61–62.

[145] See Macrides (2003) 206, citing previous bibliography.

that constituted and defined Byzantine Romania as a community of law, political unity, language, custom, history, and *ethnos*, and had separated it from other Christian nations. This unity of belief, he continues in the introduction, is what God intended when he sent Christ to mankind, so that there would not be, "in the words of the great Paul, either Greek or barbarian or Skythian or Jew or any other ethnic name, but all would be named after Christ solely." We used to be united and brotherly, he adds, but he who first divided man from God has separated us also. Would it not be better for all nations (*ethnē*) to be united in Christ?[146]

After discussing the theological issues, Akropolites concludes his treatise by wondering why there is so much strife and disunity in the Christian world. This introduces a remarkable passage that deserves to be quoted.

It seems, O Italians, that you no longer remember our ancient harmony . . . But no other nations were ever as harmonious as the Graikoi and the Italians. And this was only to be expected, for science and learning came to the Italians from the Graikoi. And after that point, so that they need no longer use their ethnic names, a New Rome was built to complement the Elder one, so that all could be called Romans after the common name of such great cities, and have the same faith and the same name for it. And just as they received that most noble name from Christ, so too did they take upon themselves the national (*ethnikon*) name [i.e., of Roman]. And everything else was common to them: magistracies, laws, literature, city councils, law courts, piety itself; so that there was nothing that was not common to those of Elder and New Rome. But O how things have changed![147]

The events of the thirteenth century had affected Akropolites' outlook after all. Instead of concentrating on what separated him from the Latins, which is what Hellenism represented for Laskaris, he looked in the Byzantine rhetorical repertoire for something that could bring them together. He professed belief in an ecumenical Roman ideal that had been synthesized long ago from two parts, the Italians and the Graikoi, who had then fallen out for reasons that Akropolites does not specify. He admits that his own people had once been Graikoi and that they had apparently become so again now. Yet no Byzantine prior to 1204 would have bothered to think such a thing. Akropolites' ideological reconstitution of Roman unity from those two constituent parts was an exercise that only the conditions of the thirteenth century made possible. Its counterpart on the Latin side can be found in the *Chronicle of the Morea*, where the

---

[146] Georgios Akropolites, *Against the Latins* 1.1 (v. II, pp. 30–31); in general, see Richter (1984).
[147] Georgios Akropolites, *Against the Latins* 2.27 (v. II, p. 64). See Magdalino (1988) 197–198; Gounaridis (1986) 250–251.

Crusaders explain that Franks and Romans (i.e., Byzantines) had once been obedient to the pope yet in time these Romans – "who were also called Hellenes . . . but had taken their name from Rome" – broke away from Rome in their arrogance. This is the same history, only viewed from the other side.[148]

Like his contemporaries, Akropolites seems not to have thought through the implications of his argument. He does not explain how his nation was simultaneously Greek and Roman. Moreover, while we can discern cultural pride in his claim that the ancient Graikoi had given science and learning to the Italians, he is vague on what the Italians had given in return. This suggests a form of Greek chauvinism. But we should not equate his position with that of Laskaris. In fact, it is antithetical in important ways, as Akropolites values being Roman over the cultural or ethnic particularities of his own "nation." And he calls his side of the Roman *oikoumenê* Graikoi rather than Hellenes, by which he elsewhere designates pagans.[149] He is willing, at least for the purposes of this treatise, to set aside the cultural differences that separated Graikoi and Italians in order to project union on a higher plane, something in which Laskaris, with his Hellenic pride, gives no sign of being interested. This more Roman ideology may be due to the fact that Akropolites was writing after the restoration of the empire to Constantinople and his siding with Michael VIII Palaiologos, who overthrew the Laskarid dynasty and whose diplomacy aimed at restoring to the Byzantines their preeminent place in the Christian world.

It seems, then, that three of the leading intellectuals of Nikaia – Laskaris, Blemmydes, and Akropolites, who knew each other well and were bound to each other through politics and pedagogy – had entirely different ideas about Greeks and Romans. There was no official Nikaian ideology of national Hellenism, only the idiosyncratic reactions of different writers. Laskaris was a Hellenic enthusiast (at least in his literary endeavors); Blemmydes an opponent of the Roman Church; and Akropolites a champion of Roman ecumenism (at least in rhetorical address to the Latins). It seems, moreover, that these men did not much discuss the issue among themselves, and probably had to work out the individual meanings of "Roman," "Hellene," and "Graikos" from the context of each other's works, just as we have to do. Still, the idea that the Byzantines were

[148] *Chronicle of the Morea* /89–800.
[149] Georgios Akropolites, *Against the Latins* 2.1 (v. II, p. 45); *Commentary on Sayings of Gregorios of Nazianzos* 6–12 (v. II, pp. 75–78); in ibid. 4 (p. 72) he uses the expression "both Hellenes and barbarians" to mean "everyone." For this, see p. 288 above.

somehow descended from the ancient Greeks was gaining ground and appears casually in the most unlikely places. In the run-up to the Council of Lyons (1274), when the pope and the emperor Michael VIII were attempting to enforce unity with Rome on the Byzantine Church and people, the patriarch Ioseph commissioned an analysis of the problems facing union. In a theoretical discussion of the meaning of names, the patriarch declared casually that "although we are Hellenes by *genos*, we call ourselves Romans, and rightly, for we have inherited this name from New Rome. We have the same personal names as many of the Italians, and we have *officia* in our *politeia*, in accordance with the words of their language." Like Akropolites, then, Ioseph had accepted the Hellenes as the ethnic ancestors of the Byzantines, and his conception of Roman identity revolved around the politically defined community of Romania, not ethnicity. The patriarch was likewise closer to Ioannes III Doukas Batatzes than to his son Laskaris in that he was far more interested in establishing the Byzantines' right to New Rome than in playing up their Greek ancestry, even though he granted it in the face of Latin polemic.[150]

We turn, finally, to the scholar and theologian Gregorios of Cyprus (1241–1290, born Georgios), who wanted to study with Blemmydes but was rejected by him; after 1261, he took up with Akropolites (his focus was on Aristotle). Eventually, he became patriarch of Constantinople (1283–1289). And yet despite his pedagogical background, he was closer to Blemmydes and even to Laskaris when it came to the issues at hand. As patriarch he was anti-Latin and rejected imperially sponsored attempts to effect union. At the beginning of his own brief autobiography (meant as a preface to his collected letters), he says that he was descended from the "Hellenic" population of the island of Cyprus, which was "enslaved by the Italians." He attended some of "the schools of the Romans," but these taught in Latin, "an alien and bastard tongue" that gave him difficulty. These "Romans," then, were Latins. That was when he decided to seek instruction in "the tongue of the Hellenes" and, against his parents' wishes, traveled to Nikaia, which he hoped would be a new Athens. He wanted to study with Blemmydes, who, he heard, was "the wisest man not only among our Hellenes (τῶν ἐφ᾽ ἡμῶν) but of all people."[151]

---

[150] Ioseph I, *Apologia* (p. 215); for the context, see the editors' introduction; Nicol (1972) V, esp. 468–470; and Gill (1979) 128–129.

[151] Gregorios of Cyprus, *Concerning his own Life* (only a few pages long); see Constantinides (1982) 25–26, 32–33; Hinterberger (1999) 354–358. For Gregorios as a scholar, Wilson (1983) 223–225; for his patriarchate, Papadakis (1996), and ch. 2 for his early life. For Cyprus, see pp. 353–354 above; for ethnic-linguistic communities there, see Moschonas (1993b).

Gregorios exhibits a "Hellenic" outlook that is slightly stronger than that of Blemmydes but does not reach the level of a Laskaris. He was certainly proud of his education, which included the virtues of "Atticism and true Hellenism" (in this context a technical term referring to vocabulary).[152] We should be cautious, however, in reading the Hellenic protestations of his autobiography, for he had openly been accused by Ioannes Bekkos, his predecessor in the patriarchate and a theological opponent, of being non-Roman. "What's wrong with you people," Bekkos had complained, "that you often revile *me* so much, who am born and raised among Romans and from Romans, and receive *that* man with praise, who was born and raised among the Italians; not only that, who only affects our dress and speech?"[153] Ethnic imputations, as we have seen, were a standard weapon in the arsenal of what were otherwise purely internal disputes in Byzantium.[154] In this context, Gregorios' emphasis on Hellenism in his autobiography serves, paradoxically, to affirm that he is a genuine Roman, because on Cyprus being Greek meant being non-Latin. "Hellenes" are now the ultimate insiders, for no foreigner could ever be that – the ultimate irony of Byzantine Hellenism!

But Gregorios' Hellenic leanings cannot entirely be explained away as defensive rhetoric. In a work on St. Georgios he notes that the saint's fatherland, Kappadokia, was distinguished because it had been settled from the start by "Hellenes, that *genos* devoted to the nature of *logos*." The rough Kappadokians made unlikely Hellenes, so what did Gregorios mean by this? That St. Georgios was a Byzantine saint rather than a Latin? That his parents were educated? The narrative, set under Diocletian, also contains references to "the conversion of the Hellenes to Christ."[155] No overview of Hellenic history is provided that would clarify these casual and somewhat contradictory references, a problem that we have encountered in many Byzantine Hellenists. Although Gregorios usually refers to Byzantines as Romans, in a work praising Andronikos II Palaiologos he claims that the emperor's *genos* was drawn from "the most illustrious of the Hellenes and the Romans of this place," i.e., of Constantinople. It is again frustrating that he does not explain the difference between the two.[156] Gregorios, like

---

[152] Gregorios of Cyprus, *Concerning his own Life* (p. 187). For "technical" Hellenism, see p. 187 above.
[153] Georgios Pachymeres, *History* 7.34 (v. III, p. 101); for the context, Papadakis (1996) 38, 74.
[154] See p. 94 above.
[155] Gregorios of Cyprus, *Praise of St. Georgios* 4, 19, 41, in *PG* CXLII (1885) 299–346, here 304, 317, 340. For stereotypes about Kappadokians, see p. 96 n. 168 above.
[156] Gregorios of Cyprus, *Encomium for Andronikos II Palaiologos*, in *PG* CXLII (1885) 387–418, here 393.

his older contemporaries surveyed above, gives us some of the answers but not the questions.

To conclude, we perceive in Gregorios, as in Laskaris, Blemmydes, and other writers of that age, a powerful ideological crisis. The Roman and Christian identities that the Byzantines had worn comfortably for 800 years had now become sources of tension. After 1204, Christianity no longer differentiated them sufficiently from their national enemies. *Roman*, like-wise, could refer to the Byzantines, but it could also refer to the Roman Church, a bitter enemy to the end. *Graikos* was also not a term that the Byzantines could easily accept, being pejorative and imposed by those outside. It could be ameliorated as "Greek-speaker" (this was attempted by Nikolaos Mesarites) and at least it avoided the semantic problems of "Hellen." *Hellen* did step in to fill the breach, providing the Byzantines with an ethnonym of which they could be proud and which clearly differ-entiated them from the Latins, but it carried with it too much baggage from a Christian point of view and implied histories that no one wanted to write. No one was yet interested in hammering out the historical and ideological problems of that word. So we see in the changes and complex-ities of its usage the *effects* of a revolution, but unfortunately we cannot see the revolution itself. An ideological crisis that churned beneath the surface of our texts tossed up Hellenes in the thirteenth century, but did not produce a satisfying explanation of where they came from, of how they were related to the ancient builders of famous cities, to the authors of that great literature, to the deluded pagans who converted to Christianity, or for that matter to the Romans of Romania. Those problems would preoccupy later generations of Byzantine thinkers, and are still with us. In due course, they produced hybrids such as *Graikoromaios* and *Graikolatinos*, *Latinellinas* and *Romaioellinas*, *Romanos* vs. *Romaios*, and also *Philoromaios* (for unionists).[157] The Greek nation would emerge again many centuries later but to do so it had to reverse the old polarities. Whereas in Byzantium Hellenism stood for the (pagan) culture of the intellectual elite of Romania, in the nineteenth and twentieth centuries "Romiosyne" stood for the demotic (orthodox) culture of the vast majority of the Greek nation. So the Byzantines were always suspicious of Hellenism, while the modern Greeks have not yet made sense of their Roman background. With few exceptions, both avoided the fundamental problems.

---

[157] See Mantouvalou (1979–1985) *passim*, esp. 182, 195; Gounaridis (1996); Politis (1998).

This paradoxical shift was caused in part by changing attitudes in the West toward the classical Greek legacy. In the thirteenth century, the Latin prelates and warlords who invaded Romania had a vague knowledge of what "Athenian wisdom" meant, as we saw above in Gregorius IX's letter to Batatzes. But this never amounted to more than rhetorical flourish; it never influenced their treatment of conquered Byzantines.[158] In the nineteenth century, by contrast, Europe had passed through several phases of intense and even culturally pathological fixation on ancient Greece, and many were eager to see in the modern Greek nation the struggling descendants of Perikles. So whereas in the thirteenth century Hellenism had allowed some Byzantine thinkers to mark off their culture from the West, in the nineteenth Hellenism served to create bridges between Greece and the West and generate support. The western market for all things Greek in turn spurred the Hellenization of the newly liberated country.

Can we speak of national Hellenism in the thirteenth century? As an elite preoccupation, Hellenism can thrive in small circles, and Attic verbs with 136 different forms create their own exclusivities. But mass dissemination is required for Hellenism to become a national identity. Unfortunately, we do not know how many Byzantines accepted the new usage. Blemmydes (an itinerant monk and popular theologian), Laskaris (an emperor who avoided the aristocracy and promoted officials from the lower class), and Gregorios of Cyprus (a patriarch who sided with the majority of Byzantines against union), would have opened the ears of many to this new Hellenism. No one who heard this new talk, from the common man to Michael Palaiologos himself, would have imagined that the referent was paganism. But what did they think *was* being said? Merely that they spoke Greek as opposed to the Italians' Latin? Or could they have imagined some kind of ethnic continuity with the ancient Greeks? Unfortunately, we will probably never know how far down the new Hellenism traveled; nor, for that matter, do we know how deeply it set roots into those who offer our conflicting evidence for it.

A major change had, however, occurred. By AD 1300 the Byzantines had overcome their Christian inhibitions regarding Greece and, in the face of Latin aggression, were prepared to reinterpret many sites of their culture. In the past, foreigners became *Romans* when they changed their dress, language, customs, faith, and mentality; by the fourteenth century, the

---

[158] See also Innocentius III, Baudouin I, and others in Lock (1995) 16, 45, 162, 214, 301; Ciggaar (1996) 90–91, 322; but cf. 260. These expressions, taken on faith from ancient Roman writers, were rare in comparison to hatred of the heretical or schismatic "Greeklings."

same process was being described as "adopting the way of thinking and the habit of a Greek."[159] Moreover, Hellenism and Christianity had previously been polar opposites, but now Byzantine writers could call their Church "Hellenic" to differentiate it from the Church of Rome.[160] Granted, we do not have direct access to the views of the majority of the population, but the casual way in which this could be done by a low-ranking churchman indicates that the new labels had caught on. The ground had been laid for deeper and more revolutionary returns and revivals.

[159] Georgios Pachymeres, *History* 12.26 (a Catalan).
[160] Georgios Pachymeres, *History* 5.8; see de Boel (2003) 174–175. For Pachymeres' use of Graikos and other terms, see Laiou (1995) 76.

# General conclusions

To the degree that Byzantium was simultaneously Roman, Christian, and Greek, it owed its existence to three traditions that originated at roughly the same time, namely in the sixth through the fourth centuries BC. That was when the Roman *res publica*, Jewish Scriptural monotheism, and Greek *paideia* all came into being. The history of their interactions in antiquity was a continuing development that pointed toward and ultimately culminated in Byzantium. Conversely, Byzantine historical awareness extended solidly back to that time of origins and beyond, to the heroic wars, migrations, and epiphanies of the second millennium BC. The Byzantines' imagined ancestors included Aeneas and the clans of the Republic, the Israelites of the Old Testament covenant, and Greek thinkers. Yet "descent" was conceived differently in each case and varied by circumstance and rhetorical effect: it could be biological, symbolic, political, or cultural.

A Byzantine could simultaneously be a Roman, a Christian, and a Greek, because those three identities defined different parts of his life. But to the degree that it was not understood as paganism, Hellenism was the least important of the three and the most rarefied. It also generated the fewest institutions. The land of Greece was always there, of course, but inspired neither enthusiasm nor loyalty. The Greek language was more important in terms of defining Byzantine identity and became an object of scrutiny especially in political and ecclesiastical debates with the Latin West. But no institutions were needed for its preservation and continuity. Greek *paideia*, by contrast, was a more exclusive possession and could become a matter of great personal importance for the learned few. In this sense, *paideia* did require maintenance and so did generate educational and cultural institutions, but these were paltry and ephemeral compared to the investment of resources in the state and Church.

On the other hand, institutions make traditions vulnerable and limit them historically, and much can be said for a tradition like that of

389

Hellenism which is capable, in any age, of generating the conditions for its own flourishing through the power of its ancient artifacts. After all, the "Romans" of Byzantium ceased to exist after the end of their empire. And Christianity, despite being a transnational faith that has proven highly mobile and adaptable, requires adherence to specific doctrines and practices, which have now (as in the past) become very vulnerable to cultural and intellectual change. The whole edifice can be undermined by the loss of a single article of faith (e.g., 1 Corinthians 15.14). There is nothing like this in the classical tradition. Hellenism, in its positive sense, does not require much by way of institutions and does not demand assent to specific beliefs, which has enabled it to weather political, cultural, and epistemological storms. No less than Christianity, it addresses fundamental questions, only instead of authoritative answers it presents the basic alternatives and invites further exploration: Achilles vs. Sokrates, Homer vs. Plato, nature vs. culture, the contemplative vs. the active life, philosophy vs. rhetoric, and others. Hellenism is the only national culture that also became a transnational ideal; moreover, it did so without ever ceasing to be rooted in the Greek language (the Roman legal tradition has had a similar trajectory, only on a more limited scale). In this way, Hellenism was taken up by many ancient peoples, in the Caliphate and Byzantium after antiquity, and later played a key role in the inauguration of modernity. Other national cultures have defined themselves in relation to it.[1] The prospects for its future relevance seem good even today, when all traditions are again facing scrutiny and revision.

I have listed the Byzantines here along with the Arabs of the Caliphate and the western modern nations to emphasize that in Byzantium Hellenism was not something natural or inevitable; it was in many ways perceived as foreign. Despite the Byzantines' easier access to the language, it is possible to imagine an alternative history in which they lose touch with the Hellenic tradition, either by allowing obscurantist forces to prevail or by not cultivating higher learning, as nearly happened in the late seventh and early eighth centuries. Having lost any sense of national or ethnic Greek identity and having condemned Hellenism as the equivalent of paganism, there was no guarantee that the Byzantines would engage with the tradition in a more positive and constructive way. The driving force that propelled the revival of Hellenism in Byzantium was the tendency of the classical Greek tradition to occupy and often monopolize the higher

---

[1] Arabic Hellenism: Gutas (1998); French: Augustinos (1994); German: Marchand (1996); American: Winterer (2002); in general, Goldhill (2002).

culture of all literate societies that are exposed to it. In this sense, the story that I have told was more comparable to that of the Renaissance and the rise of classical studies in Europe than it was to the national Greek Revolution of 1821 (though the latter was indebted in many ways to western classicism).

Certain conclusions follow regarding Byzantium and Hellenism, taking the former first.

For the past few decades, scholars have been actively and self-consciously trying to refute the image of an eternally static Byzantium, of a civilization that changed only insofar as it declined. "Change" is one of the new catchwords, and "originality" is another. This effort at rehabilitation has promoted case-studies of Byzantine originality in many spheres of life to counter the prejudice according to which its culture, and particularly its literature, consisted of nothing but sterile imitation.[2] This push has been overwhelmingly successful, among specialists at least (it is not clear how long these prejudices may linger elsewhere, perhaps too long). The present study contributes to this revision, as every step in the recovery of Greek identity and the Greek tradition represented an innovation, a creative interpretation and appropriation. Psellos, Prodromos, Choniates, and Laskaris were hardly sterile imitators and were, in addition, quite unlike each other both as individuals and in the way that they fashioned an ideology out of Hellenism to serve them in their very different personal and intellectual circumstances.

The problem is that these changes can only be seen on a large scale. We can study Psellos for the eleventh century, the sophists for the twelfth, and the Laskarids for the thirteenth, but the more detailed connections elude us, at least beyond Psellos' popularity among the Komnenian Hellenists. It is not always clear how the Byzantines moved from one stage to the next. We observe change and diversity, but not necessarily linear coherence. That part of the narrative has to be imagined, and may be imaginary. Let us consider an example. The leading intellectuals of the thirteenth century – Laskaris, Blemmydes, and Akropolites – knew each other personally but used the word *Hellen* in very different senses. It is almost as though they were living in different times or did not know (or care for) each other's works. Reading them closely, as we did, we found that their idiosyncrasies still reflected the same basic challenge facing Byzantium in that age: all three were working within traditional forms and rhetorical repertoires to cope with the rise of the West. But there was little linear development, and linear development is what we expect from intellectual history. Take

---

[2] Kazhdan and Epstein (1985) and Littlewood (1995).

another example. Tzetzes claimed to be Greek by *genos*, though it seems that he was alone among his contemporaries in saying this. And nothing quite as strong in this direction would be said before Laskaris a hundred years later, though Laskaris appears not to have known what Tzetzes wrote. Tzetzes was basically "translating" his status as a professional Hellenist into a family history, whereas Laskaris was making an argument about national pride and continuity. Their expressions are independent of each other, except in the sense that both are adaptations of the same basic sources.

Perhaps we have to fall back on a conventional view: Byzantine writing was less dated than ours. It followed traditional norms and resisted the "trends" that we want to find, trends that would give substance to cultural change. This position still allows for originality but problematizes the existence of structural change on a deep level. This has been put well regarding Byzantine poetry: it is "wrong to regard its history as an unbroken chain of literary responses."[3] It tended to fall back on the same sources repeatedly, to reinvent the wheel. So too with Hellenism, and other aspects of Byzantine literary history: it is often not an interconnected "history" at all, as any author may be responding directly to the origins of a tradition or to any later moment in it while ignoring subsequent or intermediary developments. The sources of the culture were largely fixed in late antiquity and, with a few exceptions (such as the intellectual revolution brought about by Psellos), new motions generally occurred only within those fixed parameters. About modern philosophy it is possible to say that "ideas manifest themselves slowly, unpredictably, and in labyrinthine ways, but great tidal shifts in ideas have concrete ramifications."[4] Yet it is difficult to point to any "concrete ramifications" of Hellenism in Byzantium, to the actual use of the reinvented wheel. No institutions were changed because of new ideas, and, again excepting Psellos' influence on some of the sophists, there was no point at which it was understood that something important had happened and that things had to be done differently henceforth.

Having said that, however, we cannot deny originality and change, even if they occurred against a background of solid continuity, cultural and institutional. For example, the old model of a monolithically Christian society must be finally laid to rest. We have seen that many thinkers of the middle period were led by their Hellenic researches to question the doctrines and the values of the Church. They were also suspected of doing so by their own contemporaries. Byzantium was not a closed cultural system, as it was presented in older scholarship. The Greek tradition, presenting

[3] Lauxtermann (2003) 59.    [4] Smith (1996) 6.

many tempting alternatives, was always there, as a threat or an opportunity that could, in a moment of weakness, subvert authority. Such weakness could have been historical, a period of imperial defeat perhaps, or it could have been literary. For example, when a certain cultural logic reached the limits of its ability to represent within a Christian system, it crossed over into the margins, where Hellenism was defined. The very constitution of a Christian culture harbored these antinomies. Byzantium was not, as is often said, "safely entrenched behind its own culturally and intellectually sterile demarcation lines of 'ours' and 'not ours.' "[5] The *Synodikon*, at least, which was read aloud in every church every year, proclaimed that these demarcation lines were not safe.

This allows us to correct misleading impressions about Byzantium. It is commonly asserted that in times of crisis the Byzantines turned to their faith and could become more intolerant. This certainly did happen. But we have often seen that in those same crises classical models, in recognition of their paganism, could also become normative precisely because they challenged the preconceptions of a Christian society whose foundations were wavering. Attaleiates turned to the Romans and Choniates to the Greeks, asking tough questions of their own age that could lead only to severe criticism of their society. Among the accumulating modalities of its use, then, Hellenism here appears as a cultural diagnostic and therapy, a standard for reform and inspiration. The attitude of the Fathers, who believed that one had to be "cured" of it, was not credible in these circles.

On the other hand, we must also admit that little "changed." A few intellectuals may have thought what they thought and wrote about it to each other, but there were no "concrete ramifications," or at least they are not easy to detect in our sources. To be sure, by the thirteenth and fourteenth centuries more Byzantines were calling themselves Greeks, a solid and historical "change," but what did they mean? In most cases they were trying to defend their Roman and orthodox identities in the face of Latin presumption by explaining *what kind* of Romans and Christians they were. Change was here a detour to continuity; it was adaptation. We should not look down on this and call it "static" and the like. It was, rather, a sign of great strength and the cause of an extraordinary survival. Byzantium was not some accident tossed up by circumstance. Every interlocking part of it was designed by Romans, the master-builders of history, and built to endure the centuries. Nietzsche called the Roman empire "the most grandiose form of organization under difficult conditions that has yet

[5] Lauxtermann (2003) 190, a superb study (this is a minor point).

been achieved, in comparison with which everything before and after is patchwork, bungling, dilettantism . . . its structure was calculated to prove itself by millennia."[6] He meant this as an attack on Christianity, which shows that he knew nothing of Byzantium.

The second set of general conclusions concerns Hellenism. Hellenism has often been represented as a quasi-metaphysical constant – ethnic, philosophical, cultural, or religious – though generally only by those who have an ideological stake in it, either for or against. Scholars now recognize that historical identities and cultural artifacts that operate at this level of abstraction must be approached very differently. Recognizing that the classical Greek tradition represents a range of questions and answers, forms and essences, modalities and performances, we must acknowledge its susceptibility to reinterpretation, evolution, and reversal in the history of its reception. In the fifth century BC, Hellenism was constructed as the antithesis of barbarism even while its philosophers were transcending ethnic and cultural differences. But by the fifth century AD, ironically, it could refer to the religious practices of those very barbarians. Between late antiquity and the thirteenth century, it went from being that which Byzantine writers most hated to that which most defined them. For the Church, "the Greeks" were all pagans, including Persians, Arabs, and nomads. For Psellos, they were the Platonists. For the poet of *Digenes*, they were Homer's heroes. In the thirteenth century, again, Hellenism was that which set the Greek-speaking orthodox world apart from the West, while in the nineteenth it was the bridge that brought them together. In the thirteenth, again, the Latins heaped scorn on the *Graeci*, while by the nineteenth they had come to believe that they themselves were the true heirs of Greece and not those who lived there. In Europe, Hellenism has been both the gravest threat to "our" values *and* the most promising basis for continental unity. In Greece, it is today both an abstract universal ideal *and* a set of local, exclusionary, priorities.[7] Hellenism has been defined alternately as a national, cultural, philosophical, and religious identity; it has changed its terms as different people throughout history have refracted its claims and contended its legacy.

All this can be said and truly so, yet conclusions that highlight the social and historical construction of identities and traditions have become predictable and formulaic in recent scholarship. They are, moreover,

[6] Nietzsche, *The Anti-Christ* 58.
[7] For the various Hellenisms fashioned in modern Greece, and the complexity of the traditions that made them possible, see Leontis (1995) 124. For Europe, see Voltaire in Augustinos (1994) 1.

complicit in the current philosophical project of late modernity, whose deconstructive agenda has taken on a life of its own and no longer serves the purpose of effecting a transition to postmodernity. The thesis of the "social construction of identity" is not false and has considerably shaped the methodology of this book. It is, however, one-sided and has become, well, tedious. It should no longer be adequate to deconstruct "essence" and establish "negotiation" and "representation." A supplementary thesis has therefore also been woven into the argument. The climate of scholarly opinion demands that it be given more open consideration.

The history of Hellenism has been less one of *invention* than of *selection* among the options offered up by the tradition itself, which are modified to suit present needs.[8] Their range is not limitless. It is bounded on the one hand by the very conservative nature of the Greek language. In the past 3,000 years that language has changed less than any other of which I am aware, and has preserved both its orthography and phonology (the last remained relatively stable during the Byzantine and modern periods). It has never mutated into multiple daughter languages, as happened to Latin; at any time, there has only been one Greek language. Moreover, if we set aside the gap between spoken and formal written Greek, which was already in place before the Byzantine era, and concentrate on the latter alone, we find an even more extraordinary continuity. From the age of Perikles to the beginning of the Ottoman era, so for some 2,000 years, the overwhelming majority of texts were written in more or less the same form of the language, exhibiting a better or worse quality to be sure, but variation was not such as to render texts dialectically incomprehensible. Far from it: many professional Hellenists today could simply not, on the basis of language alone, date Byzantine texts (or, often, even realize that they are Byzantine at all). There are reports that Attic Greek was spoken at the Palaiologan court, as it was in some schools in the Ottoman period.[9]

Many factors can be cited to explain this history, including the continued use of *koine* Greek in the services, literature, and administration of the Church, as well as in the bureaux of the Byzantine state. What interests us here is that the foundations of Greek *paideia* were set down by the end of the fourth century BC and changed little thereafter. Almost all men who held positions in the state and the Church, most leaders of society, and countless other men and women at any time, had learned at school the same "textbooks" and language. Being learned in the Roman and Byzantine empire meant that one had studied the classical tradition and

---

[8] Malkin (1998) 59.   [9] Wilson (1983) 5; Augustinos (1994) 248–250.

knew something of its rhetoric, poetry, and possibly philosophy, to say nothing of its more specialized fields, such as medicine and military theory. This means that all the traditions of classical scholarship remained anchored in place; flights of fancy, complete ignorance about the past, and creative naiveté there certainly were, e.g., in the *Patria* or the vernacular romances, but they never took over as they did in the West. This fact has never been fully appreciated. The West rediscovered the classics, and proudly boasts of it; Byzantium could never forget them, though it came close to that in the seventh and eighth centuries.

"Outer" wisdom was always respected and practiced professionally in Byzantium, even if some feared and hated it. To be sure, alternative, vernacular traditions developed in ecclesiastical and monastic contexts that self-consciously eschewed the classics, but they never seriously threatened the system of *paideia*. Consequently, it was not only the language that remained relatively stable but more broadly intellectual life and literature. This does not mean that nothing was added after the end of the classical period, that originality ceased, or anything like that, only that later developments looked back to the classics even as they looked to their own time and the future. Hellenism was not a fixed point, a star, so much as it was like an artfully arranged constellation; one could get bearings from it. Inevitably, some will always find this to be sterile imitation, and a case can be surely made. One can equally indict the pretentious chaos and obsessive innovation of modern literature, which, its own leading philosophers argue, lead ultimately to nihilism.

In fact, there was one moment when something new entered the tradition, and this event has shaped the analysis throughout. This was Christianity, and especially the Gospels. Among the "foreign" elements that were constantly being absorbed into Hellenism, few, or none before the advent of modernity, have had quite so dramatic an impact. I have explicated some of the consequences of this in Chapters 3, 4, and 5. Here I want to draw attention to the impact of this "barbarian wisdom" on the ongoing transformation of Greek identity, and suggest that it was an aberrant moment that has created a skewed image of the historical variability – the alleged existential relativism – of Hellenism. It was only Hellenized Jews (such as the author of 2 Maccabees) and Christians who defined Hellenism as something negative. We have already discussed how their stance could not be maintained consistently. Besides, the equation of Hellenism and paganism did not represent a good-faith effort to understand the tradition and was not fully accepted by most Byzantine thinkers anyway, or else this book could not have been written. Plato was not a "pagan." Despite being the official position of the Church, the equation failed to account for too much. Byzantine "Hellenism" was therefore always both *paideia* and paganism, both good and bad. Its history, what we have tracked in this book, is basically the process by which the former prevailed over the latter because the need to reengage with the classics was too strong. So when we remove damnation from the range of serious "renegotiations," what we are left with is Hellenism as *paideia*, philosophy, and national identity; in short, with nothing that cannot already be found in the ancient tradition itself. When all was said and done, the Byzantines more or less overcame the distorting legacy of the Fathers and returned to Hellenism as, say, Plato, Isokrates, Libanios, and Synesios had defined it. *The* question of Hellenism – in antiquity after Alexander, in Byzantium, and in modern times – is how an ancient national culture rooted in a particular and difficult language became a universal ideal, how it flourished in the most alien settings and even overcame the most bitter prejudice.

# Bibliography

## ABBREVIATIONS

| | |
|---|---|
| BF | *Byzantinische Forschungen* |
| BMGS | *Byzantine and Modern Greek Studies* |
| BS | *Byzantinoslavica* |
| BZ | *Byzantinische Zeitschrift* |
| CFHB | *Corpus fontium historiae byzantinae* |
| Cod. Just. | Codex Iustinianus (q.v. below) |
| Cod. Theod. | Codex Theodosianus (q.v. below) |
| DOP | *Dumbarton Oaks Papers* |
| EEBΣ | Ἐπετηρὶς Ἑταιρείας Βυζαντινῶν Σπουδῶν |
| GRBS | *Greek, Roman, and Byzantine Studies* |
| IJCT | *International Journal of the Classical Tradition* |
| JöB / JöBS | *Jahrbuch der österreichischen Byzantinistik / Byzantinischen Gesellschaft* |
| LCL | Loeb Classical Library. London: William Heinemann Ltd.; Cambridge, MA: Harvard University Press |
| MGH | *Monumenta Germaniae historica* |
| PG | J.-P. Migne, ed., *Patrologiae cursus completus, Series graeca* |
| PL | J.-P. Migne, ed., *Patrologiae cursus completus, Series latina* |
| REB | *Revue des études byzantines* |
| TM | *Travaux et mémoires* |
| TTH | *Translated Texts for Historians*. Liverpool University Press |

## SOURCES

The following includes translations quoted in the text or notes and editions of texts written after the seventh century (only of obscure earlier texts). Just because a translation is listed below does not mean that I have followed it. Church Fathers and late-antique authors are included only if different editions employ different numbering systems or if I cite them frequently. "Ed." means only that the publication contains the original text, not necessarily a

critical edition (though often that is the case). Byzantine authors are listed by
their family names, unless they are known by their first names. The bibliography
aims to explain my citations, not to give a comprehensive or up-to-date list of
editions and translations.

*Akathistos Hymnos.* Ed. C. A. Trypanis, *Fourteen Early Byzantine Cantica.* Vienna:
Österreichische Akademie der Wissenschaften, Kommission für
Byzantinistik, Institut für Byzantinistik der Universität Wien. 1968
(= *Wiener byzantinische Studien* v. V). 17–39.

Akropolites, Georgios, *Opera.* Ed. A. Heisenberg, *Georgii Acropolitae opera.* 2 vols.
Rev. P. Wirth. Stuttgart: Teubner. 1978.

Alexandros of Nikaia, *Letters.* Ed. J. Darrouzès, *Épistoliers byzantins du Xe siècle.*
Paris: Institut français d'études byzantines. 1960. 67–98.

Ammianus Marcellinus. Ed. and tr. J. C. Rolfe. 3 vols. LCL. 1935–1940.

Anonymous, *Monodia for Michael Choniates.* Ed. A. Papadopoulos-Kerameus,
*Noctes Petropolitanae.* St. Petersburg: V. F. Kirschbaum. 1913. 236–246.

Antiochos, Gregorios, *Encomium for the Patriarch Basileios Kamateros.* Ed. and
tr. M. Loukaki, *Grégoire Antiochos: Éloge du patriarch Basile Kametèros.* Paris:
Publications de la Sorbonne (= *Byzantina Sorbonensia* v. XIII).

*Letter to Nikolaos Hagiotheodorites.* Ed. S. P. Lambros, Μιχαὴλ Ἀκομινάτου
τοῦ Χωνιάτου τὰ σωζόμενα, v. II. Athens: Municipality of Athens. 1880.
400–409.

Antonios, patriarch of Constantinople, *Letter to the Grand Prince of Moscow.* Ed.
F. Miklosich and J. Müller, *Acta et diplomata graeca medii aevi sacra et
profana,* v. II. Vienna: C. Gerold. 1862. 188–192.

Apokaukos, Ioannes, *Letters PK.* Ed. A. Papadopoulos-Kerameus, *Noctes
Petropolitanae.* St. Petersburg: V. F. Kirschbaum. 1913. 249–294.

*Letters S.* Ed. A. Papadopoulos-Kerameus, "Συμβολὴ εἰς τὴν ἱστορίαν
τῆς ἀρχιεπισκοπῆς Ἀχρίδος," *Sbornik statei posviashchennykh pochitate-
liami akademiku i zasluzhennomu professoru V. I. Lamanskomu* 1 (1907)
227–250.

*Letters V.* Ed. Vasilievskij, "Epirotica saeculi XIII.," *Vizantijskij Vremennik* 3
(1896) 233–299.

Arethas of Kaisareia. Ed. L. G. Westerink, *Arethae scripta minora.* 2 vols. Leipzig:
Teubner. 1968–1972.

Athanasius, *Contra Gentes and De Incarnatione.* Ed. and tr. R. W. Thomson.
Oxford: Clarendon Press. 1971.

Attaleiates, Michael, *Historia.* Ed. and modern Greek tr. I. D. Polemis. Athens:
Kanaki. 1997; ed. and tr. I. Pérez Martín, *Miguel Ataliates: Historia.*
Madrid: Consejo Superior de Investigaciones Científicas. 2002 (= *Nueva
Roma* v. XV).

Balsamon, Theodoros, *Answers to questions regarding canon law posed by Markos of
Alexandria.* Ed. in *PG* CXXXVIII (1865) 951–1012.

Bardanes, Georgios, *Letter to the Patriarch Germanos II.* Ed. R. J. Loenertz, "Lettre
de Georges Bardanès, Métropolite de Corcyre, au Patriarche Oecuménique
Germain II 1226–1227 c.," *ΕΕΒΣ* 33 (1964) 87–118.

Basilakes, Nikephoros, *Or. et ep.* Ed. A. Garzya, *Nicephori Basilacae orationes et epistolae.* Leipzig: Teubner. 1984.
  *Prog. e mon.* Ed. A. Pignani, *Niceforo Basilace: Progimnasmi e monodie.* Naples: Bibliopolis. 1983.
Basileios of Kaisareia, *Address to young men on how they might profit from Greek literature.* Ed. and tr. R. J. Deferrari and M. R. P. McGuire, *Saint Basil: The Letters.* v. IV. LCL. 1934. 363–435; ed. and comm. N. G. Wilson, *Saint Basil on the Value of Greek Literature.* London: Duckworth. 1975.
Batatzes, Ioannes III Doukas, *Letter to Pope Gregorius IX.* Ed. I. Sakellion, "Ἀνέκδοτος ἐπιστολὴ τοῦ αὐτοκράτορος Ἰωάννου Δούκα Βατάτση πρὸς τὸν πάπα Γρηγόριον, ἀνευρεθεῖσα ἐν Πάτμῳ," Ἀθήναιον 1 (1872) 369–378 (faulty pagination).
Blemmydes, Nikephoros, *Basilikos Andrias.* Ed. and tr. H. Hunger and I. Ševčenko, *Des Nikephoros Blemmydes Βασιλικὸς Ἀνδριάς und dessen Metaphrase von Georgios Galesiotes und Georgios Oinaiotes: Ein weiterer Beitrag zum Verständnis der byzantinischen Schrift-Koine.* Vienna: Verlag der österreichischen Akademie der Wissenschaften. 1986 (= *Wiener byzantinische Studien* v. XVIII).
  *Letters to Theodoros II Laskaris.* Ed. N. Festa, *Theodori Ducae Lascaris epistulae CCXVII.* Florence: G. Carnesecchi e figli. 1898. 290–329.
  *Nicephori Blemmydae autobiographia sive curriculum vitae.* Ed. J. A. Munitiz. Brepols and Turnhout: Leuven University Press. 1984.
  *A Partial Account.* Tr. J. A. Munitiz. Leuven: Spicilegium Sacrum Lovaniense. 1988.
Bryennios, Nikephoros, *Materials for a History.* Ed. and tr. P. Gautier, *Nicephori Bryennii Historiarum libri quattuor (Nicéphore Bryennios: Histoire).* Brussels: Byzantion. 1975 (= *CFHB* v. IX).
*The Canons of Hippolytus.* Ed. P. F. Bradshaw and tr. C. Bebawi. Nottingham: Grove Books. 1987.
Cassiodorus, *Variae.* Tr. S. J. B. Barnish. *TTH* v. XII. 1992.
Chomatenos, Demetrios, *Various Works.* Ed. G. Prinzing, *Demetrii Chomateni ponemata diaphora.* Berlin and New York: W. de Gruyter. 2002 (= *CFHB* v. XXXVIII).
Choniates, Michael, *Catechetical Oration 14.* Ed. S. Lambros, "Μιχαὴλ Ἀκομινάτου ἀνέκδοτος κατηχητικὴ ὁμιλία," *Νέος Ἑλληνομνήμων* 6 (1909) 3–31.
  *Catechetical Oration 19.* Ed. (partial) S. Lambros, "Χωρίον Μιχαὴλ Ἀκομινάτου περὶ Εὐσταθίου Θεσσαλονίκης," *Νέος Ἑλληνομνήμων* 13 (1916) 359–361.
  *Letters.* Ed. F. Kolovou, *Michaelis Choniatae epistulae.* Berlin and New York: W. de Gruyter. 2001 (= *CFHB* v. XLI).
  *Orations.* Ed. S. P. Lambros, *Μιχαὴλ Ἀκομινάτου τοῦ Χωνιάτου τὰ σωζόμενα.* 2 vols. Athens: Municipality of Athens. 1879–1880.
Choniates, Niketas, *History.* Ed. J.-L. van Dieten, *Nicetae Choniatae Historia.* Berlin and New York: W. de Gruyter. 1975 (= *CFHB* v. XI.1–2).
  *O City of Byzantium, Annals of Niketas Choniates.* Tr. H. J. Magoulias. Detroit: Wayne State University Press. 1984.

*Or. et ep.* Ed. J.-L. van Dieten, *Nicetae Choniatae orationes et epistulae.* Berlin and New York: W. de Gruyter. 1972 (= *CFHB* v. III).

*Chronicle of Monembasia.* Ed. P. Lemerle, "La chronique improprement dite de Monemvasie: Le contexte historique et légendaire," *Revue des études byzantines* 21 (1963) 5–49, here 8–11; ed. I. Dujčev, *Cronaca di Monemvasia.* Palermo: Istituto Siciliano di Studi Bizantini e Neoellenici. 1976.

*Chronicle of Morea.* Ed. J. Schmitt. London: Methuen & Co. 1904.

*Chronicle of the Tocco.* Ed. G. Schirò, *La cronaca dei Tocco de Cefalonia di Anonimo.* Rome: Accademia nazionale dei Lincei. 1975 (= *CFHB* v. X).

Chrysoberges, Nikephoros, *Oration for the Patriarch Ioannes X Kamateros.* Ed. R. Browning, "An Unpublished Address of Nicephorus Chrysoberges to Patriarch John X Kamateros of 1202," *Byzantine Studies / Études byzantines* 5 (1978) 37–68.

Cicero, *De re publica, De legibus.* Ed. and tr. C. W. Keyes. LCL. 1928.

*Codex Iustinianus.* Ed. P. Krüger in *Corpus Iuris Civilis,* v. II. Berlin: Weidmann. 1895.

*Codex Theodosianus.* Tr. C. Pharr, *The Theodosian Code and Novels, and the Sirmondian Constitutions.* Princeton University Press. 1952.

Constantius II, *Address to the Senate Concerning Themistius.* Ed. H. Schenkl, G. Downey, and A. F. Norman, *Themistii Orationes quae supersunt,* v. III. Leipzig: Teubner. 1974. 121–128.

*Digenis Akritis.* Ed. and tr. E. Jeffreys. Cambridge University Press. 1998.

Eugenianos, Niketas, *Drosilla and Charikles.* Ed. and tr. J. B. Burton, *A Byzantine Novel.* Wauconda, IL: Bolchazy-Carducci Publishers. 2004.

(?) *Funeral Oration for his Son.* Ed. A. Sideras, 25 *unedierte byzantinische Grabreden.* Thessalonike: Paratiritis. 1990. 203–210.

Eunapios, *History.* Ed. and tr. Blockley (1981–1983) v. II, 2–150.

Eusebios, *Against Markellos.* Ed. E. Klostermann, *Eusebius Werke,* v. IV: *Gegen Marcell, über die kirchliche Theologie; Die Fragmente Marcells.* Berlin: Akademie-Verlag. 1972.

*Ecclesiastical History.* Ed. and tr. K. Lake. 2 vols. LCL. 1926–1932.

*Evangelical Preparation.* Ed. and tr. E. H. Gifford, *Eusebii Pamphili Evangelicae Praeparationis libri XV.* 4 vols. Oxford University Press; New York: H. Frowde. 1903.

Eustathios of Thessaloniki, *The Capture of Thessaloniki.* Ed. and tr. J. R. Melville Jones. Canberra: Australian Association for Byzantine Studies. 1988 (= *Byzantina Australiensia* v. VIII).

*Commentaries on Homer's* Iliad. Ed. M. van der Valk, *Eustathii commentarii ad Homeri Iliadem pertinentes.* 4 vols. Leiden: Brill. 1971–1987.

*Opera minora.* Ed. P. Wirth, *Eustathii Thessalonicensis opera minora, magnam partem inedita.* Berlin and New York: W. de Gruyter. 2000 (= *CFHB* v. XXXII).

*Opuscula.* Ed. T. L. F. Tafel, *Eustathii metropolitae Thessalonicensis opuscula.* Amsterdam: A. M. Hakkert. 1964 (reprint of the Frankfurt, 1832, ed.).

*Preface to the Commentary on Pindar.* Ed. and tr. M. Negri, *Eustazio di Tessalonica: Introduzione al Commentario a Pindaro.* Brescia: Paideia Editrice. 2000. 24–64.

Eustratios of Nikaia, *Refutation of the Monophysites.* Ed. A. K. Demetrakopoulos, Ἐκκλησιαστικὴ Βιβλιοθήκη, v. I. Hildesheim: Georg Olms. 1965 (reprint of the Leipzig, 1866, ed.). 160–198.

Frederick II Hohenstaufen, *Greek Letters.* Ed. E. Merendino, "Quattro lettere greche di Federico II," *Atti della Accademia di Scienze, Lettere, e Arti di Palermo* ser. 4, 34 (1974–1975) 293–343.

Fronto, *Epistulae.* Ed. M. P. J. van den Hout. Leipzig: Teubner. 1988.

Galenos, Ioannes, *Allegories on Hesiod's* Theogony and *Allegory on Homer,* Iliad 4.1–4. Ed. H. Flach, *Glossen und Scholien zur hesiodischen Theogonie.* Osnabrück: Biblio Verlag. 1970 (reprint of the 1876 ed.). 293–365, 420–424.

Genesios, *On the Reigns of the Emperors.* Tr. A. Kaldellis. Canberra: Australian Association for Byzantine Studies. 1998 (= *Byzantina Australiensia* v. XI).

Gennadios Scholarios, *Letter to the Empress regarding Gemistos' Book.* Ed. L. Petit, X. A. Sideridès, and M. Jugie, *Oeuvres complètes de Gennade Scholarios,* v. IV. Paris: Maison de la bonne presse. 1935. 151–155.

*Refutation of Judaism.* Ed. L. Petit, X. A. Sideridès, and M. Jugie, *Oeuvres complètes de Gennade Scholarios,* v. III. Paris: Maison de la bonne presse. 1930. 251–304.

Georgios of Alexandria, *Life of Ioannes Chrysostomos.* Ed. F. Halkin, *Douze récits byzantins sur Saint Jean Chrysostome.* Brussels: Société des Bollandistes. 1977 (= *Subsidia Hagiographica* v. LX). 69–285.

Germanos II, *Letters to the Cypriot Church.* Ed. K. Sathas, Μεσαιωνικὴ Βιβλιοθήκη, v. II. Venice: Tempus. 1873. 5–39.

*Letter to Pope Gregorios.* Ed. in ibid. 39–49.

*Orations and Letters.* Ed. N. Lagopates, Γερμανὸς ὁ Β΄ Πατριάρχης Κωνσταντινουπόλεως-Νίκαιας (1222–1240): Βίος, συγγράματα καὶ διδασκαλία αὐτοῦ, ἀνέκδοτοι ὁμιλίαι καὶ ἐπιστολαί. Tripolis: Moreas. 1913.

*Response to the Archbishop of Bulgaria.* Ed. G. Prinzing, "Die *Antigraphe* des Patriarchen Germanos II. an Erzbishof Demetrios Chomatenos von Ochrid und die Korrespondenz zum nikäisch-epirotischen Konflikt 1212–1233," *Rivista di Studi Bizantini e Slavi* 3 (1983) 21–64 (= *Miscellanea Agostino Pertusi*), here 34–36.

Grégoire de Nazianze, *Discours 4–5 contre Julien.* Ed. and tr. J. Bernardi. Paris: Les éditions du Cerf. 1983 (= *Sources chrétiennes* v. CCCIX).

Gregoras, Nikephoros, *Roman History.* Ed. L. Schopen. 3 vols. Bonn: E. Weber. 1829–1855.

Gregorios of Cyprus, *Concerning his own Life.* Ed. W. Lameere, *La tradition manuscrite de la correspondance de Grégoire de Chypre.* Brussels: Palais des Académies; Rome: Institut historique belge. 1937. 176–191.

*Letters.* Ed. S. Eustratiades, Γρηγορίου τοῦ Κυπρίου οἰκουμενικοῦ Πατριάρχου ἐπιστολαὶ καὶ μύθοι. Alexandria: Patriarchal Press. 1910.

Herodotus, *The Histories.* tr. D. Grene. University of Chicago Press. 1987.

Iakobos of Bulgaria, *Monodia for Andronikos Palaiologos and Address to Ioannes III Doukas Batatzes*. Ed. S. G. Mercati, *Collectanea Byzantina*, v. I. Bari: Dedalo. 1970. 66–73 and 81–93.

Ignatios the deacon, *Correspondence*. Ed. and tr. C. Mango with S. Efthymiadis. Washington, DC: Dumbarton Oaks Research Library and Collection. 1997 (= *CFHB* v. XXXIX).

*Life of the Patriarch Nikephoros*. Ed. C. de Boor, *Nicephori archiepiscopi Constantinopolitani opuscula historica*. Leipzig: Teubner. 1880. 139–217.

Ioannes of Antioch. Ed. U. Roberto, *Ioannis Antiocheni fragmenta ex Historia chronica*. Berlin and New York: W. De Gruyter. 2005.

Ioseph, I, patriarch of Constantinople, *Apologia*. Ed. V. Laurent and J. Darrouzès, *Dossier grec de l'union de Lyon (1273–1277)*. Paris: Institut français d'études byzantines. 1976. 134–301.

Isidoros of Pelousion, *Letters*. Ed. in *PG* LXXVIII (1864).

Jerome, *Select Letters*. Ed. and tr. F. A. Wright. LCL. 1933.

Julian, *Imp. Caesaris Flavii Claudii Iuliani epistulae, leges, poematia, fragmenta varia*. Ed. J. Bidez and F. Cumont. Paris: Les belles lettres; Oxford University Press. 1922.

*The Works of the Emperor Julian*. Ed. and tr. W. C. Wright. 3 vols. LCL. 1913–1923.

Justinian, *Digest*. Tr. ed. A. Watson. Philadelphia: University of Pennsylvania Press. 1998.

*Novels*. Tr. S. P. Scott, *The Civil Law*, v. XVI–XVII. Cincinnati: The Central Trust Company. 1932.

Kallinikos, *Life of Hypatios*. Ed. G. J. M. Bartelink, *Vie d'Hypatios*. Paris: Les éditions du Cerf. 1971 (= *Sources chrétiennes* v. CLXXVII).

Kaminiates, Ioannes, *The Capture of Thessalonike*. Ed. G. Böhlig, *Ioannis Caminiatae De expugnatione Thessalonicae*. Berlin and New York: W. de Gruyter. 1973 (= *CFHB* v. IV).

Kanaboutzes, Ioannes, *Commentary on Dionysios of Halikarnassos*. Ed. M. Lehnerdt, *Ioannis Canabutzae magistri ad principem Aeni et Samothraces in Dionysium Halicarnasensem commentarius*. Leipzig: Teubner. 1890.

Katrares, Ioannes, *Anakreontic Verses against the Philosopher among Philosophers and Most Eloquent Neophytos*. Ed. P. Matranga, *Anecdota graeca*. Rome: C. A. Bertinelli. 1850. 675–682.

Kekaumenos, *Strategikon*. Ed. and modern Greek tr. D. Tsougkarakis. Athens: Agrostis. 1993.

Kinnamos, Ioannes, *Historiarum libri VII*. Ed. in *PG* CXXXIII (1864).

*John Kinnamos: Deeds of John and Manuel Comnenus*. Tr. C. M. Brand. New York: Columbia University Press. 1976.

Komnene, Anna, *Alexiad*. Ed. D. R. Reinsch and A. Kambylis, *Annae Comnenae Alexias*. Berlin and New York: W. de Gruyter. 2001 (= *CFHB* v. XL.1–2).

*Preface to the Diataxis*. Ed. E. Kurtz, "Unedierte Texte aus der Zeit des Kaisers Johannes Komnenos," *BZ* 16 (1907) 69–119, here 93–101.

Komnenos, Alexios I, *Muses*. Ed. P. Maas, "Die Musen des Kaisers Alexios I," *BZ* 22 (1913) 348–369.

Komnenos, Isaakios, *On the Events Omitted by Homer and on the Quality and Character of the Greeks and Trojans at Troy*. Ed. H. Hinck, *Polemonis declamationes quae exstant duae*. Leipzig: Teubner. 1873. 57–88.

*On the Hypostasis of Evil*. Ed. J. J. Rizzo, *Isaak Sebastokrator's "Περὶ τῆς τῶν κακῶν ὑποστάσεως" (De Malorum Subsistentia)*. Meisenheim am Glan: A. Hain. 1971.

*Preface to Homer*. Ed. J. F. Kindstrand, *Isaac Porphyrogenitus: Praefatio in Homerum*. Uppsala: Almquist & Wiksell International. 1979.

Konstantinos VII Porphyrogennetos, *De administrando imperio (To His Own Son Romanos)*. Ed. G. Moravcsik and tr. R. J. H. Jenkins, *Constantine Porphyrogenitus: De administrando imperio*. Washington, DC: Dumbarton Oaks, Center for Byzantine Studies. 1967 (= *CFHB* v. I).

*On the Themes*. Ed. A Pertusi, *Costantino Porfirogenito de Thematibus*. Vatican City: Biblioteca Apostolica Vaticana. 1952.

*The Book of Ceremonies*. Ed. J. J. Reiske, *Constantini Porphyrogeniti imperatoris de cerimoniis aulae byzantinae*. 2 vols. Bonn: E. Weber. 1829–1830.

*What should be done when the emperor goes on campaign*. Ed. J. F. Haldon, *Constantine Porphyrogenitus: Three Treatises on Imperial Military Expeditions*. Vienna: Verlag der österreichischen Akademie der Wissenschaften. 1990 (= *CFHB* v. XXVIII). 94–151.

Kydones, Demetrios, *Advice to the Romans*. Ed. in *PG* CLIV (1866) 961–1007.

*Apologia for his Faith*. Ed. G. Mercati, *Notizie di Procoro e Demetrio Cidone, Manuele Caleca e Teodoro Meliteniota*. Vatican City: Biblioteca Apostolica Vaticana. 1931. 359–403.

Kyrillos of Alexandria, *Against Julian*. Ed. and tr. P. Burguière and P. Évieux, *Cyrille d'Alexandrie: Contre Julien*, v. I: *Livres I et II*. Paris: Les éditions du Cerf. 1985 (= *Sources chrétiennes* v. CCCXXII).

Laskaris, Theodoros II, *On Christian Theology and To the Bishop of Kotrone, Against the Latins regarding the Holy Spirit*. Ed. Ch. Krikonis, Θεοδώρου Β΄ Λασκάρεως περὶ χριστιανικῆς θεολογίας λόγοι. Thessalonike: Patriarchal Institute for Patristic Studies. 1988.

*Letters*. Ed. N. Festa, *Theodori Ducae Lascaris epistulae CCXVII*. Florence: G. Carnesecchi e figli. 1898.

*Op. rh.* Ed. A. Tartaglia, *Theodorus II Ducas Lascaris opuscula rhetorica*. Munich and Leipzig: Teubner. 2000.

*Oration on Our Surpassingly Holy Mistress, the Theotokos*. Ed. A. Giannouli, "Eine Rede auf das Akathistos-Fest und Theodoros II. Dukas Laskaris (BHG[3] 1140, CPG 8197)," *JöB* 51 (2001) 259–283.

Leon VI, *Taktika*. Ed. in *PG* CVII (1863) 669–1120.

Leon Diakonos, *History*. Ed. C. B. Hase, *Leonis Diaconi Historia*. Bonn: E. Weber. 1828.

Leon of Synada, *Letters*. Ed. and tr. M. P. Vinson, *The Correspondence of Leo, Metropolitan of Synada and Syncellus*. Washington, DC: Dumbarton Oaks Research Library and Collection. 1985 (= *CFHB* v. XXIII).

*The Life and Miracles of St. Thekla.* Ed. and tr. G. Dagron, *Vie et miracles de sainte Thècle.* Brussels: Société des Bollandistes. 1978 (= *Subsidia Hagiographica* v. LXII).

*The Life of St. Andrew the Fool.* Ed. L. Rydén. 2 vols. Uppsala: Acta Universitatis Upsaliensis. 1995 (= *Studia Byzantina Upsaliensia* v. IV).

*The Life of the Great Emperor Constantine, He who Is among the Saints and Equal to the Apostles.* Ed. F. Halkin, "Une nouvelle vie de Constantine dans un légendier de Patmos," *Analecta Bollandiana* 77 (1959) 63–107, 370–372.

Liudprand of Cremona, *The Embassy to Constantinople and Other Writings.* Tr. F. A. Wright and ed. J. J. Norwich. Rutland, VT; London: Everyman's Library. 1993.

Lydus, Ioannes, *On Powers or The Magistracies of the Roman State.* Ed. and tr. A. C. Bandy. Philadelphia: American Philosophical Society. 1983.

*On the Months.* Ed. R. Wuensch, *Ioannis Laurentii Lydi liber de mensibus.* Leipzig: Teubner. 1898.

Machairas, Leontios, *Chronicle of Cyprus.* Ed. R. M. Dawkins, *Recital concerning the Sweet Land of Cyprus Entitled "Chronicle."* 2 vols. Oxford: Clarendon Press. 1932.

Makrembolites, Eustathios, *Hysmine and Hysminias.* Ed. and tr. F. Conca, *Il romanzo bizantino del XII secolo.* Turin: Unione Tipografico-Editrice Torinese. 1994. 499–687; ed. M. Marcovich, *Eustathius Macrembolites: De Hysmines et Hysminiae amoribus libri XI.* Munich and Leipzig: Teubner. 2001.

Malakes, Euthymios. Ed. K. G. Bonis, Εὐθυμίου τοῦ Μαλάκη μητροπολίτου Νέων Πατρῶν (Ὑπάτης) τὰ σωζόμενα. Athens: Θεολογικὴ Βιβλιοθήκη εἰς μνήμην τοῦ καθηγητοῦ Χρ. Ἀνδρούτσου, v. II. 1937.

*Funeral Oration for Nikolaos Hagiotheodorites.* Ed. A. Papadopoulos-Kerameus, *Noctes Petropolitanae.* St. Petersburg: V. F. Kirschbaum. 1913. 154–162.

Malchos, *History.* Ed. and tr. Blockley (1981–1983) 401–462.

Manasses, Konstantinos, *Aristandros and Kallithea.* Ed. and tr. F. Conca, *Il romanzo bizantino del XII secolo.* Turin: Unione Tipografico-Editrice Torinese. 1994. 689–777.

*Ekphrasis of the Earth in the Form of a Woman.* Ed. O. Lampsidis, "Der vollständige Text der ΕΚΦΡΑΣΙΣ ΓΗΣ des Konstantinos Manasses," *JöB* 41 (1991) 189–205.

*Funeral Oration for Nikephoros Komnenos.* Ed. E. Kurtz, "Evstathiia Thessaloni-kiiskago i Konstantina Manassi monodii na konchinu Nikifora Komnina," *Vizantijskij Vremennik* 17 (1910) 283–322, here 302–322.

Marinos, *Proklos, or on Happiness.* Ed. and tr. H. D. Saffrey and A.-P. Segonds, *Marinus: Proclus ou sur le bonheur.* Paris: Les belles lettres. 2001.

Maurikios, *Strategikon.* Tr. G. T. Dennis, *Maurice's Strategikon: Handbook of Byzantine Military Strategy.* Philadelphia: University of Pennsylvania Press. 1984.

Mauropous, Ioannes. Ed. P. de Lagarde, *Iohannis Euchaitorum metropolitae quae in Codice Vaticano Graeco 676 supersunt.* Göttingen: *Abhandlungen der historisch-philologische Classe der königlichen Gesellschaft der Wissenschaften zu Göttingen* v. XXVIII. 1882.

*Letters*. Ed. and tr. A. Karpozilos, *The Letters of Ioannes Mauropous, Metropolitan of Euchaita*. Thessalonike: Association for Byzantine Research. 1990 (= *CFBH* v. XXXIV).

Menander Rhetor. Ed. and tr. D. A. Russell and N. G. Wilson. Oxford: Clarendon Press. 1981.

Mesarites, Nikolaos, *Description of the Church of the Holy Apostles*. Ed. and tr. G. Downey in *Transactions of the American Philosophical Association* n.s. 47 (1957) 855–924.

*Funeral Oration for his Brother Ioannes; The Disputation with the Latin Patriarch Thomas; Letter of the Clergy of Constantinople to the Emperor Theodoros; and Sermon on the Events of 1214*. Ed. A. Heisenberg, *Neue Quellen zur Geschichte des lateinische Kaisertums und der Kirchenunion, I–III*. Munich: *Sitzungsberichte der bayerischen Akademie der Wissenschaften, Philosophisch-philologische und historische Klasse*. 1922 Abh. 5; 1923 Abh. 2; and 1923 Abh. 3.

pseudo-Methodios. Eds. W. J. Aerts and G. A. A. Kortekaas, *Die Apokalypse des Pseudo-Methodius: Die ältesten griechischen und lateinischen Übersetzungen*. 2 vols. Leuvain: Peeters. 1998 (= *Corpus Scriptorum Christianorum Orientalium, Subsidia* v. XCVII–XCVIII).

Metochites, Theodoros, *Moral Maxims*. Ed. and tr. K. Hult, *Theodore Metochites on Ancient Authors and Philosophy: Semeioseis gnomikai 1–26 & 71*. Göteborg: Acta Universitatis Gothoburgensis. 2002.

Michael II of Epeiros, *Chrysoboullon for the Monastery of Hilarion*. Ed. F. Miklosich and I. Müller, *Acta et diplomata graeca medii aevi sacra et profana*, v. IV. Vienna: C. Gerold. 1871. 345–349.

Michael ὁ τοῦ Ἀγχιάλου, *Oration to emperor Manuel I, written when he was Consul of Philosophers*. Ed. R. Browning, "A New Source on Byzantine–Hungarian Relations in the Twelfth Century: The Inaugural Lecture of Michael ὁ τοῦ Ἀγχιάλου ὡς ὕπατος τῶν φιλοσόφων," *Balkan Studies* 2 (1961) 173–214.

*The Miracles of Saint Demetrios*. Ed. and tr. P. Lemerle, *Les plus anciens recueils des miracles de Saint Démétrius et la pénétration des Slaves dans le Balkans*. 2 vols. Paris: Éditions du centre national de la recherche scientifique. 1979–1981.

Nicholas of Methone, *Refutation of Proclus' Elements of Theology*. Ed. A. D. Angelou. Athens: Academy of Athens; Leiden: Brill. 1984 (= *Corpus Philosophorum Medii Aevi: Philosophi Byzantini* v. I).

Niketas Magistros, *Letters*. Ed. and tr. L. G. Westerink, *Nicétas Magistros: Lettres d'un exilé (928–946)*. Paris: Éditions du centre national de la recherche scientifique. 1973.

Niketas of Herakleia, *Apologia and Accusation: Why he does not accept the bishop of Nikaia*. Ed. J. Darrouzès, *Documents inédits d'ecclésiologie byzantine*. Paris: Institut français d'études byzantines. 1966. 276–309.

Origen, *Contra Celsum*. Tr. H. Chadwick. Cambridge University Press. 1953.

Ouranos, Nikephoros, *Letters*. Ed. J. Darrouzès, *Épistoliers byzantins du Xe siècle*. Paris: Institut français d'études byzantines. 1960. 217–248.

Pachymeres, Georgios, *History*. Ed. A. Failler, *Georges Pachymérès: Relations histor-iques*. v. I–II. tr. V. Laurent. Paris: Les belles lettres. 1984; v. III–V. tr. A. Failler. Paris: Institut français d'études byzantines. 1999–2000 (= *CFHB* XXIV.1–4).

Pakourianos, Gregorios, *Typikon*. Ed. and tr. P. Gautier, "Le typikon du sébaste Grégoire Pakourianos," *REB* 42 (1984) 5–145.

Pardos, Gregorios, *[On Composition]*. Ed. D. Donnet, *Le traité περὶ συντάξεως λόγου de Grégoire de Corinthe: étude de la tradition manuscrite, édition, traduc-tion et commentaire*. Brussels and Rome: L'institut historique belge de Rome. 1967 (= *Études de philologie, d'archéologie et d'histoire anciennes* v. X). 315–326.

Photios, *Bibliotheke*. Ed. R. Henry, *Photius: Bibliothèque*. 8 vols. Paris: Les belles lettres. 1959–1977.

*Letters*. Ed. B. Laourdas and L. G. Westerink, *Photii Patriarchae Constantinopolitani epistulae et amphilochia*, v. I–III. Leipzig: Teubner. 1983–1985.

Plethon, Georgios Gemistos, *Letter to Manuel Palaiologos regarding the Affairs of the Peloponnese*. Ed. S. P. Lambros, Παλαιολόγεια καὶ Πελοποννησιακά, v. III. Athens: Committee for the Publication of the Works Left Behind by S. Lambros. 1926. 246–265.

Porphyrios, *Against the Christians*. Ed. A. von Harnack, *Porphyrius, "Gegen die Christen," 15 Bücher*. Berlin: Verlag der königl. Akademie der Wissenschaften. 1916 (= *Abhandlungen der königlich preussischen Akademie der Wissenschaften, Philosophisch-historische Klasse* v. I).

Priskianos, *Solutiones ad Chosroem*. Ed. I. Bywater, *Prisciani Lydi quae extant*. Berlin: G. Reimer. 1886 (= *Supplementum Aristotelicum* v. I, pt. 2). 39–104.

Priskos of Panion, *History*. Ed. and tr. Blockley (1981–1983) v. II, 221–400.

Prodromos, Theodoros, *Against a dirty old hag; Against an old man with a long beard, who thinks that he is wise on that count; The ignorant man, or the grammarian on his own terms; The executioner, or the doctor; and The friend of Plato, or the tanner*. Ed. and tr. R. Romano, *La satira bizantina dei secoli XI–XV*. Turin: Unione Tipografico-Editrice Torinese. 1999. 284–335.

*Funeral Oration for Stephanos Skylitzes, Bishop of Trebizond*. Ed. R. P. L. Petit, "Monodie de Théodore Prodrome sur Etienne Skylitzès métropolitain de Trébizonde," *Izvestija Russkogo Arkheologičeskogo Instituta v Konstantinopole* 8 (1903) 1–14.

*Katomyomachia*. Ed. and tr. H. Hunger, *Der byzantinische Katz-Mäuse-Krieg. Theodoros Prodromos, Katomyomachia*. Graz, Vienna, and Cologne: H. Böhlaus. 1968.

*Letters*. Ed. in *PG* CXXXIII (1864) 1239–1292.

*The Life of Saint Meletios the Younger*. Ed. V. G. Vasil'evskij, "Nikolaja episkopa Mefonskogo i Feodora Prodroma pisatelej XII stoletija žitija Meletija Novogo," *Pravoslavnij Palestinskij Sbornik* 6 (1886) 1–69, here 40–69.

*Nuptial Oration for the Sons of the Kaisar*. Ed. and tr. P. Gautier, *Nicephori Bryennii Historiarum Libri Quattuor (Nicéphore Bryennios: Histoire)*. Brussels: Byzantion. 1975 (= *CFHB* v. IX). 339–355.

*Oration for Isaakios Komnenos*. Ed. E. Kurtz, "Unedierte Texte aus der Zeit des Kaisers Johannes Komnenos," *BZ* 16 (1907) 69–119, here 112–117.

*Poems*. Ed. in Hörandner (1974).

*Refutation of the notion that wisdom accompanies poverty*. Ed. in *PG* CXXXIII (1864) 1313–1322.

*Rhodanthe and Dosikles*. Ed. and tr. F. Conca, *Il romanzo bizantino del XII secolo*. Turin: Unione Tipografico-Editrice Torinese. 1994. 63–303; ed. M. Marcovich, *Theodori Prodromi De Rhodanthes et Dosiclis amoribus libri IX*. Stuttgart: Teubner. 1992.

Psellos, Michael, *Chronographia*. Ed. S. Impellizeri and tr. S. Ronchey, *Michele Psello: Imperatori di Bisanzio (Cronografia)*. 2 vols. Milan: Fondazione Lorenzo Valla, A. Mondadori Editore. 1984.

*De oper. daem.* Ed. J. F. Boissonade, *Michael Psellus: De operatione daemonum*. Amsterdam: A. M. Hakkert. 1964 (reprint of the Nuremberg, 1838, ed.).

*Encomium for his Mother*. Ed. and tr. U. Criscuolo, *Michele Psello: Autobiografia. Encomio per la madre*. Naples: D'Auria Ed. 1989.

*Funeral Oration for Niketas*. Ed. and tr. A. M. Guglielmino, "Un maestro di grammatica a Bisanzio nell'XI secolo e l'epitafio per Niceta di Michele Psello," *Siculorum Gymnasium* 27 (1974) 421–462.

*Hist. Byz. et alia*. Ed. K. N. Sathas, Μεσαιωνικὴ Βιβλιοθήκη (*Bibliotheca graeca Medii Aevi*), v. IV: *Pselli historia byzantina et alia opuscula*. Athens: A. Koromela Sons; Paris: Maisonneuve et cie. 1874.

*Historia Syntomos*. Ed. and tr. W. J. Aerts. Berlin and New York: W. de Gruyter. 1990 (= *CFHB* v. XXX).

*Letters A*. Ed. M. L. Agati, "Tre epistole inedite di Michele Psello," *Siculorum Gymnasium* 33 (1980) 909–916.

*Letters G*. Ed. P. Gautier, "Quelques lettres de Psellos inédites ou déjà éditées," *REB* 44 (1986) 111–197.

*Letters KD*. Ed. E. Kurtz and F. Drexl, *Michaelis Pselli scripta minora*, v. II: *Epistulae*. Milan: Vita e Pensiero. 1941.

*Letters S*. In *Misc.* 219–523.

*Letter to Ioannes Xiphilinos*. Ed. and tr. U. Criscuolo, *Michele Psello: Epistola a Giovanni Xifilino*. 2nd ed. Naples: Bibliopolis. 1990.

*Letter to Michael Keroularios*. Ed. and tr. U. Criscuolo, *Michele Psello: Epistola a Michele Cerulario*. 2nd ed. Naples: Bibliopolis. 1990.

*Misc.* Ed. K. N. Sathas, Μεσαιωνικὴ Βιβλιοθήκη (*Bibliotheca graeca Medii Aevi*), v. V: *Pselli miscellanea*. Venice: Phoenix; Paris: Maisonneuve et cie. 1876.

*Monodia for his student Ioannes the patrikios*. Ed. E. Kurtz and F. Drexl, *Michaelis Pselli scripta minora*, v. I: *Orationes et dissertationes*. Milan: Vita e pensiero. 1936. 145–154.

*Multifarious Instruction*. Ed. L. G. Westerink, *Michael Psellos: De Omnifaria Doctrina*. Utrecht: J. L. Beijers N.V. 1948.

*OFA*. Ed. G. Dennis, *Michaelis Pselli orationes, forenses et acta*. Stuttgart and Leipzig: Teubner. 1994.

*Or. Hag.* Ed. E. A. Fisher, *Michaelis Pselli orationes hagiographicae*. Stuttgart and Leipzig: Teubner. 1994.

*Or. Min.* Ed. A. R. Littlewood, *Michaelis Pselli oratoria minora*. Leipzig: Teubner. 1985.

*Phil. Min. I.* Ed. J. M. Duffy, *Michaelis Pselli philosophica minora*, vol. I: *Opuscula logica, physica, allegorica, alia*. Stuttgart and Leipzig: Teubner. 1992.

*Phil. Min. II.* Ed. D. J. O'Meara, *Michaelis Pselli philosophica minora*, vol. II: *Opuscula psychologica, theologica, daemonologica*. Leipzig: Teubner. 1989.

*Poems.* Ed. L. G. Westerink, *Michaelis Pselli Poemata*. Stuttgart and Leipzig: Teubner. 1992.

*Theol. I.* Ed. P. Gautier, *Michaelis Pselli theologica vol. I.* Leipzig: Teubner. 1989.

*Theol. II.* Ed. L. G. Westerink and J. M. Duffy, *Michael Psellos: Theologica vol. II.* Munich and Leipzig: Teubner. 2002.

*To the* vestarchês *Pothos, who asked him to write about the theological style,* and *On Ioannes Chrysostomos.* Ed. P. Levy, *Michaelis Pselli de Gregorii Theologi charactere iudicium, accedit eiusdem de Ioannis Chrysostomi charactere iudicium ineditum.* Leipzig: Typis Roberti Noske Bornensis. 1912.

*What is the difference between the novels that deal with Charikleia and Leukippe?* Ed. and tr. A. R. Dyck, *Michael Psellos: The Essays on Euripides and George of Pisidia and on Heliodorus and Achilles Tatius.* Vienna: Verlag der österreichischen Akademie der Wissenschaften. 1986 (= *Byzantina Vindobonensia* v. XVI).

Ptochoprodromos. Ed. and German tr. H. Eideneier. Cologne: Romiosini. 1991 (= *Neograeca Medii Aevi* v. V).

Robert de Clari, *La conquête de Constantinople*. Ed. P. Lauer. Paris: É. Champion. 1924.

Romanos II, *Funeral Oration for his Wife Bertha*. Ed. S. Lambros, "Ἀνέκδοτος μονῳδία Ῥωμανοῦ Β΄ ἐπὶ τῷ θανάτῳ τῆς πρώτης αὐτοῦ συζύγου Βέρθας," *Bulletin de correspondance hellénique* 2 (1878) 266–273.

Romanos Melodos, *Sancti Romani Melodi Cantica: Cantica genuina*. Ed. P. Maas and C. A. Trypanis. Oxford: Clarendon Press. 1963.

Sanudo Torsello, Marin, *History of Romania*. Ed. and tr. E. I. Papadopoulou, *Μαρίνος Σανούδος Τορσέλλο: Ἱστορία τῆς Ρωμανίας.* Athens: National Hellenic Research Foundation. 2000.

Sergios the deacon, *First Didaskalia (Encomium for the Patriarch Michael Autoreianos).* Ed. M. Loukaki, "Première didascalie de Serge le Diacre: Éloge du Patriarche Michel Autôreianos," *REB* 52 (1994) 151–173.

Skoutariotes, Theodoros, *Additions to the History of Georgios Akropolites.* Ed. A. Heisenberg, *Georgii Acropolitae opera*, v. I. Rev. P. Wirth. Stuttgart: Teubner. 1978. 275–302.

Skylitzes Continuatus. Ed. E. Th. Tsolakis, *Ἡ Συνέχεια τῆς Χρονογραφίας τοῦ Ἰωάννου Σκυλίτση (Ioannes Skylitzes Continuatus).* Thessalonike: Etaireia Makedonikon Spoudon. 1968.

Skylitzes, Ioannes, *Historical Synopsis.* Ed. J. Thurn, *Ioannis Scylitzae Synopsis Historiarum.* Berlin and New York: W. de Gruyter. 1973 (= *CFHB* v. V).

Stephanos, *Commentary on Aristotle's* Rhetoric. Ed. G. Rabe, *Anonymi et Stephani in artem rhetoricam commentaria*. Berlin: G. Reimer. 1896. (= *Commentaria in Aristotelem Graeca* v. XXI, pt. 2). 263–322.

Stethatos, Niketas, *Life of Symeon the New Theologian*. Ed. I. Hausherr and G. Horn, "Vie de Syméon le Nouveau Théologien," *Orientalia Christiana Analecta* 12 (1928) 2–228.

Stilbes, Konstantinos, *Errors of the Latin Church*. Ed. and tr. J. Darrouzès, "Le mémoire de Constantin Stilbès contre les Latins," *REB* 21 (1963) 50–100.

Straboromanos, Manuel, *Oration to Alexios Komnenos*. Ed. P. Gautier, "Le dossier d'un haut fonctionnaire d'Alexis Ier Comnène, Manuel Straboromanos," *REB* 23 (1965) 18–204.

Suetonius, *De grammaticis et rhetoribus*. Ed. and tr. R. A. Kaster. Oxford: Clarendon Press. 1995.

Symeon the New Theologian, *Ethical Discourses*. Ed. and tr. J. Darrouzès, *Syméon le Nouveau Théologien: Traités théologiques et éthiques*. 2 vols. Paris: Les éditions du Cerf. 1966–1967 (= *Sources chrétiennes* v. CXXII, CXXIX).

Synésios de Cyrène, *Correspondance*. Ed. A. Garzya and tr. D. Roques. 2 vols. Paris: Les belles lettres. 2000.

*Synodikon of Orthodoxy*. Ed. and tr. in Gouillard (1967).

Tatian, *Oratio ad Graecos and Fragments*. Ed. and tr. M. Whittaker. Oxford: Clarendon Press. 1982.

Theophanes the Confessor, *Chronographia*. Ed. C. de Boor. 2 vols. Leipzig: Teubner. 1883–1885.

Theophanes Continuatus. Ed. I. Bekker. Bonn: E. Weber. 1838.

Theophylaktos Hephaistos, *Letters*. Ed. and tr. P. Gautier, *Théophylacte d'Achrida: Lettres*. Thessalonike: Association de recherches byzantines. 1986 (= *CFHB* v. XVI.2).

*Timarion*. Ed. and tr. R. Romano, *Pseudo-Luciano: Timarione*. Università di Napoli: Cattedra di Filologia Bizantina. 1974; tr. Baldwin (1984).

Tornikes, Euthymios, *Oration for Alexios III Angelos*. Ed. J. Darrouzès, "Les discours d'Euthyme Tornikès," *REB* 26 (1968) 49–121, here 56–72.

Tornikés, Georges et Dèmètrios, *Lettres et discours*. Ed. J. Darrouzès. Paris: Éditions du centre national de la recherche scientifique. 1970.

Tzetzes, Ioannes, *Allegories from the Verse-Chronicle*. Ed. H. Hunger, "Johannes Tzetzes, Allegorien aus der Verschronik," *JöBS* 4 (1955) 13–49.

*Allegories on the* Iliad. Ed. J. F. Boissonade, *Tzetzae allegoriae Iliadis*. Paris: Dumont. 1851.

*Allegories on the* Odyssey. Ed. H. Hunger, "Johannes Tzetzes, Allegorien zur Odyssee," *BZ* 48 (1955) 4–48; 49 (1956) 249–310.

*Epilogue to the Theogony*. Ed. H. Hunger, "Zum Epilog der Theogonie des Johannes Tzetzes." In H. Hunger, *Byzantinische Grundlagensforschung*. London: Variorum. 1973. XVIII; tr. Kazhdan and Epstein (1985) 259–260.

*Epilogue to Thucydides*. Ed. and tr. W. B. Stanford, "Tzetzes' Farewell to Thucydides," *Greece and Rome* 11 (1941) 40–41.

*Epistulae*. Ed. P. A. M. Leone. Leipzig: Teubner. 1972.

*Historiae*. Ed. P. A. M. Leone. Naples: Libreria Scientifica Editrice. 1968.
*Life of Saint Loukia*. Ed. A. Papadopoulos-Kerameus, *Varia graeca sacra*. St. Petersburg: V. F. Kirschbaum. 1909. 80–101.
*Scholia on Lykophron's* Alexandra. Ed. E. Scheer, *Lycophronis Alexandra*, v. II. Berlin: Weidmann. 1958 (reprint of the 1908 ed.).
Xiphilinos, Ioannes, *Epitome of Dion of Nikaia*. Ed. U. P. Boissevain, *Cassii Dionis Cocceiani historiarum romanarum quae supersunt*, v. III. Berlin: Weidmann. 1901. 478–730.
Zonaras, Ioannes, *Chronicle*. Ed. in *PG* CXXXIV–CXXXV (1864–1887).

SECONDARY WORKS

Adams, J. N. (2004). " '*Romanitas*' and the Latin Language," *Classical Quarterly* 53: 184–205.
Aerts, W. J. (1990). "Was the Author of the Chronicle of the Morea that Bad?" In V. D. van Aalst and K. N. Ciggaar, eds., *The Latin Empire: Some Contributions*. Hernen: A.A. Bredius Foundations. 133–163.
Agapitos, P. A. (1993). " Ἡ χρονολογικὴ ἀκολουθία τῶν μυθιστορημάτων Καλλίμαχος, Βέλθανδρος καὶ Λίβιστρος." In N. M. Panagiotakis, ed., *Origini della Letteratura Neogreca (Atti del secondo congreso internazionale "Neograeca medii aevi")*, v. II. Venice: Biblioteca dell' istituto ellenico di studi bizantini e postbizantini di Venezia (v. XV). 97–134.
  (1998a). "Teachers, Pupils, and Imperial Power in Eleventh-Century Byzantium." In Y. L. Too and N. Livingstone, eds., *Pedagogy and Power: Rhetorics of Classical Learning*. Cambridge University Press. 170–191.
  (1998b). "Narrative, Rhetoric, and 'Drama' Rediscovered: Scholars and Poets in Byzantium Interpret Heliodorus." In Hunter (1998) 125–156.
  (1998c). " Ὁ λογοτεχνικὸς θάνατος τῶν ἐχθρῶν στὴν «Αὐτοβιογραφία» τοῦ Νικηφόρου Βλεμμύδη," *Ἑλληνικά* 48: 29–46.
  (1999). "Mischung der Gattungen und Überschreitung der Gesetze: Die Grabrede des Eustathios von Thessalonike auf Nikolaos Hagiotheodorites," *JöB* 48: 119–146.
  (2000). "Poets and Painters: Theodoros Prodromos' Dedicatory Verses of his Novel to an Anonymous Caesar," *JöB* 50: 173–185.
Agapitos, P. A., and D. R. Reinsch, eds. (2000). *Der Roman im Byzanz der Komnenenzeit*. Frankfurt am Main: Beerenverlag.
Agapitos, P. A., and O. L. Smith (1992). *The Study of the Medieval Greek Romance*. Copenhagen: Museum Tusculanum Press.
Ahrweiler, H. (1965). "L'histoire et le géographie de la région de Smyrne entre les deux occupations turques (1081–1317) particulièrement au XIIIe siècle," *TM* 1: 2–204.
  (1975a). *L'idéologie politique de l'Empire byzantin*. Paris: Presses Universitaires de France.
  (1975b). "L'expérience nicéenne," *DOP* 29: 21–40.

(1984). "Citoyens et étrangers dans l'Empire romain d'Orient." In *Da Roma alla terza Roma*. Studi II: *La nozione di "Romano" tra cittadinanza e universalità*. Naples: Edizioni Scientifiche Italiane. 343–350.

(1998). "Byzantine Concepts of the Foreigner: The Case of the Nomads." In Ahrweiler and Laiou 1–15.

Ahrweiler, H., and A. E. Laiou, eds. (1998). *Studies on the Internal Diaspora of the Byzantine Empire*. Washington, DC: Dumbarton Oaks Research Library and Collection.

Alexander, P. (1962). "The Strength of Empire and Capital as Seen through Byzantine Eyes," *Speculum* 37: 339–357.

(1985). *The Byzantine Apocalyptic Tradition*. Ed. D. deF. Abrahamse. Berkeley: University of California Press.

Alexiou, M. (1983). "Literary Subversion and the Aristocracy in Twelfth-Century Byzantium: A Stylistic Analysis of the *Timarion* (chs. 6–10)," *BMGS* 8: 29–45.

(1986). "The Poverty of Écriture and the Craft of Writing: Toward a Reappraisal of the Prodromic Poems," *BMGS* 10 (1986) 1–39.

(2002). *After Antiquity: Greek Language, Myth, and Metaphor*. Ithaca and London: Cornell University Press.

Alföldy, G. (1988). *The Social History of Rome*. Tr. D. Braund and F. Pollock. Baltimore: Johns Hopkins University Press.

(2001). "*Difficillima Tempora*: Urban Life, Inscriptions, and Mentality in Late Antique Rome." In T. S. Burns and J. W. Eadie, eds., *Urban Centers and Rural Contexts in Late Antiquity*. East Lansing: Michigan State University Press. 3–24.

Allen, P. (1987). "Some Aspects of Hellenism in the Early Greek Church Historians," *Traditio* 43: 368–381.

Amory, P. (1997). *People and Identity in Ostrogothic Italy, 489–554*. Cambridge University Press.

Anagnostakis, I. (1993). "Η θέση των ειδωλολατρών στο Βυζάντιο: Η περίπτωση των «Ελλήνων» του Πορφυρογέννητου." In C. A. Maltezou, ed., *Οι περιθωριακοί στο Βυζάντιο*. Athens: Ἴδρυμα Γουλανδρή-Χορν. 26–47.

(2001). "«Περιούσιος λαός»." In Kountoura-Galake 325–346.

Anagnostakis, I., and T. Papamastorakis (2004). "'Εκμανής νέος Βάκχος: The Drunkenness of Noah in Medieval Art." In Angelidi 209–256.

Anagnostou, Y. (2004). "Forget the Past, Remember the Ancestors! Modernity, 'Whiteness,' American Hellenism, and the Politics of Memory in Early Greek America," *Journal of Modern Greek Studies* 22: 25–71.

Anderson, B. (1991). *Imagined Communities: Reflections on the Origin and Spread of Nationalism*. Rev. ed. London and New York: Verso.

Anderson, G. (2003). *The Athenian Experiment: Building an Imagined Political Community in Ancient Attica, 508–490 BC*. Ann Arbor: University of Michigan Press.

Anderson, J. C., and M. J. Jeffreys (1994). "The Decoration of the Sevastokratorissa's Tent," *Byzantion* 64: 8–18.

Ando, C. (1999). "Was Rome a *polis?*" *Classical Antiquity* 18: 5–34.
 (2000). *Imperial Ideology and Provincial Loyalty in the Roman Empire*. Berkeley: University of California Press.
 (2004). "Review of T. Whitmarsh, *Greek Literature and the Roman Empire,*" *Classical Philology* 99: 89–98.
Angelidi, Ch. G., ed. (2004). *Το Βυζάντιο ώριμο για αλλαγές: Επιλογές, ευαισθησίες και τρόποι έκφρασης από τον ενδέκατο στον δέκατο πέμπτο αιώνα*. Athens: Institute for Byzantine Research, The National Hellenic Research Foundation.
Angelopoulos, A. (1977). "Τὸ γενεαλογικὸν δένδρον τῆς οἰκογένειας τῶν Καβασιλῶν," *Μακεδονικά* 17: 367–396.
Angelov, D. G. (2003). "Byzantine Imperial Panegyric as Advice Literature (1204–c. 1350)." In Jeffreys (2003a) 55–72.
 (2004). "Plato, Aristotle and 'Byzantine Political Philosophy.'" In *Mélanges de l'Université Saint-Joseph* 57 (*The Greek Strand in Islamic Political Thought*): 499–523.
 (2005). "Byzantine Ideological Reactions to the Latin Conquest of Constantinople." In A. Laiou, ed., *Urbs Capta: The Fourth Crusade and its Consequences*. Paris: Lethielleux (= *Réalités byzantines* v. X). 293–310.
Angold, M. (1972). "The Problem of the Unity of the Byzantine World After 1204: The Empire of Nicaea and Cyprus (1204–1261)." In A. Papageorgiou, ed., *Πρακτικὰ τοῦ πρώτου διεθνοῦς Κυπρολογικοῦ συνεδρίου*, v. II: *Μεσαιωνικὸν Τμῆμα*. Leukosia: Ἑταιρεία Κυπριακῶν Σπουδῶν. 1–6.
 (1975a). *A Byzantine Government in Exile: Government and Society under the Laskarids of Nicaea (1204–1261)*. Oxford University Press.
 (1975b). "Byzantine 'Nationalism' and the Nicaean Empire," *BMGS* 1: 49–70.
 ed. (1984). *The Byzantine Aristocracy: IX to XIII Centuries*. Oxford: BAR International Series v. CCXXI.
 (1989a). "The Wedding of Digenes Akrites: Love and Marriage in Byzantium in the Eleventh and Twelfth Centuries." In Ch. G. Angelidi, ed., *Ἡ καθημερινὴ ζωὴ στὸ Βυζάντιο: Τομὲς καὶ συνέχειες στὴν ἑλληνιστικὴ καὶ ρωμαϊκὴ παράδοση*. Athens: National Research Institute. 201–215.
 (1989b). "Greeks and Latins after 1204: The Perspective of Exile." In B. Abel *et al.*, eds., *Latins and Greeks in the Eastern Mediterranean after 1204*. London: Frank Cass. 63–86.
 (1995). *Church and Society in Byzantium under the Comneni, 1081–1261*. Cambridge University Press.
 (1997). *The Byzantine Empire, 1025–1204: A Political History*. 2nd ed. London and New York: Longman.
 (1999). "Autobiography and Identity: The Case of the Later Byzantine Empire," *BS* 60: 36–59.
Antonaccio, C. M. (2001). "Ethnicity and Colonization." In Malkin 113–157.
Armstrong, A. H. (1984). "The Way and the Ways: Religious Tolerance and Intolerance in the Fourth Century," *Vigiliae Christianae* 38: 1–17.

Armstrong, J. A. (1982). *Nations before Nationalism*. Chapel Hill: University of North Carolina Press.

Arrigoni, E. (1972). "Il delinearsi di una coscienza nazionale romèica nell'impero d'oriente e nell'ambito ellenòfono medievale," *Nuova Rivista Storica* 56: 122–150.

Asatrian, G. (1996). "Byzantium in New Iranian Classic Literature and Folklore." In K. Fledelius *et al.*, eds., *Byzantium: Identity, Image, Influence (Abstracts of Communications)*. Copenhagen: Danish National Committee for Byzantine Studies: Eventus. 1244.

Asmus, J. R. (1906). "Die Ethopöie des Nikephoros Chrysoberges über Julians Rhetorenedict," *BZ* 15: 125–136.

Athanassiadi, P. (1977). "Ὁ Ἰουλιανὸς τοῦ θρύλου," Ἀθηνᾶ 76: 103–154.

(1992). *Julian: An Intellectual Biography*. London and New York: Routledge.

(1994). "From Polis to Theoupolis: School Syllabus and Teaching Methods in Late Antiquity." In Θυμίαμα στη μνήμη της Λασκαρίνας Μπούρα, v. I. Athens: Benaki Museum. 9–14.

(1999). "The Chaldaean Oracles: Theology and Theurgy." In P. Athanassiadi and M. Frede, eds., *Pagan Monotheism in Late Antiquity*. Oxford: Clarendon Press. 149–183.

(2001). Ἰουλιανός· Μία βιογραφία. Tr. D. Kiritsis, rev. by author. Athens: Educational Foundation of the National Bank of Greece.

(2002). "Byzantine Commentators on the Chaldaean Oracles: Psellos and Plethon." In K. Ierodiakonou, ed., *Byzantine Philosophy and its Ancient Sources*. Oxford: Clarendon Press. 237–252.

(2006). *La lutte pour l'orthodoxie dans le Platonisme tardif de Numénius à Damascius*. Paris: Les belles lettres.

Athanassiadi-Fowden, P. (1977). "The Idea of Hellenism," Φιλοσοφία 7: 323–358.

Augustinos, G. (1992). *The Greeks of Asia Minor: Confession, Community, and Ethnicity in the Nineteenth Century*. Kent State University Press.

Augustinos, O. (1994). *French Odysseys: Greece in French Travel Literature from the Renaissance to the Romantic Era*. Baltimore and London: Johns Hopkins University Press.

Bádenas, P. (1998). "L'intégration des Turcs dans la société byzantine (XIe–XIIe siècles): Echecs d'un processus de coexistence." In S. Lambakis, ed., Η Βυζαντινή Μικρά Ασία (6ος–12ος αι.). Athens: National Hellenic Research Foundation and The Speros Basil Vryonis Center for the Study of Hellenism. 179–188.

Baldwin, B. (1982). "A Talent to Abuse: Some Aspects of Byzantine Satire," *BF* 8: 19–28.

(1984). *Timarion*. Detroit: Wayne State University Press.

Banchich, T. M. (1993). "Julian's School Laws: *Cod. Theod.* 13.3.5 and *Ep.* 42," *Ancient World* 24: 5–14.

Barber, C., and D. Jenkins, eds. (2006). *Reading Michael Psellos*. Leiden and Boston: Brill.

Barker, J. W. (1979). "Peter Charanis: A Portrait," *Byzantine Studies/Études byzantines* 6: 1–11.

Barnes, T. D. (1989). "Christians and Pagans in the Reign of Constantius," *Entretiens sur l'antiquité classique* 34 (*L'église et l'empire au IVe siècle*): 301–337.

Bartikian, Ch. (1993). " Ὀνοματοδοσίες λαῶν στὶς ἀρμενικὲς μεσαιωνικὲς πηγές." In Moschonas (1993a) 729–746.

Bartusis, M. C. (1992). *The Late Byzantine Army: Arms and Society, 1204–1453*. Philadelphia: University of Pennsylvania Press.

Barzos, K. (1984). Ἡ γενεαλογία τῶν Κομνηνῶν. 2 vols. Thessalonike: Center for Byzantine Research.

Basilikopoulou, A. (1993). "Ἡ πάτριος φωνή." In Moschonas (1993a) 103–113.

Basilikopoulou-Ioannidou, A. (1971–1972). Ἡ ἀναγέννησις τῶν γραμμάτων κατὰ τὸν ΙΒ´ αἰῶνα εἰς τὸ Βυζάντιον καὶ ὁ Ὅμηρος. Athens: Kapodistrian University of Athens, School of Philosophy.

Bassett, S. (2004). *The Urban Image of Late Antique Constantinople*. Cambridge University Press.

Bastéa, E. (2000). *The Creation of Modern Athens: Planning the Myth*. Cambridge University Press.

Beaton, R. (1987). "The Rhetoric of Poverty: The Lives and Opinions of Theodore Prodromos," *BMGS* 11: 1–28.

(1996). *The Medieval Greek Romance*. 2nd ed. London and New York: Routledge.

(2000). "The World of Fiction and the World 'Out There': The Case of the Byzantine Novel." In Smythe 179–188.

Beck, H.-G. (1959). *Kirche und theologische Literatur im byzantinischen Reich*. Munich: C. H. Beck.

(1970). *Res Publica Romana: Vom Staatsdenken der Byzantiner*. Munich: Verlag der bayerischen Akademie der Wissenschaften (= *Sitzungsberichte, philosophisch-historische Klasse* 1970, pt. 2).

(1971). *Geschichte der byzantinischen Volksliteratur*. Munich: C. H. Beck.

(1982). *Das byzantinische Jahrtausend*. Munich: Deutscher Taschenbuch Verlag GmbH & Co. KG.

Bernardi, J. (1978). "Un réquisitoire: Les *Invectives contre Julien* de Grégoire de Nazianze." In Braun and Richer 89–98.

Bidez, J., and F. Cumont (1898). "Recherches sur la tradition manuscrite des lettres de l'empereur Julien," *Mémoires couronnés et autres mémoires publiés par l'Academie Royale des Sciences, des Lettres et des Beaux Arts de Belgique* 57: 1–156.

Bingen, J. (1954). "Inscriptions d'Achaïe 1. Épigramme honorifique," *Bulletin de correspondance hellénique* 78: 74–82.

Blachakos, P. K. (2003). Νικηφόρος Γρηγοράς· Φυσικὴ γεωγραφία καὶ ανθρωπογεωγραφία στο έργο του. Thessalonike: Zitros.

Blachopoulou, F. Th. (2002). Λέων Σγουρός: Ο βίος και η πολιτεία του βυζαντινού άρχοντα της βορειοανατολικῆς Πελοποννήσου ο τις αρχές του 13ου αιώνα. Thessalonike: Herodotos.

Blank, D. L. (1998). *Sextus Empiricus: Against the Grammarians*. Oxford: Clarendon Press.

Blockley, R. C. (1981–1983). *The Fragmentary Classicising Historians of the Later Roman Empire: Eunapius, Olympiodorus, Priscus and Malchus*. 2 vols. Liverpool: Francis Cairns.

Bloom, A. (1995). "An Introduction to the Political Philosophy of Isocrates." In M. Palmer and T. L. Pangle, eds., *Political Philosophy and the Human Soul: Essays in Memory of Allan Bloom*. Lanham, MD: Rowman and Littlefield. 15–34.

Boardman, J. (2000). *Persia and the West: An Archaeological Investigation of the Genesis of Achaemenid Art*. London: Thames & Hudson.

Boatwright, M. T. (2000). *Hadrian and the Cities of the Roman Empire*. Princeton University Press.

de Boel, G. (2003). "L'identité 'romaine' dans le roman *Digénis Akritis*." In H. Hokwerda, ed., *Constructions of Greek Past: Identity and Historical Consciousness from Antiquity to the Present*. Groningen: Egbert Forsten. 157–183.

Bolton, C. A. (1968). "The Emperor Julian Against 'Hissing Christians,' " *Harvard Theological Review* 61: 496–497.

Borsari, S. (1963). *Il dominio veneziano a Creta nel XIII secolo*. Naples: Fausto Fiorentino Editore.

Børtnes, J., and T. Hägg, eds. (2006). *Gregory of Nazianzus: Images and Reflections*. Copenhagen: Museum Tusculanum Press.

Bouffartigue, J. (1991). "Julien ou l'hellénisme décomposé." In Saïd 251–266.

(1992). *L'empereur Julien et la culture de son temps*. Paris: Institut d'études augustiniennes.

Bowersock, G. W. (1969). *Greek Sophists in the Roman Empire*. Oxford: Clarendon Press.

(1990). *Hellenism in Late Antiquity*. Ann Arbor: University of Michigan Press.

Bowie, E. L. (1970). "Greeks and their Past in the Second Sophistic," *Past and Present* 46: 3–41.

(1982). "The Importance of Sophists," *Yale Classical Studies* 27: 29–59.

(1991). "Hellenes and Hellenism in Writers of the Early Second Sophistic." In Saïd 183–204.

(1998). "Phoenician Games in Heliodorus' *Aithiopika*." In Hunter 1–18.

Brague, R. (2002). *Eccentric Culture: A Theory of Western Civilization*. Tr. S. Lester. South Bend, IN: St. Augustine Press.

Braun, R., and J. Richer, eds. (1978). *L'empereur Julien de l'histoire à la légende (331–1715)*. Paris: Les belles lettres.

Braund, D. (1994). *Georgia in Antiquity: A History of Colchis and Transcaucasian Iberia, 550 BC–AD 562*. Oxford: Clarendon Press.

Bregman, J. (1982). *Synesius of Cyrene: Philosopher-Bishop*. Berkeley: University of California Press.

Brezeanu, S. (1978). "La fonction de l'idée d'*imperium unicum* chez les Byzantines de la première moitié du XIIIe siècle," *Revue des études sud-est européennes* 16: 57–64.

Brokkaar, W. G. (1972). "Basil Lecapenus." In W. F. Bakker *et al.*, eds., *Studia Byzantina et Neohellenica Neerlandica.* Leiden: Brill. 199–234.

Brown, P. (1992). *Power and Persuasion in Late Antiquity: Towards a Christian Empire.* Madison: University of Wisconsin Press.

Browning, R. (1962–1963). "The Patriarchal School at Constantinople in the Twelfth Century," *Byzantion* 32: 167–201; 33: 11–40.

   (1964). "Byzantine Scholarship," *Past and Present* 28: 3–20.

   (1971). "Review of S. Runciman, *The Last Byzantine Renaissance,*" *Journal of Hellenic Studies* 91: 214–215.

   (1975a). "Enlightenment and Repression in Byzantium in the Eleventh and Twelfth Centuries," *Past and Present* 69: 3–23.

   (1975b). "Homer in Byzantium," *Viator* 6: 15–33.

   (1983). *Medieval and Modern Greek.* 2nd ed. Cambridge University Press.

   (1989a). "Theodore Balsamon's Commentary on the Canons of the Council in Trullo as a Source on Everyday Life in Twelfth-Century Byzantium." In Ch. G. Angelidi, ed., *Ἡ καθημερινὴ ζωὴ στὸ Βυζάντιο: Τομὲς καὶ συνέχειες στὴν ἑλληνιστικὴ καὶ ρωμαϊκὴ παράδοση.* Athens: National Research Institute. 421–427.

   (1989b). "Athens in the 'Dark Age'." In R. Browning, *History, Language and Literacy in the Byzantine World.* London: Variorum Reprints. 1989. IV.

   (2002). "Greeks and Others: From Antiquity to the Renaissance." In T. Harrison, ed., *Greeks and Barbarians.* New York: Routledge. 257–277.

Brunt, P. A. (1976). "The Romanization of the Local Ruling Classes in the Roman Empire." In D. M. Pippidi, ed., *Assimilation et résistance à la culture gréco-romaine dans le monde ancien: Travaux du VIe congrès international d'études classiques.* Bucharest: Editura Academiei; Paris: Les belles lettres. 161–173.

Bryer, A. (1983). "Greeks and Turks." In T. Winnifrith and P. Murray, eds., *Greece Old and New.* London and Basingstoke: Macmillan Press. 95–110.

Buckler, G. (1929). *Anna Comnena: A Study.* Oxford University Press.

Budelmann, F. (2002). "Classical Commentary in Byzantium: John Tzetzes on Ancient Greek Literature." In R. K. Gibson and C. S. Kraus, eds., *The Classical Commentary: Histories, Practices, Theory.* Leiden: Brill. 141–169.

Buraselis, K. (1989). *ΘΕΙΑ ΔΩΡΕΑ: Μελέτες πάνω στὴν πολιτικὴ τῆς δυναστείας τῶν Σεβήρων καὶ τὴν Constitutio Antoniniana.* Athens: Academy of Athens.

Burgess, W. D. (1990). "Isaurian Names and the Ethnic Identity of the Isaurians in Late Antiquity," *Ancient World* 21: 109–121.

Burke, J., and R. Scott (2000). *Byzantine Macedonia: Identity, Image, and History.* Melbourne: Australian Association for Byzantine Studies (= *Byzantina Australiensia* v. XIII).

Burns, T. S. (2003). *Rome and the Barbarians, 100 BC–AD 400.* Baltimore and London: Johns Hopkins University Press.

Burton, J. B. (1998). "Reviving the Pagan Greek Novel in a Christian World," *GRBS* 39: 179–216.

   (2000). "Abduction and Elopement in the Byzantine Novel," *GRBS* 41: 377–409.

(2003). "A Reemergence of Theocritean Poetry in the Byzantine Novel," *Classical Philology* 98: 251–273.

Calderone, S. (1993). "Costantinopoli: La 'seconda Roma.'" In A. Momigliano and A. Schiavone, eds., *Storia di Roma*, v. III, pt. 1. Turin: G. Einaudi. 723–749.

Cameron, Al. (1982). "The Empress and the Poet: Paganism and Politics at the Court of Theodosius II," *Yale Classical Studies* 27: 217–289.

(1993). "Julian and Hellenism," *Ancient World* 24: 25–29.

Cameron, Al., and J. Long, with L. Sherry (1993). *Barbarians and Politics at the Court of Arcadius*. Berkeley: University of California Press.

Cameron, Av. (1981). "Images of Authority: Elites and Icons in Late Sixth-Century Byzantium." In M. Mullett and R. Scott, eds., *Byzantium and the Classical Tradition*. Birmingham: Center for Byzantine Studies, University of Birmingham. 205–234.

(1991). "The Eastern Provinces in the 7th Century AD: Hellenism and the Emergence of Islam." In Saïd 287–313.

(1997). "Hellenism and the Emergence of Islam," *Dialogos* 4: 4–18.

ed. (2003). *Fifty Years of Prosopography: The Later Roman Empire, Byzantium and Beyond*. The British Academy: Oxford University Press (= *Proceedings of the British Academy* v. CXVIII).

Cesaretti, P. (1991). *Allegoristi di Omero a Bisanzio: Ricerche ermeneutiche (XI–XII secolo)*. Milan: Guerini.

Chadwick, H. (1966). *Early Christian Thought and the Classical Tradition: Studies in Justin, Clement, and Origen*. Oxford University Press.

Chalk, H. H. O. (1960). "Eros and the Lesbian Pastorals of Longos," *Journal of Hellenic Studies* 80: 33–51.

Charalampopoulos, N. G. (2005). "Ένας 'πλατωνικός' διάλογος τοῦ 12ου αἰῶνος: Θεοδώρου Προδρόμου Ξενέδημος ἢ Φωναί," *Ἀριάδνη: Ἐπιστημονικὴ Ἐπετηρίδα τῆς Φιλοσοφικῆς Σχολῆς τοῦ Πανεπιστημίου Ἀθηνῶν* 11: 189–214.

Charanis, P. (1972). *Studies on the Demography of the Byzantine Empire: Collected Studies*. London: Variorum Reprints.

(1978). "The Formation of the Greek People." In S. Vryonis, ed., *The "Past" in Medieval and Modern Greek Culture*. Malibu: Undena Publications. 87–101.

(1982). "On the Question of the Evolution of the Byzantine Church into a National Greek Church," *Βυζαντιακά* 2: 95–109.

Chesnut, G. F. (1986). *The First Christian Histories: Eusebius, Socrates, Sozomen, Theodoret, and Evagrius*. 2nd ed. Macon, GA: Mercer University Press.

Cheynet, J.-C. (1990). *Pouvoir et contestations à Byzance (963–1210)*. Paris: Publications de la Sorbonne (= *Byzantina Sorbonensia* v. IX).

(2002). "Les limites du pouvoir à Byzance: Une forme de tolérance?" In Nikolaou 15–28.

(2003a). "Official Power and Non-Official Power." In Cameron (2003) 137–151.

(2003b). "Basil II and Asia Minor." In P. Magdalino, ed., *Byzantium in the Year 1000*. Leiden and Boston: Brill. 71–108.

Christou, P. K. (1996). *Ὁ «Βασιλικὸς Ἀνδριὰς» τοῦ Νικηφόρου Βλεμμύδη: Συμβολὴ στὴν πολιτικὴ θεωρία τῶν Βυζαντινῶν.* Athens: Kyromanos.

(2003). *Οἱ περιπέτειες τῶν ἐθνικῶν ὀνομάτων τῶν Ἑλλήνων.* 4th ed. Thessalonike: Kyromanos.

Chrysos, E. K. (1978). "The Title ΒΑΣΙΛΕΥΣ in Early Byzantine International Relations," *DOP* 32: 29–75.

ed. (1992). *Πρακτικά διεθνούς συμποσίου γιά τὸ Δεσποτάτο τῆς Ἠπείρου.* Arta: Musico-Philological Association of Arta "O Skoufas."

(1996). "The Roman Political Identity in Late Antiquity and Early Byzantium." In Fledelius 7–16.

(2003). "Romans and Foreigners." In Cameron 119–136.

ed. (2005a). *Τὸ Βυζάντιο ὡς Οἰκουμένη.* Athens: National Research Institute.

(2005b). "Τὸ Βυζάντιο καὶ η διεθνή κοινωνία του Μεσαίωνα." In ibid. 59–78.

Ciggaar, K. N. (1973). "Une description anonyme de Constantinople du XIIe siècle," *REB* 31: 325–354.

(1996). *Western Travellers to Constantinople: The West and Byzantium, 962–1204. Cultural and Political Relations.* Leiden: Brill.

Clark, E. G. (2001). "Pastoral Care: Town and Country in Late-Antique Preaching." In T. S. Burns and J. W. Eadie, eds., *Urban Centers and Rural Contexts in Late Antiquity.* East Lansing: Michigan State University Press. 265–284.

Clucas, L. (1981). *The Trial of John Italos and the Crisis of Intellectual Values in Byzantium in the Eleventh Century.* Munich: Institut für Byzantinistik, neugriechische Philologie und byzantinische Kunstgeschichte der Universität.

Cohen, E. E. (2000). *The Athenian Nation.* Princeton University Press.

Coleman, J. E. (1997). "Ancient Greek Ethnocentrism." In J. E. Coleman and C. A. Walz, eds., *Greeks and Barbarians: Essays on the Interactions between Greeks and Non-Greeks in Antiquity and the Consequences for Eurocentrism.* Bethesda, MD: CDL Press. 175–220.

Connor, C. L. (2004). *Women of Byzantium.* New Haven and London: Yale University Press.

Constantelos, D. J. (1998). *Christian Hellenism: Essays and Studies in Continuity and Change.* New Rochelle, NY, and Athens: A. D. Caratzas.

Constantinides, C. N. (1982). *Higher Education in Byzantium in the Thirteenth and Early Fourteenth Centuries (1204–ca. 1310).* Nicosia: Cyprus Research Center.

(2003). "Teachers and Students of Rhetoric in the Late Byzantine Period." In Jeffreys (2003a) 39–53.

Coulie, B. (1982). "Chaînes d'allusions dans les Discours IV et V de Grégoire de Nazianze," *JöB* 32.3: 137–143.

Cresci, L. R. (2001). "Parodia e metafora nella *Catomiomachia* di Teodoro Prodromo," *Eikasmos* 12: 197–204.

Criscuolo, U. (1971). "L'epistola di Michele Italico ad Irene Ducas," *EEBΣ* 38: 57–70.

(1977). "Due epistole inedite di Manuele Karanteno o Saranteno," *Bollettino della Badia Greca di Grottaferrata* 31: 103–119.

(1981). "Tardoantico e umanesimo bizantino: Michele Psello," *Koinonia* 5: 7–23.

(1982a). "πολιτικὸς ἀνήρ: Contributo al pensiero politica di Michele Psello," *Rendiconti dell'Accademia di Archeologia, Lettere e Belle Arti di Napoli* 57: 129–163.

(1982b). "Pselliana," *Studi Italiani di Filologia Classica* 4: 194–215.

(1983). *Michele Psello: Orazione in memoria di Costantino Lichudi.* Messina: Ed. Dott. Antonino Sfameni.

(1987). "Gregorio di Nazianzo e Giuliano." In U. Criscuolo, ed., *Talariskos: Studia graeca Antonio Garzya sexagenario a discipulis oblata.* Naples: M. D'Auria Editore. 165–208.

Croke, B. (1981). "The Early Byzantine Earthquakes and their Liturgical Commemorations," *Byzantion* 51: 122–147.

Cupane, C. (1974). "Un caso di giudizio di Dio nel romanzo di Teodoro Prodromo (I 372–404)," *Rivista di Studi Bizantini e Neoellenici* 10–11: 147–168.

Curta, F. (1995). "Atticism, Homer, Neoplatonism, and *Fürstenspiegel*: Julian's Second Panegyric on Constantius," *GRBS* 36: 177–211.

(2002). "Language, ἔθνη, and National Gods: A Note on Julian's Concept of Hellenism," *Ancient World* 22: 3–19.

(2004). "Barbarians in Dark-Age Greece: Slavs or Avars?" In T. Stepanov and V. Vachkova, eds., *Civitas Divino-Humana in Honorem Annorum LX Georgii Bakalov.* Sofia: Centar za izsledvaniia na balgarite Tangra TanNakRa IK. 513–550.

Curty, O. (1995). *Les parentés légendaires entre cités grecques: Catalogue raisonnée des inscriptions contenant le terme ΣΥΓΓΕΝΕΙΑ et analyse critique.* Geneva: Droz.

Cutler, A., and R. Browning (1992). "In the Margins of Byzantium? Some Icons in Michael Psellos," *BMGS* 16: 21–32.

Dagron, G. (1968). "L'empire romain d'orient au IVe siècle et les traditions politiques de l'hellénisme," *TM* 3: 1–242.

(1969). "Aux origines de la civilization byzantine: Langue de culture et langue d'État," *Revue historique* 241: 23–56.

(1974). *Naissance d'une capital: Constantinople et ses institutions de 330 à 451.* Paris: Presses Universitaires de France.

(1981). "Quand le terre tremble . . .," *TM* 8: 87–103.

(1993). "Communication et stratégies linguistiques." In Moschonas (1993a) 81–92.

(1994). "Formes et fonctions du pluralisme linguistique à Byzance (IXe–XIIe siècle)," *TM* 12: 219–240.

(2003). *Emperor and Priest: The Imperial Office in Byzantium.* Tr. J. Birrell. Cambridge University Press.

(2005a). "L'oecuménicité politique: Droit sur l'espace, droit sur le temps." In Chrysos (2005a) 47–57.

(2005b). "Byzance et la Grèce antique: Un impossible retour aux sources." In J. Leclant and M. Zink, eds., *La Grèce antique sous le regard du Moyen Âge occidental*. Paris: Diffusion de Boccard (= *Cahiers de la villa "Kérylos"* v. XVI). 195–206.

Darrouzès, J. (1962). "Notice sur Grégoire Antiochos (1160 à 1196)," *REB* 20: 61–92.

(1965). "Notes sur Euthyme Tornikès, Euthyme Malakès et Georges Tornikès," *REB* 23: 148–167.

Delacroix-Besnier, C. (1997). *Les Dominicains et la Chrétienté grecque aux XIVe et XVe siècles*. Rome: École française de Rome.

Demoen, K. (1996). *Pagan and Biblical Exempla in Gregory Nazianzen: A Study in Rhetoric and Hermeneutics*. Turnholt: Brepols (= *Corpus Christianorum, Lingua Patrum* v. II).

Dendias, M. (1953). "Διενέξεις μεταξὺ αὐτοχθόνων καὶ προσφύγων ἐν Ἠπείρῳ μετὰ τὸ 1204 καὶ ἡ ἀκολουθηθεῖσα ἐποικιστικὴ πολιτική," *Atti dello VIII Congresso internazionale di studi bizantini*, v. II. Rome: *Studi Bizantini e Neoellenici* v. VIII. 302–306.

Dennis, G. T. (2003). "Elias the Monk, Friend of Psellos." In J. W. Nesbitt, ed., *Byzantine Authors: Literary Activities and Preoccupations. Texts and Translations Dedicated to the Memory of Nicolas Oikonomides*. Leiden and Boston: Brill. 43–62.

van Dieten, J.-L. (1971). *Niketas Choniates: Erläuterungen zu den Reden und Briefen nebst einer Biographie*. Berlin and New York: W. de Gruyter.

(1990). "Das lateinische Kaiserreich von Konstantinopel und die Verhandlungen über kirchliche Wiedervereinigung." In V. D. van Aalst and K. N. Ciggaar, eds., *The Latin Empire: Some Contributions*. Hernen: A. A. Bredius Foundations. 93–125.

Dimou, B. A. (1992). "Εθνολογικά στοιχεία στο έργο του Δημητρίου Χωματιανού." In Chrysos 279–302.

Dimou, N. (1975). *Η δυστυχία του να είσαι Ελληνας*. Athens: Ikaros.

Dirven, L. (1997). "The Author of the *De Dea Syria* and his Cultural Heritage," *Numen* 44: 153–179.

Ditten, H. (1993). *Ethnische Verschiebungen zwischen der Balkanhalbinsel und Kleinasien vom Ende des 6. bis zur zweiten Hälfte des 9. Jahrhunderts*. Berlin: Akademie Verlag (= *Berliner byzantinische Arbeiten* v. LIX).

Dölger, F. (1953). "Rom in der Gedankenwelt der Byzantiner." In F. Dölger, *Byzanz und die europäische Staatenwelt*. Ettal: Buch-Kunstverlag. 70–115.

Dostálová, R. (1983). "Christentum und Hellenismus: Zur Herausbildung einer neuen Kulturellen Identität im 4. Jahrhundert," *BS* 44: 1–12.

Dubuisson, M. (1991). "*Graecus, Graeculus, graecari*: L'emploi péjoratif du nom des Grecs en latin." In Saïd 315–335.

Duffy, J. (1995). "Reactions of Two Byzantine Intellectuals to the Theory and Practice of Magic: Michael Psellos and Michael Italikos." In H. Maguire, ed., *Byzantine Magic*. Washington, DC: Dumbarton Oaks Research Library and Collection. 83–97.

(1998). "Tzetzes on Psellos." In C. F. Collatz et al., eds., *Dissertatiunculae criticae: Festschrift für Günther Christian Hansen*. Würzburg: Königshausen & Neumann. 441–445.

(2001). "Bitter Brine and Sweet Fresh Water: The Anatomy of a Metaphor in Psellos." In C. Sode and S. Takács, eds., *Novum Millennium: Studies on Byzantine History and Culture Dedicated to Paul Speck*. Aldershot: Ashgate. 88–96.

(2002). "Hellenic Philosophy in Byzantium and the Lonely Mission of Michael Psellos." In K. Ierodiakonou, ed., *Byzantine Philosophy and its Ancient Sources*. Oxford: Clarendon Press. 139–156.

Duffy, J. and E. Papaioannou (2003). "Michael Psellos and the Authorship of the *Historia Syntomos*: Final Considerations." In Βυζάντιο· Κράτος και Κοινωνία *(Μνήμη Νίκου Οικονομίδη)*. Athens: National Research Institute. 219–229.

Dujčev, I. (1980). "Some Remarks on the *Chronicle of Monemvasia*." In A. E. Laiou-Thomadakis, ed., *Charanis Studies: Essays in Honor of Peter Charanis*. New Brunswick, NJ: Rutgers University Press. 51–59.

Dunn, M. (1977). "Evangelization or Repentance? The Re-Christianization of the Peloponnese in the Ninth and Tenth Centuries," *Studies in Church History* 14 *(Renaissance and Renewal in Christian History)*: 71–86.

Dvornik, F. (1948). *The Photian Schism: History and Legend*. Cambridge University Press.

Dzielska, M. (1996). *Hypatia of Alexandria*. Tr. F. Lyra. Cambridge, MA: Harvard University Press.

Eastmond, A. (2004). *Art and Identity in Thirteenth-Century Byzantium: Hagia Sophia and the Empire of Trebizond*. Aldershot and Burlington, VT: Ashgate.

Edwards, M. (2004a). "*Romanitas* and the Church of Rome." In Swain and Edwards (2004) 187–210.

(2004b). "Pagan and Christian Monotheism in the Age of Constantine." In ibid. 211–234.

Efthimiou, M. B. (1987). *Greeks and Latins on Cyprus in the Thirteenth Century*. Brookline, MA: Hellenic College Press.

El Cheikh, N. M. (2004). *Byzantium Viewed by the Arabs*. London and Cambridge, MA: Harvard University Press.

Elton, H. (2000). "The Nature of the Sixth-Century Isaurians." In Mitchell and Greatrex 293–307.

Engels, D. (1990). *Roman Corinth: An Alternative Model for the Classical City*. University of Chicago Press.

Ferluga, J. (1972). "L'aristocratie byzantine en Morée au temps de la conquête latine," *BF* 4: 76–87.

Fink, R. O., A. J. Hoey, and W. F. Snyder (1940). "The Feriale Duranum," *Yale Classical Studies* 7: 1–222.

Fisher, E. A. (1982). "Greek Translations of Latin Literature in the Fourth Century AD," *Yale Classical Studies* 27: 173–215.

(1994). "Michael Psellos and the Literary Survival of Romulus," *Twentieth Annual Byzantine Studies Conference: Abstracts of Papers*. Ann Arbor: Byzantine Studies Conference. 75–76.

(2006). "Michael Psellos in a Hagiographical Landscape: The Life of St. Auxentios and the Encomion of Symeon the Metaphrast." In Barber and Jenkins 57–71.

# Bibliography

423

Fledelius, K., ed. (1996). *Byzantium: Identity, Image, Influence (Major Papers)*. Copenhagen: Eventus.

Flower, M. (2000). "Alexander the Great and Panhellenism." In A. B. Bosworth and E. J. Baynham, eds., *Alexander the Great in Fact and Fiction*. Oxford University Press. 96–135.

Flusin, B. (1998). "L'empereur et le Théologien: À propos du Retour des reliques de Grégoire de Nazianze (*BHG* 728)." In Ševčenko and Hutter 137–153.

Fögen, M. T. (1982). "Rechtsprechung mit Aristophanes," *Rechtshistorisches Journal* 1: 74–82.

(1998). "Reanimation of Roman Law in the Ninth Century: Remarks on Reasons and Results." In L. Brubaker, ed., *Byzantium in the Ninth Century: Dead or Alive?* Aldershot: Ashgate. 11–22.

Fortin, E. (1996). "Christianity and Hellenism in Basil the Great's Address *ad adulescentes*." In J. B. Benestad, ed., *Ernest L. Fortin: Collected Essays*, v. I: *The Birth of Philosophic Christianity: Studies in Early Christian and Medieval Thought*. Lanham, MD: Rowman and Littlefield. 137–151.

Foss, C. (1996). *Nicaea: A Byzantine Capital and Its Praises*. Brookline, MA: Hellenic College Press.

(1998). "Byzantine Responses to Turkish Attack: Some Sites of Asia Minor." In Ševčenko and Hutter 154–171.

Fowden, G. (1986). *The Egyptian Hermes: A Historical Approach to the Late Pagan Mind*. Princeton University Press.

Frankfurter, D. (1998). *Religion in Roman Egypt: Assimilation and Resistance*. Princeton University Press.

Frizzell, L. E. (1994). " 'Spoils from Egypt,' between Jews and Gnostics." In Helleman (1994a) 383–394.

Gabba, E. (1991). *Dionysius and* The History of Archaic Rome. Berkeley: University of California Press.

Gaca, K. L. (1999). "Paul's Uncommon Declaration in Romans 1:18–32 and Its Problematic Legacy for Pagan and Christian Relations," *Harvard Theological Review* 92: 165–198.

(2003). *The Making of Fornication: Eros, Ethics, and Political Reform in Greek Philosophy and Early Christianity*. Berkeley: University of California Press.

Garland, L. (1990a). " 'And His Bald Head Shone Like a Full Moon ...': An Appreciation of the Byzantine Sense of Humour as Recorded in Historical Sources of the Eleventh and Twelfth Centuries," *Parergon* n.s. 8: 1–31.

(1990b). " 'Be Amorous, But be Chaste ...': Sexual Morality in Byzantine Learned and Vernacular Romance," *BMGS* 14: 62–120.

Garnsey, P. (2004). "Roman Citizenship and Roman Law in the Late Empire." In Swain and Edwards 133–155.

Garsoïan, N. (1998). "Armenian Integration into the Byzantine Empire." In Ahrweiler and Laiou 53–124.

Garzya, A. (1967). "On Michael Psellus' Admission of Faith," *EEBΣ* 35: 41–46.

(1972). "Observations sur l' 'Autobiographie' de Gregoire de Chypre." In A. Papageorgiou, ed., Πρακτικά τοῦ πρώτου διεθνοῦς Κυπρολογικοῦ συνεδρίου, v. II: Μεσαιωνικὸν Τμῆμα. Leukosia: Ἑταιρεία Κυπριακῶν Σπουδῶν. 33–36.

(1973). "Literarische und rhetorische Polemiken der Komnenenzeit," *BS* 34: 1–14.

(1985). "Visages de l'hellénisme dans le monde byzantin (IVe–XIIe siècles)," *Byzantion* 55: 463–482.

(1992). "Byzantium." In K. J. Dover, ed., *Perceptions of the Ancient Greeks.* Cambridge, MA, and Oxford: Blackwell. 29–53.

Gasparis, C. (2005). "The Period of Venetian Rule on Crete: Breaks and Continuities during the Thirteenth Century." In A. Laiou, ed., *Urbs Capta: The Fourth Crusade and its Consequences.* Paris: Lethielleux (= *Réalités byzantines* v. X). 233–246.

Gautier, P. (1970). "La curieuse ascendance de Jean Tzetzès," *REB* 28: 207–220.

(1974). "Elogue funèbre de Nicolas de la Belle Source par Michel Psellos moine à l'Olympe," Βυζαντινά 6: 9–69.

Geiger, J. (2002). "Language, Culture and Identity in Ancient Palestine." In E. N. Ostenfeld, ed., *Greek Romans and Roman Greeks: Studies in Cultural Interaction.* Aarhus University Press. 233–246.

Gellner, E. (1997). *Nationalism.* New York University Press.

Georgiopoulou, S. (1990). "Theodore II Dukas Laskaris (1222–1258) as an Author and an Intellectual of the XIIIth Century." Dissertation: Harvard University.

Germino, E. (2004). *Scuola e cultura nella legislazione di Giuliano l'Apostata.* Naples: E. Jovene (= *Pubblicazioni della Facoltà di Giurisprudenza della Seconda Università di Napoli* v. XXVII).

Gill, J. (1977). "The Tribulations of the Greek Church in Cyprus, 1196 – c. 1280," *BF* 5: 73–93.

(1979). *Byzantium and the Papacy, 1198–1400.* New Brunswick, NJ: Rutgers University Press.

Gittings, E. A. (2003). "Civic Life: Women as Embodiments of Civic Life." In I. Kalavrezou, ed., *Byzantine Women and Their World.* Cambridge, MA: Harvard University Art Museums; New Haven and London: Yale University Press. 35–42.

Glavinas, A. A. (1972). Ἡ ἐπὶ Ἀλεξίου Κομνηνοῦ *(1081–1118)* περὶ ἱερῶν σκευῶν, κειμηλίων καὶ ἁγίων εἰκόνων ἔρις *(1081–1095).* Thessalonike: Center for Byzantine Research.

Gleason, M. W. (1995). *Making Men: Sophists and Self-Representation in Ancient Rome.* Princeton University Press.

Goldhill, S. (2002). *Who Needs Greek? Contests in the Cultural History of Hellenism.* Cambridge University Press.

Gordon, P. (1996). *Epicurus in Lycia: The Second-century World of Diogenes of Oenoanda.* Ann Arbor: University of Michigan Press.

Goudriaan, K. (1992). "Ethnical Strategies in Graeco-Roman Egypt." In P. Bilde *et al.*, eds., *Ethnicity in Hellenistic Egypt.* Aarhus University Press. 74–99.

Gouillard, J. (1967). "Le Synodikon de l'Orthodoxie: Édition et commentaire," *TM* 2: 1–316.

(1985). "Le procés officiel de Jean l'Italien: Les actes et leurs sous-entendus," *TM* 9: 133–174.

Goulet, R. (2000). "Prohérésius le païen et quelques remarques sur la chronologie d'Eunape de Sardes," *Antiquité tardive* 8: 209–222.

Gounaridis, P. (1986). "'Grecs,' 'Hellènes' et 'Romains' dans l'état de Nicée." In B. Kremmydas *et al.*, eds., Ἀφιέρωμα στὸν Νίκο Σβορώνο, v. I. Rethymno: University of Crete. 248–257.

    (1996). Γένος Ῥωμαίων: Βυζαντινές καί νεοελληνικές ἑρμηνείες. Athens: Ἱδρυμα Γουλανδρή-Χορν.

Gourgouris, S. (1996). *Dream Nation: Enlightenment, Colonization, and the Institution of Modern Greece*. Stanford University Press.

Graf, F. (1997). *Magic in the Ancient World*. Tr. F. Philip. Cambridge, MA: Harvard University Press.

Grant, R. M. (1988). *Greek Apologists of the Second Century*. Philadelphia: The Westminster Press.

Greatrex, G. (2000). "Roman Identity in the Sixth Century." In Mitchell and Greatrex 267–292.

Grierson, P. (1962). "The Tombs and Obits of the Byzantine Emperors (337–1042)," *DOP* 16: 1–63.

Grigoriadis, I. (1998). *Linguistic and Literary Studies in the* Epitome historion *of John Zonaras*. Thessalonike: Center for Byzantine Research.

Grigoriou-Ioannidou, M. (2000). "The καθ' ἡμᾶς γλῶσσα in the Mauros and Kouber episode (*Miracula S. Demetrii* 291)." In Burke and Scott 89–101.

Gruen, E. (1992). *Culture and National Identity in Republican Rome*. Ithaca, NY: Cornell University Press.

    (1998). *Heritage and Hellenism: The Reinvention of Jewish Tradition*. Berkeley: University of California Press.

    (2002). *Diaspora: Jews amidst Greeks and Romans*. Cambridge, MA, and London: Harvard University Press.

Grumel, V. (1930). "L'authenticité de la lettre de Jean Vatatzès, empereur de Nicée, au Pape Grégoire IX," *Échos d'Orient* 29: 450–458.

Grünbart, M. (1996). "Prosopographische Beiträge zum Briefcorpus des Ioannes Tzetzes," *JÖB* 46: 175–226.

Gutas, D. (1998). *Greek Thought, Arabic Culture: The Graeco-Arabic Translation Movement in Baghdad and Early 'Abbasid Society (2nd–4th/8th–10th centuries)*. London and New York: Routledge.

Habicht, C. (1998). *Pausanias' Guide to Ancient Greece*. Berkeley: University of California Press.

Hägg, T. (1983). *The Novel in Antiquity*. Oxford: Basil Blackwell.

Haldon, J. F. (1999). *Warfare, State and Society in the Byzantine World, 565–1204*. University College London Press.

    (2002). "Humour and the Everyday in Byzantium." In G. Halsall, ed., *Humour, History, and Politics in Late Antiquity and the Early Middle Ages*. Cambridge University Press. 48–71.

Hall, J. M. (1997). *Ethnic Identity in Greek Antiquity*. Cambridge University Press.

(2002). *Hellenicity: Between Ethnicity and Culture.* University of Chicago Press.

Hall, L. J. (1999). "*Latinitas* in the Late Antique Greek East: Cultural Assimilation and Ethnic Distinctions." In S. N. Byrne and E. P. Cueva, eds., *Veritatis Amicitiaeque Causa: Essays in Honor of Anna Lydia Motto and John R. Clark.* Wauconda, IL: Bolchazy-Carducci Publishers. 85–111.

Hanson, R. P. C. (1988). *The Search for the Christian Doctrine of God: The Arian Controversy, 318–381.* Edinburgh: T&T Clark.

Harder, R. E. (2000). "Religion und Glaube in den Romanen der Komnenenzeit." In Agapitos and Reinsch 55–80.

(2003). "Der byzantinische Roman des 12. Jahrhunderts als Spiegel des zeitgenössischen Literaturbetriebs." In S. Panayotakis *et al.*, eds., *The Ancient Novel and Beyond.* Leiden and Boston: Brill. 357–369.

Harris, A. (2003). *Byzantium, Britain, and the West: The Archaeology of Cultural Identity, AD 400–650.* Gloucestershire and Charleston, SC: Tempus.

Hartog, F. (2001). *Memories of Odysseus: Frontier Tales from Ancient Greece.* Tr. J. Lloyd. University of Chicago Press.

Harvey, A. (1989). *Economic Expansion in the Byzantine Empire, 900–1200.* Cambridge University Press.

Heather, P. (1988). "The Anti-Scythian Tirade of Synesius' *De Regno,*" *Phoenix* 42: 152–172.

(1998). "Themistius: A Political Philosopher." In M. Whitby, ed., *The Propaganda of Power: The Role of Panegyric in Late Antiquity.* Leiden and Boston: Brill. 125–150.

Heather, P., and D. Moncur (2001). *Politics, Philosophy, and Empire in the Fourth Century: Select Orations of Themistius. TTH* v. XXXVI.

Heisenberg, A. (1900). "Review of N. Festa, ed., *Theodori Ducae Lascaris epistulae,*" *BZ* 9: 211–222.

Helleman, W. E. ed. (1994a). *Hellenization Revisited: Shaping a Christian Response within the Greco-Roman World.* Lanham, MD: University Press of America.

(1994b). "Tertullian on Athens and Jerusalem." In ibid. 361–381.

Henaut, B. W. (1994). "Alexandria or Athens as the Essence of Hellenization: A Historian Responds to a Philosopher." In Helleman (1994a) 99–106.

Hengel, M. (1974). *Judaism and Hellenism: Studies in their Encounter in Palestine during the Early Hellenistic Period.* 2 vols. Tr. J. Bowden. Minneapolis: Fortress Press.

Herington, C. J. (1969). "Homer: A Byzantine Perspective," *Arion* 8: 432–434.

Herrin, J. (1970). "The Collapse of the Byzantine Empire in the Twelfth Century: A Study of a Medieval Economy," *University of Birmingham Historical Journal* 12: 188–203.

(1973). "Aspects of the Process of Hellenization in the Early Middle Ages," *Annual of the British School at Athens* 68: 113–126.

(1975). "Realities of Byzantine Provincial Government: Hellas and Peloponnesos, 1180–1205," *DOP* 29: 253–287.

(1976). "The Ecclesiastical Organization of Central Greece at the Time of Michael Choniates: New Evidence from the Codex Atheniensis 1371," *Actes du XVe Congrès international d'études byzantines (Athènes),* v. IV: *Histoire.* 131–137.

Herzfeld, M. (1986). *Ours Once More: Folklore, Ideology, and the Making of Modern Greece*. New York: Pella Publishing.

Hinterberger, M. (1999). *Autobiographische Traditionen in Byzanz*. Vienna: Verlag der österreichischen Akademie der Wissenschaften (= *Wiener byzantinische Studien* v. XXII).

Hoeck, J. M., and R. J. Loenertz (1965). *Nikolaos-Nektarios von Otranto, Abt von Casole: Beiträge zur Geschichte der ost-westlichen Beziehungen unter Innozenz III. und Friedrich II*. Ettal: Buch-Kunstverlag (= *Studia Patristica et Byzantina* v. XI).

Holford-Strevens, L. (1997). "Favorinus: The Man of Paradoxes." In J. Barnes and M. Griffin, eds., *Philosophia Togata II: Plato and Aristotle at Rome*. Oxford: Clarendon Press. 188–217.

Holmes, C. (2003). "Political Elites in the Reign of Basil II." In P. Magdalino, ed., *Byzantium in the Year 1000*. Leiden and Boston: Brill. 35–69.

(2005). *Basil II and the Governance of Empire (967–1025)*. Oxford University Press.

Holum, K. G. (2005). "The Classical City in the Sixth Century: Survival and Transformation." In Maas 87–112.

Honoré, T. (1975). "Some Constitutions Composed by Justinian," *Journal of Roman Studies* 65: 107–123.

(1978). *Tribonian*. Ithaca, NY: Cornell University Press.

(2004). "Roman Law AD 200–400: From Cosmopolis to Rechtstaat?" In Swain and Edwards 109–132.

Hörandner, W. (1974). *Theodoros Prodromos: Historische Gedichte*. Vienna: Verlag der österreichischen Akademie der Wissenschaften (= *Wiener byzantinische Studien* v. XI).

(1993). "Das Bild des Anderen: Lateiner und Barbaren in der Sicht der byzantinischen Hofpoesie," *BS* 54: 162–168.

(1996). "Literary Criticism in 11th-Century Byzantium: Views of Michael Psellos on John Chrysostom's Style," *IJCT* 2: 336–344.

Hornblower, S. (1982). *Mausolus*. Oxford: Clarendon Press.

Hoyland, R. (2004). "Language and Identity: The Twin Histories of Arabic and Aramaic (and: Why did Aramaic Succeed where Greek Failed?)," *Scripta Classica Israelica* 23: 183–199.

Huart, P. (1978). "Julien et l'hellénisme: Idées morales et politiques." In Braun and Richer 99–123.

Humbert, S. (1991). "Plutarque, Alexandre et l'hellénisme." In Saïd 169–182.

Hunger, H. (1954). "Allegorische Mythendeutung in der Antike und bei Johannes Tzetzes," *JöBS* 3: 35–54.

(1969–1970). "On the Imitation (ΜΙΜΗΣΙΣ) of Antiquity in Byzantine Literature," *DOP* 23–24: 17–38.

(1978). *Die hochsprachliche profane Literatur der Byzantiner*. 2 vols. Munich: C. H. Beck.

(1984). "Romanos Melodos, Dichter, Prediger, Rhetor – und sein Publikum," *JöB* 34: 15–42.

(1987). *Graeculus perfidus,* Ἰταλὸς ἰταμός: *Il senso dell'alterità nei rapporti Greco-Romani ed Italo-Bizantini.* Rome: Unione internazionale degli istituti di archeologia, storia e storia dell'arte in Roma.

(1990). "Athen in Byzanz: Traum und Realität," *JöB* 40: 43–61.

Hunt, L.-A. (1984). "Comnenian Aristocratic Palace Decoration: Descriptions and Islamic Connections." In Angold 138–156 (with plates).

Hunter, R., ed. (1998). *Studies in Heliodorus.* Cambridge: Cambridge Philological Society (Supplementary v. XXI).

Ierodiakonou, K. (2004). "The Self-Conscious Style of Some Byzantine Philosophers (11th–14th Century)." In Angelidi 99–110.

Impellizzeri, S. (1984). "Romani, Latini e barbari nell' 'Alessiade' di Anna Comnena." In *Da Roma alla terza Roma.* Studi II: *La nozione di "Romano" tra cittadinanza e universalità.* Naples: Edizioni Scientifiche Italiane. 377–383.

Inglebert, H. (2001). *Interpretatio Christiana: Les mutations des savoirs (cosmographie, géographie, ethnographie, histoire) dans l'Antiquité chrétienne, 30–630 après J.-C.* Paris: Institut d'études augustiniennes.

Ioakimidou, C. (2000). "Auch wir sind Griechen! Statuenreihen westgriechischer Kolonisten in Delpi und Olympia," *Nikephoros* 13: 63–94.

Irmscher, J. (1967). "ΦΙΛΕΛΛΗΝ im mittelgriechischen Sprachgebrauch," *BF* 2: 238–246.

(1970). "Nikäa als 'Zentrum des griechischen Patriotismus,' " *Revue des études sud-est européennes* 8: 33–47.

(1972). "Nikäa als 'Mittelpunkt des griechischen Patriotismus,' " *BF* 4: 114–137.

Jacoby, D. (1967). "Les archontes grecs et la féodalité en Morée franque," *TM* 2: 421–481.

(1973). "The Encounter of Two Societies: Western Conquerors and Byzantines in the Peloponnesus after the Fourth Crusade," *The American Historical Review* 78: 873–906.

(1989). "From Byzantium to Latin Romania: Continuity and Change." In B. Abel *et al.,* eds., *Latins and Greeks in the Eastern Mediterranean after 1204.* London: Frank Cass. 1–44.

(1993). "The Venetian Presence in the Latin Empire of Constantinople (1204–1261): The Challenge of Feudalism and the Byzantine Inheritance," *JöB* 43: 141–201.

Jaeger, W. (1961). *Early Christianity and Greek Paideia.* Cambridge, MA, and London: Harvard University Press.

Janin, R. (1969). *Le géographie ecclésiastique de l'empire byzantin,* pt. 1: *Le siège de Constantinople et la patriarcat oecuménique,* v. III: *Les églises et les monastères.* 2nd ed. Paris: Institut français d'ètudes byzantines.

Jastram, D. N. (1994). "The Praeparatio Evangelica and Spoliatio Motifs as Patterns of Hellenistic Judaism in Philo of Alexandria." In Helleman (1994a) 189–203.

Jeffreys, E. (1979). "The Attitudes of Byzantine Chronicles towards Ancient History," *Byzantion* 49: 199–238.

(1984). "Western Infiltration of the Byzantine Aristocracy: Some Suggestions." In Angold 202–210.

(1998). "The Novels of Mid-Twelfth Century Constantinople: The Literary and Social Context." In I. Ševčenko and I. Hutter, eds., *ΑΕΤΟΣ: Studies in Honour of Cyril Mango Presented to Him on April 14, 1998.* Stuttgart and Leipzig: Teubner. 191–199.

ed. (2003a). *Rhetoric in Byzantium.* Burlington, VT, and Aldershot: Ashgate.

(2003b). "Nikephoros Bryennios Reconsidered." In Vlyssidou (2003) 201–214.

(2004). "The Depiction of Female Sensibilities in the Twelfth Century." In Angelidi 73–85.

Jeffreys, E., and M. Jeffreys (1994). "Who was Eirene the Sevastokratorissa?" *Byzantion* 64: 40–68.

Jeffreys, M. (1974). "The Nature and Origins of the Political Verse," *DOP* 28: 142–195.

(1975). "The Chronicle of the Morea: Priority of the Greek Version," *BZ* 68: 304–350.

(2003c). " 'Rhetorical' Texts." In Jeffreys (2003a) 87–100.

Jenkins, D. (2006). "Psellos' Conceptual Precision." In Barber and Jenkins 131–151.

Joannou, P. (1954). "Der Nominalismus und die menschliche Psychologie Christi: Das Semeioma gegen Eustratios von Nikaia (1117)," *BZ* 47: 369–378.

Johnson, S. F. (2006). *The Life and Miracles of Thekla: A Literary Study.* Washington, DC: Center for Hellenic Studies (Harvard University Press).

Jones, A. H. M. (1940). *The Greek City from Alexander to Justinian.* Oxford: Clarendon Press.

(1959). "Were Ancient Heresies National or Social Movements in Disguise?" *Journal of Theological Studies* 10: 280–298.

(1971). *The Cities of the Eastern Roman Provinces.* 2nd ed. Oxford: Clarendon Press.

(1986). *The Later Roman Empire, 284–602: A Social, Economic, and Administrative Survey.* Baltimore: Johns Hopkins University Press.

Jones, C. P. (1978). *The Roman World of Dio Chrysostom.* Cambridge, MA, and London: Harvard University Press.

(1996). "ἔθνος and γένος in Herodotus," *Classical Quarterly* 46: 315–320.

Jouanno, C. (1989). "Nicétas Eugenianos, un héritier du roman grec," *Revue des études grecques* 102: 346–360.

(1992). "Les barbares dans le roman byzantin du XIIe siècle: Fonction d'un topos," *Byzantion* 62: 264–300.

(2000). "Discourse of the Body in Prodromos, Eugenianos, and Macrembolites." In Agapitos and Reinsch 81–93.

(2005). "A Byzantine Novelist Staging the Ancient Greek World: Presence, Form, and Function of Antiquity in Makrembolites' *Hysmine and Hysminias.*" In S. Kaklamanis and M. Paschalis, eds., Ἡ πρόσληψη τῆς ἀρχαιότητας στὸ βυζαντινὸ μυθιστόρημα. Athens: Stigmi. 17–29.

Jusdanis, G. (2001). *The Necessary Nation.* Princeton University Press.

Jüthner, J. (1923). *Hellenen und Barbaren aus der Geschichte des Nationalbewussteins.* Leipzig: Dieterich'sche Verlagsbuchhandlung.

Kahane, H. and R. Kahane (1981). "Byzantium's Impact on the West: The Linguistic Evidence," *Illinois Classical Studies* 6: 389–415.

(1982). "The Western Impact on Byzantium: The Linguistic Evidence," *DOP* 36: 127–153.

Kaimio, J. (1979). *The Romans and the Greek Language*. Helsinki: Societas Scientiarum Fennica (= *Commentationes Humanarum Litterarum* v. LXIV).

Kalavrezou, I., ed. (2003). *Byzantine Women and Their World*. Cambridge, MA: Harvard University Art Museums; New Haven and London: Yale University Press.

Kaldellis, A. (1999a). *The Argument of Psellos' Chronographia*. Leiden: Brill.

(1999b). "The Historical and Religious Views of Agathias: A Reinterpretation," *Byzantion* 69: 206–252.

(2002). Λέσβος και ανατολική Μεσόγειος κατά τη ρωμαϊκή και πρώιμη βυζαντινή περίοδο *(100 π.Χ.–600 μ.Χ.)*: Μελέτη των κοινωνικών, πολιτικών και θρησκευτικών δομών. Thessaloniki: Herodotos.

(2003). "The Religion of Ioannes Lydos," *Phoenix* 57: 300–316.

(2004a). *Procopius of Caesarea: Tyranny, History, and Philosophy at the End of Antiquity*. Philadelphia: University of Pennsylvania Press.

(2004b). "Classicism, Barbarism, and Warfare: Prokopios and the Conservative Reaction to Later Roman Military Policy," *American Journal of Ancient History* n.s. 3: forthcoming.

(2005a). "Republican Theory and Political Dissidence in Ioannes Lydos," *BMGS* 29: 1–16.

(2005b). "The Date of Psellos' Theological Lectures and Higher Religious Education in Constantinople," *BS* 63 (2005) 143–151.

(2005c). "The Works and Days of Hesychios the Illoustrios of Miletos," *GRBS* 45: 381–403.

(2006). *Mothers and Sons, Fathers and Daughters: The Byzantine Family of Michael Psellos*. South Bend, IN: Notre Dame University Press.

(2007a). "Historicism in Byzantine Thought and Literature," *DOP* 61: forthcoming.

(2007b). "A Byzantine Argument for the Equivalence of All Religions: Michael Attaleiates on Ancient and Modern Romans," *IJCT* 14: 1–20.

(2008). *The Christian Parthenon: Pilgrimage and Classicism in Byzantine Athens*. Cambridge University Press. forthcoming.

Karagiannopoulos, I. E. (1992). Η πολιτική θεωρία των Βυζαντινών. Thessalonike: Banias.

Karpozilos, A. (1973). *The Ecclesiastical Controversy between the Kingdom of Nicaea and the Principality of Epiros (1217–1233)*. Thessalonike: Center for Byzantine Research.

(1982). Συμβολή στή μελέτη τοῦ βίου καί τοῦ ἔργου τοῦ Ἰωάννη Μαυρόποδος. Ioannina: University of Ioannina, Scientific Journal of the Faculty of Arts (= *Dodone* Suppl. v. XVIII).

(1997). Βυζαντινοί ἱστορικοί καί χρονογράφοι, v. I: *405–705 αἰ.* Athens: Kanaki.

Kaster. R. A. (1988). *Guardians of Language: The Grammarian and Society in Late Antiquity*. Berkeley: University of California Press.

Katičić, R. (1957). " Ἄννα ἡ Κομνηνὴ καὶ ὁ "Ομηρος," *ΕΕΒΣ* 27: 213–223.

Katsaros, V. (1980). "Μία ἀκόμη μαρτυρία γιὰ τὴ βυζαντινὴ μονὴ τοῦ Κρεμαστοῦ," *Κληρονομία* 12: 367–388.

(1988). *Ἰωάννης Κασταμονίτης: Συμβολὴ στὴ μελέτη τοῦ βίου, τοῦ ἔργου καὶ τῆς ἐποχῆς του*. Thessalonike: Center for Byzantine Research.

(1993). "Leo the Mathematician, His Literary Presence in Byzantium during the 9th Century." In P. L. Butzer and D. Lohrmann, eds., *Science in Western and Eastern Civilization in Carolingian Times*. Basel: Birkhäuser. 383–398.

Kazanaki-Lappa, M. (2002). "Medieval Athens." In A. E. Laiou, ed., *The Economic History of Byzantium from the Seventh through the Fifteenth Century*, v. II. Washington, DC: Dumbarton Oaks Research Library and Collection. 639–646.

Kazhdan, A. (1967). "Bemerkungen zu Niketas Eugenianos," *JöBS* 16: 101–117.

(1983a). "Hagiographical Notes. 3. An Attempt at Hagio-Autobiography: The Pseudo-Life of 'Saint' Psellus?" *Byzantion* 53: 546–556.

(1983b). "Looking back to Antiquity: Three Notes," *GRBS* 24: 375–377.

(1984a). "The Aristocracy and the Imperial Ideal." In Angold 43–57.

(1984b), in collaboration with S. Franklin. *Studies on Byzantine Literature of the Eleventh and Twelfth Centuries*. Cambridge University Press; Paris: Éditions de la maison des sciences de l'homme.

(1985). "Hermitic, Cenobitic, and Secular Ideals in Byzantine Hagiography of the Ninth through the Twelfth Centuries," *Greek Orthodox Theological Review* 30: 473–487.

(2001). "Latins and Franks in Byzantium: Perception and Reality from the Eleventh to the Twelfth Century." In A. E. Laiou and R. P. Mottahedeh, eds., *The Crusades from the Perspective of Byzantium and the Muslim World*. Washington, DC: Dumbarton Oaks Research Library and Collection. 83–100.

Kazhdan, A., and G. Constable (1982). *People and Power in Byzantium: An Introduction to Modern Byzantine Studies*. Washington, DC: Dumbarton Oaks Center for Byzantine Studies.

Kazhdan, A. P., and A. W. Epstein (1985). *Change in Byzantine Culture in the Eleventh and Twelfth Centuries*. Berkeley: University of California Press.

Kelly, C. (2004). *Ruling the Later Roman Empire*. Cambridge, MA, and London: Belknap Press of Harvard University Press.

Kelly, G. (2003). "The New Rome and the Old: Ammianus Marcellinus' Silences on Constantinople," *Classical Quarterly* 53: 588–607.

Kennedy, G. A. (1983). *Greek Rhetoric under Christian Emperors*. Princeton University Press.

Kingsley, P. (1995). *Ancient Philosophy, Mystery, and Magic: Empedocles and Pythagorean Tradition*. Oxford: Clarendon Press.

Kiousopoulou, A. (1990). *Ο θεσμός της οικογένειας στην Ήπειρο κατά τον 13ο αιώνα*. Athens: A. N. Sakkoulas.

(2004). "Στοιχεία της βυζαντινής ενδυμασίας κατά την ύστερη εποχή: Τα καπέλα." In Angelidi 187–196.

Koder, J. (1976). "Arethas von Kaisareia und die sogenannte Chronik von Monembasia," *JöB* 25: 75–80.

(1990). "Byzanz, die Griechen und die Romaiosyne – eine 'Ethnogenese' der 'Römer'?" In H. Wolfram and W. Pohl, eds., *Typen der Ethnogenese under besonderer Berücksichtigung der Bayern*. Vienna: Verlag der österreichischen Akademie der Wissenschaften. 103–111.

(1996). "Byzantinische Identität – einleitende Bemerkungen." In Fledelius 3–6.

(2000). "Anmerkungen zu γραικόω," *Βυζαντινά* 21: 199–202.

(2002). "Latinoi – The Image of the Other according to Greek Sources." In C. Maltezou and P. Schreiner, eds., *Bisanzio, Venezia, e il mondo francogreco (XIII–XV secolo)*. Venice: Istituto Ellenico di Studi Bizantini e Postbizantini di Venezia, Centro Tedesco di Studi Veneziani (= *Convegni* v. V). 25–39.

(2003). "Griechische Identitäten im Mittelalter: Aspekte einer Entwicklung." In *Βυζάντιο: Κράτος και Κοινωνία (Μνήμη Νίκου Οικονομίδη)*. Athens: National Research Institute. 297–319.

(2005). *Το Βυζάντιο ως χώρος: Εισαγωγή στην ιστορική γεωγραφία της ανατολικής Μεσογείου στη βυζαντινή εποχή*. Tr. D. Stathakopoulos, rev. by author. Thessalonike: Banias.

Koder, J., and F. Hild (1976). *Hellas und Thessalia*. Vienna: Verlag der österreichischen Akademie der Wissenschaften (= *Tabula Imperii Byzantini* v. I).

Kolbaba, T. (2000). *The Byzantine Lists: Errors of the Latins*. Urbana and Chicago: University of Illinois Press.

Kolovou, F. (1999). *Μιχαὴλ Χωνιάτης: Συμβολὴ στὴ μελέτη τοῦ βίου καὶ τοῦ ἔργου του: Το corpus τῶν ἐπιστολῶν*. Athens: Academy of Athens. 1999 (= *Πονήματα* v. II).

Konstantakopoulou, A. (2002). "*Λαοί, φυλαί, γλῶσσαι:* Διακρίσεις στα Βαλκάνια τον ύστερο μεσαίωνα." In Nikolaou 327–355.

Kordoses, M. S. (1987). *Southern Greece under the Franks (1204–1262): A Study of the Greek Population and the Orthodox Church under the Frankish Dominion*. Ioannina: University of Ioannina, Scientific Journal of the Faculty of Arts (= *Dodone* Suppl. v. XXXIII).

Koukoules, Ph. I. (1932). "Κυνηγετικὰ ἐκ τῆς ἐποχῆς τῶν Κομνηνῶν καὶ τῶν Παλαιολόγων," *ΕΕΒΣ* 9: 3–33.

Kountoura-Galake, E., ed. (2001). *Οι σκοτεινοί αιώνες του Βυζαντίου (7ος–9ος αι.)*. Athens: Institute for Byzantine Research, National Hellenic Research Foundation.

Krallis, D. (2006). "Michael Attaleiates: History as Politics in Eleventh-Century Byzantium." Dissertation: University of Michigan.

Kriaras, E. (1972). "Ὁ Μιχαὴλ Ψελλός," *Βυζαντινά* 4: 53–128.

Krsmanović, B. (2003). "Αλλαγές στη δομή της κοινωνικής κορυφής μετά την εποχή του Βασιλείου Β'." In Vlyssidou 87–106.

Kuch, H. (1965). *ΦΙΛΟΛΟΓΟΣ: Untersuchung eines Wortes von seinem ersten Auftreten in der Tradition bis zur ersten überlieferten lexikalischen Festlegung*. Berlin: Akademie Verlag.

Kurmann, A. (1988). *Gregor von Nazianz Oratio 4 gegen Julian: Ein Kommentar.* Basel: F. Reinhardt Verlag.

Kustas, G. L. (1973). *Studies in Byzantine Rhetoric.* Thessalonike: Patriarchal Institute for Patristic Studies.

Kyrris, C. P. (1992). "Greek Cypriot Identity, Byzantium, and the Latins 1192–1489," Ἐπετηρὶς τοῦ κέντρου ἐπιστημονικῶν ἐρευνῶν *(of Cyprus)* 19: 169–185.

Labarre, G. (1996). *Les cités de Lesbos aux époques hellénistique et impériale.* Paris: Diffusion de Boccard.

Laiou, A. E. (1991a). "The Foreigner and the Stranger in 12th Century Byzantium: Means of Propitiation and Acculturation." In M. T. Fögen, ed., *Fremde der Gesellschaft: Historische und socialwissenschaftliche Untersuchungen zur Differenzierung von Normalität und Fremdheit.* Frankfurt am Main: Vittorio Klostermann. 71–97.

(1991b). "God and Mammon: Credit, Trade, Profit and the Canonists." In Oikonomides (1991b) 261–300.

(1995). "Italy and the Italians in the Political Geography of the Byzantines (14th Century)," *DOP* 49: 73–98.

(1998). "Institutional Mechanisms of Integration." In Ahrweiler and Laiou 161–181.

(2000). "Thessaloniki and Macedonia in the Byzantine Period." In Burke and Scott 1–11.

Lambakis, S. (2001). "Παρατηρήσεις σχετικὰ μὲ τὶς ὄψεις τῆς ἀρχαιογνωσίας στὸ ἔργο τοῦ Ἰγνατίου Διακόνου." In Kountoura-Galake 109–132.

(2004). *Γεώργιος Παχυμέρης, πρωτέκδικος καὶ δικαιοφύλαξ· Εἰσαγωγικὸ δοκίμιο.* Athens: National Research Institute.

Lamberton, R. (1986). *Homer the Theologian: Neoplatonist Allegorical Reading and the Growth of the Epic Tradition.* Berkeley: University of California Press.

Lambropoulos, K. (1988). *Ἰωάννης Ἀπόκαυκος· Συμβολή στην έρευνα του βίου και του συγγραφικού έργου του.* Athens: Basilopoulos.

Lampsidis, O. (1980). "La rivalité entre l'état des Grands Comnènes et celui de Nicée à propos de l'héritage de l'idée byzantine," *Actes du XVe Congrès international d'études byzantines (Athènes),* v. IV: *Histoire.* 186–191.

(1988). "Zur Biographie von K. Manasses und zu seiner Chronike Synopsis (CS)," *Byzantion* 58: 97–111.

Lanata, G. (1984). *Legislazione e natura nelle Novelle giustinianee.* Naples: Edizioni Scientifiche Italiane.

(1989). "L'immortalità artificiale. Appunti sul proemio della Novella 22 di Giustiniano," *Serta Historica Antiqua* 2: 259–263.

Langdon, J. S., *et al.*, eds. (1993). *TO ΕΛΛΗΝΙΚΟΝ: Studies in Honor of Speros Vryonis, Jr.*, v. I: *Hellenic Antiquity and Byzantium.* New Rochelle, NY: A. D. Caratzas.

Lasithiotakis, M. (2005). "παύσασθαι γράφειν Ὅμηρον... / ἃ Ὅμηρος ἐψεύσατο: Παρατηρήσεις στὸν πρόλογο τοῦ «μυθιστορήματος τοῦ Διγενῆ» (G IV 27 κ.ἑ. / Ε 718 κ.ἑ.)." In S. Kaklamanis and M. Paschalis, eds., Ἡ πρόσληψη τῆς ἀρχαιότητας στὸ βυζαντινὸ μυθιστόρημα. Athens: Stigmi. 49–72.

Latacz, J. (2004). *Troy and Homer: Towards a Solution of an Old Mystery.* Tr. K. Windle and R. Ireland. Oxford University Press.

Lauxtermann, M. D. (1999). "Ninth-Century Classicism and the Erotic Muse." In L. James, ed., *Desire and Denial in Byzantium.* Brookfield, VT, and Aldershot: Ashgate. 161–170.

(2003). *Byzantine Poetry from Pisides to Geometres: Texts and Contexts*, v. I. Vienna: Verlag der österreichischen Akademie der Wissenschaften (= *Wiener byzantinische Studien* v. XXIV.1).

Lechner, K. (1954). *Hellenen und Barbaren im Weltbild der Byzantiner: Die alten Bezeichnungen als Ausdruck eines neuen Kulturbewusstseins.* Munich: Inaugural-Dissertation, Ludwig-Maximilians-Universität.

Lemerle, P. (1986). *Byzantine Humanism: The First Phase (Notes and Remarks on Education and Culture in Byzantium from its Origins to the 10th Century).* Tr. H. Lindsay and A. Moffatt. Canberra: Australian Association for Byzantine Studies (= *Byzantina Australiensia* v. III).

Leontis, A. (1995). *Topographies of Hellenism: Mapping the Homeland.* Ithaca and London: Cornell University Press.

Leontsini, M. (2001). "Θρησκευτικές πεποιθήσεις και γλωσσική διατύπωση τον 7ο αιώνα." In Kountoura-Galake 73–87.

Lepelley, C. (1994). "Le musée des statues divines: La volonté de sauvegarder le patrimoine artistique païen à l'époque théodosienne," *Cahiers archéologiques* 42: 5–15.

Liebeschuetz, W. (1995). "Pagan Mythology in the Christian Empire," *IJCT* 2: 193–208.

(2001). *Decline and Fall of the Roman City.* Oxford University Press.

Lightfoot, J. L. (2003). *Lucian, On the Syrian Goddess.* Oxford University Press.

Lilie, R.-J. (1984). "Des Kaisers Macht und Ohnmacht: Zum Zerfall der Zentralgewalt in Byzanz vor dem vierten Kreuzzug," *Poikila Byzantina* 4 (1984) 9–120.

Linnér, S. (1983). "Psellus' *Chronographia* and the *Alexias*: Some Textual Parallels," *BZ* 76: 1–9.

Littlewood, A. (1980). "A Byzantine Oak and its Classical Acorn: The Literary Artistry of Geometres, *Progymnasmata 1*," *JöB* 29: 133–144.

(1981). "The Midwifery of Michael Psellos: An Example of Byzantine Literary Originality." In M. Mullett and R. Scott, eds., *Byzantium and the Classical Tradition.* Birmingham: Centre for Byzantine Studies, University of Birmingham. 136–142.

(1988). "A Statistical Survey of the Incidence of Repeated Quotations in Selected Byzantine Letter-Writers." In J. Duffy and J. Peradotto, eds., *Gonimos: Neoplatonic and Byzantine Studies Presented to Leendert G. Westerink at 75.* Buffalo, NY: Arethusa. 137–154.

ed. (1995). *Originality in Byzantine Literature, Art, and Music: A Collection of Essays.* Oxford: Oxbow Books.

(1999). "The Byzantine Letter of Consolation in the Macedonian and Komnenian Periods," *DOP* 53: 19–41.

(2006). "Imagery in the *Chronographia* of Michael Psellos." In Barber and Jenkins 13–71.

Livanos, C. (2006). "Michael Choniates, Poet of Love and Knowledge," *BMGS* 30: 103–114.

Ljubarskij, J. N. (1992a). "Man in Byzantine Historiography from John Malalas to Michael Psellos," *DOP* 46: 177–186.

(1992b). "The Fall of an Intellectual: The Intellectual and Moral Atmosphere in Eleventh-Century Byzantium." In S. Vryonis, ed., *Byzantine Studies: Essays on the Slavic World and the Eleventh Century*. New Rochelle, NY: A. D. Caratzas. 175–182.

(1993). "Some Notes on the Newly Discovered Historical Work by Psellos." In Langdon *et al.* 213–228.

(2000). "John Kinnamos as a Writer." In C. Scholz and G. Makris, eds., *Polypleuros Nous: Miscellanea für Peter Schreiner zu seinem 60. Geburtstag*. Munich and Leipzig: K. G. Saur. 164–173.

(2004a). *Η προσωπικότητα και το έργο του Μιχαήλ Ψελλού: Συνεισφορά στην ιστορία του βυζαντινού πολιτισμού*. Tr. A. Tzelesi. Athens: Kanaki.

(2004b). "Byzantine Irony: The Example of Niketas Choniates." In Angelidi (2004) 287–298.

Lock, P. (1995). *The Franks in the Aegean, 1204–1500*. London and New York: Longman.

Lounghis, T. (1990). *Κωνσταντίνου Ζ΄ Πορφυρογέννητου De administrando imperio (Πρὸς τὸν ἴδιον υἱὸν Ῥωμανόν): Μία μέθοδος ανάγνωσης*. Thessalonike: Banias.

Lutz-Bachmann, M. (1992). "Hellenisierung des Christentums?" In C. Cople *et al.*, eds., *Spätantike und Christentum: Beiträge zur Religions- und Geistesgeschichte der griechisch-römischen Kultur und Zivilisation der Kaiserzeit*. Berlin: Akademie Verlag. 77–98.

Lyman, R. (2003). "The Politics of Passing: Justin Martyr's Conversion as a Problem of 'Hellenization.'" In K. Mills and A. Grafton, eds., *Conversion in Late Antiquity and the Early Middle Ages: Seeing and Believing*. University of Rochester Press. 36–60.

Maas, M. (1986). "Roman History and Christian Ideology in Justinianic Reform Legislation," *DOP* 40: 17–31.

(1992). *John Lydus and the Roman Past: Antiquarianism and Politics in the Age of Justinian*. London and New York: Routledge.

(1995). "Fugitives and Ethnography in Priscus of Panium," *BMGS* 19: 146–160.

(2003). "'Delivered from their Ancient Customs': Christianity and the Question of Cultural Change in Early Byzantine Ethnography." In K. Mills and A. Grafton, eds., *Conversion in Late Antiquity and the Early Middle Ages: Seeing and Believing*. University of Rochester Press. 152–188.

ed. (2005). *The Cambridge Companion to the Age of Justinian*. Cambridge University Press.

McCail, R. C. (1971). "The Erotic and Ascetic Poetry of Agathias Scholasticus," *Byzantion* 41: 205–267.

McCormick, M. (1986). *Eternal Victory: Triumphal Rulership in Late Antiquity, Byzantium and the Early Medieval West.* Cambridge University Press.

(1998). "The Imperial Edge: Italo-Byzantine Identity, Movement and Integration, AD 650–950." In Ahrweiler and Laiou 17–52.

McCoskey, D. E. (2003). "By Any Other Name? Ethnicity and the Study of Ancient Identity," *The Classical Bulletin* 79: 93–109.

MacCoull, L. S. B. (1988). *Dioscorus of Aphrodito: His Work and his World.* Berkeley: University of California Press.

McGuckin, J. A. (2001). *St Gregory of Nazianzus: An Intellectual Biography.* Crestwood, NY: St. Vladimir's Seminary Press.

(2006). "Gregory: The Rhetorician as Poet." In Børtnes and Hägg 193–212.

McInerney, J. (1999). *The Folds of Parnassos: Land and Ethnicity in Ancient Phokis.* Austin: University of Texas Press.

(2001). "Ethnos and Ethnicity in Early Greece." In Malkin 51–73.

McLynn, N. (2006). "Among the Hellenists: Gregory and the Sophists." In Børtnes and Hägg 213–238.

MacMullen, R. (1990). *Changes in the Roman Empire: Essays in the Ordinary.* Princeton University Press.

(1997). *Christianity and Paganism in the Fourth to Eighth Centuries.* New Haven and London: Yale University Press.

(2000). *Romanization in the Time of Augustus.* New Haven and London: Yale University Press.

Macrides, R. (1981). "Saints and Sainthood in the Early Palaiologan Period." In S. Hackel, ed., *The Byzantine Saint.* London: Fellowship of St. Alban and St. Sergius. 67–87.

(1985). "Poetic Justice in the Patriarchate: Murder and Cannibalism in the Provinces." In L. Burgmann *et al.*, eds., *Cupido Legum.* Frankfurt am Main: Löwenklau Gesellschaft. 137–168.

(2000). "The Pen and the Sword: Who Wrote the *Alexiad*?" In T. Gouma-Peterson, ed., *Anna Komnene and Her Times.* New York and London: Garland Publishing. 63–81.

ed. (2002). *Travel in the Byzantine World.* Aldershot and Burlington, VT: Ashgate.

(2003). "George Akropolites' Rhetoric." In Jeffreys (2003a) 201–211.

(2004). "The Ritual of Petition." In D. Yatromanolakis and P. Roilos, eds., *Greek Ritual Poetics.* Washington, DC: Center for Hellenic Studies (Harvard University Press). 356–370.

Macrides, R., and P. Magdalino (1992). "The Fourth Kingdom and the Rhetoric of Hellenism." In P. Magdalino, ed., *The Perception of the Past in Twelfth-Century Europe.* London and Rio Grande: The Hambledon Press. 117–156.

Magdalino, P. (1981). "The Byzantine Holy Man in the Twelfth Century." In S. Hackel, ed., *The Byzantine Saint.* London: Fellowship of St. Alban and St. Sergius. 51–66.

(1983). "Aspects of Twelfth-Century Byzantine *Kaiserkritik*," *Speculum* 58: 326–346.

(1984). "Byzantine Snobbery." In Angold 58–78.

(1985). "Die Jurisprudenz als Komponente der byzantinischen Gelehrtenkultur des 12. Jahrhunderts." In L. Burgmann *et al.*, eds., *Cupido Legum*. Frankfurt am Main: Löwenklau Gesellschaft. 169–177.

(1988). "The Phenomenon of Manuel I Komnenos," *BF* 13: 171–199.

(1989). "Honour Among the Romaioi: The Framework of Social Values in the World of Digenes Akrites and Kekaumenos," *BMGS* 13: 183–218.

(1991a). "Hellenism and Nationalism in Byzantium." In P. Magdalino, *Tradition and Transformation in Medieval Byzantium*. Aldershot: Variorum; Brookfield, VT: Gower. XIV.

(1991b). "Constantinople and the ἔξω χῶραι in the Time of Balsamon." In Oikonomides (1991b) 179–197.

(1991c). "Enlightenment and Repression in Twelfth-Century Byzantium: The Evidence of the Canonists." In Oikonomides (1991b) 357–373.

(1992). "Eros the King and the King of *Amours*: Some Observations on *Hysmine and Hysminias*," *DOP* 46: 197–204.

(1993). *The Empire of Manuel I Komnenos, 1143–1180*. Cambridge University Press.

(1996a). "Innovations in Government." In M. Mullett and D. Smythe, eds., *Alexios I Komnenos*, v. I: *Papers*. Belfast: Belfast Byzantine Enterprises. 146–166 (= *Belfast Byzantine Texts and Translations* v. IV.1).

(1996b). "Eustathios and Thessalonica." In C. N. Constantinides *et al.*, eds., *ΦΙΛΕΛΛΗΝ: Studies in Honour of Robert Browning*. Venice: Istituto Ellenico di Studi Bizantini e Postbizantini di Venezia. 225–238.

(1996c). *The Byzantine Background to the First Crusade*. Toronto: Canadian Institute of Balkan Studies.

(1997). "In Search of the Byzantine Courtier: Leo Choirosphaktes and Constantine Manasses." In H. Maguire, ed., *Byzantine Court Culture from 820 to 1204*. Washington, DC: Dumbarton Oaks Research Library and Collection. 141–165.

(1998). "Paphlagonians in Byzantine High Society." In S. Lambakis, ed., *Η Βυζαντινή Μικρά Ασία (6ος–12ος αι.)*. Athens: National Hellenic Research Foundation and The Speros Basil Vryonis Center for the Study of Hellenism. 141–150.

(2000). "Constantinople and the Outside World." In Smythe 149–162.

(2002). "A History of Byzantine Literature for Historians." In P. Odorico and P. A. Agapitos, eds., *Pour une "nouvelle" histoire de la littérature byzantine: Problèmes, méthodes, approches, propositions*. Paris: Centre d'études byzantines, néo-helléniques et sud-est européennes, École des Hautes Études en Sciences Sociales. 167–184.

(2003a). "Prosopography and Byzantine Identity." In Cameron 41–56.

(2003b). "The Porphyrogenita and the Astrologers: A Commentary on *Alexiad* VI.7.1 7." In C. Dendrinos *et al.*, eds., *Porphyrogenita: Essays on the History and Literature of Byzantium and the Latin East in Honour of Julian Chrysostomides*. Aldershot: Ashgate. 15–31.

Magoulias, H. J. (1964). "A Study in Roman Catholic and Greek Orthodox Church Relations on the Island of Cyprus between the Years AD 1196 and 1360," *The Greek Orthodox Theological Review* 10: 75–106.

Majercik, R. (1989). *The Chaldean Oracles: Text, Translation, and Commentary.* Leiden: Brill.

Malkin, I. (1998). *The Returns of Odysseus: Colonization and Ethnicity.* Berkeley: University of California Press.

ed. (2001). *Ancient Perceptions of Greek Ethnicity.* Washington, DC: Center for Hellenic Studies (Harvard University Press).

Maltese, E. V. (1994). "Michele Psello commentatore di Gregorio Nazianzo: Note per una lettura dei *Theologica*." In ΣΥΝΔΕΣΜΟΣ: *Studi in onore di Rosario Anastasi*, v. II. Università di Catania: Facoltà di lettere e filosofia. 289–309.

Maltezou, C. A. (1990). Ἡ Κρήτη στὴ διάρκεια τῆς περιόδου τῆς Βενετοκρατίας (1211–1669). Crete: Association of Local Unions, Municipalities, and Communities of Crete.

(1993). "Diversitas Linguae." In Moschonas (1993a) 93–102.

(1999). "Ἡ διαμόρφωση της ελληνικής ταυτότητας στη λατινοκρατούμενη Ελλάδα," *Études balkaniques* 6 (*Byzance et l'hellénisme: L'identité grecque au Moyen-Âge*): 103–119.

Mango, C. (1963). "Antique Statuary and the Byzantine Beholder," *DOP* 17: 53–75.

(1965). "Byzantinism and Romantic Hellenism," *Journal of the Warburg and Courtauld Institutes* 28: 29–43.

(1973). "Eudocia Ingerina, the Normans, and the Macedonian Dynasty," *Zbornik Radova Vizantološkog Instituta* 14–15: 17–27.

(1980). *Byzantium: The Empire of New Rome.* New York: Scribner.

(2005). "Constantinople: Capital of the *Oikoumene?*" In Chrysos (2005a) 319–324.

Mantouvalou, M. (1979–1985). "Romaios-Romios-Romiossyni: La notion de 'Romain' avant et après la chute de Constantinople," Ἐπιστημονική Ἐπετηρίδα τῆς Φιλοσοφικῆς Σχολῆς τοῦ Πανεπιστημίου Ἀθηνῶν 28: 169–198.

Marchand, S. L. (1996). *Down from Olympus: Archaeology and Philhellenism in Germany, 1750–1970.* Princeton University Press.

Markus, R. (1990). *The End of Ancient Christianity.* Cambridge University Press.

Marrou, H. I. (1956). *A History of Education in Antiquity.* Tr. G. Lamb. Madison: University of Wisconsin Press.

Martin, J.-M. (2002). "*O Felix Asia!* Frédéric II, l'empire de Nicée et le 'Césaropapisme,'" *TM* 14: 473–483.

(2005). "Hellénisme politique, hellénisme religieux et pseudo-hellénisme à Naples (VIIe–XIIe siécle)," Νέα Ῥώμη: *Rivista di Ricerche Bizantinistiche* 2 (= Ἀμπελοκήπιον: *Studi di amici e colleghi in onore di Vera von Falkenhausen* v. II): 59–77.

Matalas, P. (2002). Ἔθνος και ορθοδοξία: Οι περιπέτειες μιάς σχέσης από το «Ελλαδικό» στο βουλγαρικό σχίσμα. Herakleio: University of Crete Press.

Matthews, J. (1989). *The Roman Empire of Ammianus*. London: Duckworth.
  (1994). "The Origin of Ammianus," *Classical Quarterly* 44: 252–269.
Mauromatis, L. (1987). "'Ρωμαϊκή ταυτότητα, 'Ελληνική ταυτότητα (ΙΓ –
  ΙΕ'αἰ.)," *Σύμμεικτα* 7: 183–191.
Merendino, E. (1975). "Federico II e Giovanni III Vatatzes," *Byzantino-Sicula II: Miscellanea di scritti in memoria di Giuseppe Rossi Taibbi*. Palermo: Istituto Siciliano di Studi Bizantini e Neoellenici (= *Quaderni* 8). 371–383.
Mertzios, K. D. (1949). "Ἡ συνθήκη 'Ενετῶν-Καλλέργη καὶ οἱ συνοδεύοντες αὐτὴν κατάλογοι," *Κρητικὰ Χρονικὰ* 3: 262–292.
Messis, C. (2004). "Deux versions de la même 'vérité': Les deux vies d'Hosios Mélétios au XIIe siècle." In P. Odorico and P. A. Agapitos, eds., *Les Vies des Saints à Byzance: Genre littéraire ou biographe historique?* Paris: Centre d'études byzantines, néo-helléniques et sud-est européennes, École des Hautes Études en Sciences Sociales. 303–345.
Metzler, K. (2006). "Eustathios von Thessalonike und sein Publikum." In M. Kaplan, ed., *Monastères, images, pouvoirs et société à Byzance*. Paris: Publications de la Sorbonne (= *Byzantina Sorbonensia* v. XXIII). 49–60.
Meunier, F. (1991). "Théodore Prodrome: 'Rhodantè et Dosiklès'. Roman grec ou roman byzantin?" *Rivista di Bizantinistica* 1: 195–227.
Meyendorff, J. (1993). "Universalist Ideologies and Historical Realities in the Orthodox Church." In Langdon 229–252.
Millar, F. (1977). *The Emperor in the Roman World (31 BC–AD 337)*. Ithaca, NY: Cornell University Press.
  (1987a). "The Problem of Hellenistic Syria." In A. Kuhrt and S. Sherwin-White, eds., *Hellenism in the East: The Interaction of Greek and non-Greek Civilizations from Syria to Central Asia after Alexander*. London: Duckworth. 110–133.
  (1987b). "Empire, Community and Culture in the Roman Near East: Greeks, Syrians, Jews and Arabs," *Journal of Jewish Studies* 38: 143–164.
  (1993). *The Roman Near East, 31 BC–AD 337*. London and Cambridge, MA: Harvard University Press.
  (1997). "Porphyry: Ethnicity, Language, and Alien Wisdom." In J. Barnes and M. Griffin, eds., *Philosophia Togata II: Plato and Aristotle at Rome*. Oxford: Clarendon Press. 241–262.
  (1998). "Ethnic Identity in the Roman Near East, 325–450: Language, Religion, and Culture," *Mediterranean Archaeology* 11: 159–176.
Miller, D. (1995). *On Nationality*. Oxford: Clarendon Press.
Miller, T. S. (1997). *The Birth of the Hospital in the Byzantine Empire*. 2nd ed. Baltimore and London: Johns Hopkins University Press.
  (2003). *The Orphans of Byzantium: Child Welfare in the Christian Empire*. Washington, DC: Catholic University of America Press.
Millett, M. (1990). *The Romanization of Britain: An Essay in Archaeological Interpretation*. Cambridge University Press.
Missiou, D. (2000). "The Importance of Macedonia during the Byzantine Era." In Burke and Scott 102–110.

*Bibliography*

Mitchell, S. (1993). *Anatolia: Land, Men, and Gods in Asia Minor*, v. I: *The Celts and the Impact of Roman Rule*. Oxford: Clarendon Press.

(2000). "Ethnicity, Acculturation and Empire in Roman and Late Roman Asia Minor." In Mitchell and Greatrex 117–150.

(2003). "The Galatians: Representation and Reality." In A. Erskine, ed., *A Companion to the Hellenistic World*. Oxford: Blackwell Publishing. 280–293.

Mitchell, S., and G. Greatrex, eds. (2000). *Ethnicity and Culture in Late Antiquity*. London: Duckworth.

Moles, I. N. (1969). "Nationalism and Byzantine Greece," *GRBS* 10: 95–107.

Momigliano, A. (1971). *Alien Wisdom: The Limits of Hellenization*. Cambridge University Press.

Moore, P. (2005). *Iter Psellianum*. Toronto: Pontifical Institute of Medieval Studies.

Moorhead, J. (2001). *The Roman Empire Divided, 400–700*. London: Longman.

Morris, R. (1995). *Monks and Laymen in Byzantium, 843–1118*. Cambridge University Press.

Moschonas, N. G., ed. (1993a). Ἡ ἐπικοινωνία στὸ Βυζάντιο. Athens: National Research Institute.

(1993b). "Ετερόγλωσσοι πληθυσμοί και επικοινωνία στο φραγκικό βασίλειο της Κύπρου." In ibid. 125–144.

Most, G. (1997). "Atene come scuola della Grecia." In S. Settis, ed., *I Greci: storia, cultura, arte, società*, v. II: *Una storia greca, pt. 2: Definizione (VI–IV secolo a.C.)*. Turin: G. Einaudi. 1339–1352.

Mpazaiou-Barabas, Th. (1993). "Θαλάσσιοι δρόμοι: Δυνατότητες και δυσκολίες της θαλάσσιας επικοινωνίας σε βυζαντινά λόγια κείμενα." In Moschonas (1993a) 435–443.

Mullett, M. (1984). "Aristocracy and Patronage in the Literary Circles of Comnenian Constantinople." In Angold 173–201.

(1995). "Originality in the Byzantine Letter: The Case of Exile." In Littlewood 39–58.

(1997). *Theophylact of Ochrid: Reading the Letters of a Byzantine Archbishop*. Aldershot and Brookfield, VT: Variorum (= *Birmingham Byzantine and Ottoman Monographs* v. II).

(2002). "In Peril on the Sea: Travel Genres and the Unexpected." In Macrides 259–284.

Munitiz, J. A. (1981). "Self-Canonization: The 'Partial Account' of Nikephoros Blemmydes." In S. Hackel, ed., *The Byzantine Saint*. London: Fellowship of St. Alban and St. Sergius. 164–168.

(1991). "Review of Psellos, *Theol. I* and *Phil. Min. II*" (q.v. above), *The Classical Review* 41: 229–230.

Musti, D. (1963). "Sull' idea di συγγένεια in iscrizioni greche," *Annali della Scuola Normale Superiore di Pisa* 32: 225–239.

Nagy, G. (1990). *Pindar's Homer: The Lyric Possession of an Epic Past*. Baltimore and London: Johns Hopkins University Press.

Nardi, E. (2002). *Né sole né lune: L'immagine femminile nella Bisanzio dei secoli XI e XII*. Florence: Leo S. Olschki: Fondazione Carlo Marchi (= *Quaderni* v. XVI).

Neratzi-Varmazi, V. (1997). "The Identity of the Byzantine Province in the 12th Century," Ἐπετηρίδα τοῦ κέντρου ἐπιστημονικῶν ἐρευνῶν (Λευκωσία) 23: 9–14.

Neville, L. (2004). *Authority in Byzantine Provincial Society, 950–1100*. Cambridge University Press.

Nicol, D. M. (1957). *The Despotate of Epiros*. Oxford: Basil Blackwell.

(1972). *Byzantium: Its Ecclesiastical History and Relations with the Western World*. London: Variorum Reprints.

(1979a). *Church and Society in the Last Centuries of Byzantium*. Cambridge University Press.

(1979b). "Symbiosis and Integration: Some Greco-Latin Families in Byzantium in the 11th to 13th Centuries," *BF* 7: 113–135.

Nicolaou-Konnari, A. (2005). "Greeks." In A. Nicolaou-Konnari and C. Schabel, eds., *Cyprus: Society and Culture, 1191–1374.* Leiden and Boston: Brill. 13–62.

Nietzsche, Friedrich (1966). *Beyond Good and Evil: Prelude to a Philosophy of the Future*. Tr. W. Kaufmann. New York: Vintage Books.

(1967). *The Will to Power*. Tr. W. Kaufmann and R. J. Hollingdale. New York: Vintage Books.

(1990). *Twilight of the Idols/The Anti-Christ*. Tr. R. J. Hollingdale. London: Penguin Classics.

Nikolaou, K., ed. (2002). Ἀνοχή καὶ καταστολή στοὺς Μέσους Χρόνους· Μνήμη Λένου Μαυρομμάτη. Athens: Institute for Byzantine Research, National Hellenic Research Foundation.

Nikolov, A. (2006). "Empire of the Romans or Tsardom of the Greeks? The Image of Byzantium in the Earliest Slavonic Translations from Greek (End of Ninth–Eleventh Century)." In E. Jeffreys, ed., *Proceedings of the 21st International Congress of Byzantine Studies*, v. II: *Abstracts of Panel Papers*. Aldershot and Burlington, VT: Ashgate. 173.

Nimmo Smith, J. (2001). *A Christian's Guide to Greek Culture: The Pseudo-Nonnus Commentaries on Sermons 4, 5, 39 and 43 by Gregory of Nazianzus*. *TTH* v. XXXVII.

Nixon, C. E. V., and B. S. Rodgers (1994). *In Praise of Later Roman Emperors: The Panegyrici Latini*. Berkeley: University of California Press.

Ober, J. (1996). *The Athenian Revolution: Essays on Ancient Greek Democracy and Political Theory*. Princeton University Press.

Obolensky, D. (1971). *The Byzantine Commonwealth: Eastern Europe, 500–1453*. London: Weidenfeld & Nicholson Ltd.

(1972). "Nationalism in Eastern Europe in the Middle Ages," *Transactions of the Royal Historical Society* 22: 1–16.

Oikonomides, N. (1967). "Cinq actes inédits du patriarche Michel Autôreianos," *REB* 25: 113–145.

(1991a). "The Holy Icon as an Asset," *DOP* 45: 35–44.

ed. (1991b). *Τὸ Βυζάντιο κατὰ τὸν 12ο αἰώνα· Κανονικὸ δίκαιο, κράτος καὶ κοινωνία*. Athens: Society of Byzantine and Post-Byzantine Studies.

(1999). "L''unilinguisme' officiel de Constantinople byzantine (VIIe–XIIe s.),"
Σύμμεικτα 13: 9–22.

(2004). "Όψιμη ιεραποστολή στη Λακωνία." In V. Konti, ed., *Ο μοναχισμός
στην Πελοπόννησο, 405-1505 αι.* Athens: Institute for Byzantine Research,
The National Hellenic Research Foundation. 29–35.

O'Meara, D. J. (1998). "Aspects du travail philosophique de Michel Psellus
(*Philosophica minora*, vol. II)." In C.-F. Collatz *et al.*, eds., *Dissertatiunculae
criticae: Festschrift für Günther Christian Hansen*. Würzburg: Königshausen &
Neumann. 431–439.

Ostrogorsky, G. (1969). *History of the Byzantine State*. Tr. J. Hussey, rev. ed. New
Brunswick, NJ: Rutgers University Press.

Papadakis, A. (1996). *Crisis in Byzantium: The Filioque Controversy in the
Patriarchate of Gregory II of Cyprus (1283–1289)*. Rev. ed. Crestwood, NY:
St. Vladimir's Seminary Press.

Papadopoulos, C. A. (1935). *Συμβολαὶ εἰς τὴν ἱστορίαν τοῦ μοναχικοῦ βίου ἐν
Ἑλλάδι*, v. II: *Ὁ ὅσιος Μελέτιος «ὁ νέος» (περ. 1035–1105)*. Athens: Phoenix.

Papaioannou, E. N. (1998). "Das Briefcorpus des Michael Psellos vorarbeiten zu
einer kritischen Neuedition," *JöB* 48: 67–117.

(2000). "Michael Psellos' Rhetorical Gender," *BMGS* 24: 133–146.

Papamastorakis, T. (2004). "The Discrete Charm of the Visible." In Angelidi
111–127.

Paparrigopoulos, K. (1970). *Προλεγόμενα*. Ed. K. Th. Dimaras. Athens: Ermis.

Papoulia, V. (1993). "Ἡ τροπὴ τῶν ἐθνικῶν ὀνομάτων σὲ γεωγραφικά: Ἡ
περίπτωση τῆς Μακεδονίας." In Moschonas (1993a) 685–700.

(2003). "Vers une identité byzantine: La mobilité sociale et la mobilité culturelle
comme facteurs de la transformation de l'état romain en état byzantin." In
*Byzantina-Metabyzantina: La périphérie dans le temps et l'escape*. Paris: Centre
d'études byzantines, néo-helléniques et sud-est européennes, École des
Hautes Études en Sciences Sociales (= *Dossiers byzantins* v. II). 25–55.

Parry, K. (2006). "Reading Proclus Diadochus in Byzantium." In H. Tarrant
and D. Baltzly, eds., *Reading Plato in Antiquity*. London: Duckworth.
223–235.

Parsons, P. (1993). "Identities in Diversity." In A. Bulloch *et al.*, *Images and
Ideologies: Self-Definition in the Hellenistic World*. Berkeley: University of
California Press. 152–170.

Pattenden, P. (1983). "The Byzantine Early Warning System," *Byzantion* 53: 258–299.

Pazdernik, C. (2005). "Justinianic Ideology and the Power of the Past." In Maas
185–212.

Peckham, R. S. (2001). *National Histories, Natural States: Nationalism and the
Politics of Place in Greece*. London and New York: I. B. Tauris.

Pelikan, J. (1993). *Christianity and Classical Culture: The Metamorphosis of Natural
Theology in the Christian Encounter with Hellenism*. New Haven and London:
Yale University Press.

Penella, R. J. (1993). "Julian the Persecutor in Fifth-Century Church Historians,"
*Ancient World* 24: 31–43.

Pitsakis, G. (1991). "Conceptions et éloges de la romanité dans l'Empire romain d'Orient: Deux thèmes 'byzantins' d'idéologie politique." In P. Catalano and P. Siniscalco, eds., *Seminario Internazionale di Studi Storici "Da Roma alla terza Roma,"* v. X: *Idea giuridica e politica di Roma e personalità storiche,* v. I. Rome: Herder. 95–139.

(1995). "Universalité et nationalisme: La Nouvelle Rome. Quelques points de repère à travers les textes grecs." In *Umanità e nazioni nel diritto e nella spiritualità da Roma a Costantinopoli a Mosca (Rendiconti del XII Seminario Internazionale di Studi Storici "Da Roma alla terza Roma")*. Rome: Herder. 25–42.

(1997). "À propos de la citoyenneté romaine dans l'Empire d'Orient: Un survol à travers les textes grecs," *Méditerranées* 12: 73–100.

(2005). " Ἡ οἰκουμενικότητα τοὺ βυζαντινοῦ δικαίου." In Chrysos (2005a) 141–182.

Podskalsky, G. (2003). "Humanismus und Theologie in Byzanz: Ein vernachlässigtes Kapitel. Die humanistischen Theologen des 11. Jahrhunderts, insbesondere Michael Psellos." In Vlyssidou 317–329.

Pohl, W. (1998). "Telling the Difference: Signs of Ethnic Identity." In W. Pohl and H. Reimitz, eds., *Strategies of Distinction: The Construction of Ethnic Communities, 300–800.* Leiden: Brill. 17–69.

(2005). "Justinian and the Barbarian Kingdoms." In Maas 448–476.

Polemis, D. I. (1968). *The Doukai: A Contribution to Byzantine Prosopography.* London: The Athlone Press.

(1983). "Remains of an Acoluthia for the Emperor John Doukas Batatzes," *Harvard Ukrainian Studies* 7: 542–547.

Politis, A. (1998). "From Christian Roman Emperors to the Glorious Greek Ancestors." In D. Ricks and P. Magdalino, eds., *Byzantium and the Modern Greek Identity.* Aldershot: Ashgate. 1–14.

Pontikos, I. N. (1992). *Anonymi Miscellanea Philosophica: A Miscellany in the Tradition of Michael Psellos (Codex Baroccianus Graecus 131).* Athens: The Academy of Athens; Paris: J. Vrin; Brussels: Éditions Ousia (= *Corpus Philosophorum Medii Aevi: Philosophi Byzantini* v. VI).

Poole, R. (1999). *Nation and Identity.* London and New York: Routledge.

Pratsch, T. (2005). "Zur Herkunft des Niketas Magistros (*um 870–†frühestens 946/947) aus Lakonien," *Byzantion* 75: 501–506.

Preka, M. (1992). "Η εθνικότητα στο Χρονικό των Τόκκο." In Chrysos 303–308.

Price, S. R. F. (1984). *Rituals and Power: The Roman Imperial Cult in Asia Minor.* Cambridge University Press.

Pricoco, S. (1980). "L'editto di Giuliano sui maestri (*CTh* 13, 3, 5)," *Orpheus* n.s. 1: 348–370.

Radošević N. (1993). "The Emperor as the Patron of Learning in Byzantium." In Langdon *et al.* 267–287.

Rahner, H. (1963). *Greek Myths and Christian Mystery.* Tr. B. Battershaw. New York and Evanston: Harper & Row.

Rapp, C. (2004). "Hagiography and Monastic Literature between Greek East and Latin West in Late Antiquity," *Settimane di Studio della Fondazione Centro Italiano di Studi sull'Alto Medioevo* 15 (*Cristianità d'Occidente e Cristianità d'Oriente*): 1221–1280.

Rappe, S. (2001). "The New Math: How to Add and to Subtract Pagan Elements in Christian Education." In Y. L. Too, ed., *Education in Greek and Roman Antiquity*. Leiden: Brill. 405–432.

Reardon, B. P. (1974). "The Second Sophistic and the Novel." In G. W. Bowersock, ed., *Approaches to the Second Sophistic*. Philadelphia: The American Philological Association. 23–29.

(1984). "The Second Sophistic." In W. Treadgold, ed., *Renaissances Before the Renaissance: Cultural Revivals of Late Antiquity and the Middle Ages*. Stanford University Press. 23–41.

Reinert, S. W. (1998). "The Muslim Presence in Constantinople, 9th–15th Centuries: Some Preliminary Observations." In Ahrweiler and Laiou 125–150.

Reinink, G. J. (1992). "Ps.-Methodius: A Concept of History in Response to the Rise of Islam." In A. Cameron and L. I. Conrad, eds., *The Byzantine and Early Islamic Near East*, v. I: *Problems in the Literary Source Material*. Princeton, NJ: The Darwin Press. 149–187.

Reinsch, D. R. (1996). "Ausländer und Byzantiner im Werk der Anna Komnene," *Rechtshistorisches Journal* 8: 258–274.

(2000). "Women's Literature in Byzantium? – The Case of Anna Komnene." In T. Gouma-Peterson, ed., *Anna Komnene and her Times*. New York and London: Garland Publishing. 83–105.

Renfrew, C. (1988). "The Minoan–Mycenean Origins of the Panhellenic Games." In W. J. Raschke, ed., *The Archaeology of the Olympics: The Olympics and Other Festivals in Antiquity*. Madison: University of Wisconsin Press. 13–25.

Reynolds, S. (1998). "Our Forefathers? Tribes, Peoples, and Nations in the Historiography of the Age of Migrations." In A. C. Murray, ed., *After Rome's Fall: Narrators and Sources of Early Medieval History. Essays Presented to Walter Goffart*. University of Toronto Press. 16–36.

Rhoby, A. (2001). "Untersuchungen zu Psellos' Περὶ τῶν Ἀθηναϊκῶν τόπων καὶ ὀνομάτων," *Göttinger Beiträge zur byzantinischen und neugriechischen Philologie* 1: 75–91.

(2002). "Studien zur Antrittsrede des Michael Choniates in Athen," *Göttinger Beiträge zur byzantinischen und neugriechischen Philologie* 2: 83–111.

Richter, G. (1984). "Des Georgios Akropolites Gedanken über Theologie, Kirche, und Kircheneinheit," *Byzantion* 54: 276–299.

Robinson, C. (1979). *Lucian and his Influence in Europe*. London: Duckworth.

Rochette, B. (1997). *Le latin dans le monde grec: Recherches sur la diffusion de la langue et des lettres latines dans les provinces hellénophones de l'Empire romain*. Brussels: Latomus.

Rochow, I. (1991). "Der Vorwurf des Heidentums als Mittel der innenpolitischen Polemik in Byzanz." In M. Salamon, ed., *Paganism in the Later Roman Empire and in Byzantium*. Cracow: Universitas. 133–156.

Roilos, P. (2000). "Amphoteroglossia: The Role of Rhetoric in the Medieval Greek Learned Novel." In Agapitos and Reinsch 109–126.

(2005). *Amphoteroglossia: A Poetics of the Twelfth-Century Medieval Greek Novel.* Washington, DC: Center for Hellenic Studies (Harvard University Press).

Romanides, I. S. (2002). Ρωμηοσύνη, Ρωμανία, Ρούμελη. 3rd ed. Thessalonike: Pournara.

Romeo, I. (2002). "The Panhellenion and Ethnic Identity in Hadrianic Greece," *Classical Philology* 97: 21–40.

Rösch, G. (1978). *ONOMA ΒΑΣΙΛΕΙΑΣ: Studien zum offiziellen Gebrauch der Kaisertitel in spätantiker und frühbyzantinischer Zeit.* Vienna: Verlag der österreichischen Akademie der Wissenschaften (= *Byzantina Vindobonensia* v. X).

Roueché, C. (1988). "Byzantine Writers and Readers: Storytelling in the Eleventh Century." In R. Beaton, ed., *The Greek Novel, AD 1–1985.* London: Croom Helm. 123–133.

(2000). "Defining the Foreign in Kekaumenos." In Smythe 203–214.

Rowe, W. V. (1994). "Adolf von Harnack and the Concept of Hellenization." In Helleman (1994a) 69–98.

Rubenson, S. (2006). "The Cappadocians on the Areopagus." In Børtnes and Hägg 113–132.

Ruether, R. R. (1969). *Gregory of Nazianzus: Rhetor and Philosopher.* Oxford: Clarendon Press.

Russell, B. (1957). *Why I Am Not a Christian and Other Essays on Religion and Related Subjects.* New York: Simon and Schuster.

Russell, N. (1979–1980). "Anselm of Havelberg and the Union of the Churches," *Sobornost* 1.2: 19–41; 2.1: 29–41.

Ruzicka, S. (1992). *Politics of a Persian Dynasty: The Hecatomnids in the Fourth Century BC.* Norman and London: University of Oklahoma Press.

Saïd, S., ed. (1991). *ΕΛΛΗΝΙΣΜΟΣ: Quelques jalons pour une histoire de l'identité grecque.* Leiden: Brill.

(2001). "The Discourse of Identity in Greek Rhetoric from Isocrates to Aristides." In Malkin 275–299.

(2002). "Greeks and Barbarians in Euripides' Tragedies: The End of Differences?" In T. Harrison, ed., *Greeks and Barbarians.* New York: Routledge. 62–100.

Salmeri, G. (2000). "Dio, Rome, and the Civic Life of Asia Minor." In S. Swain, ed., *Dio Chrysostom: Politics, Letters, and Philosophy.* Oxford University Press. 53–92.

Sansaridou-Hendrickx, T. (1999). Το Χρονικόν του Μορέως και η έννοια του εθνικισμού κατά τον Μεσαίωνα: Σχέσεις των Ελλήνων με Φράγκους, Τούρκους και άλλους λαούς. Athens: Demiourgia.

Saradi, H. (1995). *Aspects of the Classical Tradition in Byzantium.* Toronto: Canadian Institute of Balkan Studies.

(1997). "The Use of Ancient Spolia in Byzantine Monuments: The Archaeological and Literary Evidence," *IJCT* 3: 395–423.

Saradi-Mendelovici, H. (1990). "Christian Attitudes toward Pagan Monuments in Late Antiquity and their Legacy in Later Byzantine Centuries," *DOP* 44: 47–61.

Sarikakis, Th. Ch. (1998). Ἡ Χίος στήν ἀρχαιότητα. Athens: Eriphyle.

Sarris, B. A. (1995–1997). "Ἡ σάτιρα τῆς ἐξουσίας στή συγγραφή τοῦ ἀρχιεπισκόπου Εὐσταθίου," Βυζαντινός Δόμος 8–9: 15–29.

Sartre, M. (2005). *The Middle East under Rome*. Tr. C. Porter and E. Rawlings. Cambridge, MA: Harvard University Press.

Sathas, K. N. (1888). *Documents inédits relatifs à l'histoire de la Grèce au Moyen-Âge*, v. VII. Paris: Maisonneuve et cie.

Savvides, A. G. K. (1987). Βυζαντινὰ στασιαστικὰ καὶ αὐτονομιστικὰ κινήματα στὰ Δωδεκάνησα καὶ στή Μικρὰ Ἀσία, 1189–c.1240 μ.Χ. Athens: Domos.

Schaefer, D. L. (1990). *The Political Philosophy of Montaigne*. Ithaca, NY: Cornell University Press.

Scheer, T. S. (2003). "The Past in a Hellenistic Present: Myth and Local Tradition." In A. Erskine, ed., *A Companion to the Hellenistic World*. Oxford: Blackwell Publishing. 216–231.

Schmalzbauer, G. (2004). "Überlegungen zur Idee der Oikumene in Byzanz." In W. Hörandner *et al.*, eds., *Wiener Byzantinistik und Neogräzistik*. Vienna: Verlag der österreichischen Akademie der Wissenschaften (= *Byzantina et Neogreca Vindobonensia* v. XXIV). 408–419.

Schmitz, D. (1993). "Schimpfwörter in der Invektiven des Gregor von Nazianz gegen Kaiser Julian," *Glotta* 71: 189–202.

Schott, J. M. (2003). "Founding Platonopolis: The Platonic Πολιτεία in Eusebius, Porphyry, and Iamblichus," *Journal of Early Christian Studies* 11: 501–531.

(2005). "Porphyry on Christians and Others: 'Barbarian Wisdom,' Identity Politics, and Anti-Christian Polemics on the Eve of the Great Persecution," *Journal of Early Christian Studies* 13: 277–314.

Schouler, B. (1991). "Hellénisme et humanisme chez Libanios." In Saïd 267–285.

Schucan, L. (1973). *Das Nachleben von Basilius Magnus "ad adolescentes." Ein Beitrag zur Geschichte des christlichen Humanismus*. Geneva: Librairie Droz.

Schwartz, S. (2001). *Imperialism and Jewish Society, 200 BCE to 640 CE*. Princeton University Press.

Seibt, W. (2003). "Stärken und Schwächen der byzantinischen Intergationspolitik gegenüber den neuen armenischen Staatsbürger im 11. Jahrhundert." In Vlyssidou 331–347.

Setton, K. M. (1944). "Athens in the Later Twelfth Century," *Speculum* 19: 179–207.

Ševčenko, I. (1980). "A Shadow Outline of Virtue: The Classical Heritage of Greek Christian Literature (Second to Seventh Century)." In K. Weitzmann, ed., *The Age of Spirituality: A Symposium*. New York: Metropolitan Museum of Art; Princeton University Press. 53–73.

(1981). "Levels of Style in Byzantine Prose," *JöB* 31: 289–312.

Ševčenko, I., and I. Hutter, eds. (1998). *ΑΕΤΟΣ: Studies in Honour of Cyril Mango Presented to Him on April 14, 1998*. Stuttgart and Leipzig: Teubner.

Shahîd, I. (1981). "On the Titulature of the Emperor Heraclius," *Byzantion* 51: 288–296.

(1998). "Miles Quondam et Graecus." In Ševčenko and Hutter 299–305.

Shaw, B. (1990). "Bandit Highlands and Lowland Peace: The Mountains of Isauria-Cilicia," *Journal of the Economic and Social History of the Orient* 33: 199–270.

Shaw, G. (1995). *Theurgy and the Soul: The Neoplatonism of Iamblichus.* University Park: Pennsylvania State University Press.

Shawcross, T. (2003). "Re-Inventing the Homeland in the Historiography of Frankish Greece: The Fourth Crusade and the Legend of the Trojan War," *BMGS* 27 (2003) 120–152.

Shepard, J. (1979). "Tzetzes' Letters to Leo at Dristra," *BF* 6: 191–239.

(2006). "Byzantium's Overlapping Circles." In E. Jeffreys, ed., *Proceedings of the 21st International Congress of Byzantine Studies,* v. I: *Plenary Papers.* Aldershot and Burlington, VT: Ashgate. 15–55.

Shukurov, R. (2001). "Turkoman and Byzantine Self-Identity: Some Reflections on the Logic of the Title-Making in Twelfth- and Thirteenth-Century Anatolia." In A. Eastmond, ed., *Eastern Approaches to Byzantium.* Brookfield, VT, and Aldershot: Ashgate. 259–276.

Sider, R. D. (1980). "Credo quia absurdum?" *Classical World* 73: 417–419.

Simeonova, L. (2001). "Constantinopolitan Attitudes toward Aliens and Minorities, 860s–1020s (Part Two)," *Études balkaniques* 2001 (1): 83–98.

Simpson, A. (1999). "Byzantine 'Latinophobia': Some Explanations Concerning the Central Aspect of Byzantine Popular Attitudes towards the Latins in the XII Century," *Mésogeios* 3: 64–82.

Skopetea, E. (1988). *Τὸ «Πρότυπο Βασίλειο» καὶ ἡ Μεγάλη Ἰδέα· Ὄψεις τοῦ ἐθνικοῦ προβλήματος στὴν Ἑλλάδα (1830–1880).* Athens: Polytypo.

Smith, A. D. (1986). *The Ethnic Origins of Nations.* Malden, MA, and Oxford: Blackwell.

(1991). *National Identity.* Reno and Las Vegas: University of Nevada Press.

(2003). *Chosen Peoples: Sacred Sources of National Identity.* Oxford University Press.

Smith, B. G. (1996). *Nietzsche, Heidegger, and the Transition to Postmodernity.* University of Chicago Press.

Smith, R. (1995). *Julian's Gods: Religion and Philosophy in the Thought and Action of Julian the Apostate.* London and New York: Routledge.

Smythe, D. C., ed. (2000). *Strangers to Themselves: The Byzantine Outsider.* Aldershot and Burlington, VT: Variorum.

Snyder, C. A. (2003). *The Britons.* Oxford: Blackwell Publishing.

Spawforth, A. (2001). "Shades of Greekness: A Lydian Case Study." In Malkin 375–400.

Speck, P. (1975). "Eine byzantinische Darstellung der Antiken Stadt Athen," *Ἑλληνικά* 28: 415–418.

Spiteris, G. (1977). "I dialoghi di Nicolas Mesarites coi Latini: Opera storica o finzione letteraria?" *Orientalia Christiana Analecta* 204: 181–186.

Stadtmüller, G. (1934). *Michael Choniates, Metropolit von Athen: ca. 1138 ca. 1222.* Rome: Pont. Institutum Orientalium Studiorum (= *Orientalia Christiana Analecta* v. XCI).

Stavridou-Zaphraka, A. (1990). Νίκαια και Ἤπειρος τον 130 αιώνα· Ιδεολογική αντιπαράθεση στην προσπάθεια να ανακτήσουν την αυτοκρατορία. Thessalonike: Banias.

Stephanou, P. É. (1949). *Jean Italos, philosophe et humaniste*. Rome: Pont. Institutum Orientalium Studiorum (= *Orientalia Christiana Analecta* v. CXXXIV).

Stephenson, P. (2000a). *Byzantium's Balkan Frontier: A Political Study of the Northern Balkans, 900–1204*. Cambridge University Press.

(2000b). "Byzantine Conceptions of Otherness after the Annexation of Bulgaria." In Smythe 245–257.

(2003). *The Legend of Basil the Bulgar-Slayer*. Cambridge University Press.

Stolte, B. (1991). "The Past in Legal Argument in the Byzantine Canonists of the Twelfth Century." In Oikonomides (1991b) 199–210.

(1999). "Desires Denied: Marriage, Adultery, and Divorce in Early Byzantine Law." In L. James, ed., *Desire and Denial in Byzantium*. Brookfield, VT, and Aldershot: Ashgate. 77–86.

Stone, A. F. (2001a). "On Hermogenes's Features of Style and Other Factors Affecting Style in the Panegyrics of Eustathios of Thessaloniki," *Rhetorica* 19: 307–339.

(2001b). "Eustathian Panegyric as a Historical Source," *JöB* 51: 225–258.

Stoppie, K. (2003). "The Macedonians before the Death of Alexander the Great: A People in the Shadow of the Hellenic *Ethnos*." In H. Hokwerda, ed., *Constructions of Greek Past: Identity and Historical Consciousness from Antiquity to the Present*. Groningen: Egbert Forsten. 47–62.

Stroumsa, G. G. (1999). "Philosophy of the Barbarians: On Early Christian Ethnological Representations." In G. G. Stroumsa, *Barbarian Philosophy: The Religious Revolution of Early Christianity*. Tübingen: Mohr Siebeck. 57–84.

Svoronos, N. (1989). "Τὸ νόημα καὶ ἡ τυπολογία τῶν κρητικῶν ἐπαναστάσεων τοῦ 13ου αἰ.," *Σύμμεικτα* 8: 1–13.

(2004). *Το ελληνικό έθνος· Γένεση και διαμόρφωση του Νέου Ελληνισμού*. Athens: Polis.

Swain, S. (1996). *Hellenism and Empire: Language, Classicism, and Power in the Greek World AD 50–250*. Oxford: Clarendon Press.

(1999). "Defending Hellenism: Philostratus, *In Honour of Apollonius*." In M. Edwards *et al.*, eds., *Apologetics in the Roman Empire: Pagans, Jews, and Christians*. Oxford University Press. 157–196.

Swain, S., and M. Edwards, eds. (2004). *Approaching Late Antiquity: The Transformation from Early to Late Empire*. Oxford University Press.

Talbot, A.-M. (1993). "The Restoration of Constantinople under Michael VIII," *DOP* 47: 243–261.

Tanoulas, T. (1997). Τὰ Προπύλαια τῆς Ἀθηναϊκῆς Ἀκρόπολης κατὰ τὸν Μεσαίωνα. Athens: Βιβλιοθήκη τῆς ἐν Ἀθήναις Ἀρχαιολογικῆς Ἑταιρείας v. CLXV.

Tăpkova-Zaimova, V. (1993). "L'emploi des ethnica et les problèmes de la communication à Byzance." In Moschonas (1993a) 701–709.

Tarnanidis, I. (2000). "The Macedonians of the Byzantine Period." In Burke and Scott 29–49.

Telelis, I. (2003). "Οἱ λόγιοι του πιου αἰώνα και ο Ἀριστοτελισμός: Η περίπτωση των «Μετεωρολογικών»." In Vlyssidou 425–442.

Thiriet, F. (1959). *La Romanie vénitienne au Moyen Age: Le développement et l'exploitation du domaine colonial vénitien (XIIe–XVe siècles)*. Paris: Éditions de Boccard.

Thomas, R. (2000). *Herodotus in Context: Ethnography, Science and the Art of Persuasion*. Cambridge University Press.
(2001). "Ethnicity, Genealogy, and Hellenism in Herodotos." In Malkin 213–233.

Thompson, D. J. (2001). "Hellenistic Hellenes: The Case of Ptolemaic Egypt." In Malkin 301–322.

Tinnefeld, F. H. (1989). "Michael I. Kerullarios, Patriarch von Konstantinopel (1043–1058). Kritische Überlegungen zu einer Biographie," *JöB* 39: 95–127.

Tomadakis, N. B. (1956–1957). "Ἦσαν βάρβαραι αἱ Ἀθῆναι ἐπὶ Μιχαὴλ Χωνιάτου;" Ἐπιστημονικὴ Ἐπετηρὶς τῆς Φιλοσοφικῆς Σχολῆς τοῦ Πανεπιστημίου Ἀθηνῶν 7: 88–105.

Too, Y. L. (1995). *The Rhetoric of Identity in Isocrates: Text, Power, Pedagogy*. Cambridge University Press.

Topping, P. (1977). "Co-Existence of Greeks and Latins in Frankish Morea and Venetian Crete." In P. Topping, *Studies on Latin Greece, AD 1205–1715*. London: Variorum Reprints. XI.

Toynbee, A. (1973). *Constantine Porphyrogenitus and his World*. Oxford University Press.

Tozer, H. F. (1881). "Byzantine Satire," *Journal of Hellenic Studies* 2: 233–270.

Trapp, E. (2003). "The Role of Vocabulary in Byzantine Rhetoric as a Stylistic Device." In Jeffreys (2003a) 137–149.

Travlos, I. N. (1993). Πολεοδομικὴ ἐξέλιξις τῶν Ἀθηνῶν ἀπὸ τῶν προϊστορικῶν χρόνων μέχρι τῶν ἀρχῶν τοῦ 19ου αἰῶνος. 2nd ed. Athens: Kapon.

Treadgold, W. (1980). *The Nature of the Bibliotheca of Photius*. Washington, DC: Dumbarton Oaks Center for Byzantine Studies.
(1984). "The Macedonian Renaissance." In W. Treadgold, ed., *Renaissances Before the Renaissance: Cultural Revivals of Late Antiquity and the Middle Ages*. Stanford University Press. 75–98.
(1988). *The Byzantine Revival, 780–842*. Stanford University Press.
(1995). *Byzantium and Its Army, 284–1081*. Stanford University Press.
(1998). "Observations on Finishing a General History of Byzantium." In Ševčenko and Hutter 342–353.
(2005). "Standardized Numbers in the Byzantine Army," *War in History* 12: 1–14.

Treu, M. (1892). "Ein Kritiker des Timarion," *BZ* 1: 361–365.

Troianos, S. (2004a). "Latinitas Graeca." In Angelidi 168–176.

(2004b). "Η γλώσσα χωρίζει ή ενώνει το Βυζάντιο και την Ευρώπη." In E. Grammatikopoulou, ed., *Το Βυζάντιο και οι απαρχές της Ευρώπης*. Athens: The National Hellenic Research Foundation. 155–187.

Trombley, F. R. (2001). *Hellenic Religion and Christianization, c. 370–529*. 2 vols. 2nd ed. Boston and Leiden: Brill.

Tsolakis, E. Th. (1990). "Τιμαρίων, μία νέα ανάγνωση." In *Μνήμη Σταμάτη Καρατζά: Ερευνητικά προβλήματα νεοελληνικής φιλολογίας και γλωσσολογίας*. Thessalonike: Aristotelian University of Thessalonike. 109–117.

Tsougarakis, D. (1995). "Cultural Assimilation through Language Infiltration: Some Early Examples from Venetian Crete," *BF* 21: 181–194.

(2001). "Venetian Crete and the Myth of Novel Ideas," *Thesaurismata* 31: 43–64.

Turlej, S. (1998). "The So-Called Chronicle of Monemvasia: A Historical Analysis," *Byzantion* 68: 446–468.

Urbainczyk, T. (1997). *Socrates of Constantinople: Historian of Church and State*. Ann Arbor: University of Michigan Press.

Usher, S. (1993). "Isocrates: Paideia, Kingship and the Barbarians," *Nottingham Classical Literature Studies* 2: 131–145.

Vakalopoulos, A. E. (1974). *Ἱστορία τοῦ Νέου Ἑλληνισμοῦ*, v. I: *Ἀρχὲς καὶ διαμόρφωσή του*. Rev. ed. Thessalonike: n.p.

Van Dam, R. (2002). *Kingdom of Snow: Roman Rule and Greek Culture in Cappadocia*. Philadelphia: University of Pennsylvania Press.

(2003). *Becoming Christian: The Conversion of Roman Cappadocia*. Philadelphia: University of Pennsylvania Press.

Vercleyen, F. (1988). "Tremblement de terre à Constantinople: L'impact sur la population," *Byzantion* 58: 155–173.

Viscuso, P. (2005). "Theodore Balsamon's Canonical Images of Women," *GRBS* 45: 317–326.

Vlyssidou, V. N., ed. (2003). *Η αυτοκρατορία σε κρίση (;) Το Βυζάντιο τον 11ο αιώνα (1025–1081)*. Athens: The Speros Basil Vryonis Center for the Study of Hellenism and the Institute for Byzantine Research of the National Hellenic Research Foundation.

Voliotis, N. A. (1988). *The Tradition of Isocrates in Byzantium and His Influence on Modern Greek Education*. Athens: National and Capodistrian University of Athens, School of Philosophy.

Volk, R. (1990). *Der medizinische Inhalt der Schriften des Michael Psellos*. Munich: Institut für Byzantinistik und neugriechische Philologie der Universität München.

Voltaire, *Philosophical Dictionary*. Ed. and tr. T. Besterman. London: Penguin Books. 1972.

de Vries-van der Velden, E. (1996). "Psellos et son gendre," *BF* 23: 109–149.

Vryonis, S. (1971). *The Decline of Medieval Hellenism in Asia Minor and the Process of Islamization from the Eleventh through the Fifteenth Century*. Berkeley: University of California Press.

(1978). "Recent Scholarship on Continuity and Discontinuity of Culture: Classical Greeks, Byzantines, Modern Greeks." In S. Vryonis, ed., *The 'Past' in Medieval and Modern Greek Culture*. Malibu: Undena Publications. 237–256.

(1992). "Byzantine Civilization, a World Civilization." In A. E. Laiou and H. Maguire, eds., *Byzantium: A World Civilization*. Washington, DC: Dumbarton Oaks Research Library and Collection. 19–35.

(1999). "Greek Identity in the Middle Ages," *Études balkaniques* 6 (*Byzance et l'hellénisme: L'identité grecque au Moyen-Âge*): 19–36.

Walker, J. (2004). "These Things I Have Not Betrayed: Michael Psellos' Encomium of His Mother as a Defense of Rhetoric," *Rhetorica* 22: 49–101.

Wallace-Hadril, A. (1998). "To Be Roman, Go Greek: Thoughts on Hellenization at Rome." In M. Austin *et al.*, eds., *Modus Operandi: Essays in Honour of Geoffrey Rickman*. University of London. 79–92.

Watts, E. (2005). "An Alexandrian Christian Response to Fifth-Century Neoplatonic Influence." In A. Smith, ed., *The Philosopher and Society in Late Antiquity: Essays in Honour of Peter Brown*. Swansea: The Classical Press of Wales. 215–229.

Weitzmann, K. (1981). "The Survival of Mythological Representations in Early Christian and Byzantine Art and their Impact on Christian Iconography." In K. Weitzmann, *Classical Heritage in Byzantine and Near Eastern Art*. London: Variorum. VI.

Wendel, C. (1948). "Tzetzes." In A. Pauly, G. Wissowa, and W. Kroll, eds., *Real-Encyclopädie der klassischen Altertumswissenschaft* 7A: 1959–2011.

Westerink, L. G. (1986). "Leo the Philosopher: Job and Other Poems," *Illinois Classical Studies* 11: 193–222.

Whitmarsh, T. (1998). "The Birth of a Prodigy: Heliodorus and the Genealogy of Hellenism." In Hunter 93–124.

(2001). *Greek Literature and the Roman Empire: The Politics of Imitation*. Oxford University Press.

Whittaker, J. (1979). "Christianity and Morality in the Roman Empire," *Vigiliae Christianae* 33: 209–225.

Wickham, C. (1998). "Ninth-Century Byzantium through Western Eyes." In L. Brubaker, ed., *Byzantium in the Ninth Century: Dead or Alive?* Aldershot: Ashgate. 245–256.

Widmann, F. (1935–1936). "Die Progymnasmata des Nikephoros Chrysoberges," *Byzantinisch-neugriechische Jahrbücher* 12: 12–41, 241–299.

Wilken, R. L. (1983). *John Chrysostom and the Jews: Rhetoric and Reality in the Late 4th Century*. Berkeley: University of California Press.

(1984). *The Christians as the Romans Saw Them*. New Haven and London: Yale University Press.

Williams, P. (1980). *A New History of the Organ from the Greeks to the Present Day*. Bloomington: Indiana University Press.

Wilson, N. G. (1983). *Scholars of Byzantium*. London: Duckworth.

452          *Bibliography*

Winterer, C. (2002). *The Culture of Classicism: Ancient Greece and Rome in American Intellectual Life, 1780–1910*. Baltimore and London: Johns Hopkins University Press.

Wirth, P. (1979). "Die Bevölkerungspolitik der Komnenen- und Laskaridenkaiser," *BF* 7: 203–212.

Wolff, R. L. (1957). "Greeks and Latins before and after 1204," *Ricerche di Storia Religiosa: Rivista di Studi Storico-Religiosi* 1: 320–334.

(1976). *Studies in the Latin Empire of Constantinople*. London: Variorum Reprints.

Wolfram, H. (1988). *History of the Goths*. Tr. T. J. Dunlap. 2nd ed. Berkeley: University of California Press.

Woodhouse, C. M. (1995). *Rhigas Velestinlis: The Proto-Martyr of the Greek Revolution*. Euboia: Denise Harvey Publisher.

Woolf, G. (1994). "Becoming Roman, Staying Greek: Culture, Identity and the Civilizing Process in the Roman East," *Proceedings of the Cambridge Philological Society* 40: 116–143.

(1998). *Becoming Roman: The Origins of Provincial Civilization in Gaul*. Cambridge University Press.

Xanthoudides, S. A. (1902). "Συνθήκη μεταξὺ τῆς Ἐνετικῆς Δημοκρατίας καὶ Ἀλεξίου Καλλιέργου," Ἀθηνᾶ 14: 283–331.

(1939). Ἡ Ἐνετοκρατία ἐν Κρήτῃ καὶ οἱ κατὰ τῶν Ἐνετῶν ἀγῶνες τῶν Κρητῶν. Athens: Texte und Forschungen zur byzantinisch-neugriechischen Philologie v. XXXIV.

Zakythinos, D. A. (1980). "Two Historical Parallels: The Greek Nation under Roman and Turkish Rule." In E. A. Laiou-Thomadakis, ed., *Charanis Studies: Essays in Honor of Peter Charanis*. New Brunswick, NJ: Rutgers University Press. 312–328.

Zambelios, S. (1857). *Βυζαντιναὶ μελέται περὶ πηγῶν νεοελληνικῆς ἐθνότητος ἀπὸ Η΄ ἄχρι Ι΄ ἑκατονταετηρίδος μ.Χ*. Athens: Ch. N. Philadelphos.

Zilliacus, H. (1935). *Zum Kampf der Weltsprachen im oströmischen Reich*. Helsingfors: Mercators Tryckeri Aktiebolag.

(1937). "Das lateinische Lehnwort in der griechischen Hagiographie," *BZ* 37: 302–344.

# Index

Achaian League 52, 57
Achaians
  Bronze Age ethnonym 13, 167
  Byzantines as 336
Achilles 132, 150, 242, 243, 244, 248
Adeimantos (Plato's *Republic*) 273
Aemilius Paulus 89
Aeneas, as national ancestor, 62, 89, 99,
  299–300, 355, 389
Agamemnon 244, 304
Agathias of Myrina 177
Ailianos, sophist, 32
Aimilianos, patriarch of Antioch, and Psellos
  207, 209, 211
Aineias of Gaza 175–176, 290
Aischines 35
Aischylos 20, 306
Akathistos hymn 178–179
Akropolis: *see* Parthenon
Akropolites, Georgios, 81, 87, 352, 357, 366, 369,
  373, 377, 381–383
  *Against the Latins* 381–383
  and Blemmydes 381, 383
  on creation of Roman nation 52, 382
  *History* 381
  and Theodoros II Laskaris 381–383
Akropolites, Konstantinos, on *Timarion*, 277,
  281, 282
Albanians 94
Albucius, Titus, 31
Alexander the Great 89, 270, 373, 380
  and brotherhood of man 48
  compared to Manuel I Komnenos 285–286
  compared to Theodoros I Laskaris 343
  as end of classical period 36, 37
  and Greeks and barbarians 24–25
  as Hellenizer 26
  as historical marker 13–14, 18, 21,
    23, 25, 38
  and Julian 153
  as medieval folk hero 248–249, 284

Alexandria 65, 70, 194
  Hellenistic 22
  and Julian 59, 150
Alexandros I of Makedonia
  at Olympic games 16
  in Persian Wars 15
  "Philhellene" 16
Alexios I Komnenos 89, 92, 233–234, 242, 293
  and Anna's education 232, 245
  and Bohemond 289
  cites Perikles 256–257
  and Orphanotropheion 290–291
  and trial of Ioannes Italos 228–230, 282
Alexios III Angelos 340
  classicizing letter to Genoa 256
Alkaios 20
Alkibiades 38
Amazaspos, Hellenized Kolchian, 53
Ambrakiots 18
Ambrosius of Milan, admits praise
  of Julian, 145
Ammianus Marcellinus 70, 72
  as *Graecus* 115
  on Julian's laws 149
Amphilochian Argives 18
Anastasios, emperor, 175
Anatolikon (theme) 96
Andronikos I Komnenos 247, 248, 318, 367
Andronikos II Palaiologos 350
  his ancestry 385–386
Anselm of Havelberg 297
Antioch 70, 71, 98
  Hellenistic 22
  and Julian 59
Antiochos I 89
Antiochos IV and Maccabean revolt 28–29
Antiochos, Gregorios, 240
  on Athens 324
  as Constantinopolitan 88, 99
  his genealogy 89
Antiphon, sophist, 20

Antonios IV 100
  equates Romans and Christians 104–105, 107
Anysios, Synesios' correspondent, 3
Aphrodite
  in Byzantine texts 217
  *ethopoeia* of her mourning for Adonis 175
Aphthonios, rhetor, 260
Apokaukos, Ioannes, 344–345, 346, 362, 363,
    365, 368
  classicising legal decision 256
  hatred of Latins 345–345, 362
  on *Hellenes/Graikoi* 344–345, 369
Apollinarioi, response to Julian, 157, 162, 163
Apollinarios, apologist, 127
Apollo, in Komnenian literature, 245–247
Apollonios of Tyana 65, 171
*Apostolic Constitutions* 141
Aquinas, Thomas, 198
Arabia 34
Arabs
  on Byzantine "unity" 111
  conquests 179
  claim to Hellenism 118, 185, 220–221, 390
  as *Hellenes* 122
Aramaic 21, 28, 31, 67
Archimedes
  and Psellos 204
  and St Loukia 305
Ares, in Komnenian literature, 245–247, 270, 292
Arethas
  and *Chronicle of Monembasia* 117–118
  against Julian 144
  against Leon Choirosphaktes 144
Argos
  and Alexandros I of Makedonia 16
  and Xerxes 16, 38
Aristagoras of Miletos 15
Aristainetos, erotic letters, 177
Aristeides, Ailios, 36, 40, 227
  classical dreams 37
  *Defense of Rhetoric* 151
  *Panathenaic Oration* 19, 38, 58
  *Roman Oration* 56–58, 82, 86
  and Themistios 72
  and *Timarion* 283
Aristeides the Just 319–320, 326
Aristenos, Alexios
  compared to ancients 286–287
  genealogy 89
Aristoboulos the Philhellene 29
Aristophanes, in Byzantium, 196, 250, 252, 256
Aristotle
  adviser of Alexander 24–25
  in Byzantium 187, 188, 194, 204, 230–231, 244,
    245, 249, 321

  on foreigners 60
  on Greek nation 20, 52
  on pride 134, 137
Armenians 90, 91, 97, 98, 229, 339
Arrianos of Nikomedeia 37, 56, 227
Arsakes the Parthian 89
"artificiality" of Byzantine literature 239, 252
Asklepios, in *Timarion*, 279–280
"Assyrians": *see* "Syrians"
Athanasios of Alexandria
  anti-intellectualism in *Life Antonios* 155
  on Greeks 130
Athena
  displaced from Akropolis 298, 329
  in Komnenian literature 245–247, 256,
    270, 274
Athenaios, sophist, 37, 40
Athenians
  autochthony 17, 19
  praised by Blemmydes 380
  purity of descent 284
  receive Spartan envoys 15, 17, 166, 167, 184
Athens 31, 32
  attacked by Christians 178–179, 181
  in Byzantium 94, 176, 178, 194, 222–223, 295,
    298, 323–334, 376–377
  and Gregorios of Nazianzos 159
  as ideal 2, 38, 57, 178
  invents "the barbarian" 19
  and Ioannes Chrysostomos 134
  and Julian 59
  as nation 77, 80
  new home of Arrianos 56
  Panathenaia 278
  praised by Aristeides 58
  and Roman law 48–49
  and St Paul 129–130
  as standard of *paideia* 31, 32–33, 36, 54–55, 58, 59
  and Synesios 59–60
  *see also:* Choniates, Michael; Parthenon
Attaleiates, Michael, 89, 242–243, 288
  critic of monasticism 213, 254
  interest in Republic 62
  "new man" in Constantinople 88
  Romanocentric *History* 295, 317–318, 321,
    323, 331
  on temple of Kyzikos 185
  on *translatio imperii* 61
Augustus 143
  as Hellenizer 26
  as Romanizer 52, 79
Ausones
  Byzantines as Romans 63, 221, 303, 355, 374
  Italians 221, 339
  Normans 299

Ausonius of Bordeaux 175
autopsies, in Byzantium, 249
Auxentios, St, and Psellos, 254
Avars, in Greece, 117
Axouch, Ioannes, Byzantine of "Persian" descent, 92

Baal, equated with Jewish God, 28
Balkan and Slavic nationalisms 82–83, 109–110, 123, 345
Balsamon, Theodoros, 100, 252, 254
  on cunnilingus 248
  equates Romans and Orthodox 104–105
  on Komnenian *erotomaniacs* 247–248
  as native Constantinopolitan 88
"barbarian wisdom" 122, 124–126, 133, 139–140, 152–153, 165, 168–171
barbarization, fear of,
  in antiquity 25–26
  in Byzantium 267–271, 293–295, 333, 340
Bardanes, Georgios, 345–346, 362, 365
  and Apokaukos 345
Basilakes, Konstantinos, "both Greek and Roman," 296
Basilakes, Nikephoros, 89, 240, 252–253, 258, 291, 296
  *basilakizein* 238
  between inner and outer wisdom 253
  encomia 243, 286–287
  *progymnasmata* 258–260
  satires 253
  and Sophokles 244, 259
Basileios I 90, 337
  genealogy 89
  and Slavs in Greece 116
Basileios II 90, 189, 214
  at Athens 325
Basileios of Kaisareia 144, 207, 231
  *Address to Young Men* 133–134, 164–165
  on Athens 165
  and Eustathios 314
  and Gregorios of Nazianzos 159, 164
  and Julian 164–165
  on prose of Scripture 139–140
Basileios of Patra, genealogy, 60
Basileios of Thessalonike, debate with Anselm of Havelberg, 297
*basileus* 65–66;
  *see also:* emperor
Batatzes, Ioannes, 218
Batnai, and Julian, 152
Belisarios 339
Bemarchios, sophist, 156
Benedictus, cardinal, 357
*Beowulf* 264–265

Berossos, and Christian apologists, 126
Bertha-Eudokia 90, 92
Berthold of Hohenburg 374
Berytos 70
Blemmydes, Nikephoros, 368, 373, 375, 377, 379–381, 384, 387
  *Basilikos Andrias* 379–380
  on *genos* and *patris* 88
  *Partial Account* 380–381
  on Romans and Greeks 380–381, 383, 384, 385
Boethius 175
Bohemond
  and Anna Komnene 249
  and treaty of Diabolis 289
Boïlas, Eustathios, on Armenians, 98
Bonditza, city, 345
Bonifatius, marquis of Montferrat, 334
Borysthenes (Olbia) 25
Bostra 34
Boukellarioi theme, as *ethnos*, 88
Bourtzes, Georgios, letter from Tornikes, 297–298
Bronze Age, Greek, 13, 16, 112, 167
Brutus 220
Bryennios, Nikephoros, 89, 227, 235, 276, 300
  Homeric values of *History* 242, 244
Bulgarians 90, 94, 96, 98, 363, 365–366
"Byzantine Commonwealth" 109–110, 357–358, 362
"Byzantines" as Constantinopolitans 42, 96, 356–357
Byzantium
  under Basileios II 189
  and "Christendom" 106, 110–111
  as city-state 80–82
  its "Dark Age" 179
  decline in late twelfth century 330–331
  and Latin rule 334–379
  as "multi-ethnic empire" 75, 78–79, 82–100, 109
  not monolithically Christian 392–393
  "official languages" 65–68
  "originality" and literature 391–392
  as Roman nation-state 5, ch. 2, 296, 335, 360–368
  as "western" civilization 2–3, 120
  *see also:* "ecumenical ideology"; Komnenian regime

Caesar, Julius, 65, 300
  in Byzantine view of history 62
  in Komnenian rhetoric 299, 339
Caliphate
  outlived by Byzantium 111
  recognized by Byzantium 102

Caracalla 47–48
Carthage, as base of Herakleios, 97
Cassiodorus, on Odysseus, 165
Cato
  in Byzantium 220, 227, 270, 287–288
  *see also:* Tzetzes
Cecilia, St, Roman saint, 355, 358
Chairemon 198
Chaironeia (Boiotia) 55, 71
Chaldaeans/*Chaldaean Oracles* 124, 169–170, 171
  and Iamblichos 169–170
  and Julian 152–153
  and Proklos 171
  and Psellos 196–198, 206
  *see also:* Berossos
Chalkokondyles, Laonikos, 378
Charanis, Peter, 42–43, 111–112
Chinese as *Hellenes* 122
Choirosphaktes, Leon
  and Arethas 144
  and Julian 144
  praised Leon the Philosopher 183
Chomatenos, Demetrios, 365–366
  on *Graikoi* 353
  on Psellos 227
  on Roman union 362–363, 364, 366
Choniates, Michael, 35, 240, 298, 317–334, 346, 355, 361
  *Address to Demetrios Drimys* 318–319
  against the Latins 364
  and Aristotle 321
  as Athenian 322, 324
  as bishop 322, 332
  and Byzantine Athenians 328–329
  and decline of Athens 318–319, 323, 331, 333–334, 377–378
  disappointed in his flock 326–327, 332–333
  and Eustathios 301, 309, 310, 313, 315, 318, 321, 326, 346
  Greeks and Christians 310, 319–320, 326, 327, 331–332
  Greeks and Latins 340
  *Inaugural Address* 328–333
  and Leon Sgouros 322, 364–365
  letter to Demetrios Drimys 318, 319–320, 322, 328, 331, 332, 380
  on Michael Psellos 227
  as *philologos* 321, 322, 327, 328, 333
  and Themistios 73
Choniates, Niketas, 240, 323, 341–344, 346, 361
  on Anna Komnene 249
  on Byzantines as *Graikoi/Hellenes* 341–344, 346, 369
  on Byzantines vs. Latins 95, 336, 341
  on Constantinopolitans 94

on custom vs. *genos* 76
*History* 341–344, 346, 365, 368
on Ioannes Axouch 92
on Komnenian empire 233–234, 248, 252, 341
on Leon Sgouros 365
on monks 254
on peasants and refugees 346, 348
Chorikios of Gaza 175
Christ: *see* Jesus
Christianity
  aspects prefigured in Maccabean revolt 27–30, 127, 135
  as barrier to Hellenic ethnonym 45, 54, 58, 61
  and definitions of the "West" 1–2
  effects on Roman world 135–136
  and Hellenism ch. 3
  "Hellenists" vs. "Hebrews" 129, 168
  virtues in New Testament 132–133
  *see also:* "barbarian wisdom"; Byzantium and "Christendom"; "ecumenical ideology"
*Chronicle of Cyprus*, on Greeks and Romans, 351–352
*Chronicle of Monembasia*, on Greeks and Avars, 117–118
*Chronicle of the Morea*, on Greeks and Romans, 351, 382–383
*Chronicle of the Tocco*, on Romans and others, 351
Chrysoberges, Nikephoros
  against Julian 161
  on Euphrosyne as Greek 340–341
  *progymnasmata* 258–260
Cicero 31, 34, 46, 64
  in Byzantium 227, 286, 300, 364
  compared to Gregorios of Nazianzos 162
  and Jerome 139, 181
  on *res publica* 76
  on two *patriae* 99
citizenship, Roman, 47–48, 57, 85
Classical Studies
  in Byzantium 180–181, 189, 236–237, 243, 255, 301
  from Byzantium to the West 4, 6–7, 41, 156, 190, 236, 387
  and Christianity 155–156, 174–179
  and Hellenism in Byzantium 5–6, 118–119, 174, 186–187, 226, 232, ch. 5
  and Second Sophistic 40–41
Claudianus 70
Claudius I 65, 66
Clement of Alexandria 127–128, 131–132, 138
Constantine 70, 79, 81, 89, 143, 148
  cited by Ioannes III Batatzes 370
  legends in Byzantium 91
  Stilbes on why Latins hate him 358–359

Constantinople
  as Byzantion 42, 96, 221
  Hagia Sophia 177, 178, 202, 356
  Holy Apostles 145, 235–236, 237
  as imperial capital 79–82
  inhabitants 92–93, 94, 99
  Latin in sixth century 70
  lost in thirteenth century 361–362, 367–368
  as New Rome 44, 52, 59, 61–62, 71–72, 81–82
  pagan art 156, 241
  resented in fourth century 71–72
  resented in twelfth century 319–321,
    322–323, 328
  see also: theatra
Constantinus III, renames his sons Constans and
    Julian, 145
Constantius I 91
Constantius II 59, 72–73, 155
Consul of the Philosophers
  Ioannes Italos 228, 277
  Michael III *ho tou Anchialou* 230, 237, 285
  Michael Psellos 193, 196, 277
  Theodoros of Smyrne 277
Coptic 122
Corinth
  destruction by Romans 46
  and Favorinus 32–33, 184
Corippus 70
cosmopolitanism 20–21
Crete, revolts against Venice, 347, 349–351
Crusaders 87, 92, 97, 107, 295, 317, 321–323,
    334–336, 339, 342, 348
  Byzantine views of 87–88, 335–336, 369–371
Cyclops, in Komnenian literature, 245, 254
Cyprus, Greeks and Romans in, 352, 353–354,
    384–385

Danube frontier 97–98
Daphnomeles, Eustathios, 96
Delphi 15, 37, 173
  last oracle 161
Demetrios, king, 279
Demetrios, St, in *Timarion*, 277, 278–279, 302
Demetrios, theologian from Lampe, 96
Demokritos 253
Demonax 56
Demosthenes
  and Julian 147
  standard of Atticism 36, 227, 258, 286–288
demotic Greek literature 238–239
Diabolis, treaty of, 289
*Digenes Akrites* 238
  attitude to Homer 248
  on becoming Roman 107
  and Komnenian society 248–249, 269

Diocletian 70, 79, 305, 385
Diodoros of Sicily, on indigenous Sicilians, 22
Diogenes the Cynic, in *Timarion*, 282
Diogenes Laertios 37
  champion of Hellenism 170–171
Diogenes of Oinoanda 20–21
Diomedes 244
Dion Chrysostomos 35, 36, 40, 54
  on Borysthenes (Olbia) 25
  *Dion* by Synesios 60
Dionysios of Alexandria, on author of
    Revelation, 140
Dionysios of Halikarnassos
  and Atticism 36, 39
  commentary by Ioannes Kanaboutzes 339–340
  on Greek origin of Rome 25, 57, 59, 65
  on moral qualities of Rome 50
  on Thucydides 151
Dionysos
  Euhemerized as Noah 307
  in Nonnos' *Dionysiaka* 176
  in romance novels 265–266, 270, 274
Dioskoros of Aphrodito 176
Dominicans in Constantinople, on Greeks,
    359–360
Dorians 17
  and Synesios 60, 86, 172
Doukas family
  genealogy 89, 299, 371–372
  and Ioannes Italos 228
  and Psellos 193
Doukas, Ioannes, 215
Dracontius 175
Drimys, Demetrios, and Michael Choniates,
    318–320
Dyrrachion 297

"ecumenical ideology" 75, 77, 79, 100–111, 381–383
Egilbald-Georgios 90
Egypt 22, 33–34, 53, 185
  not fully Romanized 52
  Orthodox Church in 104
  Thrakians in 23–24
Egyptians
  Arab Egyptians 220
  in Christian polemics 124, 127, 129, 130
  and Diogenes Laertios 171
  Hermetic literature 169–170
  in Herodotos 17
  and Iamblichos 170
  and Julian 152
  as pagan *Hellenes* 122
  and Psellos 197–198
  "spoiling the Egyptians" 138
  see also: Manethon

emperor, Roman-Byzantine conception, 49–51,
    52–53, 75, 103, 105–106, 363–364
Ennius 32
Epeiros, Byzantine state, 338, 341, 344, 347,
    361–363, 366
Ephoros 137
Ephraim the Syrian 127
Epikouros/Epicureans 20, 31, 37, 197
    and Leon the Philosopher 182
    viewed by Christians 134, 138
Epiphanios of Salamis
    on Hellenism 130
    against Origenes 141
Erasmus 118–119
Eratosthenes of Kyrene, debate with Strabon,
    24–25
Eros, in Komnenian literature, 247–249, 259–270
ethnicity 70, 115
    in Byzantium 43–44, 54, 75, 78–79, 82–100,
        345, 365
    in classical Greece 15
    Julian's views on 58–59
    modern Greek views of 112–114, 118, 338, 360
    in Roman empire 48, 54
*ethnikoi* 87, 90, 124
*ethnos* 15–16, 19, 62, 80, 81, 87–88, 95, 98, 106, 112,
    116, 117, 312, 356, 357, 358, 360, 364, 370, 382
Etruscans 87
Euagrios Pontikos, on monasticism, 137
Euagrios Scholastikos
    models and methods 137
    mythological images 176
Eudokia, Homeric centones, 157
Eugenianos, Niketas, *Drosilla and Charikles*,
    260–270
Eunapios of Sardeis, student of Prohairesios, 149
Euphrosyne, empress, her Greek blood, 340–341
Euripides 17, 175, 242, 277, 333
Eusebia, empress, her Greek descent, 152
Eusebios of Kaisareia 30
    on authors of Scripture 140
    on Christians 131
    on Greeks 130
    historiographical ideals 137, 176, 244
    on Origenes 141
    and Plato 126
Eustathios of Thessalonike 35, 87, 236, 240, 252,
    284, 286, 307–316, 332
    on Athens 324, 326–327
    and Basileios of Kaisareia 314
    *Capture of Thessalonike* 246–247, 307, 342
    on debate with Anselm of Havelberg 297
    on friendship 244
    on Greeks, pagans, and barbarians 288, 297,
        301, 309–313

Homeric allegories 246, 315
Homeric commentaries 313–315
    on laughing and crying 253
*Life of Philotheos* 254
    and Manuel I Komnenos 91, 243–244, 294,
        307–308
    Pindaric commentaries 310
    and Psellos 227, 297, 308
    reform of monasticism 137, 253–255, 307, 315
    scholarship 301–302
    on slavery, Venice, and drama 307–308
    *see also:* Choniates, Michael
Eustratios of Nikaia 229, 231, 240
Euthydemos, Karian notable, 23

Fabii family 89
Favorinus of Arelate 32–33, 34, 35, 59, 184
Flamininus 35
Franks: *see* Latins
Fravitta, Gothic *Hellen*, 151–152
Frederick II Hohenstaufen
    on Byzantine Church–state relations 107
    letters to Byzantines 372
French vernacular romances 261

Gadara, and Meleagros, 21
Galenos
    and Byzantine doctors 286
    and small town life 55
    in *Timarion* 280
Galenos, Ioannes, commentaries, 246
"Galilaians": *see* Julian
*Gallogreci* 84
Gaul/Gauls/Gallic/Celts 31, 32, 35, 58, 59, 67, 84,
    152, 184, 340
    Romanized 46
Gaza orators 40, 175–176
genealogies, in Byzantium, 89, 290
Gennadios Scholarios 96
Genoa/Genoese 256, 337
*genos* 15, 18, 26, 31, 37–38, 57–59, 76, 87–93, 95–96,
    99, 115, 124, 151, 197, 223, 289, 290, 355–360,
    364–366, 370, 374–375, 384, 385
Georgians 98, 302–303
Georgios of Alexandria, *Life of Ioannes
    Chrysostomos*, 134
Georgios of Pisidia 177, 236
Germanos II 362, 363
    on Constantinopolitans 94
    on Greeks and Romans 353–354, 355
Gilakios, Ioannes, Armenian in Italy, 98
Glaukon (Plato's *Republic*) 20, 273
Glykas, Michael, 238
Gnostics, attacked by Plotinos, 169
Gothic Bible 133

Goths 58–59, 60, 98, 133, 151
*Gotthograikoi* 85
Graces, in Komnenian literature, 245–247, 270
*Graeculus* 32, 58
*Graikoi* 52, 68, 115–116, 129, 186, 296, 312, 336–338,
    341–345, 349–360, 369, 372, 382–383, 386
Greece, Byzantine, 115, 184–185, 311, 318, 342, 389
Greece, modern, 9, 13–14, 74, 78, 79, 105, 110–111,
    311, 334, 376–377, 386–387
Greek language 13, 73, 92, 98, 112–113, 116, 118–119,
    167, 174
  and *Invectives* of Gregorios of Nazianzos
    160–161, 167
  Latin views of 297
  made one a "Greek" 185–186, 290–291,
    296–297, 312, 342, 355–356, 368, 387
  as "Roman" language 113–114, 167, 174, 186,
    291, 351, 365–366
  separates Byzantines from Latins 296, 389
  shaped by Latin 61, 69–70, 73
  in twelfth-century *paideia* 236–240, 258, 269,
    290–291
  *see also:* demotic Greek literature
"Greeklings" 43, 64, 312
Greeks, modern
  and Europe 1, 105, 110
  use of *ethnikoi* 87
  views of Byzantium 8, 43–44, 63, 82–83,
    112–114, 123
Gregoras, Nikephoros, 361
  on *indicia* of Roman identity 107
Gregorios Dekapolites, identifies himself, 108
Gregorios of Cyprus 384–386, 387
  on ancestry of Andronikos II Palaiologos
    385–386
  attacked as un-Roman 107, 385
  on Greeks, Romans, and Latins 384–385
Gregorios of Nazianzos 144, 158–164, 175, 227,
    231, 236
  admits praise of Julian 145
  and Athens 159, 325
  and Basileios of Kaisareia 159, 164
  between Hellenism and Christianity, rhetoric
    and philosophy 158–164
  buried with Julian 145
  compared to Cicero 162
  and Gregorios of Nyssa 159
  and Himerios 161
  hysteria of *Invectives* 158
  on Kappadokians 84
  on Latin 69
  and Libanios 163
  and Maximos the Cynic 159
  and Psellos 200, 207–209, 217–218
  response to Julian 147, 149, 158–164, 167

Gregorios of Nyssa
  and Gregorios of Nazianzos 159
  stylistic ambitions 140
Gregorios Thaumatourgos 127
Gregorius I, pope, intercedes for Trajan, 380
Gregorius IX, pope, 81
  letter from Germanos II 353–354
  letter from Ioannes III Batatzes 369–372

Hadrian 52, 73, 79
  *Graeculus* 32, 37, 58
  and Panhellenion 38
Hagiotheodorites, Nikolaos, 324, 326
Hasmonean dynasty 29
Hebrew 26, 27
Hegias, philosopher, 60
Hekataios of Abdera, on Jews, 28
Hekatomnid dynasty (Karia) 23
Heliodoros, *Aithiopika*, 125–126
Helladikoi, Byzantine inhabitants of Greece,
    173–174, 184
Hellanikos, historian, 20, 239
Hellen, son of Deukalion, 16, 18
Hellenion (Naukratis) 16
*Hellenismos*, technical rhetorical term, 187, 385
Henri, Latin emperor, 348, 353, 357
Herakleios 177
  as Armenian or Libyan 97
  and Byzantine "official language" 65–69, 116
Herakleitos 253
Herakles 320
  ancestor of Synesios 60, 172
  in Komnenian literature 245–247
Hermes
  and Julian 147
  in Komnenian literature 262, 270, 274, 292
Hermes Trismegistos 170
Hermetic texts 34
  and Iamblichos 169–170
Hermogenes 260
Herod, king, 29
Herodes Attikos, sophist, 36, 38
  and *Timarion* 283
Herodotos 9, 125, 239, 327
  on Athens 17, 19
  on Greek identities 15, 17, 20, 25
  and Julian 147
  and *Miracles of St Thekla* 176
  on Pelasgians 17
  on Persian Wars 15, 166–167, 184
heroic genealogies 15–17
Heron 204
Hesiod
  and Julian 147, 151
  in twelfth century 246, 256, 294

Hesychios of Miletos
  a pagan 176–177
  on *translatio imperii* 61
Himerios 40
  and Gregorios of Nazianzos 161
*hippiatrika* 69
Hippokrates
  and Byzantine doctors 290
  in *Timarion* 279–280
Hittites 13
Homer 140, 239
  in Borysthenes (Olbia) 25
  Christian centones 157
  as component of ancient *paideia* 22, 26
  on Greek ethnonyms 13, 167
  and Julian 58, 147, 151, 153, 161, 171
  and Karians 24
  and Panhellenism 15
  and Psellos 201
  in Thucydides 18
  in twelfth century 232, 236, 237,
    240, 242–243, 246–251, 257, 258,
    277, 306–307, 340
  *see also:* Eustathios; Tzetzes
Horapollon 34
hospitals, Byzantine, 3a
humanism, Byzantine, 215–216, 250, 266
Hybreas, Karian notable, 23
Hypatia 59, 172
  taught pagans and Christians 148
Hypatios, abbot, 140

Iakobos of Ochrid 372
Iamblichos, *The Babylonian Story*, 125
Iamblichos of Chalkis 169–170
  and barbarian wisdom 169–170
  and Julian 151, 170
  and Psellos 194, 198, 200
Iason of Kyrene (= 2 Maccabees) 29
iconoclasm 179, 229, 280
Ignatios the deacon 179–180
  and Gregorios of Nazianzos 163
  imitation of Platonic dialogues 180
Illyria/Illyrians 58
Ingerina, Eudokia, 90
Innocentius III, and Constantinopolitan
    clergy, 353
Innocentius IV, on Greeks, 349
Io, in *progymnasma*, 259
Ioannes II Komnenos 76, 92, 243, 249, 284,
    285, 301
Ioannes III Doukas Batatzes 81, 95, 352, 364,
    365, 369–372, 373
  and Frederick II Hohenstaufen 372
  letter to pope Gregorius IX 369–372, 384

Ioannes VII the Grammarian, condemned as
    Hellene, 182
Ioannes X Kamateros 356–357
Ioannes XI Bekkos 107, 385
Ioannes Chrysostomos 144
  at Athens 134
  between Hellenism and Christianity 136,
    142–143, 155
  on Roman laws 48–49
  on title *basileus* 66
Ioannes Geometres, on Athens, 325
Ioannes Lydos 69
  compared to Pausanias 73–74
  on Latin 67–68
  a pagan 176–177
  on Roman history 62, 73–74
Ioannes of Antioch, praises Julian, 145
Ioannes of Chalkedon 104
Ioannes the Kappadokian 67, 74, 94
Ionian revolt 15
Ionians 17
Ioseph I, on Greeks and Romans, 384
Ioulianos the theurgist 198
Isaakios I Komnenos 214
Isaakios II Angelos, on Latin, 69
Isauria/Isaurians 96
  not fully Romanized 52, 85
Ises, Ioannes, Byzantine of "Persian" descent, 91
Isidoros of Pelousion, on inner and outer
    wisdom, 165–166
Isokasios, pagan professor, 138
Isokrates
  on assimilation 93
  on dissimulation 237
  on Greeks and barbarians 18–19
  and Julian 147
Italians/*Italoi* 68, 69, 74, 107, 108
Italos, Ioannes, 90, 220–221, 277
  in *Timarion* 282
  trial of 228–230
Italy, in Byzantine ideology, 62–63, 87, 89, 103,
    248, 297–298, 300, 303, 339, 384

al-Jāḥiẓ 118
Jean de Brienne, Latin emperor, 369
Jerome 129
  between learning and faith 139, 181
Jerusalem 379
  as ideal 2
  and Maccabean revolt 28–29, 184
Jesus
  appears to Jerome in dream 139
  heals Syro-Phoenician *Hellenis* 124
  Herakles as 246
  and Komnenian emperors 243–244

miracles parodied by Prodromos 273–274
rejected by Julian 144–145
words on marriage in romance novels 265–266
Jews
  in Byzantium 92, 99
  their Greek names, 30
  on Hellenism as derivative 126, 170
  on Hellenism as enemy 127, 138
  in Hellenistic age 26–30, 35, 38, 157
  and Psellos 197
  in Roman empire 85, 167
Jones, A. M. H., on effects of Christianity, 135
Josephos
  and Christian apologists 126–127
  on Hellenization of names 27
  the survival of his writings 30
Judaea 28–29
Julian 143–167, 332
  accepts Hellenic label 122, 167
  against monks 137, 213
  *Against the Galilaians* 144, 148, 149–150, 152,
    160, 163, 178, 280, 282, 325
  anti-Christian measures 149
  and Athens 325
  before Ktesiphon 153
  buried in Holy Apostles 145
  Christian responses to 147–148, 149, 157–165
  on Christians as barbarians 140
  "edicts" on education 146–149
  on ethnicity, Greeks, and Romans 58–59, 152
  and Gregorios of Nazianzos 145, 147, 149,
    158–164
  Hellenism and Christianity 121, 133–134,
    143–166
  and Homer 153, 171
  *Hymn to King Helios* 152
  and Iamblichos, Chaldaeans 151, 152, 170, 184
  and last oracle of Delphi 161
  *Letter to Arsakios* 152
  on myth 246
  notions of Hellenism 151–154, 167, 283
  as potential Hellenizer of Persia 26
  and Prohairesios 148–149
  remembered in Byzantium 144, 161, 183,
    202, 284
  and Themistios 72
jurists, Severan, 48, 52, 79
Justin, apologist, 127
Justinian 65, 74, 230, 257, 339, 378
  on Aeneas, Romulus, and Numa 62, 89
  against the Platonists 325
  burial with Julian 145
  issues Greek edicts 67
  radical imperial ideology 100, 102–103, 107, 110
Juvenal 239

Kabasilas, Konstantinos, 223–224
Kallerges, Alexios, Cretan rebel, 350
Kamateros, Ioannes, letter from Tornikes,
    292–293
Kaminiates, Ioannes, against Greek learning, 181
Kanaboutzes, Ioannes, commentary on
    Dionysios of Halikarnassos, 339–340
Kappadokia/Kappadokians 22, 94, 117, 152,
    277, 302, 385
  regional stereotype 84
Karia/Karians 18, 23, 24, 84, 124
Karneades, philosopher, 26, 296
Kassia, and bridal show, 249
Kassios Dion 53–54, 63, 64, 115
Kataphloron, Nikolaos, on Athens, 324
Katrares, Ioannes, 94
Kekaumenos
  on the ancients 286
  genealogy 89–90
  limited *paideia* 186
  on Vlachs 92
Kekrops 184
Kelsos, against Christians, 128, 142–143
Kephalas, Konstantinos, 166, 182
Kerberos, in *Timarion*, 279
Keroularios, Michael
  and Psellos 193, 196, 212, 220, 302
  and Tzetzes 302
Kilikia/Kilikians 24, 84, 88
Kinnamos, Ioannes, 91
Klearchos, Hellenized Jew, 35, 168
Kleomenes of Sparta 15
Kommagene 23
Komnene, Anna, 87, 89, 90, 235, 256–257, 293
  boasts of Hellenism 187, 232, 258, 291
  on body and sexuality 249
  and Bohemond 249
  Byzantium as ecumenical vs. exclusive 106
  on Greeks and barbarians 288–290
  Homeric qualities of *Alexiad* 242–243, 288
  language 238, 239, 288–289
  mythology in *Alexiad* 245
  parents and her education 232, 245
  and Psellos 227, 232
  on *translatio imperii* 61–62
Komnenian regime 189, 233–234, 241–242,
    247–248, 293–294
Komnenos, David, 247
Komnenos, Isaakios, author, 231, 232, 270
Komnenos, Isaakios, and Tzetzes, 302–303, 305
Komnenos, Nikephoros, 284
Konstantinos VII Porphyrogennetos 90, 93, 97
  on ceremonies 69
  *De administrando imperio* 93
  different levels of style 186

Konstantinos VII Porphyrogennetos (cont.)
  on Greek and Latin 68
  on history of Asia Minor 96
  on Roman *archê* 61
  on Slavs, *Hellenes*, and *Graikoi* 116
Konstantinos IX Monomachos, and Psellos,
  192–193, 195, 204, 204–205, 217
Konstantinos X Doukas 193
Kos 21
Ktesiphon 153
Kydones, Demetrios
  and "Byzantine Commonwealth" 110
  on Greeks and barbarians 289
Kyrillos of Alexandria, against Julian, 144
Kyros, king, 380
Kyros of Panopolis 67
Kyzikos, Greek temple, 185

Lampsakos, under Latin rule, 347
Latin empire of Constantinople 323, 335,
  337–338, 347
Latin language
  Byzantine views of 3, 68–69, 74, 186, 296, 298,
    300, 335, 384
  in Byzantium 55, 58, 62, 64–71, 91, 116, 296, 337
  and demotic Greek 61, 69–70, 73
  and modern Europe 1
  and Romanization 45
"Latins"
  as barbarians 268
  conquer Byzantium 334–335, 338, 347–348
  Demetrios Kydones on 289
  Georgios Akropolites against 381–383
  and Greeks after conquest 347–360
  ideological challenge of 295, 335–336, 353
  and Manuel I Komnenos 294
  and pagan–Christian distinction 289
  religious polemic against 240, 295, 335, 339,
    348, 358–359, 374–376, 381–383
  spur Hellenism in Byzantium 295–300, 312,
    340–341, 343, 352, 387
  study in Constantinople 290–291
  Theodoros II Laskaris against 374–376
  views of Byzantium 336–338, 343
  *see also:* Crusaders
law, Roman, 48–49, 51, 52, 59, 64, 66, 69, 71, 78,
  102, 104, 189
Lazaros, in *progymnasma*, 259
Leichoudes, Konstantinos, and Psellos, 213
Lemnos 42, 111
Leon VI, on Basileios I, 116
Leon of Chalkedon, on temple properties, 257
Leon of Synada 181
Leon the Philosopher 182–183
Lesbos, as alternative Hellenism, 19–20

Libanios 40, 71–73, 166, 184, 236, 260
  on "cities of the Greeks" 114
  and Gregorios of Nyssa 140, 163
  on monks 137, 213, 255
  on Seleukos 26
  teaches Christians 148
  and Themistios 72–73, 156
Libellios, Petros, 98
Liudprand of Cremona 337
Livius 64
Livius Andronicus 32
Louis II, and Basileios I, 337
Loukas of Steiris 185
Lucian of Samosata 36, 56
  and Apokaukos 256
  compared to Tatianos 124–125
  multiple identities 31, 35
  and Prodromos 251–252, 258
  read by Leon the Philosopher 182
  and *Timarion* 277
Lucullus 220
Lyons, Council, 384
Luke, St
  improves St Mark's style 140
  and Julian 147
Lydia/Lydian, antiquarian revivals, 84
Lykaonians/Lykaonian 84–85, 96
Lykia/Lykians 20–21
  banned from high office 94
Lysias, and Julian, 147

Maccabean revolt 27–29, 127, 135, 184
Machairas, Leontios, *Chronicle of Cyprus*, 351–352
Magistros, Niketas, 94
Makedonia/Makedonians 39, 96, 117, 152, 302, 311
Makrembolites, Eustathios, *Hysmine and
  Hysminias*, 231, 250, 260–270
Malakes, Euthymios
  on Eustathios 315
  on monks 254
Malalas, Ioannes, 116
Malchos: *see* Porphyrios
Manasses, Konstantinos, 258
  *Aristandros and Kallithea* 260
  on Hellenic descent 284
Manethon, and Christian apologists, 126
Manglabites, Nikolaos, 366
Mani (Peloponnese) 116–117
Manuel I Komnenos 231, 233–235, 237,
  243–244, 300
  compared to Alexander 285–286
  hires Latins 294
  and Justinian 103
  pursuits 247–248
  settles barbarians 91

Manzikert, battle, 193
Marathon, battle, 19
Marcus Aurelius 65, 270
  Julian compared to 145, 153
Mardonios, Gothic pedagogue, 58–59
Maria of Alania, and Tzetzes, 302
Marius Victorinus of Rome, 175
  and Julian 148
Mark, St, style improved by St Luke, 140
Markos of Alexandria 104
Massilia 32
Matthew, St, and Julian, 147
Maurikios 177
  military manual 69, 76
Mauropous, Ioannes
  against Julian 144
  pleads for Plato and Plutarch 216
  and Psellos 202, 216
Maussollos 23
Maximos the Cynic 159
Meleagros of Gadara 21
Melenikon (city) 366
Menandros Rhetor, on Roman law, 48
Mesarites, Ioannes, in debates of 1204, 354, 356–357
Mesarites, Nikolaos, 365, 386
  description of Holy Apostles 236, 237
  dossier on debates of 1204–1206 354–358
Methodios, patriarch, 180
Metochites, Theodoros, 8–9
  on Philon and Josephos 30
Michael I Doukas of Epeiros 348
Michael II Doukas of Epeiros 92, 372
Michael III, on Latin, 68, 186, 296
Michael III *ho tou Anchialou* 230, 237, 240, 285–286
Michael IV 217
Michael IV Autoreianos 361
  Roman nationalism of 366–367
Michael V 223
Michael VII Doukas
  and Maria of Alania 302
  and Psellos 145–146, 193, 204, 219
  and Robert Guiscard 105
Michael VIII Palaiologos 381, 383, 384, 387
millet of Rum, Ottoman, 44
Miltiades, ancestor of Herodes Attikos, 38
Miltiades, apologist, 127
*Miracles of Saint Demetrios* 113–114, 115–116, 181
monasticism, questioned in twelfth century, 253–255
Morea, Latin principality, 348–349, 351
Morosini, Latin patriarch, 356
Moschos, Ioannes, use of ethnonyms, 115
Moses
  Nikolaos Mouzalon compared to 287
  and Psellos 199, 201

Mouzalon, Georgios, 373
Muses
  and Ioannes Kaminiates 181
  and Julian 147, 151
  in Komnenian literature 245–247, 269, 292, 315
Mycenaean Greece: *see* Bronze Age, Greek
Mylasa (Karia) 23
Mysian 84–85
mythology, in twelfth century, 232–233, 245–247, 263–264, 270, 279–280, 285
Mytilene, and Pompeius, 53

Nabataeans 34
Naukratis (Egypt) 16
Nazianzos 158
Nearchos, *Indika*, 239
Neoplatonists: *see* Platonists
Nicolaus I, and Michael III, 68–69, 186, 296
Nietzsche
  on burden of Greece 334
  and Christianity 120, 140, 143, 165
  on Roman empire 393–394
Nikaia
  empire 108, 189, ch. 6 *passim*, esp. 360–384
  as new Athens 375–376, 384
  as new New Rome 81, 367–368
Nikephoros III Botaneiates 242, 302
  genealogy 89
Niketas, friend of Psellos, 200, 213
Niketas of Herakleia 229
Nikolaos Mouzalon, praised by Basilakes, 286–287
Nikolaos of Methone 231, 240
Nikomedeia 194, 204
Nikostratos of Kilikia 24
Nonnos of Panopolis 157, 176
Noumenios 125
Numa 62

Obolensky, D., see: "Byzantine Commonwealth"
Odysseus
  in Basileios' *Address to Young Men* 164–165
  and Julian 153
Oinoanda (Lykia) 20
Olympia 15, 173
  as standard of Hellenism 16, 22
Olympieion (Athens) 37
Olympiodoros, philosopher, 177
Olympus, in Bithynia and Greece, 213
Oribasios 161
Origenes 127, 138
  against Kelsos 142–143
  legacy debated 140–141
  and Porphyrios 128–129
Orphanotropheion 290–291
Orpheus, and Kaminiates, 181

Orthodoxy and Byzantine identity 75, 103–104, 107, 109, 357–358, 362–367
Ottoman period 42, 44, 83, 99, 123
Oumbertopoulos, Konstantinos, 90
Ouranos, Nikephoros, on Greeks, Christians, and barbarians, 289
Ouzas 90
Oxylos, ancestor of Basileios of Patras, 60

Pachymeres, Georgios
    on becoming Greek 387–388
    on Byzantines under Latin rule 107–108
Pakourianos, Gregorios, 98
Palestine, Hellenistic, 28
Palladas, and Themistios, 156
Pamphilians 96
*Panhellenion*, in Byzantion, 292–293, 375
Panhellenism 15, 17, 20, 184
Paphlagonians 96, 97, 184
Pardos, Gregorios, on Psellos, 226–227
Parthenon (Athenian), conversion of, 176, 256, 325, 327, 328, 333
Pasiphae, in *progymnasma*, 259
Patras, and *Chronicle of Monembasia*, 117
"Patriarchal Academy" 230, 235
Patrikios, Homeric centones, 157
Patroklos 244
Paul, St
    1 Corinthians 132–133, 138
    and Athens 129–130, 298, 329
    on Chonai 327–328
    Christ and Belial 139
    and Clement of Alexandria 138
    on Greeks and Jews 129, 382
    and Jerome 139
    as Roman and Jew 92
    and Sokrates of Constantinople 163
    Stilbes on why Latins distrust him 358–359
Paulos the Greek, monk, 115
Pausanias 24, 37, 166, 184
    compared to Ioannes Lydos 73–74
Pediadites, Basileios, blasphemous verses, 252
Pelagius, cardinal, 355–356, 357
Pelasgians 17, 18
    Byzantines as 336
Peloponnese 185
Pelops 284
Perboundos, Slav in Thessalonike, 113–114
Perikles 38, 222, 256–257, 291, 300, 329, 331, 387
Perseus, hero, 16, 38
Persia/Persians 26, 185
    cultural influence in Hellenistic age, 23
    Julian's war against 143, 153, 158
    recognized by Byzantium 102
    wars with Byzantium 179

Persian Wars 9, 14–15, 166, 184
Petrarch 378
Philip of Makedonia 89
Philon of Alexandria 26–27, 28, 127
    on Augustus 26
    survival of writings 30
Philopoimen, and Plutarch, 37
philosophy, mistaken for the whole of Hellenism, 122–123, 132
Philostorgios 133
Philostratos 32, 65
    champion of Hellenism 170–171
    on Second Sophistic 35–36
Philotheos 69
Phoenicia/"Phoenicians"/Phoenician 21, 22, 28–29, 35, 67, 86, 124, 125, 194, 287
Phoinix, *ethopoeia* of mourning for Achilles, 175
Phokas family 89
Phokion 287
Photios 105, 358–359
    *Bibliotheke* 180, 181
    on erotic literature 123
    and Latin language 68–69
    reaction to pagan rituals 123–124
    and St Paul's ethnicity 92
Phrygia/Phygians/Phrygian 22, 83, 84–85, 96, 111
*phylon* 87–88, 93, 106, 357, 358, 360, 364–366, 373
Pindar 239
    Eustathios' commentary 310
Pisidians 96, 97
Plataians 19
Plato
    and Anna Komnene 187
    attacked as derivative 126, 170
    in Byzantium 181, 216, 229–231, 281, 289, 290, 304–305, 310, 320
    and Christians 150
    on cultural diffusion under Persia 23
    and Eusebios of Kaisareia 126
    on Greeks and barbarians 20, 126
    imitated by Ignatios the deacon 180
    and Julian 150, 151
    and Leon the Philosopher 182
    and Origenes 128
    and Plotinos 168–169
    *Republic* and Synesios 60
    *Republic* and *Timarion* 282
    ridiculed by Gregorios of Nazianzos 160
    as standard of Atticism 36, 37, 236
    *Timaios* and Proklos 171
    vs. rhetorical tradition 120
    *see also:* Psellos; Prodromos

Platonists
  and barbarian wisdom 125–126, 152–153, 165,
    168–171
  and Christians 123, 132, 134, 142
  and Homer 153
  Ioannes Lydos 67
  Julian 60, 144, 150, 168
  Kelsos 142
  Olympiodoros 177
  Origenes 127, 141
  Philippos of Opous (?), *Epinomis*, 168
  Plethon 121
  Plotinos 168–169
  Porphyrios 128, 169
  Prodromos 230–231, 271
  reactions to Julian 145
  Simplikios 177
  Stephanos of Alexandria 177
  Synesios 3, 59–60, 172
  Tribonianus 67
  *see also:* Justinian; Psellos; Prodromos
Plethon, Georgios Gemistos, 8–9, 121, 173, 183,
    185, 378
Plinius, on Athens, 327
Plotinos 194
  philosophical Hellenism 168–169, 198
Plutarch 38, 216, 300, 305, 310
  on Alexander 26
  on Demetria festival 278–279
  on Greeks and Romans 55–56
  Libanios compared to 71, 166
  *Lives* 37
Polemarchios, Demetrios, 90
Polemon, Antonios, sophist, 36
  and Panhellenion 38
  in *Timarion* 283
*politeial res publica*: *see* Romania
Polybios 79, 137
  on Achaian League 52, 57
  as Byzantine source for Rome 64
Polybios, target of Lucianic anecdote, 56
Pompeius 53
Pomponius Atticus, Titus, 31–32
Porphyrios 169, 194
  against Origenes 128–129, 141
  as "Phoenician" etc. 35, 125, 169
  on prose of Scripture 139–140
  refutation of Zoroastrian texts 169
Priscianus 70
Priskos, at the court of Attila, 75–76, 115
Prodromos, Theodoros, 235, 236, 238, 240, 291
  as author and satirist 250–252, 270–276
  *Katomyomachia* 251
  on the Komnenoi 233, 242–245, 251, 254, 270,
    272–273, 285, 300–301

*Life of Meletios* 251, 254
  and Lucian 251, 258, 271
  and Plato 230–231, 271, 273, 275–276, 287
  on poverty and wisdom 287
  *Rhodanthe and Dosikles* 260–262, 264, 267,
    269–276, 305
  satire of Jesus' miracles 273–274
  *Xenedemos, or Voices* 251–252
  *see also:* Ptochoprodromos
*progymnasmata* 258–260
Prohairesios of Athens 175
  and Julian 148–149
Proklos 171, 175
  and Psellos 194, 198–202
  in twelfth century 231
Prokopios of Gaza 175
Prokopios of Kaisareia 75, 96
  on *Graikoi* 115–116
  on Greeks and Romans 68, 115
  a pagan 177
Prosouch, Byzantine of "Persian" descent, 91
Psellos, Michael, ch. 4
  accused of heterodoxy 183, 193, 195–196
  addicted to autobiography 191
  against asceticism 209–219, 254
  and Athens 222–223, 324
  authorial strategies 191–192, 205–209, 237, 251
  biography 192–193
  body-and-soul humanism 192, 209–219, 248,
    253, 255, 287
  *Chronographia* 193–194, 200, 204–208, 211,
    217–220, 222–224, 227–228, 341
  commentaries on Aristotle 198, 227, 264
  as Consul of the Philosophers 193, 196, 277
  debunks miracles etc. 204–205
  on earthquakes 203, 205–206, 207
  *Encomium of his Mother* 195–196, 211, 217,
    226–227
  *eros* for knowledge 146, 196, 281
  on "ethnic" magicians 95, 114
  *Funeral Oration for Ioannes* 217
  and Greek science 199, 202–207, 221
  on Greeks and Romans 219–224, 294
  on Greeks, Romans, and Jews 3, 219
  and Gregorios of Nazianzos 200, 207–209,
    217–218
  Hellenism as philosophy 169
  *Historia Syntomos* 62, 143, 145–146, 219
  Homeric allegories 201, 246
  intellectual autobiography 193–194
  and Ioannes Italos 220–221
  and Ioannes Xiphilinos 192, 196, 201, 203, 207
  and Julian 143, 145–146
  and Michael Keroularios 193, 196, 212, 222
  and monk Elias 218

Psellos, Michael (cont.)
  on non-Greek philosophies 197–198
  Platonism and Christianity 198–202
  Platonist 194–195, 196, 198–202, 203, 207, 210,
    214, 216
  political philosophy 213–214, 218–219
  range of interests 195–196
  revives learning 180, 193–194
  and Sokrates 196, 200, 202, 209
  and St Auxentios 254
  and Themistios 73, 215, 227
  in *Timarion* 277, 281–283
  in the twelfth century 225–228, 241, 243, 247,
    284, 297, 299
  as Typhon 192, 219, 231
pseudo-Methodios, *Apocalypse*, 63
Ptochoprodromos 238, 249–250, 251,
    252, 254
Ptolemaios I, as founder of Alexandria, 150
Pythagoras
  and eastern wisdom 170
  in *Timarion* 282

Republic, Roman, Byzantine interest in, 62, 64,
    74, 75, 306
Roman Church 67–68, 335, 339, 347, 353–357, 359,
    370, 380–381, 383, 386, 388
Roman identity, post-Byzantine, 42–44
Roman legacy
  denied to Byzantium by the medieval West
    63–64, 312, 336–338
  denied to Byzantium by modern scholarship 3,
    43, 47, 83, 112–114, 338, 367
  and "the West" 1–2, 43
romance novels 151
  Christian views of 123–124, 134
  Hellenism in 267–270
  in twelfth century 261–276
Romania (Byzantium) ch. 2, 336–337, 349–351,
    352, 357–368
Romanization, different views of, 45–46, 49,
    54–55, 82, 85, 112
"Romanoi" vs. "Romaioi" 339–340
Romanos II
  and Bertha-Eudokia 90, 92
  and Konstantinos VII 93
Romanos IV Diogenes 193
Romanos Melodos
  against Athens 178, 325
  anti-intellectualism 155
Rome
  ethnic conceit at 54, 87
  and Greek *paideia* 31–32, 65
  as ideal 2
  occupied by Belisarios 339

as *patria* 46, 48, 49, 54–55, 59, 61, 72, 73, 75, 82,
    99, 365–366
  and the Second Sophistic 38–39
*romiosyne* 42, 73, 386
Romulus 62, 74, 219
Rus' 104–105
  as *Hellenes* 122
Russell, Bertrand, 154

Sabines 87
Salamis, battle, 19
Saloustios, Gallic *Hellen*, 59, 152, 153
Samaritans 85
Samians 19
Samosata (on Euphrates) 31, 56
Samuel of Bulgaria 90
Sanoudo Torsello, Marin, on Greeks,
    348–349
Sappho 20
Sasima (city) 158
Sathas, K. N., 183
satire, in twelfth century, 251–253, 255, 271
  *see also: Timarion*
Saturninus, Gaius Iulius, 53
Scipio Africanus 89
Scripture
  alternative to Greek *paideia* 141,
    165, 178
  barbaric prose 139–140
  Julian on 147, 150
  and Psellos 199–201
  put into Greek genres by Apollinarioi 157
Second Sophistic 30–41
  and Church Fathers 40, 159
  and classical tradition 40–41
  its Hellenism misleading 168
  legacy in Byzantium 72–73, 177, 186, ch. 5
Seleukos I, as Hellenizer, 26
Serblias, Nikephoros, and Tzetzes, 304
Sergios the deacon 361
Sgouros, Leon, 322
  as Roman 364–365
Sicily, its Hellenization, 22
Sikeliotai 22
Simplikios 177
*Sirach*, on translating Hebrew, 34
Sirens, in Christian thought, 164–165, 181,
    299, 314
Skepticism 134
Skoutariotes, Theodoros, 369
"Slavic face" 94
Slavs
  in Greece 117
  "Hellenized" 113, 116
  potential allies of Byzantium, 110

Sokrates
  on Greeks and barbarians 20, 126
  on *logos* in *Phaedo* 321
  and Prodromos 252
  and Psellos 192, 196, 200, 202, 209, 221
  and Themistios 156
Sokrates of Constantinople
  historiographical methods 137, 176
  response to Julian 163
Solon 319, 326, 344
  ancestor of Hegias 60
  ridiculed by Gregorios of Nazianzos 160
Song of Songs, in romance novels,
    265–266
Sophists 20
sophists, Komnenian, 235–241
Sophokles 20, 244–245, 259
Sozomenos, between eloquence and
    monasticism, 141
Sparta/Spartans
  ancestors of Synesios 60
  barbarians compared to Athens 19
  in Byzantium 94
  envoys to Athens 15, 17
  and Hellenistic Judaism 38
Spartakos 222
Stephanos of Alexandria/Athens 177
Stephanos (Skylitzes?)
  on Constantinopolitans 92–93
  teacher in Orphanotropheion 291
Sthenelos 244
Stilbes, Konstantinos, on Greeks and Latins,
    358–359
Strabon of Amaseia
  on Athens 324
  debate with Eratosthenes 24–25
  on Karia 23, 24, 84
Straboromanos, Manuel, 291
Strategopoulos, Alexios, 352
Straton of Sardeis 166
Symeon Metaphrastes 73
Symeon of Bulgaria, Greek *paideia*, 186
Symeon the New Theologian
  decides not to Hellenize 186
  on *indicia* of Roman identity 107
Synesios of Kyrene 3, 59–61, 86, 178, 183, 208,
    213, 283
  *Dion* 60
  on Greeks and Romans 59–61
  last Hellene 171–172
  and Libanios 71
  *On Kingship* 60
  and Plato's *Republic* 60
*Synodikon of Orthodoxy* 229–230,
    258, 393

Syria/Syriac 34, 63, 84, 85, 125
  terms for pagans and Greeks 127
"Syrians" 21, 31, 35, 85, 86, 95, 98, 124, 125,
    170, 220, 353

Tarasios, patriarch, 179–180
Tarsos 145
Tatianos, *Address to the Greeks*, 124–128
Temple (Jerusalem) 28–29, 361
Tertullianus
  on Athens and Jerusalem 139
  on idolatry 128, 151
*theatra* of Constantinople 235–236, 239, 292, 295,
    323, 352, 368
Thekla, St
  *Miracles* modeled on Herodotos 176
  pleased by eloquence 140
Themistios
  between pagans and Christians 156
  controversy of career 72–73
  and Latin 69, 72
Themistokles 222
Theodora, empress (daughter of Konstantinos
    VIII), 223
Theodora of Arta 92
Theodoretos of Kyrrhos, between Hellenism and
    Christianity, 138
Theodoros I Laskaris 354–355, 357, 361,
    366–367
  compared to Alexander 343
Theodoros II Laskaris 108, 366, 369, 372–379, 387
  as Athenian 376
  and Blemmydes 379–381
  on Constantinople 81–82
  on Hellenic nation 373–379, 383, 384
  on Ioannes III Batatzes 373, 377
  and Michael Choniates 377–378
  on Roman unity 95
  on ruins of Pergamos 376–378
Theodoros Doukas Komnenos of Epeiros
    344–345, 363, 364, 366
Theodoros Eirenikos, Nikaian patriarch, 356
Theodoros of Smyrne, in *Timarion*, 277–283
Theodosius I, and pagan temples, 156
Theophanes of Mytilene 53
Theophilos, emperor
  and bridal show 249
  in *Timarion* 280–281
Theophylaktos Hephaistos 292
  on Bulgarians 98, 294
  on Psellos 226
  on Zeus and God 257
Theophylaktos Simokattes 177
Theopompos 137
Theseus 318

Thessalonike
  in *Timarion* 277–279, 302
Thessaly/Thessalians 15, 96
Thoth 170
Thrake/Thrakians 22, 58, 96, 111, 117, 152, 184
  in Hellenistic Egypt 23–24
Thucydides 20, 239, 258, 301
  account of plague 324
  on Greek ethnonyms 13
  on Greek identity 18
  and Julian 147, 150, 151, 161
*Timarion* 258, 276–283, 302
  and Ioannes Italos 282
  and Plato 282
  and Psellos 282–283
Tiridates the Armenian 89
Titans, allegorized, 246
Torah 27, 28
Tornikes, Georgios
  on Anna Komnene 232, 249, 290
  letter to Georgios Bourtzes 297–298
  letter to Ioannes Kamateros 292–293
  turns down see of Corinth 345
Trajan, Blemmydes' ideal of kingship, 380
Trebizond, empire, 361, 367
Tribonianus
  invents nations 67, 86, 95
  a pagan 176–177
Troy/Trojans/Trojan War 18, 62, 87, 337
Turkey and Europe 2
Turks
  in Asia Minor and Balkans 76, 110, 233, 285,
    295, 296, 312, 317, 342–343
  as barbarians 268
Typhon, Sokrates and Psellos as, 192
Tyre 21, 22, 99
Tzetzes, Ioannes, 64, 184, 235, 240, 301–307
  advises revenge 244
  against monks 254, 306
  as author 251, 252, 301
  and Cato 300, 303, 305–306
  as classicist 301–307
  and foreign languages 21, 294
  Greek and Georgian ancestry 301–307
  *Histories* and *Letters* 302, 304, 305
  Homeric allegories 246, 306–307, 315
  *Life of Loukia* 305, 306, 309
  and Plato 304–305
  and Plutarch 305
  and Psellos 227, 307
  scholia on Lykophron 304
  as versifier 239, 301, 304

Ulfila 133
Ulpianus 67
  as "Phoenician" 125
  and Tyre 99

Valens, and Themistios, 156
Varangians 98
Venetians/Venice 97, 337, 347, 354–356
  see: Crete
virginity 135
Vlachs 92, 94

Wales, not fully Romanized, 52
"western civilization," defined, 1–2, 120

Xenophon 327
  *Education of Kyros* 272, 275
  as model of Arrianos 37
  in *progymnasmata* 259
Xerxes 15
  and Argos 16, 38
  in Byzantium 285
Xiphilinos, Ioannes, epitomator, 63
Xiphilinos, Ioannes, patriarch, and
    Psellos, 192–193, 196, 201,
    203, 207

Zacharias of Mytilene, *Ammonios*
  constrasted to *Theophrastos*,
    175–176
Zeus
  equated with Christian God 246,
    257, 265
  equated with Jewish God 28
  equated with Psellos 213
  Euhemerized 306–307
  Eustathios on 310
  in *progymnasma* 259
  in romance novels 265, 274
Zoe, empress, 205, 217, 223
Zonaras, Ioannes, 115, 227, 240
  interest in the Republic
    62–63, 300
  on Komnenian empire 233–234
Zoroastrians
  dismissed by Diogenes Laertios 171
  as *Hellenes* 122
  texts debunked by Porphyrios 169
Zosimos
  and foreign mercenaries 60
  on Fravitta 151–152
  and Julian 151